MACROECONOMIC THEORY
AND POLICY

MACROECONOMIC THEORY AND POLICY

THIRD EDITION

William H. Branson
Princeton University

HARPER & ROW, PUBLISHERS, New York
Grand Rapids, Philadelphia, St. Louis, San Francisco,
London, Singapore, Sydney, Tokyo

1817

Sponsoring Editor: John Greenman
Project Editor: Ellen MacElree
Cover Design: Joseph Cavalieri
Text Art: Fineline Illustrations Inc.
Production Manager: Jeanie Berke
Production Assistant: Beth Maglione
Compositor: TAPSCO, Inc.
Printer and Binder: R. R. Donnelley & Sons Company
Cover Printer: Phoenix Color Corp.

Macroeconomic Theory and Policy, Third Edition

Copyright © 1989 by Harper & Row, Publishers, Inc.

Library of Congress Cataloging in Publication Data

Branson, William H.
    Macroeconomic theory and policy / William H. Branson. — 3rd ed.
        p.   cm.
    Includes bibliographies and index.
    ISBN 0-06-040932-0
    1. Macroeconomics.   I. Title.
HB172.5.B73   1989
339—dc19   88-32622
                                                                CIP

89   90   91   92   9   8   7   6   5   4   3   2

Contents

Preface

The first edition of *Macroeconomic Theory and Policy* grew out of my lectures at the advanced undergraduate and graduate levels, in the late 1960s, at Princeton University. Similarly, the new and revised material in the second edition was developed as a result of teaching macroeconomic courses at Princeton, and as a visitor at the University of Stockholm and the Institute for Advanced Studies in the Social Sciences in Vienna during the turbulent 1970s. The new material and extensive revisions in the third edition reflect the rise in importance of rational expectations and intertemporal maximization in the 1980s. The basic objectives and methodology of the first two editions are retained, but the third edition is thoroughly revised, with two new chapters, to reflect the macroeconomic events and theoretical developments of the 1980s.

In this third edition, I still try to meet three objectives concerning substance (*what* material is presented), while adhering to three principles concerning methodology (*how* the material is presented). Concerning substance, I want first to give the reader a fairly thorough discussion of the structure of the macroeconomic system and the theoretical questions and controversies concerning this basic structure before getting down to the details of empirical estimates of the precise shape of the economy. So the first substantive objective is to display to the reader the skeleton of the macroeconomy and how its parts interact, before we get into controversies concerning the precise measurement of the body. This basic theoretical overview is accomplished in Part Two, after three brief introductory chapters deal with the national income accounts and basic multiplier models from the principles course.

The second substantive objective is to provide a fairly thorough review of the empirical work that has been done to date on the various sectors of the economy that we discuss in skeletal form in Part Two. This review includes development of alternative theories concerning consumer behavior, investment demand, and so on; the empirical estimates that have been developed on the basis of these theories; and the modifications of the basic structure that these estimates require. This basic empirical review, which is meant to acquaint the student with typical quantitative relationships in the U.S. economy, is accomplished in Part Three.

Finally, I have integrated the static theory of income determination with modern growth theory and with the recent work in medium-term dynamics.

In Part Four, several of the dynamic mechanisms that take the economy from the short-run equilibrium of Part Two to the long-run growth paths of Part Five are discussed. In Part Five, I introduce the readers to some of the important results from growth theory, such as the "turnpike theorems" of optimal growth, and also to some of the problems of growth theory, such as the unexplained "residual" in economic growth. Thus, integration of static general equilibrium theory and growth models comes in Parts Four and Five.

Concerning methodology, my first principle is to present a general equilibrium view of the macroeconomy, in which we analyze supply and demand in several aggregate markets, impose the equilibrium condition that supply equals demand at the equilibrium price, and then study the interrelationships between the sectors as policy variables change. This approach is clear in Part Two, where the macroeconomy is developed from the single market model of the Keynesian multiplier (in which only the product market for goods and services is considered), to a multisector model which includes product, money, and labor markets. At the end of Part Two, in the new Chapter 11, the behavior of the model with rational expectations, is explicitly contrasted to the case of adaptive expectations. Near the end of Part Three we add a foreign exchange market and the exchange rate in developing the foreign sector.

The second methodological principle I follow is to develop the aggregate macroeconomic functions from basic microeconomic principles. For example, in Chapter 12 the aggregate consumption function is developed from the microeconomic theory of consumer behavior. This principle is followed both to give the reader an intuitive feeling for the relation of the macroeconomic functions to observed individual behavior and to erase the imaginary boundary between micro- and macroeconomics that develops in many economics curricula.

The final methodological, or expositional, principle is to juxtapose verbal (or literary), graphical, and algebraic discussions of the material. This technique developed naturally in the Princeton lectures in response to a division among the students roughly into one group with a good economics background but little mathematics and another—mostly engineers—with mathematical training but little economics. This kind of parallel development makes the material easily accessible to students with or without mathematical training. At the same time, this technique may help to interest nonmathematicians in mathematical modes of analysis, while permitting students with a mathematical background to develop new insights into "real-world" economics.

The book focuses on policy questions and the current "state of the art" in macroeconomics, bringing in doctrinal controversies only where they are relevant to current problems. I have not footnoted references in the text; whenever theories or results associated with particular individuals are discussed, the appropriate references are included in the selected readings.

Revisions in the second edition reflected both advances in macroeconomic theory and the macroeconomic events of the 1970s. The major macroeconomic events were the deep worldwide recession of 1974–1975 and the subsequent "stagflation"—persistence of inflation with high unemployment. This led macroeconomic research to shift to an emphasis on the supply side of the economy, and the second edition reflected this shift. An important theoretical development in macroeconomics during the 1970s was the reinterpretation of the static equilibrium model of Part Two as a short-run model of general equilibrium with price rigidities, nonclearing markets, and quantity rationing. A complete exposition of the model when markets do not clear is retained in Chapter 18, adapted by John Muellbauer and Richard Portes from their paper published in the *Economic Journal*. I want to thank them for the care they took in integrating this new approach into the text.

The revisions in the third edition reflect mainly the increase in importance of expectations and intertemporal decision making in macroeconomic theory in the 1980s. Time and expectations are introduced explicitly in the new Chapter 6 on labor markets, and adaptive expectations in the new Chapter 7 on aggregate supply. These split Chapter 6 of the second edition into two. A completely new Chapter 11, on rational expectations, appears in the third edition. There rational and adaptive expectations are compared, and the role of multiperiod wage contracts is discussed. Chapter 20 on wage dynamics and unemployment discusses the expectations-augmented Phillips curve, and applies it to an analysis of the inflation cycle in the United States from 1960 to 1988.

Intertemporal choice problems are discussed explicitly in Chapters 12 and 13 on consumption and investment in the third edition. The discussion of the transactions model of money demand is updated in Chapter 14, and the choice between the money stock and the interest rate as instruments of monetary policy is analyzed in Chapter 15. Finally, all the discussion of trend growth in Chapters 1, 22, and 27 is updated to reflect the slowdown in productivity growth in the United States since the mid-1970s.

In preparing the third edition, I have incorporated suggestions from correspondents too numerous to mention here. I want to thank them all. I have, of course, learned a lot from colleagues and students at Princeton who have used the text. Among my colleagues, particular thanks go to Stephen Goldfeld, Dwight Jaffee, and Alan Blinder. Special thanks go to Heidi Schmitt and Lenore Denchak, who prepared the manuscript, and to Princeton graduate students Yoonjae Choe, Daniel Hardy, and Elie Canetti, who provided valuable assistance at various stages of the revision. The editors at Harper & Row have been helpful and expert, as ever. The third edition remains dedicated to my children Kris, Bill, and Emily; may they finish college and prosper in the world!

William H. Branson

one

AN INTRODUCTION TO MACROECONOMICS

chapter 1

Actual and Potential GNP: Fluctuations and Growth

In *micro*economic theory, full employment of resources is generally assumed, so that the focus of the analysis is on the determination of relative prices and the allocation of scarce resources among alternative uses. On the other hand, *macro*economics focuses on the level of utilization of resources—especially the level of employment—and the general level of prices. In addition, within macroeconomics we consider the question of what determines the rate of growth of resources—the growth of potential output—as well as the determinants of their level of utilization at any one time.

The focus of classical microeconomics on the allocation of scarce resources for their best uses implicitly assumes that full employment—scarcity of resources—is the normal state of the economy. If the economy is operating at substantially less than full employment, resources are, at least temporarily, really not scarce, and the opportunity cost of additional output of almost any kind is about zero—more total output can be produced by simply reducing unemployment. Because the U.S. economy, for example, suffered major recessions or depressions with high unemployment in the years 1907–1908, 1920–1921, and 1930–1939, the relevance of classical microeconomics was bound to be questioned by more than just the hard-core skeptics.

THE DEVELOPMENT OF MACROECONOMICS

Partly as a reaction to the Great Depression—that's what the historians call it, even though one suspects the people living then didn't think it was so great—of the 1930s, and with the publication of Keynes' *The General Theory of Employment, Interest and Money* in 1936, modern macroeconomics has developed as an analytical framework for understanding what causes large, and sometimes prolonged, fluctuations in the level of employment.

From 1950 to the early 1970s post-Keynesian macroeconomic analysis focused almost exclusively on those fluctuations in employment that had their origins in fluctuations in aggregate demand. Implicit in this demand-oriented analysis, and soon made explicit, was the explanation of how to prevent such fluctuations, that is, how to keep the economy operating near full employment. Once this was understood, in the period from World War II to 1972, the economy was kept operating reasonably close to its full-employment level, with exceptions in 1949, 1954, 1958, 1961, and 1970. These recessions were mild, compared with unemployment rates of 15 to 25 percent in the 1930s.

In 1974 a deep recession developed that had its origins in a shift in aggregate supply, mainly from the first oil price increase. This possibility was largely ignored by previous macroeconomic analysis. By 1975 the unemployment rate reached 9 percent and the rate of inflation reached 10 percent. This shift in the source of fluctuations moved macroeconomics on to the study of the supply side, completing the earlier story begun on the demand side. This work is included at several points in this book to integrate both demand and supply disturbances into the analysis of fluctuations in employment. In 1980, demand expansion and the second oil price increase pushed inflation back above 10 percent. The deep recession of 1982 brought unemployment above 10 percent, but reduced inflation surprisingly quickly. This illustrated the important role of inflation expectations in the economy. Since the 1970s macroeconomists have increasingly integrated expectations into their analysis of the economy. This book continues that trend.

One important consequence of the development of modern macroeconomics, which has taught us reasonably well how to maintain full employment, is that it restores the importance of classical microeconomics, as suggested by Samuelson's term the *neoclassical synthesis*. If the economy is operating near full employment, the theory of the optimum allocation of scarce resources is once again valid and crucially important. Increases in output under these conditions do have opportunity costs; for example, a $25 billion increase in defense spending from mid-1965 to mid-1967, once the economy had reached roughly full employment in 1965, had to come from reduced output *somewhere*. In that case, it came mainly from reduced output of housing and consumers' durables, at a time when family formation was soaring.

Another result of approximate mastery of the theory of income determination was the turn of the macroeconomist's attention to dynamic questions of growth in the 1960s, and the medium-term dynamics that move the economy from initial equilibrium towards a long-run growth path in the 1970s.

Growth theory studies the questions of what determines the level and rate of growth of potential of full-employment output. Medium-term dynamics studies the dynamic mechanisms that would tend to bring the economy toward the potential growth path.

The acceleration of inflation in the 1970s, and development of theoretical models in which inflation expectations are generated from the model itself, shifted the emphasis of macroeconomists toward incorporation of rational expectations into their analysis of fluctuations in output and inflation. Rational expectations are *model consistent* in the sense that the economist uses his or her own model to generate expectations of future values of the variables of interest. With rational expectations came a re-emphasis on sticky prices and wages as a fundamental source of fluctuations. This was in a way a return to Keynes' original analysis.

ACTUAL AND POTENTIAL OUTPUT

Most of macroeconomic theory focuses on two main questions:

1. What determines the path—level and rate of growth—of full employment or potential output? This is the question of growth theory.
2. What determines the level of actual output relative to potential at any one time? This is the question of income determination or stabilization theory.

A third question concerning the behavior of the price level—the rate of inflation—can be added to the second of these two central questions, and it too occupies a good deal of space here.

Theory and Policy

Implicit in these two questions, and inextricably bound up with them, are questions of policy. If we know, for example, that the level of actual output depends, at least in part, on the level of the money supply, then we also know, at least in part, how to change the level of output if it is unsatisfactorily low. Thus, it is almost impossible to talk about theory without implying possibilities for policy, and the best way to approach policy is probably by studying theory and its empirical applications.

In this book we deal with the two main questions in inverse order, mostly because, as is suggested earlier, much more is known about stabilization theory and, especially, policy than about growth theory and its applications. For this reason, the traditional macroeconomics course focuses on the problem of income determination and its implications for stabilization policy. Before we go on to a brief preview of the methods we use in Parts II–IV, it should be useful to review the movement of actual and potential gross national product (GNP), unemployment, and prices in the U.S. economy since 1960. This is to give the reader a feeling for the relationships between these variables and for the context in which this book is set.

The Record: 1960–1987

Movements of actual and potential output—or *real* GNP—are shown in Figure 1-1(a) for the period 1960–1987. The movement of the unemployment rate—the fraction of the labor force that is unemployed—is shown in Figure 1-1(b). Finally, in Figure 1-1(c), we show the rate of increase of the GNP deflator—the comprehensive price index for GNP.

The potential real GNP line in Figure 1-1(a) shows the real GNP that would be produced with an unemployment rate of about 5 percent in the 1960s, drifting up to 6 percent in the 1980s. This is an estimate of the unemployment rate that is consistent with a non-inflationary labor market equilibrium, given the fact that literal full employment is impossible. The potential GNP line has a slope that reflects the rate of growth of potential output. The current rate of 2.5 percent may be derived by taking the average growth rate in labor supply, 1.7 percent during the last decade, and subtracting the annual 0.2 percent decline in the work week. Adding to this a 1.0 percent growth rate in labor productivity gives a rate of 2.5 percent for growth of potential output. The actual GNP line in Figure 1-1(a) is just that—the *real* GNP actually produced. The difference between potential and actual GNP is the GNP *gap*—the amount of output lost when actual output falls short of potential and unemployment rises above the current 6 percent full employment rate.

Figure 1-1(b) plots the unemployment rate corresponding to the gap in Figure 1-1(a). In general, the larger the GNP gap is, the greater the unemployment rate will be. A rule of thumb characterizing this relationship was developed by Arthur Okun. Roughly, *Okun's law* states that a 3 percent increase in real GNP will yield a 1 percentage-point decrease in the unemployment rate. Figure 1-1(c) shows the percentage (annual) rate of change of the GNP deflator—the rate of inflation—corresponding to the GNP gap and unemployment-rate series. Comparison of Figures 1-1(b) and 1-1(c) shows that, in general, as the unemployment rate is reduced, the rate of inflation rises. This is the *Phillips curve* relationship between unemployment and the rate of inflation that is discussed in Chapter 20. It is also interesting that from 1961 to early 1965, as the unemployment rate gradually came down, there was no perceptible increase in the rate of inflation. But the further drop in unemployment from early 1965 to 1966 brought a sharp increase in the rate

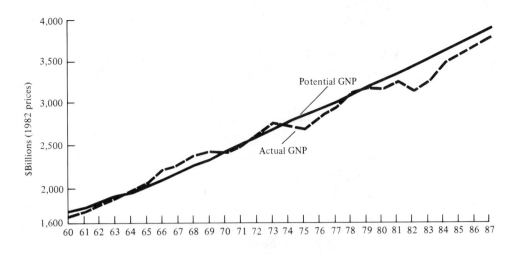

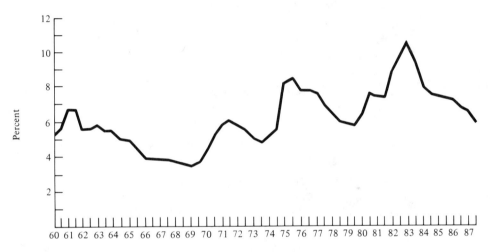

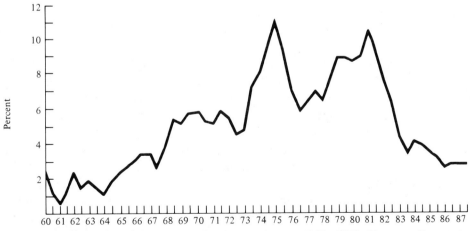

Figure 1-1 The GNP gap, unemployment, and inflation, 1960–1988. (*Sources:* Economic Report of the President, February 1988; and Robert J. Gordon, *Macroeconomics,* 4th ed. (Boston: Little, Brown and Company, 1987).

of inflation, and the maintenance of a level of demand pressure that kept unemployment below 4 percent from 1966 through 1969 generated a continuing inflation that only showed faint signs of slowing by mid-1970.

The 1960s opened with unemployment at a cyclical peak of 7 percent in the second quarter of 1961 (1961 II), and, correspondingly, actual real GNP at a cyclical trough with a GNP gap of $70 billion in 1982 dollars. The price level was very stable as a result of the maintenance of slack demand conditions since 1958. The gradual closing of the GNP gap and reduction of unemployment from 1962 to mid-1965 was due to increased demand for output, stimulated by a series of expansionary fiscal policy actions combined with a mildly expansionary growth of the money supply. In 1961 the Administration increased federal government expenditures to stimulate the economy, and in 1962 revisions of the investment tax laws to liberalize depreciation allowances and provide a tax credit on purchases of new equipment stimulated investment demand. When in late 1962 the rate of growth and the unemployment rate flattened out, the Administration proposed a tax cut in January 1963 to give the economy a further boost. The tax cut was passed in March 1964, adding to consumer demand. This stimulus, along with a continued expansion of the money supply, took the economy almost up to full employment by the end of 1964, as can be seen in Figure 1-1(a).

At this point, at the end of 1964, the story of stabilization policy in the 1960s was a success story. Fiscal and monetary policy had reduced the GNP gap to zero, unemployment was 5 percent, and the rate of inflation, while beginning to rise, was still under 2 percent. To be sure, the stabilization problem in 1961 was fairly easy, or seems so with the advantage of hindsight. With stable prices, a large GNP gap, and high unemployment, the right direction for policy was obvious: Expand! The expansion was carried out in a gradual, noninflationary way; the only real difference of opinion that appeared was whether the fiscal stimulus proposed in 1963 should come from a tax cut, boosting consumer spending, or from an increase in public spending on housing, health, and other programs. The decision came down on the side of a tax cut, partially for political expediency. Considering the difficulty that the Administration later had in first deciding to propose, and then getting Congress to pass a tax increase when excess demand appeared, it seems clear to this author that the increased-spending route would have been preferable. But the record is hard to fault in terms of stabilization policy, per se.

In 1965 the demand expansion associated with the Vietnam War began a long inflation cycle that ended only in the 1980s. This is analyzed in some detail in Chapter 20. In mid-1965 the expansion of the Vietnam War began an extremely rapid increase of federal purchases of goods and services in the defense sector. In 1965 III, these expenditures stood at $50 billion; by 1966 III they had risen to $63 billion, and by 1967 III they stood at $73 billion—

an increase of nearly $25 billion, or 50 percent, in two years. This huge stimulus to demand was not balanced by the tax increase needed to reduce private-sector demand, and money supply growth continued from mid-1965 to mid-1966. So with no offset to the large and unexpected (from the point of view of economic policy makers) increase in demand from the federal budget, unemployment fell below 4 percent in 1966, and the rate of inflation rose to 4 percent, as shown in Figure 1-1(c).

To slow the rising inflation, in the middle of 1966 the Federal Reserve tightened monetary policy, reducing the rate of growth of the money supply to zero from June 1966 to January 1967. Credit tightness reduced housing demand substantially by restricting mortgage credit, and business investment fell off in late 1967. These steps reduced the growth of demand and actual output, and the reduction in demand pressure brought the unemployment rate up slightly in late 1967. The rate of inflation also flattened as a result of eased demand pressure.

With the economy slowing in late 1966, the Federal Reserve eased monetary policy. To balance this expansionary move, in January 1967 the Administration requested a temporary income tax increase, to become effective in July 1967, to slow down the growth in consumer demand. However, the tax increase was not passed until July 1968, and by then the combination of continued money supply growth and further increases in Federal government purchases had pushed the unemployment rate back down to 3.6 percent and raised the rate of inflation to 5.1 percent. Passage of the explicitly temporary income tax increase of about 2 percent in July 1968 did little to dampen demand, while money supply growth continued into early 1969.

Finally, in late 1968 and early 1969 the growth of government purchases slowed; there was almost no increase in purchases from 1968 III into 1970. At the same time the growth of the money supply was again slowed in early 1969. Even with the expiration of the income tax increase—half in January 1970 and half in July 1970—this shift to a restrictive monetary and fiscal policy slowed the growth of demand in late 1969, generating a recession in 1970. By the end of 1970 a GNP gap of about $35 billion reappeared. The unemployment rate was up to 6 percent at the end of 1970, and the first signs of a slowdown in the rate of inflation were appearing.

Thus, in early 1971, it appeared that the economy, in a way, was coming back to a position similar to its starting point in 1960, but with a smaller GNP gap relative to potential GNP, and an unemployment rate around 6 percent instead of the 7 percent of 1961. The reduction in demand seemed to be slowing the rate of inflation, so that in 1971 the economy might begin another gradual expansion with stable prices and slowly falling unemployment.

However, this pleasant scenario, written for the first edition of this book in early 1971, did not describe the actual developments that followed. In mid-

1971 the unemployment rate peaked at 6 percent. The rate of inflation also peaked at 6 percent, and began falling after mid-year. This fall in the inflation rate was not apparent at the time, and in August 1971 the Administration began the first phase of wage and price controls, which continued into 1974.

With the controls in place, the Administration provided a substantial stimulus to demand in 1972 (an election year). Federal purchases and money growth both increased. The result, with a lag, was a drop in the unemployment rate from its 6 percent peak in mid-1971 to under 5 percent in mid-1973. This rapid expansion put upward pressure on the rate of inflation again, and the supply shocks in the form of a shortfall of agricultural output in 1972 and the oil price increases of 1973 and 1974 resulted in a sudden jump in the inflation rate. Monetary and fiscal policy shifted to neutrality in 1973 and were drastically tightened in 1974 in reaction to the jump in inflation.

The effect of the monetary and fiscal squeeze in 1974 was apparent in the unemployment rate, which rose to 9 percent, and in the rate of inflation, which was about 7 percent by the end of 1975. At that point, however, the recession hit bottom, and gradual expansion began once again. Although economic recovery started in the second half of 1975, the 1973 pre-recession level of GNP was not reached until 1976. With the economic stimulus of tax cuts and monetary growth, overall unemployment declined, hovering between 7 and 8 percent during 1976 and falling under 7 percent by mid-1977. With a more stable oil price, the rate of inflation fell below 6 percent by the end of 1976. Continued economic growth seemed possible for the remainder of the decade, assuming a continuous but gradual recovery during 1977–79, but full employment by 1980 or 1981 was not assured.

This much was written for the second edition of the book. However, in fact aggregate demand policy again became overly expansive in the late 1970s, driving the unemployment rate below 6 percent by the end of 1978. The second oil price increase of 1979 added to the inflationary pressure, taking inflation again over 10 percent in the election year of 1980. During 1979 monetary policy tightened dramatically in the face of the rising inflation. The shift toward monetary tightness, supplemented by some fiscal cuts, drove the economy into a small recession in 1980, and a major one in 1982. This time the Federal Reserve seemed determined to hold on until the inflation rate was reduced definitively.

In the recession of 1982, the unemployment rate reached a post-War peak of nearly 11 percent. As we can see in Figures 1-1(a) and 1-1(c), the prolonged recession and high unemployment *did* reduce inflation, and rapidly. From 10 percent at the beginning of 1981, inflation fell to under 4 percent in 1983. This major disinflation of the 1980s is a striking example of the effects of demand policy on unemployment and inflation.

By 1983, the tax cuts and defense spending increases of the Reagan budgets began the recovery that has lasted to 1988. The Federal Reserve accommodated the recovery by easing growth of the money supply. Inflation continued to fall, to the 2–3 percent range in 1987, and the unemployment rate fell to under 6 percent by the end of 1987. In terms of inflation and unemployment, the recovery seemed complete by mid-1988. Indeed, the unemployment rate was below the current estimate for full employment, and inflation seemed to be creeping up. The risk was that demand policy would overdo the expansion once again, after having ended the inflation cycle that began back in 1964–65.

Some Implications for Macroeconomic Theory

From our brief description of the main macroeconomic events of the period, and from a study of the data in Figure 1-1, certain relationships between the aggregate economic variables should be apparent. First, the relationship between actual output and the unemployment rate suggests that the level of output is a function of employment. This *production function* relationship is developed in Chapter 6 and is used throughout the rest of the book.

Second, as suggested above, there appears to be an inverse relationship between the level of unemployment and the rate of inflation as the economy fluctuates because of demand-side disturbances. This Phillips curve relationship is introduced in Chapter 20 as an important part of the economy's medium-term dynamics.

Finally, we have the notion of actual output regulated by the level of demand, which is, in turn, strongly affected by monetary and fiscal policy changes—movements in the money supply, government purchases, and tax rates. Much of Parts II and III focuses on the effects of changes in these variables, singly or in combination, on the level of output, employment, and the price level. We begin analysis of the effects of stabilization policy changes with a review of simple multiplier analysis in Chapter 3 and then carry that analysis to increasing levels of complexity in Chapters 5, 9, and 16.

AN ANALYTICAL APPROACH TO MACROECONOMICS

In Parts II and III, we use an aggregate general equilibrium approach to build a theory explaining movements in output, employment, and the price level. We introduce, in turn, a *product market* for goods and services, a *money market,* and a *labor market.* Together with the production function linking output and employment, demand-and-supply equilibrium conditions in these three markets jointly determine the equilibrium levels of four key variables— output, employment, the price level, and the interest rate.

In general, what happens in one market affects all markets in a general equilibrium framework. Therefore, in Part II, where we focus on the skeletal analytic framework of the system, the emphasis is on simultaneity and interaction between markets.

An Example of Simultaneity Between Markets

Consider a major increase in the efficiency of a transactions mechanism—the introduction of a widely held and accepted credit card system. This is "like" an increase in the money supply in that a given stock of money will finance an increase in annual transactions. This will tend to reduce interest rates, since people can reduce cash holdings and buy interest-earning bonds. The increase in bond demand brings bond prices up and interest rates down. The drop in interest rates essentially raises investment demand by making borrowing cheaper. Increased investment demand raises sales and income and pulls the price level up. The increase in output and the price level raises employment.

In the meantime, higher income and price levels tend to raise the demand for money, so that to a certain extent the effect of the original stimulus of the credit card is offset. Eventually, the system settles to a new equilibrium with higher levels of output, prices, and employment, and a lower interest rate. The initial disturbance in the money market has spread through the other markets in the "model," as it would spread through the entire economy in the real world. The important point in Part II is developing an intuitive understanding of this kind of simultaneity.

Connection to the "Real World" Through Empirical Results

The discussion of empirical findings in Part III is designed to add richness of texture to the analytical framework of Part II. We see what both theory and practical experience with economic data tell us, for example, about how long it takes for one variable, say, investment demand, to react to changes in another variable, say, the interest rate. We also discuss whether temporary tax changes have different effects on the level of consumer spending than permanent ones.

While Part II is meant to help develop an understanding of the bare analytics of the macroeconomic system, Part III should help in developing a kind of quantitative intuition concerning the relationships between the basic macroeconomic variables: How long do things take to react and how large will the reactions be?

To begin at the beginning, we need a brief review of the national income accounts, which both define many of our key macroeconomic variables—consumption, investment, and so on—and provide a social accounting framework for later analysis. This review is presented in Chapter 2. Part I then closes with a brief review in Chapter 3 of the basic income determination analysis from the initial economic principles course.

SELECTED READINGS

P.K. Clark, "A New Estimate of Potential GNP" (Council of Economic Advisers, 1977; processed).

Council of Economic Advisers, *Annual Reports* (Washington, D.C.: Government Printing Office), January 1962, pp. 39–56; January 1980, pp. 88–90.

R.J. Gordon, *Macroeconomics,* 4th Ed. (Boston: Little, Brown and Company, 1987).

R.J. Gordon, "Unemployment and Potential Output in the 1980s," Brookings Papers on Economic Activity, vol. 15, no. 1, 1984, pp. 132–145.

A.M. Okun, "Potential GNP: Its Measurement and Significance," in A.M. Okun, *The Political Economy of Prosperity* (Washington, D.C.: The Brookings Institution, 1970), pp. 132–145.

A.M. Okun, "The Gap Between Actual and Potential Output," in A.M. Okun, ed., *The Battle Against Unemployment* (New York: W. W. Norton, 1965).

chapter *2*

A Review of the National Income and Product Accounts

The National Income and Product Accounts—frequently referred to as NIPA—are the official measurement of the flow of product and income in the economy. The accounts are maintained by the Office of Business Economics (OBE) of the Department of Commerce and are published in a monthly OBE publication called the *Survey of Current Business.* Many of the economic aggregates, such as consumer expenditure and business investment, that this book deals with are defined in the accounts, which also provide a framework for analyzing the level of economic activity. So we begin our analysis of income determination with a brief review of the accounts.

The *product* side of the national accounts measures the flow of *currently produced* goods and services in the economy. The *income* side of the accounts measures the *factor incomes* that are earned by U.S. workers in current production. On the product side, the flow of goods and services currently produced by U.S. workers is measured by expenditures on these goods and services by consumers, businesses, government, and foreigners. The counterpart to this flow of expenditures on final product is national income, which measures income received by factors of production—compensation of employees, profits paid to owners of capital, earnings of proprietors, and so on—in compensation for producing the final product.

This means that the product and income sides are two different measures of the same continuous flow. The product side measures expenditures on output. These expenditures then become payments compensating the factors that produced the output. These factor incomes then are disposed of in consumer expenditure, tax payments, saving, and transfer payments to foreigners. Thus, we can view gross national product (GNP) in three different ways—all measuring identically the same flow. The first is GNP measured by expenditure on final product; the second is GNP measured by the type of income generated in production; and the third is GNP measured by the way this income is used or disposed of. The first and third of these measurements give us the basic *GNP identity* that is fundamental to the study of economics on an aggregate— or "macro"—level:

$$C + I + G + (X - M) \equiv \text{GNP} \equiv C + S + T + R_f. \qquad (1)$$

The left-hand side of this identity measures GNP by expenditures on final product. Here C is consumer expenditure; I is business expenditure on plant, equipment, inventories, and residential construction, all aggregated into gross private domestic investment; G is total (federal, state, and local) government purchases of goods and services; and $(X - M)$ is net exports.

The right-hand side of (1) measures GNP by the way income earned in production is disposed of. Here C, again, is consumer expenditure; S is total saving by consumers and by businesses in the form of depreciation allowances and retained earnings; T is net tax payments (total tax receipts less transfer, interest, and subsidy payments by all levels of government); and R_f is transfer payments to foreigners by private citizens, for example, in private pension plans or donations to international relief efforts.

Much of this chapter shows how expenditures on final product, the left-hand side of (1), are translated into the disposition of income earned in production, the right-hand side of (1), through the income accounts. This exercise serves several purposes. First, it explicitly justifies the identity (1), which is basic to all the macroeconomic theory that follows, by showing the reader how the National Income and Product Accounts "hang together." Second, it is designed to give the reader a feel for the quantities involved. Macroeconomic theory, like all theory, involves a great deal of abstraction, and it will be useful for the reader to be able to translate the theory, more or less continuously, back into the relevant national accounts categories. Finally, a review of the accounts introduces the reader to the categories of economic variables commonly dealt with in macroeconomic theory. The theory deals with aggregated variables; a tour through the accounts makes clear what these aggregated categories are.

The next section of this chapter discusses some basic principles underlying the accounts. We then introduce the idea of a circular flow of product and income behind the GNP identity (1). Next, we describe the major expenditure aggregates on the product side of the accounts and trace the income flows back to the income side. We finish this description of the accounts by looking at both the saving-investment balance in the economy and the distinction between nominal, or money, GNP measured in current prices and real GNP measured in base-year prices. Next, since much of our later discussion of policy focuses on the government budget, we take a closer look at the government sector of the accounts and compare it to the federal unified budget that the President submits annually to Congress. Finally, we end the chapter by raising some questions about the use of GNP as a measure of national welfare.

SOME PRINCIPLES BEHIND THE ACCOUNTS

A few basic ideas that underlie the construction of the accounts should be kept in mind as we go through them. Here, four of these ideas, which seem particularly relevant to our purposes, are briefly discussed. Keeping an eye on them will help prevent confusion in the later discussion.

The first point is that the accounts should aggregate economic variables in a way that is useful for economic analysis. In general, this means that "like" expenditures, or incomes, should be aggregated together, and "unlike" expenditures should be separated. On the product side of the accounts, this principle means that sectors of expenditure should be aggregated by who does the spending, that is, into expenditures by consumers, businesses, governments, and foreigners. This is a useful way to aggregate, since presumably each of these different kinds of expenditure is related to a different set of motivations, and thus to a different set of other economic variables. For example, consumer spending is probably related to consumer income and perhaps wealth, as we see in some detail in Chapter 12; business investment may be related to such variables as expected sales, profits, and the cost of capital, as Chapter 13 shows; government spending is determined by a political process only distantly related to consumer and business spending decisions; and net exports depend to a great extent on foreign incomes and prices.

Second, the accounts measure the expenditure and income stream that comes from *current* production of goods and services. Transactions that transfer ownership of *existing* assets are, in general, not reflected in the accounts because they do not involve current production. For example, an individual's purchase of a used car will enter the accounts only insofar as the purchase price exceeds the sale price of the previous owner, reflecting some value added to the car by the services and facilities of the used car dealer, which presumably facilitate trading and thus add to output. In a case where the owner sells directly, the transaction involves only the trade of one existing asset—the car—for another, presumably cash or checking account deposits, with no value added by a used car dealer. The transaction *involving purely an asset exchange* has no *direct* effect on current production and thus does not enter into the national income accounts. Of course, it may have *indirect* effects on consumer expenditure since the mixture of assets on both sides has changed. The seller now has liquid funds that may increase his or her spending, while the buyer may reduce spending for just the opposite reason. But these are indirect effects that would be observed, to the degree they occur, in current consumer expenditure items.

The last two points are related to the orientation of the accounts toward the measurement of total output as an (obviously imperfect) indicator of welfare. Consistent with an individualistic view of welfare, consumer expenditure is counted as final demand, rather than as an input to the labor force. This treatment of consumer expenditure may seem obvious here. However, in any forced-labor economy, such as a slave state, the consumption by the labor force would be treated as a cost of maintaining the capital stock, just as is the cost of maintaining plant and equipment in the United States. While the forced-labor economy example is an extreme case, arguments have been made, for example, to count the cost of transportation to and from work as a business cost rather than a consumer expenditure.

The other related point is that, where possible, output is valued at market price. This reflects the conclusion from microeconomics that, in a competitive economy, the market price of a good represents its marginal utility to the buyers, and the market price of a labor service represents its marginal disutility to the sellers.

The procedure of valuing output at market price even in a competitive economy can hold only for the output of the business sector; most government services are not sold, and it is hard to measure output in the household sector. Thus, these two sectors measure output as equal in value to input, while the accounts measure business output, which is about 85 percent of GNP, at market price.

THE CIRCULAR FLOW OF PRODUCT AND INCOME

The flow of product and income in a simple two-sector economy with only households and firms is shown in Figure 2-1. The top pair of arrows represents *product* markets, in which the households exchange money for goods and services provided by the firms. The dashed "Product measure" line cutting these two arrows represents the product-side measure of GNP. This measures the flow of output by the total expenditure by households on that flow.

The bottom pair of arrows represents *factor* markets, in which the firms exchange money for the services provided by the households—wage payments for labor services, profits for capital services. Again, the dashed "Income measure" line represents the income side of GNP. It measures the flow of services provided by households by the factor incomes they receive. These two flow measures should give the same reading for GNP: output = GNP = income.

Here we should point out the importance of not double-counting when

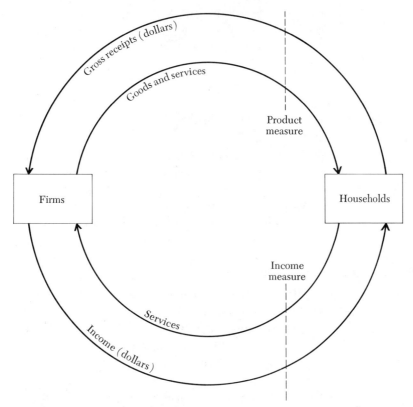

Figure 2-1 The circular flow of product and income.

we measure GNP, that is, of not adding the product and income measures together. The GNP loop of Figure 2-1 says that we can measure GNP by final output *or* by total input; intermediate goods must not be counted in the final output measure.

Another term for total input, measured by total factor income, is *value added*. GNP measured by final output should be equal to GNP measured by value added, as shown by the following example illustrated in Figure 2-2, which traces the steps from the coal and iron mines to the final sale of a (all steel?) car to a consumer. Suppose manufacture of a $10.0 thousand car measured at retail value takes $7.0 thousand worth of steel, which in turn requires $2.0 thousand of coal and $4.0 thousand of iron to manufacture. Then we have the chain of events shown in Figure 2-2, in which the mines, using only capital and labor inputs, sell $6.0 thousand of output to the steel firm, which adds $1.0 thousand in capital and labor costs to produce $7.0 thousand of steel. The auto manufacturer adds another $2.5 thousand to make an auto for $9.5 thousand, and the dealer adds $0.5 thousand in services to sell it at $10.0 thousand to the consumer.

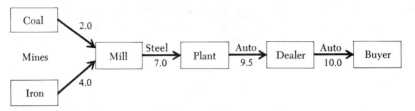

Figure 2-2 Value added and final output.

Now GNP in this case can be measured either by the value of the final sale, $10.0 thousand, which represents an upper loop transaction in Figure 2-1, or by value added in production, which represents the lower loop in Figure 2-1. In the example, total value added is $6.0 thousand by the mines, $1.0 thousand at the mill and $2.5 at the auto plant, and $0.5 by the dealer, for a total of $10.0 thousand, the same as the final output measure of GNP. Thus, when we look at the product-side measure of GNP, we should remember that we're looking at final output; the income side measures value added.

Figure 2-1 obviously could be expanded to include a government, which buys goods and services from firms and services from households in exchange for money, and receives tax receipts, implicitly in exchange for government services. We will not go into this expansion here, because the point on double-counting can be made most easily in the context of Figure 2-1 as it stands. We now turn to a description of U.S. national income and product as actually measured in the official accounts, working toward a verification of the identity of equation (1).

GNP ON THE PRODUCT SIDE

On the product side of the accounts, GNP can be measured as total expenditure in final U.S. output, the upper loop of Figure 2-1. The accounts break down this expenditure by four major sectors—consumer expenditure, business investment, government purchases, and exports. U.S. output can go to U.S. consumers' purchases of consumption goods output, C_d; U.S. business purchases of plant and equipment output plus residential investment, I_d; U.S. federal, state, and local governments' purchases of U.S. output, G_d; and total exports, X. Thus, we have as an allocation of total output,

$$GNP = C_d + I_d + G_d + X. \tag{2}$$

But U.S. consumers' purchases of *domestic* output are equal to *total* consumer expenditure C less *imports* of consumer goods, M_c; U.S. business investment purchases of equipment are equal to total equipment purchases I less capital goods imports, M_i; and government purchases of U.S. output are equal to total government purchases, G, less purchases of foreign goods and, especially, services, such as maintaining U.S. embassies or armed forces abroad, for example, M_g. Thus, we also have as an allocation of total output,

$$\text{GNP} = (C - M_c) + (I - M_i) + (G - M_g) + X$$
$$= C + I + G + (X - M), \tag{3}$$

where M is total imports. Equation (3) is the basic product-side identity in which *total* consumer expenditure, investment, government purchases, and *net* exports add up to GNP. Another way to see the relation between the two identities in (2) and (3) is shown in Table 2-1, where $M_c + M_i + M_g$ add up to total imports. Read across, this table shows the relations between total expenditures, domestic expenditures, and imports by sector, and, read down, the table shows GNP.

The major product-side components of U.S. GNP for 1987 are shown in Table 2-2. Besides scanning the numbers to get an idea of the relative size of the sectors, the reader should notice several items. First, about 15 percent of consumer expenditures are on durable goods, with a lifetime over one year. There is some question concerning whether these should be treated as a separate investment category, with the output of the goods entered as investment goods, and consumer use of their services, measured by depreciation or an implicit rental price, entered in consumer expenditure on services. For example, if all consumer durables were owned by leasing firms, as is sometimes the case with autos, sales of the goods would enter into business investment and the rental price would enter into consumer expenditures.

A second related point is that around 30 percent of total investment is in residential structures. Houses, of course, are the most important single consumer durable, and they are treated in the accounts in exactly the way suggested above for all consumer durables. All residential structures are entered in the accounts as investment as they are being built—the Census Bureau measures quarterly the value of residential construction put in place. In the case of rental housing, rents enter consumer expenditure on services. For owner-occupied housing, the OBE imputes a gross rental value to the house and adds it to consumer expenditures on services; on the income side an imputed *net* rental income is added.

Table 2-1   GNP ON THE PRODUCT SIDE

$$C_d = C - M_c$$
$$I_d = I - M_i$$
$$G_d = G - M_g$$
$$X = X$$

$$\text{GNP} = C + I + G + (X - M)$$

Table 2-2   GNP AND ITS MAJOR COMPONENTS, 1987 ($ BILLION)

GROSS NATIONAL PRODUCT (GNP)	$4527
PERSONAL CONSUMPTION EXPENDITURES	3012
Durable goods	422
Nondurable goods	998
Services	1592
GROSS PRIVATE DOMESTIC INVESTMENT	713
Business fixed investment	447
Structures	140
Producers' durable equipment	307
Residential structures	227
Change in business inventories	39
NET EXPORTS OF GOODS AND SERVICES	−123
Exports	428
Imports	551
GOVERNMENT PURCHASES OF GOODS AND SERVICES	925
Federal	382
National defense	295
Other	87
State and local	543

Source: Survey of Current Business, July 1988.

Figures may not sum to totals due to rounding.

The last thing to notice about the investment component in this brief review is that it includes investment in business inventories. This is the *change* in the stock of inventories from the beginning of the accounting period to the end. The change in inventory component is perhaps the most volatile sector of the accounts, at least on the product side, and it is important in our discussion in Chapter 3 on the relationship between two interpretations of equation (1): as an *identity* that *always* holds and as an *equilibrium condition* that is true *only* when income and product are in equilibrium.

Finally, the breakdown of total government purchases of goods and services between the federal defense, federal nondefense, and state and local categories should be noticed. Total state and local government purchases are larger than total federal purchases. In addition, about 80 percent of federal purchases are for national defense. This is because almost all federal *defense expenditures* are *purchases* of goods and services—such items as tanks and military pay—while only about 10 percent of nondefense expenditures are purchases. The rest of these expenditures are transfer payments, interest payments, and grants to state and local government. These are *not* payments for currently produced goods and services, and thus do not enter GNP directly. Rather, they are recorded on the income side as offsets to tax receipts—as negative tax payments—as we will see in the discussion of the disposition of national income.

GNP BY TYPE OF INCOME, AND NATIONAL INCOME

The translation of GNP at market price—the product-side measure of GNP as measured by expenditure—to national income (NI)—the sum of factor incomes earned in producing GNP—is shown in Table 2-3. Starting from GNP, capital consumption allowances (CCA)—depreciation of plant, equipment, and residential structures—are subtracted to obtain net national product (NNP). CCA, of course, are part of business cash flow and also are a major part of gross business saving, as we will see shortly. To state the basic identity (1), which is in terms of GNP, in terms of NNP, we can subtract CCA from *I,* making investment *net,* instead of *gross,* and from *S,* reducing the business saving component of *S* to *net,* instead of *gross,* business saving.

There are one major and three very minor items between NNP and national income. The major item is indirect business tax (IBT) payments. These represent the difference between what buyers pay for final product and what sellers receive—the receipts from excise and sales taxes. Since it is the amount that sellers receive, net of IBT, that is converted into factor payments, IBT must be subtracted from NNP to go to national income, which is essentially NNP measured at factor cost, rather than market price. IBT will enter the *T* component of the income side of the GNP identity (1).

The first of the minor items between NNP and NI, business transfer payments, is mainly business gifts to nonprofit foundations and write-offs of

Table 2-3   GNP BY TYPE OF INCOME, 1987 ($ BILLION)

GROSS NATIONAL PRODUCT (GNP)	$4527
less Capital consumption allowances	480
NET NATIONAL PRODUCT (NNP)	4047
less indirect business taxes	366
Business transfer payments	28
Statistical discrepancy	−8
plus Net subsidies to government enterprises	18
NATIONAL INCOME (NI)	3679
Compensation of employees	2683
Proprietors' income	313
Rental income of persons	18
Corporate profits	310
Net interest	354

Source: Survey of Current Business, July 1988.

Figures may not sum to totals due to rounding.

bad debts. These must be subtracted because they are a part of business receipts from sales that are not passed on as factor incomes. Later, in Table 2-4, we will see that business transfers are added back in as we go from national income to personal income.

The statistical discrepancy is the difference between GNP measured on the income and product sides due to the fact that the statistical bases for the two measurements are independent of, or at least different from, one another. The income-side measure comes from such items as personal and corporate tax returns and employment tax returns—payments into the social security and unemployment compensation funds. The product-side measure is built up from sales, inventory, and shipments data. The two measures will never exactly coincide. A negative discrepancy says that the income-side measure is greater than the product side. The statistical discrepancy is included in saving in the GNP identity; measured income that does not show up in product-side expenditures is assumed to be saved.

The other minor item between NNP and NI is net subsidies paid by governments to government enterprises, such as the Tennessee Valley Authority (TVA) or state liquor stores. These enterprises are in the business sector, so on the product side their output is measured as sales value. But if they incur losses, on balance, their payments to factor incomes for current production exceed the value of their output by the amount of the loss, which is, in turn, made up by a net subsidy from government. So these net subsidies must be added in to NNP to get NI. These net subsidies enter the basic GNP identity (1) as negative tax payments on the income side.

The last five lines of Table 2-3 show the breakdown of national income by factor shares, before direct tax payments. These are, then, gross factor incomes. The categories of factor incomes should be self-explanatory. In an effort to measure only real contributions to GNP, proprietors' income, rental income, and corporate profits are adjusted for depreciation through capital consumption allowances. Proprietors' income and corporate profits are also shown net of capital gains due to price increases on existing inventory holdings by including inventory valuation adjustments.

If we exclude proprietors' income, the share of national income going to compensation of employees in 1987 was about 80 percent, with 20 percent for property income. Therefore, these would be the shares of national income to labor and capital if proprietors' income were divided proportionately to total national income. It is, however, very difficult to determine what fraction of proprietors' income is due to the store-owner's capital and what fraction is due to his or her labor. If it were all capital income, the labor share would have been about 73 percent in 1987; if it were all labor income, the labor share would have been about 81 percent.

THE DISPOSITION OF NATIONAL INCOME

The final step in our review of the accounts is to allocate GNP and national income among the income-side components of the GNP identity, consumer expenditure C, saving S, tax payments T, and private transfers to foreigners R_f. We do this by going down the income side from GNP to national income to personal income to disposable personal income to consumer expenditure, allocating each item that is taken out of GNP along the way to S, T, or R_f, so that at the end, when only C is left, we have a sum $C + S + T + R_f$ that equals GNP.

The steps from GNP down to consumer expenditure on the income side are shown in Table 2-4, allocated among S, T, and R_f. The reader should notice that since the components $C + S + T + R_f$ add up to GNP, the items that are *added* in going down the income side from GNP at the top of Table 2-4 to consumer expenditure at the bottom are either *subtracted* in the allocation of the items to S, T, and R_f or *canceled out* by subtraction farther down in the progression to consumer expenditure.

The three items that are subtracted in allocation to an income-side category are net subsidies to government enterprises—"Net subsidies" in Table 2-4—government transfer payments, and government interest, which are all offsets to tax revenues T. Thus, the total for T on the income side is the *net* tax revenue—the *net* withdrawal from the income stream caused by the combined tax receipts less transfer payments of the federal, state, and local governments. Viewed another way, government transfer payments for such items as social security, unemployment compensation, and public assistance are *not* payments for current output, and therefore not in G, but rather negative tax payments to be included with a minus sign in T.

The other *plus* items going from GNP to consumer expenditure—personal interest payments and business transfer payments—are canceled by subtraction of items elsewhere in the same chain from GNP to consumer expenditure. Thus, the sum $C + S + T + R_f$ does, in fact, add up to GNP.

In the last section we discussed the items between GNP and NI. Here we can briefly discuss the items in Table 2-4 between NI and consumer expenditure. Going from NI to personal income (PI) involves subtracting factor incomes that do not get passed on to persons as gross before-tax income and adding items that enter PI but are not in NI. The fourth item under NI in Table 2-4, net business saving, is linked to the first item, corporate profits, by the following definition:

$$\text{Net business saving} \equiv \text{Corporate profits} - \text{Corporate profits tax} - \text{Dividends.} \qquad (4)$$

Table 2-4   ALLOCATION OF GNP ON THE INCOME SIDE, 1987 ($ BILLION)

GNP	$4527	——— Y	4527
less Capital consumption allowances	480		
NNP	4047		
less indirect business taxes	366		
Business transfer payments	28		
Statistical discrepancy	−8		
plus Net subsidies	18$^{(-)}$	S	657
NI	3679		
less Corporate profits	310		
Corporate profits tax	134		
Dividends	96		
Net business saving	81		
Net interest	354		
Contributions for social insurance	399		
Dividends received by government	7		
plus Government transfer payments	521$^{(-)}$		
Personal interest income	527	T	856
Net interest	354		
Interest paid by government to persons and business	192$^{(-)}$		
less Interest received by government	110		
Interest paid by consumers to business	92		
Dividends	89		
Business Transfer Payments	28		
PERSONAL INCOME (PI)	3780		
less Personal tax payments	570		
DISPOSABLE PERSONAL INCOME (DPI)	3210		
less Personal saving	104		
Transfers to foreigners	1	——— R_f	1
Interest paid by consumers to business	92		
CONSUMER EXPENDITURE	3012	——— C	3012

Source: Survey of Current Business, July 1988.

Figures may not sum to totals due to rounding

Thus, net business saving is the same as retained earnings, the fraction of profits not paid out in taxes or dividends. Net business saving plus CCA is gross business saving.

Contributions for social insurance (CSI) include both employer and employee payments of social security taxes, unemployment compensation taxes, and the like. These are taken out going from NI to PI and are part of government receipts in the accounts.

As shown above, government transfers and interest payments are added to NI and are treated as negative entries in T. These payments redistribute income between the (overlapping) groups who pay taxes, on the one hand,

and those who receive transfer payments and interest on government debt, on the other hand.

The rest of the entries are straightforward. Personal interest, business transfers, and dividends are canceled elsewhere. Personal tax payments, allocated to T, take us from PI to disposable personal income (DPI), which is personal income after taxes. Personal tax payments also include expenditures for such items as tolls and licenses. DPI is divided into personal saving which enters S, transfers to foreigners—remittances to relatives in the old country, personal interest payments that cancel the previous addition going from NI to PI, and consumer expenditure.

SUMMARY OF THE GNP IDENTITY

The final allocation of DPI finishes the allocation of GNP to the income-side components $C + S + T + R_f$. In Table 2-2 we show the composition of GNP on the product side of the accounts. Table 2-3 shows the translation from GNP to NI and the composition of NI by factor incomes. Finally, Table 2-4 demonstrates how GNP and NI are allocated between the income-side components. This verifies the basic GNP identity.

$$C + I + G + (X - M) \equiv \text{GNP} \equiv C + S + T + R_f, \tag{5}$$

which plays an important analytical role throughout the rest of this book. Two other versions of this identity, the saving-investment balance and the real GNP identity, are also important in our analysis; so we will introduce them here.

The Saving-Investment Balance

Implied in the GNP identity of equation (5) is another identity that shows the equality between, roughly speaking, saving and investment in the economy. This saving-investment identity will become an important analytical concept in Chapter 3, so it is useful to introduce it here as a natural derivative from the GNP identity.

If we subtract consumer expenditure C from both sides of the GNP identity (5), we obtain the saving-investment identity,

$$I + G + (X - M) \equiv S + T + R_f. \tag{6}$$

The sum on the left-hand side of (6) represents total output *not* going to consumer expenditure, and the right-hand sum gives total income of consumers that is not spent. If we loosely identify nonconsumed output as investment of one kind or another, and income not going to consumer expenditure as saving, then equation (6) can be interpreted as an investment = saving identity.

In a closed economy, or one in which net exports and private transfer payments to foreigners are small, the $(X - M)$ and R_f terms can be dropped from equation (6) for analytical purposes. If we do this, and move government purchases G over to the right-hand side, we obtain

$$I \equiv S + (T - G), \qquad (7)$$

as another version of the saving-investment identity. This says that private investment I must be equal to the sum of private saving S plus net government saving $T - G$. The latter is the total federal, state, and local government surplus. Output going to business investment plus residential construction must be equal to the sum of private saving—after-tax income not spent—plus the net government surplus.

Nominal and Real GNP

GNP can be measured either at current prices, as we have assumed implicitly up to this point, or in *real* terms using some base-year prices. Nominal, or money, GNP, measured at current prices, is simply the total national output in dollar terms. Real GNP must be built up by dividing by the relevant price index each subsector of nominal GNP such as consumer expenditure on durables or business purchases of electrical equipment.

When each GNP component is thus "deflated" by the relevant price index, we have the real GNP identity,

$$\text{gnp} = c + i + g + (x - m). \qquad (8)$$

Here we are establishing the convention of using capital letters to denote nominal values, while small letters denote real values. If P_I is the price index for investment, for example, then $I \equiv P_I \cdot i$, and real investment i in equation (8) is obtained by dividing nominal investment I by P_I.

Dividing real GNP from equation (8) into nominal GNP gives us the *implicit deflator* for GNP, the comprehensive price index P defined by

$$P \equiv \frac{\text{GNP}}{\text{gnp}}. \qquad (9)$$

This relationship is extremely important to our analysis of income determination in Part II. There we explain movements in real output, gnp, and the price level, P. Changes in nominal GNP are determined analytically by the identity $\text{GNP} = P \cdot \text{gnp}$.

This completes our survey of the GNP accounts and the basic identities they contain. All three identities—income equals product, saving equals investment, and nominal GNP equals real gnp times the price index—are important for later analysis of employment level and price level determination.

Now we can turn to another important aggregate in the accounts, the federal government budget.

THE GOVERNMENT SECTOR IN THE ACCOUNTS

Since much of our discussion of macroeconomic policy in the following chapters focuses on the results, under various conditions, of changing government spending and tax decisions, the next few pages of this chapter concentrate on the (total) government sector in the national income accounts and the relation between the federal NIPA sector and the unified budget that is presented to Congress by the President in January each year as the budget plan of the United States. First, we take a closer look at the government sector and identify the G and T variables in the basic GNP identity,

$$C \;+\; I \;+\; G \;+(X - M) \equiv \text{GNP} \equiv \; C \;+\; S \;+\; T \;+\; R_f,$$

$$\text{\$3012} \quad 713 \quad 925 \quad -123 \qquad 4527 \quad 3012 \quad 657 \quad 856 \quad 1$$

$$(10)$$

where the values of the major GNP components in 1987 are shown.

Table 2-5 shows the combined federal, state, and local government sector in the accounts for 1987. The entries in Table 2-5 must be consistent with those of the product- and income-side Tables 2-2 and 2-4. Our focus here is on the definition of G and T in the basic GNP identity (10).

On the product side, measuring expenditure on current output of goods and services, the G entry is total government purchases of goods and services only—$925 billion in 1987—*not* total government expenditure. The reader should verify this in Table 2-2. On the income side, the tax entry T is *net* tax

Table 2-5 GOVERNMENT SECTOR IN THE NIPA, 1987 ($ BILLION)

Expenditures		Receipts	
Purchase of goods and services	$925	Personal tax	$570
Transfer payments	533	Corporate profits tax	134
To persons	521	Indirect business tax	366
To foreigners	12	Contributions for social insurance	399
Interest paid	216		
To persons and business	192		
To foreigners	24		
Less interest received	110		
Less dividends received	7		
Net subsidies	18		
Total Expenditures	1574	Total Receipts	1469

Source: Survey of Current Business, July 1988.

Figures may not sum to totals due to rounding.

receipts—$856 billion in 1987. This number can be obtained by subtracting from gross tax receipts—$1469 billion—the sum of transfer payments "to persons," net interest paid to residents, and net subsidies less dividends received by government—$613 billion. The reader should be able to locate each of these entries in Table 2-5. These items are government additions to the income stream, *not* in compensation for currently provided services. The tax item on the income side, *T,* thus measures *net withdrawals* by government from the income stream. Of the $1469 billion gross tax receipts in 1987, $613 billion was returned to the public in a pure redistribution of income.

We should note here that $36 billion government interest and transfer payments to foreigners—foreign aid and retirement for foreigners—are *not* netted against gross tax receipts in calculating *T.* This is because transfers to foreigners are not payments returned to the U.S. income stream but are funds transferred abroad. While these funds may indirectly stimulate U.S. exports, the transfer itself does not enter the accounts.

The federal government sector of the accounts is shown in Table 2-6. With one exception, the items in Table 2-6 can be subtracted from those in Table 2-5 to get the state and local government sector. The one exception is the federal expenditure item, "Grants-in-aid," which are federal grants to state and local governments under such varied programs as the highway trust fund and public assistance. In general, under the grant programs, the federal government provides funds to "match" state and local expenditures for the specified program under a fixed formula. For example, the federal government provides about $30 for every $10 of state funds in the child welfare services program. These grants, which are entered as expenditures in the federal ac-

Table 2-6 FEDERAL GOVERNMENT SECTOR IN THE NIPA, 1987 ($ BILLION)

Expenditures		Receipts	
Purchases of goods and services	$382	Personal tax	$406
Transfer payments	414	Corporate profits tax	106
To persons	402	Indirect business tax	54
To foreigners	12	Contributions for social insurance	351
Grants-in-aid	103		
Interest paid	163		
To persons and business	138		
To foreigners	24		
Less interest received	19		
Net subsidies	32		
Total Expenditures	1074	Total Receipts	917

Source: Survey of Current Business, July 1988.

Figures may not sum to totals due to rounding.

count, are entered as receipts in the state and local account. When the two accounts are consolidated into the total government account, as is done in Table 2-5, this intragovernment transfer payment cancels out and the grants item disappears.

The federal sector in the national income accounts is not a budget in the legislative, accounting, or control sense. It is more a record of the economic activity of the federal government in the national accounts. However, the federal NIPA sector is very close, both in coverage and measurement, to the *expenditure account* of the *unified budget,* which is now presented in January of each year for the fiscal year beginning the following October 1. Before fiscal year 1977, the budgeting period ran from July 1 to June 30. The federal NIPA sector and the unified budget totals for fiscal year 1987, which ran from October 1986 through October 1987, are shown in Table 2-7.

The unified budget separates expenditures and tax receipts, in the expenditure account, from loan activities, in the loan account. This corresponds to the NIPA exclusion of asset transfers. The unified budget then records a total surplus that is the difference between the expenditure account surplus and net lending. The latter item is added to (or subtracted from) expenditures to make up "Outlays."

Generally, the differences between the unified budget measure of federal receipts and expenditures and that of the federal NIPA sector are in the timing with which various transactions are recorded. Both budgets ideally record expenditures as they accrue and receipts as they become liabilities to the government. In practice, a few differences remain.

Expenditures other than purchases of goods and services—transfers, interest, grants, and subsidies—are recorded in both budgets when checks are

**Table 2-7   FEDERAL NIPA SECTOR AND UNIFIED BUDGET,
FISCAL YEAR 1987 ($ BILLION)**

NIPA		Unified Budget	
		EXPENDITURE ACCOUNT	
Receipts	$906	Receipts	$854
Expenditures	1055	Expenditures	1005
		Surplus	−151
		LOAN ACCOUNT	
		Net lending	−6
		TOTAL BUDGET	
		Receipts	854
		Outlays	999
Surplus	−149	Surplus	−145

Source: Economic Report of the President, Table B-78, Washington, D.C.: Government Printing Office, February 1988.

issued. However, purchases are recorded in the unified budget as they accrue, while in the NIPA sector they are recorded upon delivery, with the exception of construction, which is recorded as it is put in place. The accrual–delivery lag can make a significant difference in the case of items such as ships and other large hard goods.

In these cases, the unified budget records the accrual of expenditures through progress payments made to contractors. The federal NIPA sector, however, subtracts a factor related to progress payments from total purchases as the item is being built, and then records the total value as an expenditure upon delivery. Thus, while the item is under construction, it adds to inventories in the national income accounts through work-in-progress inventories. When it is delivered, inventories are reduced and federal purchases go up by the inventory reduction plus the addition to value in the final accounting period. Thus, the federal NIPA sector treatment does not affect the level of GNP, but it does affect the distribution of federal hard-goods purchases between inventory investment and federal purchases while items are under construction and progress payments are being made.

On the receipts side, both budgets record corporate profits taxes as the liabilities accrue. The unified budget, however, records personal taxes and contributions for social insurance as they are paid, while the federal NIPA sector estimates their accrual. This can make a difference when tax laws are changing—as was the case in 1968 with the income tax surcharge. Since the personal tax period is generally the calendar year, the federal sector in the accounts spread the 1968 personal tax liability due to the surcharge enacted in July 1968 over the entire year of 1968, while the unified budget counted the receipts in the second half of 1968 as all falling within fiscal year 1969. This was, of course, during the period when the fiscal year ran from July to June. Aside from these fairly small differences, the unified budget—the legislated financial control document—is now fairly close to the economic measure of the federal government's impact on the economy in the national income accounts.

GNP AS A WELFARE MEASURE

There are difficulties on at least two levels in interpreting GNP as a welfare measure. The objective of this book is to describe the theory of the determinants of the level of employment and the rate of growth of national output and not to evaluate any particular indicator of social welfare. Since there are fairly clear statistical and analytical relationships between real GNP, the price level, and the unemployment rate, all as presently measured, real GNP as currently measured is a satisfactory concept for our purposes. But the subject of this book isn't the only important subject in economics, and we should not leave the reader thinking that real GNP is a satisfactory general measure of economic welfare, even though it will adequately serve our analytical ends.

Market and Nonmarket Transactions

The most obvious deficiency of the accounts is that they exclude nonmarket transactions. If two people exchange services in a barter arrangement, the output involved is not measured in GNP. But if they incorporate and sell each other the services, the output is counted. Thus, the accounts are sensitive to the extent to which transactions are conducted through established markets in the monetary sector, as opposed to individual barter transactions.

The main instance of the exclusion of nonmarket transactions in the accounts is the fact that housewives' services are not counted, since no market transaction is involved in the provision of the services. Presumably housewives' services are worth the average wage in the economy in the absence of discrimination against women. Thus, if their services were correctly valued, the measured output of the household sector of the economy would rise by perhaps $440 billion—about 25 million women aged 16–64 and not in the labor force working 8 hours a day at home for an average wage of $8.98 an hour.

As long as the ratio between the volume of market and nonmarket transactions is fairly stable, a change in measured real GNP will correspond to a change in actual market and nonmarket output. But as a country develops with increasing labor specialization, the ratio of market to nonmarket transactions will rise. This will bring an increase in measured GNP due simply to the increase in the monetary, or market, sector of the economy. Real output will rise, but the extent of this increase will be overstated by the shift from a largely nonmarket economy to a largely market economy.

Externalities and the Social Value of Output

Another problem involved in using real GNP as a welfare measure has to do with the assumption that market prices approximate the social value of output. Suppose a steel plant produces both steel, which enters GNP at market price, and smoke, which is given away free—that is, the steel company doesn't have to pay the consumers for its ill-effects—and thus doesn't enter GNP. In this case the social value of the plant's output is less than the private value to the steel firm that enters GNP.

In the case of these *externalities* where undesirable output is produced but private costs are not assessed for it—it is not *internalized* to the producer— measured real GNP will overstate the social value of output. If firms were required to absorb the costs of not polluting, nominal GNP might not immediately change, but the costs and price of private output would rise so that measured real GNP would fall. The drop in real GNP would correspond to the deduction from the value of private output that would come from recognizing the negative value of the output of pollution.

The measurement of real GNP in the case of externalities, as well as nonmarket transactions, could be adjusted to reflect true social values. The costs of pollution can be estimated, and a value can be imputed to nonmarket output, so that a rough adjustment to GNP can be made for these factors. As economic data are improved, the implicit value of work in the home is recognized, and the costs of pollution are internalized, measured GNP should become a better approximation of social welfare.

This completes our brief survey of the National Income and Product Accounts and the federal budget. We will now use the product = GNP = income identity expressed in equation (1) to begin analysis of the determination of the level of national output and income.

SELECTED READINGS

O. Morgenstern, *National Income Statistics: A Critique of Macroeconomic Aggregation* (San Francisco: The Cato Institute, 1979).

W.D. Nordhaus and J. Tobin, *Is Growth Obsolete?* (New York: National Bureau of Economic Research, 1972).

R. Ruggles, "The United States National Income Accounts, 1947–1977: Their Conceptual Basis and Evolution," in M.F. Foss, ed., *The U.S. National Income and Product Accounts: Selected Topics* (Chicago: The University of Chicago Press, 1983).

P.A. Samuelson and W.D. Nordhaus, *Economics,* 12th Ed. (New York: McGraw-Hill, 1985), chapter 6.

P.A. Samuelson, "The Evaluation of Social Income," in F. Lutz and D. C. Hague, eds., *The Theory of Capital* (London: Macmillan, 1961).

U.S. Department of Commerce, *Survey of Current Business* (December 1985), National Income Accounts Revision Article, pp. 1–19.

chapter 3

Introduction to Income Determination: The Multiplier

In the national income accounts, GNP can be viewed as a flow of either *product* or *income*. In either case the total value (at market prices) of goods and services produced in the economy is the same, so that we have the basic GNP identity,

$$C + I + G + (X - M) = \text{GNP} = C + S + T + R_f, \qquad (1)$$

where

$C \equiv$ total value of consumption expenditure

$I \equiv$ total value of investment expenditure

$G \equiv$ government purchases of goods and services

$(X - M) \equiv$ net exports of goods and services

$S \equiv$ gross private saving (business saving + personal saving + depreciation)

$T \equiv$ net tax revenues (tax revenue minus domestic transfer payments, net interest paid, and net subsidies)

$R_f \equiv$ total private transfer payments to foreigners

Since the foreign sector in the U.S. economy is very small (as we saw in Chapter 2), for analytical purposes here we consider the United States to be a closed economy. The foreign sector is reintroduced in Chapter 17, in terms of both flows of goods and services and monetary flows. But for the present, eliminating the relatively minor foreign component from the GNP identity (1) gives us the following version of that identity,

$$C + I + G = Y = C + S + T, \qquad (2)$$

where Y is the standard symbol for national income, or GNP.

Equation (2) can be interpreted as a GNP identity, a net national product (NNP) identity, or a national income (NI) identity. If Y is defined as GNP, then C, I, and G are valued at market prices, including indirect business taxes (IBT) which, on the other side of the identity, are included in T. Also, if Y is defined as GNP, I is gross private investment and S is gross private saving. If we subtract capital consumption allowances both from I to get net investment and from S to get net private saving, equation (2) is an identity for $Y = \text{NNP}$. If, in addition, we value C, net I, and G at factor prices, subtracting IBT from both sides of the identity, equation (2) becomes an identity for $Y = \text{NI}$. This chapter, all of Part II, and a good deal of Part III focus on the problem of the determination of the equilibrium level of national income and product (or output). For analytical purposes it will not matter much whether we define Y, national income, and output, to include or exclude depreciation and IBT. Thus, in these chapters Y stands for both income and output.

National income, Y, is measured at current price levels and is frequently referred to as *money* or *nominal* GNP. Nominal Y can be broken down into a *price component, P*, and a *real output component, y;* so that $Y = P \cdot y$. In the national income accounts, discussed in Chapter 2, real output is measured on a disaggregated basis by dividing (or "deflating") the various components of output in nominal terms by the relevant price indices. These disaggregated real c, i, and g components then are added up to total real output y. This is then divided into total nominal output Y to obtain the *implicit price deflator for GNP, P*. Thus, we have a real output identity,

$$c + i + g = y = c + s + t, \tag{3}$$

corresponding to the nominal GNP identity of equation (2). We will use this notation throughout Parts II to IV: capital letters stand for nominal amounts, and small letters stand for real amounts, so that, for example, $Y = P \cdot y$.

This breakdown of nominal output into price and real output components is essential for the analysis of income determination in Parts II and III. Changes in employment and unemployment are related to changes in real output y, while, in a way, changes in the price level P are what we mean by inflation or deflation. In this chapter, and in Chapters 4 and 5 in Part II, we look at the effects of shifts in demand factors on the level of real output assuming the price level P is fixed. In the rest of Part II, Chapters 6 through 11, we investigate the factors determining the price level in the economy, so that by the end of Part II we have a fairly complete economic system which determines both P and y. In this chapter we review the simplest models of income determination and multipliers from the principles course starting with the basic identity

$$c + i + g = y = c + s + t. \tag{3}$$

THE SAVING-INVESTMENT BALANCE

Subtracting the real consumption component from each side of equation (3) gives us

$$y - c = i + g \quad \text{and} \quad y - c = s + t,$$

so that

$$i + g = s + t \tag{4}$$

is just another way to express the basic real identity (3). Equation (4) expresses the *saving-investment* balance implicit in the basic GNP identity. On the product side, $i + g$ is the amount of real output that does not go to consumer expenditure, while on the income side, $s + t$ is the amount of consumer income that is not spent. These two sums are the same, by definition, in the accounts. The use of resources in the private sector to produce output *not* for sale to consumers—$i + g$—must equal the amount of income that consumers do not spend—$s + t$.

By moving the g term to the right-hand side of (4), we obtain another expression for the saving-investment balance,

$$i = s + (t - g). \tag{5}$$

Here i is total private investment (gross or net, depending on the definition of y), s is total private saving, and $(t - g)$ is the government surplus, which may be thought of as net government saving. The sum of private saving and the government's surplus must, by definition, equal private investment in the national income accounts.

PLANNED AND REALIZED INVESTMENT

Embedded in the investment component i of equations (3) and (4) are both intended investment, $\bar{\imath}$, that is, investment that is part of producers' plans, and unintended investment, that is, unforeseen changes in inventories, Δinv, that come about because of unexpected changes in the level of consumption demand, or, in general, final sales. Intended investment $\bar{\imath}$ can, of course, include some *planned* amount of inventory accumulation; in a growing economy *desired* inventories would probably grow in line with final sales. But in addition to planned inventory accumulation, total investment will include an unplanned (and undesired) inventory change, Δinv, which can be positive, negative, or zero, depending on whether sales are smaller, greater, or no different than expected. This gives us for the investment component in equation (4),

$$i = \bar{\imath} + \Delta inv. \tag{6}$$

Replacing the investment component in the saving-investment balance (4) gives us

$$\bar{\imath} + \Delta inv + g = s + t, \tag{7}$$

and adding real consumer expenditure c back into (7) converts it back into the national income identity

$$c + \bar{\imath} + \Delta inv + g = y = c + s + t. \tag{8}$$

this is the first step toward converting the *accounting identities* of equations (3) and (4) into *equilibrium conditions* determining the level of income y.

The Δinv component is now a balancing item in the GNP identity (8). If, for example, people suddenly decide to reduce saving and increase consumer expenditure, the increase in spending will bring a drop in inventories as sellers meet the unexpected increase in demand by selling from inventory so that $\Delta inv < 0$. This is an *unexpected* or *involuntary decumulation* of inventories. The negative Δinv entry in (8) will balance, initially, the c increase on the output side, while the c and s changes balance on the income side, maintaining the GNP identity at the preexisting level of income.

But this involuntary drop in inventories will cause sellers to increase orders to meet the higher sales level, leading to an increase in production and a change in y. Thus, the preexisting level of income is no longer at an equilibrium level. It is only when producers and retailers are selling as expected, so that $\Delta inv = 0$ and realized investment i equals planned investment $\bar{\imath}$, that income is at an equilibrium level. In that case, there is nothing in the current situation to change producers' or sellers' behavior, and thus to change the level of income.

THE TAX, CONSUMPTION, AND SAVING FUNCTIONS

The next step in developing the conditions for income to be in equilibrium is recognition that tax payments, consumer spending, and saving are all likely to depend on the level of income. Each of these will be an increasing function of the level of income. In particular, tax revenue is a function of gross income y,

$$t = t(y); \qquad t' > 0, \tag{9}$$

and consumer expenditure and saving are functions of disposable (after-tax) income $y - t(y)$,

$$c = c(y - t(y)); \qquad c' > 0; \tag{10}$$

$$s = s(y - t(y)); \qquad s' > 0. \tag{11}$$

Equation (9) gives the level of tax revenue for any given level of income y. This function comes from the country's tax law. The slope of the tax function, giving the change in tax revenue with a change in income, $t' = dt/dy$, is positive. Equations (10) and (11) give the split of disposable income between consumption and saving, both of which increase with disposable income, so that both c' and s' are positive. If saving and consumer spending exhaust disposable income, then $c' + s' = 1$, since all of a change in disposable income must be allocated between c and s.

The tax, consumption, and saving schedules are shown in Figure 3-1, which plots total income on the horizontal axis and uses of income—t, c, and s—on the vertical axis. Since the sum of uses of income must equal income, for any income level like y_0 in Figure 3-1 we can add up the uses of income to the 45° line where, by construction, uses = total income. At income level y_0 in Figure 3-1, the government takes tax revenue $t(y_0)$ and consumers split their disposable income, $y_0 - t(y_0)$, between consumer expenditure, c, and saving, s, as shown. As income increases along the horizontal axis, each of the wedges showing t, c, and s gets wider, so that, in general, an increase in y will increase t, c, and s. In particular, saving rises with the level of before-tax income y, so that as y increases the sum $(s + t)$ also increases. We can compute the expression for the change in $(s + t)$ as y changes, $d(s + t)/dy$ as follows. Starting with

$$s + t = s(y - t(y)) + t(y),$$

we can compute the total differential of this equation,

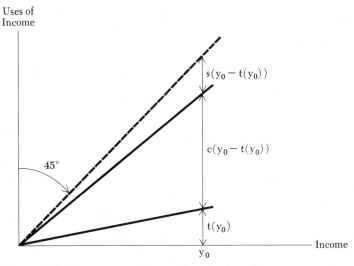

Figure 3-1 Tax, consumption, and saving functions.

$$d(s + t) = s' \cdot (dy - t' \, dy) + t' \, dy$$
$$= s' \cdot (1 - t')dy + t' \, dy,$$

so that

$$\frac{d(s + t)}{dy} = s' \cdot (1 - t') + t'.$$

If total private saving is about 20 percent of national income less tax revenue, and tax revenue is also about 20 percent of national income, then the slope of this total social saving function is

$$\frac{d(s + t)}{dy} = 0.2(1 - 0.2) + 0.2 = 0.36,$$

that is, about 36 percent of an increase in income will go to taxes and saving. The important point here, however, is just that as y rises $(s + t)$ also increases. This fact is crucial for the stability of equilibrium income.

DETERMINATION OF EQUILIBRIUM INCOME

We can now bring together the material developed in the last two sections into a simple model of the determination of equilibrium income. The national income accounts identity (7) gave us the saving-investment balance equation,

$$\bar{\imath} + \Delta inv + g = s + t,$$

where Δinv is unexpected, or involuntary, inventory changes. This equation is true, by definition, all the time. But income is at its *equilibrium* level—that is, sales are going as expected—only when $\Delta inv = 0$, and

$$\bar{\imath} + g = s(y - t(y)) + t(y). \tag{12}$$

Equation (12) is an *equilibrium* condition for income y. When income is at the level where saving plus tax revenue (as functions of income) equal *planned* investment plus government spending, then unexpected Δinv equals zero, sales expectations are being realized, and there is no tendency for income and output to change. If income is higher than that level which satisfies equation (12), $(s + t)$ will exceed planned $(\bar{\imath} + g)$, sales will be low, and Δinv will be positive. The identity (7) will still hold with $\Delta inv = (s + t) - (\bar{\imath} + g)$, but income will not be at its equilibrium level because sellers will be cutting back orders to reduce unwanted inventory stocks, and production and income will be falling. This will continue until income falls enough to bring $(s + t)$ down to $(\bar{\imath} + g)$ and reduce Δinv to zero, bringing sales expectations and realizations back in line with each other.

Thus, from equation (7), if at an initial level of income y_0, $(s + t)$ exceeds $(\bar{\imath} + g)$, $\Delta inv > 0$. If this is the case, the economy is not in equilibrium because final sales are less than producers and sellers expected. Therefore, producers will reduce their expectations and begin to reduce production. As they do that, income will fall so that its time rate of change is negative, that is, $dy/dt < 0$. (Here dy/dt is the rate of change of income, where t equals time. While there is some potential for confusion because we are using t for time and $t(y)$ for the tax function, it seemed best to use this standard notation. The text is explicit as to the use of t where it is necessary to avoid confusion.) Conversely, if $(s + t) < (\bar{\imath} + g)$, Δinv must be negative, producers will expand output to meet the unexpected increase in demand, and income will rise, that is, $dy/dt > 0$.

The Stability of Equilibrium Income

The determination of the equilibirum level of income is shown graphically in Figure 3-2. In Figure 3-2(a), $s + t$ has a positive slope because of the assumption that both s and t are increasing functions of y, described in the previous section. We have also assumed that $\bar{\imath}$ and g are fixed independently of the level of y, so that the $\bar{\imath} + g$ line is horizontal. The point at which $s + t = \bar{\imath} + g$, that is, where the two lines cross, determines the equilibrium level of income y_E that satisfies equilibrium condition (12).

We can further see that this equilibrium is a *stable* one. In other words, if outside forces cause the system to move away from the equilibrium point, it will tend to settle back to equilibrium at y_E. At a level of income y_0 in Figure 3-2(a), to the right of y_E, saving plus tax revenue is greater than planned $\bar{\imath} + g$. This means that people are buying less than sellers expected at that level of income, causing an unexpected inventory accumulation of amount Δinv_0. The inventory accumulation is just enough to maintain the saving-investment balance in the national income accounts, since at y_0,

$$\bar{\imath} + g + \Delta inv_0 = s(y_0 - t(y_0)) + t(y_0).$$

But since $\Delta inv_0 > 0$, producers will cut back on production, causing income to decrease toward y_E. Conversely, to the left of y_E, where income is at y_1, saving plus tax revenue is less than $\bar{\imath} + g$. This means that people are buying more than sellers anticipated, causing an unexpected reduction of inventories of amount Δinv_1. Producers will then expand production to satisfy this greater demand, causing income to increase toward y_E. Thus, the equilibrium level of income y_E, is stable.

This situation is demonstrated in the *phase diagram* of Figure 3-2(b), which plots the rate of change of income over time dy/dt, on the vertical axis against the level of income itself on the horizontal axis. As has been described

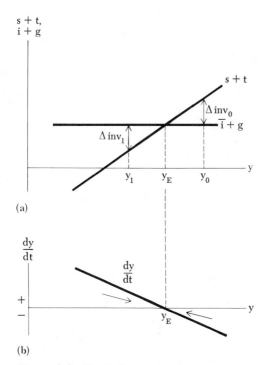

(a)

(b)

Figure 3-2 Equilibrium national income.

in the last few paragraphs, to the left of y_E, where $y < y_E$, the phase diagram shows dy/dt positive, so y is increasing. To the right of y_E, dy/dt is negative, so y is decreasing. Thus, any disturbance of y, moving it away from y_E, will be followed by a movement back toward y_E through the inventory mechanism described above; y_E is a *stable* equilibrium.

In general, in a phase diagram such as Figure 3-2(b), *equilibrium* is reached at the level of income (or whatever variable is plotted on the horizontal axis) where the phase curve crosses the axis and the rate of change is zero. If y reaches y_E, it has no tendency to move away from y_E since dy/dt is zero. Moreover, if the phase curve crosses the horizontal axis moving down from left to right, the equilibrium will be *stable*, since if y begins below y_E, as in Figure 3-2(b), dy/dt is positive, so y rises; if y begins above y_E, dy/dt is negative, so y falls. If the phase curve had a positive slope at y_E, the equilibrium would be *unstable;* once y moved away from y_E initially, it would continue to move away. To sum up, in Figure 3-2(b), at y_E where $\Delta inv = 0$, the rate of change of income dy/dt is 0, and the system is in equilibrium. To the left of y_E, where $\Delta inv < 0$, income tends to increase, hence $dy/dt > 0$. To the right of y_E, where $\Delta inv > 0$, income decreases and $dy/dt > 0$. Thus, y_E is a stable equilibrium.

This explanation of the equilibrium level of income contains one important oversimplification. At y_0 unexpected inventories accumulated, causing producers to decrease their production until there was no further unexpected inventory accumulation at y_E, where $\Delta inv = 0$. However, although no new unwanted inventories are accumulated at y_E, producers and sellers are still faced with that unwanted stock of inventories that accumulated before they made their adjustments. In order to work off that stock, they may cut *intended* inventory accumulation slightly, shifting the $\bar{i} + g$ line of Figure 3-2(a) down a bit as excess inventories are reduced. Eventually, however, the desired level of inventory accumulation included in $\bar{i}$ will return to its original level, and equilibrium income will be restored at y_E.

Shifts in the Saving Function

Now that we have seen that the equilibrium level of income determined by equation (12) is stable, it is useful to look at the effects of shifts in the saving function to see better how this simple model of income determination works. In particular, consider the effect of an increase in the desire to save. This can be shown graphically as an upward shift in the $s + t$ function to $s_1 + t$ in Figure 3-3. At any given level of income, people now save more than before. In Figure 3-1, this shift would be shown by a widening of the saving wedge at the expense of the consumption wedge. At the initial equilibrium level of income y_0, with the new saving function, $s + t$ exceeds planned $\bar{i} + g$, which results in an unintended increase in inventories of Δinv_0. As we have seen, this will cause producers to cut production until $\Delta inv = 0$, where y reaches a new equilibrium at y_1, which brings a return to the original level of saving, but at a *lower* level of income. Thus, in a situation where $\bar{i} + g$ is fixed exogenously, an exogenous increase in the desire to save leads to an unchanged level of $s + t$ but at a lower level of income.

If we change the assumption that $\bar{i}$ and g are fixed independently of y,

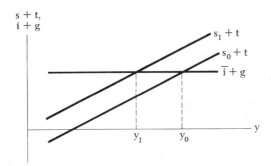

Figure 3-3 Shifts in saving behavior.

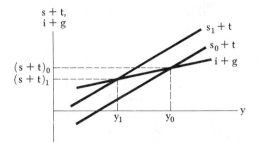

Figure 3-4 The "paradox of thrift."

we can observe the possibility of what has been called the *paradox of thrift*. Suppose that, as shown in Figure 3-4, $\bar{i} + g$ is an increasing function of income. That is, as the level of income increases, planned investment and or government purchases rise. This gives the $\bar{i} + g$ line a positive slope in Figure 3-4. Now we can see that an autonomous shift upward in saving to $s_1 + t$ not only causes a decrease in the level of income from y_0 to y_1, but also brings a *decrease* in the level of realized $s + t$. Thus, an *increase* in the desire to save can lead ultimately to a *decrease* in the realized level of $s + t$, since the drop in income reduces planned investment. This is the so-called paradox of thrift.

Finally, suppose that it is not the saving function that shifts autonomously but the level of planned investment, $\bar{i}$. In Figure 3-5, this is represented by an upward shift in the $\bar{i} + g$ line to $\bar{i}_1 + g$. This shift causes $s + t$ to be less than planned $\bar{i} + g$ at the initial equilibrium level of income y_0 by the amount $(-\Delta inv_0)$, representing an unexpected sell-off of inventory. As a result, orders and production increase, bringing an increase in the level of income toward the new equilibrium level y_1. (The same effect would occur, of course, as a result of a *downward* shift in the saving or tax function.) The size of the increase in income caused by an autonomous increase in $\bar{i}$ or g depends on the slope of the $s + t$ function. In Figure 3-6, with the flat $(s + t)_0$ function, income rises from y_0 to y_1 with an investment shift from $\bar{i}_0$ to $\bar{i}_1$. With the very steep

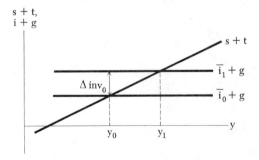

Figure 3-5 An increase in planned investment.

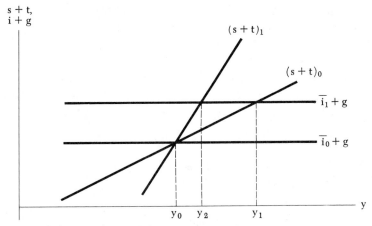

Figure 3-6 Investment shifts and the $s + t$ function.

$(s + t)_1$ function, implying a large increase in saving plus tax revenue with a change in y, the investment shift raises y only to y_2. This relationship between the slope of the $s + t$ function and the size of the increase in equilibrium income following from a given increase in exogenous investment demand or government purchases takes us to consideration of the multiplier.

DERIVATION OF THE EXPENDITURE MULTIPLIER

We have just seen how a change in planned investment from $\bar{i}_0$ to $\bar{i}_1$ changes equilibrium y from y_0 to y_1, and that the relationship of the change in y, $dy = y_1 - y_0$, to the initial change in investment, $d\bar{i} = i_1 - i_0$, depends on the slope of the $s + t$ schedule. The ratio $dy/d\bar{i}$, which gives the change in equilibrium y per unit change in $\bar{i}$, is the *multiplier* for investment expenditure. Here we will develop the multipliers for changes in investment and government purchases, and also for shifts in the tax schedule, beginning with the simplest economy in which taxes are levied as lump-sum amounts, not sensitive to the level of income.

Lump-Sum Taxes

In order to make the analytics of the multiplier process as clear as possible, we begin with a case where tax revenues are a fixed sum, $\bar{t}$. This is the real tax revenue to be collected, regardless of the level of income. In this case we have the basic equilibrium condition,

$$c(y - \bar{t}) + \bar{i} + g = y = c(y - \bar{t}) + s(y - \bar{t}) + \bar{t}. \tag{13}$$

Subtracting c from each of the three parts of this expression gives us the alternative version of the equilibrium condition,

$$\bar{\imath} + g = y - c(y - \bar{t}) = s(y - \bar{t}) + \bar{t}. \tag{14}$$

To find the change in equilibrium income following a change in planned investment in this case, we can differentiate the left-hand equation in equilibrium condition (13), holding g and $\bar{t}$ constant, to obtain

$$c' \, dy + d\bar{\imath} = dy \quad \text{and} \quad dy(1 - c') = d\bar{\imath},$$

so that the investment multiplier giving the change in equilibrium income dy relative to the change in investment $d\bar{\imath}$ is

$$\frac{dy}{d\bar{\imath}} = \frac{1}{1 - c'}. \tag{15}$$

If the slope c' of the consumption function is, say, 0.7, so that, with taxes fixed, 70 percent of an addition to income goes to consumption, then the multiplier $1/(1 - c')$ is $1/0.3 = 3.3$. A \$1 billion increase in investment demand will yield a \$3.3 billion increase in income.

The multiplier can be related to the $s + t = \bar{\imath} + g$ diagrams of the previous section by observing that, from the right-hand equation of (14),

$$dy - c' \, dy = s' \, dy \quad \text{and} \quad 1 - c' = s'.$$

Thus, the value of the multiplier is also $1/s'$, since $s' + c' = 1$. Also, in this model with $\bar{t}$ fixed, the slope of the $s + t$ function, $d(s + t)/dy$, is simply s'. An increase in y does not change $\bar{t}$, and it changes s by s'. Thus, in Figure 3-7, the increase in planned investment by $d\bar{\imath}$ from $\bar{\imath}_0$ to $\bar{\imath}_1$ raises y from y_0 to

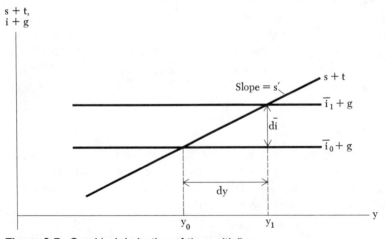

Figure 3-7 Graphical derivation of the multiplier.

y_1. The ratio of the $\bar{i}$ increase to the y increase is the slope of the $s + t$ function, s'. That is, $d\bar{i}/dy = s'$, so that $dy/d\bar{i} = 1/s'$, as was shown algebraically above.

We can also view the multiplier in a dynamic setting as the sum of a stream of expenditure increases following from a $d\bar{i}$ increase. When expenditure is first raised by $d\bar{i}$, income and output rise directly by the amount $d\bar{i}$; more investment goods are produced, and the incomes of the factors producing them go up. With taxes fixed, the *net* income of these factors rises by $d\bar{i}$. But they in turn spend $c'\, d\bar{i}$ (in the previous example, $0.7\, d\bar{i}$) for groceries, shoes, and so on, so that the output and income of the grocers go up by $c'\, d\bar{i}$, adding another term to the income increase generated by the initial investment change. Again, the recipients of this increment of spending $c'\, d\bar{i}$ will spend c' of it, adding a term of $c'^2\, d\bar{i}$ to the income increase. This will go on indefinitely with the increments becoming smaller and smaller as c'^n tends toward zero as n gets large. The increase in output and income, dy, given by this process is

$$dy = d\bar{i} + c'\, d\bar{i} + c'(c'\, d\bar{i}) + \cdots,$$

or

$$dy = d\bar{i}(1 + c' + c'^2 + c'^3 + \cdots). \tag{16}$$

From elementary algebra, we know that dividing $1 - c'$ into 1 will give us the expression in parentheses in equation (16), that is,

$$\frac{1}{1 - c'} = 1 + c' + c'^2 + c'^3 + \cdots,$$

so that we can replace the expansion term in equation (16) by $1/(1 - c')$ to obtain the multiplier given in equation (15).

This is essentially all there is to the multiplier. It can be viewed as the result of a convergent expansion (or contraction) of income as the economy adjusts to an exogenous increase (or decrease) in expenditure. It can be derived by differentiating the equation giving the equilibrium condition for income and solving for the change in income. It can also be derived by careful consideration of the slope of the curve along which the economy adjusts from one equilibrium position to the next. In the rest of this section we first see what happens to the multiplier as we allow g and $\bar{i}$ to change, and then we look at a multiplier for tax *rate* changes. This manipulation of the basic equilibrium model should bring out a few interesting relationships and also make the reader more familiar with the type of analysis to be used in Part II.

The Balanced-Budget Multiplier

Returning to the basic equilibrium condition (13) with taxes exogenously given as $\bar{t}$,

$$y = c(y - \bar{t}) + \bar{i} + g,$$

we can obtain a general expression giving changes in y as a function of changes in $\bar{t}$, $\bar{i}$, and g by differentiating (13) to obtain

$$dy = c' \cdot (dy - d\bar{t}) + d\bar{i} + dg$$

and

$$dy \cdot (1 - c') = -c' \, d\bar{t} + d\bar{i} + dg,$$

so that

$$dy = \frac{-c' \, d\bar{t} + d\bar{i} + dg}{1 - c'} \tag{17}$$

is a general multiplier expression. To obtain the multiplier for $d\bar{i}$, we can set $d\bar{t}$ and dg equal to zero and divide by $d\bar{i}$. This gives the multiplier $1/(1 - c')$ of equation (15). The same multiplier would also apply to dg, holding $\bar{i}$ and $\bar{t}$ constant.

Suppose now we ask what happens to y if we raise government purchases and tax revenues by the same amount, holding $\bar{i}$ fixed. Substituting $dg = d\bar{t}$ into equation (17) and setting $d\bar{i} = 0$ gives us

$$dy = \frac{-c' \, dg + dg}{1 - c'} = dg \, \frac{1 - c'}{1 - c'},$$

so that the *balanced-budget multiplier* is given by

$$\frac{dy}{dg} = \frac{1 - c'}{1 - c'} = 1. \tag{18}$$

An equal increase in $\bar{t}$ and g with investment $\bar{i}$ fixed, leaving the government surplus or deficit unchanged, will raise equilibrium y by the dg increase, that is, $dy = dg$. Thus, in this simple case, the balanced-budget multiplier is one.

One explanation for this comes from the income expansion chains considered earlier. In the case of government purchases, dg raises net (or gross, for that matter) national product by the amount dg *directly* and then *indirectly* through the multiplier chain, giving a dy effect of

$$dy = dg(1 + c' + c'^2 + \cdots).$$

But the tax increase only enters net national product when the cut in disposable income by $d\bar{t}$ reduces consumer expenditure by $c' \, d\bar{t}$. Thus, the dy effect of the tax increase is given by

$$dy = -d\bar{t}(c' + c'^2 + \cdots).$$

The difference between the two, which gives the net effect on y, is $dg \, (= d\bar{t})$, since the initial direct increase in NNP is missing from the tax multiplier. A $10 billion increase in g has an immediate $10 billion impact on NNP, while a $10 billion increase in $\bar{t}$ affects NNP only when consumers reduce their spending in reaction to the change.

Taxes as a Function of Income

Next, we can return to the original specification of the tax function, which is $t = t(y)$; tax revenues are an increasing function of income. In this more realistic case, the basic equilibrium condition for income determination is

$$c(y - t(y)) + \bar{i} + g = y = c(y - t(y)) + s(y - t(y)) + t(y), \quad (19)$$

and subtracting $c(y - t(y))$ from each part of equation (19) gives us the alternative form

$$\bar{i} + g = y - c(y - t(y)) = s(y - t(y)) + t(y). \quad (20)$$

To obtain the general form of the multiplier with a given tax structure, we can differentiate the left-hand equation in the equilibrium condition (19) to obtain

$$dy = c' \cdot (dy - t' \, dy) + d\bar{i} + dg$$

and

$$dy = c' \cdot (1 - t')dy + d\bar{i} + dg,$$

so that the multiplier expression is given by

$$dy = \frac{di + dg}{1 - c'(1 - t')}. \quad (21)$$

Introducing a tax function has *reduced* the multiplier. As tax revenue rises with income (with fixed tax *rates*), the increase in disposable income that a person can either save or spend is smaller than the increase in total income. A little is thus siphoned off of each round of expenditure by the existence of the tax schedule, thereby reducing the size of the multiplier.

This can be related to the $s + t = \bar{i} + g$ diagram of Figure 3-8 by differentiation of the right-hand equality in equation (20):

$$dy - c' \cdot (1 - t')dy = s' \cdot (1 - t')dy + t' \, dy$$

and

$$1 - c' \cdot (1 - t') = s' \cdot (1 - t') + t'.$$

Thus, the denominator of the multiplier expression in (21) is equal to $s'(1 - t') + t'$, which is the increase in saving plus tax revenue that comes

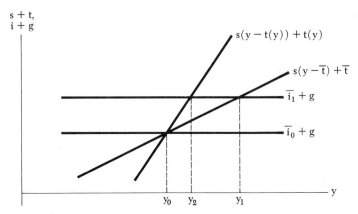

Figure 3-8   Tax revenues as a function of income.

from an increase in y. Earlier, on page 46, this was shown as the slope, $d(s + t)/dy$, of the $s(y - t(y)) + t(y)$ curve in Figure 3-8. With tax revenue fixed at $\bar{t}$ in Figure 3-8, an increase in investment demand from i_0 to i_1 raises equilibrium income from y_0 to y_1. If tax revenues are an increasing function of income, that is $t = t(y)$, then the same $\bar{i}$ increase only raises y to y_2 from y_0. The presence of the tax function reduces the increases in disposable income relative to those in total income at each stage in the expansion, reducing the eventual increase in y from y_1 to y_2 in Figure 3-8. The tax system thus functions as a *built-in stabilizer,* reducing the changes in income that are induced by exogenous changes in investment. If investment demand had shifted down, the steeper $s(y - t(y)) + t(y)$ function would have cushioned the fall in y since disposable income would fall less than total income with a reduction in tax payments.

The Tax Rate Multiplier

To conclude our discussion of multipliers, we can develop the multiplier for a tax rate change. This is the model most relevant to stabilization policy decisions involving tax changes; the government controls the tax rates, and their relation to the state of the economy determines the level of tax revenues.

Here we simplify the tax function by assuming that tax revenues are proportional to income, so that $t(y) = \tau y$, where τ is a percentage tax rate, such as, perhaps, 20 percent. This proportional tax schedule is shown in Figure 3-9. With this tax schedule, we can write the basic equation for equilibrium income as

$$y = c(y - \tau y) + \bar{i} + g. \tag{22}$$

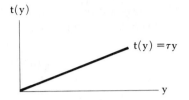

Figure 3-9 Proportional tax schedule.

Since $d(\tau y)$ is approximately equal to $\tau\, dy + y\, d\tau$, the differential of equilibrium condition (22) can be written as

$$dy = c' \cdot (dy - \tau\, dy - y\, d\tau) + d\bar{\imath} + dg$$

and

$$dy = c' \cdot (1 - \tau)dy - c'\, y\, d\tau + d\bar{\imath} + dg,$$

so that the multiplier expression with tax rates $\bar{\imath}$ and g all changing is given by

$$dy = \frac{d\bar{\imath} + dg - c'\, y\, d\tau}{1 - c' \cdot (1 - \tau)}. \tag{23}$$

With the exception of the odd-looking term $c'\, y\, d\tau$, this is the same as the general multiplier expression of equation (21), since with $t(y) = \tau y$, $t' = \tau$. The expression $-c'\, y\, d\tau$ simply gives the *exogenous* consumer expenditure change, analogous to the $d\bar{\imath}$ and dg changes, that comes from a tax rate change. If tax rates are raised by $d\tau$, then $-y\, d\tau$ gives the drop in disposable income that comes directly from the tax change, and c' times $-y\, d\tau$ gives the direct effect on consumer expenditure. This is a direct, policy-induced change in consumer expenditure c, as opposed to the endogenous changes that result from changes in income. From this point on, we refer to this type of expenditure change, which comes as a *direct* effect of a policy change before any adjustment to a changing level of income is considered, as a *policy-induced* change in expenditure. Thus, the tax rate multiplier just translates a tax rate change into a direct impact on consumer spending and then multiplies it by the usual multiplier, $1/(1 - c' \cdot (1 - \tau))$. The difference between the multipliers is in the source of the exogenous expenditure change.

CONCLUSION TO PART I

The three introductory chapters have reviewed the basics of income determination as they generally appear under the name "Keynesian model" in introductory texts. The multipliers developed in this chapter show the changes in equilibrium income and output that follow changes in investment demand, savings behavior, government purchases, and tax rates in a world in which investment is given exogenously, the money supply plays no role, and real output y can change with no effect on the price level P. In Part II we first introduce the money supply and interest rates and then the labor market and price level. The multipliers of this chapter are revised in Chapters 5 and 9 to reflect these increasing levels of complexity. This procedure of comparing the operation of the system through changes in the multipliers, as well as through graphical and verbal explanation, will, it is hoped, give the reader additional insight into how the various parts of the economy are interconnected.

SELECTED READINGS

R.G.D. Allen, *Macroeconomic Theory* (New York: St. Martin's Press, 1967), chapter 2.

W.A. Salant, "Taxes, Income Determination, and the Balanced Budget Theorem," in R. A. Gordon and L. R. Klein, eds., *Readings in Business Cycles* (Homewood, Ill.: R. D. Irwin, 1965).

P.A. Samuelson, "The Simple Mathematics of Income Determination," in *Income, Employment, and Public Policy: Essays in Honor of Alvin Hansen;* reproduced in M. G. Mueller, ed., *Readings in Macroeconomics* (New York: Holt, Rinehart and Winston, 1966).

two

NATIONAL INCOME DETERMINATION: THE STATIC EQUILIBRIUM MODEL

chapter *4*

Demand-Side Equilibrium: Income and the Interest Rate

In Part II we develop, step by step, the basic model of income determination. This shows how the price level, the interest rate, and the levels of output and employment are determined in an economy that typically operates with more or less full employment. Most of the industrial economies of North America, Europe, and Japan fit into this category. The various pieces of this model—the consumption function, the investment function, and so on—are kept as simple as possible here, so that we can focus on how the various sectors of the economy interact. Further investigation of the details of these various sectors, then, is the subject of Part III.

Since macroeconomics is really just aggregated microeconomics—the trick being to aggregate the zillions of microactivities and markets in a way that improves our understanding of how the economy works—it is only natural that we approach determination of equilibrium values of the interest rate, the price level, output, and employment by identifying supply and demand functions in the various markets and then finding equilibrium price and output in each. What we find, as we might expect, is that changing conditions in one market, for example, shifting the demand for money, changes the outcomes in the other markets—equilibrium output and employment, for example. The point of Part II is to see just how this system hangs together.

In this chapter we develop the *demand side* of the economy. This involves finding the equilibrium values of interest rate and of *output demanded* by consumers, business, and government, given the price level. At the end of the chapter, we are able to develop a *demand curve* for the economy that shows how these equilibrium demand-side variables change as the price level changes.

After introducing monetary and fiscal policy and its effect on demand conditions in the economy, we then go on to develop, in Chapters 6 and 7, a simple model of the labor market and the *supply side* of the economy. This shows how the equilibrium values of *output produced* and employment are determined, again given the price level. Varying the price level then gives us an economy-wide *supply curve.* Combining the demand curve and the supply curve gives us the equilibrium price level which equates the quantity of output demanded, from the demand side, to that produced, on the supply side.

This can all be put very simply in mathematical terms. On the demand side we have two equations, expressing equilibrium conditions in the *product* and *money* markets, in three variables: the level of income (or real national product) y; the interest rate r; and the price level P. On the supply side we have two equations, a production function and a labor market equilibrium condition, in three variables: y, P, and the level of employment N. Combining these gives us four equations in four variables: y, N, P, and r. The work of Part II is to expose, as simply as possible, the relationships between these variables (the equations) and just how their equilibrium values are determined.

EQUILIBRIUM INCOME AND THE INTEREST RATE
IN THE PRODUCT MARKET

In Chapter 3 we reviewed the simplest model of income determination, in which both the price level and the level of investment are taken as given. This model is essentially one equilibrium condition—total expenditure as a function of income equals income—in one variable, income. This equation, developed in Chapter 3, is

$$y = c(y - t(y)) + i + g, \tag{1}$$

or

$$y - c = s(y - t(y)) + t(y) = i + g,$$

where y is real GNP, c is real consumer expenditure as a function of real disposable income, and s is real saving; t is real tax revenue as a function of real GNP, i is real investment demand, and g is real government purchases of goods and services.

Investment Demand and the Interest Rate

In equation (1) each element is at a planned or *ex ante* level. Thus, i is the level of *planned* fixed investment and inventory investment. In Chapter 3, we took i as exogeneously given. Now we turn to the question of what determines i. To begin with, we can speculate that the level of fixed investment planned by a firm might depend on the market interest rate, r. Intuitively, this seems reasonable because, in order to invest, a firm must either borrow or use its own funds. In either case, the cost of borrowing can be measured by the interest rate the firm has to pay or to forego receiving in case it uses its own funds.

In deciding whether to invest in a given project, a firm might utilize a concept known as the *present discounted value* (*PDV*) of future income from the investment. To compute the *PDV* of any investment project, a firm weighs the stream of future net returns, that is, net incomes, R_t, from the project, discounted by the rate of interest $[R_{t+1}/(1 + r)$ and so on], against the cost, C, of the project, using the formula,

$$PDV_t = -C + R_t + \frac{R_{t+1}}{1 + r} + \frac{R_{t+2}}{(1 + r)^2} + \cdots + \frac{R_{t+n}}{(1 + r)^n}. \qquad (2)$$

In this calculation of the present value of the future income stream, the interest rate r is used in evaluating, in the present, the "worth" of each future return. For example, if A were to offer B $104, payable in one year, in exchange for cash now, B would have to decide how much that $104 a year from now is worth to her now. If she knew that she could lend money in the market and receive a 4 percent return on it, she would decide that $104 in one year was worth $100 now. Therefore, she would give A $100 now in exchange for $104 in a year. This is her way of valuing future payments at the present time. This can be expressed mathematically as in equation (2):

$$PDV \text{ of } \$104 \text{ now: } PDV_t = \frac{\$104}{1.04} = \frac{R_{t+1}}{1 + r}.$$

If the money were to be returned in two years, the present discounted value of this repayment would be

$$PDV_t = \frac{R_{t+2}}{(1 + r)^2},$$

and so on. It can be seen that the further in the future B expects to be paid, the less that payment is worth to her now.

This description simplifies reality somewhat. In the first place, returns (*R*'s) are *expected future returns*. While we take these as given, in reality future returns will vary with changes in current business conditions. This additional complication is added in Chapter 13, where we discuss investment demand in more detail. Furthermore, a firm is faced, in reality, with several interest rates in different kinds of bond and securities markets. These different interest rates, however, will probably move together when there are changes in monetary conditions, so that for simplicity we can treat them as one generalized interest rate r.

Now firms can rank various projects in order of their PDV's, as shown in Figure 4-1. With an elastic supply of investment funds, firms will invest in all projects with $PDV > 0$ (that is, having positive net returns). This would push the level of investment shown in Figure 4-1 to i_0. If a firm had only limited investment funds, it would invest them in the most productive projects (highest PDV's) until its funds ran out, at a point somewhere to the left of i.

Thus, in Figure 4-1, applying the PDV formula of equation (2) to its potential investment projects using r_0, the firm comes to an investment level i_0. If the interest rate were higher, all the entries in the PDV formula for each project would have a larger denominator, so the PDV of each project would be smaller. Therefore, as interest rates rise, all PDV's fall and the PDV curve of Figure 4-1 shifts down, reducing the level of planned investment.

This gives us the simplest investment model,

$$i = i(r), \tag{3}$$

with $i' < 0$ as shown in Figure 4-2. Increasing the interest rate r from r_0 to r_1 reduces the level of planned investment i from i_0 to i_1. Now, substituting the investment function (3) into the original equilibrium equation gives us the product-market equilibrium condition,

$$y = c(y - t(y)) + g + i(r). \tag{4}$$

Derivation of the *IS* Curve

Equation (4) now describes pairs of y and r values that will maintain equilibrium in what we will call the "product market." We can analyze the nature

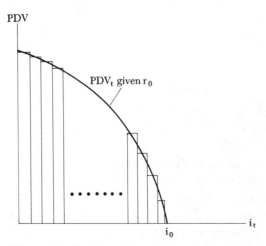

Figure 4-1 Ranking investment projects.

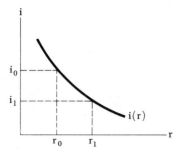

Figure 4-2 The investment demand function.

of these equilibrium pairs of y and r in several ways. First graphically: Figure 4-3 is by now familiar, with a fixed level of $i + g$ and with $s + t$ increasing with the level of income. From Figure 4-2 we know that an increase in r from r_0 to r_1 will cause a decrease in i. This decrease is represented in Figure 4-3 as a downward shift in the $i(r) + g$ line by the amount $\Delta i = i_1 - i_0$. At the original level of $i(r) + g$, with $r = r_0$, equilibrium income was at y_0. With the increase in r to r_1, equilibrium shifts to y_1, a lower level of income, due to the drop in planned investment. This relationship between equilibrium r and y can be represented directly as shown in Figure 4-4. As the interest rate r rises, the level of investment in Figure 4-3 falls, reducing equilibrium income through the multiplier. Thus, the line describing equilibrium pairs of r and y must be negatively sloped, as in Figure 4-4. This curve, showing equilibrium r, y points in the product market, is labeled *IS*. It describes the r, y combinations that maintain equality between planned $i + g$ and planned $s + t$.

The slope of the *IS* curve can also be derived with some simple mathematics. Totally differentiating equation (4) holding g constant gives us

$$dy = c' \cdot (dy - t'\, dy) + i'\, dr.$$

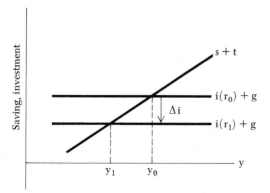

Figure 4-3 Equilibrium income with a change in the interest rate.

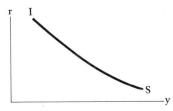

Figure 4-4 The *IS* curve: equilibrium *r* and *y* in the product market.

This equation does *not* represent a movement away from equilibrium, but rather gives changes in *y* and *r* that can occur simultaneously and *keep* the product market in equilibrium. Thus, it is also an equilibrium condition. Isolating terms containing dy and dr gives us

$$dy(1 - c'(1 - t')) = i' \, dr \quad \text{and} \quad \frac{dr}{dy} = \frac{1 - c'(1 - t')}{i'}$$

along the product-market equilibrium curve *IS*. Since we know that $1 - c'(1 - t') > 0$, and $i' < 0$, it is clear that $(dr/dy) < 0$. This shows that the slope of the *IS* curve in Figure 4-4, which represents the product-market equilibrium condition of equation (4), is negative. So now in the product market we have a whole series of equilibrium income levels, each corresponding to a given interest rate. We cannot find the equilibrium value for *r* or *y* without positing a value for the other.

All of the relationships discussed so far that contribute to the location of equilibrium pairs of *r* and *y* in the product market are summarized in the four-quadrant diagram in Figure 4-5. The southeast quadrant in Figure 4-5 is an "upside down" version of a graph similar to that shown in Figure 4-3 giving saving plus tax revenues as a function of income. To make the drawing easier, we have assumed that both savings and taxes are proportioned to income, so the $(s + t)$ schedule goes through the origin. No significant loss of generality is incurred by making use of this convenience. In the northwest quadrant we have plotted government spending, which is fixed by the budget and therefore a vertical line, plus investment, which is a decreasing function of *r*. The $i(r)$ line is similar to the one shown in Figure 4-2 but rotated 90°. The values of g and $i(r)$ are summed horizontally in this quadrant to give the $i(r) + g$ lines, which represent total expenditure on *i* plus *g* as a function of *r*. In the southwest quadrant we have drawn a 45° line from the origin. This line is used to equate $s + t$ from the southeast quadrant to $i + g$ in the northwest quadrant. Thus, it directly represents the equilibrium condition in the product market, given by equation (1).

It is the line in the northeast quadrant, the *IS* curve, representing equilibrium pairs of *r* and *y*, that we can now derive from these three other relationships. If we choose a level of income on the *y*-axis, we can trace through

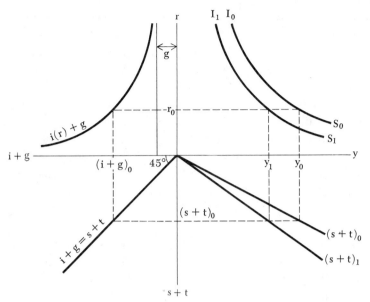

Figure 4-5   The *IS* curve: a shift in saving.

the three quadrants following the dashed line to locate the equilibrium interest rate for that level of income. For example, at income y_0 in equilibrium we would have planned $s + t$ at $(s + t)_0$. To generate an equal amount of $(i + g)_0$ the interest rate would have to be at r_0. This can be done for any level of y to give a corresponding level of r. Or, conversely, we can take the level of r as given and locate the equilibrium income level associated with that interest rate.

In other words, *the IS curve represents the pairs of r and y that will keep the product market in equilibrium, in the sense that planned investment plus government purchases equals planned saving plus tax revenue at that level of income.*

Shifting the *IS* Curve

The four-quadrant diagram is useful for studying the effects of changes in exogenous variables like g, or shifts in the investment, saving, or tax functions on the product-market equilibrium r and y levels.

For example, an increase in the desire to save, that is, a decrease in consumption demand at any given income level, can be shown as a downward rotation of the $s + t$ function to the $(s + t)_1$ function in Figure 4-5. This gives a higher level of $s + t$ for any given y. At the original level of the interest rate r_0, and planned $(i + g)_0$, this decrease in consumption demand will reduce equilibrium income through the multiplier process. Graphically, at old equilibrium r_0 and thus the old level of $i + g$, with the new $s + t$ function, we will trace out a new, lower equilibrium y_1 in Figure 4-5. Thus, the increase in the desire to save, reducing total demand at any given interest rate level, has shifted the *IS* curve to the left, giving a lower equilibrium y for any given r, or lower equilibrium r for any given y.

As another example of the use of the *IS* four-quadrant diagram, consider the effects of increasing government purchases, g, on the equilibrium r, y pairs, shown in Figure 4-6. The increase in g can be shown as an outward shift in the $i + g$ function in the northwest quadrant. This increase in g, as we saw in Chapter 3, will increase y through the multiplier, assuming investment is unchanged. Thus, in Figure 4-6, the increase in g from g_0 to g_1 ($= dg$) would raise y from y_0 to y_1 ($= dy$) at the initial interest rate r_0. Since $i = i(r)$, holding r constant here holds i constant.

For any initial level of r, the g increase has increased equilibrium y, shifting the *IS* curve to the right, as shown in Figure 4-6. At any given r, implying again an unchanged i, the ratio of the increase in y to the increase in g, dy/dg, is simply the multiplier of Chapter 3.

EQUILIBRIUM INCOME AND THE INTEREST RATE IN THE MONEY MARKET

So far we have developed one equilibrium equation in two variables, y and r, which gives us an infinity of potential equilibrium points known as the *IS* curve. In order to be able to locate a single equilibrium level of income and

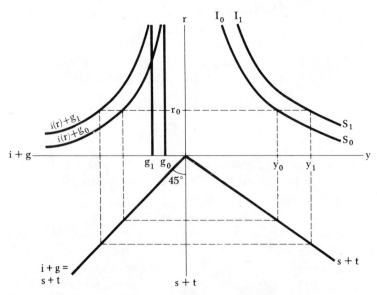

Figure 4-6 The *IS* curve: an increase in g.

the interest rate, we need another equation in the same two variables that can be solved simultaneously with our product-market equation. In order to obtain this second equation, we now introduce a *money market.*

We begin by defining money, *M,* as currency in circulation plus demand deposits, that is, checking account deposits in commercial banks. A more thorough and detailed analysis of the money supply is to be found in Chapter 15. Both kinds of money share the features of being an accepted unit of exchange and bringing a very low return. Currency, of course, earns no interest, and demand deposits earn almost zero after allowing for inflation and bank charges. On the other hand, most other kinds of liquid assets, which we will lump into a general category called *bonds,* do bring a return to the holder and cannot be used directly as a medium of exchange. With liquid assets thus defined as consisting of two categories, money and bonds, a person who has liquid assets can choose to put them into either money or bonds.

Demand for Money and Real Balances

The money market, like all other markets, has both a demand side and a supply side. We will first examine the demand side. Since people can put their liquid assets into either money or bonds, we might expect that an increase in the interest rate, or the rate of return on bonds, would tempt them to put more of their assets into bonds and less into money. Conversely, a decrease in the interest rate should induce them to shift some assets out of bonds and into money.

This inclination to hold more or less money depending on the interest rate on bonds we will call the speculative demand for money:

$$\text{Speculative demand} \equiv l(r).$$

Hence, *l* might stand for *liquidity preference,* as discussed in Chapter 14. Because the speculative demand for money will probably go down as interest rates go up, $l' < 0$.

There is another reason to hold money, creating another kind of demand for money. People hold money in order to bridge the time gap between their receipt of income and payments they have to make, that is, to smooth out the difference between monthly paychecks and daily payments for food and other items. As incomes rise, both income and expenditure streams grow, and these balances held to smooth out the cash flow must also grow. Therefore, this second kind of demand for money, which we call a *transactions demand,* increases with the level of income, or

$$\text{Transactions demand} \equiv k(y) \quad \text{and} \quad k' > 0.$$

Both components of the demand for money, the transactions demand and the speculative demand, should be stated as demand for real money balances, $M/P = m$. This is fairly evident in the transactions balance case. Suppose with a given real income y, the price level P doubles overnight so that money income Y and money expenditures also double. In this case, we should expect the transactions demand for money balances M also to double, since the money transactions which these balances are financing have doubled. Thus, the transactions demand $k(y)$ is for *real* balances; the demand for money balances is $P \cdot k(y)$.

Speculative demand should also be a demand for real balances. This is a little less obvious than the transactions balance case, but perhaps the following thought experiment will make things more clear. Suppose one night you go to bed holding a given amount of money depending on present interest rates and your expectation concerning the bond market. Overnight, the government changes currency units from old francs to new francs, with 10 old francs = 1 new franc. When you wake up in the morning, you find your salary is now 1,000 new francs, where it was previously 10,000 old francs, all prices in new francs are one-tenth of old franc prices, and your new franc money balances are one-tenth of their old franc value. Is there any reason for you to change your demand for money? No. All prices, incomes, and wealth values have changed proportionately, reduced to one-tenth their former values. Nothing really has changed.

But this is the same as if the price level just changed overnight by the same amount! With all prices changed, your income, in (new) money terms, is smaller, your expenditures are smaller, and your wealth is smaller; again, no real change has occurred. Thus, the speculative demand $l(r)$ is also a demand for real balances; the money balance demand would be $P \cdot l(r)$.

Summing the two components of the demand for money, we have the demand function for real balances, with $l' < 0$ and $k' > 0$.

$$\frac{M}{P} = l(r) + k(y) \tag{5}$$

In general, we should recognize that the speculative and transactions demands cannot be separated. For example, as the interest rate on bonds rises we would expect transactions balances to be reduced as people recognized the increasing opportunity cost of holding idle cash balances and squeezed them down. Thus, the demand-for-money function, in general, might be written as

$$\frac{M}{P} = m(r, y), \tag{6}$$

with $(\partial m/\partial r) < 0$ and $(\partial m/\partial y) > 0$, removing the separation of speculative and transactions demands. But for the time being we will stick with the approximation to $m(r, y)$ given in equation (5), mainly because it helps the graphical analysis of the next few chapters a good deal.

Figure 4-7 shows the money demand function of either equation (5) or (6). When we plot the demand for real balances against the interest rate r, we get a different curve for each level of income y. At any given level of y, say, y_0, which (more or less) fixes transactions demand, as r rises the speculative demand falls, reducing total demand. Also, at any given r, say, r_0, fixing speculative demand, as y rises transactions demand also rises, increasing total demand.

It may be useful here to discuss briefly the probable shape and curvature of the demand-for-money function. These will play an important role in the discussion of the relative effectiveness of monetary and fiscal policy in the next chapter. It also relates to the discussion in Chapter 8 of the infamous liquidity trap. At very high interest rate levels, speculative balances should be squeezed down to some irreducible minimum, giving a minimum demand for money with rising interest rates. At the other end, as interest rates fall lower and lower, people may become indifferent between holding, for example, 2 percent bonds and 0 percent money. Thus, the demand for money may become very flat at low interest rates. So the demand-for-money map might be drawn as in Figure 4-7, with the demand curves converging at both extremely high and extremely low interest rate levels.

On the supply side of the money market, we will assume that the amount of currency and demand deposits in the economy are fixed by institutional arrangements between the commercial banking system and the Federal Reserve Board. This is discussed in much more detail in Chapter 15. Thus, the money supply is fixed exogenously: $M = \bar{M}$.

Figure 4-8 is a graphic representation of the demand and supply situation we have so far described. Given the price level, the real money supply is fixed at the level $\bar{M}/P$. As in Figure 4-7, the demand for money is represented by

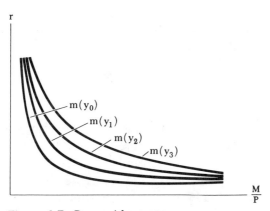

Figure 4-7 Demand for money.

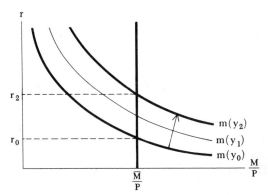

Figure 4-8 Demand and supply in the money market.

the functions $m(y_0)$, $m(y_1)$, and $m(y_2)$. At any given rate of interest, say, r_2, the total demand depends on the level of income.

From Figure 4-8 we see that as income rises from y_0 to y_1 to y_2, the money market equilibrium interest rate also rises, given the level of the real money supply. When income goes up, there is an increase in the transactions demand for money. Some present holders of interest-earning bonds need to shift into money due to their higher transactions needs. This reduction in demand in the bond market drives bond prices down and interest rates up. Thus, the excess demand for money at the old interest rate r_0 and the new income level y_2 drive interest rates up until supply equals demand at the new, higher, level of income y_2 and interest rate r_2.

Equating the money demand function to the exogenously fixed supply gives us the equilibrium condition in the money market:

$$\frac{\bar{M}}{P} = m(r, y) \approx l(r) + k(y). \tag{7}$$

Separating the speculative and transactions balances gives us a convenient way to represent money market equilibrium in another four-quadrant diagram that summarizes the money market relationships we have just discussed.

Derivation of the *LM* Curve

In the southeast quadrant of Figure 4-9 the line $k(y)$ gives transactions demand as an increasing function of income, measured downward. In the northwest quadrant is the curve representing the speculative demand as a function of the interest rate. This curve has a slope $l' < 0$, as we have seen in Figures 4-7 and 4-8. In the southwest quadrant we have used another geometric "trick," which represents the equilibrium condition (7), equating total supply of money

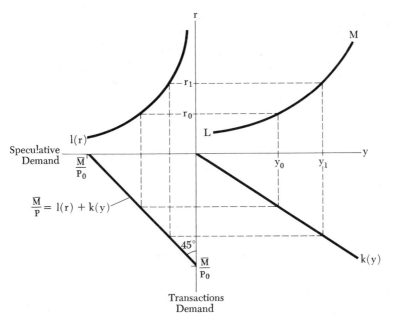

Figure 4-9 The *LM* curve: equilibrium *r* and *y* in the money market.

to total demand. This time we have drawn a line between the transactions demand axis and the speculative demand axis, at a 45° angle to each axis. The line is drawn at a distance from the origin on each axis equal to the total exogenously given real money supply, $\bar{M}/P_0$. Because of the geometric nature of the 45° triangle, the transactions demand and the speculative demand always add up to the total money supply on each axis, so that this 45° line directly represents money market equilibrium condition (7). Any point on this 45° line gives a transactions demand plus a speculative demand that just add up to the total money supply.

We can now locate in the northeast quadrant of Figure 4-9 the *r, y* pairs that maintain the money market in equilibrium. At a given level of income such as y_0, we can find transactions demand for money from the $k(y)$ function. By following the dashed line, we subtract this from supply, $\bar{M}/P_0$, to see what level of speculative demand this implies if the money market is to be in equilibrium. This level of speculative demand shows us, in turn, the level of interest rate r_0 that will maintain the money market in equilibrium with income level y_0. Having located one money market equilibrium pair, (r_0, y_0), we can locate another by beginning with y_1 in Figure 4-9. Repeating this process traces out the line that describes the set of *r, y* pairs that maintains money market equilibrium. This is the *LM* curve in Figure 4-9.

Thus, we can see that *the LM curve represents the pairs of r and y that will keep the money market in equilibrium with a given level of the money supply, M, and a given price level, P.*

By differentiation of the equilibrium condition, equation (7), and inspection of the results, we can see that the slope of the *LM* curve is positive:

$$\frac{\bar{M}}{P_0} = l(r) + k(y); \qquad 0 = l' \, dr + k' \, dy.$$

Thus,

$$\frac{dr}{dy} = -\frac{k'}{l'}$$

along the money market equilibrium curve *LM*. Since $k' > 0$ and $l' < 0$, $(dr/dy) > 0$, that is, the *LM* curve is positively sloped.

Shifting the *LM* Curve

This four-quadrant diagram is useful in analyzing the effects of changes in exogenous variables or shifts in the speculative demand or transactions demand functions on the equilibrium values of *r* and *y* in the money market. Looking back to Figure 4-8, for example, we see that an increase in the money supply creates an excess supply of money at the old level of income and interest rate. This excess supply pushes the equilibrium interest rate down, given the income level.

In Figure 4-9, an increase in the money supply will shift the $\bar{M}/P_0$ line out. With the increase in the real money supply, at any given level of income, corresponding to a given level of transactions demand, there is room within the money supply for an increased speculative demand. This implies, for money market equilibrium, a lower interest rate at each income level. This increase in the money supply thus shifts the *LM* curve to the right.

Here we should point out that a change in the price level, *P*, works symmetrically opposite to a change in the money supply, $\bar{M}$. For example, an increase in *P* reduces the supply of real balances, shifting the $\bar{M}/P$ line in Figure 4-9 in toward the origin. This reduction in the real money supply creates excess demand in the money market at the initial income and interest rate levels, causing interest rates to rise to clear the market. Thus, for any given level of income *y*, an increase in *P* raises the money market equilibrium *r*, shifting the *LM* curve to the left. This movement can be traced out in the four-quadrant diagram of Figure 4-9; it will play an important role in the derivation of the economy's demand curve later in this chapter.

EQUILIBRIUM IN THE PRODUCT AND MONEY MARKETS

We have now derived two pieces of geometric apparatus. One gives the equilibrium pairs of r and y in the product market—the IS curve—and the other gives the equilibrium pairs of r and y in the money market—the LM curve. By placing these two curves in the same quadrant, that is, by solving equations (4) and (7) simultaneously, we can find the single r, y pair that gives equilibrium in both markets, the intersection of the IS and LM curves. If the interest rate, income pair is at r_0, y_0 in Figure 4-10, both markets are in equilibrium, and there is no reason for either r or y to be changing. This is what is meant by *equilibrium*.

How the economy moves toward equilibrium if it begins from disequilibrium depends in general on how fast financial markets, including the money market, and goods markets react to disequilibrium. Financial markets have prices that adjust very rapidly; interest rates move every minute to equate supply and demand in the bond market. Goods markets react much more slowly. Sellers adjust price only occasionally in the face of unexpected changes in demand. So we think of the economy as being more or less continuously on the LM curve, moving gradually toward the IS curve.

This pattern of adjustment is shown in Figure 4-11. Beginning at an initial equilibrium r_0, y_0, suppose the money supply is increased so that the LM curve shifts from L_0M_0 to L_1M_1. (Go back to Figure 4-9 to see how this shift occurs!) At the initial equilibrium level of income y_0, the interest rate that clears the money market falls to r_1 (check this against Figure 4-8). At

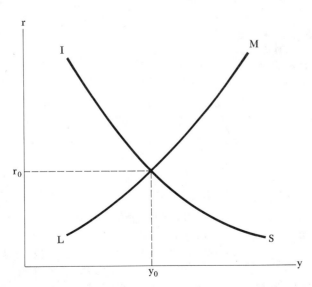

Figure 4-10 Equilibrium in the product and money markets.

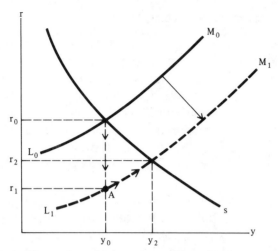

Figure 4-11 Adjustment to disequilibrium.

income level y_0 and interest rate r_1, the economy is to the left of the *IS* curve in Figure 4-11. The lower level of the interest rate r_1 means that investment $i(r)$ is larger than in the original equilibrium at r_0, y_0; *ex ante* $(i + g) >$ $(s + t)$, so inventories are falling and y is rising. Thus, at point A in Figure 4-11, output and income y are rising. This pulls up the demand for money, so as y rises, r also increases along the *LM* curve. This process continues until the economy reestablishes equilibrium at r_2, y_2.

The product and money markets thus interact to bring the economy toward the equilibrium intersection. Their interaction can be described as follows, using Figure 4-11:

increase in
money supply $\rightarrow$ fall in r $\rightarrow$ rise in i $\rightarrow$ increase in y $\rightarrow$ increase in
money demand

Eventually, the increase in income reestablishes equilibrium at r_2, y_2, with a higher level of income and a lower interest rate than the original equilibrium r_0, y_0.

Effect of an Increase in g

To see the effects of an increase in government spending, let's look at a case in which the government decides to increase spending in order to raise incomes. By using a diagram such as Figure 4-6, we can see that this shifts the *IS* curve out, giving a higher product-market equilibrium y for any given r. This shift is represented by the shift to I_1S_1 in Figure 4-12. At the initial level of the interest rate r_0, income begins to rise through the multiplier process. The increase in income causes an increase in the demand for transactions balances.

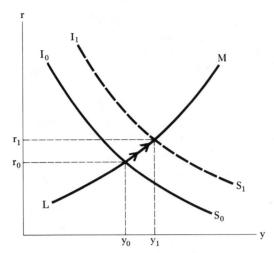

Figure 4-12　Increasing *g: IS* curve.

This creates excess demand in the money market, raising r. Eventually, a new equilibrium is reached at r_1, y_1.

　　Because investment is a function of r and $i' < 0$, the increase in equilibrium r leads to a reduction in equilibrium i. In other words, the increase in government spending causes a partial displacement of private investment. This displacement is smaller than the magnitude of the original increase in g, because both r and y rise from their initial equilibrium position.

　　Another way to look at the effect of the increase in g is that the government decision to spend more means it will have to increase borrowing. It does this by selling government bonds. To get people to buy the additional bonds, the government has to offer higher interest rates. Interest rates go up along with incomes, and the movement shown in Figure 4-12 begins. We see that equilibrium income goes up because of the increase in g. This means that more tax revenue will accrue to the government than at the earlier equilibrium level. This increase in tax revenue will cover part of the increased government expenditure, so that the amount the government borrows will be less than the increment to expenditure.

Effect of an Increase in *M*

As an alternative to increasing g to increase income, the government might increase the money supply. By examination of Figure 4-9, we can see that this will result in an outward shift of the *LM* curve, which will move the economy toward higher income at lower interest rates. This was shown in Figure 4-11. The increase in the money supply creates excess supply in the money market, pushing r down. This, in turn, increases investment demand, raising y. The increase in income will, of course, increase the demand for money. But the increase in demand will not offset the increased supply, so that interest rates will still go down. Thus, the main difference between the effects of increasing g or increasing M to raise the level of income in the economy is where the interest rate ends up. An increase in government spending raises interest rates, while an increase in the money supply lowers interest rates. For this reason, the two "tools"—fiscal policy changes in g or tax rates and monetary policy changes in M—are usually used together to achieve a desired mix of income expansion and control of interest rates. Chapter 5 looks at the effects of monetary and fiscal policy on the demand side of the economy in more detail. First, we will derive the economy's demand curve from the *ISLM* apparatus.

INCOME AND THE PRICE LEVEL ON THE DEMAND SIDE

In the previous section we saw how the intersection of the *IS* and *LM* curves determines the equilibrium level of income and the interest rate, *given the price level* P_0. Now we can derive the economy's demand curve by varying P and seeing what happens to the equilibrium real income level, y.

The two equilibrium conditions we have developed so far, for the product and money markets, are

$$s(y - t(y)) + t(y) = i(r) + g \tag{8}$$

and

$$\frac{\bar{M}}{P} = l(r) + k(y). \tag{9}$$

These are two equations in three variables, y, r, and P. In the *ISLM* analysis we assumed P to be given exogenously, eliminating one variable, and then solved for the equilibrium values of y and r at the intersection of the *IS* curve—equation (8)—and the *LM* curve—equation (9).

To analyze the effects of price level changes on equilibrium y on the demand side of the economy, we can use Figure 4-11. This reproduces the money market four-quadrant diagram behind the *LM* curve and then superimposes on it the *IS* curve of equation (8) to locate equilibrium r_0, y_0, given the initial price level P_0. We use the complete *LM* diagram with a given *IS* curve here because the price level P does not enter into equation (8), the *IS* product-market equilibrium condition, but it does enter equation (9). Thus, a change in P will not affect the position of the *IS* curve in this model, but it will shift the *LM* curve.

Suppose, now, from the initial price level P_0 in Figure 4-12, which gives equilibrium r_0, y_0, the price level *increases* to P_1, reducing the real money supply to $\bar{M}/P_1$. As can be seen in Figure 4-13, this shifts the *LM* curve to the left to L_1M_1 and moves the equilibrium point to r_1, y_1. Why is this?

The price level increase reduces the real money supply. This means that at any given real income level, the transactions demand for money rises, reducing the money free for speculative demand. For the market to clear, then, the interest rates must be higher for any given income level than they were with the initial price P_0. So when the price level increases—for whatever reason—the real money supply shrinks and excess demand is created in the money market. This can be seen by increasing P in Figure 4-8. This excess demand raises interest rates, reducing investment demand and equilibrium income. Gradually, the economy settles toward a new r_1, y_1 equilibrium with the new higher price level P_1. As Figure 4-13 shows, the new equilibrium y_1 is smaller than the initial y_0 because of the increase in P from P_0 to P_1.

If, from P_0, we had reduced the price level in Figure 4-13, increasing the real money supply, the equilibrium r, y point would have moved down the stationary *IS* curve, increasing the equilibrium y level. Thus, varying the (exogenously given, for the time being) price level produces opposite variations in the equilibrium level of output demanded in the economy: As P rises, y falls, and vice versa. This relationship is shown as the *economy's demand curve* of Figure 4-14. This curve is created by changing the price level in Figure 4-13 (from P_0 to P_1) and plotting against the price level the change in income

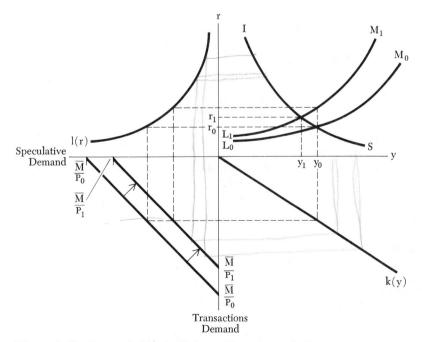

Figure 4-13 Demand-side equilibrium with a change in P.

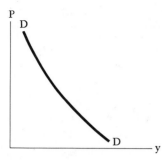

Figure 4-14 The economy's demand curve.

(from y_0 to y_1) caused by the shifting *LM* curve. The Figure 4-13 demand curve shows that *as the price level P increases, the equilibrium output y demanded in the economy decreases.*

The demand curve is derived by asking what happens to equilibrium output demanded as the price level changes, allowing other variables, such as the interest rate, also to adjust to their equilibrium levels. This brings out an important point. Changes in equilibrium variables on the demand side of the economy as a result of price changes are *movements along the demand curve.* Changes in exogenous variables on the demand side, such as *g* or *M* or the tax schedule, or shifts of functions like the saving function or the transactions demand for money, *shift the demand curve.* This distinction will become important when we have developed the supply side of the economy and can analyze how changes in exogenous variables *shift* the demand or supply curve, creating excess demand (or supply) and causing price changes that bring further adjustments *along* the demand and supply curves.

The other important point to notice about the Figure 4-14 demand curve is that it does *not* reflect the ordinary substitution effect of a rising price-reducing demand. Rather, the rising aggregate price level *P* reduces equilibrium output demanded, *y,* by tightening the money market, raising the interest rate, and thus reducing investment.

In the next chapter we use the algebraic and graphical representations of demand-side equilibrium to discuss the effects of monetary and fiscal policy changes. This offers us a chance to give our simple model a "workout," which is really the only way to learn the workings of the economy thoroughly.

SELECTED READINGS

R.G.D. Allen, *Macroeconomic Theory* (New York: St. Martin's Press, 1967), chapters 6–7.

A. Hansen, *Monetary Theory and Fiscal Policy* (New York: McGraw-Hill, 1949), chapter 12.

J.R. Hicks, "Mr. Keynes and the Classics," *Econometrica* (April 1937).

chapter *5*

An Introduction to Monetary and Fiscal Policy

Monetary and fiscal policies are generally thought of as *demand-management* policies. Since they deal with demand management, we can discuss their effects fairly thoroughly now before we go on to the supply side in Chapters 6 and 7. The purpose of monetary and fiscal policy, taken together, is to maintain output near full employment in the economy and to maintain the existing price level. The appearance of excess demand will probably cause inflation, while an insufficiency of demand will bring at least temporary unemployment and deflation.

In Chapter 4 we derived the economy's demand curve by finding, in the *ISLM* diagram, the equilibrium level of output demanded at each price level. This demand curve is shown as D_0D_0 in Figure 5-1. Thus, if the initial price level is P_0, the equilibrium output demanded will be y_0. Now suppose the economy has full-employment output level, y_F, which is determined by the existing labor force and capital stock. (The determination of the level of y_F is discussed at some length later in Part II and in Part IV.) If, as shown in Figure 5-1, equilibrium output demanded, y_0, is more than full-employment output, y_F, there will be excess demand in the economy, measured by $y_0 - y_F$, and the price level will be bid up, causing inflation. In this case the object of demand management (monetary and fiscal) policy would be to shift the demand curve down to D_1D_1 to eliminate the excess demand without inflation.

The case of deficient demand is shown in Figure 5-2. Suppose the demand curve D_0D_0 is initially lower than was shown in Figure 5-1, due, perhaps, to

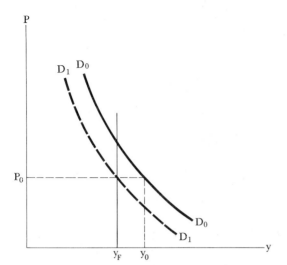

Figure 5-1 Excess demand and inflation.

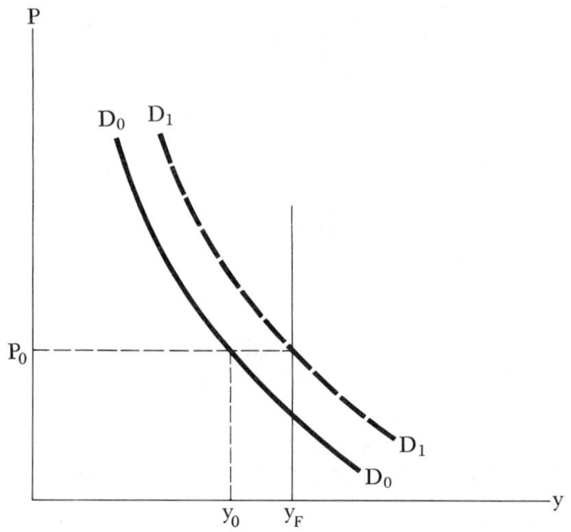

Figure 5-2 Deficient demand and unemployment.

lower investment demand. Then at the initial price level P_0, equilibrium output demanded could be less than full-employment output y_F, creating excess supply, or deficient demand, in the economy. This would tend to push prices down, and, at least temporarily, cause unemployment corresponding to the shortfall in demand measured by $y_F - y_0$ in Figure 5-2. In this case the objective of demand-management policy would be to shift the demand curve up to $D_1 D_1$, eliminating the deflationary gap and maintaining full employment.

The government can shift the economy's demand curve by manipulating its monetary and fiscal *policy instruments*. In the case of deficient demand in Figure 5-2, the demand curve can be shifted up by (a) a fiscal policy increase in government purchases, g; (b) a fiscal policy cut in the tax rate; (c) a monetary policy increase in the money supply, $\bar{M}$; or some combination of purchases, tax, and money supply changes. Thus, in this analysis, the instrument of monetary policy is the money supply, and the instruments of fiscal policy are the level of government purchases and the tax rate.

In Chapter 4 we briefly described how changes in the money supply shift the *LM* curve, while changes in the fiscal policy instruments shift the *IS* curve. Each of these changes also shifts the demand curve. Here we describe in more detail the effects of monetary and fiscal policy changes on the level of demand, both graphically, and algebraically. We see how the simple multipliers of Chapter 3 are modified by the introduction of the money market and how the size of these multipliers depends on whether the economy is initially near full employment or in a recession. We also discuss the effects of changes in monetary and fiscal policy on the composition of output at full employment—the division of output between c, i, and g—and take an initial look at some current issues in macroeconomic stabilization policy.

FISCAL POLICY EFFECTS ON DEMAND

In analyzing the effects of fiscal policy changes in g or tax rates on equilibrium output demanded, we use the four-quadrant diagram for the *IS* curve, shown in Figure 5-3. Since fiscal policy changes do not affect any of the curves underlying the *LM* curve, we can just add a fixed *LM* curve to the r, y quadrant in Figure 5-3, giving an initial equilibrium point r_0, y_0, corresponding to an initial price level. Fiscal policy changes will then shift the *IS* curve along the given *LM*, changing equilibrium output demanded, y, and the interest rate as well. Since the initial price level is held constant throughout, these changes in equilibrium output demanded, at a given price level, represent horizontal shifts in the demand curve equal to the change in equilibrium output. Thus, in analyzing fiscal policy shifts, we will also refer to Figure 5-4, which shows the demand curve D_0D_0 which corresponds to the initial *IS* curve in Figure 5-3, I_0S_0, with initial P_0 and y_0 corresponding to y_0 in Figure 5-3.

Now suppose with the initial level of government purchases g_0 and tax schedule t_0 in Figure 5-3, the resulting output level y_0 is below full employment. Then fiscal policy can increase equilibrium output, shifting the demand curve to the right, either by increasing g or by shifting the tax schedule down.

Changes in Government Spending, *g*

Consider first an increase in government purchases by Δg from g_0 to g_1 with the tax schedule unchanged at $t_0(y)$, as shown in Figure 5-3. The increase in g adds directly to real GNP and, through the multiplier, further increases y.

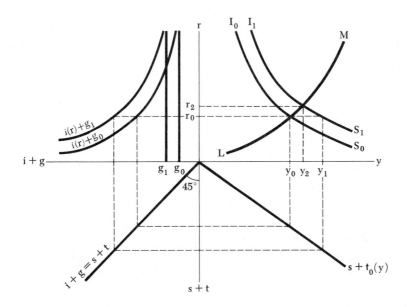

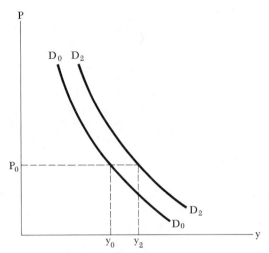

Figure 5-4 Fiscal policy change in *g:* demand curve.

If the interest rate did not rise from the initial level r_0 in Figure 5-3, so that investment $[i = i(r)]$ was not affected, equilibrium y would rise from y_0 to y_1. This measures the outward shift in *IS,* since y_1 is the new equilibrium y if the old interest rate had been maintained. As we see in the next section, the ratio $(y_1 - y_0)/\Delta g$ is the multiplier of Chapter 3, which assumed investment to be fixed exogenously, the equivalent of a constant r here.

But the interest rate must rise from r_0 following the Δg. With a fixed level of real money balances $(=\bar{M}/P_0)$, the increase in y raises the demand for money, pulling interest rates up along the *LM* curve. In the background, the g increase raises the government deficit, increasing the amount of bonds the government sells. To sell more bonds, that is, buy more money to finance the Δg increase, the government must raise the interest rate it pays. In general, the increase in bond supply raises interest rates in the bond market, the other side of the coin to the money market rise in r, shown in Figure 5-3.

The increase in interest rates, along *LM,* reduces the level of investment demand, tending to offset the increase in government spending. Again, in the bond market the increase in government borrowing squeezes out borrowing by corporations buying plant and equipment and especially borrowing by house builders, reducing the level of investment. The reduced level of investment moves the new equilibrium level of output demanded down from y_1 to y_2, with the interest rate rising from r_0 to r_2. This increase in equilibrium demand-side y is reflected in the shift in the Figure 5-4 demand curve from $D_0 D_0$ to $D_2 D_2$, with y rising from y_0 to y_2 at the initial price level P_0.

Here we can summarize the results of the fiscal policy increase in g on the demand side. With income increased and the tax rate unchanged, both disposable income and consumer spending are higher. Government purchases have risen, and, with an interest rate increase, the level of investment has fallen, partially offsetting the g increase. We know the offset is only partial because for y to go up in the end, the $i + g$ sum must have risen. Thus, increasing g to raise equilibrium y shifts the mix of output away from investment and toward g, and also raises consumer spending.

Changes in the Tax Schedule, $t(y)$

Much the same effects on the level of y and r [and thus $i(r)$] could be obtained by permanently reducing tax rates or increasing transfer payments instead of raising government purchases. The main difference between these two expansionary fiscal policy steps is in the resulting mix of output: With an equal effect on y, r, and investment, a tax reduction favors consumer expenditure, while a g increase obviously increases the government share of output.

The result of a tax reduction is shown in the four-quadrant diagram of Figure 5-5. Here we essentially assume that the tax schedule is proportional, that is,

$$t_0(y) = \tau_0 y, \tag{1}$$

so that tax revenues $t_0(y)$ are a constant fraction, τ_0, of y. Then the tax cut just reduces the proportional tax rate from τ_0, say, 25 percent, to τ_1, say, 20 percent. This simplification will come in handy when we compute the tax rate multiplier a bit later.

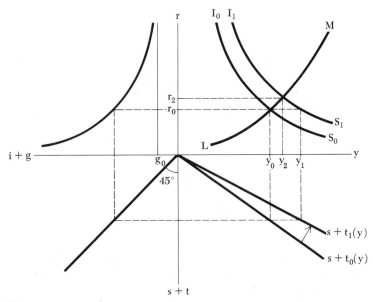

Figure 5-5 Fiscal policy change in $t(y)$: *IS* curve.

The downward rotation of the tax schedule increases the level of equilibrium income at any given interest rate. The alert observer might notice that since the Δg level is the same regardless of the y level while the $t(y)$ change is bigger at higher y levels, the tax change will result in a slightly flatter slope of the IS curve.

From the basic equilibrium condition

$$i(r) + g = y - c(y - t(y)) = s(y - t(y)) + t(y), \tag{2}$$

we can see that if $i(r_0)$ and g are unchanged, and the tax cut raises disposable income $y - t(y)$, raising consumption, y must increase to maintain $y - c$ equal to $i(r) + g$. Essentially, with a given r_0 maintaining i fixed, the change in disposable income at the initial income level y_0, that is, $t_0(y_0) - t_1(y_0)$, generates a policy-induced increase in consumer spending that has the same effects as the Δg considered earlier. If r_0 were maintained, equilibrium output demanded would rise to y_1 through the multiplier effect.

But the increase in income again creates excess demand in the money market, raising r along LM. In the bond markets, the increase in the deficit generated by the tax cut increases the supply of bonds as the government increases borrowing. This squeezes out borrowing for plant and equipment investment and house building, reducing investment to offset partially the exogenous increase in consumer spending. In the end, equilibrium demand-side output rises to y_2 and the interest rate rises to r_2. The demand curve shifts out much the same as in Figure 5-3, with equilibrium y increasing from y_0 to y_2 at the initial price level P_0.

The main difference between the effects of a government purchases increase and a tax cut that yield about the same final level of y and r is in the composition of the final y. Since r rises about the same in both cases, the final level of investment is the same. But where in the Δg case government purchases rose, providing the initial fiscal policy stimulus, here g has remained the same throughout. The stimulus here has come from the initial increase in consumer spending following the tax cut, and this has increased the consumers' share of output. In fact, since the secondary multiplier effects of policy-induced c and g changes are the same in this fairly simple model, the entire difference in the final composition of output is that the increase in g in the first case has been replaced by an increase in c in this tax policy case, giving the same level of final y and i in the final equilibrium.

The Multiplier for g Changes

The last section described the effects of government spending and tax rate changes using mainly the $ISLM$ diagram. The IS curve represents the product-market equilibrium condition

$$y = c(y - t(y)) + i(r) + g, \tag{3}$$

and the *LM* curve represents the money market equilibrium condition

$$\frac{\bar{M}}{P_0} = l(r) + k(y). \tag{4}$$

The various functions in equations (3) and (4) are shown in Figure 5-6(a)–(e). Both the tax and consumption functions have slopes that are positive but less than one, that is, $0 < c', t' < 1$. The slopes of the investment and speculative demand for money functions are negative; i' and $l' < 0$. The transactions demand function has a positive slope, $k' > 0$.

As we saw graphically in the previous section, the increase in y following an increase in g will be smaller in this two-equation model than it was in the simple multiplier models of Chapter 3. We can see this more precisely by developing an expression for the government purchases multiplier that includes this money market effect on i and r. Differentiating the *IS* equation (3), we obtain

$$dy = c' \cdot (dy - t' \, dy) + i' \, dr + dg = c'(1 - t')dy + i' \, dr + dg.$$

Differentiating the *LM* equation (4), holding $\bar{M}/P_0$ constant, we get

$$0 = l' \, dr + k' \, dy,$$

so that

$$dr = -\frac{k'}{l'} \, dy.$$

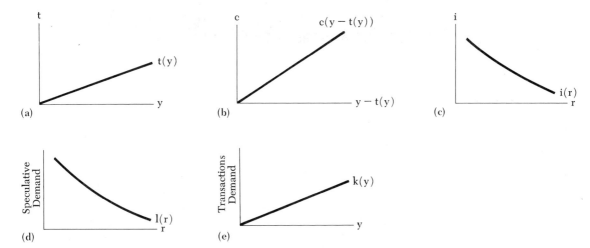

Figure 5-6 Basic function library.

Notice here that the expression $-(k'/l')$ is simply the slope of the LM curve. The last equation tells us how much r must rise along the LM curve to maintain market equilibrium with a given increase in income.

Substituting this expression for dr into the IS differential, we get

$$dy = c'(1 - t')dy - \frac{i'k'}{l'}\,dy + dg,$$

so that the final multiplier expression is

$$dy = \frac{1}{1 - c'(1 - t') + \dfrac{i'k'}{l'}}\,dg. \tag{5}$$

Since $c'(1 - t')$ is less than one and $(i'k')/l'$ is positive (both i' and l' are negative), the multiplier is positive.

The g multiplier developed in Chapter 3 was simply $1/[1 - c'(1 - t')]$. The multiplier in (5) is smaller than this because of the additional positive term in the denominator. What is the meaning of this term?

First, since $-k'/l'$ is the slope of LM, it gives the increase in r that is needed for money market equilibrium with the increase in y. Second, since i' gives the change in i that comes from a change in r, the expression $(i'k')/l'$ then gives the decrease in investment that comes from the interest rate increase as y and r rise along the LM curve.

If the LM curve were flat with zero slope, so that $-(k'/l') = 0$, the multiplier in (5) would be the same as the original multiplier of Chapter 3. In Figure 5-7, the distance from y_0 to y_1 is measured by the multiplier $1/[1 - c'(1 - t')]$ with no money market effects, that is, with the interest rate held constant. The distance from y_0 to y_2 is given by the full multiplier of equation (5), which includes the money market effect on i in the denominator.

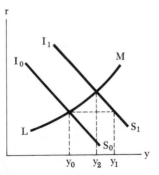

Figure 5-7 Money market effects on the fiscal multiplier.

To give a rough idea of the magnitude of the multiplier, suppose that the marginal propensity to consume (c') is 0.8 and that the marginal tax rate is 0.25. The interest rate effect on investment is probably quite small, say $i' = -0.02$, at least in the short run. Following the research of Stephen Goldfeld (reported more fully in Chapter 14), a rough estimate of the income sensitivity of money demand would be 0.1, while the interest rate derivative (l') might equal about -0.05. Substituting these values into equation (5) gives us

$$dy = \frac{1}{1 - (0.8)[1 - (0.25)] + \dfrac{(-0.02)(0.1)}{(-0.05)}} dg$$

$$= \frac{1}{1 - 0.6 + 0.04} dg$$

$$= \frac{1}{0.44} dg = 2.275\, dg.$$

Thus, the multiplier for changes in government spending is a bit over two in the short run of perhaps two years.

The Effectiveness of Fiscal Policy

The multiplier formula of equation (5) also points out that the size of the fiscal policy multiplier itself, or the effectiveness of fiscal policy, depends on whether the fiscal policy change is initiated at a low or high level of output relative to full-employment output. This point is illustrated in Figure 5-8 which shows the differing effect on y of a given IS shift, depending on where on the LM curve the action begins.

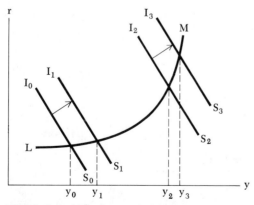

Figure 5-8 Effectiveness of fiscal policy.

At the initial equilibrium y_0, the LM curve is relatively flat, so that its slope, $-(k'/l')$, is nearly zero. This gives a large fiscal policy multiplier, nearly equal to $1[1 - c'(1 - t')]$, the simple value without any money market effects. But at the initial equilibrium point y_2, the LM curve is nearly vertical, with a slope $-(k'/l')$ that is very large. In this case the fiscal policy multiplier is extremely small, approaching zero as the LM curve becomes vertical.

Thus, the size of the fiscal policy multiplier depends on the slope of the LM curve at the initial equilibrium point. A given increase in g and shift in IS will yield a large increase in y, if the economy begins at a point of high unemployment and low interest rates. But if the g increase comes in a tight economy near full employment, there will be little effect on y, with a large increase in r squeezing out an amount of investment demand nearly equal to the g increase.

The economic explanation of this difference is as follows: With a given supply of real money balances $\bar{M}/P_0$ (which fixes the position of the LM curve), at the low level of r and y, there is, loosely speaking, a lot of money in speculative balances that can be drawn out to finance a higher level of transactions, that is, a higher y, by a small increase in interest rates. But at the higher level of r and y, at y_2 in Figure 5-8, the amount of funds in speculative balances is very small, and the increase in demand for money from a rising y serves mostly to raise r, reducing investment, rather than bringing funds out of speculative balances in any substantial amount.

The main point of this section is that the size of the Δg multiplier itself depends on the initial cyclical position of the economy. Thus, it is not surprising that some investigators have found the multiplier "unstable" looking at data, say, since World War II. Of course it is unstable; the data include the initial conditions of the 1958 recession with unemployment at 7 percent and short-term interest rates at 1.8 percent, as well as the boom conditions of 1968 with unemployment at 3.5 percent and short-term rates at 5.3 percent. But the conclusion should not be that fiscal policy is not effective because the multiplier seems unstable. Rather, its effectiveness varies over the cycle, and in anticipating the effects of any given Δg at any given time, a prudent analyst must take into consideration the initial state of the economy rather than simply relying on a multiplier like the $1/[1 - c'(1 - t')]$ of Chapter 3.

The Multiplier for Tax Rate Changes

With the development of the multiplier for Δg behind us, we can go fairly quickly through the tax rate multiplier. To begin with, we make the simplifying assumption that the tax system is proportional and that we are looking at a proportional change in all tax rates. This simplifies the algebra considerably, with no effects whatsoever on the qualitative results. This tax assumption is illustrated in Figure 5-9. We assume the tax function $t(y)$ is τy, that is, a tax rate τ times income y. With this tax function we can easily develop the effects of changing (here reducing) the tax rate from τ_0 to τ_1 in Figure 5-9.

Again, we begin with the *IS* and *LM* equilibrium equations,

$$y = c(y - \tau y) + i(r) + g \tag{6}$$

and

$$\frac{\bar{M}}{P_0} = l(r) + k(y). \tag{7}$$

Differentiating the *IS* equation (6) gives us

$$dy = c' \cdot (dy - \tau_0\, dy - y\, d\tau) + i'\, dr + 0$$

$$= c'(1 - \tau_0)dy - c'y\, d\tau + i'\, dr.$$

The last two terms in the disposable income $(y - \tau y)$ differential come from the approximation that $d(\tau y) = \tau\, dy + y\, d\tau$. Again, from the *LM* equation (7) we have

$$dr = -\frac{k'}{l'}\, dy,$$

so that substitution into the dy equation gives us

$$dy = c'(1 - \tau_0)dy - c'y\, d\tau - \frac{i'k'}{l'}\, dy$$

and

$$dy = \frac{-c'y}{1 - c'(1 - \tau_0) + \dfrac{i'k'}{l'}}\, d\tau. \tag{8}$$

The numerator of the tax rate multiplier in (8) simply converts the tax change into the policy-induced change in consumer expenditure. The term $y\, d\tau$ is the change in disposable income that comes directly from the tax rate

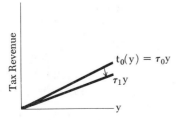

Figure 5-9 Proportional tax function.

change, $d\tau$. Then the term $c' \, y \, d\tau$ is the change in consumption spending that comes from this change in disposable income, and the minus sign says that when tax rates go up, the policy-induced consumption change is negative.

The simplifying assumption for the tax multiplier of equation (8) that the tax function $t(y) = \tau y$ means that the slope of the tax function t' is τ, in this special case $(dt(y)/dy = \tau)$. This makes the denominator of the tax multiplier (8) the same as the denominator of the government purchases multiplier (5). Since these two are the same, interpreting the numerator of the tax multiplier $-c'y \, d\tau$ as the direct change in consumption following from a tax change makes the multipliers for tax changes and g changes essentially the same. To get the effect of a g change, dg, or a consumption change induced by $d\tau$, $-c'y \, d\tau$, on equilibrium demand-side income and output, we multiply by

$$\frac{1}{1 - c'(1 - \tau) + \dfrac{i'k'}{l'}} .$$

The similarity between the g and t multipliers tells us that the effects of fiscal policy changes in g or t on the level of total output y will be roughly the same. But there are two major differences between fiscal policy changes in g and in tax rates. First, there will be a difference in the composition of the new equilibrium output. Expanding output by increasing g also will increase the government's share of output. But a tax cut shifts the initial stimulus to a policy-induced increase in consumer spending, raising the share of output going to consumers. Thus, the choice between cutting taxes or increasing government purchases to expand output and reduce unemployment will in part depend on a judgment on the relative social benefits of more consumer expenditure as opposed to more resources going into the production of public goods. This was one of the points of debate within the Kennedy Administration prior to the proposal of the 1964 tax cut. With unemployment near 6 percent and the economy expanding too slowly, the debate was whether to increase government purchases g, increasing the provision of public goods, or to cut taxes, placing more emphasis on consumer spending.

The second major difference between g and t changes stems from the fact that a tax cut will affect the economy only if consumers increase their spending as a result, so that the direct policy-induced consumption stimulus does, in fact, appear. There is always the possibility that consumers will save the additional disposable income, leaving the total $s + t(y)$ schedule unchanged with no effect on y. To a certain extent, but in the other direction, this happened with the income tax surcharge in 1968. When the surcharge was passed, raising taxes, consumers paid about half of the additional tax out of saving and half out of consumption, thus reducing the effect on y.

This problem does not occur with g changes though, since the government can make sure that g changes by the desired amount. Thus, there is more certainty of achieving the desired effect on y if fiscal policy changes come in government purchases, rather than in tax and transfer payment changes. Also, it seems likely that permanent tax rate changes will have a greater effect than temporary changes that may well be compensated by temporary changes in saving.

The Balanced-Budget Multiplier

The balanced-budget multiplier for equal changes in g and tax revenues is also reduced from its value of unity in Chapter 3 by the introduction of money market effects. To see this, we will introduce a different simplifying assumption on the tax schedule, namely, that tax revenues are fixed exogenously: $t(y) = \bar{t}$. This makes the analysis of the effects of an equal change in g and $\bar{t}$ fairly simple. Again, we begin with the IS and LM equations,

$$y = c(y - \bar{t}) + i(r) + g \qquad (9)$$

and

$$\frac{\bar{M}}{P_0} = l(r) + k(y). \qquad (10)$$

Differentiation of (9) gives us

$$dy = c' \cdot (dy - d\bar{t}) + i' \, dr + dg$$
$$= c' \, dy - c' \, d\bar{t} + i' \, dr + dg.$$

The LM equation (10) gives us $dr = -(k'/l')dy$, and substitution into the dy equation yields

$$dy = c' \, dy - c' \, d\bar{t} - \frac{i'k'}{l'} \, dy + dg$$

and

$$dy = \frac{dg - c' \, d\bar{t}}{1 - c' + \dfrac{i'k'}{l'}}.$$

If the government purchases and tax increases are of equal size, so that $dg = d\bar{t}$, the last expression gives us the expanded balanced-budget multiplier:

$$dy = \frac{1 - c'}{1 - c' + \dfrac{i'k'}{l'}} \, dg. \qquad (11)$$

Introduction of money market effects on investment through the last term in the denominator in (11) has reduced the value of the balanced-budget multiplier. If the LM curve were flat at the initial value of y, that is, if r and $i(r)$ were fixed, then the slope of LM, $- k'/l'$ would be zero and the balanced-budget multiplier in (11) would be $(1 - c')/(1 - c') = 1$. But with the introduction of the money market, we see that as y rises with a balanced change in government purchases and revenues, the demand for money for transactions purposes goes up, raising the interest rate and reducing investment. This partially offsets the initial increase in y, giving a final expansion of y that is less than the initial $dg = d\bar{t}$.

MONETARY POLICY EFFECTS ON DEMAND

To analyze the effects of monetary policy changes in the money supply, $\bar{M}$, we will use the four-quadrant LM diagram, shown in Figure 5-10. Since in this section we will be holding the fiscal policy variables and the saving and investment functions behind the IS curve constant, we can add a fixed IS curve to Figure 5-10. This establishes initial equilibrium values of y_0 and r_0, given the price level P_0 and the initial level of the money supply $\bar{M}_0$.

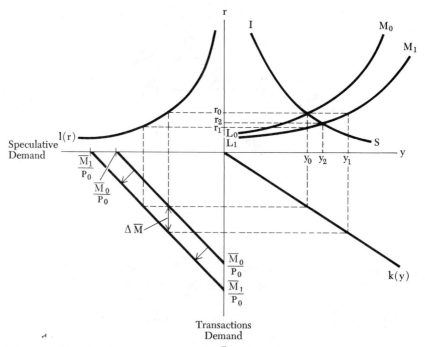

Figure 5-10 Monetary policy change in $\bar{M}$: LM curve.

Monetary policy changes in $\bar{M}$ will now shift the LM curve along the given IS curve, changing the interest rate and the equilibrium output demanded. These changes in output demanded, *at the given price level,* produce horizontal shifts in the economy's demand curve. This was shown in Figure 5-4 and is reproduced here as Figure 5-11. The $D_0 D_0$ demand curve corresponds to the fixed IS in Figure 5-10 and the initial level of the money supply, $\bar{M}_0$. The initial y_0 and P_0 of Figure 5-11 are the same as those of Figure 5-10.

Changes in the Money Supply, $\bar{M}$

If the initial equilibrium value of real output y_0 is below full-employment output, the demand curve can be shifted to the right by fiscal policy changes, as we have seen above, or by an increase in the money supply. This is illustrated in Figure 5-10, where the money supply is increased by $\Delta \bar{M}$ from $\bar{M}_0$ to $\bar{M}_1$. At the initial equilibrium level of output and income, y_0, this increase in the money supply would push the interest rate down to r_1 to maintain equilibrium in the money market. Thus, the $\Delta \bar{M}$ shifts the LM curve down (or to the right) by an amount measured by $r_0 - r_1$ at the initial y_0 level.

Another way to measure the LM shift is to assume that the interest rate remains at r_0, fixing the level of speculative demand for money. In this case, all of the $\Delta \bar{M}$ increase would be available for transactions balances to support a higher level of y. The increase in y that would absorb the money supply increase into transactions balances at the old r_0 is shown in Figure 5-10 as $y_1 - y_0$. Thus, the point r_0, y_1 would also maintain the money market in equi-

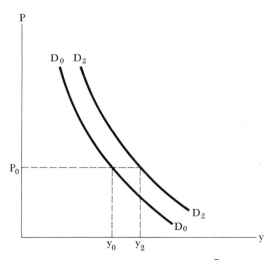

Figure 5-11 Monetary policy change in $\bar{M}$: demand curve.

librium and is on the new LM curve, L_1M_1. The distance $y_1 - y_0$ measures the outward shift in LM at the initial interest rate r_0.

When the money supply is increased, initially the interest rate will tend to fall toward r_1 at the initial y_0 in Figure 5-10. But this drop in r increases investment demand, raising the level of output and income, moving the economy from r_1, y_0 over toward the IS curve. The income increase, in turn, raises the transactions demand for money, pulling the interest rate back up. In the end, the economy comes to the equilibrium point r_2, y_2 with both the product market and money market in equilibrium.

In the bond market in the background, the central bank increases the money supply by buying bonds (selling money). This increase in bond demand raises bond prices, reducing interest rates. Firms find it easier (and cheaper) to borrow to finance investment projects, so investment demand goes up, moving the economy toward equilibrium at r_2, y_2.

The movement from the old equilibrium y_0 to the new y_2 at the original price level P_0 is also reflected in a shift of the demand curve in Figure 5-11 to D_2D_2, giving a higher level of equilibrium output demanded at any given price level. Here monetary policy has shifted the demand curve; back in Figure 5-4 it was fiscal policy. The same increase in income could be achieved by an appropriately sized change in any of the three major policy instruments: g, t, or $\bar{M}$.

The monetary policy increase in $\bar{M}$ has reduced the interest rate and raised investment and equilibrium output and income. The income increase, with a given tax schedule, has increased consumer spending, while government purchases remain unchanged. Thus, monetary policy has a different effect on the composition of output than do fiscal policy changes in g or $t(y)$. Here the policy-induced expenditure effect comes through a change in investment demand. Government purchases remain unchanged, and consumer expenditure goes up only endogenously. We can summarize these compositional effects by looking at the basic national income identity,

$$y = c + i + g. \tag{12}$$

For a given increase in income and output, y, each of the policies gives about the same endogenous consumption increase through the multiplier. The difference lies in the source of the policy-induced expenditure change. An increase in government spending raises g and reduces i somewhat, raising the proportion of g in the use of output relative to c or i in the final equilibrium position. A tax cut gives a direct c increase and also reduces i somewhat, raising the proportion of c. Finally, a money supply increase gives a policy-induced increase in i, raising the fraction of investment in the final equilibrium position. Thus, a choice of which policy instrument to use to *expand* (or contract) output will, in part, depend on how the policy maker wants the *composition* of output to change.

The Multiplier for Changes in $\bar{M}$

As usual, we can develop the multiplier for changes in $\bar{M}$ on y beginning with the IS and LM equilibrium equations. The product-market equation is

$$y = c(y - t(y)) + i(r) + g. \tag{13}$$

The money market equation is

$$\frac{\bar{M}}{P_0} \equiv m = l(r) + k(y). \tag{14}$$

Since we are focusing on equilibrium demand-side output and employment in this chapter, we are holding P_0 constant. This enables us to introduce a new variable in (14), $m \equiv \bar{M}/P_0$. Since $dm = d\bar{M}/P_0$, we can conduct the analysis in terms of a change in real balances, dm, which is the same as the change in nominal money supply, $d\bar{M}$, with the price level held constant. Differentiating the LM equation (14) gives us

$$\frac{d\bar{M}}{P_0} = dm = l' \, dr + k' \, dy$$

and

$$dr = \frac{dm}{l'} - \frac{k'}{l'} \, dy.$$

As usual, differentiation of the IS equation yields

$$dy = c'(1 - t')dy + i' \, dr,$$

with g constant so that $dg = 0$. Substituting the previous expression for dr, we have

$$dy = c'(1 - t')dy + \frac{i'}{l'} \, dm - \frac{i'k'}{l'} \, dy$$

and

$$dy = \frac{\dfrac{i'}{l'}}{1 - c'(1 - t') + \dfrac{i'k'}{l'}} \, dm \tag{15}$$

as the multiplier expression for the money supply change, dm.

The denominator of the multiplier in (15) is the same as that for the g and t multipliers. But how is the numerator to be interpreted? From the discussion in the previous section, we might expect this to turn out to be the change in investment induced directly by dm. Referring back to the money market equilibrium condition, (14), which is also the demand equation for real balances m set equal to a fixed supply $\bar{m}$, we see that the partial derivative of m with respect to r is l', so that in (15) the expression dm/l' is the drop in r initially induced by the dm increase. Then, since i' is the increase in investment with a drop in r, $i' \cdot dm/l'$ is the investment increase resulting from the drop in r induced by dm—the policy-induced investment change. So the $\bar{M}$ multiplier in (15) is the usual multiplier

$$\frac{1}{1 - c'(1 - t') + \dfrac{i'k'}{l'}}$$

times the initial i change induced directly by dm.

We can calculate a rough and ready estimate of the monetary policy multiplier by recalling the fiscal multiplier estimated on page 83. As a first approximation, we have already from the fiscal policy calculation,

$$dy = \frac{1}{1 - c'(1 - t') + \dfrac{i'k'}{l'}} \, dg = \frac{1}{0.44} \, dg = 2.275 \, dg.$$

The estimates for i' and l' in equation (15) were given there as $i' = -0.02$ and $l' = -0.05$. So, substituting into equation (15) for the money multiplier, we obtain

$$dy = \frac{(-0.02)/(-0.05)}{0.44} \, dm$$

$$= \frac{0.04}{0.44} \, dm = 0.91 \, dm.$$

This value of dy/dm of about unity is consistent with a fairly constant income velocity of money (y/m) over time.

The multiplier on m in equation (15) can be interpreted further with the help of Figure 5-12. At the initial level of income, y_0, the shift in the LM curve due to dM would reduce r to r_1. If the LM curve were flat, so that $(k'/l') = 0$, the subsequent increase in y to y_1 would be equal to

$$\frac{i'/l'}{1 - c'(1 - t')} \, dm.$$

But with the positive slope of the new LM curve, L_1M_1, the y change is reduced to $y_2 - y_0$ with the introduction of the $i'k'/l'$ term in (15).

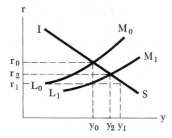

Figure 5-12 The money supply multiplier.

The Effectiveness of Monetary Policy

As was the case with fiscal policy, the effectiveness of monetary policy will vary with the cyclical position of the economy. As Figure 5-13 shows, with a given slope of the *IS* curve, a given shift in the *LM* curve due to an increase in the money supply will have a greater effect on y at high levels of y and r than at low levels.

This can also be seen from the *dm* multiplier in equation (15). Multiplying both numerator and denominator of (15) by l', which is negative, gives us

$$dy = \frac{i'}{l'[1 - c'(1 - t')] + i'k'} \, dm. \qquad (16)$$

Note here that since i' and l' are both negative, the multiplier dy/dm given by equation (16) is still positive, with both the numerator and denominator negative.

Now, if l' is a very large negative number, approaching minus infinity, the denominator of (16) will be very large, so that an increase in m will have very little effect on y. From the four-quadrant diagram of Figure 5-14, it is

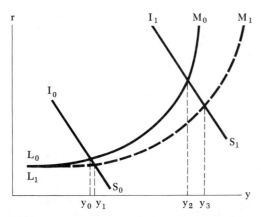

Figure 5-13 The effectiveness of monetary policy.

clear that when the $l(r)$ curve is very flat, the LM curve is flat and the economy is at a low level of y and r. At that low level of r, people may be relatively indifferent between holding money and bonds, so that speculative balances absorb an increase in $\bar{M}$ with little effect on r and thus little effect on i and y.

On the other hand, if l' is a very small negative number, approaching zero, the first term in the denominator of (16) will be near zero, so that the multiplier will approach the value $i'/(i'k') = 1/k'$. From Figure 5-14, it is clear that at high interest rates where the $l(r)$ curve is steep, the LM curve is nearly vertical. Thus, in this area of the LM curve, the effect of an increase in $\bar{M}$ on y will be greatest, since the first term in the denominator of (16) will be nearly zero. In this area of r, y speculative balances have been squeezed to a minimum by the high r, so that almost all of $\bar{M}$ is used to finance transactions, and the limit on y is the availability of $\bar{M}$. Since k' is the increase in transactions demand with a unit increase in y, $1/k'$, the value of the multiplier when LM is vertical gives the increase in y that is possible with a $d\bar{M}$ increase if it all goes to finance additional y. So monetary policy has its maximum effectiveness when the economy is at high r, y levels and is utilizing almost all of the money supply to finance transactions, that is, to support y.

THE INTERACTION OF MONETARY AND FISCAL POLICIES

In the previous sections of this chapter, we discussed the relative effectiveness of monetary and fiscal policies in relation to the cyclical position of the economy. The likelihood that the policy instruments g, $t(y)$, and $\bar{M}$ differ in the certainty of their results was also mentioned. In addition, it should by now be

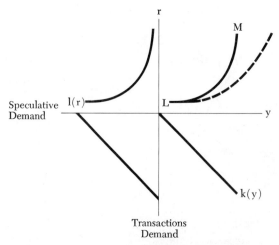

Figure 5-14 The slope of $l(r)$ and the LM curve.

apparent that changes in these policy instruments can be combined in many different ways to achieve a desired position of the economy's demand curve. We end this introductory chapter on monetary and fiscal policy as demand-management tools first by summarizing what has already been said on relative effectiveness and certainty of results. Then we look at the interaction between monetary and fiscal policies in two important cases: first, where they work in opposite directions to change the interest rate and the composition of output at a given level of output; and second, where they work in the same direction to achieve a desired shift in the demand curve and change in y, given P_0.

The Effectiveness and Certainty of Monetary and Fiscal Policy

The relative effectiveness of monetary and fiscal policy, depending on the shape of the LM curve and the economy's initial position, can be summarized by reference to Figure 5-15. If the economy is in an initial position such as r_1, y_1 of Figure 5-15, an expansionary monetary policy, shifting LM right, may have little effect on y, since at that low interest rate the additional money would be absorbed by speculative balances and not become available to finance a substantial increase in y. On the other hand, at r_1, y_1, a shift in the IS curve will be relatively effective in raising y, since a small increase in the interest rate will release a substantial amount of funds from speculative balances to support an increase in y.

At the other extreme, where the economy is very taut with high r and y at r_2, y_2, a fiscal policy shift in IS will be relatively ineffective in changing equilibrium demand-side y. With interest rates very high, speculative balances will be squeezed to a minimum with most of the real money supply already financing transactions. An increase in demand by, say, an increase in g will raise the interest rate enough that the initial g increase will be nearly fully offset by a drop in investment demand, giving little increase in y. In this case, however, an expansion of the money supply will be very effective in shifting

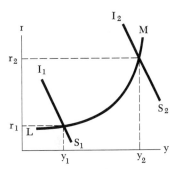

Figure 5-15 The effectiveness of monetary and fiscal policy.

the economy's demand curve. With the level of output and income y limited by the money available for transactions purposes, an $\bar{M}/P_0$ increase will permit a commensurate increase in y. Thus, when the economy is near full employment with very tight credit conditions, monetary policy will be most effective in shifting the demand curve.

In developing the multiplier expressions for changes in the policy instruments g, t, and $\bar{M}$, we were able to separate the multipliers into two pieces. The first was the multiplier for an exogenous expenditure change,

$$\frac{1}{1 - c'(1 - t') + \dfrac{i'k'}{l'}} . \tag{17}$$

This was the same in all cases.

The second part, which differed from case to case, was the expression for the directly induced expenditure change that follows from a change in a policy instrument. In the case of a change in government purchases this was just dg, since the dg change is itself a change in exogenous expenditure. In the case of a change in the tax rate t, the policy-induced change in consumer expenditure was given by $-c'y\,dt$. Finally, in the case of a change in $\bar{M}$, or in real balances m, the policy-induced change in investment demand was given by $(i'/l')dm$. These last three expressions can be used to rank the policy instruments in terms of the certainty of the results.

The highest degree of certainty seems to come in the dg case, since here the government actually exogenously changes spending. In the two other cases, the direct expenditure effect depends on the reaction of private spending to a change in one of its determinants. Tax changes will be effective only if consumer spending reacts. Since it is possible that consumers will offset tax changes, particularly temporary ones, by changing saving behavior, the results of tax changes aren't as certain as those of g changes.

Money supply changes will be effective only if (a) the change affects the interest rate and credit conditions facing investors, and (b) if these changes affect investment spending. Since both of these steps are uncertain, it seems likely (although this would be hard to prove) that the effects of $\bar{M}$ changes may be less certain than those of tax changes. This is very likely the case for permanent tax changes but less likely for temporary tax changes.

These considerations of uncertainty might lead to the following kind of stabilization policy formula. First, keep $\bar{M}$ growth fairly smooth, since the results of $\bar{M}$ changes in the short run may be fairly unpredictable. Second, use permanent tax changes to set the *IS* curve at a desired *long-run normal level*, depending on the long-run desired level of g. Third, use small g changes for short-run *fine-tuning* stabilization policy since their results are most certain.

The Monetary-Fiscal Policy Mix

From the discussion of the effects of monetary and fiscal policy changes in this chapter, it should be clear that changes in the policy variables can be used to change the level of the interest rate and the composition of output without shifting the demand curve, that is, without changing equilibrium demand-side y at the given P_0.

For example, in Figure 5-16, it may be that at the going price level P_0, the level of output y_0 yields roughly full employment. But the r_0 level may be too high because it gives a level of investment that is too low. In this case, the interest rate may be reduced by putting in a permanent tax increase, shifting IS to I_1S_1, and reducing consumption demand. This could be balanced by a money supply increase, lowering the interest rate and stimulating investment demand, bringing the economy back to y_0 at the lower interest rate r_1. This shift in the *monetary-fiscal policy mix,* tightening the budget and easing the money supply, has shifted the composition of the equilibrium y_0. With g fixed, consumer expenditure has been reduced and investment increased. Thus, the policy variables can be changed in opposite directions to change composition without shifting the demand curve.

Working the policy variables against each other in this way creates substantial uncertainty about the outcome, especially since the *amount* of change in each variable will depend on the initial position of the economy. For example, in the early 1980s a mix shift was attempted, with the Reagan administration's tax cuts and a shift to monetary tightness. With the economy running at very low unemployment and historically high interest rates, we might say that it was in the *vertical* region of the *LM* curve when the mix change began. Then the monetary tightening shifted the vertical *LM* curve to the left, while the tax cuts shifted the *IS* curve up. This resulted in a shift of the economy's demand curve to the left, causing a recession and reduction in inflation, while interest rates remained at record levels. Thus, while the policy instruments can be used against each other to change composition, the amounts by which

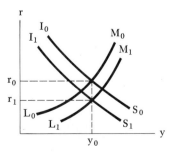

Figure 5-16 A shift in the mix.

the instruments should change will depend on the economy's initial position. This should be carefully taken into account before such a mix shift is attempted.

The various levels of uncertainty associated with the policy instruments also suggest that if the objective is to shift the demand curve, it might be best to use all the instruments in the same direction, giving the highest probability of success in changing y. This strategy, of course, maximizes the uncertainty as to where r will come out, since if, for example, in a restrictive move the fiscal policy change "bites" but the monetary policy change doesn't, r will fall, while if the monetary change bites but the fiscal doesn't, r will rise.

This section is meant to temper, at least a bit, the air of determinateness and certainty that the calculation of multipliers gives stabilization policy. The theory is fairly clear, as the multipliers show. But the actual reaction in the economy to changes in g, $t(y)$, and $\bar{M}$ is uncertain, so that the exact results of any given policy change will be hard to forecast. The chapters in Part III discuss the sectors of the economy in more detail, trying to reduce this level of uncertainty.

MULTIPLIERS AND THE AGGREGATE DEMAND CURVE

The fiscal policy multiplier was derived from the IS and LM curves by taking the money stock and the price level as fixed. We worked out the monetary policy multiplier under the assumption that g and P_0 were constant.

In Figures 5-4 and 5-11 we saw that fiscal or monetary policy will shift the aggregate-demand curve; in Chapter 4 we saw that the effects of a change in the price level on demand are movements along the aggregate-demand curve. Here we will bring together the multipliers as demand shifts and the expression for the slope of the aggregate-demand curve, solving for the total differential dy as g, M, or P changes. We start from the product-market equation (3), reproduced here as

$$y = c(y - t(y)) + i(r) + g. \tag{18}$$

Total differentiation, including movements in y, r, or dg, gives us the familiar IS differential

$$dy = c'(1 - t')dy + i' \, dr + dg. \tag{19}$$

The money market equilibrium condition is the LM curve

$$\frac{\bar{M}}{P_0} = l(r) + k(y). \tag{20}$$

Total differentiation of equation (20) with respect to M, P, r and y, gives the *LM* differential

$$\frac{1}{P_0} d\bar{M} - \frac{\bar{M}}{P_0^2} dP = l' \, dr + k' \, dy.$$

Rearranging, we can solve this for r along the *LM* curve:

$$dr = \frac{1}{l' \cdot P_0} d\bar{M} - \frac{\bar{M}}{l' \cdot P_0^2} dP - \frac{k'}{l'} dy.$$

Substituting this expression into the *IS* differential, equation (19), we obtain

$$dy = c'(1 - t')dy + i' \left[\frac{1}{l'P_0} d\bar{M} - \frac{\bar{M}}{l'P_0^2} dP - \frac{k'}{l'} dy \right] + dg,$$

which can be sorted out as

$$\left[1 - c'(1 - t') + \frac{i'k'}{l'} \right] dy = \frac{i'}{l'P_0} d\bar{M} - \frac{i'\bar{M}}{l'P_0^2} dP + dg. \tag{21}$$

Recall that the real money supply m equals $\bar{M}/P_0$; also, for the sake of neatness, we "normalize" the initial price level to unity, that is, scale the price index so that $P_0 = 1$. With these simplifications in equation (21), we arrive at the total derivative of the aggregate-demand curve:

$$dy = \frac{1}{1 - c'(1 - t') + \dfrac{i'k'}{l'}} \cdot \left[\frac{i'}{l'} dm + dg - \frac{i'}{l'} m \, dP \right], \tag{22}$$

with again, P_0 set equal to 1.

The components of equation (22) are easily interpreted. The first is the usual multiplier, first seen back in equation (5), which is the same no matter what the source of the disturbance to aggregate demand. Next, we have the numerators from the monetary and fiscal policy multipliers. Finally, we have the price term, which gives the slope of the aggregate-demand curve shown, for instance, in Figure 5-11. Algebraically, the slope is

$$\frac{dy}{dP} = \frac{-\dfrac{i'}{l'} \cdot m}{1 - c'(1 - t') + \dfrac{i'k'}{l'}}, \tag{23}$$

which is negative as expected. Thus, the total derivative dy is the sum of the partial derivatives of y with respect to M, y and P. Any change in output demanded can be traced to some linear combination of changes in the money supply, government spending, and the price level, given stable functions for consumption and investment. Equation (21) for the aggregate-demand curve gives us equilibrium output demanded for a given P_0 and for given values of $\bar{M}$ and g. Changes in the latter shift the aggregate-demand curve. To close our skeletal macromodel, we must turn to the supply side of the economy and relax the assumption that the price level P_0 is fixed.

SELECTED READINGS

E.C. Brown, "Fiscal Policy in the '30's," *American Economic Review,* December 1956.

R.A. Musgrave and P.B. Musgrave, *Public Finance in Theory and Practice,* 4th Ed. (New York: McGraw-Hill, 1984), Chapters 27–29.

Appendix: Matrix Algebra

This text uses only algebraic manipulations to solve problems in comparative statics, for instance, by differentiating the LM equation (4), holding $\bar{M}/P_0$ constant, and substituting the expression for dr into the IS differential in order to get the fiscal policy multiplier. However, the same result can be obtained using *matrices*. This method can be very elegant, and it is essential in larger problems where direct substitutions become extremely unwieldy. In order to use matrices, we begin by sorting out derivatives of endogenous and exogenous variables in each equation, and then we can move around these blocks of derivatives using the rules of matrix algebra.

An essential ingredient is the rule for inverting a matrix. With a two-by-two matrix

$$\underline{A} = \begin{pmatrix} a_{11} & a_{12} \\ a_{21} & a_{22} \end{pmatrix},$$

where the a_{ij} terms are numbers or derivatives, the inverse of $\underline{A}$ is defined as that matrix which transforms $\underline{A}$ into the identity matrix:

$$\underline{A}^{-1} \cdot \underline{A} = I = \begin{pmatrix} 1 & 0 \\ 0 & 1 \end{pmatrix}.$$

It turns out that the inverse of $\underline{A}$ is

$$\underline{A}^{-1} = \frac{1}{a_{11}a_{22} - a_{12}a_{21}} \begin{pmatrix} a_{22} & -a_{12} \\ -a_{21} & a_{11} \end{pmatrix}. \tag{1}$$

The term $(a_{11}a_{12} - a_{12}a_{21})$ is known as the determinant of $\underline{A}$ and is often designated by $|\underline{A}|$.

Let us now see how the inversion rule may be applied, taking as an example the simple fixed price model developed in this chapter. Our starting point is equations (3) and (4), rewritten here as

$$y = c(y - t(y)) + g. \tag{2}$$

$$\bar{M}/P = l(r) + k(y). \tag{3}$$

We'll use as our example a change in government spending. Differentiating totally equations (2) and (3) gives us

$$dy = c'(dy - t'\,dy) + i'\,dr + dg.$$

$$0 = l'\,dr + k'\,dy.$$

Sorting out endogenous and exogenous variables, we can rewrite these two linear total differentials as

$$(1 - c'(1 - t'))dy - i'\,dr = dg; \tag{4}$$

$$k'\,dy + l'\,dr = 0. \tag{5}$$

These in turn can be written in matrix form as

$$\begin{pmatrix} (1 - c'(1 - t')) & -i' \\ k' & l' \end{pmatrix} \begin{pmatrix} dy \\ dr \end{pmatrix} = \begin{pmatrix} 1 \\ 0 \end{pmatrix} dg. \tag{6}$$

Let the matrix on the left-hand side be called $\underline{A}$. Then equation (6) can be written

$$\underline{A} \begin{pmatrix} dy \\ dr \end{pmatrix} = \begin{pmatrix} 1 \\ 0 \end{pmatrix} dg. \tag{7}$$

From the inversion rule of equation (1), the inverse of the $\underline{A}$ matrix is

$$\underline{A}^{-1} = \frac{1}{|\underline{A}|} \begin{bmatrix} l' & i' \\ -k' & (1 - c'(1 - t')) \end{bmatrix}. \tag{8}$$

The determinant $|\underline{A}|$, in turn, is given by

$$|\underline{A}| = l'(1 - c'(1 - t')) + i'k'. \tag{9}$$

To solve for dy/dg and dr/dg, we can invert $\underline{A}$ as follows:

$$\underline{A}^{-1} \cdot \underline{A} \cdot \begin{pmatrix} dy \\ dr \end{pmatrix} = \underline{A}^{-1} \begin{pmatrix} 1 \\ 0 \end{pmatrix} dg,$$

but $\underline{A}^{-1} \cdot \underline{A}$ equals the identity matrix, so that

$$\begin{pmatrix} dy \\ dr \end{pmatrix} = \underline{A}^{-1} \cdot \begin{pmatrix} 1 \\ 0 \end{pmatrix} dg, \quad \text{or} \quad \begin{pmatrix} dy \\ dr \end{pmatrix} = \frac{1}{|\underline{A}|} \begin{pmatrix} l' & i' \\ k' & 1 - c'(1 - t') \end{pmatrix} \begin{pmatrix} 1 \\ 0 \end{pmatrix} dg.$$

Using the vector of coefficients of dg, we can simplify this to

$$\begin{pmatrix} dy \\ dr \end{pmatrix} = \frac{1}{|\underline{A}|} \begin{pmatrix} l' \\ -k' \end{pmatrix} dg, \tag{10}$$

where the determinant of the $\underline{A}$ matrix of derivatives is given by equation (10). The explicit solution for dy from the matrix equation (10) is

$$dy = \frac{l'}{|\underline{A}|} \, dg. \tag{11}$$

Substituting for the determinant from equation (9), we get

$$dy = \frac{1'}{l'(i - c'(1 - t')) + i'k'} \, dg,$$

or

$$dy = \frac{1}{1 - c'(1 - t') + \dfrac{i'k'}{1'}} \, dg. \tag{12}$$

This is the same as the text equation (5), which was derived by substitution. We can use the same method to find the multiplier for r, dr/dg.

   For more complex problems, finding the inverse for the matrix of derivatives $\underline{A}$ becomes immensely tiresome. We therefore resort to a mathematical trick known as Cramer's Rule. Suppose we want to find dy/dg. Go back to equation (6) and notice that the terms in the first column of $\underline{A}$ are the coefficients of dy in equations (4) and (5). Then substitute the vector of coefficients of dg into the place of that vector of coefficients of dy, which produces a matrix

$$\begin{pmatrix} 1 & -i' \\ 0 & l' \end{pmatrix}. \tag{13}$$

Then Cramer's Rule says that dy/dg equals the ratio of the determinant of the matrix (13) to the determinant of the matrix $\underline{A}$. In algebraic terms,

$$\frac{dy}{dg} = \frac{\begin{vmatrix} 1 & -i' \\ 0 & l' \end{vmatrix}}{|\underline{A}|}, \quad \text{and} \quad \frac{dy}{dg} = \frac{l'}{|\underline{A}|},$$

which is the same as equation (11) earlier.

   To find dr/dy, we substitute the vector of coefficients of dg into the second column of $\underline{A}$, that is, we replace the coefficients of dr by the coefficients of dg. Then we take the ratio of determinants, leaving us with

104

$$\frac{dr}{dg} = \frac{\begin{vmatrix} 1 - c'(1 - t') & 1 \\ k' & 0 \end{vmatrix}}{|A|}$$

$$= \frac{-k'}{|A|},$$

which is the correct answer.

SELECTED READING

A.C. Chiang, *Fundamental Methods of Mathematical Economics,* 3rd Ed. (New York: McGraw-Hill, 1984), Chapters 4–5.

6

Demand and Supply in the Labor Market

The last two chapters developed the demand side of the economy taking the price level P as exogenously determined. The product market equilibrium condition,

$$IS: \quad y = c(y - t(y)) + i(r) + g, \tag{1}$$

and the money market equilibrium condition,

$$LM: \quad \frac{\bar{M}}{P} = l(r) + k(y), \tag{2}$$

are two equations that determine the equilibrium values of the level of output y and the interest rate r for any given value of P. Changing the level of P changes equilibrium y and r through changes in real money supply, $m = (\bar{M}/P)$. Graphically, this effect comes through shifts in the LM curve. Varying the exogenous P assumption gives us the economy's demand curve, shown in Figure 6-1 as DD.

This chapter begins our discussion of the supply side of our skeletal macroeconomy by introducing demand and supply in the labor market. Chapter 7 will build on this analysis to develop an aggregate supply curve for the economy. In subsequent chapters we will therefore be able to equate supply and demand for output to analyze endogenously determined equilibrium values of output and the price level.

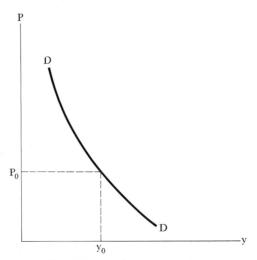

Figure 6-1 The aggregate-demand curve.

We begin here with a brief discussion of a simple depression model of the economy with a rigid price level. This topic will be taken up again in more detail in Chapter 10. Here it is used to introduce the role of the labor market. The main sections of the chapter develop demand, supply, and equilibrium in the labor market. We will finish the chapter with a brief discussion of equilibrium unemployment.

THE SIMPLE DEPRESSION MODEL

To begin with, let's look for the moment at an economy such as that of the depression in the 1930s. The labor supply is more or less unlimited, so that a demand increase can expand output y and employment N without raising the price level. This essentially gives us as a supply curve a horizontal line at P_0 in Figure 6-1, with equilibrium output then at y_0. We can next introduce a short-run production function for real output,

$$y = y(N; \bar{K}); \qquad \frac{\partial y}{\partial N} > 0, \tag{3}$$

which says simply that in the short run the level of real output y depends on labor input N only. All other factor inputs, included in $\bar{K}$ (K for *Kapital*), are either fixed in the short run, like the capital stock, or vary in direct proportion to labor input, like materials input. For any given level of y, the production function gives the level of employment N needed to produce this y.

This gives us a complete, if somewhat unsatisfactory, *depression model.* The presence of massive unemployment means that a demand increase can increase output and employment without pulling up wages and prices to any significant degree. This situation is represented by the horizontal supply curve at P_0 in Figure 6-1. Production of the resulting equilibrium output y_0 gives employment to N_0 persons in Figure 6-2, presumably far less than the total labor force. (Unemployment peaked at 25 percent in 1933.) In this case, if government purchases were increased, the *IS* curve would shift out, and the demand curve of Figure 6-1 would shift to $D_1 D_1$ in Figure 6-3. Equilibrium output would rise to y_1, and employment would rise to N_1 in Figure 6-2.

Formally, this depression model adds the exogenous P assumption,

$$P = P_0, \tag{4}$$

to equations (1)–(3) to form a four-equation system in four variables: y, r, P, and N.

The main difficulty with this analysis is that the assumption of a fixed price level is not acceptable if labor supply is not perfectly elastic. We know this from empirical observation. In the 1930s, when widespread unemployment prevailed, an increase in demand could have expanded production without resulting in much of a price increase. Even after 1961, when unemployment was about 7 percent, demand increases expanded output without causing much of an increase in prices. After 1965, however, with unemployment below 4 percent, the continued expansion of demand brought a rise in prices that continued to the early 1970s. This is a case where demand expansion pulled prices up. The 1980s provide an example of a demand reduction ending an inflation. Monetary policy, which was aimed at cutting demand, reduced output from 1980 to 1982, and the unemployment rate increased from 6 to 10.5 percent. The inflation rate, which had been pushed up to 11.5 percent by 1980 following a series of supply shocks (more on these later), fell to 4 percent by the end of 1982. Thus, the empirical record suggests that increasing demand leads to rising prices and that reduction in demand slows inflation or reduces the price level.

Intuitively we should be able to imagine the qualitative relationship between prices, wages, and the level of employment that would occur when an

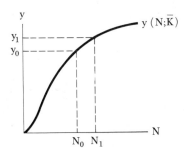

Figure 6-2 The short-run production function.

economy is at or near full employment. If the demand for goods should suddenly rise above the available supply, prices would begin to rise. Higher prices would mean increased profits for producers, and they would expand their production in order to make even greater profits. To do so they would try to hire more labor; thus, higher prices would lead to an increased demand for labor. The increased demand for labor would take the form of employers offering higher money wages to hire more labor.

Presumably, however, workers are interested in the purchasing power of their wages—what they can buy with their income. What they can buy depends not only on the level of money wages, but also on the prices of goods and services. Thus, an increase in prices would lower the real wages earned by workers and might cause a reduction in the supply of labor offered at a given money wage. Another way to look at this is that the effect of an increase in demand for labor stimulated by an increase in the price level is likely to be dampened by the reduction in labor supply caused by the falling real wage. Thus, common sense tells us that there is a close relationship between prices, wages, and the level of employment, and that this relationship is more complicated than the simple depression model outlined above.

We have already developed the product market and money market equilibrium conditions, (1)–(2):

$$y = c(y - t(y)) + i(r) + g$$

and

$$\frac{\bar{M}}{P} = l(r) + k(y),$$

and introduced the production function, (3):

$$y = y(N; \bar{K}).$$

These three equations have four endogenous variables: y, r, P, and N. So the system as it stands is *underdetermined;* it has fewer equations than unknowns.

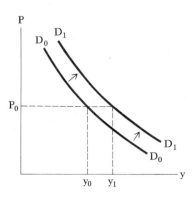

Figure 6-3 Demand shift in the depression model.

In order to find equilibrium solutions for y, r, P, and N, we have to find another equation that includes at least some of these variables and is a bit more sensible than the exogenous P assumption in (4) above. We will find this equation by looking at a third market, the *labor market,* and deriving from it an aggregate supply curve relating P and y on the supply side.

THE DEMAND FOR LABOR

We have already introduced a simple production function, equation (3), which describes real output y as a function of labor input N, with the level of the capital stock and of other inputs held constant or varying in direct proportion to labor in the short run. This function is shown graphically in Figure 6-4(a). The shape of the production function $y(N; \bar{K})$ shows y increasing with each increase in labor input. Thus, $\partial y/\partial N > 0$. However, y increases at an increasing rate with the first additions of labor to the fixed capital stock. But after some level of employment, shown as N_1 in Figure 6-4, y begins to increase at a decreasing rate—showing diminishing marginal returns—as the capital stock is spread over more and more workers. Eventually, a point may be reached where no addition to output would come from added labor [where $y(N; \bar{K})$ would flatten out] or even where output would be diminished by adding labor [where $y(N; \bar{K})$ would turn down].

There are some interesting functions to be derived from this production function, shown in Figure 6-4(b). One is average labor productivity, y/N, also known as the average product of labor (APL). This is represented by the

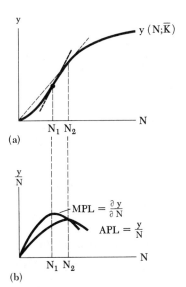

(a)

(b)

Figure 6-4 The production function and its derivatives.

slope of a line from the origin to any point on the production function. It can be seen that as employment increases, the average product of labor first increases and then decreases. This relationship between *APL* and the level of employment is shown in Figure 6-4(b). The other curve in Figure 6-4(b), derived from the production function, is the marginal product of labor (*MPL*). This is the slope of the production function, $\partial y / \partial N$, and in Figure 6-4(a) would be shown by the slope of a tangent to the production function at each point N.

Three points about the *APL* and *MPL* curves should be apparent from Figure 6-4. With the production function first convex, showing increasing returns, and then concave, showing diminishing returns, the *MPL* curve will reach a maximum at the N level where the production has an inflexion point, that is, changes from convex to concave. This is shown as N_1 in Figure 6-4. The maximum *APL* comes at the N level where a ray from the origin in Figure 6-4(a) is just tangent to the production function, N_2 in Figure 6-4. Since *MPL* is given by the slope of $y(N; \bar{K})$, at maximum *APL*, *MPL* = *APL*. Finally, to the left of maximum *APL*, *MPL* > *APL*; to the right, *MPL* < *APL*.

Now as a firm increases employment, the resulting increase in output is given by the *MPL*, $\partial y / \partial N$. For a competitive firm, facing a given price level, the revenue increase from employment increase is

$$\Delta R = P \cdot \frac{\partial y}{\partial N} \cdot \Delta N,$$

where $P \cdot (\partial y / \partial N)$ is the marginal value product of labor. The increase in cost, ΔC, to the firm hiring an additional increment of labor is simply the money wage rate W times ΔN. This gives us the firm's equilibrium employment condition and the demand-for-labor function, as follows. If an addition to the labor force is such that $\Delta R > \Delta C$, a profit-maximizing firm will hire the additional labor. If $\Delta R < \Delta C$, the firm will not hire. The firm will continue to hire labor until $\Delta R = \Delta C$ and

$$W = P \cdot \frac{\partial y}{\partial N}, \tag{5a}$$

or

$$w \equiv \frac{W}{P} = \frac{\partial y}{\partial N}, \tag{5b}$$

where w is the *real wage rate*.

We can develop the demand-for-labor function from equations (5) in the following way. Suppose the competitive firm is faced with market wage W_0. It will then extend employment until $P \cdot (\partial y / \partial N) = W_0$. If W falls, the firm will increase employment to maintain condition (5). This gives us the interpretation of equations (5) as (a) the real wage the firm will offer, $w = \partial y / \partial N$, or (b) the money wage the firm will offer, $W = P \cdot (\partial y / \partial N)$, for employment N. These relationships are shown in Figure 6-5.

If $W_0 / P < (\partial y / \partial N)$ or $W_0 < P \cdot (\partial y / \partial N)$, the firm will hire additional labor. If the direction of the inequality is reversed, firms will reduce the amount of labor hired.

The Monopolistic Case

The monopolistic firm's demand for labor will be qualitatively similar to that of the competitive firm, and we can develop it briefly here. The difference between the two cases is that, where the competitive firm faces a given price determined by the market, so that the marginal revenue product of labor $= P \cdot MPL$, the monopolist can choose the price-quantity combination that maximizes profit along the firm's demand curve. We can write the demand curve as

$$P = P(y(N; \bar{K})); \qquad P' < 0, \tag{6}$$

with price as a declining function of quantity sold.

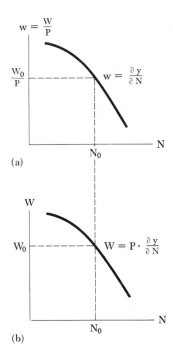

(a)

(b)

Figure 6-5 Competitive firm's demand for labor.

In this case total revenue is given by

$$R = y(N; \bar{K}) \cdot P(y(N; \bar{K})), \tag{7}$$

or quantity y times price P. To obtain an expression for the change in revenue, dR, that follows from a small change in employment, dN, we can differentiate (7):

$$\frac{dR}{dN} = y \frac{dP}{dy} \frac{\partial y}{\partial N} + P \frac{\partial y}{\partial N}$$

$$= P \frac{\partial y}{\partial N} \left(1 + \frac{y}{P} \frac{dP}{dy} \right).$$

The last term inside the parentheses is simply the elasticity of demand, so that the marginal revenue product of labor for a monopolist is

$$\frac{dR}{dN} = P \left(1 + \frac{1}{e} \right) \frac{\partial y}{\partial N}, \tag{8}$$

where e is the (negative) elasticity of demand along the demand curve given by equation (6).

The marginal cost of hiring a new worker in this simple model is still W, the wage rate. The monopolist will maximize profit by hiring additional labor until the marginal revenue is reduced to the level of marginal cost, or

$$W = P \left(1 + \frac{1}{e} \right) \frac{\partial y}{\partial N}. \tag{9}$$

This gives the monopolist's demand for labor curves shown in Figure 6-6. These are simply the competitive firm's curves of Figure 6-5 shifted left by the factor $1 + (1/e)$. A value of -1.5 for e would put each point on the monopolist's curve one-third of the horizontal distance to the vertical axis to the left of the competitive firm's curve.

The Aggregate Demand for Labor

In an economy with a mixture of monopolistic and competitive elements, the aggregate demand for labor will be a horizontal sum of many individual demand curves, some looking like Figure 6-5 and others like Figure 6-6. With a given technology, so that each firm's $\partial y / \partial N$ curve is stable, this aggregate labor-demand curve will be fairly stable if product market demand changes do not substantially alter either the output mix between the monopolistic and

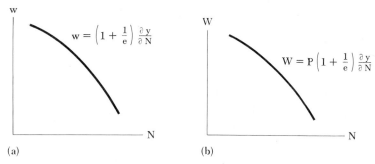

Figure 6-6 Monopolistic firm's demand for labor.

competitive sectors, or the average elasticity of demand within the monopolistic sector. Under these conditions, the aggregate demand for labor is given by

$$w \equiv \frac{W}{P} = f(N), \tag{10a}$$

or

$$W = P \cdot f(N), \tag{10b}$$

where $f'(N) < 0$. The aggregate demand curve (10) is shown in Figure 6-7, following the same format as Figure 6-5 and 6-6.

     There are two important things to notice about the aggregate labor-demand curve. First, its negative slope is due to diminishing marginal productivity of labor as more labor is added to a fixed capital stock. In a perfectly competitive economy with a fixed output mix, the demand curve $f(N)$ would be the aggregate MPL, $\partial y / \partial N$. Second, since profit-maximizing firms are interested in the real wage they pay—the price of the labor input relative to the price of output—the price level enters the money wage version of the demand function (10b) multiplicatively. We write $W = P \cdot f(N)$, rather than $W =$

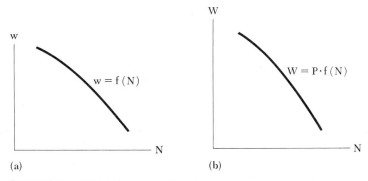

Figure 6-7 Aggregate demand for labor.

$f(P, N)$. This distinction will be important when we examine the effects of price changes shifting the labor-demand and labor-supply curves.

THE SUPPLY OF LABOR

In developing the aggregate demand for labor in Figure 6-7, we did not make any explicit assumption about price or wage expectations of the employers on the demand side of the labor market. This is because we assume that an employer has good information on, or perhaps control of, the particular prices charged and the wage rates paid. Thus, he or she is in a position to know the real product wage at each point in time. For the employer, this is the money wage deflated by the employer's particular product price. A worker, however, must deflate a known wage income by a price index, such as the CPI, that covers a wide range of products to arrive at an estimate of the real wage w. Thus, his or her information concerning the price level (and subsequently the real wage) is not as good as that of employers, and an explicit assumption linking worker expectations of the price level P^e to the actual price level P is needed. The importance of this asymmetry between firms on the demand side and workers on the supply side will become evident as we proceed with the analysis of aggregate supply.

In developing the supply side of the labor market, two important questions must be answered at the outset. The first has to do with expectations and the other with the nominal wage rate W, which up to now was taken to be fixed.

1. How rapidly and completely do workers' expectations of the future price level P^e adjust to changes in the actual price level P?
2. Is the nominal wage rate rigid or flexible over time?

The assumptions made regarding the correct answers to these questions will be important for the operation of our skeletal macromodel. In Chapter 10 we will explore the meaning and implications of wage rigidity. In the rest of Chapter 6 we will analyze labor market equilibrium and aggregate supply under a range of assumptions between the polar cases of (a) immediate and correct adjustment of P^e to changes in P, and (b) no adjustment at all. Assumption (a) results in the *classical* case in which the supply of labor depends only on the real wage w. This polar case is called "classical" because it stems from the traditional theory of consumer behavior and was at the root of the pre-Keynesian school of macroeconomic thinking, which Keynes dubbed "classical" in 1936. We will find that while the hypothesis that labor supply is a function only of the real wage w may be correct (but very difficult to verify) in the long run, assumption (b), which makes the labor supply a function of the money wage W, may be a more useful hypothesis for explaining actual short-run variations in employment. This is the extreme Keynesian case.

Time and Expectations

From our introductory comments on labor supply, it is clear that expectations about the price level will be important. The relevant measure of the price level here is the price of the worker's consumption basket. This is the Consumer Price Index (CPI). The worker facing a nominal wage offer W must make an estimate of the expected real wage W/P^e, where P^e is the expected value of the CPI. So the workers must form price expectations, which we generally denote by P^e.

To handle expectations carefully, we need to introduce some additional notation that makes time sequences explicit. We need to specify *what* is expected and *when*. This notation will be useful when we focus on expectations; when it is not useful, we'll skip it. Here we introduce notation for expected prices and show how price expectations enter labor supply. Later, we will discuss how expectations might be formed.

At any point in time which we will call period t, the price level in that period will be P_t. A person may have expectations of what the price level will be in this period. However, others may have shakier beliefs and guesses, and in advance they know only that P_t might be distributed in some way across a range of possible values. Knowing this distribution at the end of period $t-1$, they can calculate the mean or expected value of the price level for the period t, which we will denote by $_{t-1}P_t$. They may know full well that the price level may change at t from P_{t-1} to any one of an infinite number of possibilities, each with its own probability of occurrence, but the weighted average of all these possibilities is a particular number $_{t-1}P_t$. Thus, the expected value of the price level for period t, with the expectation being made at the end of period $t-1$, is the variable $_{t-1}P_t$. This is the price index the worker would use to calculate an expected real wage for period t.

In general, when we discuss price expectations here and in following chapters, we will refer to $_{t-1}P_t$ as "the expected price level" and simply call it P^e. Unless special reference is made to expectations formed in some earlier period, like $_{t-2}P_t$, or to expectations of the price level at a later period, like $_{t-1}P_{t+1}$, the variable P^e will stand for the usual current-period price expectation $_{t-1}P_t$. To minimize the complexity and potential confusion of notation, we will generally refer to the actual equilibrium price level in an initial period t as P_0, and the price level that was expected for that period, $_{t-1}P_t$, as P^e. These are the P_0 and P^e that we see, for example, in Figure 6-10 on page 118.

The Individual's Work-Leisure Decision

To develop the labor-supply function, we again borrow some basic ideas from microeconomics. We assume that a worker wants to achieve the mix of real income and leisure that is anticipated to be most satisfactory to him or her. Assuming a worker can allocate hours to work, thus earning expected real income y^e, or to leisure S, the limits or constraints on his or her ability to achieve maximum satisfaction, or, as we will refer to it, *utility U,* are the number of hours in the day and the real wage rate. Thus, the worker's utility function is

$$U = U(y^e, S); \qquad \frac{\partial U}{\partial y^e}, \frac{\partial U}{\partial S} > 0 \qquad (11)$$

and is to be maximized subject to the constraint that

$$y^e = \frac{W}{P^e} \cdot (T - S) = w^e \cdot (T - S), \qquad (12)$$

where T is the total hours available to the worker, so that $T - S = n$ gives the number of working hours. Since we assume the worker is uncertain about the price level to use to convert nominal income into real income, the *expected price level* P^e enters the calculation of *expected* real wage w^e and *expected* real income y^e.

The work-leisure decision is shown in Figure 6-8. Each U (indifference) curve shows all the combinations of y^e and S that yield the same level of satisfaction or utility. The points on U_1 represent a higher level of utility than those on U_0. The entire y^e, S space is filled with such curves, none crossing any other. The worker-consumer wants to reach the highest indifference curve possible. The limit of his or her ability to move toward the northeast in the y^e, S space is given by the straight line; its location is determined by the number of hours available to the person and by the real wage faced. Thus, if the worker has T hours to allocate and chooses to have no income at all, he or she will have T hours of leisure. At expected real wage w_0^e, if the worker chooses to have no leisure at all, he or she will have $w_0^e \cdot T$ income, and leisure can be traded for income along the *budget line* connecting these two points. All points on or below the budget line are attainable, or *feasible;* those above it are not. From the budget constraint $y^e = w^e \cdot (T - S)$, we have $dy^e = -w^e \cdot dS$, so that the slope of the budget line, dy^e/dS, is $-w^e$.

With a given expected real wage rate, the worker will reach maximum utility at the point where the straight line is just tangent to an indifference curve, such as y_0^e, S_0 in Figure 6-8. This will be the highest indifference curve, and thus the highest level of utility, attainable. As the real wage rate changes, the slope of the budget line changes. For example, if the wage rate were increased to w_1^e, the budget line would swing up to meet the y-axis at $w_1^e T$, and the equilibrium point would move to y_1^e, S_1.

As we have drawn the indifference curves, it can be seen that increasing the expected wage rate, that is, increasing the slope of the budget line from an

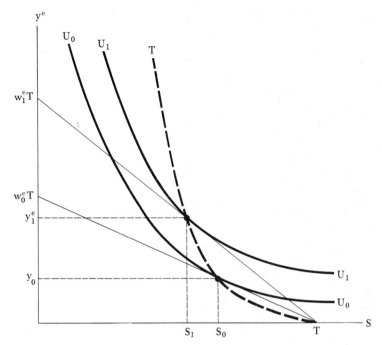

Figure 6-8 The work-leisure decision.

initial low level, initially reduces the amount of leisure consumed by the individual, or conversely, increases the number of hours worked, $T - S$. By
connecting all the points of tangency of the budget line and indifference curves
for various real wage rates with T held constant, we get the dashed labor-
supply curve TT of Figure 6-8.

The Aggregate Labor-Supply Curve

Since leisure S is just T minus the number of hours of labor offered n, we can
redraw the relationship between the expected real wage rate w^e and the amount
of labor n_i offered by the individual as in Figure 6-9(a), which shows an
individual labor-supply curve that eventually bends backwards. This suggests
that once wage rates reach a certain high level, increases in wages may cause
some workers to begin to increase leisure rather than working time, as the
income effect of higher wages overcomes the substitution effect. If we assume
a homogeneous labor force with a single wage rate, we can sum all the individual
labor-supply curves to get the aggregate labor-supply curve for the entire economy. This is shown in Figure 6-9(b). In Chapter 10 we drop the assumption
of a homogeneous labor supply and deal with the problem of a labor force
disaggregated both by geography and by skills. This does not change our qual-

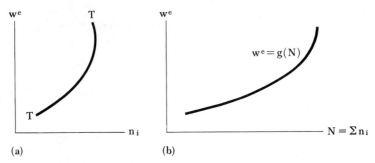

(a)   (b)

Figure 6-9   Labor-supply curves.

itative conclusions about the aggregate level of employment, but it does help
to explain the distribution of unemployment.

For a given value of P^e, the aggregate labor-supply curve shown in Figure
6-9(b) can be represented mathematically as $N = N(w^e)$, or

$$w^e \equiv \frac{W}{P^e} = g(N); \qquad g' > 0, \tag{13a}$$

or

$$W = P^e \cdot g(N). \tag{13b}$$

Equation (13b) can be used to draw a labor-supply curve in the W, N space
of Figure 6-10(b). To draw the labor-supply curve on the w, N space of Figure

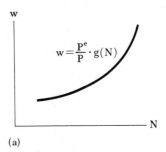

(a)

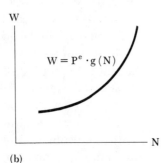

(b)   **Figure 6-10**   Aggregate supply of labor.

6-10(a), we must convert equation (13a) into a relation between the actual real wage w and N. Since we know by definition that

$$w = \frac{W}{P^e} \cdot \frac{P^e}{P},$$

we can use equation (13a) to substitute $g(N)$ for W/P^e in the above identity and get

$$w = \frac{P^e}{P} \cdot g(N), \tag{14}$$

which is plotted in the w,N space of Figure 6-10(a).

The supply curves of Figure 6-10 follow the same format as our illustrations of the demand for labor.

EQUILIBRIUM IN THE LABOR MARKET

We have now derived equations for both the demand and the supply of labor.

$$\text{Demand:} \quad w = f(N); \tag{15}$$

$$\text{Supply:} \quad w = \frac{P^e}{P} \cdot g(N). \tag{16}$$

Equating demand to supply gives the labor market equilibrium condition

$$f(N) = \frac{P^e}{P} \cdot g(N); \tag{17a}$$

or

$$P \cdot f(N) = P^e \cdot g(N). \tag{17b}$$

The graphical solution of labor market equilibrium is represented by the intersection of the two curves in Figure 6-11. The actual equilibrium value of the price level is P_0; in our general time-oriented notation it would be P_t. The price level that was expected for this period is P^e; in the general notation it would be $_{t-1}P_t$. Workers formed expectations of this period's price level at the end of the last period. This is P^e. The actual equilibrium price level P_0 then appeared via the equilibration processes that will be discussed at length later. The result is the equilibrium level of employment N_0 and the nominal and real wage rates W_0 and w_0, respectively. Let us now see what happens to labor market equilibrium as the price level P changes under the extreme classical and Keynesian assumptions regarding the reaction of P^e to changes in P, namely,

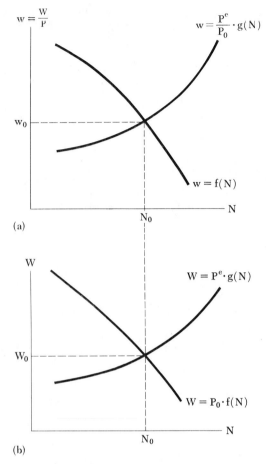

Figure 6-11 Equilibrium in the labor market.

(**a**) complete and correct adjustment of P^e to P (classical case).
(**b**) no adjustment of P^e to P (extreme Keynesian case).

In the complete adjustment case (a), as P rises from P_0, P^e moves by the same proportion, leaving the ratio P^e/P unchanged. It is evident from Figure 6-11(a) that this movement in P, with the expected price P^e fully adjusting to actual changes in P, would leave the initial labor market equilibrium values w_0, N_0 undisturbed. This is the classical result, in which movements of the price level do not affect equilibrium employment N. The same results can be obtained, but less obviously, from Figure 6-11(b). There the equiproportional increases in P and P^e shift both labor demand and supply up by the same amounts, again leaving N_0 undisturbed. The nominal wage W then rises by the same proportion as P (and P^e), leaving the real wage w_0 also unchanged. Thus, in the *classical* case, labor demand and supply move together as the price level changes, leaving employment and the real wage unchanged.

In the zero-adjustment case (b), an extreme example of the *Keynesian* model, as P rises from P_0 there is no adjustment of P^e. Therefore, in Figure 6-11(b) the demand for labor shifts up along an unchanged supply curve, raising equilibrium employment and the nominal wage W. Since there is no shift in the supply curve with P^e fixed, the nominal wage rises less than the price level, and the real wage w falls. This is evident in Figure 6-11(a). There the rise in P with P^e unchanged reduces P^e/P, shifting the labor-supply curve in w, N space down. This gives an increase in employment with a drop in the real wage w. This is an extreme example of the *Keynesian* model, in which an increase in the price level results in an increase in employment. The rigidity of price expectations P^e on the supply side of the labor market permits a reduction of the actual real wage w as the price level rises, inducing an increase in employment.

From these two polar cases, it is clear that the relation of expected price changes to movements in the actual price level is crucial. At one extreme, a change in the actual price level has no effect on equilibrium employment; at the other extreme it does. So we should analyze this relationship of P^e to P, and its implications for aggregate supply of output, more rigorously in order to see what should be our normal expectation about the effect of an increase in the price level on aggregate supply: How great is the effect and what is the time horizon? This question will be at the center of our discussion of the aggregate supply in Chapter 7.

EQUILIBRIUM UNEMPLOYMENT

The labor-supply function shown in Figure 6-11 gives employment N as a function of the money wage W and the expected price level P^e. Implicitly, N was measured in worker-hours of employment or the product of the number of people employed E and the average number of hours worked $\bar{n}$:

$$N = E \cdot \bar{n}. \tag{18}$$

Changes in N are generally reflected in changes in both E and $\bar{n}$. Thus, the slope of the labor-supply curve combines two effects. As the wage rate rises, persons already employed will offer increasing hours of work. More importantly here, a wage rate increase will increase the number of people employed E and reduce the number of workers unemployed, $U = L - E$, with a given size of the labor force L.

The Supply of Workers and Hours

The change in both $\bar{n}$ and E along the labor-supply function as N goes up can be explained by the existence of a customary minimum number of working hours n^* that is acceptable to employers. For example, employers may require at least 35 hours per week of their employees, and not be willing to hire anyone offering less. The effect of this institutional rigidity on labor supply is shown in Figures 6-12 and 6-13.

In Figure 6-12 we see the work-leisure decision for an individual who has nonlabor income $\bar{y}$ and must work at least $n^* = T - S^*$ hours to obtain employment. Nonlabor income might come from property, transfer payments, or another worker in the same family unit. The worker is maximizing the usual utility function of equation (11): $U = U(y^e, S)$, subject to the budget constraint $y^e = \bar{y} + w^e(T - S)$. T is total hours available, to be divided between work n and leisure S. With the minimum n constraint, only points to the left of the vertical S^* line are permissible; the worker has to sacrifice at least S^* hours of leisure to get a job.

At wage rates below w_0^e in Figure 6-12, the worker prefers no employment to an n^*-hour job. When the wage rises to w_0^e, he or she takes an n^*-hour job, and his or her labor supply stays at the n^* "corner solution" until the wage rises to w_*^e. At wage rates above w_*^e, the labor-supply curve moves to interior tangencies, becoming the expansion path $h_i(n_i)$. Along $h_i(n_i)$ the worker supplies additional labor at a decreasing rate. This individual labor-supply curve is shown in the w^e, N space of Figure 6-13. Below w_0^e the worker supplies zero

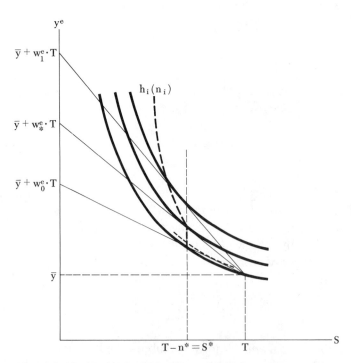

Figure 6-12 Work-leisure decision with minimum hours n^*.

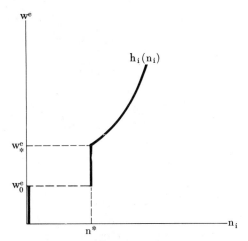

Figure 6-13 Individual labor-supply curve.

hours of labor. At w_0^e supply jumps to $n*$, and stays there up to w_*^e, when the usual $h_i(n_i)$ function takes over.

When the individual labor-supply curves of Figure 6-13 are aggregated over the labor force, the slope of the resulting aggregate labor-supply curve, then, has the two components pointed out at the beginning of this section: as w rises, first more workers' w_* thresholds are passed, and E rises; and second, the number of hours worked by those employed rises, raising $\bar{n}$, average hours worked. The first of these effects gives us the supply curve of workers shown in Figure 6-14.

The shape of the aggregate worker-supply curve can be explained as follows. As the wage rate rises from very low levels, increasing numbers of workers become employed as their w_* thresholds are passed, so that at low wage levels, the curve is concave. But after most of the primary workers—working heads of households and single males—are employed, further w increases call forth diminishing increases in the supply of workers, so that the curve turns convex and becomes nearly vertical at a high wage level where virtually all potential workers are employed.

The Labor Force and Unemployment

The aggregate worker-supply curves of Figure 6-14, with positive and increasing slopes in the range that is relevant for our analysis, provide a natural definition of full employment. As wages rise, the labor-supply curve becomes vertical at some maximum level of feasible employment, which we will identify as the labor force. Thus, in Figure 6-14 we can define the labor force L as that level of employment at which the labor-supply curve becomes vertical. The difference between the total labor force L and the equilibrium level of employment,

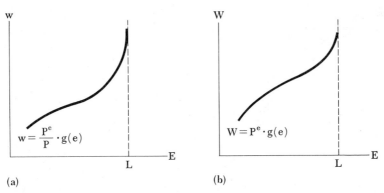

Figure 6-14 Aggregate worker supply curves.

E_0 in Figure 6-14 is then the level of unemployment—the number of unemployed people who would be willing to work if a suitable job were available:

$$U_0 = L - E_0. \tag{19}$$

Voluntary and Involuntary Unemployment

We now have a reasonable explanation of fluctuations in unemployment in an economy that is generally operating near full employment, such as the U.S. economy since World War II with unemployment rates between 3 and 10 percent, as compared with the 15 to 25 percent of the 1930s. Even so, this explanation has one troublesome aspect: It implies that the unemployed are unemployed more or less by choice. Looking back to Figure 6-13 we see that the cause of their unemployment is that the wage rate (for their skill class and geographical area) is below their threshold w_0. In a way, it is their definition of what is a suitable job—one paying at least w_0—that keeps them unemployed.

In an economy generally operating near full employment, this can certainly be the case, even if there are pockets of local unemployment running as high as 15 percent. Examples of these are Appalachia, many areas in our major central cities, and, in general, areas where there has been a major drop in industrial output. When industrial output declined in steel- and auto-producing areas like Pittsburgh or Detroit in the 1980s, unemployment in those areas went up. The industrial boom in the high-tech Research Triangle of North Carolina or Silicon Valley in northern California did not do much to alleviate unemployment in Pittsburgh or Detroit. This kind of large-scale local structural unemployment is due to local labor market rigidities, the lack of job information, and the cost of moving, and can, in time, be alleviated by government action to remove these impediments. It is still consistent with our Figure 6-15 explanation of unemployment in an economy that is, in the aggregate, operating near full employment.

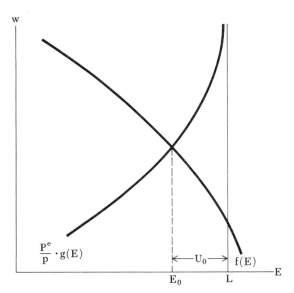

Figure 6-15 Equilibrium in the market for workers.

But this view of unemployment will not hold up well in a case in which there is clearly widespread involuntary unemployment, such as in the 1930s when people would take work at almost any wage, but no work was available. The labor market equilibrium pictures of Figure 6-15 include unemployment of people who can't find *suitable* work, not of people who can't find *any* work. So the model of Figure 6-15 can't, by itself, explain the massive involuntary unemployment of the 1930s, although it does represent the operation of the postwar economy fairly well.

To explain aggregate, or economy-wide, involuntary unemployment, we will introduce the notion of *wage rigidity*—when labor market demand falls and wages don't fall, so that the equilibrium labor market outcome is off the labor-supply curve. In Chapter 10 we look at the aggregate labor markets with rigid wages and the spillovers that may occur as rigidities in one sector of the economy lead to distortions elsewhere.

SELECTED READINGS

R.J. Barro, *Macroeconomics,* 2nd Ed. (New York: John Wiley & Sons, 1987), Chapters 2 and 6.

J.H. Power, "Price Expectations, Money Illusion and the Real Balance Effect," *Journal of Political Economy,* April 1959.

W.L. Smith, "A Graphical Exposition of the Complete Keynesian System," in W.L. Smith and R.L. Teigen, eds., *Readings in Money, National Income, and Stabilization Policy* (Homewood, Ill.: R.D. Irwin, 1970).

chapter 7

Supply-Side Equilibrium: Output and the Price Level

In Chapter 6 we began development of the supply side of our skeletal macro-model by considering demand and supply in the labor market. There we saw that equilibrium employment depends on the actual price level P_0 and the expected price level P^e, for example, in Figure 6-11. In this chapter we go on to derive an aggregate supply curve from that analysis of the labor market, as well as a production function that relates the supply of output y to employment N. The aggregate supply and demand curves can then be put together in Chapter 8 to determine economy-wide equilibrium in our skeletal macromodel.

It is clear from Chapter 6 that the effects of movements in the price level on equilibrium employment, as well as on output, will depend crucially on how price expectations react to movements in the actual price level. We begin by specifying an assumption about how price expectations P^e relate to the actual price level P. This specification will allow for a full range of reactions of P^e to P, from no adjustment to 100 percent adjustment. The no adjustment case will be interpreted both as a very *short-run* model where expectations have no opportunity to adjust and as an extreme *Keynesian* model where labor supply depends only on the nominal wage. The case of 100 percent adjustment will be interpreted on a *long-run* model and as the extreme *classical* case where labor supply depends only on the real wage. The reality in most relevant situations where we study fluctuations in output and employment over a period of one or two years is probably in between.

With specification of the dependence of P^e on P, we can derive the aggregate supply curve under various assumptions about adjustment of P^e to movements in P. Then in the section introducing expectations formation, we explore the microeconomic underpinnings of determination of P^e, and relate these to the short-run and long-run interpretations of the aggregate supply curve.

EXPECTATIONS AND AGGREGATE SUPPLY

Implicit in our discussion of expectations on the supply side of the labor market is a functional relation between the expected price level P^e and the actual price level P. Here we will specify that relationship a little more precisely in order to derive the aggregate supply curve and to see exactly how it is affected by the expectations assumption. Later in this chapter we will look at a particular model of expectations adjustment that would give us the relation of P^e to P that is simply assumed in equation (1).

Relation of P^e to P

The expectations function that makes P^e dependent on P can be written as

$$P^e = p(P); \qquad 0 \le p' \le 1. \tag{1}$$

Here P^e depends on P, and the slope of the p function lies between zero and unity. The extreme value of $p' = 0$ defines the case of no adjustment of the expected price level as the actual price level changes. This case is one of complete *money illusion,* following the usage of the economics literature. With P^e constant as P moves, the labor-supply function depends only on the money wage rate W. This is also known as the extreme *Keynesian* case in the literature, usually with the added, but unnecessary, assumption that the money wage rate is rigid. The money illusion assumption might be appropriate for very short-run movements in aggregate demand, when the labor force has not had time to absorb new price information to adjust P^e.

The other extreme value $p' = 1$ defines the case of full adjustment of expectations over the period under consideration. This case could be labeled *perfect foresight* to conform with the economics literature. Since P^e adapts to changes in P, labor supply in this case depends only on the real wage rate w, and the economy follows the extreme *classical case* in which movements in P do not affect employment. This assumption is probably most appropriate for long-run movements in which there is enough time for the labor force to process fully new information on P.

For values of p' between zero and unity, we have a general short-run model with some degree of money illusion, and labor supply dependent on both the money wage rate W *and* the real wage rate w. As we will see below, in this general model movements on the price level do cause changes in equilibrium employment. The size of the change in N depends on both the degree of money illusion and the length of the period of adjustment.

Aggregate Supply Curve: Extreme Keynesian Case

We can begin our derivation of the aggregate supply curve in the extreme Keynesian case of complete money illusion with the labor market equilibrium condition written as

$$P \cdot f(N) = P^e \cdot g(N). \qquad (2)$$

This is equation (17b) from Chapter 6, and is illustrated in Figure 7-1(a). With P^e given and not responsive to changes in actual P ($p' = 0$), this labor market equilibrium condition gives us equilibrium employment N depending on the price level P. By varying the (so far) exogenously determined price level, we can see how equilibrium employment will vary. Then, using the production function in Figure 7-1(b), we can determine the variation in equi-

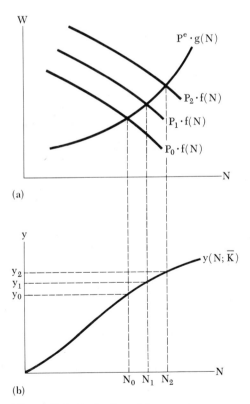

Figure 7-1 Derivation of the supply curve, extreme Keynesian case.

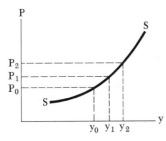

Figure 7-2 The aggregate-supply curve, extreme Keynesian case.

librium output supplied as the price level changes. This gives us the economy's aggregate supply curve.

Figure 7-1(a) illustrates the effect on equilibrium employment in the labor market as the price level rises from P_0 to P_1 to P_2. Since this shifts the labor-demand curve, but not the labor-supply curve with P^e fixed, employment rises from N_0 to N_1 to N_2. Figure 7-1(b) shows the changes in equilibrium output on the supply side as employment changes. As N rises in Figure 7-1(b), equilibrium output, in turn, rises from y_0 to y_1 to y_2. This gives the aggregate supply curve of Figure 7-2. This supply curve can be combined with the economy's demand curve from Chapter 4 to show determination of equilibrium price and output in the economy.

The important thing to see in Figures 7-1 and 7-2 is that the positive slope of the aggregate supply curve of Figure 7-2 comes from the fact that as P increases, shifting labor demand up in Figure 7-1(a), labor market equilibrium employment N moves up along the given labor-supply curve. The money-illusion assumption that $p' = 0$ holds the labor-supply curve constant as P rises, generating the increase in employment and output in Figure 7-2.

Aggregate Supply Curve: Classical Case

To derive the aggregate supply curve in the classical case of perfect foresight with $p' = 1$, we can focus on the labor market equilibrium condition written as

$$f(N) = \frac{P^e}{P} \cdot g(N). \tag{3}$$

This is equation (17a) in Chapter 6 illustrated in Figure 7-3(a). Equilibrium in W, N space, using equation (2) is shown in Figure 7-3(b). Again, we can derive the aggregate supply curve in this classical case with $p' = 1$ by asking what happens to equilibrium employment as the price level moves exogenously.

With P^e moving along with P, Figure 7-3(a) shows no effect on equilibrium employment as P rises. The mechanism holding employment constant is seen more clearly in Figure 7-3(b). There the exogenous increase in actual P_0 to P_1 to P_2 shifts the labor-demand curve up. With $p' = 1$, P^e moves by equal amounts, from P^e_0 to P^e_1 to P^e_2. Thus, the labor-supply curve shifts up

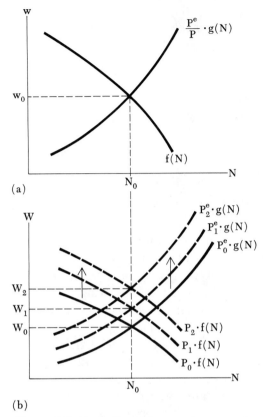

Figure 7-3 Derivation of the supply curve, classical case.

proportionately to the demand curve shifts, holding equilibrium employment at N_0. The nominal wage rate rises proportionately to the originating increase in the price level P, holding the real wage constant at w_0 in Figure 7-3(a). The result is no movement in employment and output as the price level rises in the classical case with $p' = 1$.

The resulting aggregate supply curve in the classical case is shown in Figure 7-4. With employment fixed at N_0 in Figure 7-3, output is fixed at $y_0 = y(N_0; \bar{K})$ as P rises from P_0 to P_1 to P_2. So in this classical case the aggregate supply curve is vertical; on the supply side, equilibrium output and employment are insensitive to movements in the price level under the assumption of perfect foresight.

General Short-Run Model: Imperfect Foresight

The extreme Keynesian and classical cases result from two polar assumptions about price expectations as formulated by equation (1): $p' = 0$ in the extreme

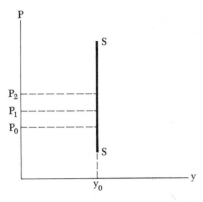

Figure 7-4 The aggregate-supply curve, classical case.

Keynesian case and $p' = 1$ in the classical case. These two assumptions give very different results for the aggregate supply curves of Figures 7-2 and 7-4. Now we can derive the aggregate supply curve in the general short-run static model in which $0 < p' < 1$. This is the model in which expectations adjust to changes in the actual price level, but not fully. It could be labeled the *imperfect foresight* model.

In Figure 7-5, adjustment of the labor market equilibrium to an exogenous increase in the price level from P_0 to P_1 is shown, with $0 < p' < 1$, so that P^e adjusts by an amount less than the exogenous change in P. In Figure 7-5(a), the increase in P reduces the ratio of expected to actual price level from P_0^e/P_0 to P_1^e/P_1 since $p' < 1$. This shifts the labor-supply curve down in w, N space, reducing the real wage and increasing employment from N_0 to N_1.

The same movement is also shown in the W, N space of Figure 7-5(b). There we see the increase in P shifting the demand curve up while the rise in P^e shifts the supply curve up, but less than the movement in the demand curve, since $p' < 1$. The excess demand for labor at W_0 pulls up the nominal wage to W_1, an increase less than proportionate to the P increase since $dP^e < dP$. Thus, employment rises to N_1. The movement in employment is translated to the change in output in Figure 7-5(c), using the production function.

So, in the imperfect foresight model, with $p' < 1$, the exogenous increase in the price level from P_0 to P_1 increases equilibrium output supplied from y_0 to y_1 in Figure 7-5(c). This movement is traced in the aggregate supply curve of Figure 7-6, where the (P_0,y_0) and (P_1,y_1) pairs lie along the positively sloped supply curve SS. The assumption of less-than-perfect foresight eliminates the verticality of the supply curve, making the curve positively sloped.

We can derive the slope of the aggregate supply curve algebraically using labor market equilibrium condition (2), rewritten as

$$P \cdot f(N) = P^e \cdot g(N) = p(P) \cdot g(N). \qquad (4)$$

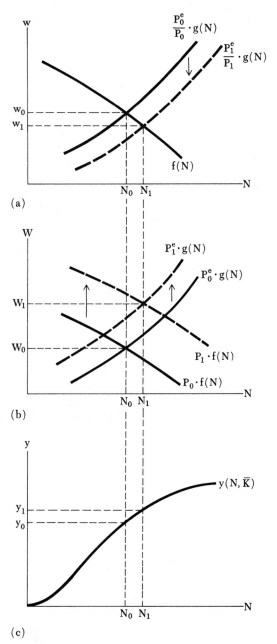

Figure 7-5 Derivation of the aggregate supply curve, general short-run model.

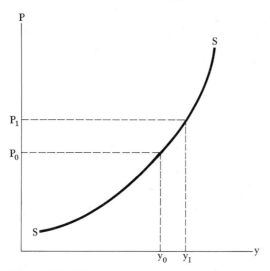

Figure 7-6 The aggregate-supply curve, general case.

The total differential of the equilibrium condition is

$$P \cdot f' \, dN + f(N)dP = P^e \cdot g' \, dN + g(N) \cdot p' \, dP.$$

To simplify this expression, let us assume that $P^e = P = 1$ initially. That is, suppose expectations are correct initially and set the price index $P = 1$, so that $f(N) = g(N) = w$ initially. Remember that the equilibrium condition in the labor market from equations (14)–(17) in Chapter 6 can be written as

$$w = \frac{P^e}{P} \cdot g(N) = f(N). \qquad (5)$$

This means that

$$f(N) = g(N) \quad \text{if} \quad P^e = P.$$

Now the total differential giving movements in N as P changes, maintaining labor market equilibrium, simplifies to

$$f' \, dN + w \, dP = g' \, dN + wp' \, dP.$$

This can be rearranged to give dN/dP along the supply curve

$$\frac{dN}{dP} = \frac{w \cdot (1 - p')}{g' - f'} \geq 0. \qquad (6)$$

With $0 < p' < 1$, $g' > 0$ and $f' < 0$, dN/dP is at least zero. To convert (6) into an expression for the aggregate supply curve in y,P space, we use the marginal product relationship $dy = (\partial y/\partial N) \cdot dN$. Thus, from (6) we have the slope of the aggregate supply curve as P changes.

$$\frac{dy}{dP} = \frac{\partial y}{\partial N} \cdot \frac{w \cdot (1 - p')}{g' - f'} \geq 0. \tag{7}$$

This says the slope of the aggregate supply curve of Figure 7-6 is vertical or positive. The inverse of equation (7),

$$\left(\frac{dy}{dP}\right)^{-1} = \frac{dP}{dy}\bigg|_S = \frac{1}{\partial y/\partial N} \cdot \frac{g' - f'}{w \cdot (1 - p')},$$

defines the reaction of P as y changes. This will be useful in extending the multiplier analysis of Chapter 5 to include supply as well as demand.

The slope of the supply curve in the extreme classical and Keynesian cases can be obtained by setting $p' = 1$ and 0, respectively, in (7). In the *classical* case, $p' = 1$, and $dy/dP = 0$ from (7), as shown in Figure 7-4. In the extreme *Keynesian* case with $p' = 0$, $dy/dP = w/(g' - f')$, the slope of the curve in Figure 7-2. In general, with some adaptation of P^e to changes in P, but with imperfect foresight, the slope of the Figure 7-6 supply curve is given by (7), with p' as an important parameter. Since in general the slope of the aggregate supply curve is positive, except in the extreme case where $p' = 1$, it is useful to think of the classical case as the extreme, while in general $dy/dP > 0$. The extreme Keynesian case gives the flattest version of the supply curve, but in all cases except the classical perfect foresight case, the curve is nonvertical.

Aggregate Supply in the Short Run and Long Run

It makes sense to think of the aggregate supply curve as being more nearly vertical, the longer the adjustment period after a disturbance. In other words, we expect p' to be smaller in the short run than in the long run. Consider a disturbance to aggregate demand that pulls up the price level, such as an increase in M or g from Chapter 5. In the very short run, the economy will move along a relatively flat supply curve with p' near zero. As time passes, and labor force price expectations adjust, p' will rise, steepening the supply curve. In the very long run p' might approach unity, restoring the original values of y and N.

This progression from short run to long run is sketched in Figure 7-7. An initial shift in aggregate demand from $D_0 D_0$ to $D_1 D_1$ would move income and the price level from (P_0, y_0) to (P_1, y_1) along the short-run supply curve $S_s S_s$, with a slope given by (7) and p' close to zero. Then as the labor force begins to react to the price increase, p' rises and the supply curve becomes steeper. In the longer run, p' moves closer to unity, and the supply curve looks

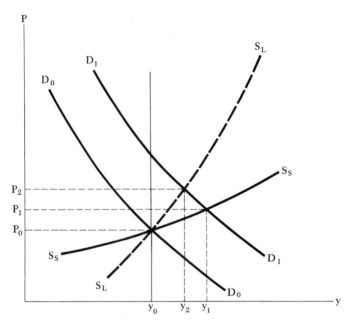

Figure 7-7   Aggregate supply in the short and long run.

more like the dashed $S_L S_L$ curve in Figure 7-7. The price level continues to rise, but the short-run increase in y is reduced as the economy moves to P_2, y_2. In the extreme classical case, y would return to y_0 and P to a yet higher P_3 on a vertical supply curve. But in the short run on which policy makers focus, the result of the shift in DD is an increase in P and y along the short-run supply curve.

INTRODUCTION TO THE FORMATION OF EXPECTATIONS

How might the price expectation function $p(P_t)$ and its derivative p' be specified? This question will assume greater importance in chapters to come, but for the moment let us try a rather simple relationship that has a certain intuitive appeal. The derivation of the function $p(P_t)$ will require both a mechanism to describe how expectations are formed and some knowledge about what happens to P_t over time.

Imagine now that you are a worker who has arrived at the end of some period $t - 1$, and you can look back over the economic history of that period and of previous periods. You have noticed that in the past the price level has moved jerkily up and down without (we assume for the moment) any overall trend or drift. Then you might adopt an *error correction* method for making *adaptive expectations*. Your guess about the future price level would be composed of two parts. One is the actual price level when you make your forecast, and the other is a term that adjusts for your error in the previous forecast. Formally, we can write

$$_{t-1}P_t = P_{t-1} + \lambda(_{t-2}P_{t-1} - P_{t-1}). \qquad (8)$$

The first term is the actual price level at $t-1$, and the second is an adjustment factor λ times the error you made in forecasting the price level in $t-1$. Typically, we imagine that λ lies between 0 and 1. At the zero extreme you ignore past erroneous anticipations, placing all the weight on the last period's actual price level; with λ = unity, you never change your expectations at all.

We now want to see that if expectations are adjusted by an error correction mechanism such as the one given in equation (8), the implication is that this period's expected price $_{t-1}P_t$ depends solely on the history of past prices. This makes it exogenous to this period's actual price determination. It is useful here to perform a little trick, known as a Koyck transformation. Changing time subscripts appropriately, we see that equation (8) also describes how expectations were formed about periods $t-1$, $t-2$, and so on. For example, at the end of $t-2$ the worker works out this equation for the expected price for period $t-1$:

$$_{t-2}P_{t-1} = P_{t-2} + \lambda(_{t-3}P_{t-2} - P_{t-2}).$$

We can take this last equation, multiply it by λ, and add to equation (8). In symbols

$$_{t-1}P_t = (1 - \lambda)P_{t-1} + \lambda(1 - \lambda)P_{t-2} + \lambda^2{}_{t-3}P_{t-2}.$$

The procedure can be repeated to eliminate $_{t-3}P_{t-2}$ and then on backwards again and again. A pattern rapidly emerges:

$$_{t-1}P_t = (1 - \lambda)P_{t-1} + \lambda(1 - \lambda)P_{t-2}$$
$$+ \lambda^2(1 - \lambda)P_{t-3} + \lambda^3(1 - \lambda)P_{t-4} + \cdots \qquad (9)$$

We are now in a position to investigate the consequences of adaptive expectations for the relationship between P_t and $_{t-1}P_t$. For a start, suppose that the price level had been constant for a long time at P_0. Then, suppose that at the beginning of a certain time T (subscript t is a variable, indicating some time period; subscript T is like the proper name of a particular period), the price level jumps up to P_1 and stays there indefinitely. At the beginning of T, all the terms on the right-hand side of equation (9) are equal to P_0, so the expected price for period T is given by P_0, that is, $_{T-1}P_T = P_0$:

$$_{T-1}P_T = (1 - \lambda)P_0 + \lambda(1 - \lambda)P_0 + \lambda^2(1 - \lambda)P_0 + \cdots = P_0.$$

Here we have the extreme Keynesian case during the first period after the price shift.

Once T is over, however, expectations are formed by equation (9) with t set equal to $T + 1$. Hence, the first term on the right-hand side for period $T + 1$ is P_1 and not P_0:

$$_TP_{T+1} = (1 - \lambda)P_1 + \lambda(1 - \lambda)P_0 + \lambda^2(1 - \lambda)P_0 + \cdots$$

Since $P_1 > P_0$, by assumption, it is easy to verify that

$$P_1 > {_TP_{T+1}} > {_{T-1}P_T} = P_0.$$

There is some correction in $T + 1$ for the error made at T, but it is incomplete. Then at the start of the following period, $t = T + 2$ in equation (9) and two of the right-hand terms contain P_1. The remaining error is again partly corrected, but because the error is smaller than during the first period, the absolute value of the correction is less. The size of each step depends on the parameter λ and on the time elapsed since the price level jump. This process continues indefinitely, with the remaining error becoming smaller and smaller. In equation (8), the second term on the right diminishes over time to make the difference $(P_t - {_{t-1}P_t})$ arbitrarily small.

Graphically, the evolution of the price level and of price level expectations following a one-time jump in P is shown in Figure 7-8. Table 7-1 sets out the change in expectations following a one-unit rise in the price level ($P_1 - P_0 = 1$) at time T, as a function of the time (i) after that increase. Also illustrated is the deviation of expectations from the current price level. In a discrete setting, $_{T+i-1}P_{T+i} - {_{T-2}P_{T-1}}$ corresponds to the derivative p' from $P^e = p(P)$. Clearly, it is rising across time; we start from the extreme Keynesian case and approach the classical case over time.

The adaptive adjustment of price expectations over time is the basis for our analysis of short-run and long-run adjustment of aggregate supply. The extreme Keynesian case with $_{T-1}P_T = P_0$ yields the flattish short-run aggregate supply curve of Figure 7-2. The classical case with P^e approaching P_1 is the vertical long-run supply curve.

Let us close this section with a brief discussion of the merits and demerits of adaptive expectations. Adaptive expectations have the advantage of being relatively straightforward to operate as a "rule of thumb," but isn't it silly not to correct fully at time $T + 1$? And isn't it even sillier to make the same error in expectations time after time, to underestimate the true price level consistently? Even worse could happen if at T the price level did not jump just once but started to rise each period along a trend. If the rate of inflation were high enough, the divergence would grow and grow without limit.

Simple adaptive expectations are at best appropriate in a stable world where the price level is not subject to inexorable inflation or deflation. In addition, the partial adjustment mechanism is more plausible in a world with a series of random movements in the price level, rather than one-time shifts.

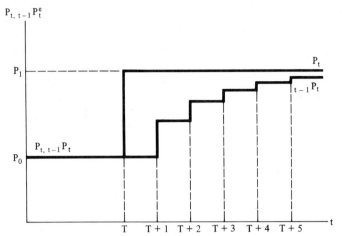

Figure 7-8 Adaption of expectations after a permanent change in the price level.

Suppose that at $T + 1$, P_t goes back down again. Then adaptive expectations would be below the actual price level during T but above the actual level during $T + 1$, $T + 2$, ... With the risk of being in error in either direction, we would not want to commit ourselves to belief in the permanence of any changes. Indeed, a smaller adjustment parameter λ corresponds to a smaller chance that a given change is permanent.

So adaptive expectations can make sense in an economic environment in which the price level moves up and down in a fairly random fashion, with the possibility of somewhat more permanent shifts in the background. This is the basic assumption about the economic environment in any static equilibrium model of the economy. We analyze the consequences for changes in output and the price level of generally unanticipated exogenous disturbances that can be interpreted as randomly distributed before they actually occur. Adaptive expectations seem appropriate in this environment.

Table 7-1.   ADAPTIVE ADJUSTMENT OF EXPECTATIONS

i	P_{T+i}	ΔP^e $_{T+i-1}P_{T+i} - _{T-2}P_{T-1}$	Forecasting error $P_{T+i} - _{T+i-1}P_{T+1}$
-1	P_0	0	0
0	$P_0 + 1$	0	1
1	$P_0 + 1$	$(1 - \lambda)$	λ
2	$P_0 + 1$	$(1 - \lambda) + \lambda(1 - \lambda)$	λ^2
3	$P_0 + 1$	$(1 - \lambda) + \lambda(1 - \lambda) + \lambda^2(1 - \lambda)$	λ^3

Here we assume that $\Delta P = (P_1 - P_0) = 1$ and $0 < \lambda < 1$.

SUPPLY-SIDE DISTURBANCES

The aggregate supply curve of equation (7) gives the reaction of equilibrium *output supplied, y*, as the price level changes, with a given production function $y(N; \bar{K})$, marginal product of labor function $f(N)$, and labor-supply function $g(N)$. A change in any of these relationships will shift the aggregate supply curve in P,y space. It is worth examining three "pure" cases by changing in turn each of these functions while holding the others constant. This exercise should point the way for more complicated cases in which more than one

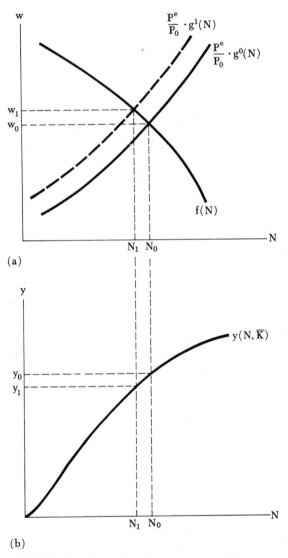

(a)

(b)

Figure 7-9 Shift in labor supply.

of these functions shifts, such as a change in technology that shifts both $y(N; \bar{K})$ and $f(N)$.

Shift in Labor Supply

The effect of an upward shift in the labor-supply function is illustrated in Figures 7-9 and 7-10. In Figure 7-9(a) the labor-supply curve shifts up from $g^0(N)$ to $g^1(N)$. This could be the result of a change in labor force tastes between income and leisure, an increase in unionized real wage demands, or an increase in unemployment benefits. The upward shift in the labor-supply function reduces equilibrium employment to N_1 in Figure 7-9(a), at the preexisting values of actual and expected price levels, P_0 and P^e. In Figure 7-9(b) the reduction in equilibrium employment reduces output supplied from y_0 to y_1 along the production function $y(N; \bar{K})$, again at the preexisting values of P_0 and P^e.

The shift in the aggregate supply function is shown in Figure 7-10. At the initial price level P_0, equilibrium output supplied falls from y_0 to y_1. This shift of the functional relationship between P and y on the supply side is shown as the shift of the supply curve from $S_0 S_0$ to $S_1 S_1$. For any initial price level, equilibrium output is reduced by the shift in labor supply; the shift at P_0 is an illustration.

Shift in the Production Function

The effect of an upward shift in the production function is illustrated in Figures 7-11 and 7-12. The shift could be due to a technical improvement that increases

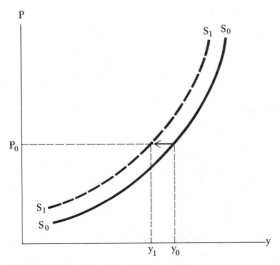

Figure 7-10 Effect on the supply curve.

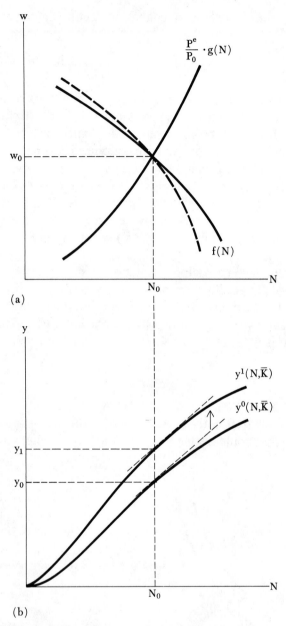

Figure 7-11   Shift in the production function.

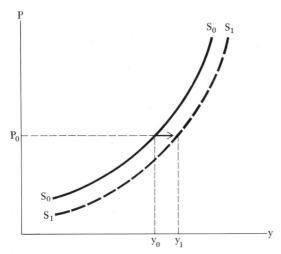

Figure 7-12 Effect on the supply curve.

capital efficiency. It could also result from an increase in the capital stock. The illustration in Figure 7-11(b) shows the slope of the production function (= marginal product of labor or *MPL*) unchanged at the initial employment level N_0. We focus on this particular case in order to keep the effects of a shift in the production function separate from the effect of a shift in labor demand (=*MPL*).

The shift in the production function leaves the labor market equilibrium undisturbed in Figure 7-11(a), since the *MPL* is unchanged by assumption. But at equilibrium N_0, the equilibrium level of output supplied rises from y_0 to y_1, in Figure 7-11(b). This shifts the aggregate supply function out from $S_0 S_0$ to $S_1 S_1$ in Figure 7-12 at the initial price level P_0. The technical improvement increases equilibrium output supplied at any price level.

Figures 7-9 to 7-12 provide a good illustration of a basic principle in comparative static analysis. When we want to examine the effects of an exogenous event, we go to the shift in the underlying supply or demand function (as in Figure 7-9), or technical relationship (as in Figure 7-11) and trace the movement from there. This insures against mistakes arising from beginning the analysis "in the middle of the story."

Shift in Labor Demand

A technical change that alters the *slope* of the production function without changing y/N at the initial equilibrium N_0 can be represented as a pure shift in the labor-demand function $f(N)$. The results can be worked through with a pair of figures such as 7-9 and 7-10. An *increase* in the slope of the production function, for example, shifts $f(N)$ up, increasing N and y at the initial value of *P*. This shifts the aggregate supply function out, increasing equilibrium output supplied at any value of *P*, as in Figure 7-12.

These examples conclude our analysis of the supply side of our skeletal macromodel. They illustrate shifts in output supplied, given *P*, while earlier sections showed the effects of movements in *P*, given the underlying relationships. We can now combine the demand analysis of Chapters 4 and 5 with the supply analysis of Chapters 6 and 7 to study general equilibrium determination of *y, P, r,* and *N* in this basic short-run static model.

SELECTED READINGS

P. Cagan, "The Monetary Dynamics of Hyper Inflations," W.M. Friedman, Ed., *Studies in the Quantity Theory of Money* (Chicago: University of Chicago Press, 1956).

Z. Griliches, "Distributed Lags: A Survey," *Econometrica,* January 1967.

chapter 8

Equilibrium in the Static Model

In Chapters 4 and 5 we developed the demand side of our skeletal macromodel, taking the price level P as exogenous. In Chapters 6 and 7 we turned to the labor market and the supply side, and derived the economy's supply curve, still taking P as exogenous. Now, in Chapter 8, we combine demand and supply to determine equilibrium values for the price level P and output ($=$ income) y, and for employment N and the interest rate r. In Figure 8-1, the intersection of the supply and demand curves gives us equilibrium P_0 and y_0. We can take those equilibrium values back to the IS or LM curves on the demand side to find equilibrium r_0, and to the labor market equation or production function on the supply side to find equilibrium N_0.

This chapter analyzes the general equilibrium determination of the four key variables y, N, r, and P, and the reaction of these equilibrium values to exogenous shocks, both on the demand side and on the supply side. Working carefully through the analysis of the reactions to exogenous disturbances will give the student the beginning of an intuitive understanding of how the macro economy "hangs together." Then in Chapter 9 we will work through the effects of monetary, fiscal, and incomes policies in this skeletal macro economy.

DETERMINATION OF EQUILIBRIUM y, N, r, AND P

The demand side of Chapters 4 and 5 was summarized in the equilibrium conditions for the product market and the money market. These are written as

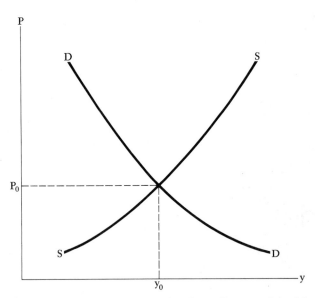

Figure 8-1   Aggregate demand and supply: general model.

$$\text{Product market:} \quad y = c(y - t(y)) + i(r) + g; \quad (\text{the } IS \text{ curve}). \quad (1)$$

$$\text{Money market:} \quad \frac{\bar{M}}{P} = l(r) + k(y); \quad (\text{the } LM \text{ curve}). \quad (2)$$

These two equilibrium conditions were combined in Chapter 4 to give the economy's demand curve in P, y space, as shown in Figure 8-1. The supply side of Chapter 6 added a production function and a labor market equilibrium condition to the model:

$$\text{Production function:} \quad y = y(N; \bar{K}); \quad (3)$$

$$\text{Labor market:} \quad P \cdot f(N) = P^e \cdot g(N) = p(P) \cdot g(N). \quad (4)$$

In Chapter 7 we discussed the error correction, or partial adjustment, mechanism for price expectations. In that model, in the short run P^e is unresponsive to movements in the actual price level P; it takes time for expectations to adjust. So in the short run, p' is near zero, and we have the relatively flat aggregate supply curve of Figure 7-2. In the long run, expectations adjust more fully, so p' approaches unity. This gives us a steeper aggregate supply curve. The extreme case in the long run is $p' = 1$, resulting in the classical case with a vertical aggregate supply curve as shown in Figure 7-4. In the discussion of equilibrium in the static model here, we will focus on two cases: a *short-run* model where $0 < p' < 1$ and the aggregate supply came in positively sloped, and the *classical* case, where $p' = 1$, and the aggregate supply curve is vertical. Here we identify the classical case with the longer run. In Chapter 11 we will see cases where *rational expectations* collapses the longer run classical case into the short run.

The three equilibrium conditions (1), (2), and (4) and the production function (3) give us four equations in our *short-run model* to determine values for four unknowns: y, N, r, and P. In general, the model is *nonseparable:* it is simultaneous enough to require all three equilibrium conditions to solve for all the variables. Substituting N for y from the production function (4), we can see that the product market equilibrium condition includes the variables N and r, and the money market includes N, P, and r. On the supply side, the labor market equilibrium condition includes N and P. Thus, the general model is completely simultaneous, as seen in Figure 8-1.

The model becomes *separable,* or *dichotomous,* when we use the *classical* assumption that $p' = 1$. If we begin with a full equilibrium where P and P^e are indexed to 1, so $P^e = P = 1$, then the classical assumption of $p' = 1$ makes $P^e = P$ throughout the analysis. But if we substitute $P^e = P$ into the left-hand version of the labor market equilibrium condition (4), we have the classical condition,

$$\text{Classical labor market:} \quad f(N) = g(N). \qquad (4a)$$

The classical assumption that $p' = 1$ *dichotomizes* the model. The classical labor market equilibrium condition (4a) is one equation with one unknown, N. As shown in Figure 7-3, this determines equilibrium employment N_0 with no influence from aggregate demand. With N_0 determined by condition (4a), we can find equilibrium output using equation (3) as $y_0 = y(N_0; \bar{K})$. This gives us an aggregate supply curve that is vertical at $y = y_0$, as shown in Figure 7-4.

The separability, or dichotomy, of the classical model is shown in Figure 8-2. There the demand curve has the usual negative slope implied by the *IS* and *LM* curves of equation (1) and (2), and derived in Chapter 4. However, the supply curve in Figure 8-2 is vertical at y_0. The labor market condition (4a) and the production function (3) fix y_0 independently of demand. In Figure 8-2, the position of the aggregate demand curve determines only the price level P_0. With y_0 and P_0 fixed, we can go back to the *IS* curve *or* the *LM* curve to find r_0. Remember that they each give the same value for r_0 because the aggregate demand curve *DD* was derived from movements of *ISLM* intersections where the r,y pair is the *same* on both curves.

REACTION TO DEMAND DISTURBANCES

Let us now look at a graphical solution of the complete system in the short-run static model, using labor market condition (4) with $p' < 1$. Figure 8-3(a) shows the product and money market equilibrium, while Figure 8-3(b) shows

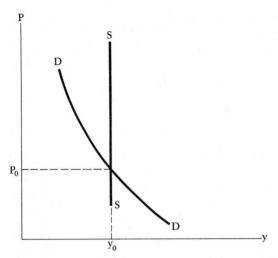

Figure 8-2 Aggregate demand and supply: classical case.

the labor market. The initial equilibrium level of output y_0 in Figure 8-3(a) must correspond to N_0 in Figure 8-3(b) through the production function. Initial equilibrium y_0, P_0 is shown in the supply and demand diagram of Figure 8-4. The Figure 8-4 value y_0 is the same as that of Figure 8-3(a), and P_0 is the initial equilibrium price level fixing the position of the LM curve of Figure 8-3(a), through $\bar{M}/P$, the labor-demand curve of Figure 8-3(b), and the labor-supply curve, through $P^e = p(P)$.

Adjustment in the Short-Run Model

To see how equilibrium is reached, we will now assume that there is a sudden exogenous increase in the level of investment demand in the economy, due, perhaps, to an increase in expected returns from investment. It should by now be clear from the four-quadrant diagram behind IS that this shift in $i(r)$ will lead to an outward shift in the IS curve. This is shown in Figure 8-3(a) by the IS shift from $I_0 S_0$ to $I_1 S_1$, changing equilibrium output on the demand side of the economy to y_1. Equilibrium output supplied remains at y_0, corresponding to N_0, on the supply side at the initial price level P_0. In Figure 8-4 the increase in investment demand shifts the demand curve up to $D_1 D_1$. At the initial price level P_0, this shows a new equilibrium output demanded of y_1, the same as the new demand-side equilibrium y_1 in Figure 8-3(a). Thus, the shift in investment demand $i(r)$ creates an excess demand for goods and services which would be magnified by the multiplier process to give excess demand at the initial price level of $y_1 - y_0$. The excess demand leads to a rise in prices. This, in turn, on the demand side reduces the level of the real money

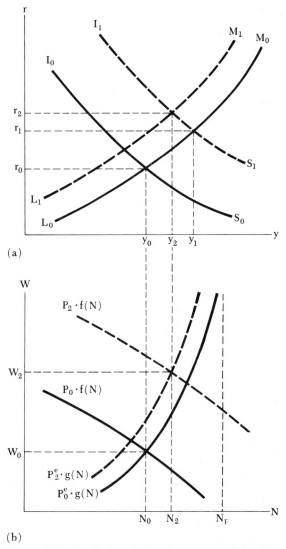

(a)

(b)

Figure 8-3 Equilibrium in the short-run model.

supply $m = \bar{M}/P$ (or increases the demand for nominal balances), shifting the LM curve up toward L_1M_1 in Figure 8-3(a). This reduction in equilibrium output demanded in the economy as the price level rises is represented in Figure 8-4 by movement up along the new demand curve D_1D_1 from y_1 toward y_2.

In the labor market the rise in prices stimulates employers to expand production by offering higher wages to hire more labor. This increase in demand for labor is represented in the labor market diagram of Figure 8-3(b) by upward shifts of the demand curve from $P_0 \cdot f(N)$ toward $P_2 \cdot f(N)$. At the same time, as the labor force begins to perceive the rise in the price level, the expected price level P^e rises, shifting up the labor-supply curve $P^e \cdot g(N)$ in Figure 8-3(b). In the short run with p' near zero, the shift in labor supply will be small compared to the shift in demand. Thus, in the short run equilibrium employment would rise toward N_2 in Figure 8-3(b).

In Figure 8-4, this increase in equilibrium output supplied is represented by moving up the original supply curve from y_0 toward y_2. Thus, the price increase raises equilibrium output on the supply side from y_0 toward y_1 and reduces it on the demand side from y_1 toward y_2. The price increase will continue until the excess demand, measured by the difference between equilibrium y on the demand side and on the supply side in Figure 8-4, is eliminated. Thus, at the final equilibrium output y_2, which is greater than the original level y_0, the excess demand for goods and services has been eliminated, stopping the rise in prices, and the excess demand for labor has been eliminated, stopping the increase in wages. The excess demand for money that was created in the background has also been eliminated, stopping the rise in the interest rate at r_2.

Since y has increased, we know from the production function $y = y(N; \bar{K})$ that employment has increased as shown in Figure 8-3(b). Also, the increase in prices has caused the interest rate r to increase.

The increase in demand has increased equilibrium employment from N_0 to N_2 in this short-run model with $p' < 1$. The rise in prices has reduced the

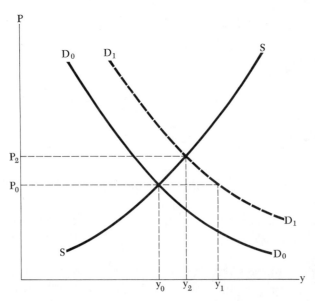

Figure 8-4 Demand shift in the short-run model.

equilibrium output demanded from y_1, but it has also *increased* equilibrium supply-side output from y_0 and employment from N_0, as opposed to the independence of N from demand conditions in the classical case with $p' = 1$.

Higher prices have brought higher wages by creating excess labor market demand, raising W from W_0 to W_2 in Figure 8-3(b). From the labor-demand function

$$W = P \cdot f(N) \quad \text{or} \quad \frac{W}{P} = f(N); \quad f' < 0, \tag{5}$$

we can see that the increase in worker-hours means that the real wage $w = W/P$ has been reduced. This was necessary to induce employers to take on additional labor. Thus, since the real wage is lower, the rise in wages has not been as great as the rise in prices.

It should be useful here to summarize the effects of the exogenous increase in investment demand in the short-run model. First, the increase in demand has tightened money market and credit market conditions both by raising y at the initial price level, pulling r up to r_1 in Figure 8-3(a), and by raising prices, accounting for a further increase in r to r_2. But this increase in the interest rate has not been sufficient to choke off the initial increase in investment demand. From the product market equilibrium condition, equation (1) (p. 146), we have

$$y - c(y - t(y)) = i(r) + g. \tag{6}$$

With an increase in y, the endogenous increase in c will be smaller than the y increase, so that the left-hand side of (6) must increase from the old to the new equilibrium. With no change in g, this means i must have risen also, on balance. This just reflects the fact that, if y is to increase, there must be, on balance, an *exogenous* or *policy-induced* increase in some expenditure component.

While on the demand side of the economy the price increase tends to reduce equilibrium output through money market effects, on the supply side the price increase tends to increase equilibrium output in this model. With price perceptions or expectations not adjusting fully to the actual price increase in the short run, that is, $p' < 1$, the price rise increases employment by increasing the demand for labor, the money wage rises less than the price level, and so the real wage rate goes down.

Adjustment in the Classical Case

In the classical case with $p' = 1$, the increases in the price level and interest rate squeeze the initial increase in demand completely out of the system. The initial demand shift is the same as in the short-run model with $p' < 1$. In

Figure 8-5(a) the IS curve shifts up to $I_1 S_1$ with the initial increase in investment demand. At the initial price level P_0, equilibrium output demanded rises to y_1. This is shown as a shift in the aggregate demand curve of Figure 8-6, where the increase from y_0 to y_1 on the demand side is the same as in Figure 8-5(a).

    The shift of the demand curve produces an excess demand gap of $y_1 - y_0$, so the price level begins to rise. This shifts the LM curve in Figure 8-5(a) up, raising the interest rate further and reducing investment demand. In Figure 8-5(c), the price increase shifts labor demand up as firms bid for more employees to increase output when they see prices rise. But with $p' = 1$, the labor-supply curve shifts up as much as demand, so that while an excess demand gap appears on the labor market, pulling up the money wage, there is no movement in employment or output, which remain fixed at N_0, y_0. This is seen explicitly in Figure 8-5(b) where the ratio P^e/P remains unchanged, leaving $N = N_0$.

    How long does the price increase continue in this classical case? The price level rises until demand is reduced to the original level y_0, as seen in Figure 8-6. At that point demand is again equal to the fixed supply, so excess demand is eliminated. In Figure 8-5(a), the LM curve shifts up until equilibrium output demanded is back to y_0. In Figure 8-5(c) the money wage W rises as much as the price level, so that in Figure 8-5(b) the real wage is unchanged.

    What has happened to investment demand? From the product market equilibrium condition (1), we again have

$$y - c(y - t(y)) = i(r) + g.$$

If y remains unchanged at y_0 and there has been no change in g, investment i must return to its original value before the exogenous shift. The price increase to P_2 raises the interest rate r just enough to move total investment back to its original value. Only then is total demand equal to y_0.

    This result follows from the classical assumption that $p' = 1$, which makes the aggregate supply curve of Figure 8-6 vertical at y_0. The vertical supply curve in the classical case is just a graphical representation of the dichotomy between the labor market, where equilibrium N_0 is determined, and demand conditions in the economy. It is this dichotomy that leads us to question the relevance of the classical assumption for explaining short-run macroeconomic developments. It is clear in reality that exogenous shifts in demand, such as the i change discussed above, will usually generate partially offsetting reductions in investment demand through the money market. But wide fluctuations in the level of employment and unemployment also have been observed in reality, with unemployment reaching 25 percent in 1933 and varying between 10 and 3 percent since World War II. While the classical model says that the level of employment is not sensitive to changes in demand conditions in the economy,

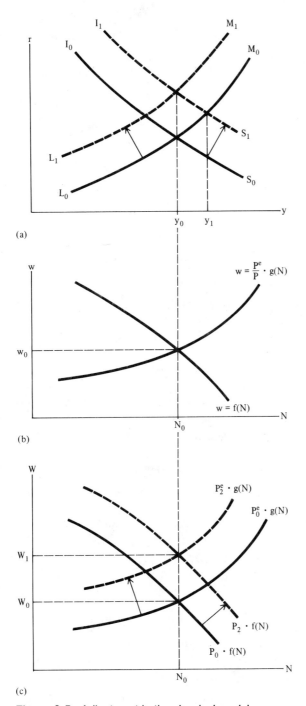

Figure 8-5 Adjustment in the classical model.

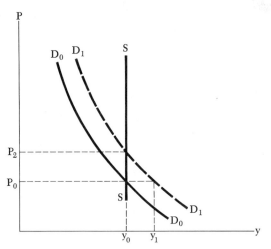

Figure 8-6 Aggregate supply and demand in the classical case.

these fluctuations in the level of employment in reality have been related to demand conditions.

The Liquidity Trap

The liquidity trap suggested by Keynes is a special circumstance in which the classical case has no equilibrium solution. Keynes used the liquidity trap to score a debating point against the classical case; we can use it here to illustrate a conceptual difference between the classical case and the short-run model with a positively sloped aggregate supply curve.

We saw in Chapter 5 that the speculative demand-for-money curve, $l(r)$, may become very flat at low interest rates. If $l(r)$ becomes horizontal at some low r_{min}, the LM curve will also be horizontal at that value of r. The theoretical importance of this point in the classical case is shown in Figures 8-7 and 8-8. If, from initial equilibrium y_0 in Figure 8-7(a), investment demand collapses so that the IS curve shifts to $I_1 S_1$, the price level will begin to fall. In the classical labor market of Figure 8-7(b), the price drop will not change equilibrium N_0; the price change affects labor supply and demand symmetrically, since both depend on the real wage alone.

On the demand side, in Figure 8-7(a), the price drop shifts the LM curve out. But since IS has fallen to an intersection with the horizontal segment of the LM curve, the price change does not increase demand-side equilibrium output from y_1, so that excess supply $y_0 - y_1$ remains. Thus, as Keynes pointed out, the classical model may be *inconsistent* at low interest rates. This inconsistency is brought out in Figure 8-8, which shows the demand curve shifting to $D_1 D_1$, corresponding to the IS shift to $I_1 S_1$. With no intersection of the

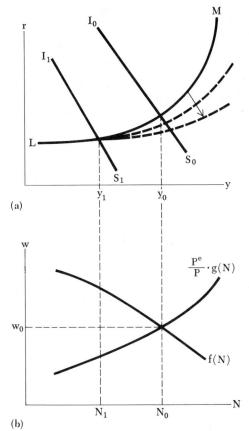

Figure 8-7 The liquidity trap: the classical case.

supply and demand curves, the classical model has no equilibrium solution, and seems to suggest that wages and prices would fall continuously if the economy were to get stuck in this liquidity trap where people are indifferent between holding bonds that earn r_{min} and money that earns nothing.

Various writers since Keynes have removed this inconsistency in the classical model. A. C. Pigou suggested that falling prices would increase consumers' real wealth, increasing consumer spending and reducing saving, shifting $s(y - t(y))$ down. This would shift *IS* up to eventual demand-side equilibrium. This wealth effect has been confirmed by subsequent research, as discussed in Chapter 12 on the consumption function. Also, empirical work on the demand for money has found no evidence that it does, indeed, become absolutely flat at very low interest rates, as we discuss in Chapter 14 on the demand for money.

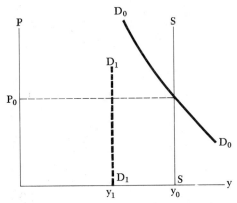

Figure 8-8 Supply and demand in the liquidity trap: the classical case.

These solutions to the "inconsistency" in the classical model generally imply that, after a long period of falling wages and prices, equilibrium will be reestablished at the original N_0, y_0 point. But in the 1930s, the U.S. economy seemed to reach a different result: a fairly stable low level of employment with wages and prices dropping to a fairly stable level.

This result is consistent with the short-run model which does not have the liquidity-trap inconsistency. The problem in the classical model was that neither equilibrium output supplied nor demanded responded to the price drop in the liquidity-trap case. In the short-run model of Figures 8-9 and 8-10 the price drop reduces the demand for labor, reducing equilibrium supply-side output from y_0 to y_1, along the positively sloped SS curve of Figure 8-10.

Thus, in this depression case, the short-run model establishes a new equilibrium at y_1, N_1, P_1, W_1, with a drop in employment, as experienced in the 1930s, and a new, but lower, equilibrium, price, and wage level. The short-run model seems to be a better framework for understanding the events of the 1930s than the classical case with the liquidity trap.

REACTION TO SUPPLY DISTURBANCES

Discussion of demand-side disturbances, or exogenous shocks, is simplified by the fact that once the disturbance is translated into an impact effect on expenditure, the results can be analyzed independently of the source of the disturbance. As we saw in the multiplier analysis of Chapter 5, any demand-side shock works through the same multiplier [equation (17) of Chapter 5] as any other disturbance, once we have accounted for the impact effect on expenditure.

For supply-side disturbances, the analysis is not quite so simple, because an event changing both the *level* and the *slope* of the production function will

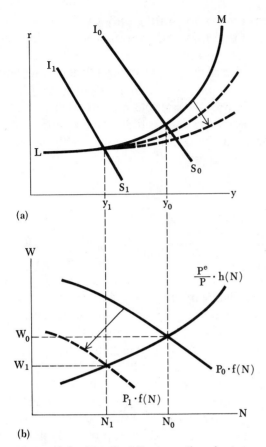

(a)

(b)

Figure 8-9 The liquidity trap: the short-run model.

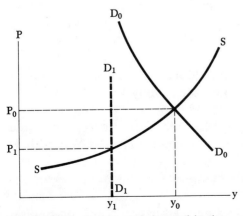

Figure 8-10 Supply and demand in the liquidity trap: the short-run model.

have different results from an event shifting only the level, or only the slope. This is because a change in the slope of the production function ($=MPL$) will shift the labor-demand curve as well as the production function.

An exogenous shock that shifts the production function without changing MPL at the initial level of employment is hard to imagine. So here we will focus on shocks that shift both, for example, bad weather or an oil embargo, and in passing note the differences that would appear if MPL did not change. In Chapter 9 we will look at the effect of exogenous shifts in labor supply under the heading of *incomes policy*.

Impact Effects

To make the analysis as clear as possible, we should begin by isolating the source of the supply curve shift and then go on to the economy's reaction to the shift. Let's consider a shock that reduces the supply of some factor that cooperates with capital and labor in producing output. This could be a run of bad weather that reduces the supply of agricultural output, such as we had in 1972, a shift in the supply curve of an intermediate input, such as the oil embargo in 1974, or the price rise in 1979, or even a bombing raid that reduces the capital stock (not neutron bombs, presumably).

The effects of a reduction in the supply of a cooperating factor such as raw materials or energy on the aggregate supply curve are shown in Figures 8-11 and 8-12. In Figure 8-11(b), the reduction in supply of, say, energy shifts the production function down. With a given input of labor and capital, less output can be produced. In Figure 8-11(a), the demand for labor also shifts down, on the assumption that the marginal product of labor $f(N)$ falls. This would be the case with any multiplicative production function such as $y = AK^\alpha L^\beta E^{(1-\alpha-\beta)}$ where E stands for energy supply. A partially additive production function such as $y = AK^\alpha L^{(1-\alpha)} + bE$ would be needed to give a change in E availability with no change in MPL.

At the initial values for P_0 and P^e, the reduction in energy supply from E_0 to E_1 reduces equilibrium output supplied in Figure 8-11(b) from y_0 to y_2. A drop from y_0 to y_1 would result simply from the shift in the production function at N_0. The original level of employment would produce less output with less E input. The additional drop to y_2 comes from the fall in MPL, which reduces equilibrium employment at P_0 from N_0 to N_2 in Figure 8-11(a). Thus, the supply curve shift in Figure 8-12, from (P_0, y_0) to (P_0, y_2) comes from two factors: the production function shift at $N_0(y_0 \rightarrow y_1)$, and the change in employment to $N_2(y_1 \rightarrow y_2)$. As we will now see, the shift in demand for labor (MPL) is crucial, because the final outcome for employment depends on it.

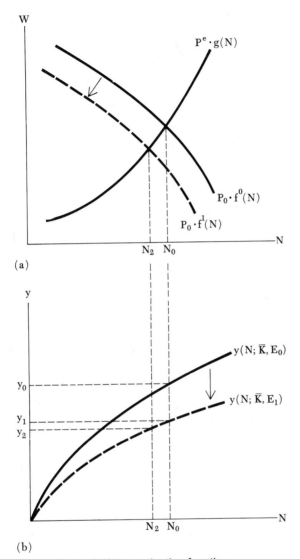

(a)

(b)

Figure 8-11 Shift in production function.

Equilibrium Reactions in the Short-Run Model

The drop in available energy input shifts the supply curve left in Figures 8-12 and 8-13. This creates an excess demand gap equal to $y_0 - y_2$ in those two figures. Notice that in this case the excess demand came from a reduction of supply, where in the earlier section on demand disturbances it came from an increase in demand. There is an important point to be understood here. Once it is established whether a given exogenous shock generates excess demand (pulling P up) or excess supply (pushing P down), the analyses of reactions

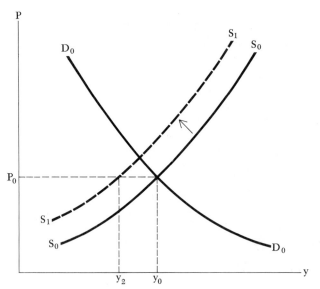

Figure 8-12 Shift in aggregate supply.

in the supply and demand sides are independent of *where* the shock originates. The origin of the shock is important in telling us how *DD* or *SS* shifts in Figure 8-13. Once we have established that, we know whether excess demand or supply appears. At that point we know whether *P* rises or falls as a consequence, and the analysis proceeds independently of the source of the shock.

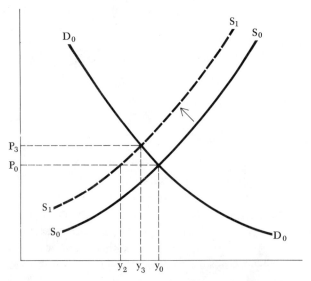

Figure 8-13 Reaction to a shift in aggregate supply.

In the short-run model with $p' < 1$, the rise in prices from P_0 to the new equilibrium P_3 in Figure 8-13 raises equilibrium employment to N_3 in Figure 8-14(a). With $p' < 1$, the shift of labor supply from $P_0^e \cdot g(N)$ to $P_3^e \cdot g(N)$ is smaller than the shift in demand from $P_0 \cdot f^1(N)$ to $P_3 \cdot f^1(N)$. Output supplied increases along the new production function $y(N; \bar{K}, E)$ and along the new supply curve $S_1 S_1$ in Figure 8-13 from y_2 to y_3 as P rises.

On the demand side, the rise in the price level from P_0 to the new equilibrium P_3 reduces equilibrium output *demanded* from y_0 to y_3. As P rises the *LM* curve shifts up, raising the interest rate and reducing output demanded. This process continues as long as P rises, that is, until equilibrium is reestablished at y_3 with the excess demand gap eliminated. The rise in the interest rate has reduced investment, and the fall in income has reduced consumption.

It is useful to look at the final outcome for employment in some detail to see the importance of the *MPL* shift. Given the supply curve shift of Figure 8-13 it is inevitable that equilibrium output is reduced. All that this requires is a negatively sloped demand curve. But the outcome for employment is not so clear. As the price level rises to eliminate excess demand, equilibrium employment on the supply side rises from N_2. Figure 8-14 and the text assume the intuitively likely outcome that N settles below N_0. But this is not necessarily the case. If the aggregate demand curve were very steep, the needed P increase could shift equilibrium N *above* N_0. For example, y_4 in Figure 8-14(b) gives a higher level of employment than N_0, but is still below y_0. Thus, we cannot be sure that *employment* goes down in response to the reduction in energy supply; only that *output* falls.

What is happening here? There are two effects at work. The drop in output reduces demand for all inputs at given factor-input ratios. This is the equivalent of an income effect. But in the case at hand, energy prices rise relative to wages, causing employers to attempt to substitute labor for energy. If substitution is *easy,* the *MPL* drop in Figures 8-11(a) and 8-14(a) is *small.* And if the aggregate demand curve is very *steep,* the price increase will be large and the output drop *small.* In that case, the substitution effect could outweigh the output effect, and employment would rise.

An extreme example should make this point clear. Suppose the production function had shifted with no change in *MPL.* Then the initial level of equilibrium employment in Figure 8-14(a) would not have been affected by the *impact effects.* But as P rose to eliminate excess demand, equilibrium N would then have clearly risen.

This illustrates the complexity of analysis of supply-side shocks that we mentioned above. While the results for output are clear, we have to know the exact specification of the production function *and* the slope of the demand curve before we can say something definitive about employment. So for this analysis we must turn to econometric models, which unfortunately have not yet concentrated enough on the supply side to give us clear results.

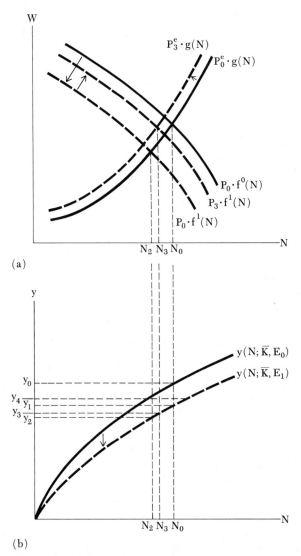

(a)

(b)

Figure 8-14 Supply-side reactions.

Summary of the Classical Case

In the classical case, the impact effect of a drop in energy supply is to shift the vertical supply curve of Figure 8-15 left. Returning to Figures 8-11 and 8-12, we see that the impact effect of a drop in energy supply is to reduce equilibrium employment to N_2, and output *supplied* to y_2, shown also as y_2 in Figure 8-15. This, as usual, creates the excess demand gap $y_0 - y_2$ in Figure 8-15.

But as the price level rises in reaction to excess demand, with $p' = 1$, the equilibrium level of employment and output on the supply side remain at N_2, y_2. This should be clear by now; the vertical supply curve has shifted from

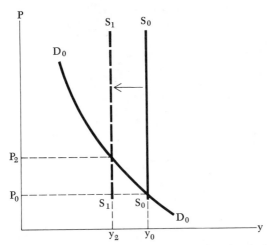

Figure 8-15 Supply and demand in the classical case.

$S_0 S_0$ to $S_1 S_1$ in Figure 8-15. All the equilibrium adjustment to a supply shock after the impact effects in the classical case comes on the demand side, as equilibrium output demanded is reduced to y_2 in Figure 8-15.

The analysis of reaction to supply disturbances in the classical case thus does not result in the ambiguity of the general model, since there is no adjustment of equilibrium N, y on the supply side beyond the impact effects. This gives us a useful insight into the long-run effects of a change in energy availability. However, for the short run we have the likely outcome of Figures 8-13 and 8-14. In the short run the impact effects of a supply-side shock are only partially offset by the equilibrating price movement that follows. It is only in the classical case that the impact effects are also the final equilibrium effects.

SELECTED READINGS

R.W. Clower, "The Keynesian Counter-Revolution: A Theoretical Appraisal" in R.W. Clower, ed., *Monetary Theory: Selected Readings* (Harmondsworth, Middlesex, England: Penguin Books Ltd., 1969).

M. Friedman, "A Theoretical Framework for Monetary Analysis," *Journal of Political Economy,* March/April 1970.

J.M. Keynes, *The General Theory of Employment, Interest and Money* (New York: Harcourt, Brace and Company, 1936), Chapter 15.

D. Patinkin, *Money, Interest and Prices,* 2nd ed. (New York: Harper & Row, 1965), Chapters 9–10.

D. Patinkin, "Price Flexibility and Full Employment," in M.G. Mueller, ed., *Readings in Macroeconomics* (New York: Holt, Rinehart and Winston, 1966).

A.C. Pigou, "The Classical Stationary State," *Economic Journal,* December 1943.

chapter *9*

Monetary, Fiscal, and Incomes Policy

In Chapter 8 we joined the demand side of the economy, developed in Chapters 4 and 5, with the supply side, developed in Chapters 6 and 7, to study general equilibrium determination of the key variables y, P, r, and N in the short run. Now we turn to the analysis of aggregate demand and supply policy in the static model.

In this chapter we return to the issues of Chapter 5. Suppose the government, in its wisdom, decides that the existing equilibrium levels of y, P, r, and N are not satisfactory. For example, suppose the level of output and employment yields an unemployment rate of 10.5 percent as in mid-1983. Or the problem could be an excess demand gap caused by an upward shift in the supply curve, analyzed in Chapter 7, that is pulling the price level up (i.e., inflation). The instruments the government has to deal with these problems are *monetary policy, fiscal policy,* and perhaps *incomes policy.*

Monetary policy changes in the money supply $\bar{M}$ and fiscal policy changes in government purchases g or the tax schedule t operate to shift the aggregate demand curve, as we saw in Chapter 5. Incomes policy attempts to shift the aggregate supply curve by shifting labor supply vertically; it changes the nominal wage rate W demanded by the labor force to supply any given amount of labor N, given the price level P_0. Incomes policy is generally used to slow down the rate of price increase in a situation where the labor-supply curve is shifting up because of workers' expectations of real wage increases. Dynamic aspects of incomes policy will be discussed in Chapter 20 of Part IV; here we include it in the static model as a shift in the labor-supply curve.

In most of Part II, we take policy instruments such as $\bar{M}$ or g as given, positioning the relevant demand or supply curves, and then solve for the equilibrium values of our key variables. Then, in Chapters 5 and 9 we study the effects on these key variables of changes in the policy instruments. This procedure is inverted in the formal study of the theory of economic policy. There the desired values for the key endogenous variables y, P, r, and N are given as the *policy targets*. The basic static model is then inverted to solve for the values of the *policy instruments* $\bar{M}$, g, t, and α [where α is an incomes policy instrument that shifts the labor force's price-expectations function, $P^e = p(P, \alpha)$]. Thus, where we generally take $\bar{M}$, g, t, and α as given (α generally $= 0$) and solve for y, P, r, and N, the theory of policy would solve the model the other way round to get values for the policy instruments necessary to hit the desired policy targets. A full discussion of the theory of policy would take too much time to develop here, but the student who has followed the analysis carefully to this point should be able to see how the four-equation system of Chapter 8, repeated below, can be inverted to solve for desired instrument settings, given policy targets.

MONETARY AND FISCAL POLICY IN THE STATIC MODEL

On the demand side of the economy, the equilibrium conditions for the product market,

$$IS: \quad y = c(y - t(y)) + i(r) + g, \tag{1}$$

and for the money market,

$$LM: \quad \frac{\bar{M}}{P} = l(r) + k(y), \tag{2}$$

are shown in the r,y space of Figure 9-1(a) as $I_0 S_0$ and $L_0 M_0$. The investment and saving functions and level of government purchases fix the position of the *IS* curve. The demand-for-money function and the level of real balances $m = \bar{M}/P$ fix the position of the *LM* curve. Varying the price level shifts the *LM* curve in Figure 9-1(a), tracing out the demand curve $D_0 D_0$ in Figure 9-2.

On the supply side we have the labor market equilibrium condition developed in Chapter 6,

$$P \cdot f(N) = P^e \cdot g(N) = p(P) \cdot g(N); \quad 0 < p' < 1, \tag{3}$$

shown in Figure 9-1(b). This gives equilibrium employment N as a function of the price level. Employment is translated into output y by the production function,

$$y = y(N; \bar{K}). \tag{4}$$

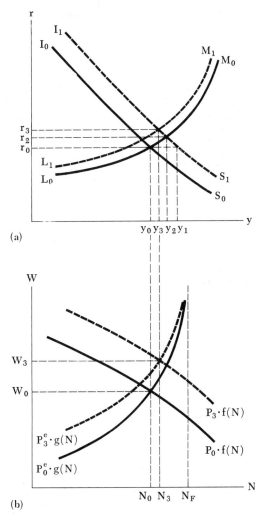

Figure 9-1 Equilibrium in the static model: an increase in *g*.

The model of equations (1)–(4) is, of course, the same as in equations (1)–(4) in Chapter 8. There we focused on equilibrium itself; here we look at the effects of policy.

In this model, changes in P shift both the demand and supply curves in Figure 9-1(b), changing equilibrium employment N. This, in turn, changes equilibrium output on the supply side through the production function, tracing out the supply curve $S_0 S_0$ of Figure 9-2. Thus, the *IS* and *LM* equations give us a demand relationship between P and y, and the labor market equation and the production function give us a supply relationship between the same

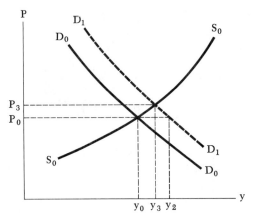

Figure 9-2   Supply and demand with an increase in g.

two variables. On the most aggregate level we have two equations in the two unknowns, P and y, shown in Figure 9-2. The solution to those two equations—the intersection of the demand and supply curves of Figure 9-2—is equilibrium P_0, y_0, which we can trace back to W_0, N_0 in Figure 9-1(b) and r_0, y_0 in Figure 9-1(a).

The Effects of a Fiscal Policy Stimulus

In the initial equilibrium position employment is at N_0 in Figure 9-1(b). Suppose the political judgment is made that unemployment $N_F - N_0$ is excessive; so government purchases g are increased by dg to increase employment. This shifts the IS curve up to I_1S_1 in Figure 9-1(a) just like the shift in investment demand earlier in Figures 8-3 and 8-4 (pp. 149–50). The increased government purchases increase GNP directly, and, through the multiplier process, increase GNP indirectly by increasing consumption. At the initial price level P_0 *and interest rate* r_0, equilibrium output on the demand side would rise to y_1 in Figure 9-1(a). The ratio of $y_1 - y_0$ to dg is given by the simple g multiplier of Chapter 3, $1/[1 - c'(1 - t')]$, which assumes that investment, and thus implicitly the interest rate, are fixed.

But the increase in output, even with the price level unchanged, will increase the demand for money, raising the interest rate along L_0M_0 and reducing investment demand. This partially offsets the g increase, so that at the initial price level, equilibrium output on the demand side would rise to y_2 in Figures 9-1(a) and 9-2, with the interest rate rising to r_2. Thus, the g increase has shifted the demand curve to $D_1 D_1$ in Figure 9-2, creating excess demand $y_2 - y_0$ in the economy. At the initial price level P_0, consumers, businesses, and government would demand y_2 output, but producers are supplying only y_0, so prices rise.

On the demand side of the economy, the price increase tightens the money market by increasing the demand for money $\bar{M}$ or, what is the same thing, reducing the supply of real balances m. This shifts the LM curve up toward $L_1 M_1$ in Figure 9-1(a), reducing equilibrium output demanded from y_2 along the new demand curve $D_1 D_1$ in Figure 9-2. Again, the reader should notice that the price increase reduces equilibrium output demanded indirectly; it tightens the money market, raising r and reducing investment.

On the supply side, the price increase raises the demand for labor, shifting the demand curve in Figure 9-1(b) up toward $P_3 \cdot f(N)$. It also shifts the labor-supply curve up toward $P_3^e \cdot g(N)$, but if $p' < 1$ the supply shift is smaller than the demand shift, so equilibrium employment increases from N_0 toward N_3. This is represented in Figure 9-2 by a movement along the supply curve $S_0 S_0$ from y_0 toward y_3.

The price increase continues until excess demand has been eliminated at P_3, y_3 in Figure 9-2. Employment rises to N_3 and the money wage rises to W_3. The real wage rate is reduced somewhat, but if the elasticity of demand for labor is greater than one at the initial equilibrium point, real labor income rises. Presumably, this was the point of the g increase in the first place.

The interest rate rises from r_0 to r_3 following the g increase. The increase in government spending is partially offset by an increase in tax revenues as both P and y rise, but the government has to increase its borrowing in the bond market somewhat to finance the increase in its deficit. This increased supply of bonds reduces bond prices and raises yields, giving the bond market counterpart to the money market increase in r. The r increase reduces investment demand with $i = i(r)$, but by less than the initial g increase, so that on balance the g increase directly induces an increase in expenditure, raising y from y_0 to y_3.

A permanent tax cut would have much the same effect as the g increase, assuming that consumers react by spending a large fraction of the increase in disposable income. The tax cut would shift the IS curve and demand curve out, raising the price level and the interest rate. Employment and output would rise, and the tax cut would yield the same y increase as the alternative dg increase if tax rates were reduced by an amount that gives a policy-induced consumer expenditure increase—$c'y\, dt$, equal to dg.

The difference between a tax cut and a g increase, as usual, is in the composition of final output. The tax cut favors increased consumer spending, while the g increase favors increased output of public goods.

The Effects of a Money Supply Increase

Instead of a fiscal policy stimulus through a government purchases increase or a tax cut, employment could be raised from the initial level N_0 by the monetary policy stimulus of an increase in $\bar{M}$. Putting aside the problem of the certainty of results, discussed in Chapter 5, a desired increase in equilibrium output and employment can be achieved with an $\bar{M}$ change equivalent to the necessary g change if fiscal policy were to be used. The difference in outcomes will be in the composition of final output. An $\bar{M}$ increase pushes down interest rates, stimulating investment, whereas the fiscal policy stimuli either increases g or consumer spending directly raises interest rates.

The effects of a money supply increase are shown in Figures 9-3 and 9-4. Figures 9-3(b) and 9-4 are exactly the same as Figures 9-1(b) and 9-2; the only difference between the analyses of a g increase and an $\bar{M}$ increase lies in the origin of the demand shift in Figure 9-3(a).

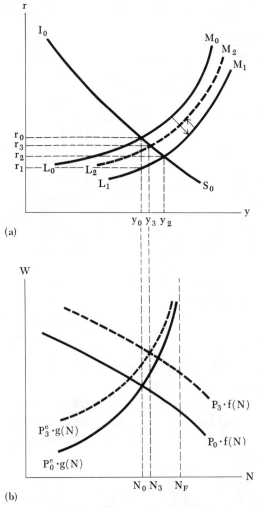

(a)

(b)

Figure 9-3 Equilibrium in the static model: an increase in $\bar{M}$.

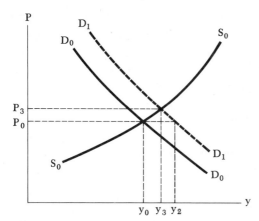

Figure 9-4 Supply and demand with an increase in $\bar{M}$.

The increase in the money supply shifts the LM curve from $L_0 M_0$ to $L_1 M_1$ in Figure 9-3(a). At the initial income level y_0, the interest rate would be pushed down to r_1 by the appearance of excess supply in the money market. This drop in the interest rate would stimulate investment demand, increasing equilibrium demand-side y. This, in turn, would increase the demand for money, pulling the interest rate back up again. At the initial price level P_0, equilibrium demand-side output after the $\bar{M}$ increase would be y_2 with the interest rate at r_2. This is shown in Figure 9-4, where the money supply increase has shifted the demand curve out and created excess demand $y_2 - y_0$ in the economy. In equilibrium with $P = P_0$, consumers, business, and government would purchase y_2 level of output, but producers are still supplying only y_0, employing N_0 worker-hours.

The excess demand raises the price level in Figure 9-4 toward P_3. On the demand side of the economy, the price level increase tightens the money market, shifting LM back up toward $L_2 M_2$. This brings an increase in r and a drop in equilibrium demand-side output toward y_3. In Figure 9-4, equilibrium output on the demand side falls along the new demand curve, $D_1 D_1$ toward y_3.

On the supply side, the situation is exactly the same as with the increase in g. The price increase shifts the labor-demand curve up toward $P_3 \cdot f(N)$ and the labor-supply curve up toward $P_3^e \cdot g(N)$. The latter supply shift is smaller than the demand shift by hypothesis, so employment rises toward N_3. In Figure 9-4, the employment increase is represented by a movement of equilibrium supply-side output up the supply curve $S_0 S_0$ from y_0 toward y_3.

The price level stops rising when the excess demand gap has been eliminated at P_3, y_3 in Figure 9-4. Employment has risen to N_3 in Figure 9-3(b).

The interest rate first fell from r_0 to r_1 in Figure 9-3(a) under the initial monetary stimulus, and then rose back to r_3, still below the initial r_0. With g constant and i higher due to the drop in r from r_0 to r_3, output and income have risen, and consumer expenditure, with tax rates unchanged, has risen endogenously. Again, the difference between equivalent doses of monetary or fiscal policy stimulants is in the composition of final output.

MONETARY AND FISCAL POLICY IN THE CLASSICAL CASE

The effects of fiscal policy in the classical model can be seen in Figures 9-5 and 9-6, which reproduce Figures 8-5 and 8-6. A fiscal stimulus acts just like any other exogenous impulse on the demand side. The excess demand $y_1 - y_0$ leads to a rise in the price level, which moves the LM curve upwards. Similarly, in the labor market, increased demand at the initial nominal wage W_0 from the higher demand for goods is matched by a vertical shift in the labor-supply function as workers raise their price expectations in line with the actual price level. There is no effect on real output, so that the fiscal stimulus is translated entirely into a higher interest rate and price level. On the product side, the higher interest rate reduces investment just enough to counterbalance exactly the higher government spending. In the money market, with the money supply $\bar{M}$ fixed and the price level rising, the supply of real balance shrinks. Thus, in the LM equation, $\bar{M} = P[l(r) + k(y)]$, the rise in P must be matched by an equiproportional fall in the term within square brackets. Since y is fixed by the vertical aggregate supply curve of Figure 9-6, r must rise enough to equilibriate the money market. Note that real money demand falls, implying a change in the velocity of circulation (see Chapters 14 and 15).

It should now be easy to anticipate the consequences of an expansion of the money supply. Real output y is fixed by the vertical aggregate supply function of Figure 9-6. In the product market, savings and government spending are constant; therefore, for equilibrium the level of investment rate must remain the same. Hence, in the money market, real money demand $[1(r) + k(y)]$ remains constant, and the higher money supply can go only into an equiproportional rise in the price level.

These changes are shown in Figure 9-7. The increase in the money stock shifts up the demand curve in Figure 9-7(c). This pulls the price level up proportionately, with P^e rising as much as P in Figure 9-7(d). The result is no change in y or N in Figures 9-7(a) and (b). The increase in the price level just offsets the increase in nominal money, leaving the real money stock unchanged. Money, then, is completely "neutral" in the classical case. Real output and incomes, the real interest rate, real wages, and employment are all left unchanged by an increase in the money supply. Even the demand for real money balances does not shift, implying a constant velocity of circulation.

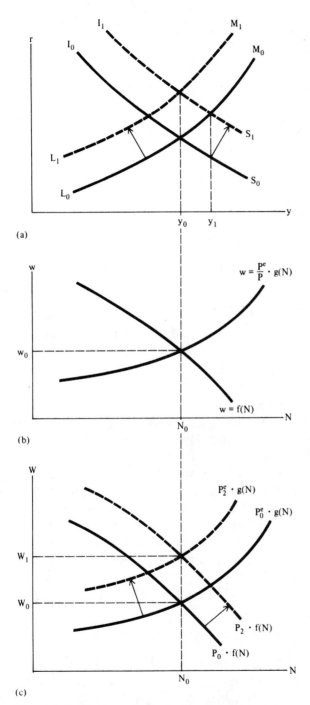

Figure 9-5 Fiscal expansion in the classical model.

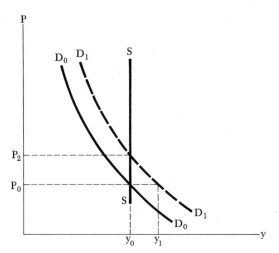

Figure 9-6 Aggregate supply and demand in the classical case.

You may wonder how the price level makes this neat jump, or who makes sure that the economy stays in the initial real equilibrium in the classical case. For some intuition on this point, it is worth imagining that the economy functions according to the short-run model over some time scale and then adjusts toward the classical case, as we distinguished between aggregate supply in the short run and the long run in Chapter 7. Upon impact, the *LM* curve shifts downwards, there is an incipient reduction in the interest rate and real wages, and excess demand develops. Temporarily, markets are out of long-run equilibrium, allowing some kind of *tâtonnement* (literally, a "groping") process in the various markets toward that long-run state. The microeconomic fable evokes a "Walresian auctioneer" who calls out prices until equilibrium is reached before any trading actually takes place. The extreme classical case is distinguished by the assumption that the "long run" is reached almost immediately, or equivalently, that trading is briefly suspended until the *tâtonnement* process is completed. In Chapter 11, we will see that *rational expectations* can collapse this classical long run into the short run, as agents in the economy anticipate the movement to long-run equilibrium.

FISCAL AND MONETARY MULTIPLIERS IN THE STATIC MODEL

In Chapter 5 we developed multipliers that gave the effects of changes in the monetary and fiscal policy instruments—$\bar{M}$, g, and tax rates t—on equilibrium output under the assumption that the price level was fixed. This was equivalent to assuming that the supply curve of Figure 9-8 is horizontal like the dashed line at P_0. Then with a shift in the demand curve from $D_0 D_0$ to $D_1 D_1$, induced

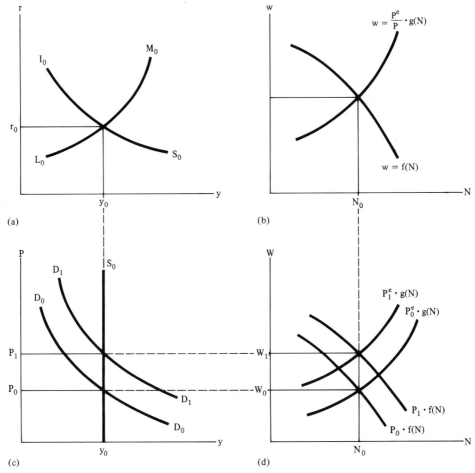

Figure 9-7 Monetary expansion in the classical case.

by a change in a policy instrument, the $y_1 - y_0$ increase in y is given by the change in the policy variable times the relevant Chapter 5 multiplier.

But if the supply curve is positively sloped, like $S_0 S_0$ in Figure 9-8, the same policy change would raise equilibrium output to only y_2, an increase of $y_2 - y_0$. Thus, introduction of the supply side and a price response to changes in demand conditions reduces the size of the multiplier.

Two general points should be noted about the modification of the Chapter 5 multipliers needed to extend them to the complete model. First, the fiscal and monetary policy multipliers apply to situations in which changes in policy variables shift the demand curve, and price and income adjust along the supply curve, for example, from P_0, y_0 to P_1, y_2 in Figure 9-8. This means that the change in the Chapter 5 multipliers needed to allow for price change along the supply curve will involve the slope of the supply curve, particularly in the

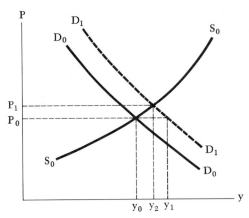

Figure 9-8 Multipliers in the static model.

form of dP/dy—the change in P needed to restore equilibrium on the supply side. An expression for

$$\left.\frac{dP}{dy}\right|_S$$

—the slope of the supply curve—was developed in Chapter 7 as

$$\left.\frac{dP}{dy}\right|_S = \frac{1}{\partial y/\partial N}\cdot\frac{g'-f'}{w\cdot(1-p')}. \tag{5}$$

For convenience we will use $\left.\dfrac{dP}{dy}\right|_S$ to represent this expression. Remember that in the short-run model, $p' < 1$, so that dP/dy in equation (5) is positive. If p' approaches unity as in the classical case, dP/dy approaches infinity. In that case the aggregate supply curve is vertical.

The change in price along the supply curve will then enter the multiplier expression through its effect in the money market on interest rates and then on investment. This is shown graphically by the secondary shift in the LM curves of Figures 9-1(a) and 9-3(a). So the price change enters the multiplier through the following chain:

$$\left.\frac{dP}{dy}\right|_S \rightarrow \Delta r \rightarrow \Delta i \quad \text{(Endogenous investment change)}.$$

The second point is that, as we suggested in the first section, the difference between the effects of the three aggregate demand policy instruments is in where the initial *policy-induced* expenditure stimulus appears. Once the excess demand is created, for example, $y_2 - y_0$ in Figures 9-2 and 9-3, the adjustment of the model through the price mechanism is the same in all cases. This means that, as in Chapter 5, all the multipliers here should contain the *same* price adjustment terms shown in the chain above, appearing in the denominator of the multipliers. The differences, again, will be in the policy-induced expenditure terms in the numerators of the multipliers.

In the following subsections we will first develop the multiplier for changes in government purchases. It is the simplest because the policy-induced expenditure change is simply dg. The tax and $\bar{M}$ multipliers are more complicated because they depend on the private sector to provide the direct expenditure change. These multipliers have the same denominator as the g multiplier, so we can simplify the analysis all around by focusing on the g multiplier first.

The Multiplier for Changes in Government Purchases

As usual, to derive the expression for the equilibrium multiplier for the impact of changes in g on y, we totally differentiate the set of equations giving the equilibrium values of y, N, P, and r, set $d\bar{M} = 0$, and solve for dy/dg. While this could be simply a mechanical exercise, its value here is hopefully that the *way* the multiplier is developed will add to our understanding of how the parts of the static model are linked together.

To begin with, we repeat the three market equilibrium conditions and the production functions, equations (1), (2), (3), and (4), for easy reference:

$$IS: \qquad y = c(y - t(y)) + i(r) + g;$$

$$LM: \qquad \frac{\bar{M}}{P} = m = l(r) + k(y);$$

$$\text{Production function:} \qquad y = y(N; \bar{K});$$

$$\text{Labor market:} \quad P \cdot f(N) = p(P) \cdot g(N).$$

Differentiation of the product market (*IS*) equilibrium condition gives us

$$dy = c' \cdot (1 - t')dy + i' \, dr + dg. \tag{6}$$

The next step is to find an expression giving the change in r, dr, between equilibria. From the money market (*LM*) equation, allowing P to vary (along the supply curve) but holding $\bar{M}$ constant, we obtain

$$d\left(\frac{\bar{M}}{P}\right) = -\frac{\bar{M}}{P^2} \, dP = l' \, dr + k' \, dy,$$

and solving for dr yields

$$dr = -\frac{k'}{l'} \, dy - \frac{\bar{M}}{P^2 \cdot l'} \, dP \tag{7}$$

as the expression for r changes keeping the money market in equilibrium as both y and P change. The first term in (7) gives the effect of a y change on r *along* a given LM curve; $-k'/l'$ is the slope of the LM curve holding M/P constant. The second term in (7) gives the effect of the P change, *shifting LM,* on r. A price level increase dP shifts the LM curve up, and at any given y, so that for $dy = 0$, the r increase is given by $dr = [-\bar{M}/(P^2 \cdot l')]dP$, which is positive since $l' < 0$.

The next step is to replace dP in (7) by our expression for the slope of the aggregate supply curve, which gives the price change needed to restore equilibrium for a given change in y on the supply side. With P and y rising along the supply curve of Figure 9-8, the increase in P is given by

$$dP = \frac{dP}{dy}\bigg|_S \cdot dy. \tag{8}$$

Substituting (8) into (7) for dP gives us

$$dr = -\left[\frac{k'}{l'} + \frac{\bar{M}}{P^2 \cdot l'} \cdot \frac{dP}{dy}\bigg|_S \right] dy, \tag{9}$$

for the change in r with a change in y. Again, the first term inside the brackets gives the r change due to the y change, directly along the LM curve; the second term gives the r change due to the P change needed to restore equilibrium on the supply side.

In equation (9) we have replaced dP by a term in dy. We can substitute (9) for dr into equation (6) to obtain

$$dy = c' \cdot (1 - t')dy - i'\left[\frac{k'}{l'} + \frac{\bar{M}}{P^2 \cdot l'} \cdot \frac{dP}{dy}\bigg|_S \right] dy + dg,$$

and, for the g multiplier expression,

$$dy = \frac{1}{1 - c' \cdot (1 - t') + i'\left[\dfrac{k'}{l'} + \dfrac{\bar{M}}{P^2 \cdot l'} \cdot \dfrac{dP}{dy}\bigg|_S \right]} dg. \tag{10}$$

Since later multipliers will have the same denominator as (10), we will simply designate the entire denominator as D, so that $dy = (1/D)dg$.

The multiplier of equation (10) differs from that of Chapter 5 only in the final term in the denominator, which reduces the multiplier's size—y_0 moves to y_2 instead of y_1 in Figure 9-8. The term dP/dy gives the price increase (shifting LM) between equilibria with a dg increase; multiplying that by $M/(P^2 \cdot l')$ gives the effect of this LM shift on r, for example, $r_3 - r_2$ in Figure 9-1(a); multiplying again by i' gives the endogenous effect on investment of including the supply side and price changes in the model.

Referring back to equation (5), which gives the expression for dP/dy along the supply curve, we can recall in the classical case $p' = 1$. Therefore, in this case $dP/dy = \infty$, that is, the supply curve is vertical. In that case, D in (21) $= \infty$ and $dy/dg = 0$. Again, in the classical case, fiscal policy does not affect the level of output. In an extreme Keynesian case, $p' = 0$ in equation (5) for dP/dy, giving the slope of the supply curve its minimum value, and maximizing the equilibrium multiplier dy/dg. Finally, if the economy is operating near full employment, where g', the slope of the labor-supply curve, approaches infinity, the slope of the aggregate supply curve will again become nearly vertical. An increase in g will not change equilibrium y appreciably, but simply raise prices and interest rates, reducing investment by as much as g increased. The reader is left to investigate the effects of setting other slopes in the multiplier expression in equation (10) at their extreme values or introducing the effects of wage rigidities. We will move on to the tax multiplier.

The Multiplier for Changes in Tax Rates

As in Chapter 5, here we will assume that the tax function is proportional; $t(y) = \tau y$ where τ is the fraction of national income, say, 20 percent, that is turned in as tax revenue. This will simplify calculation of the tax rate multiplier without affecting the qualitative conclusions.

With the proportional tax schedule we can rewrite the *IS* equation as

$$y = c(y - \tau y) + i(r) + g. \tag{11}$$

To calculate the tax rate multiplier, one can differentiate (11) to obtain

$$dy = c' \cdot (dy - \tau \, dy - y \, d\tau) + i' \, dr$$

and

$$dy = c' \cdot (1 - \tau)dy - c'y \, d\tau + i' \, dr.$$

The term $-c'y \, d\tau$ gives the policy-induced effect of a tax rate change on consumer expenditure. At the initial level of income y, $- y \, d\tau$ gives the change in disposable income resulting directly from the tax rate change. If τ is raised, disposable income is reduced. Then c' times $(-y \, d\tau)$ gives the amount that this changes consumer expenditure.

Aside from the substitution of $-c'y \, d\tau$ for dg as the exogenous expenditure change, the multipliers for g and t are exactly the same. We can substitute the expression for dr given by (9) into the dy equation here, collect terms in y, and obtain the tax rate multiplier

$$dy = \frac{-c'y}{D} \, d\tau, \tag{12}$$

where, again, D is the denominator of the g multiplier in (10), with τ replacing t'.

The Multiplier for Changes in the Money Supply

A change in the money supply $\bar{M}$, in our simple static model, affects the level of output by changing investment demand through money market effects on the interest rate. To obtain the policy-induced investment effect that corresponds to the shift in the LM curve, we can differentiate the LM equation

$$\frac{\bar{M}}{P} = l(r) + k(y),$$

to obtain

$$-\frac{\bar{M}}{P^2}\,dP + \frac{d\bar{M}}{P} = l'\,dr + k'\,dy$$

and

$$dr = -\frac{k'}{l'}\,dy - \frac{\bar{M}}{P^2 \cdot l'}\,dP + \frac{d\bar{M}}{P \cdot l'}. \tag{13}$$

The first two terms in (13) are the usual effects of changing income and prices on the interest rate, developed earlier. The third term gives the interest rate effect of the increase in M *at the original price and income levels*—the drop from r_0 to r_1 in Figure 9-3(a). At the original price level $d\bar{M}/P$ gives the increase in the real money supply, and $1/l'$ times this gives the drop in the interest rate needed to maintain short-run money market equilibrium with a given P and y.

Expression (13) for dr with a money supply change can be substituted into the IS differential to obtain

$$dy = c' \cdot (1 - t')dy - i'\left[\frac{k'}{l'} + \frac{\bar{M}}{P^2 \cdot l'} \cdot \frac{dP}{dy}\Big|_S\right]dy + \frac{i'}{P \cdot l'}\,d\bar{M}.$$

The first two terms on the right-hand side of this expression for dy are the same as those in the multiplier for dg. The last term gives the policy-induced investment effect of the dM change. If $d\bar{M}/(P \cdot l')$ gives the interest rate effect at the initial income and price level, then i' times this gives the effect on investment at the initial income and price level. Collecting terms in dy gives us the multiplier for $\bar{M}$ changes:

$$dy = \frac{i'/P \cdot l'}{D}\,d\bar{M}, \tag{14}$$

where $i'/(P \cdot l')$ translates the change in the money supply into an exogenous investment effect. From there on, as we saw in Figures 9-3 and 9-4, the multiplier, $1/D$, is the same as that for g and t changes. The difference lies in the source of the expansionary effect.

The multipliers developed in this section show how introduction of the supply side of the economy affects the y change that follows from any given change in a policy variable. The reader should again be able to confirm our earlier conclusions about the relative effectiveness of monetary and fiscal policies in special situations by writing out the multipliers with D from equation (10) written out in full. A little manipulation then should show, for example, that in the liquidity-trap case where $l' \to \infty$, $dy/d\bar{M} = 0$ and dy/dg is just $1/[1 - c'(1 - t')]$ again. This is because the price level change does not affect the interest rate and thus generates no endogenous effect on investment. The point here, however, is that the multiplier expressions show how the parts of the economy are interrelated. They point up both similarities and differences between the workings of the major macroeconomic policy variables, and they make explicit the way in which special assumptions—the classical case with a vertical supply curve or the liquidity trap—affect the likely behavior of the economy.

Here we can point out an interesting long-run as opposed to short-run interpretation of the labor-supply function $p(P) \cdot g(N)$. As demand goes up in the short run, employment expands along the short-run labor-supply curve, with p' close to zero. But as time passes, the price increase that followed the demand increase is translated, at least partially, into wage demands, shifting the labor-supply function and the economy's supply curve up; in the longer run, p' rises toward unity. This will lead to an inflation cycle in which a price increase due to a demand increase (demand pull) leads to an upward shift in the supply curve, bringing a further price increase (cost-push). This interpretation provides a link to the discussion of inflation in Chapter 20, in Part IV, on medium-term dynamics.

INCOMES POLICY IN THE STATIC MODEL

One clear implication of our analysis of monetary and fiscal policy is that expansionary aggregate demand policy will pull up the price level as a side effect. This result has led policy makers to search for additional policy instruments that could shift the aggregate supply curve, to eliminate the price (inflationary) effects of movements in aggregate demand. The Council of Economic Advisers' guideposts for wage and price behavior in 1962 were an early example of incomes policy. (See Chapter 19 for an explicit analysis of the guideposts.)

During the 1974–1975 recession, in which a supply-side disturbance caused the unhappy combination of rising prices *and* rising unemployment, the search for an effective *incomes policy* that would shift the aggregate-supply curve down intensified in most countries. The United States had tried wage and price controls in 1971–1973, and most European countries had been tinkering with incomes policies for decades. But the partially supply-induced 1974–1975 recession brought incomes policy to the forefront of macroeconomic policy.

Essentially, incomes policy is a euphemism for wage restraints. In exchange for a promise of less price increase later, the authorities ask the labor force for less nominal wage increase now. In terms of our basic static model, they ask the labor force for a downward shift in the labor-supply curve, through a decrease in price expectations P^e given P. Most attempts at incomes policy have been unsuccessful, because the promise of a future slowdown in the rate of price increase has not been believed (and correctly so). The failure of incomes policy owing to rapid price increase is discussed in Chapter 19.

Here we analyze incomes policy in the static model as a policy that shifts the labor-supply curve down. This translates into a downward shift in the aggregate supply curve and a downward pressure on the price level. If the policy began from an initial situation of excess demand disequilibrium, it would be aimed at stopping or slowing an incipient inflation.

Aggregate Supply Shift

To represent incomes policy in the labor-supply curve, we add a shift parameter α to the expectations function, so that the latter is now $P^e = p(P, \alpha)$. An increase in α represents an increase in the expected price level for any given value of P. A reduction in α, representing a successful incomes policy, reduces P^e, given P. The effect of an incomes policy change, shifting the aggregate supply curve, is shown in Figures 9-9 and 9-10. There P^e is reduced from P_0^e to P_1^e directly by incomes policy. This would shift the labor-supply curve down at any initial price level P_0 in Figure 9-9(a), increasing equilibrium employment at the initial values of P_0 from N_0 to N_1. This in turn increases equilibrium output supplied from y_0 to y_1 in Figure 9-9(b).

The increase in equilibrium output supplied at the initial price level P_0 is shown as an outward shift in the aggregate supply curve in Figure 9-10. The objective of incomes policy is generally stated as shifting the supply curve down, but with the positively sloped SS we can interpret the shift as down in terms of P, given y_0 or out in terms of y, given P_0.

INCOMES POLICY AND EXCESS DEMAND

Incomes policies are usually tried during periods of excess demand in an attempt to forestall incipient price increases. Frequently, an incomes policy is added to expansionary aggregate demand measures as a means of eliminating the inflationary consequences of demand expansion. For example, in both

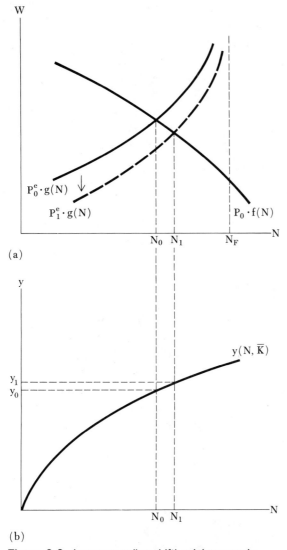

Figure 9-9 Incomes policy shifting labor supply.

1962 and 1971 the economy was beginning to come out of recession, and monetary and fiscal policies were being used to stimulate demand. In 1962 the Council of Economic Advisers published the wage-price guideposts as an attempt to shift the supply curve in order to get the expansionary effects on N and y without prices increasing. In 1971 the Administration applied a wage-price freeze as an extreme measure to control inflation as demand was expanded.

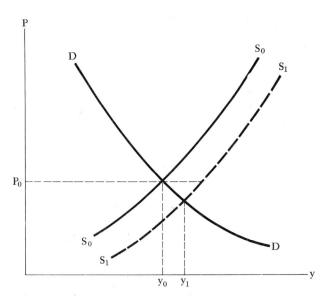

Figure 9-10   Supply curve shift.

The coupling of incomes policy with expansionary demand policy is illustrated in Figure 9-11. An expansionary monetary or fiscal policy move, as discussed earlier in this chapter, would shift the demand curve out to $D_1 D_1$. This would increase equilibrium output in the general Keynesian model to y_1, but would also pull the price level up to P_1. To eliminate the price increase, incomes policy could attempt to shift the supply curve out to $S_1 S_1$, taking the

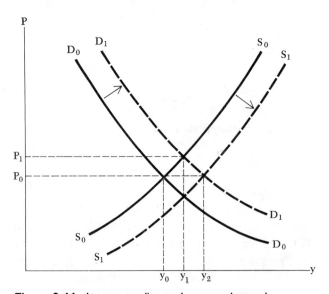

Figure 9-11   Incomes policy and excess demand.

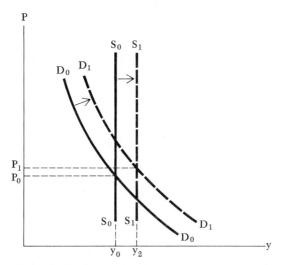

Figure 9-12 Incomes policy in the classical case.

economy to the new equilibrium P_0, y_2. The incomes policy in this case would increase the change in equilibrium output while holding the price constant. Clearly, if y_1 was the target for income, a smaller dose of both policies could take the supply-demand intersection to P_0, y_1.

In the classical case, incomes policy would have effects somewhat different from those in the short-run model. In Figure 9-12 we show an excess demand gap eliminated by the shift in the vertical classical supply curve. At the initial price level P_0, aggregate demand shifts to $D_1 D_1$. As we saw earlier, in the classical case this would result in the price level rising to P_1 with no change in output. To obtain a change in output, the vertical supply curve must shift; incomes policy is one way to do this. In Figure 9-12, incomes policy moves equilibrium output, while demand policy controls the price level. Thus, in the classical case, movements in aggregate demand move the price level, and incomes policy offers one way to move equilibrium output.

SELECTED READINGS

A. S. Blinder, "Can Income Tax Increases Be Inflationary? An Expository Note," *National Tax Journal,* June 1973.

A. S. Blinder, *Economic Policy and the Great Stagflation* (New York: Academic Press, 1979), Chapter 6.

F. Modigliani, "The Monetary Mechanism and Its Interaction with Real Phenomenon," *Review of Economics and Statistics,* Supplement, February 1963.

chapter 10

Search, Wage Rigidity, and Unemployment

In Chapter 8 we combined the demand and supply sides into a skeletal general equilibrium model of the macroeconomy. In this *general static* model, movements in aggregate demand affect the equilibrium level of employment in the economy. We are naturally led to the questions: How is the *un*employment rate related to this equilibrium level of employment, and how does it change when demand conditions change? As we see in this chapter, there are several ways to answer these questions.

First, we interpret movements in employment in the general static model as changes in the proportion of job-seekers taking employment. If we take an unemployment rate of 6 percent as being "full employment," then at any given time there are about 7.2 million unemployed persons in the United States seeking jobs. Half will find jobs within a month or so. Shifts in aggregate demand affect how rapidly these job-seekers find employment.

In the period since the publication of Phelps et al. (1970), labor economists and macroeconomists have focused on models of search in the labor markets to explain equilibrium unemployment. These are surveyed in the first section below. They provide the theoretical underpinning for the model of equilibrium unemployment presented in Chapter 6.

Next, we introduce wage rigidities into the picture, both in the sense of an economy-wide average wage floor and in the sense of local labor market rigidities. Downward rigidity of the money wage W is a prime candidate from recent research as the cause of involuntary unemployment. While the relevance of an economy-wide wage floor is questionable, the hypothesis of local wage rigidity is useful. We also briefly introduce the possibility of a downwardly rigid price level. Finally, we summarize a view of unemployment that draws on all of these elements.

LABOR MARKET SEARCH AND EMPLOYMENT

The labor market is always in a state of flux, even when the economy is at an equilibrium position, as in Chapter 8. With a civilian labor force of about 120 million persons and a full-employment unemployment rate of about 6 percent, there is a monthly average of about 7 million persons actively looking for jobs in the U.S. labor market. Moreover, these are not the same people every month, so the monthly average does not come close to measuring the rate of job search and turnover. In a full-employment year such as 1987, just under half of the unemployed in any given month found jobs with less than 5 weeks of unemployment; about 25 percent remained unemployed more than 15 weeks. Thus, with a monthly average of 7 million unemployed job-seekers at full employment, about 3 million find jobs in a month and are replaced by other job-seekers. This gives us a picture of a labor market in constant turnover, with workers searching for better, or at least different, jobs, and employers continuously screening applicants for newly open positions. It is in this context that we must understand movements in employment and implicitly in unemployment in the basic static model of Chapter 8.

Aggregate Demand and Employment

In Chapter 8 we saw that fluctuations in aggregate demand will cause fluctuations in employment in the general short-run model with $P^e = p(P)$ and $p' < 1$. This story is fully consistent with a view of the labor market which has a stock of unemployed job-seekers that is turning over frequently. In Figure 10-1 we see the labor market results of an increase in aggregate demand in the short-run model. As we saw in Chapter 8, an increase in aggregate demand generates excess demand in the product market, pulling up the price level.

In Figure 10-1 the price increase shows up in the labor market as a shift in demand to $P_1 \cdot f(N)$ and in supply to $P_1^e \cdot g(N)$. The resulting excess demand in the labor market pulls the nominal wage rate up to W_1. The increase in the wage rate is greater than the increase in P^e (since $p' < 1$). As a result, workers searching for employment perceive an improvement in the employment opportunities available to them, that is, W/P^e rises. So an increased fraction of the job-seekers accepts employment, and total employment increases to N_1. The effect of the increase in W/P^e on the decisions of job-seekers to take employment is simply the movement along the new labor-supply schedule from N_0 to N_1.

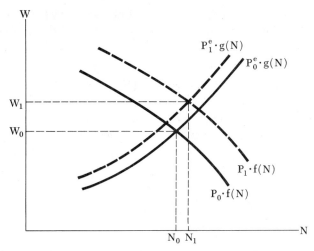

Figure 10-1 Demand shifts and employment changes.

The effect of a drop in aggregate demand in this job search model would be just the opposite of Figure 10-1. With the price level P falling, the wage rate would fall more than P^e, so W/P^e would go down. This deterioration in the number of job offers would result in a smaller fraction of job-seekers accepting employment, and a drop in equilibrium N.

This search model incorporating the effect of aggregate demand on employment has two key features. The first is the existence of a stock of job-seekers looking at employment opportunities at any point in time. The second is uncertainty about the price level. If workers could perceive the price level accurately, and adjust their expectations fully, we could then apply the extreme classical case with $p' = 1$, and we would see no movement in employment in Figure 10-1. Thus, our search model depends on workers' uncertainty about the future price level, as explained in Chapter 6.

Alternative Job Search Models

There are numerous alternative stories about search in the labor market that make employment sensitive to fluctuations in aggregate demand. One can focus on workers and model cases in which they are uncertain about alternative wage offers or about the general level of money wages. Or one can focus on employers seeking workers, uncertain about alternative wage offers available to the workers, or about the price at which they can sell their product. Many such models can be found in the volumes edited by Phelps and by Brunner and Meltzer. The key ingredient common to all the models is that one side—either worker or employer—is searching and is uncertain about either W or P.

A worker, or a whole section of the work force engaged in a particular activity, may not have any choice about whether or not to search for a job. Since individual firms and sectors of the economy are in constant change, sometimes growing and sometimes declining, some workers are always being laid off permanently and have to "get on [their] bikes," as the British Employment Minister Norman Tebbit once remarked. An individual may also choose to search for a new job, either remaining on the job while doing so or quitting to search more intensively. Voluntary searching behavior is only relevant for the level of unemployment if it is indeed optimal for a worker to leave one job before having found another. In either case, the costs and benefits of job search can be categorized as follows: first, there are the direct costs of changing jobs, including not only moving expenses but also such financial penalties as loss of pension rights. Second, there can be direct search costs, such as travel expenses and the foregone income of those who quit in order to search. On the plus side, there is the expected extra income from the new job, discounted back across the time which it is expected to take to find the new job. The solution to this problem of deciding whether to embark on a job search, if we are to introduce any degree of realism, becomes quite complicated. But this very complexity adds plausibility to the assumption that workers may be rather badly informed about conditions elsewhere in the economy.

As an example of a search story that is complementary to our model, consider the case of a worker who is considering one job offer and is uncertain about the wages paid in alternative jobs. If demand for its output rises, the wage offered by the firm under consideration will rise. If the job-seeker does not expect other wages and the price level to rise, he or she will perceive an increased wage offer relative to other employment possibilities and to P. This will increase the probability of accepting the job under consideration. If this situation characterizes a substantial fraction of all job-seekers, the result will be an increase in employment as aggregate demand rises.

SEARCH COSTS AND WAGE RIGIDITY

While search by individuals and firms is inevitable and desirable in a world of diverse markets, there may be ways of cutting down on the search and turnover costs involved. In this subsection, we suggest some ways in which these costs, along with other features of the labor market, may lead to wage rigidities.

The first is contracts. It is possible that the time and effort involved in constantly changing employment, or in frequent renegotiations, is so great that firms and workers prefer to commit themselves in advance to a certain set of wages and conditions. The same complexities that promote the use of contracts may also ensure that these contracts are relatively simple, perhaps even leading to agreements set in nominal terms. The difficulties of enforcing contracts, especially when not all circumstances are observable to every party or to an impartial arbitrator, also tend to make the contracts fairly straightforward. The other role of contracts is to provide a kind of "home-made insurance" to workers. If firms are less averse to risk or have better access to capital markets, then workers should be willing to trade off lower expected income for greater stability. The insurance motive suggests that real unemployment compensation should not be very sensitive to cyclical variations. Indeed, profits are much more variable than wages. For insurance purposes, workers are concerned about real labor income as deflated by the CPI, but the particular firm can only control its product price, at best. The result of the asymmetry could be nominal wage stickiness in a generally noninflationary environment.

The second rationale for wage inflexibility is more directly connected to search costs in poorly coordinated markets. In the jargon of economists, one might say that information is transmitted slowly in the labor market, and therefore adjustment is slow. For example, people may have only a very vague idea about the true marginal revenue product of labor, so that, when negotiating a contract, the bargainers rely primarily on other recent contracts to set a benchmark. In countries with annual wage negotiations with uncoordinated timing across sectors, such as Britain, it is quite clear that certain agreements early in the season become trend-setters. To preempt a little the discussion in the next chapter, everyone could be acting fully rationally and yet in effect have slowly adaptive expectations when their main source of information is past nominal wage contracts.

To construct another and more subtle example, suppose that the price level falls equally in each sector of the economy. If all prices fell at once, followed by a nominal wage cut for everybody, then employment and real output would be unchanged. But if prices fell at different times in different markets, then the fear of turnover costs could put firms in a bind. Say the output price for firm A falls first; if firm A immediately cuts its nominal wage, then its workers will emigrate to all the other, higher paying firms. Once some new long-term equilibrium is reached, firm A will have rehired the initial number of workers, but everybody will have incurred substantial costs in the meanwhile. So firm A leaves its nominal wage unchanged or adjusts it only a little. Then, say firm B's price falls, and it is put in a similar position. Hence, B's nominal wage is also sticky downwards, and so on for each firm in sequence. Nobody wants to be the first to cut wages. It is possible eventually to reach a new long-term equilibrium with all nominal values reduced, but the process could take a long time.

Search models connect the analytics of Chapters 6 and 7 and Figure 10-1 to the real world of the labor market, which has constant turnover and search on both demand and supply sides. There are many such models corresponding to different situations facing employers and workers. The supply-side model of Chapter 7 is meant to be representative of these search- and uncertainty-based models in the context of our skeletal static macroeconomic model.

WAGE RIGIDITY IN THE AGGREGATE LABOR MARKET

The possibility that the money wage rate is "sticky" or "rigid" in a downward direction was introduced in the 1930s as an explanation for unemployment within the framework of the classical real wage model. It provides a rationalization for the existence of large-scale aggregate unemployment. Suppose that once the money wage rate rises to an equilibrium level W_0, it cannot fall from that level due to institutional imperfections in the labor market. Perhaps employers don't like the idea of wage cuts, labor contracts make it impossible to reduce wages, or the lack of information makes wages sticky. This downward wage rigidity will give us an explanation of involuntary unemployment on an economy-wide scale.

Wage Rigidity in the General Static Model

Downward wage rigidity in the general static model is shown in Figure 10-2. There, labor supply is $W = P^e \cdot g(N)$, with $p' < 1$, and the demand function

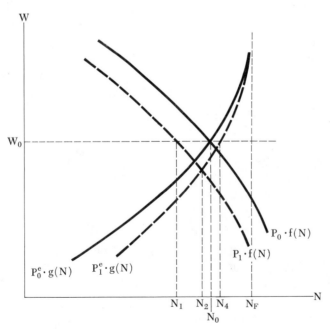

Figure 10-2 Wage rigidity in the general model.

is $W = P \cdot f(N)$, as developed in Chapter 6. In the initial equilibrium situation employment is at N_0, with equilibrium unemployment of $N_F - N_0$. The money wage rate is W_0, and, by hypothesis, it cannot fall from W_0.

If, starting from the initial equilibrium W_0, N_0, aggregate demand falls off creating excess supply in the product market, prices will fall. This will, in turn, shift the demand curve for labor in Figure 10-2 down toward $P_1 \cdot f(N)$ and the supply curve down toward $P_1^e \cdot g(N)$. If P_1 is the new equilibrium price level in the sense that the product and money markets come into equilibrium at P_1, employment will drop to N_1 at wage rate W_0. If the wage rate were able to fall, the price level drop to P_1 would have reduced equilibrium employment only to N_2 along the supply curve, although, as we will see shortly, a further price drop would actually have been required to restore equilibrium.

The wage rigidity would replace the segment of the labor-supply curve $P^e \cdot g(N)$ below W_0, N_0 with the horizontal line at W_0. As the price level falls, equilibrium employment falls along the W_0 horizontal line instead of along the shifting supply curve in Figure 10-2. Therefore, a given price level drop causes a bigger drop in N (to N_1, for example) with the wage rigidity than without it (to N_2, for example).

This is shown in the supply and demand diagram of Figure 10-3. The segment of the supply curve SS below the initial equilibrium P_0, y_0 point is replaced by ss, which corresponds to the horizontal line at W_0 in Figure 10-2. When demand drops from $D_0 D_0$ to $D_1 D_1$, the price level falls from P_0 to P_1, and output falls from $y_0 = y(N_0; \bar{K})$ to y_1. At P_1 without the wage rigidity, equilibrium output supplied would have been y_2, corresponding to

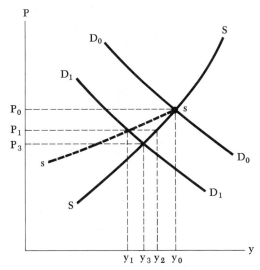

Figure 10-3   Demand and supply with rigid wages: the general model.

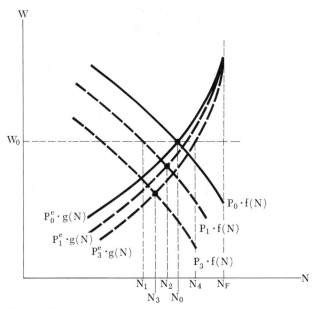

Figure 10-4 Labor market equilibrium with rigid wages.

N_2 in Figure 10-2. This still would have left excess supply measured by $y_2 - y_1$ in the product market, requiring a further price drop to P_3 to establish a new equilibrium at y_3.

Thus, with the wage rigidity the downward shift in demand gives a new equilibrium at P_1, y_1, W_0, N_1 in Figures 10-2 and 10-3, with y falling along ss. Without the wage rigidity the new equilibrium would be P_3, y_3 in Figure 10-3. N would be at N_3 in Figure 10-4, between N_1 and N_2 in Figure 10-2, and the price level would be at P_3 in Figures 10-3 and 10-4, lower than P_1. Introduction of the wage rigidity has increased the magnitude of the decrease in y and reduced the magnitude of decrease in P needed to restore equilibrium with a given downward demand shift. In other words, the slope of the supply curve, dy/dP, has been flattened by the substitution of ss for the lower segment of SS in Figure 10-3.

This can be seen in mathematical terms using the expression for the slope of the supply curve given by equation (7) in Chapter 7:

$$\frac{dy}{dP} = \frac{\partial y}{\partial N} \cdot \frac{w(1 - p')}{g' - f'}, \tag{1}$$

along the supply curve in the general static model. In this equation, introduction of the wage rigidity has reduced g' to zero below W_0 in Figures 10-2 and 10-4. The slope of SS is given by (5); the slope of ss is given by

$$\frac{dy}{dP} = \frac{\partial y}{\partial N} \cdot \frac{w(1 - p')}{-f'}.$$

Adopting the view of equilibrium unemployment developed in Chapter 6 Figures 10-2 and 10-4 measure equilibrium unemployment in the initial equilibrium. But strictly speaking, there was no aggregate *involuntary* unemployment in that equilibrium since, on average, the unemployed people in the labor force were in that circumstance by choice. They were searching for jobs at the existing wage rate. Similarly, if wages were flexible so that employment stabilized at N_3 in Figure 10-4, $N_F - N_3$ would measure a kind of voluntary unemployment.

With the wage rigidity fixing the wage rate at W_0 in Figures 10-2 and 10-4, *involuntary* unemployment measured by the gap between labor market supply and demand equal to $N_4 - N_1$ shows up in the new equilibrium. At the existing wage rate, the gap measures the number of people willing to work who cannot find jobs. Of total unemployment $N_F - N_1$, $N_4 - N_1$ is involuntary in this sense. However, the involuntary unemployment of $N_4 - N_1$ is not a measure of the effect of the wage rigidity. With flexible wages, employment would have fallen to N_3; the wage rigidity has caused an additional drop in worker-hours employed of $N_3 - N_1$.

Whether or not the new equilibrium on the *ss* curve at w_0, P_1, N_1, y_1 in Figures 10-2 and 10-3 is a true equilibrium position is a question that has been debated in the economics literature since the 1930s. From Figure 10-2 it is clear that at this new "quasi-equilibrium" point the labor force is off its supply curve. This is just another way of saying that points on *ss* in Figure 10-3 are not on *SS*. If the definition of equilibrium requires that all economic actors are on their relevant supply and demand curves, then the quasi-equilibrium P_1, y_1 of Figure 10-3 is an outcome, but not an equilibrium outcome. It seems more reasonable, however, to define an equilibrium situation as one that will not change of itself if it is left undisturbed. Is there a tendency in the model for the point P and y to move from P_1, y_1? The answer has to be "no" if the money wage is really rigid. Once the economy reaches P_0, y_0 in Figure 10-3, if W_0 really cannot fall, then the true supply curve below P_0 becomes *ss* in this definition of equilibrium. Thus, whether P_1, y_1 is an equilibrium position depends on your definition of equilibrium. The view taken here is that the better definition is one that focuses on whether the situation tends to change if left alone, so that P_1, y_1 is an equilibrium outcome.

Wage Rigidity in the Classical Case

Downward wage rigidity in the classical case is shown in Figure 10-5. There the labor-supply function is $g(N)$, drawn to become vertical at full-employment worker-hours N_F, corresponding to the employment of the entire labor force L at average hours $\bar{n}$.

Figure 10-5 shows an initial equilibrium at real wage w_0 with money wage W_0, price level P_0, and equilibrium employment N_0. $N_F - N_0$ measures

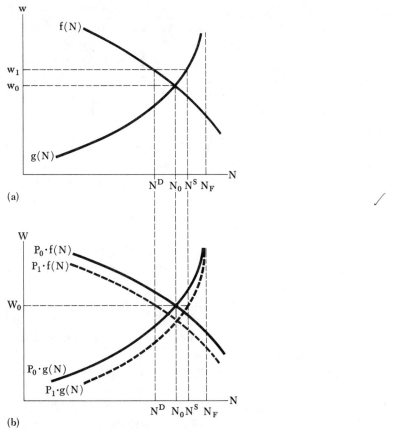

Figure 10-5 Wage rigidity in the classical case.

unemployment in the initial equilibrium. But strictly speaking, there is no aggregate *involuntary* unemployment since, on average, the people in the labor force out of work are in that circumstance by choice.

Now suppose the money wage rate is fixed at W_0, and aggregate demand drops because of, say, a collapse in investment demand and a large shift of the *IS* curve to the left. This creates excess supply in the economy, and the price level falls to P_1. In Figure 10-5(a), the real wage, with W stuck at W_0, rises to w_1, creating an excess supply of labor equal to $N^S - N^D$. Similarly, in Figure 10-5(b) both the supply and demand curves of labor shift down, giving the same excess supply. If there is no mechanism to force employers to hire more labor than they want to, employment will fall to N^D in Figure 10-5. If P_1 is the new equilibrium price level, assuming that W_0 is fixed, then employment has dropped to N^D and output has dropped to $y_1 = y(N^D; \bar{K})$. This is shown in the supply and demand diagram of Figure 10-6.

The "true" supply curve *SS* is, as usual in the classical case, vertical in

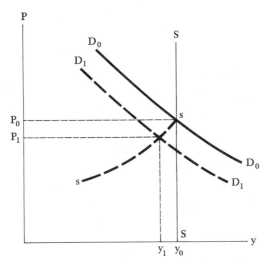

Figure 10-6 Supply and demand with rigid wages:
the classical case.

Figure 10-6, with output fixed in the labor market at $y_0 = y(N_0; \bar{K})$. The intersection of the original demand curve $D_0 D_0$ and the supply curve determined the initial equilibrium price level P_0 of Figure 10-5. Given w_0, this determined the initial, and now rigid, money wage rate W_0.

Now if W_0 is rigid downward, as the price level falls in Figure 10-5 raising the real wage, employment and output will fall along the labor-demand curve. This is best illustrated in Figure 10-5(a); as P falls from P_0 with W fixed at W_0, employment falls along the $f(N)$ demand curve. This again gives us the dashed ss segment of the supply curve in Figure 10-5, which replaces the segment of the true supply curve below the initial equilibrium. The downward shift in the demand curve from $D_0 D_0$ to $D_1 D_1$ now creates excess supply and reduces the price level to P_1 with observed output $y_1 = y(N^D; \bar{K})$.

If we now ask how many more worker-hours will be offered at the going wage than are employed, the answer is $N^S - N^D$, the measure of aggregate involuntary unemployment. Thus, the introduction of the rigid wage provides an explanation for truly involuntary unemployment in the classical case, as well as in the general static model.

Several points should be noticed here. First, unemployment in the sense of an externally measured labor force minus actual employment has risen from $N_F - N_0$ to $N_F - N_D$ in Figure 10-5, while truly involuntary unemployment has risen from zero to $N_S - N_D$ *at real wage* w_1. This is emphasized because $N^S - N^D$ does not measure the "effect" of the wage rigidity. If the rigidity were removed, employment would return to N_0 in this model, an increase of $N_0 - N^D$, not $N^S - N^D$, which overstates the effect of the rigidity by $N^S - N_0$.

Second, from the supply and demand diagram of Figure 10-6, it should be clear that the rigid wage hypothesis provides another solution to the liquidity-trap problem, if the trap exists in the first place. If the demand curve shifts to the left and becomes vertical because price decreases won't increase equilibrium output demanded, an inconsistency appears in the classical case; there is no intersection between the demand and supply curves, and prices and wages can fall continuously without restoring equilibrium. With a rigid wage rate, however, the original vertical supply curve below the initial equilibrium point is replaced by the positively sloped supply curve ss. Now if the classical economy falls into the liquidity trap, equilibrium will be reached at a new P_1, y_1 point as shown in Figure 10-7, at the intersection of ss and the vertical $D_1 D_1$ demand curve.

Finally, a point of contrast should be noticed about the effects of wage rigidity in the general model and in the classical case. Wage rigidity changed the fundamental character of the classical case. Without wage rigidity the labor market equilibrium condition in the real wage model is

$$f(N) = g(N), \tag{2}$$

and employment is determined in the labor market alone; (2) is one equation in one unknown. Wage rigidity replaces this equilibrium condition by

$$W_0 = P \cdot f(N), \tag{3}$$

one equation in two unknowns, P and N. This eliminates the dichotomy of the real wage model. It makes the supply curve in Figure 10-7 the positively sloped ss instead of a vertical SS, and the model becomes simultaneous, with interaction between demand and supply sides.

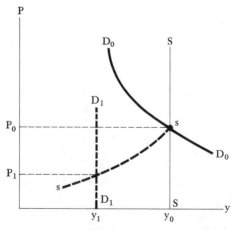

Figure 10-7   The liquidity trap with rigid wages.

In the general model, with (3) replacing the flexible wage equilibrium condition,

$$P \cdot f(N) = P^e \cdot g(N) = p(P) \cdot g(N), \qquad (4)$$

the fundamental character of the model is not changed. Both (3) and (4) include the variables P and N; both SS and ss in Figure 10-3 have positive slopes. Wage rigidity just changes the positive slope of the supply curve in an already simultaneous general static model.

LOCAL WAGE RIGIDITIES AND AGGREGATE UNEMPLOYMENT

The previous section analyzed the effects of wage rigidity in the general static model and in the classical case partially to take advantage of an opportunity to look at those models from a new angle. The best way to understand how the economy "hangs together" is to look at it from several different aspects, and asking how wage rigidity affects its operation is one useful way to do this. But these labor market models with an economy-wide rigid wage probably have little relevance to the actual explanation of unemployment in the United States. This is because, at least in the short run, labor mobility between local labor markets, disaggregated by geography or skill class, is very low. Thus, the notion of an economy-wide downward-rigid wage has to be based on the assumption that all local wage rates—for steelworkers in Pittsburgh, computer technicians in Houston, electricians in Los Angeles, and so on—are rigid downward. But if this is the case, for an economy-wide wage index literally not to fall as demand and employment fall implies both that every local market where demand falls has a wage rigidity, and that demand falls the same proportion in each, so that the wage index isn't reduced by a shift in the mix of employment from high-wage to low-wage areas. Since one major cause of a downward-rigid wage, at least in the short run, would be the existence of a union contract, the fact that only 20 percent of the U.S. labor force is unionized suggests that local rigidities aren't so frequent that the first of these conditions is very likely to be met.

One might expect the economy-wide labor-supply curve to have a horizontal rigid wage floor at the level of the minimum wage, or at the average unemployment or public assistance benefit level. But the minimum wage—the highest of these three levels(!)—is $3.35 (in 1986), compared to average gross hourly earnings in manufacturing of $9.70. So this floor is so far below the normal operating range of the economy that it cannot explain existing economy-wide unemployment, although it might explain some unemployment among marginal workers such as teenagers.

A more plausible role for wage rigidity to play in explaining unemployment is in the presumption that some local labor markets have rigid wages, particularly those most unionized in the manufacturing and mining sectors, and some have flexible wages, particularly those in services. If this is the case, as aggregate demand rises, the money wage rate and employment will generally rise with the impact on particular local labor markets, depending on the source of the demand increase. But when demand falls, W and N fall along the supply curve in markets with flexible wages, but in markets with rigid wages, N falls along the initial W_0 line. This will give us a positively sloped economy-wide labor-supply curve, but the supply curve will be steeper as W and N rise to any point W_0, N_0 than it is as W and N fall from that point.

This kind of local wage rigidity curve is shown in Figure 10-8. There $P^e \cdot g(N)$ is the usual supply curve. As demand increases, W and N rise to an equilibrium point like W_0, N_0. If demand falls from that level, W and N will fall along $s_0 s_0$, not along $P^e \cdot g(N)$, due to rigid wages in some local markets. If demand rises beyond W_0, N_0, W and N increase along $P^e \cdot g(N)$ to the new equilibrium, say, W_1, N_1, establishing a new, higher, rigid wage. If demand then falls from W_1, N_1, it falls along $s_1 s_1$, not along $P^e \cdot g(N)$. Thus, as demand expands, an ss curve is established at each equilibrium point, replacing the supply curve $P^e \cdot g(N)$ below that point. When demand does fall, then, literal involuntary unemployment appears (or increases) in the markets with rigid wage rates.

Another feature of this kind of partial local-wage-rigidity model is interesting. Suppose demand shifts from a product that is manufactured in rigid-wage market i, to any other product (since all markets are assumed to have *up*ward-flexible wages) manufactured in, say, market j, with no drop in aggregate real demand. Then, in the rigid-wage market N_i will fall but W_i won't.

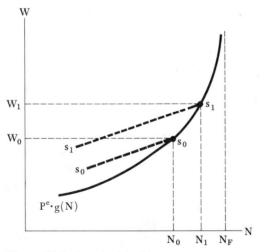

Figure 10-8   Local wage rigidities.

But in the other market j, both N_j and W_j will rise, and since W_j rises, N_j will probably rise less than N_i fell. Thus, the demand shift would raise average W and reduce total employment while maintaining the same level of aggregate demand. As long as all markets have upward-flexible wage rates, but some have downward-rigid wages, as demand continually shifts there may be a bias toward both wage and unemployment increases.

PRICE STICKINESS AND THE AGGREGATE SUPPLY FUNCTION

Not only nominal wages, but also prices may be sticky. It can be directly costly for firms to change their prices, because new catalogs must be printed and labels exchanged. Some aspects of the market discourage frequent price changes. For example, if consumers engage in costly and lengthy searching for "a good deal," comparing the prices of different brands, then they will be very annoyed if prices change too quickly. Perhaps you will restrict your purchases if, after checking six dealers, the offer made by the first one is no longer valid. On the firms' side, advertising is negated by frequent price revisions. Furthermore, in (partially) cartellized markets, any one firm may not want to change its own price for fear of setting off a price war.

Let us look, then, at what happens when both the nominal wage and the level are sticky. Suppose the initial price level is P_0, the nominal wage W_0 and the real wage w_0, as shown in Figures 10-9 and 10-10. If demand rises, then the price level and the nominal wage can rise to bring us to a new long-run equilibrium. If, however, aggregate demand were to fall (to $D_1 D_1$), the price level would have to fall in Figure 10-9 to P_1 and the nominal wage to fall equiproportionately, in order to restore initial output y_0 and employment N_0.

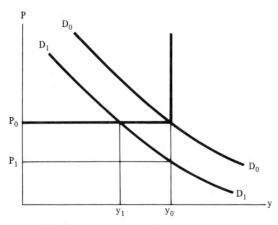

Figure 10-9 Aggregate supply and demand with price stickiness.

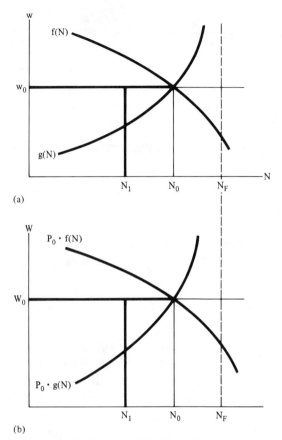

(a)

(b)

Figure 10-10 Wage and rigidity in the labor market.

However, with the price level fixed at P_0, firms want to supply y_0 while demand and sales fall to y_1. Eventually, output then falls along the horizontal line to y_1 in Figure 10-9. There is excess supply ($y_0 - y_1$).

With output limited to y_1 in Figure 10-9, firms will restrict their employment to the numbers of workers needed to produce y_1. Let's call this number N_1 in Figure 10-10; clearly, $N_1 < N_0$ since $y_1 < y_0$. In the sticky-wage version of the classical case, shown in Figure 10-5, labor demand fell because the real wage rose as the price level fell. Here, causation runs from excess supply in the goods market to a lower demand for labor. Labor demand is just that amount required to produce output y_1, rather than being given by the usual demand function $w = f(N)$.

Since the real wage is unchanged, the labor-supply function in Figure 10-10 is unaffected. Hence, excess supply of goods causes involuntary unemployment ($N_0 - N_1$). Total unemployment is ($N_F - N_1$), of which only ($N_F - N_0$) is voluntary. Price stickiness creates a horizontal aggregate supply function at P_0, altering labor demand as output demand falls. Wage and price stickiness together create an effective labor-supply function that is horizontal at w_0 in Figure 10-10(a).

Let's now put together the vertical long-run supply curve, the positively sloped supply curve with sticky nominal wage, and the flat supply schedule when both prices and wages are sticky, as shown in Figure 10-11. When the price level rises above P_0, output reaches its long-term equilibrium level y_0 and can go no higher. In a range of lower prices, from P_1 to P_0, wage stickiness is the important "distortion" from the long-term equilibrium, and we have the upward-sloping supply schedule ss shown in Figure 10-3. The supply curve has a positive slope, even though expectations are fulfilled exactly. Finally, once the price level reaches P_1 and output is down to y_1, price stickiness becomes binding and the supply function becomes horizontal. Both the nominal wage and the price level are above the levels required to clear the labor and the goods markets. Up to output y_1, firms are willing to meet any demand at price P_1, and correspondingly labor demand depends on actual output rather than the real wage.

SUMMARY: AN ECLECTIC VIEW OF UNEMPLOYMENT

In an economy operating at fairly high levels of resource utilization, unemployment can be explained without appeal to wage rigidity, as the first part of this chapter showed. With the labor market in equilibrium in the sense that demand and supply are equal, there will be search unemployment with a rotating stock of workers unemployed and looking for work. At any point in time the voluntarily unemployed job-seekers can be considered to be above

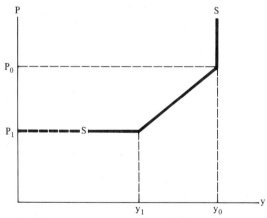

Figure 10-11 Aggregate supply with wage and price floors.

the going wage on their supply curves. The general static model explains how changes in demand conditions alter this equilibrium level of unemployment.

While this explanation of aggregate unemployment might be sufficient when the economy is operating at high levels of employment, it needs help in cases of widespread involuntary unemployment. Here the hypothesis that wages are rigid in the downward direction in local labor markets seems more useful than a hypothesis that there is an economy-wide rigid wage. The hypothesis of local wage rigidity can explain the appearance of widespread involuntary unemployment as demand drops substantially. In addition, combined with shifting industrial mix and immobility between labor markets, the hypothesis of local wage rigidity can explain the existence of local high-unemployment areas in a generally full-employment economy.

SELECTED READINGS

J-P. Benassy, *The Economics of Market Disequilibrium* (New York: Academic Press, 1982), Part III.

K. Brunner and A. H. Meltzer, eds., *The Phillips Curve and Labor Markets* (Amsterdam: North Holland, 1976).

R.E. Hall, "Why Is the Unemployment Rate So High at Full Employment?" *Brookings Papers on Economic Activity,* vol. 3, 1970.

N.G. Mankiw, "Small Menu Costs and Large Business Cycles: A Macroeconomic Model of Monopoly," *Quarterly Journal of Economics,* May 1985.

A.M. Okun, *Prices and Quantities* (Washington, D.C.: The Brookings Institution, 1981), Chapter 2.

E.S. Phelps et al., *Microeconomic Foundations of Employment and Inflation Theory* (New York: W.W. Norton, 1970), Part I.

J. Rotemberg, "Sticky Prices in the United States," *Journal of Political Economy,* December 1982.

C.L. Schultze, "Recent Inflation in the United States," Study Paper No. 1, Joint Economic Committee, 86th Congress, September 1959.

chapter 11

Rational Expectations and Demand Policy

The discussion of monetary and fiscal policy in Chapter 9 was based on the general static model in which the expected price level could deviate from the actual price level in the short run. In this case the aggregate supply curve is nonvertical in the short run. Chapter 7 ended with a discussion of *adaptive expectations* as a model compatible with the distinction between a relatively flat short-run aggregate supply curve and a more vertical longer run version. Demand policy makes most sense in a world where the aggregate supply curve is fairly flat. Then demand fluctuations create fluctuations in output and employment, which are to be avoided. The role of monetary and fiscal policy is to offset private-sector fluctuations in demand and to stabilize output. The positively sloped (nonvertical) aggregate supply curve could be based on lags in expectations, such as in Chapter 9, or on wage rigidities, as in Chapter 10. In both cases, we have a role for monetary or fiscal policy as a stabilizer of aggregate demand.

In this chapter we discuss a very different model of expectations formation called *rational expectations,* and explore its consequences for what we think about policy. As an alternative to adaptive expectations, suppose that economic agents, namely the workers here, form expectations using our skeletal macro-model. We can ask what happens if expectations are taken from the model instead of an error correction mechanism as in Chapter 7. We will see that in the absence of wage rigidities, only the part of demand policy that is not anticipated by the private sector moves output. The aggregate supply curve may become vertical in the short run in the face of predictable demand policy, with *rational expectations.* Thus, the rational expectations hypothesis could have quite radical implications for the way we think about demand policy.

After a few technical preliminaries, we will look at a version of a rational expectations model that comes straight out of the basic static model of Chapter 9. A little additional notation and simplification can transform the aggregate demand curve of equation (22) in Chapter 5 and the supply curve in equation (7) of Chapter 7 into a fairly typical example of a rational expectations model. In the absence of wage or price rigidities, the aggregate supply curve of Chapter 7 is the *Lucas supply function* of the *new classical* economics. It is nonvertical only if the expected price level can deviate from the actual price level. So we can go directly from the basic static model to a rational expectations example by comparing the effects of policy with exogenous price expectations to the effects with expectations based on the model. The latter is our version of rational expectations, while exogenous price expectations comes from the adaptive expectations mechanism.

After the example of the consequences of rational, or *model-consistent,* expectations for the effects of policy is clear, we can go on to a more precise definition of rational expectations and the conditions for its being a reasonable operating assumption. Finally, we see that wage rigidity in the form of multiperiod contracts restores the nonvertical slope of the aggregate supply curve, even with rational expectations. Thus, with no wage or price rigidity, thoroughgoing rational expectations will verticalize the aggregate supply curve against predictable demand policy in the short run, but multiperiod wage contracts will flatten it again.

TWO PRELIMINARIES

Whenever expectations are involved in an economic model, it is critical to sort out the temporal sequence of events and expectations. Therefore, we introduced a system of time subscripts in Chapter 7. A subscript small "t" at the bottom right of a variable indicates in which time period we will evaluate the variable, and a subscript before the variable shows when the expectation of that value was made. So the expression $_{t-1}P_t$, which we will use for the sake of its compactness, can be read as "the expectation, formed at $t - 1$, of P at time t." In Chapter 7 and subsequently, we suppressed much of this notation when we could do so without ambiguity, writing P for P_t and P^e for $_{t-1}P_t$. It is useful to be reminded of the fuller notation because we will have to use some of it later in this chapter.

Besides our usual collection of variables (P_t, y_t, etc.) and parameters, we will often add terms at the end of equations to represent random shocks or, borrowing a phrase from econometrics, error terms. These represent the chance events that are always occurring, for example, because of the weather, accidents, natural disasters, random shifts in tastes, technology or income distributions, or manna from heaven. When doing comparative statics in past chapters, we often posited, for example, an exogenous change in investment; such changes could also be counted as random shocks. In the structural equations of a model, such as the production function or the consumption function, these shifts and jumps will have two essential characteristics. First, they are exogenous, that is, they are not determined from within the model. Second, their expected values are all zero, so that a shock is as likely to be positive as negative. For example, when you throw sand on the ground, a physicist can work out where the center of gravity of the sand will land, but the distance of any single grain from the center of mass is a random number of mean zero. One could say that each grain receives some random shock which sends it out a certain distance from the mean. Throwing sand is literally stochastic, the word *stochastic* coming from the Greek for scattering or spreading, with the position of any one grain being decomposable into a mean plus a random component following a probability distribution. The random component is also known as "white noise," a term from electroengineering describing the meaningless hiss that electronic systems tend to generate.

Once we start manipulating the structural equations of a model, the shocks combine in a variety of ways, so that in the *reduced form* equations the error terms need not have an expected value of zero and they are not entirely exogenous. Typically, we get a linear combination of shocks from different parts of the economy (e.g., production and the money supply) and from different time periods. The latter is important in producing persistence (econometrically, serial correlation) in economic fluctuations.

THE BASIC MODEL WITH EXOGENOUS EXPECTATIONS

To illustrate the importance of how price expectations are modeled, we will first look at a simplified version of the basic static model with exogenous price expectations, then solve it with expectations that are formed using the model, and finally compare the two results. This will produce the basic insight or result from the rational expectations hypothesis. We will begin with the aggregate supply curve of Chapter 7, equation (7), with P^e exogenous, couple this with the aggregate demand curve of Chapter 5, equation (22), and see what the equilibrium result is for output y.

Aggregate Supply Once Again

The labor market equilibrium condition from Chapter 7, equation (2), is reproduced here:

$$P \cdot f(N) = P^e \cdot g(N). \tag{1}$$

In the initial equilibrium we will index the price level P to unity and assume that $P^e = P = 1$. This implies from equation (1) that in the initial equilibrium $f(N) = g(N)$. Changes in employment, the price level, and the expected price level are related by the total differential of (1), which is

$$f \cdot dP + Pf' \, dN = g \cdot dP^e + P^e g' \, dN.$$

Remembering that $P = P^e = 1$ and $f = g$ in the initial equilibrium, we can rewrite the labor market differential as

$$dN = \frac{f}{g' - f'} (dP - dP^e). \tag{2}$$

Here $dN/dP > 0$ and $dN/dP^e < 0$. Finally, we can use the production function to convert equation (2) into an aggregate supply curve. The production function is

$$y = y(N; \bar{K}), \tag{3}$$

so that changes in y and N are related by

$$dy = y' \cdot dN = f(N) \cdot dN. \tag{4}$$

Remember that $f(N)$ is the marginal product of labor $\partial y / \partial N$. Substituting for dN from equation (4) into equation (2), we get the aggregate supply curve from Chapter 7:

$$dy = \frac{f^2}{g' - f'} [dP - dP^e]. \tag{5}$$

In equation (7) of Chapter 7, the assumption that dP^e is exogenous means $p' = 0$. If we also recognize there that in the initial equilibrium $\partial y / \partial N = w = f$, we get equation (5) here. The labor market equilibrium of equations (2) and (5) is illustrated in Figure 11-1. The top panel shows how N will move following $dP - dP^e$ from equation (2), and the bottom panel shows the determination of movements in y.

The aggregate supply curve from the basic static model, equation (5), can be rewritten in the explicitly time-subscripted form of the expectations-oriented literature. Suppose we consider changes from time $t - 1$ to time t. Then the change in y in equation (5) is actually

$$dy = y_t - y_{t-1} \tag{6}$$

The change in the actual price level is given by

$$dP = P_t - P_{t-1}, \tag{7}$$

and the expected change in the price level is given by

$$dP^e = {}_{t-1}P_t - P_{t-1}. \tag{8}$$

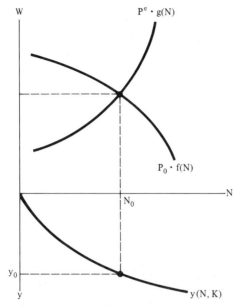

Figure 11-1 Aggregate supply and the labor market.

Here P_{t-1} is known at the end of period $t - 1$, and $_{t-1}P_t$ is the price expected for period t. If we call the coefficient in equation (5)

$$\beta \equiv \frac{f^2}{g' - f'},$$

and substitute from equations (6)–(8) into (5), we get the Lucas supply function:

$$y_t = y_{t-1} + \beta(P_t - {}_{t-1}P_t).$$

To represent random or unanticipated shocks to the supply curve, we will add a random error term ϵ_t to it, which will give us the final form of aggregate supply here:

$$y_t = y_{t-1} + \beta(P_t - {}_{t-1}P_t) + \epsilon_t. \qquad (9)$$

If we think of the $t - 1$ period as the initial equilibrium, the aggregate supply curve (9) says that output this period, y_t, will increase from the initial equilibrium y_{t-1} by an amount proportional to the increase of the price level P_t relative to its expected level $_{t-1}P_t$. In addition, there is a random supply shock ϵ_t with an average value of zero over time. This simply represents the fact that there are unpredictable elements behind aggregate supply. The econometrician's best estimate still has a nonzero standard error.

The aggregate supply curve of equation (9) is shown as SS in Figure 11-2. The slope is $dP_t/dy_t = 1/\beta$, and an increase in expected price $_{t-1}P_t$ shifts

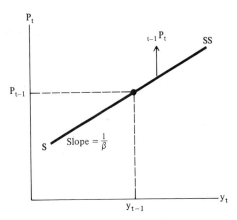

Figure 11-2 Aggregate supply.

it up. The random error term provides for our uncertainty about precisely where SS will be located at any point in time.

Aggregate Demand

The total differential of the aggregate demand curve in the basic static model was given in equation (22) of Chapter 5 as

$$dy = \frac{1}{\delta}\left[dg + \frac{i'}{l'}\frac{dM}{P} - \frac{i'}{l'}\frac{M}{P}\frac{dP}{P}\right].\qquad(10)$$

Here $\delta = i - c'(1 - t') + \dfrac{i'k'}{l'}$, the denominator of the standard demand

multiplier in the basic static model. The terms in dg and dM give the shift in the aggregate demand curve as g or M changes, and the dP term gives the slope.

We can convert the total differential in equation (10) into a time-subscripted aggregate demand curve with a few simplifying assumptions. First, since the object here is to see the implications of alternative assumptions about price expectations, there is no need to carry along both dg and dM in the analysis. These two policy variables are important because they provide a shift in the aggregate demand curve. Since both do that, we need only one to make the analytical points here. So we'll hold g constant, setting $dg = 0$, and focus on the effects of monetary policy characterized by dM in equation (10).

The total differentials in (10) can be interpreted as the change from period $t - 1$ to period t in each variable, with period $t - 1$ taken as the initial equilibrium. The initial level of the price level P_{t-1} has already been set at unity (indexed to $P_{t-1} = 1.0$) in the discussion of aggregate supply. To further simplify, we will also set the initial level of the money stock M_{t-1} at unity. This means that the changes in y will be measured implicitly in multiples of the initial real money stock. This simplification permits us to proceed without carrying along multiplicative terms in M_{t-1}, which would only make the analysis messy. These simplifications eliminate the initial levels of M and P from equation (10), since both equal unity. The dy and dP terms can be interpreted as $y_t - y_{t-1}$ and $P_t - P_{t-1}$, respectively, and we add that

$$dM = M_t - M_{t-1}. \tag{11}$$

With dg set equal to zero, we now have a new interpretation of equation (10):

$$y_t - y_{t-1} = \frac{i'}{\delta l'} [M_t - M_{t-1} - (P_t - P_{t-1})]. \tag{12}$$

With both M_{t-1} and P_{t-1} indexed to unity, those terms now cancel out in (12). It will be convenient for doing the solutions for aggregate demand and supply to write the aggregate demand curve with P_t on the left-hand side. Thus, inverting (12) to make it an equation for P_t, and adding a random error term μ_t to represent demand shocks, from (12) we finally obtain the demand curve

$$P_t = -\alpha(y_t - y_{t-1}) + M_t + \mu_t. \tag{13}$$

Here $\alpha = \delta l'/i'$, the slope of the aggregate demand curve. Since both P and M are indexed to unity, the coefficient of M in (13) is also one. An equal increase in M and P will leave output demanded y_t unchanged.

The aggregate demand curve in equation (13) is shown as DD in Figure 11-3. The slope is $-\delta l'/i'$, the same as in Chapter 5, equation (22), with

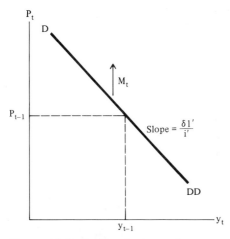

Figure 11-3 Aggregate demand.

$M = P = 1$. An increase in M shifts the demand curve up. The random error term μ_t expresses our uncertainty about precisely where AD will be at any point in time.

Equilibrium Output with Exogenous Expectations

The aggregate supply curve of equation (9) and the aggregate demand curve of equation (13) can now be combined to get an explicit solution for equilibrium output y_t, given y_{t-1}, M_t, and expected price $_{t-1}P_t$, which here we are assuming is given exogenously. This will be the y solution with adaptive expectations, for example. The aggregate model of equations (9) and (13) is essentially the same as the starting point in the Sargent and Wallace paper on rational expectations. One of the main aims of going through the conversion of SS from the form of equation (5) to the form in (9), and of DD from equation (10) to equation (13), is to show explicitly that the basic static model in Chapters 4–9 is the same as the model underlying the literature on rational expectations.

For convenience, we rewrite AS and AD together here.

$$SS: \quad y_t = y_{t-1} + \beta(P_t - _{t-1}P_t) + \epsilon_t; \tag{9}$$

$$DD: \quad P_t = -\alpha(y_t - y_{t-1}) + M_t + \mu_t. \tag{13}$$

To obtain the solution for y_t with exogenous $_{t-1}P_t$, we can substitute the DD expression for P_t into the SS curve. Now it should be clear why it was convenient to write DD with P_t on the left-hand side! After we do that substitution and solve for y_t, we get the *reduced-form* expression for y_t,

$$y_t = y_{t-1} + \frac{\beta}{1 + \alpha\beta}(M_t - _{t-1}P_t) + \frac{1}{1 + \alpha\beta}(\beta\mu_t + \epsilon_t). \tag{14}$$

This is the basic static model's solution for y_t in its linearized Sargent-Wallace form with exogenous price expectations. It is illustrated in Figure 11-4, which is the same as Figure 8-1 in Chapter 8. All we have done here is

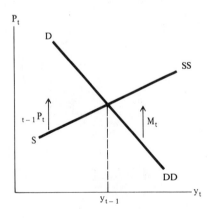

Figure 11-4 Equilibrium output, exogenous expectations.

to make expectations more explicit and convert to a linear form of the model in order to get an explicit algebraic solution. An increase in M_t shifts the DD curve up and increases y_t by $\beta/(1 + \alpha\beta)$ times the increase in M. A rise in price expectations $_{t-1}P_t$ shifts the SS curve up and reduces y_t by the same proportion. Equal increases in M_t and $_{t-1}P_t$ leave output unchanged at y_{t-1}; they shift DD and SS up equally. Notice that since M_{t-1} and P_{t-1} were set at unity, equal changes in M_t and $_{t-1}P_t$ are equiproportionate changes, too. The last term in equation (14) gives the effects of random demand or supply shocks in y_t. A positive drawing for μ_t is an upward shift in DD; a positive drawing for ϵ_t is an outward shift of SS.

The reduced-form solution for y_t in equation (14) contains nothing essentially new. It is an explicit solution of the basic static model of Chapter 8, after we have cast it in a linear form so that an explicit solution can be obtained. It shows explicitly the role of exogenous price expectations. More importantly, it shows how monetary policy moves y_t by shifting the aggregate demand curve. If we had kept fiscal policy dg in the picture, it would enter equation (14) in essentially the same way as monetary policy.

The important aspect of the solution for y_t given in (14) will be seen when we compare it to the alternative solution when $_{t-1}P_t$ is taken from the model itself, instead of being formed exogenously. In (14) we should notice two things. First, actual M_t is what moves y_t; in equation (14) we make no distinction between anticipated and unanticipated changes in monetary policy. This distinction is crucial in the alternative expectations model that is coming up. Second, if price expectations $_{t-1}P_t$ and M_t change by the same amount in (14), there is no effect on y_t. We will now explore this result more carefully.

THE BASIC MODEL WITH EXPECTATIONS ENDOGENOUS

The solution for y_t given in equation (14) is based on the assumption that price expectations, represented by $_{t-1}P_t$, are exogenous. In Chapter 7 we discussed adaptive expectations as a reasonable example that is consistent with exogenous price expectations. At the time of a policy shift in M_t, the adaptive expectations mechanism is still looking at past prices, and so $_{t-1}P_t$ is exogenous. Then in subsequent periods, actual price movements begin feeding into the adaptive expectations mechanism, adjusting P^e toward the long run. The adaptive expectations hypothesis makes sense if the price level is fluctuating more or less randomly around some equilibrium average level.

In the past 10 to 15 years, macro research has concentrated on the alternative hypothesis: that expectations are formed by using the model rather than by looking into the past. It seems natural to suggest that if economic agents expect monetary policy to expand, for example, they use some kind of macromodel to predict what will happen to the price level. In Chapters 4–9 we have developed a model that includes price determination. Let's see what happens if we assume that price expectations are formed using this model. This will give us the basic result of the rational expectations revolution in macroeconomics. Later, we'll turn to a more explicit examination of rational expectations itself.

Equilibrium Output with Endogenous Expectations

Again, we begin with the aggregate supply and demand curves, repeated here for convenience:

$$SS: \quad y_t = y_{t-1} + \beta(P_t - {}_{t-1}P_t) + \epsilon_t, \tag{9}$$

$$DD: \quad P_t = -\alpha(y_t - y_{t-1}) + M_t + \mu_t. \tag{13}$$

We now want to use the model itself to get an expression for ${}_{t-1}P_t$ to put into the SS curve as we solve for y_t. One way to arrive at the solution is the following. First, use the DD curve to see what the expected price should be, given expected output. Then use the SS curve to get expected output. This will give us an expression for ${}_{t-1}P_t$ which eliminates all other endogenous variables. Then put that plus (13) for P_t itself into (9) and solve for y_t. We will get a result that stands in striking contrast to the reduced-form equation (14)!

So, to obtain an endogenous expression for the price expectation ${}_{t-1}P_t$, we shift the demand curve back one period and ask what P_t should have been expected to be in period $t-1$. From the DD curve (13) we get

$$_{t-1}P_t = -\alpha[{}_{t-1}y_t - y_{t-1}] + {}_{t-1}M_t. \tag{15}$$

From the vantage point of period $t-1$, we have to put our expectations of y_t and M_t into the DD curve, since we don't know the realized values yet. The expected value of the error term is zero, so μ_t drops out of (15).

Now equation (15) has an expected ${}_{t-1}y_t$ in it. We can use the SS curve to see that expected output is just going to be

$$_{t-1}y_t = y_{t-1}. \tag{16}$$

We know that there will be some deviation $(P_t - {}_{t-1}P_t)$ once we see what happens in period t. But from the point of view of period $(t-1)$, the expected value of that error in predicting P_t is zero. We know we'll be wrong, but we don't know in advance which way. Essentially, the *expected* prediction error is zero: ${}_{t-1}(P_t - {}_{t-1}P_t) = 0$. The expected value of the random supply shock ϵ_t is also zero.

Next we can use (16) for ${}_{t-1}y_t$ in (15) to see that the expected price movement is just the expected movement in money (remember that we set $P_{t-1} = M_{t-1} = 1$),

$$_{t-1}P_t = -\alpha(y_{t-1} - y_{t-1}) + {}_{t-1}M_t = {}_{t-1}M_t. \tag{17}$$

The structure of the solution for $_{t-1}P_t$ should be clear. Since the expected value of the price prediction error in the *SS* curve (9) is zero, the *expected* y_t is equal to y_{t-1}. But then in the *DD* curve (13), the *expected* deviation $y_t - y_{t-1}$ is also zero. This gives us equation (17) for $_{t-1}P_t$.

To obtain the reduced-form solution for y_t, we can now substitute into the *SS* curve (9): first, the expression in the *DD* curve (13) for P_t, and second, $_{t-1}M_t$ for $_{t-1}P_t$ from (17). When we make those substitutions, and then solve for y_t, we obtain the reduced-form solution for y_t with endogenous price expectations taken from the model:

$$y_t = y_{t-1} + \frac{\beta}{1 + \alpha\beta}(M_t - {}_{t-1}M_t) + \frac{1}{1 + \alpha\beta}(\beta\mu_t + \epsilon_t). \qquad (18)$$

Comparison of the two reduced-form expressions (14) and (18) shows that the difference is the substitution in (18) of $_{t-1}M_t$ for $_{t-1}P_t$ in (14).

How do we interpret this new reduced-form equation for y_t? Essentially, it says that the difference between actual M_t and expected $_{t-1}M_t$ moves output. Consider equations (14) and (17) together. In (14) with exogenous price expectations, it was the difference between actual money M_t and expected prices $_{t-1}P_t$ that moved y_t. Then in equation (17) we saw that with expectations taken from the model, expected price movements are determined by expected money movements. This means in (18) that, with endogenous expectations, it becomes the deviations of actual from expected money movements that drive output. Equation (18) is the basis of the now-famous "policy ineffectiveness" result that, under rational expectations, it is the deviations of actual policy from the public's expectations of it that have an effect on output.

In equation (18), current output y_t deviates from its classical equilibrium level y_{t-1} only because of random shocks to demand and supply, μ_t and ϵ_t, and unanticipated policy. This result comes from combining the assumptions of complete wage and price flexibility and model-consistent or "rational" expectations. These two assumptions are the basis of the *new classical economics* and the policy ineffectiveness result. The classical model had a vertical aggregate supply curve in the long run. In the new classical model it is effectively vertical in the short run, too.

Anticipated Versus Unanticipated Policy

Before we go on to examine the idea of rational expectations in more precise detail, we should pause to consider the economics that lie under the policy ineffectiveness conclusion. The basic idea is as follows. If the public, which in the basic model is the labor force, expects an expansion in the money supply, they, or their economic consultants, can use the model to calculate an expectation of what this will do to the price level. This expected $_{t-1}P_t$, conditioned on their expected $_{t-1}M_t$, gets built into the aggregate supply curve, shifting it up in Figure 11-4. Then when the actual increase in money comes along, it shifts the demand curve up by the same amount. If all the calculations were done right, and the actual M_t comes through as expected, then the two shifts will be equal and nothing will happen to y_t. If mistakes in expectations about movement in M or its consequences for P are random with zero means, then the $(y_t - y_{t-1})$ movements themselves become random. It is only the surprise movements in money or prices that give movements in output.

This result is built on two essential assumptions. First, expectations must be "rational" in the way just described; no systematic errors are made in predicting price movements. Second, wages and prices must be flexible. The way expected price movements $_{t-1}P_t$ get into the SS curve is by shifting labor supply and moving the wage rate. This was clear in the labor market analysis of Chapter 6. If wages are fixed by multiperiod contracts, for example, they will not be able to respond quickly (in one period) to changes in price expectations. This would break the link from price expectations to the shift in the SS curve in Figure 11-4. So before we place too much emphasis on the result of equation (18), we have to explore these assumptions a bit more carefully.

THE RATIONAL EXPECTATIONS HYPOTHESIS

In the last section we looked at a very simple model of aggregate demand and supply and worked out the consequences of taking expectations from the model. These expectations are said to be *rational* or *model-consistent* because it is as if everyone knows the model and uses this knowledge fully. In the practice of economic research, this means that when you put forward an economic model you assume that agents acting in that model know as much about it as you do. They know the functional forms of the equations, they know parameter values, and they know the distributions of the exogenous shocks. They are just as good at working out the implications of the model as you are.

Let us get closer to a definition of rational expectations. In Chapter 7 we posited an expectations function $_{t-1}P_t = p(P_t)$. Rational expectations are usually presented the other way around as

$$P_t = {}_{t-1}P_t + \epsilon_t, \tag{19}$$

with

$$_{t-1}\epsilon_t = 0. \tag{20}$$

That is, the realized price level (or whatever variable you are predicting) equals the predicted price level, plus a stochastic error term with mean zero. Your prediction in (19) is said to be *unbiased*. If the price level is random, that is, a nonzero ϵ_t is a possibility, with a given distribution across possible values but mean zero as in (20), then your expected value of the price level is the true mean of this distribution. Your subjectively held expectation for p_t in (19) equals the objective mean (often called the population mean). Furthermore, full, "strong form," rational expectations require that your prediction be the best you can make, as measured perhaps by the variance of the error term. Creating the best predictor involves incorporating all information currently available. The policy ineffectiveness result holds in qualitative terms with "weak form" rational expectations that require only unbiasedness. Typically, if forecasting errors still have mean zero but variance greater than that which is warranted by exogenous shocks, then output will become more variable as well. But *anticipated* monetary policy will still be ineffective in stabilizing output. Going from strong form to weak form rational expectations affects the variance of the error term in equation (18) on p. 215.

The Law of Iterated Expectations

An implication of the unbiasedness of rational expectations is that the expected value of all prediction errors is zero. The difference between the realization of a variable and its forecast, say, $(P_t - {}_{t-1}P_t)$, equals a stochastic term with mean zero. Even though some error is inevitable, it is as likely to be positive as negative. Therefore, no one can say in advance what sign the error will have.

Unbiasedness implies that the expected prediction error is zero for all future periods. For example, your forecast of the difference $(P_{t+1} - {}_{t-1}P_{t+1})$, the difference between the actual value and the prediction two periods earlier, is also a random variable with mean zero and a given variance. Typically, the variance of the errors increases as the forecasting horizon lengthens, but the expected value is always zero.

Rational expectations applies not only to variables such as the price level or real output, but also to the predictions themselves. Consider the relationship between the realization of the price level at $t + 1$ and the forecasts made one and two periods in advance. If the forecasts are unbiased, then

$$P_{t+1} = {}_{t-1}P_{t+1} + \epsilon_{2t+1}, \quad \text{and} \quad P_{t+1} = {}_t P_{t+1} + \epsilon_{1t+1},$$

so that

$$ {}_t P_{t+1} = {}_{t-1}P_{t+1} + \epsilon_{1t+1} - \epsilon_{2t+1}. \tag{21}$$

Here ϵ_{1t+1} and ϵ_{2t+1} are two independent "white noise" error terms. If we take expectations through equation (21) as of time $t - 1$, then the two error terms drop out and the term ${}_{t-1}P_{t+1}$ is unchanged. We are left with

$$ {}_{t-1}({}_t P_{t+1}) = {}_{t-1}P_{t+1}. \tag{22}$$

The left-hand expression in (22), $_{t-1}(_tP_{t+1})$, is the expectation, made in period $t-1$, of the prediction that will be made at time t about $t+1$. The right-hand expression, $_{t-1}P_{t+1}$, is the actual prediction in $t-1$ of P_{t+1}. So, equation (22) says that the expected forecast equals the current forecast, a relationship known as *the law of iterated expectations.* This follows from unbiasedness of expectations. The idea is that if you now have a reason to believe that your forecast will be revised in a particular direction, then you should revise it immediately. Otherwise you will be predicting worse than you could be, even though the means of improvement are immediately at hand. To take an extraneous example, if a bettor came up to you and said, "I expect Flying Finish to win the 3.30 at Belmont, but I also expect that just before the race I'll expect Bumble Bee to come in first," you would think him a stupid gambler indeed.

The law of iterated expectations may not be intuitively obvious because you also know that expectations are almost always revised. Quite right, but the law of iterated expectations tells us that the mean of these revisions is zero, that they are not expected to raise or lower your expectation systematically. In the jargon of rational expectations, your expectation at t already allows for all the information you have at t. Your forecast is only revised in response to *new* information, which is inevitably unpredictable. The law of iterated expectations is a consequence of the fact that the rational expectations forecasting error has a zero mean, over one period and thus over any time span, and that this also applies to the forecasting of forecasts.

Rational Versus Adaptive Expectations

The adaptive expectations of Chapter 7 were first presented in the context of a one-time change in the price level, which resulted in prediction errors for a long time as expectations shifted slowly toward the new value of P.

This partial adjustment mechanism does not seem too bad when the price level does not jump just once, but goes up and down repeatedly, that is, when the price level is subject to stochastic shocks. On the other hand, the persistent errors implied by adaptive expectations are unappealing, especially because the error could become larger and larger if the price level started rising along a fast trend. This persistence implies that expectations made by an error correction mechanism do not fulfill the law of iterated expectations. The change in expectations from one period to the next is not a random variable with mean zero, but depends on the past realizations of variables relative to past expectations. Therefore, objective observers could forecast expectations better using this history than they could if the law of iterated expectations held. With adaptive expectations, expected forecasts are not identically equal to current forecasts.

Those who form their expectations rationally conform to the law of iterated expectations because they use all available information and incorporate all "news" as it comes in. News would come from personal experience in buying and selling, from private contacts, or from such public sources as the daily newscast or *The Wall Street Journal,* and from one's own past prediction errors. The last resource is especially important, for it brings out the difference between rational and adaptive expectations. If forecasts are fully rational, then the prediction error in one period is already taken into account in forming the next period's prediction. Therefore, no one can look at the forecasting errors and find that one error helps to predict the next. An econometrician would say that the errors are serially uncorrelated or that the expected value of the product of two errors is zero.

These contrasts can be brought out in a more formal context using the example from Chapter 7 of an unanticipated one-unit rise in the price level. In the example, we assume that the objective reality is that any change in the price level will be unique and permanent, but that its *timing* is unknown in advance. The actual change occurs at some time T, when the price level jumps from P_0 to $P_1 = P_0 + 1$.

Expectations are rational or model-consistent if they allow for the structure of the example. In particular, with rational expectations, agents would adjust their expectations of the price level fully, once the jump occurred. *Ex ante,* the timing of the price rise was unknown, so that up to period T no change was expected:

$$_{t-2}P_{t-1} = {_{t-1}}P_t = P_0, \qquad t \le T. \tag{23}$$

Then at time T in our example, the one-unit rise in P from P_0 to P_1 occurs, implying a forecasting error in period T of

$$P_T - {_{T-1}}P_T = P_1 - P_0 = 1. \tag{24}$$

Here the difference $(P_1 - P_0)$ is the innovation in P, the surprise term, which is zero in expected value. Furthermore, with rational expectations one observes the change at T and knows it to be permanent. Thus, the rise in P is exactly mirrored in the next period's expectations:

$$_{T}P_{T+1} = P_1,$$

and for every subsequent period

$$_{t}P_{t+1} = P_1, \qquad t > T.$$

The forecasting error occurs only when the (intrinsically unforecastable) change in P actually takes place.

With rational expectations, the expected error is always zero, and the errors are not linked in any way by serial correlation. In addition, once the forecast has been revised at time T, we know in this example that we will never have to change it again. This means that, for instance,

$$_T(_{T+1}P_{T+2}) = P_1,$$

or

$$_T(_{T+1}P_{T+2}) = {}_TP_{T+2},$$

which conforms to the law of iterated expectations.

In contrast, under adaptive expectations, we get serial correlation of forecast errors, implying a violation of the law of iterated expectations. The adaptive adjustment formula given in equation (8) of Chapter 7 is

$$_{t-1}P_t^a = P_{t-1} + \lambda(_{t-2}P_{t-1}^a - P_{t-1}). \tag{25}$$

For the rest of this section, a superscript "a" will be used to denote an adaptive expectation. At time T, just after the price increase, the forecast error equals one, as for rational expectations, but in period $T + 1$ the error is λ and at $T + 2$ the error is λ^2, and so on:

$$P_t - {}_{T-1}P_T^a = P_1 - P_0 = 1; \tag{26a}$$

$$P_{T+1} - {}_TP_{T+1}^a = P_1 - (P_0 + 1 - \lambda) = \lambda; \tag{26b}$$

$$P_{T+2} - {}_{T+1}P_{T+2}^a = P_1 - (P_0 + 1 - \lambda^2) = \lambda^2. \tag{26c}$$

So the forecast errors are serially correlated, and we can write in general that

$$(P_{t+1} - {}_tP_{t+1}^a) = \lambda(P_t - {}_{t-1}P_t^a).$$

Correspondingly, the forecasting errors subsequent to the initial surprise at time T are predictably different from zero. For example, if we take expectations through equation (26c) as of time T, we obtain

$$_TP_{T+2} - {}_T(_{T-1}P_{T+2}^a) = \lambda^2. \tag{27}$$

From this equation it follows immediately that the law of iterated expectations is broken:

$$_T(_{T-1}P_{T+2}^a) = {}_TP_{T+2} - \lambda^2,$$

and forecasts evolve in a predictable way.

The contrast between adaptive and rational expectations is shown in Figure 11-5, which reproduces Figure 7-8 showing the paths of the price level and adaptive expectations, with the addition of the path of rational expectations. Adaptive and rational expectations are the same until T, and then they both entail a one-unit prediction error at T corresponding to the genuine price shock. The two paths diverge subsequently as the rational expectation leaps up to match the new price level, and the adaptive expectation adjusts slowly toward it.

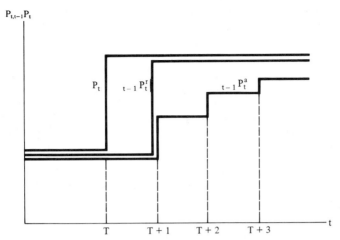

Figure 11-5 Adaptive versus rational expectations after a one-time price rise.

The Pros and Cons of Rational Expectations

Rational expectations have great appeal to economists, for this hypothesis comes closest to our vision of *homo economicus,* a person of thoroughgoing rationality in pursuit of his or her maximum expected utility. If we propose that people and firms are very acute in choosing what to do in any one period, then they ought to be equally acute in allowing for the future. Each individual has an interest in devoting at least some time and effort to making good predictions, as more foreknowledge cannot leave you worse off. It will usually allow you to make better decisions, and even if adaptive expectations, say, lead to optimal actions, then with rational expectations you could simply reproduce that behavior. Or if your rational expectations are more pessimistic than your adaptive ones, given that the rational expectations are unbiased predictions of what will happen, you might at least have a chance to mitigate the bad events to come.

By the same token, the rational expectations hypothesis assumes that errors are truly errors as opposed to a form of blindness toward one's own mistakes. As shown in Chapter 7, adaptive expectation implies that the forecaster can underestimate the true price level time and time again without reacting to such an obvious pattern. Rational expectations seem to grant a more realistic measure of flexibility in people's response to "the slings and arrows of outrageous fortune" which constantly assail them, unlike a mechanical rule for projecting forward from the present.

To back up this argument, one may add that there is just one way to be rational but any number of ways to fall below this standard. Some people may use naive adaptive expectations, others rely on Data Resources, Inc. (DRI) forecasts, and perhaps still others read Tarot cards. Since irrationalities in one direction are, in some sense, likely to balance out irrationalities in another, we might as well assume that everyone forecasts just as well as everybody else.

The main problem with rational expectations is that, in a model of any complexity, they demand a fantastic devotion to forecasting on the part of people and firms, especially if we require that people make the best possible forecast. It is conceivable that a large firm or an agent in the financial markets has enough incentive to make this effort, but not that the average worker or small business will. Perhaps we can get around this objection by supposing that people operate a sophisticated form of adaptive expectations, or that most people can purchase forecasts very cheaply through newspapers or the published results from large computer simulations of the economy. Furthermore, for many results unbiasedness is sufficient. It was mentioned before that "weak-form" rational expectations are sufficient to make anticipated policy ineffective. In more sophisticated examples, excessive variance in forecasting errors could matter.

The objection, however, goes deeper, for the amount of resources you ought to devote to making forecasts is itself a matter for economic decision making. It costs real resources to collect, distill, and disseminate information, and there may be good reasons why the market for information is far from perfect, so maybe people rationally choose not to have "rational" expectations.

This problem is, indeed, made especially clear in the new classical models that first popularized the rational expectations hypothesis, because they emphasized the importance of news. Now, rational expectations have also been dubbed "model-consistent expectations," as was mentioned above, because it is assumed that agents know everything about the relationships making up the model. Yet, news does not take the form simply of stochastic error terms added on to the end of equations; there can also be unanticipated changes in parameter values and even in the functional forms describing the behavior of the economy. In fact, the economy does not just oscillate around some one equilibrium, but rather it constantly moves into areas where it has not been before. For example, no one in living memory had experienced the kind of major supply shock brought on by the oil price rise of 1973. Therefore, people are not just making predictions from a given model, but they are also constantly reviewing that same model. Since there are not only a mixture of, for instance, permanent and temporary shocks, but also more or less enduring "structural changes," perfect model consistency at each moment may be too much to hope for even from *homo economicus.* The rational, economically optional response may depend on a learning process. Such fundamental changes may be occurring all the time, implying that the method of expectation formation may always fall behind full "rationality."

It is difficult enough to impose perfect model consistency on everyone, but even worse to start making arbitrary distinctions between people and firms as to who knows what. In the literature, one often finds models in which one group lacks some information possessed by others, when that information is equally important to both. Back in Chapter 6, we assumed that firms were better informed about future prices than workers were. This assumption was justified by the belief that firms may find it cheaper than workers to learn about their local prices because each is directly engaged in selling a limited number of goods. Although it is prohibitively expensive for any individual to compute a private price index, it is very cheap to buy a newspaper and read about the economic projections of skilled econometricians. One criterion for selecting among rational expectations models, then, is to determine the validity of the rationales behind their informational assumptions.

ONE-PERIOD CONTRACTS AND AGGREGATE SUPPLY

The rational expectations example given earlier in this chapter showed the potential ineffectiveness of aggregate demand policy in changing the level of output, especially in stabilizing it around the full-employment level. The example was based on the model of aggregate supply given in Chapter 6. There all prices and wages are flexible. Thus, the wage rate can adjust to the *anticipated* consequences of demand policy, like monetary expansion, potentially eliminating its effect on output. If wages are fixed by labor contracts, we can see the potential for stabilizing demand policy re-appearing. It is possible that wages then would not be able to react to the anticipated price effects of demand policy fast enough to fully eliminate its effect on output. Essentially, if the wage contract period is longer than the time it takes policy to react to a disturbance, then policy can smooth out their effects on output. It is this quicker reaction time that gives government an advantage over the private sector, and restores the potential stabilizing role of government demand policy.

In this section we set up the two-period contract example by briefly introducing one-period wage contracts into the supply rule of Chapter 7 and the example given earlier in this chapter. We can then contrast the situation in which the contract wage is exogenous with the case in which it is set equal to the expected price. We will see that one-period contracts with the wage set by the expected price level, and the latter expectation taken from the model, give basically the same rational expectations result as flexible wages. In this setting, one-period contracts don't make much of a difference. But the point here is just to set up the contrast for the two-period example.

In the next section we will go through the example of a labor market structure with two-period wage contracts to show how a one-period policy reaction time allows demand policy to influence output. The model is basically a formalization of the ideas of wage rigidity discussed in Chapter 10. We will end up with an aggregate supply curve like the one depicted in Figure 10-3. The example is based on the research of Stanley Fischer and John B. Taylor.

Exogenous One-Period Wage Contracts

Let's begin with the idea that all labor contracts are of a one-period (say, one-year) duration, with the wage $\bar{W}$ fixed at the beginning of the period. In fact, in many U.S. labor agreements, contracts are signed for up to three years, and the late Arthur Okun argued in *Prices and Quantities* (that) "implicit contracts" bind workers and employers for even longer. But here we begin with one-period contracts, both to see how to work them into the model and to provide the contrast for longer term contracts.

A one-period wage contract would set the nominal wage at some negotiated level $\bar{W}_t$ for the period t, replacing the labor-supply curve in Figure 11-6 with a horizontal line at $\bar{W}$. For the one-period t the horizontal line at $\bar{W}$ would supercede the dashed labor-supply schedule in Figure 11-6. The work force agrees to supply all the hours the employer wants at wage $\bar{W}$. The labor market equilibrium condition is now given by

$$\bar{W} = P \cdot f(N), \tag{28}$$

with $\bar{W}$ replacing the supply function $P^e \cdot g(N)$ in equation (1) at the beginning of the chapter. In the example here, we will index $\bar{W}$ and P to unity initially, so by definition $f(N) = 1$ initially, also.

To get an expression for the aggregate supply curve with the contract wage, we can totally differentiate (28) to obtain

$$d\bar{W} = f \, dP \cdot \; + P f' \, dN. \tag{29}$$

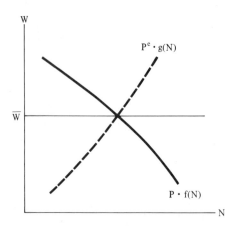

Figure 11-6 Labor market with a nominal wage contract.

With $P = f = 1$, this gives the labor market differential

$$dN = -\frac{1}{f'}(dP - d\bar{W}). \tag{30}$$

It is useful to contrast this equation with equation (2) for dN with a flexible wage. In place of dP^e we have $d\bar{W}$. The numerator of the coefficient of $(dP - d\bar{W})$ is unity; earlier, we could have set $f = g = 1$, but it was not necessary for the clarity of the derivation. The denominator in (30) is f' instead of $g' - f'$ in (2). The wage contract wipes out the slope of the labor-supply curve in Figure 11-6. A given increase in the price level from P_0 to P_1 in Figure 11-7 will move employment from point A to point B with a wage contract. With a flexible wage, the equilibrium would move to point C with a rise in the wage and less increase in employment.

The aggregate supply function can be obtained from the labor market differential (30) by using the production function relationship given in equation (4) earlier:

$$dy = y' \cdot dN = f(N) \cdot dN = dN. \tag{4}$$

Here, since we have normalized the marginal product of labor $f(N)$ at unity, changes in y are measured in labor units. Thus, the slope of the aggregate supply function here is the same as the labor market differential in (30):

$$dy = -\frac{1}{f'}(dP - d\bar{W}). \tag{31}$$

Notice that in contrast to the aggregate supply curve of equation (5) earlier, here the exogenous price variable is $d\bar{W}$ instead of dP^e. The inverse slope of the aggregate supply curve in (5), with exogenous P^e, is given by

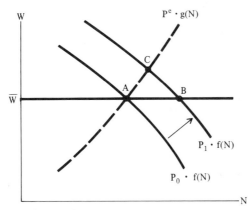

Figure 11-7 Employment reaction with nominal wage contract.

$1/(g' - f') > 0$. Note that here again we have applied the additional normalization that $f(N) = 1$. The inverse slope of the aggregate supply curve here is $-1/f' > 0$, giving a flatter SS curve. This is because the wage contract wipes out the labor-supply curve and its slope term in (5) earlier, g'. The result, with a wage contract and the wage exogenous, is the flat dashed ss schedule of Figures 10-3 and 11-8. The expression from equation (5) is the steeper SS curve. Thus, the wage contract specification here simply formalizes the model of Chapter 10. If the contract wage $\bar{W}$ is exogenous to the model, the aggregate supply schedule in (31) is the flatter ss curve of Figure 11-8. An increase in the contract wage would shift it up.

Contracts Based on Price Expectations

The aggregate supply curve of equation (31) is a comparative-static supply curve, the supply curve of the basic static model with an exogenous one-period wage contract. We can rewrite it in the explicitly time-subscripted form of the expectations-oriented literature by replacing dy and dP in (31) using equations (6) and (7) earlier, and by noting that the change in contract wage $d\bar{W}$ can be written as

$$d\bar{W} = \bar{W}_t - \bar{W}_{t-1}. \tag{32}$$

With these replacements for dy, dP, and $d\bar{W}$, equation (31) becomes

$$y_t = y_{t-1} - \frac{1}{f'}[P_t - P_{t-1} - (\bar{W}_t - \bar{W}_{t-1})].$$

If we remember that we indexed P and $\bar{W}$ to unity initially, we have $P_{t-1} = \bar{W}_{t-1} = 1$. If we also call the coefficient in equation (31) $\beta' = -1/f'$—to make an analogy to the earlier supply curve in equation (9)—we get another version of the Lucas supply function:

$$y_t = y_{t-1} + \beta'(P_t - \bar{W}_t).$$

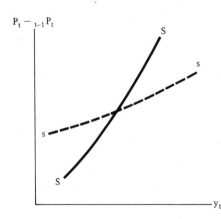

$P_t - {}_{t-1}P_t$

Figure 11-8 Aggregate supply with a nominal wage contract.

Adding the random error term ϵ_t gives us the aggregate supply function analogous to equation (9) with flexible wages:

$$y_t = y_{t-1} + \beta'(P_t - \bar{W}_t) + \epsilon_t. \tag{33}$$

Here $\bar{W}_t$ has replaced $_{t-1}P_t$ (but not for long) in (9), and we have a flatter slope coefficient $\beta' > \beta$ in equation (9).

Now let us consider what wage contract workers are likely to agree on. Suppose in period $t - 1$ the labor market was in equilibrium, including workers being on their supply schedule. Then in period $t - 1$ we would have

$$\frac{\bar{W}_{t-1}}{P_{t-1}} = g(N). \tag{34}$$

To be in equilibrium, workers would have had to set a contract wage in period $t - 1$ that gave a real wage $w_{t-1} = \bar{W}_{t-1}/P_{t-1}$, on the labor-supply schedule. Again, let us index $\bar{W}_{t-1} = P_{t-1} = 1$, so in addition $g(N) = 1$.

Now in the absence of any disturbance to underlying labor-supply parameters in productivity, to stay in this equilibrium workers would demand a contract wage increase equal to the expected price increase. This would maintain the expected real wage at its initial equilibrium. It would also satisfy employers, who were initially in equilibrium too. Hence, a good candidate for the specification of the movement in the nominal wage contract is that

$$\bar{W}_t - \bar{W}_{t-1} = {}_{t-1}P_t - P_{t-1};$$

the contract wage moves with the *expected* price change. If we remember that $\bar{W}_{t-1}$ and P_{t-1} were indexed at unity, this gives us the nominal contract wage as equal to the expected price level:

$$\bar{W}_t = {}_{t-1}P_t. \tag{35}$$

Once in equilibrium, workers and employers try to stay there by setting a wage contract that moves along with the expected price level.

What does the wage-contract idea in equation (35) imply for aggregate supply? Go back to equation (33), and substitute from (35) for $\bar{W}_t$. The result is the aggregate supply curve with wage contracts given by (35):

$$y_t = y_{t-1} + \beta'(P_t - {}_{t-1}P_t) = \epsilon_t. \tag{36}$$

This equation is the same as equation (9) with a larger β' reflecting the existence of one-period contracts rather than flexible wages. The one-period contract disappears into a more general form of the aggregate supply equation.

This result comes from assuming that nominal contracts are not negotiated out of the blue sky, with no reference to expected inflation. If contracts are set to match expected price increases, then we get back the price-expectation term in the aggregate supply equation (36), via the nominal wage contracts.

Equilibrium Output with Exogenous Versus Endogenous Price Expectations

Now that we have introduced one-period wage contracts and keyed them to price expectations, we have arrived at the aggregate supply curve of equation (36), as compared with equation (9) in the flexible-wage case. The only difference is the flatter ss curve in Figure 11-8, with the coefficient β' in equation (36) greater than β in equation (9). To see the implications for the effect of demand policy in this model with one-period wage contracts based on price expectations, we simply go back to the earlier analysis with flexible wages.

In the case of exogenous price expectations, we can put the aggregate supply curve of equation (36) in for the SS expression in equation (9) (p. 212). Then we can proceed using the DD equation (13) to obtain a reduced-form expression that is the same as (14) with β' in place of β. All else is the same, including the conclusion that the deviation of actual M_t from the expected price level $_{t-1}P_t$ moves output. But now $_{t-1}P_t$ enters by setting $\bar{W}_t$.

In the case of endogenous expectations, we can again substitute equation (36) for equation (9), this time on p. 214. Again, the only change is substitution of β' for β. Then we can proceed through the steps of equations (15)–(17) to get a new version of equation (18) with β' in place of β. Again, it is the *deviations* of actual M_t from expected M_t that matter for output. How? Expected M drives price expectations, and these drive the contract wage $\bar{W}$, shifting the aggregate-supply curve. Unexpected movements as M move aggregate demand *relative* to aggregate supply.

The basic result with one-period wage contracts should now be clear. An anticipated increase in the money supply can be fed through the model to produce an estimate of the expected price increase. This will move the wage contract, shifting the ss curve of Figure 11-9 up. When the actual increase in the money stock comes along, it shifts the DD curve up in Figure 11-9. As in the flexible-wage case, if the calculations were done right, the two shifts would

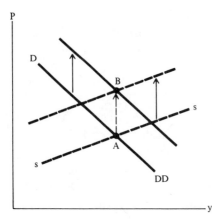

Figure 11-9 Endogenous expectations and one-period wage contracts.

be equal, and there would be no effect on output. Prices would rise as expected, and the real wage would remain unchanged. So the one-period contract result is essentially the same as the flexible-wage case.

This equivalence is due to the fact that one-period contracts do not introduce enough wage rigidity to give the policy authority an advantage in reaction time. If the Federal Reserve decides in period $t - 1$ to expand the money supply in period t, *and the public knows it,* they can form price expectations and base new contracts on them. Thus, the public can act as fast as the Federal Reserve. This produces the result that one-period wage contracts are essentially the same as flexible wages.

LONG-TERM CONTRACTS AND ECONOMIC POLICY

The simple new classical model that has been developed so far relies on most agents having full flexibility at the start of each period. The only limitation is in the labor market, where workers sign one-period contracts. By the end of every period, therefore, not only are expectations brought up to date, but also people are able to use their expectations. With recontracting every period, the real wage can differ from its equilibrium level for at most one period, and therefore a price surprise has only a very short-term effect. That is why systematic economic policy has no influence on real variables. In this section we give an example of how policy can have a stabilizing role when the government has some advantage over private agents. Specifically, we construct a simple model with two-period contracts that set the nominal wage at the beginning of period t and that bind workers to provide as much labor as firms demand at that wage until the end of $t + 1$ when a new contract is formulated. These kinds of contracts exist, and in the United States their term is usually three years. In reality, of course, different groups sign contracts at different times, and so we have almost a continuum of overlapping agreements. But the point can be made most clearly if we imagine that the entire labor force recontracts together every two periods. The government can revise its decisions in every period.

Two-Period Wage Contracts

To simplify further, we eliminate any inflationary trend, implying that $_{t-1}P_t = {_{t-1}}P_{t+1}$. With no inflation expected, it seems reasonable that contracts will not be indexed. That is, they do not include a clause allowing the nominal wage to move along with the price level. Then, as in the last section, we set the nominal wage equal to the expected price level at the time contracts are signed:

$$\bar{W}_t = \bar{W}_{t+1} = {_t}P_{t+1} = {_{t-1}}P_{t+1}. \tag{37}$$

Equation (37) is now one of our basic equations, replacing equation (35) with one-period contracts. We can use it to replace $\bar{W}_t$ in the supply equation (33) to get

$$y_t = y_{t-1} + \beta'(P_t - {}_{t-1}P_t) + \epsilon_t, \tag{38a}$$

$$y_{t+1} = y_t + \beta'(P_{t+1} - {}_{t-1}P_{t+1}) + \epsilon_{t+1}. \tag{38b}$$

We now have enough to solve for the rational expectations equilibrium. Starting from the unchanged demand equation (13) will give us P_t and P_{t+1} as

$$P_t = -\alpha(y_t - y_{t-1}) + M_t + \mu_t, \tag{39a}$$

$$P_{t+1} = -\alpha(y_{t+1} - y_t) + M_{t+1} + \mu_{t+1}. \tag{39b}$$

We can substitute these demand equations into the supply relationships (38a) and (38b) and solve for y_t and y_{t+1}:

$$y_t = y_{t-1} + \frac{\beta'}{1 + \alpha\beta'}(M_t - {}_{t-1}P_t) + \frac{1}{1 + \alpha\beta'}(\beta'\mu_t + \epsilon_t), \tag{40a}$$

$$y_{t+1} = y_t + \frac{\beta'}{1 + \alpha\beta'}(M_{t+1} - {}_{t-1}P_{t+1}) + \frac{1}{1 + \alpha\beta'}[\beta'\mu_{t+1} + \epsilon_t + 1], \tag{40b}$$

as when deriving equation (14). Next, we derive the endogenous, rational expectations of P_t and P_{t+1} from the demand relationships, taking expectations as of time $t - 1$ for *all* variables including those dated $t + 1$:

$$_{t-1}P_t = -\alpha({}_{t-1}y_t - y_{t-1}) + {}_{t-1}M_t, \tag{41a}$$

$$_{t-1}P_{t+1} = -\alpha({}_{t-1}y_{t+1} - {}_{t-1}y_t) + {}_{t-1}M_{t+1}. \tag{41b}$$

Here we have used the fact that the expected value of all shock terms is always zero. As in the first section of this chapter, the expressions for aggregate supply imply that output is not expected to change, even when viewed across two periods from $t - 1$ to $t + 1$, so

$$_{t-1}y_{t+1} = {}_{t-1}y_t = y_{t-1}. \tag{42}$$

Again, the expected value of the prediction error is zero, even though we know that some error will be made. Using equation (42), equations (41a) and (41b) become

$$_{t-1}P_t = -\alpha(y_{t-1} - y_{t-1}) + {}_{t-1}M_t = {}_{t-1}M_t, \tag{43a}$$

$$_{t-1}P_{t+1} = -\alpha({}_{t-1}y_t - {}_{t-1}y_t)_{t-1}M_{t+1} = {}_{t-1}M_{t+1}. \tag{43b}$$

Since the expected value of the price prediction error in the supply equations (22a) and (22b) is zero, the expectations of y_t and y_{t+1} as of $t - 1$ are equal to y_{t-1}. Therefore, the *expected* output deviations $(y_t - y_{t-1})$ and $(y_{t+1}$

$- y_t$) in the demand equations (39a) and (39b), respectively, are also zero. So prices are expected to change exactly in line with the money supply, as expressed in equations (43a) and (43b), and in equation (17) in the earlier example (p. 214). These last two relations are substituted into equations (40a) and (40b) to obtain the complete reduced-form solutions for y_t and y_{t-1}:

$$y_t = y_{t-1} + \frac{\beta'}{1 + \alpha\beta'} (M_t - {}_{t-1}M_t) + \frac{1}{1 + \alpha\beta'} (\beta'\mu_t + \epsilon_t), \qquad (44a)$$

$$y_{t+1} = y_t + \frac{\beta'}{1 + \alpha\beta'} (M_{t+1} - {}_{t-1}M_{t+1}) + \frac{1}{1 + \alpha\beta'} (\beta'\mu_{t+1} + \epsilon_{t+1}). \qquad (44b)$$

So far it appears that two-period contracts have made scarcely any difference, but let's look closer. Equation (44a) is much the same as the reduced form of the flexible-wage example in equation (18) (p. 215). Equation (28b) is very similar, but the relevant monetary "surprise" is over two periods. In the second period of the contract, output is affected by total monetary innovation over the whole time span. People can improve their expectations during period t, so ${}_t M_{t+1}$ is not equal to ${}_{t-1}M_{t+1}$ and ${}_t P_{t+1}$ is not the same as ${}_{t-1}P_{t+1}$. But because of the existence of two-period wage contracts, they are unable to use this improvement to update $\bar{W}_{t+1}$. Therefore, policy can be stabilizing during the second period.

During the first period of the contract, the economy behaves just as if contracts lasted for a single period; equation (44a) is the same as equation (18). Systematic monetary policy has no leverage in this first period because both the contract and policy depend just on variables from period $t - 1$ and earlier, so the government has no advantage over the private sector.

At the start of the next period, time $t + 1$, contracts are still based on what was anticipated at $t - 1$ while the government can adapt monetary policy to the events of period t. This will be useful because two-period contracts introduce serial correlation into the behavior of y, as can be seen by substitution of equation (44a) for y_t into equation (44b):

$$y_{t+1} = y_{t-1} + \frac{\beta'}{1 + \alpha\beta'} (M_t - {}_{t-1}M_t) + \frac{\beta'}{1 + \alpha\beta} (M_{t+1} - {}_{t-1}M_{t+1})$$

$$+ \frac{1}{1 + \alpha\beta'} (\beta'\mu_t + \epsilon_t) + \frac{1}{1 + \alpha\beta'} (\beta'\mu_{t+1} + \epsilon_{t+1}). \qquad (45)$$

The shocks from time t, μ_t and ϵ_t, enter the expression for y_{t+1} as well as helping to determine y_t, so y_t and y_{t+1} are positively related. Even rule-based monetary policy is effective in stabilizing y_{t+1} because the choice of M_{t+1} can depend on the observed realization of y_t, and thus indirectly on the actual shocks μ_t and ϵ_t. Workers and firms may anticipate the stabilizing policy fully as of time t, but by then they are locked in to their contracts and cannot undo its effectiveness (which they would with one-period contracts, as shown in the previous section). When the government acts on the new information received at time t, it can offset the effect of the period t shocks, $(\beta'\mu_t + \epsilon_t)/(1 + \alpha\beta')$, on output at $t + 1$. Since the expected value of the shocks is zero, no one can predict before t what the stabilizing response will be. Policy that is foreseen in $t - 1$ is ineffective, a fact that equation (45) makes clear. But once y_t is observed, and knowing that y_t and y_{t+1} are positively correlated, corrective action can be taken. The optimal monetary policy would exactly negate this carryover from one period to the next. At time t, government must accept M_t, $_{t-1}M_t$ and $_{t-1}M_{t+1}$ as given, and it does not yet know μ_{t+1} or ϵ_{t+1}. It can, however, set M_{t+1}, so as to cancel out the $(\beta'\mu_t + \epsilon_t)/(1 + \alpha\beta')$ term in equation (45).

Long-term contracts, then, give us the persistence in economic fluctuations missing from the simplest flexible-wage or one-period contract model. The best policy works to eliminate this serial correlation, reducing money supply when output in the previous period was especially high and vice versa. Mean real output is unaffected, but the variance around it is reduced. The longer contracts make the economy diverge more and for a longer time from the classical equilibrium employment level of output, which is the best we can hope for. Optimal policy is directed toward undoing the effects of the two-period contracts.

Here we see that policy tends to be most effective when there is most to be achieved. When shocks have an effect for only one period, the economy adjusts too quickly for monetary authorities to do anything worthwhile, but by the same token these ups and downs are brief and not very large. With two-period contracts, shocks have a lasting impact and are correspondingly more important, and yet we can do something about them in order to make the economy behave as in the simple new classical model.

Overlapping Contracts

We have emphasized that the labor market is constantly changing, with workers changing jobs, firms growing and shrinking, and contracts ending and beginning all the time. With overlapping contracts, output is serially correlated in every period because there are always some workers bound by their contracts, unlike the example just given here where everyone's contracts change at once. For example, if contracts last for two periods and some proportion of workers recontract every period, then the aggregate supply function becomes, in general,

$$y_t = y_{t-1} + \beta(P_t - {}_{t-1}P_t) + u_t + \lambda u_{t-1}. \tag{46}$$

Here u_t and u_{t-1} are some combination of supply and demand shocks from periods t and $t - 1$, respectively. Because the shocks of one period hold over into the next and those shocks are known when policy is formulated, money supply can be adjusted to stabilize output in every period. There are always some workers whose nominal wage is fixed two periods before the present. Thus, the monetary authorities can intentionally move those workers' real wage closer to its long-term expected equilibrium level. Therefore, employment and output are held closer to their equilibrium employment levels, and the persistence of economic fluctuations is reduced.

Local and Aggregate Price Surprises

Long-term contracts are one way to go from the "price surprise" aggregate supply function to a model in which policy can play a stabilizing role. In general, the reduced-form description of the economy depends on the details of the contract and on the government's freedom of action relative to that of the private sector.

There are other possible routes to the same result. For example, in Chapter 6 we emphasized that firms are concerned about their own individual prices, rather than the general price level. Suppose that both local prices and the aggregate price levels are subject to stochastic shocks, whereas contracts last for just one period so that they set $W_t = {}_{t-1}P_t$, that is, wages depend on the price index. A firm will want to raise its output when its *own* price rises relative to others, but not when its own price goes up due to general inflation. The firm has a difficulty because, in a given period, it can observe only its local price, and it cannot immediately tell relative from general price movements. The optimal solution to this *inference problem* is to assign a proportion of any observed price movement to inflation and to treat the remainder as a relative price shift. Output reacts only to the latter. The exact solution to this problem is rather complex, but the result is quite intuitive: the share of the price movement attributed to aggregate price level movements equals the share of aggregate price variability in total price variability. This share will be smaller, the smaller the variance of the inflation rate and the greater the variance of the local price. Since only its relative price matters to a firm, its output response to a given total price movement will be negatively related to aggregate price variability and positively related to its sectoral price variability. Relative prices are moving all the time, and individual sectors of the economy are rising and falling. The Lucas supply function comes about because no one firm is entirely sure about how to interpret its local signals, and when we aggregate them together there is a "mistake" overall.

All this suggests another way in which the reduced forms can be misleading to policy makers. Not only does systematic macro policy affect the reduced forms through the expected price level, but also government action can alter the parameters in the equations which describe private-sector behavior. For example, if the money supply becomes less variable, so will the price level. Therefore, the share of observed price movements regarded as sector-specific relative price changes will rise. Hence, aggregate output will become more sensitive to what inflation surprises there are.

Not only macro policy, but also microeconomic policy can have major effects on how workers and firms react. A perfect substitute for the stabilizing monetary rule of the last section is the imposition of one-period contracts, which brings us back to the simple, new classical model presented earlier in the chapter. One can also imagine that the provisions of the tax code and welfare schemes could alter the magnitude and durability of the effects of exogenous shocks.

CONCLUSION: RATIONAL EXPECTATIONS AND THE NEW CLASSICAL VIEW

The new classical doctrine that developed in the last 15 years or so is a rigorous and innovative school of thought, and one that has had some political influence. It went beyond the old classical approach by stressing and investigating the intrinsically intertemporal nature of economic activity, and by modeling explicitly endogenous expectations as a driving force in macroeconomics. The new classicist can also be credited with being the first to apply rational expectations seriously in macroeconomics. But the rational expectations hypothesis is not synonymous with the new classical results on policy ineffectiveness. Most economists now accept some form of rational expectations, or at a minimum treat the formation of expectations as an important element in any explanation of economic phenomena. The new classical view of policy ineffectiveness comes from a model that assumes not only rational expectations, but also wage and price flexibility to maintain full equilibrium and a costless and symmetric flow of information through the economy. Critics of new classicism have shown how deviations from the classical paradigm may be the inevitable result of, for example, inference problems and the problems of asymmetric information in general.

Our discussion of wage and price rigidities and contracts also suggested that expectations may be rational and that the results can diverge from new classicism. It is also unclear whether slight deviations from full rationality, either in aggregate or by some substantial share of the population, have a major or a minor impact on overall performance. For example, if expectations themselves are distributed through the population around their rational mean, it is not obvious that we can treat the economy as if everyone uniformly predicted without bias and as well as they possibly could. Perhaps at this stage the most we can say is that there is no need to accept without reservation full-blown rational expectations, especially when the economy is pushed into areas that are outside historical data, and that the case for the new classical policy results is necessarily weaker than that for rational expectations.

SELECTED READINGS

D.K.H. Begg, *The Rational Expectation Revolution in Macroeconomics* (Baltimore: The Johns Hopkins University Press, 1982).

A.S. Blinder, "Keynes, Lucas, and Scientific Progress," *American Economic Review,* May 1987.

S. Fischer, "Long-Term Contracts, Rational Expectations, and the Optimal Money Supply Rule," *Journal of Political Economy,* February 1977.

R.E. Lucas, Jr., "Some International Evidence on Output-Inflation Tradeoffs," *American Economic Review,* June 1973.

B.T. McCallum, "The Significance of Rational Expectations Theory," *Challenge,* 1–2/1980.

A.M. Okun, *Prices and Quantities* (Washington, D.C.: The Brookings Institution, 1981), Chapters 3–4.

T.J. Sargent and N. Wallace, "Rational Expectations and the Theory of Economic Policy," *Journal of Monetary Economics,* April 1976.

J.B. Taylor, "Staggered Wage Setting in a Macro Model," *American Economic Review,* May 1979.

three

SECTORAL DEMAND FUNCTIONS AND EXTENSIONS OF THE STATIC MODEL

chapter 12

Consumption and Consumer Expenditure

In Part II, consumer expenditure is simply assumed to be a function of income less taxes:

$$c = c(y - t(y)) \qquad 0 < c' < 1, \tag{1}$$

where c is real consumer expenditure, y is real income, and $t(y)$ is the tax function. This general formulation was sufficient for the qualitative analysis of income determination introduced in Part II. We turn now to a closer examination of the nature of the consumption function.

The consumption function provides an excellent illustration of a typical sequence in the development of knowledge in economics. This sequence involved first a conceptual breakthrough by Keynes in 1936, after which it was fairly obvious that a key relationship in macroeconomic analysis for some time to come would be the relationship between income and consumer expenditure. The importance of this relationship should be clear from Part II. The second step in the sequence involved the development of statistical information about consumer behavior and the relationships between consumption, saving, and income. This work, reasonably complete by the end of World War II, turned up an interesting and seemingly contradictory fact: The ratio of consumer expenditure to income varies inversely with the level of income both cyclically and across families at any given time, but on average this ratio does not tend to fall as income rises over a long period. The next step in the sequence of research into the consumption function was the development of more rigorous and elaborate theories that could explain the facts. Three different theories were suggested by Duesenberry in 1949, Friedman in 1957, and a series of papers by Ando, Brumberg, and Modigliani beginning in the early 1950s. These theories have their similarities and differences, and differ in their implications for stabilization policy. The next step in this sequence which began in the mid-1930s was further statistical testing of the theories and the inclusion of statistically estimated consumption functions in econometric models of the economy.

This chapter traces that sequence. After we look at the background and the facts as they were known around 1945, we develop the microeconomic basis for the consumption function. Then we study three major approaches to the theory of consumer behavior based on this microeconomic model. Here we encounter distinctions between labor and property income, and current and permanent income, the consumption life-cycle, and the role of rational expectations. The next section discusses alternative approaches to the ones based on the microeconomic maximizing model. These emphasize the role of liquidity constraints and the idea that consumers care about relative income positions. The subsequent section discusses an interpretation of a consumption function derived from a disequilibrium situation with wage and price rigidity. This interpretation improves our understanding of the short-run dynamics of the multiplier. Then, returning to the equilibrium framework, we present current empirical work on the consumption function, especially concerning the lag of consumer expenditure behind changes in income. The last two sections of the chapter draw the implications of the theoretical and empirical work, first for the operation of the static model of Chapter 8, and second for economic policy.

BACKGROUND: CROSS SECTIONS, CYCLES, AND TRENDS

Consumer expenditure runs about 65 percent of GNP in the United States; so any analysis of the factors determining the level of GNP must be concerned with consumer expenditure at some point. Analytically, in 1936 Keynes made the consumption function the basic element in the income-expenditure approach to the determination of national income. We have seen in Part II that the consumption function is the principal building block in multiplier analysis.

The short-run consumption function that Keynes introduced is shown in Figure 12-1, which plots real consumer expenditure c against real income y. This function reflects the observation that as incomes increase people tend to spend a decreasing percentage of income, or conversely tend to save an increasing percentage of income. The slope of a line from the origin to a point on the consumption function gives the *average propensity to consume* (APC), or the c/y ratio at that point. The slope of the consumption function itself is

Figure 12-1 Keynes' consumption function.

the *marginal propensity to consume (MPC)*. Using the notation of Part II, if $c = c(y)$, $MPC \equiv c'$. From the graph it should be clear that the marginal propensity to consume is less than the average propensity to consume. If the ratio c/y falls as income rises, the ratio of the increment to c to the increment to y, c', must be smaller than c/y. Keynes saw this as the behavior of consumer expenditure in the short run over the duration of a business cycle. He reasoned that as income falls relative to recent levels, people will protect consumption standards by not cutting consumption proportionally to the drop in income, and conversely as income rises, consumption will not rise proportionally.

The same kind of reasoning can also be applied to cross-sectional budget studies. Given a social standard of consumption, one would expect the proportion of income saved to rise as income rises. In the late 1930s cross-sectional budget studies were examined to see if Keynes' assumption that "rich people save proportionally more" was borne out. In general, these budget studies seemed to verify the theory.

Acceptance of the theory that $MPC < APC$, so that as income rises c/y falls, led to the formation of the *stagnation thesis* around 1940. It was observed that if consumption followed this pattern, the ratio of consumption demand to income would decrease as income grew. The problem for fiscal policy that the stagnation thesis poses can be seen as follows. If

$$y = c + i + g, \quad \text{or} \quad 1 = \frac{c}{y} + \frac{i}{y} + \frac{g}{y},$$

is the condition for equilibrium growth of real output y, and there is no reason to assume that i/y will rise as the economy grows, then g/y must increase to balance the c/y drop to maintain full-employment demand as y grows. In other words, unless government spending increases at a faster rate than income, the economy will not grow but will stagnate.

During World War II, as government purchases soared, the economy did expand rapidly. However, many economists, following the stagnation thesis, feared that when the war ended and government spending was reduced, the economy would plunge back into depression. Yet precisely the opposite occurred. Private demand increased sharply when the war ended, causing inflation rather than recession. Why did this happen? One plausible explanation is that during the war people had earned large increases in income but consumer expenditure was curbed by rationing. Consumers put their excess funds, the savings "forced" by rationing, into assets in the form of government bonds. When the war ended, people had an excess stock of assets that they converted into increased consumption demand. This phenomenon suggests that assets, as well as level of income, have something to do with consumption. In other words, for a given level of income, consumption may also be a function of *assets* or *wealth.*

In 1946 Simon Kuznets published a study of consumption and saving behavior dating back to the Civil War. Kuznets' data pointed out two important things about consumption behavior. First, it appeared that on average over the long run the ratio of consumer expenditure to income, c/y or *APC,* showed no downward trend, so the marginal propensity to consume equaled the average propensity to consume as income grew along trend. This meant that along trend the $c = c(y)$ function was a straight line passing through the origin, as shown in Figure 12-2. Second, Kuznets' study suggested that years when the c/y ratio was below the long-run average occurred during boom periods, and years with c/y above the average occurred during periods of economic slump.

This meant that the c/y ratio varied inversely with income during cyclical fluctuations, so that for the short period corresponding to a business cycle empirical studies would show consumption as a function of income to have a slope like that of the short-run functions of Figure 10-2 rather than the long-run function.

Thus, by the late 1940s it was clear that a theory of consumption must account for three observed phenomena:

1. Cross-sectional budget studies show s/y increasing as y rises, so that *in cross sections of the population, MPC < APC.*
2. Business cycle, or short-run, data show that the c/y ratio is smaller than average during boom periods and greater than average

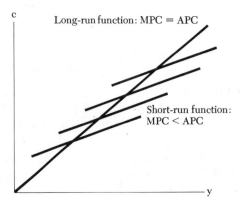

c

Long-run function: MPC = APC

Short-run function:
MPC < APC

Figure 12-2 Long-run and short-run consumption functions.

y

during slumps, so that *in the short run, as income fluctuates,* MPC < APC.

3. Long-run trend data show no tendency for the c/y ratio to change over the long run, so that *as income grows along trend,* MPC = APC.

In addition, a theory of consumption should be able to explain the apparent effect of wealth on consumption that was observed after World War II.

THE BASIC MODEL OF CONSUMER BEHAVIOR

The theories developed by Duesenberry, Friedman, and Modigliani et al. to explain these phenomena all have a basic foundation in the microeconomic theory of consumer choice. In particular, both Friedman and Modigliani begin with the explicit common assumption that observed consumer behavior is the result of an attempt by rational consumers to maximize utility by allocating a lifetime stream of earnings to an optimum lifetime pattern of consumption. So we can begin a discussion of these theories at their common point of departure in the theory of consumer behavior, and then follow them individually as they diverge.

Optimizing Consumption: A Two-Period Example

Following the original work of Irving Fisher, we can begin with a single consumer with a utility function

$$U = U(c_0, \ldots, c_t, \ldots, c_T), \tag{2}$$

where lifetime utility U is a function of his real consumption c in all time periods up to T, the instant before he dies. The consumer will try to maximize his utility, that is, obtain the highest level of utility, subject to the constraint that the present value of his total consumption in life cannot exceed the present value of his total income in life; that is,

$$\sum_0^T \frac{c_t}{(1+r)^t} = \sum_0^T \frac{y_t}{(1+r)^t}, \tag{3}$$

where T is the individual's expected lifetime. The notion of present discounted value is discussed in Chapter 4, pp. 57–58. This constraint says that the consumer can allocate his income stream to a consumption stream by borrowing and lending, but the present value of consumption is limited by the present value of income. For this restriction to hold as a strict equality, we assume that if the person receives an inheritance, he passes on a bequest of an equal amount.

We thus have an individual with an expected stream of lifetime income who will want to spread that income over a consumption pattern in an optimum way. We might imagine that his expected income stream begins and ends low, with a rise in midlife, and he wants to smooth it out into a more even consumption stream.

2 period model To capture the essence of this problem, let us consider as an example a two-period case in which the individual has an income stream y_0, y_1 and wants to maximize $U(c_0, c_1)$ subject to the borrowing-lending constraint

$$c_0 + \frac{c_1}{1 + r} = y_0 + \frac{y_1}{1 + r}.$$

In Figure 12-3 the income stream y_0, y_1 locates the point A. This point shows the amount of income the individual will earn in period 0, y_0, and the amount of income he will earn in period 1, y_1. We assume that he can either lend or borrow money at the interest rate r. Thus, if his income in period 0 is greater than the value of goods and services he wants to consume in that period, he can lend, that is, save, his unspent income:

$$s_0 = y_0 - c_0 \equiv \text{money lent in period 0.} \qquad (4)$$

By lending this amount, he will receive in period 1 an amount equal to $s_0(1 + r)$, so that his consumption in period 1 can exceed his income by that amount, which is his period 1 *dissaving*, s_1:

$$s_1 = -(1 + r)s_0 = y_1 - c_1. \qquad (5)$$

The minus sign enters equation (5) because the dissaving in period 1 is of the opposite sign to the saving in period 0, and $c_1 > y_1$. Dividing the expression for s_1 by that for s_0 yields the trade-off between present and future consumption

$$\frac{s_1}{s_0} = - \frac{s_0(1 + r)}{s_0} = \frac{y_1 - c_1}{y_0 - c_0}. \qquad (6)$$

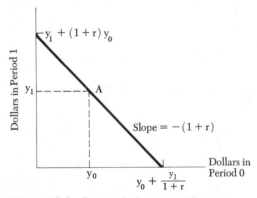

Figure 12-3 Two-period consumption case.

From the right-hand equality in (6), by canceling the s_0's and multiplying through by $(y_0 - c_0)$, we obtain

$$y_1 - c_1 = -(1 + r)(y_0 - c_0). \tag{7}$$

This says that by reducing consumption in period 0 below income by the amount $s_0 = y_0 - c_0$, the consumer can enjoy in period 1 consumption in excess of income, $c_1 - y_1$, by the amount $(1 + r)s_0$. In other words, the consumer can trade from a y_0, y_1 income point in Figure 12-3 to a c_0, c_1 consumption point along a budget constraint that has a slope of $-(1 + r)$.

Another way to construct this budget line is to suppose that the individual wants to consume 100 percent of his income stream in period 0, by borrowing against his period 1 income. The maximum amount he can consume in period 0 will then be $y_0 + y_1/(1 + r)$, which is the intercept of the budget line on the period 0 axis. Conversely, if he decides that he will consume nothing in period 0, putting off all consumption until period 1, the maximum he can consume in period 1 will be $y_1 + (1 + r)y_0$, which is the intercept of the budget line on the period 1 axis. Thus, the budget line in Figure 12-3 bounds the consumption possibilities open to the individual with an income stream y_0, y_1 facing an interest rate r. His consumption point c_0, c_1 cannot be above the budget line.

From the individual's utility function $U = U(c_0, c_1)$, we can obtain a set of indifference curves that show the points at which he is indifferent between additional consumption in period 1 or period 0 at each level of utility. These curves—U_0, U_1, U_2 in Figure 12-4—are conceptually similar to those introduced in Chapter 6, pp. 115–117. Movement from U_0 to U_1 to U_2 raises the individual's level of utility.

Now, as pointed out above, all points on or below the budget line in Figure 12-4 are attainable. That is, the individual may consume at any level

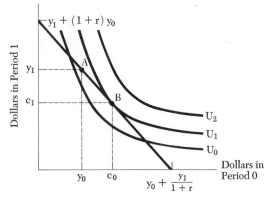

Figure 12-4 Two-period consumption case: utility maximization added.

in either period up to the budget constraint. In order to maximize utility, he will consume at a point on the budget line where it is just tangent to an indifference curve, such as point B in Figure 12-4. At point B, the individual's consumption pattern is c_0, c_1. Since his income flow is skewed toward period 1 (y_1 is much greater than y_0), he borrows $c_0 - y_0$ in period 0 at interest rate r. In period 1, he pays back $y_1 - c_1 = (1 + r)(c_0 - y_0)$. The consumer's pattern of consumption, including present consumption c_0, is determined by the position of his budget line and the shape of his indifference curves.

The position of the budget line in Figure 12-4 is determined by three variables—the income in each period and the interest rate. This can be seen by noting that point A on the budget line has coordinates (y_0, y_1), the value of income in each period. The slope of the budget line, $-(1 + r)$, is determined by the interest rate. If the consumer's income should increase in *any* period, the present value (PV) of his income stream will increase since point A would move horizontally or vertically, moving the period 0 intercept and the budget line out with an unchanged slope. Thus, any increase in current or expected income will shift the budget line up parallel to the old budget line. This will make it possible for the consumer to reach a new, higher level of utility at a new c_0, c_1 point.

If consumption is not in any period an *inferior good,* that is, one with a negative income effect, then whenever *any* period's income rises, consumption in *all* periods rises. For example, an increase in y_1 in Figure 12-4, shifting the budget line up, would raise both c_0 and c_1. The level of present consumption rises with a rise in future (expected) income.

One implication of this analysis is that current-period consumption will vary less than does income. In the two-period case of Figure 12-4, an increase in y_0 would be spread across an increase in both c_0 and c_1. The change in c_0 would equal that in y_0 only if point B moved directly to the right with the y_0 increase. If we extend the analysis to many periods, say, 25 years, spreading a y_0 increase over 25 years of consumption increments would give a c_0 increase that is very small relative to the y_0 increase. If, for example, the consumer allocates his income to equal consumption in each of 25 years—in the two-period case this would put point B of Figure 12-4 on a 45° line from the origin, so that $c_0 = c_1$—the c_0 increment would be only 4 percent ($= \frac{1}{25}$) of the y_0 increment.

The relationship between the present value of the income stream and current consumption from Figure 12-4 gives us the first general formulation of the consumption function,

$$c_t = f(PV_t); \qquad f' > 0, \tag{8}$$

where PV_t, the present value of current and future income at time t, is

$$\sum \frac{y_t}{(1 + r)^t}.$$

This says simply that an individual's consumption in time t is an increasing function of the present value of his income in time t.

We now turn to an explicit, but still fairly general, multiperiod model of consumer behavior. The end result will be essentially the same as (8), but the model provides a clearer understanding of the analytics involved and an introduction to the style of modern theorizing about consumer behavior.

An Intertemporal Optimizing Model of Consumption

Most specific theories of the consumption functions and savings behavior are based on a very general model of optimizing household behavior over time. We have just reviewed a two-period example. The specific theories differ in how they modify this model to make it testable against observed data and to emphasize different aspects of the policy implications of the model. Here we will lay out a fairly simple, analytically tractable version of the many-period optimizing model, of which we have already seen the two-period version. This will give us the general conclusions from this line of thinking about consumer behavior that we can consider as we study the specific models of Ando-Modigliani, Friedman, and Hall. The model we discuss here is the basic framework for modern optimizing analyses of consumer behavior.

To get into the model, let's consider an individual at some time 0 who expects to live until time T. At time 0, that is, now, she has to choose a level of current consumption that will maximize expected utility over the current and all future periods, given her current and expected income and current wealth, A. Solving the problem at the present requires consideration of the future because income not consumed immediately, that is, what is saved, contributes to future resources available for future consumption. For convenience we assume that no one wishes to leave a bequest to future generations, so everyone aims to use up all wealth and income by the end of their lives. We can get the same results with a fixed amount of individual bequests.

Along with Friedman, Modigliani, and before them, Irving Fisher, we can begin with a consumer with a utility function already given as equation (2):

$$U = U(c_0, \ldots c_t, \ldots c_T).$$

To make the problem analytically tractable, we will take as an example a particular form of the utility function. Let us assume first that the underlying utility function is logarithmic, that is,

$$u(c) = \ln c.$$

This utility function has the usual properties that marginal utility is positive, $u'(c) = 1/c$, and diminishing in consumption, $u''(c) = -1/c^2$. (Readers not familiar with differentials of logarithms may want to consult the Appendix to Chapter 19.) Second, we will assume that the utility function is additively separable over time. This means that each period's marginal utility is independent of the consumption in all other periods. Third, we assume that future utilities are discounted at the subjective rate δ. For the moment we will ignore uncertainty to avoid the complications of expectations notation. These three assumptions give us the particular specification of utility function of equation (2):

$$u = \ln c_0 + \frac{\ln c_1}{1 + \delta} + \cdots + \frac{\ln c_t}{(1 + \delta)^t} + \cdots + \frac{\ln c_T}{(1 + \delta)^T}$$

$$= \sum_0^T \frac{\ln c_t}{(1 + \delta)^t} \, . \tag{9}$$

The constraint on the consumer's choices in this many-period case comes from total resources available: current plus all future income. With no bequests, the *intertemporal budget constraint* over the remaining T years of life is

$$c_0 + \frac{c_1}{1 + r} + \cdots + \frac{c_T}{(1 + r)^T} = y_0 + \frac{y_1}{1 + r} + \cdots + \frac{y_T}{(1 + r)^T} \, ,$$

or in more compact notation,

$$\sum_0^T \frac{c_t}{(1 + r)^t} = \sum_0^T \frac{y_t}{(1 + r)^t} \, . \tag{10}$$

This is the intertemporal budget constraint of equation (3), interpreted at an arbitrary initial starting point 0. We want our theory to be able to explain consumer behavior beginning with any given initial conditions, or at any given point in time. In (10), r is the interest rate available to the consumer for saving or borrowing.

The consumer faces the problem of maximizing the utility function given by (9), subject to the constraint given by (10). This is usually written in the form:

$$\max_{c_t} \sum_0^T \frac{\ln c_t}{(1 + \delta)^t} \, ,$$

subject to the constraint that

$$\sum_0^T \frac{c_t}{(1 + r)^t} = \sum_0^T \frac{y_r}{(1 + r)^t} \, .$$

To solve this problem and obtain the maximizing stream of consumption $c_0, \ldots, c_T$, we will use the method of *Lagrange multipliers*. We incorporate the constraint and the objective together into one expression:

$$\max_{c_t, \lambda} L = \sum_0^T \frac{\ln c_t}{(1 + \delta)^t} + \lambda \left[\sum_0^T \frac{y_t}{(1 + r)^t} - \sum_0^T \frac{c_t}{(1 + r)^t} \right]. \qquad (11)$$

The *Lagrange multiplier* λ is a positive constant that will turn out to measure the marginal utility of an additional unit of wealth.

Having followed Lagrange in reformulating the maximization problem, we can move toward the solution by partially differentiating L with respect to all c's and λ, and setting these differentials equal to zero. This gives us the *first-order conditions*

$$\frac{\partial L}{\partial c_0} = \frac{1}{c_0} - \lambda = 0 \qquad (12a)$$

$$\frac{\partial L}{\partial c_t} = \frac{1}{(1 + \delta)^t} \cdot \frac{1}{c_t} - \frac{\lambda}{(1 + r)^t} = 0 \qquad (12b)$$

$$\begin{matrix} \cdot & \cdot & \cdot & \cdot & \cdot & & \cdot \\ \cdot & \cdot & \cdot & \cdot & \cdot & & \cdot \end{matrix}$$

$$\frac{\partial L}{\partial c_T} = \frac{1}{(1 + \delta)^T} \cdot \frac{1}{c_T} - \frac{\lambda}{(1 + r)^T} = 0 \qquad (12c)$$

$$\frac{\partial L}{\partial \lambda} = \sum_0^T \frac{y_t}{(1 + r)^t} - \sum_0^T \frac{c_t}{(1 + r)^t} = 0. \qquad (12d)$$

There will be T marginal conditions like (12a)–(12c), one for each c in (c_0, $\ldots, c_t, \ldots, c_T$). Equation (12d) just gives us back the budget constraint. Let's now use the first-order conditions to this maximization problem to see what the consumption path looks like.

First, we'll compare time 0 consumption c_0 to time t consumption, which represents any of the future periods. If we move the terms in λ to the right-hand sides of (12a) and (12b), and then divide equation (12a) by (12b), we get

$$\frac{c_t}{c_0} = \left(\frac{1 + r}{1 + \delta} \right)^t, \qquad (13)$$

and in general for any two adjacent periods we would have

$$\frac{c_t}{c_{t-1}} = \frac{1 + r}{1 + \delta}, \quad \text{or} \quad c_t = \left(\frac{1 + r}{1 + \delta} \right) c_{t-1}. \qquad (14)$$

Before we discuss the implications of the intertemporal consumption relations (13) and (14), let's interpret them in terms of marginal utility relationships. Remember that to simplify our example here, we assumed that $u(c) = \ln c$, so that $u'(c) = 1/c$. This means that in general the expression in equation (14) could be written as

$$\frac{u'(c_t)}{u'(c_{t-1})} = \frac{1+\delta}{1+r}. \qquad (14a)$$

In our particular example, because $u'(c) = 1/c$ this ratio in equation (14) is the inverse of c_t/c_{t-1} in (14). Thus, the first-order conditions give the result that the ratio of marginal utilities of consumption in each two adjacent periods over time is equal to the ratio of the market interest rate to the consumer discount rate.

These *intertemporal consumption relations* have some interesting implications. First, from (13) or (14) we see that whether consumption rises or falls over time depends on whether the market rate of return is larger or smaller than the individual's discount rate, that is, whether $r \gtrless \delta$. From the technical solutions we see that if $r > \delta$, the consumption path would be rising over time. This makes sense. The market interest rate r measures the return in additional saving, whereas the discount rate δ gives the individual's loss from waiting to consume. If $r > \delta$, it pays to save to consume later; if $r < \delta$, it pays to consume more now, less later. This gives us the time profiles of consumption in this simple example shown in Figure 12-5. Each consumption path is constrained by the period 0 present value, defined already as

$$PV_0 \equiv \sum_0^T \frac{y_t}{(1+r)^t},$$

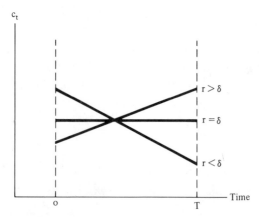

Figure 12-5 Alternative time profiles of consumption.

the right-hand side of the constraint in equations (3) and (9). This is total resources available in time 0. The discounted integral of consumption from time 0 to time T cannot exceed PV_0; this is what the constraint says. Therefore, a consumption path that begins high because $r < \delta$ must cross one that begins low because $r > \delta$. Their integrals must equal the same constraint. This is what is shown in Figure 12-5.

A remarkable implication, which we'll explore more fully in the discussion of Hall's work below, is that if we know c_{t-1}, we can predict c_t from equation (14). If the consumer is on an optimal consumption path at time $(t - 1)$, using all the information he or she has about future income prospects, we can use c_{t-1} to predict c_t. There is no need for other variables for forecasting, because all their information is already in the c_{t-1} decision.

Finally, from the discussion of Figure 12-5, it should be intuitively clear that new information about future incomes y_t would lift the entire consumption path in Figure 12-5. Whether r is greater or less than δ for a given individual, an unexpected increase in present value in equation (14) would raise the c_t in all periods. This same point was made in discussing Figure 12-4 in the two-period case. The implication is that current consumption can be stated in terms of PV_0 since the entire path depends on PV. Let's see how this result can be obtained from the first-order conditions equations (12).

Consumption and the Present Value of Future Income

The explicit relation between present value and consumption can be obtained from the constraint of the maximization problem, which is reproduced by the Lagrange technique as equation (12d), and equation (13), which we can rewrite as the following relation between c_0 and c_t:

$$\frac{c_t}{(1 + r)^t} = \frac{c_0}{(1 + \delta)^t}. \tag{13a}$$

Notice that from the first-order conditions equations (12), this relationship holds for all c_t periods.

Let's now rewrite the constraint from equation (12d), using the definition of present value:

$$\sum_0^T \frac{c_t}{(1 + r)^t} = \sum_0^T \frac{y_t}{(1 + r)^t} = PV_0.$$

We can pull c_0 out of the left-hand summation, noting that $(1 + r)^0 = 1$, to rewrite this as

$$c_0 + \sum_1^T \frac{c_t}{(1 + r)^t} = PV_0.$$

Now from equation (13a), which followed from the first-order conditions, we can substitute for each $c_t/(1 + r)^t$ under the summation $c_0/(1 + \delta)^t$, to get

$$c_0 + \sum_1^T \frac{c_0}{(1 + \delta)^t} = PV_0.$$

Factoring out c_0, we obtain the final result,

$$c_0 \left(1 + \sum_1^T \frac{1}{(1 + \delta)^t} \right) = PV_0 \quad \text{or} \quad c_0 = \left[\frac{1}{1 + \Sigma[1/(1 + \delta)^t]} \right] PV_0, \qquad (15)$$

where the summation runs from 1 to T. This says that for a given discount rate δ, consumption is proportional to the present value of future income, with the coefficient given in brackets in equation (15). This will hold for any point t along the consumption paths of Figure 12-5. It is the same as equation (8), with a bit more specification for the functional form $f(PV)$. Clearly, an unexpected increase in PV_0, due to new information about future y's, will shift up the entire consumption path proportionately. Again, this is the same result as in the two-period case of Figure 12-4.

To summarize, out of the first-order conditions for the lifetime (0 to T) maximization problem, we have obtained several results that will appear in various forms in the specific theories of consumption that we examine in the next section.

1. The slope of the consumption path depends on r relative to δ (see Figure 12-5), with any two adjacent consumptions related by equation (14).
2. Along an optimal consumption path, c_{t-1} is a good predictor for c_t.
3. Consumption at any time t is proportional to the present value of future income PV_0 at that period, from equation (15).

With these results from the basic life-cycle optimizing model in mind, let's now turn to an examination of the development of three major lines of thinking about consumption that generally fit into this framework.

THREE THEORIES OF THE CONSUMPTION FUNCTION

Within the general framework set out in the last section, researchers on consumption make further assumptions to make the model more testable. In this section we discuss three important lines of research, each of which emphasizes different aspects of consumption behavior. We start with the analysis of Ando-

Modigliani and then turn to that of Friedman, which differ mainly in the treatment of the *PV* of future income term, especially in how they relate this term to observable economic variables for the statistical testing of their hypotheses. Finally, in this section we look at a very different way of looking at the consumption function, that of Hall, which is based on rational expectations and the concept of "news."

The Ando-Modigliani Approach: The Life-Cycle Hypothesis

To explain the three observed consumption function relationships discussed earlier in this chapter, Ando and Modigliani postulate a *life-cycle* hypothesis of consumption. According to this hypothesis, the typical individual has an income stream that is relatively low at the beginning and end of her life. This "typical" income stream is shown as the *y* curve in Figure 12-6 where *T* is expected lifetime.

On the other hand, the individual might be expected to maintain a more-or-less constant, or perhaps slightly increasing, level of consumption, shown as the *c* line in Figure 12-6, throughout her life. This corresponds to the $r > \delta$ path in Figure 12-5. The constraint on this consumption stream, equation (3), is that the present value of her total consumption does not exceed the present value of her total income. This model suggests that in the early years of a person's life, the first shaded portion of Figure 12-6, the person is a net borrower. In the middle years, she saves to repay debt and provide for retirement. In the late years, the second shaded portion of Figure 12-6, she dissaves.

Now if the life-cycle hypothesis is correct, if one is to undertake a budget study by selecting a sample of the population at random and classifying the sample by income level, the high-income groups will contain a higher-than-average proportion of persons who are at high-income levels *because* they are in the middle years of life, and thus have a relatively low *c*/*y* ratio. Similarly, the low-income groups will include relatively more persons whose incomes are low *because* they are at the ends of the age distribution, and thus have a high *c*/*y* ratio. Thus, if the *life-cycle* theory is true, a cross-sectional study will show *c*/*y* falling as income rises, explaining the cross-sectional budget studies showing *MPC* < *APC*.

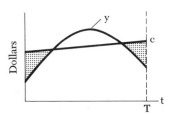

Figure 12-6 "Life-cycle" hypothesis of consumption.

Next, it was shown in the last section, equation (15), that under reasonable assumptions consumption in any one period will not be favored over that in any other. Thus, for representative consumer i if PV^i rises, all his c_t^i rise more or less proportionately. In algebra, for consumer i, this means that we can write the Ando-Modigliani version of equation (8) as

$$c_t^i = k^i(PV_t^i); \qquad 0 < k^i < 1. \tag{16}$$

Here k^i, which is the coefficient of PV in the example of equation (15), is the fraction of consumer i's PV that she wants to consume in period t. It depends on the shape of her indifference curves, embedded in the utility function of the last section, as well as in the interest rate and the consumer's personal discount rate. Equations (15) and (16) say that if an increase in any income entry, present or expected, raises the consumer's estimate of PV, she will consume the fraction k^i of the increase in the current period.

If the population distribution by age and income is relatively constant, and tastes between present and future consumption (that is, the average shape of indifference curves) are stable through time, we can add up all the individual consumption functions (9) to a stable aggregate function,

$$c_t = k(PV_t). \tag{17}$$

The kind of gradual changes in age and income distribution that we have seen in the United States since World War II certainly meets the Ando-Modigliani stability assumptions.

The next step in developing an operational consumption function from (17) is to relate the PV term to measurable economic variables. This is the crucial step in empirical investigations of the consumption function, as it is in almost any empirical study in economics. The theory involves consumption as a function of *expected* income, which of course cannot be measured. The problem is to link expected income back to measured variables by making further assumptions. Choosing the right assumptions and making the right linkage is the crucial art in empirical economics. The work of Ando and Modigliani provides an excellent example of the practice of this art. Ando and Modigliani begin to make the PV term operational by noting that income can be divided into income from *labor* y^L and income from assets or *property* y^P. Thus,

$$PV_0 = \sum_0^T \frac{y_t^L}{(1+r)^t} + \sum_0^T \frac{y_t^P}{(1+r)^t},$$

where time 0 is the current period, and t ranges from zero to the remaining years of life, T. Now if capital markets are reasonably efficient, we can assume that the present value of the income from an asset is equal to the value of the asset itself, measured at the beginning of the current period. That is,

$$\sum_0^T \frac{y_t^P}{(1+r)^t} = a_0,$$

where a is real household net worth at the beginning of the period. Furthermore, we can separate out *known* current labor income from unknown, or expected, future labor income. This gives us for PV_0,

$$PV_0 = y_0^L + \sum_1^T \frac{y_t^L}{(1+r)_t} + a_0.$$

The next step in this sequence is to determine how expected labor income $y_1^L, \ldots, y_T^L$ might be related to current observable variables. First, let us assume that there is an average expected labor income in time 0, y_0^e, such that

$$y_0^e = \frac{1}{T-1} \sum_1^T \frac{y_t^L}{(1+r)^t},$$

where $T-1$ is the average remaining life expectancy of the population and the term $1/(T-1)$ averages the present value of future labor income over $T-1$ years. Then the expected labor income term in the expression for present value PV_0 can be written as

$$\sum_1^T \frac{y_t^L}{(1+r)^t} = (T-1)y_0^e.$$

This gives us an expression for the present value of the income stream,

$$PV_0 = y_0^L + (T-1)y_0^e + a_0, \tag{18}$$

which has only one remaining variable that is not yet measurable—average expected labor income y^e. We now need a final hypothesis linking average expected labor income to a current variable—current labor income.

    Several assumptions might be tested to see how they fit the data coming from observations of the real world. The simplest assumption would be that average expected labor income is just a multiple of present labor income:

$$y_0^e = \beta y_0^L: \qquad \beta > 0.$$

This assumes that if current income rises, people adjust their expectation of future incomes up so that y^e rises by the fraction β of the increase in y^L. We might note here that this assumption assigns great importance to movements in current income as a determinant of current consumption. If an increase in current income shifts the entire expected income stream substantially it will have a much larger effect on current consumption than it would if the expected income stream did not shift, leaving the increment to current income to be allocated to consumption over the remaining years of life.

Ando and Modigliani tried a number of similar assumptions, and found that the simplest assumption that $y^e = \beta y^L$ fits the data as well as any. Thus, substituting βy_0^L for y_0^e in equation (18) for PV, we obtain

$$PV_0 = [1 + \beta(T - 1)]y_0^L + a_0,$$

as an operational expression for PV, in that both y^L and a can be measured statistically. Substitution of this expression into equation (16) for consumption yields

$$c_0 = k[1 + \beta(T - 1)]y_0^L + ka_0, \tag{19}$$

as a statistically measurable form of the Ando-Modigliani consumption function. The coefficients of y^L and a in equation (19) were estimated statistically by Ando and Modigliani using annual U.S. data. A typical result of their procedures is

$$c_t = 0.7y_t^L + 0.06a_t, \tag{20}$$

which says that an increase of $1 billion in real labor income will raise real consumption by $0.7 billion—the marginal propensity to consume out of labor income is 0.7. Similarly, the marginal propensity to consume out of assets is 0.06.

Comparing the estimates of the coefficients in (20) with the derived coefficients in (19), we can see from the coefficient of a in (20) that k is 0.06. This suggests, from equation (10), that on aggregate, households consume about 6 percent of net worth in a year. Using this value for k and 45 years as a rough estimate of average remaining lifetime T, we can also obtain the value of β from equation (18) that is implicit in the estimate of the y^L coefficient in (20):

$$0.7 = k[1 + \beta(T - 1)] = 0.06(1 + 44\beta),$$

so that β is about 0.25. This suggests that when current labor income goes up by $100, in the aggregate, estimates of average expected labor income rise by $25.

The Ando-Modigliani consumption function of equation (19) is shown in Figure 12-7 which graphs consumption against labor income. The intercept of the consumption-income function is set by the level of assets a_t. The slope of the function—the marginal propensity to consume out of labor income—is the coefficient of y^L in the Ando-Modigliani consumption function. In short-run cyclical fluctuations with assets remaining fairly constant, consumption and income will vary along a single consumption-income function. Over the longer run, as saving causes assets to rise, the consumption-income function shifts up as a_t increases.

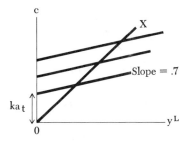

Figure 12-7 Estimated consumption function: Ando and Modigliani.

Thus, over time we may observe a set of points such as those along the line OX in Figure 12-7, which shows a constant consumption-income ratio along trend as the economy grows. This constancy of the trend c/y ratio can be derived from the Ando-Modigliani function as follows. We can divide all the terms in equations (20) by total real income to obtain

$$\frac{c_t}{y_t} = 0.7\frac{y_t^L}{y_t} + 0.06\frac{a_t}{y_t}. \tag{21}$$

If the c/y ratio given by this equation is constant as income grows along trend, then the line OX, which gives the average propensity to consume c/y, will go through the origin in Figure 12-7. The c/y ratio will be constant if y^L/y—the labor share in total income—and a/y—the ratio of assets, or capital, to output—are roughly constant as the economy grows along trend. The observed data for the United States confirm that both of these terms are fairly constant. Over time the labor share of income has remained around 75 percent with a slight tendency to drift up, and the ratio of assets to income has been roughly constant at about 3 with a slight tendency to drift downward over time.

Inserting these typical values into equation (21) for the c/y ratio, we obtain

$$\frac{c_t}{y_t} = (0.7)(0.75) + 0.06(3) = 0.53 + 0.18 = 0.71.$$

Thus, the average propensity to consume out of total income is constant at about 0.7, which implies that the line OX in Figure 12-7 is a straight line passing through the origin with a slope of 0.7. A spot check of the data for 1987 shows that consumption expenditure was about $3.0 trillion and national income was about $3.7 trillion, giving a c/y ratio of 0.8, high by historical standards.

Thus, the Ando-Modigliani model of consumption behavior explains all three of the observed consumption phenomena. It explains the $MPC < APC$ result of cross-sectional budget studies by the life-cycle hypothesis: it provides an explanation for the cyclical behavior of consumption with the consumption-income ratio inversely related to income along a short-run function in Figure

12-3, and it also explains the long-run constancy of the c/y ratio. In addition, it explicitly includes assets as an explanatory variable in the consumption function, a role that was observed in the post-World War II inflation.

The Ando-Modigliani model is attractive because it remains close to the original Fisherian formulation of intertemporal optimization. It brings out the importance of demographics for trends in aggregate consumption patterns. For example, with no bequests, no trend in economic growth, and a static population, the life-cycle hypothesis implies that net aggregate saving is zero. The saving by the middle-aged is exactly offset by the dissaving of the young and the old. If, in contrast, the population is aging, on average, with many middle-aged high earners now, then the savings rate will be positive. Likewise in a growing economy, because younger cohorts live during a richer era, their savings are greater than the dissavings from the poorer old folks, and again aggregate savings are positive. On the other hand, an increase in prospective government retirement (social security) benefits may reduce gross private-sector savings now, matched by an equal reduction in gross private dissavings when current savers retire. Such fairly stable features of societies help explain why the Japanese save twice as much, in proportional terms, as Americans do.

There remains a question concerning the role of current income in explaining current consumption in the Ando-Modigliani model. The analysis of the relationship of current consumption to the present value of the entire future income stream suggested that a change in current income not accompanied by a change in expected future income would cause a relatively small change in current consumption. To a certain extent, the Ando-Modigliani analysis obscures this point by *assuming* that expected average income depends on current income, raising the leverage of current income on current consumption. Literal acceptance of the Ando-Modigliani results, typified by equation (21), would mean that all increases in labor income would tend to raise current consumption by 70 percent of the income change. But one can think of income changes that should have no effect on expected future income, for example, an explicitly temporary income tax surcharge such as that enacted in July 1968. In this case, simple application of the Ando-Modigliani marginal propensity to consume to obtain the direct policy-induced consumption effect of the tax change would probably be (and in fact was) misleading. The consumption reduction should be far less than 70 percent of the disposable income cut. Thus, the econometric results should be used carefully with an eye on their underlying assumptions, which sometimes won't hold true.

The Friedman Approach: Permanent Income

Let us now turn to Friedman's model of consumption. Friedman also begins with the assumption of individual consumer utility maximization which gives us the relation between an individual's consumption and present value, corresponding to equation (8) earlier,

$$c^i = f^i(PV^i); \qquad f' > 0. \tag{22}$$

Friedman differs from Ando-Modigliani beginning with his treatment of the PV term in (21). Multiplying PV by a rate of return r gives us Friedman's *permanent income*,

$$y_p^i = r \cdot PV^i. \tag{23}$$

This is the permanent income from the consumer's present value which includes his *human capital*—the present value of his future labor income stream—which is included along with a_0 in PV in (23). Friedman, along with Ando-Modigliani, assumes that the consumer wants to smooth his actual income stream into a more or less flat consumption pattern. This gives a level of *permanent consumption, c_p^i,* that is proportional to y_p^i:

$$c_p^i = k^i y_p^i. \tag{24}$$

The individual ratio of permanent consumption to permanent income k^i presumably depends on the interest rate—the return on saving—individual tastes shaping the indifference curves, and the variability of expected income. If there is no reason to expect these factors to be associated with the level of income, we can assume that the average k^i for all income classes will be the same, equal to the population average $\bar{k}$. Thus, if we classify a sample of the population by income strata, as is done in the cross-sectional budget studies, we would expect that the average permanent consumption in each income class i (using *sub*scripts for income classes as opposed to *super*scripts to denote individuals) would be $\bar{k}$ times its average permanent income:

$$\bar{c}_{pi} = \bar{k}\bar{y}_{pi}, \tag{25}$$

for all income classes i.

Next, we can observe that total income in a given period is made up of permanent income y_p^i which the individual has imputed to himself, plus a transitory random transitory income component y_t^i which can be positive, negative, or zero, and really represents current income deviations from permanent income. Notice here that the subscript t refers to "transitory," not "time," as in the previous section. This is the standard notation for transitory income in the literature. Transitory income can be thought of as the random component of the income stream. This gives us measured income as the sum of the permanent and transitory components:

$$y^i = y_p^i + y_t^i. \tag{26}$$

Similarly, total consumption in any period is permanent consumption c_p^i plus a random transitory-consumption component c_t^i, which represents positive, negative, or zero deviation from the "normal" or permanent level of consumption. Thus measured, consumption is the sum of permanent and transitory consumption:

$$c^i = c_p^i + c_t^i. \tag{27}$$

Next comes a series of assumptions concerning the relationships between permanent and transitory income, permanent and transitory consumption, and transitory income and consumption. The assumptions concerning these relationships give the explanation in the Friedman theory of the cross-sectional result that $MPC < APC$.

First, Friedman assumes that there is no correlation between transitory and permanent incomes. In other words, y_t is just a random fluctuation around y_p, so that the covariance of y_p^i and y_t^i across individuals is zero. This assumption has the following implication for cross-sectional budget study results: Suppose we take a sample of families from a roughly normal income distribution and then sort them out by observed income classes. Since y_p and y_t are not related, the income class that centers on the population average income will have an average transitory-income component $\bar{y}_t$ equal to zero, and for that income class $\bar{y} = \bar{y}_p$. As we go up from the average in income strata, we will find, for each income class, more people in that group because they had unusually high incomes that year, that is, because $y_t^i > 0$, than people who were in that class because they had unusually low incomes that year. This happens because in a normal distribution, for any income class above the average, there are more people with permanent incomes *below* that class who can come up into it because $y_t^i > 0$ in any one year than there are people *above* that class who can fall down due to $y_t^i < 0$. Thus, for income classes above the population average, $\bar{y}_t > 0$, and observed $\bar{y} > \bar{y}_p$.

Similarly, below the average income level, for any given income class, there are more people who can fall into it due to having a bad year so that $y_t^i > 0$, than people who come up into it by having a good year so that $y_t^i > 0$. Thus, for income classes below the average, $\bar{y}_t < 0$, and $\bar{y} < \bar{y}_p$. This result—that when sorted by measured income, groups above the population mean have $\bar{y}_t > 0$ and groups below the mean have $\bar{y}_t < 0$—is important for Friedman's analysis, as we will see shortly.

Next, Friedman assumes that there is no relationship between permanent and transitory consumption, so that c_t is just a random variation around c_p. Thus, the covariance of c_p^i and c_t^i is zero.

Finally, Friedman assumes that there is no relationship between transitory consumption and transitory income. In other words, a sudden increase in income, due to a transitory fluctuation, will not contribute immediately to an individual's consumption. This assumption is intuitively less obvious than the previous ones, but it seems fairly reasonable, because we are dealing with *consumption* as opposed *to consumer expenditure.* Consumption includes, in addition to purchases of nondurable goods and services, only the "use" of durables—measured by depreciation and interest cost—rather than expenditures on durables. This means that if a transitory or windfall income is used to purchase a durable good, this would not appreciably affect current consumption. Thus, Friedman assumes that the covariance of c_t and y_t is also zero.

The last two assumptions, that transitory consumption is not correlated with either permanent consumption or transitory income, mean that when we sample the population and classify the sample by income levels, for each income class the transitory variations in consumption will cancel out so that for each income class $\bar{c}_{ti} = 0$, and average permanent consumption is the population average:

$$\bar{c} = \bar{c}_{pi}. \tag{28}$$

We can now bring this series of assumptions together into an explanation of the cross-sectional result that *MPC < APC,* even when the basic hypothesis of the theory is that the ratio of permanent consumption to permanent income is a constant $\bar{k}$. Consider a randomly selected sample of the population classified by income levels. A group i, with average observed income $\bar{y}_i$ *above* average population income, will have a positive average transitory-income component $\bar{y}_{ti} > 0$. For this above-average group, then, observed average income will be greater than average permanent income, that is, $\bar{y}_i > \bar{y}_{pi}$.

All income groups will have average permanent consumption given by $\bar{c}_{pi} = \bar{k}\bar{y}_{pi}$. But since $\bar{c}_{ti}$ is not related to either $\bar{c}_{pi}$ or $\bar{y}_{ti}$, all groups, including the above-average income group, will have a zero average transitory-consumption component, so that $\bar{c}_i = \bar{c}_{pi}$. Linking these two consumption conditions gives us

$$\bar{c}_i = \bar{c}_{pi} = \bar{k}\bar{y}_{pi}. \tag{29}$$

Thus, the above-average income group will have average measured consumption equal to permanent consumption, but average measured income greater than permanent income, so that its measured $\bar{c}_i/\bar{y}_i$ ratio will be less than $\bar{k}$. Similarly, a below-average income group j will have a measured $\bar{c}_j/\bar{y}_j$ ratio greater than $\bar{k}$.

These results are illustrated in Figure 12-8. The solid line $\bar{k}$ represents the relationship between permanent consumption and income. The point $\bar{y}$ is the population average measured income, and if the sample is taken in a "normal" year when measured average income is on trend, average transitory income will be zero, so that $\bar{y} = \bar{y}_p$. The point $\bar{c}_p$ is the population average measured and permanent consumption.

First, consider sample group i, with average income above population

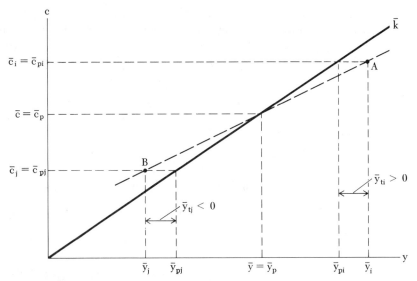

Figure 12-8 Friedman's consumption function.

average, so that $\bar{y}_i > \bar{y}$. This group has a positive average transitory-income component $\bar{y}_{ti}$, so that $\bar{y}_{pi} < \bar{y}_i$, as shown in Figure 12-8. To locate average consumption, both measured and permanent, for group i, we multiply $\bar{y}_{pi}$ by $\bar{k}$ to obtain $\bar{c}_i = \bar{c}_{pi}$ along the $\bar{k}$ line. Thus, for an above-average income group i, we observe $\bar{c}_i$ and $\bar{y}_i$ at the point A which lies below the permanent consumption line $\bar{k}$ in Figure 12-8.

Next, observing lower-than-average income group j, we see that the average income of the group y_j is less than the national average income $\bar{y}$, so that the average transitory income of the sample group, $\bar{y}_{tj}$, is less than zero. Furthermore, we observe $\bar{c}_j$ and know that $\bar{c}_j = \bar{c}_{pj} = \bar{k}\bar{y}_{pj}$ along the $\bar{k}$ line. The location of $\bar{c}_j$ and y_j gives us the point B lying above the $\bar{k}$ line for the below-average income group j. Connecting the points A and B, we obtain the cross-sectional consumption function that connects observed average income-consumption points. This function has a smaller slope than the underlying permanent function, so that in cross-sectional budget studies, we expect to see $MPC < APC$ if (but not only if) the Friedman permanent income hypothesis is correct.

Over time, as the economy and the national average permanent income grow along trend, the cross-sectional consumption function of Figure 12-8 shifts up. What we observe in a long-run time series are movements of national average consumption and income along the line $\bar{k}$, giving a constant c/y ratio. As the economy cycles about its trend growth path, the average $\bar{c}/\bar{y}$ point will move above and below the long-run $\bar{k}$ line. In a boom year when $\bar{y}$ is above trend, the average transitory income of the population will be positive, so that

$\bar{y} > \bar{y}_p$. But average transitory consumption will be zero, so that $\bar{c} = \bar{c}_p = \bar{k}\bar{y}_p$. Thus, when $\bar{y}$ is above trend, $\bar{c}/\bar{y}$ will be less than $\bar{c}_p/\bar{y}_p = \bar{k}$. Similarly, in a year when y is below trend, $\bar{y}_t$ will be negative, $\bar{y} < \bar{y}_p$, and the $\bar{c}/\bar{y}$ ratio will be greater than $\bar{k}$.

This cyclical movement is illustrated in Figure 12-9, with a slight reinterpretation of the horizontal axis. Instead of showing a cross section of income, we interpret it to show national income at various points in time. Now transitory components are cyclical swings, while permanent income and consumption move up along the trend growth path given by $\bar{k}$. In an average year, when $\bar{y}_t = 0$, the $\bar{c}_0, \bar{y}_0$ point falls on the long-run k line. In a year with above-trend income $\bar{y}_1$, transitory income is positive, so that $\bar{y}_{p1} < \bar{y}_1$, and the $\bar{c}_1, \bar{y}_1$ point is below the $\bar{k}$ line of Figure 12.9. In a year with below-trend income $\bar{y}_2$, the $\bar{c}_2, \bar{y}_2$ point is above the $\bar{k}$ line, giving us the short-run function of Figure 12-9. The difference between Figures 12-8 and 12-9 is just that in Figure 12-8 the variation in income and consumption is in a cross section at any one time, while in Figure 12-9 the variation is an average c and y over the business cycle.

Thus, Friedman's model also explains the cross-sectional budget studies and short-run cyclical observations that indicate $MPC < APC$, as well as the long-run observation that the c/y ratio is fairly constant, that is, $APC = MPC$. His model is somewhat less satisfactory than the Ando-Modigliani model in that assets are only implicitly taken into account as a determinant of permanent income. In addition, it relies on less observable aspects of income—"permanent" income and "transitory" income—than the Ando-Modigliani model, which separates out the observable components—labor income and value of assets.

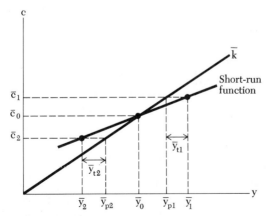

Figure 12-9 Friedman's consumption function: cyclical movements.

Nevertheless, the two models are closely related. Families with transitorily high income in Friedman's analysis could be families in the middle years in the Ando-Modigliani life-cycle, and families with negative transitory income could be the ones at the ends of the life-cycle. Thus, the life-cycle hypothesis could be one explanation of the distribution of Friedman's transitory incomes.

The two models are similar in the starting point of the analysis in the consumption–present value relationship given in equation (22)

$$c^i = f^i(PV^i),$$

and in the explanation of cross-sectional results. The Ando-Modigliani model might be more useful to econometric model-builders and forecasters since it explicitly includes measured current income and assets to explain consumption. However, it may also need careful interpretation in cases where income changes are clearly temporary, and permanent income considerations are more relevant.

Permanent Income and Adaptive Expectations

The Ando-Modigliani life-cycle hypothesis was summarized in equation (19): consumption depends on current labor income and wealth. Wealth acts as a "shift parameter" in the short-run consumption function of Figure 12-7. As Figure 12-9 hints, the permanent income hypothesis of Friedman can be put in the same form, with the last period's consumption acting as the shift parameter. Developing this analogy more explicitly will give us some additional insight into the similarities between the models of Ando-Modigliani and Friedman. The results will be useful when we discuss Robert Hall's rational expectations approach below.

To explore a bit further the relationship between the life-cycle hypothesis and permanent income, it is useful to look more closely at what permanent income means. The permanent component of income is not somehow marked or branded, even for the recipient of the income stream, much less for an econometrician trying to study consumption and distinguish between the permanent income and life-cycle hypothesis. The problem for the income recipient and the observing econometrician alike is to infer from a given income stream $(y_t, \ldots, y_{t-1}, \ldots, y_0)$, and in the case of the econometrician, from the consumption stream $(c_t, \ldots, c_{t-1}, \ldots, c_0)$, what permanent income is and how it behaves over time.

Friedman approached this problem along the lines of adaptive expectations, which we first discussed in Chapter 7. As in the case of adaptive expectations, the problem is to find a sensible rule for adjusting one's estimate of permanent income y^p using the information from the realizations of actual income y. Note that here we switch notation to using superscripts p and t for permanent and transitory, respectively, in order to go back to using subscripts for time periods. At any point in time t, the individual has a realization of actual income y_{t-1} and his or her past estimate of permanent income y_{t-1}^p. One mechanism akin to adaptive expectations is to assume that the stream of permanent income is smoother than actual income, since the actual income includes transitory income. This would imply adjusting actual income y_{t-1} by a fraction of its excess over the estimate of permanent income y_{t-1}^p in translating it into the next period's estimate of permanent income. Following this reasoning, we can write Friedman's process for extracting an estimate of permanent income from the time series of actual income as the following:

$$y_t^p = y_{t-1} + \lambda(y_{t-1}^p - y_{t-1}). \tag{30}$$

Here $0 < \lambda < 1$ is the fraction of last period's error that is subtracted from y_{t-1} in forming the estimate of y_t^p. (Note λ is *not* a Lagrange multiplier here! Another change in notation.) The assumption is that if actual y was above y_{t-1}^p, it is also above y_t^p, but by a fraction λ. Thus, equation (30) smooths the actual y stream into a permanent income stream.

To develop the analogy to Ando-Modigliani, we rewrite equation (30) as

$$y_t^p = (1 - \lambda)y_{t-1} + \lambda y_{t-1}^p.$$

In Friedman's permanent income hypothesis, expressed in equation (24), permanent consumption is a fraction k of permanent income, and transitory consumption is randomly distributed around permanent consumption. So, given the data of time period $t - 1$, expected actual consumption c_t in period t is permanent consumption, given by

$$c_t^p = k(1 - \lambda)y_{t-1} + k\lambda y_{t-1}^p. \tag{31}$$

Since by the same model $c_{t-1}^p = ky_{t-1}^p$, for y_{t-1}^p in (31) we can substitute c_{t-1}^p/k to obtain the Ando-Modigliani analogy in the Friedman theory:

$$c_t^p = k(1 - \lambda)y_{t-1} + \lambda c_{t-1}^p. \tag{32}$$

Here the shift parameter in the Friedman version is λc_{t-1}^p.

Obviously, equation (32) is very similar to Ando-Modigliani's equation (19) describing the life-cycle hypothesis. The difference between the two theories rests mainly in the specification of the shift parameter. Furthermore, we saw in equation (15) that consumption should be expected to be highly correlated with wealth, so the two variables c_{t-1} and a_t are going to have very similar time-series properties. The net result is that the permanent income and life-cycle hypotheses are extremely difficult to distinguish in empirical tests.

The Hall Approach: Rational Expectations

The consumption models of Ando-Modigliani and Friedman concentrate on the structural relationship between expected lifetime income and current consumption. They differ in their approach to empirical implementation of the theory. More recently, Robert Hall has reformulated consumption theory by adding the assumption of rational expectations to the first-order conditions equations (12) of the intertemporal optimizing model of consumer behavior. This approach goes around structural relationships, moving directly to a reduced-form forecasting equation. It does so by assuming that the values of the fundamental determinants of consumption behavior are known to the consumer, who acts on them at any point in time. In this case the consumption decision at point $t - 1$, c_{t-1}, takes into account known information and the consumer's expectations about the future income stream as of $t - 1$. Then a first-order condition like equation (14) can be used to predict c_t, given c_{t-1}. The error in predicting c_t will be any new information about the future income stream that was received between period $t - 1$ and period t.

Let's state Hall's insight somewhat more carefully in terms of the intertemporal consumption model. Equation (14) earlier, taken from the first-order conditions, says that along the optimal consumption path, for a given expectation of future income,

$$c_{t+1} = \left(\frac{1 + r}{1 + \delta}\right)c_t. \qquad (14)$$

Remember that this is a specific example of the general case where we have assumed $u = \ln c$, so that $u'(c) = 1/c$. In the general case then, the first-order equations give a relationship between current and expected marginal utility of consumption that was shown in equation (14a):

$$u'(c_{t+1}) = \left(\frac{1 + \delta}{1 + r}\right)u'(c_t). \qquad (14b)$$

Again, since $u'(c) = 1/c$ when $u = \ln c$, the coefficient ratio is inverted going from (14) to (14b).

The intertemporal consumption equation (14) can be interpreted both in terms of the permanent income hypothesis and econometrically, applying the assumption of rational expectations. The equation gives the expected value of the next period's consumption c_{t+1}, conditional on this period's consumption c_t, which is already known. The permanent income interpretation is that when the consumer makes this period's consumption choice, c_t, he or she has incorporated the best estimate of permanent income into the decision. The consumption predicted by equation (14) is then c_{t+1}^p. The *expected value* for consumption is permanent consumption; transitory consumption is the random term around it. With this interpretation, we would rewrite equation (14) as

$$c_{t+1}^p = \left(\frac{1 + r}{1 + \delta}\right)c_t, \tag{14c}$$

and add transitory consumption c_t^t to get the expression for total consumption

$$c_{t+1} = \left(\frac{1 + r}{1 + \delta}\right)c_t + c_t^t. \tag{33}$$

Here transitory consumption is a random component around the path of permanent income given in (14c), and $c_t = c_t^p + c_t^t$. Hence, following the permanent income hypothesis, equation (14) can be interpreted as a forecasting equation for permanent income.

If the present value of actual consumption c_t indeed incorporates the consumer's best estimate of permanent income in an unbiased way, then his or her *expectations* of permanent income are *rational,* and the transitory component in equation (13) will indeed be random over time. Thus, the econometrician estimating a consumption relationship such as (31) using time-series data on consumption would see random residuals c_t^t from the estimated equation. Furthermore, no lagged values of other relevant variables like c_{t-1} or y_{t-1} would have any extra explanatory power in a regression of (31). Why not? Because by the rational expectations hypothesis, c_t has incorporated all the relevant information embodied in these variables.

An econometric test of the permanent income/rational expectations approach, as applied by Hall, would be that a regression of (31) would yield random residuals and that no lagged variables would have added significance once c_t was included in the regression for c_{t+1}. Hall's hypothesis cannot be rejected on U.S. quarterly data, but it has not held up so well on data from other countries. There (and in later tests on U.S. data as well) lagged values of income and other variables have been significant.

The weak point in Hall's approach is the application of rational expectations to the process consumers use to estimate permanent income. Friedman simply assumed that an adaptive expectations mechanism made sense. In Chapter 7 we saw that it does when the variable we are trying to predict shows random movements like transitory income around a stable trend like permanent income. If adaptive expectations is used to form estimates of permanent income, we have already seen in the last section that the equation for permanent consumption can have lagged income in it. This represents partial adjustment of estimated permanent income to past movement in actual income.

To see the point clearly, let us move equation (32) (p. 265) ahead one period and add transitory consumption c_{t+1}^t to both sides of it to get an equation that looks like Hall's (33):

$$c_{t+1} = \lambda c_t^p + k(1 - \lambda)y_t + c_t^t. \tag{34}$$

Here the lagged value of y represents the adaptive, rather than rational, expectations assumption. Leaving it out of the regression would introduce non-randomness in the estimated error terms unless the time series of y were itself random.

Hall's work adds the rational expectations assumption to the basic Fisherian intertemporal model underlying both Ando-Modigliani and Friedman. This gives us a reduced-form forecasting equation for consumption in the form of (33). This equation is, of course, consistent with the basic structural relationship of this whole body of theory: current consumption depends on the present value of the entire future income stream. This is the common starting point for all the variants we have discussed. The jury is still out on the role of rational expectations, however.

TWO ALTERNATIVES IN CONSUMPTION THEORY

The approaches to consumption theory set out in the last section all started from the intertemporal maximization model. The assumptions of that model are not sacrosanct, however. Their empirical validity is open to question and to econometric verification. The consumption literature includes two major alternatives to the pure intertemporal maximizing model, which we will discuss here. The first alternative modifies the budget constraint of equation (3). It is generally referred to as a "liquidity-constraint" model. The second introduces an alternative utility function to equation (2) that recognizes that individuals care about their relative position in the income distribution and their relative consumption levels, as well as the absolute level of consumption. James Duesenberry developed a theory built on this idea in the 1940s. It can be traced to Thorstein Veblen's ideas about conspicuous consumption which date from the beginning of the 1900s. Let's begin with liquidity constraints.

The Role of Liquidity Constraints

In discussing both the two-period and many-period intertemporal maximizing model, we made heavy use of the intertemporal budget constraint of equation (3):

$$\sum_0^T \frac{c_t}{(1 + r)^t} = \sum_0^T \frac{y_t}{(1 + r)^t}.$$

This budget constraint assumes that the consumer can in fact move resources through time in both directions. He or she can save today for consumption tomorrow, or can borrow today to consume against future income. The second case is the one illustrated in Figure 12-4. Both saving (lending) and borrowing are assumed to be possible at the same rate of interest. It is obvious, just from everyday experience, that this assumption does not hold generally at the level of the individual household. Many households cannot borrow freely for consumption against future income. They are constrained in their consumption decisions by current liquidity—current income plus existing assets. Thus, the term *liquidity constraint.*

There are two basic causes of liquidity constraints in the form of banks' unwillingness to lend for consumption against repayment out of future income. One is the uncertainty that both bank and borrower feel about future income. The second is the risk of default by the borrower. The combination of these uncertainties causes banks to place credit limits on borrowers, so that they cannot borrow freely against future income. It may be possible to borrow against the purchase of durable goods, such as houses and cars, because they provide collateral. The bank owns the item until the loan is paid off. Banks will lend against education because in many cases the government guarantees repayment of the loan. In this case public policy is attempting to break the liquidity constraint on investment in education.

Generally, however, these limits apply to how far you can go in borrowing to consume. If the borrower goes beyond a reasonable limit in committing uncertain future income to repayments, he or she faces the possibility of bankruptcy. Once faced with that situation, the borrower may as well go broke on a grand scale, enjoying life in the short run. This possibility adds to banks' reluctance to lend for consumption.

The extreme case of liquidity constraint would be characterized by a level of consumption limited by current liquidity. For these consumers, the budget constraint would be

$$c_t^i \leq y_t^i + a_t^i, \tag{35}$$

where y_t is current net income (net of past repayment obligations). In an economy with a mixture of consumers, some constrained by liquidity as in (35) and some under the usual intertemporal constraint of equation (3), the aggregate consumption function would then resemble that of Ando and Modigliani:

$$c_t = \alpha_0 y_t + \alpha_1 a_t, \quad \text{with} \quad \alpha_0, \alpha_1 \lessgtr 1. \tag{36}$$

Pervasive liquidity constraints would therefore lead us back to a "Keynesian" consumption function with an important role for current wealth.

The existence of liquidity constraints would not eliminate life-cycle patterns in consumption and saving, since the constraint is one-sided. It would constrain borrowing at the young end of the life-cycle. But saving in the middle years for retirement would still be optimal. So the consumption path would

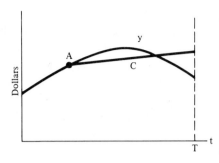

Figure 12-10   Liquidity-constrained life cycle.

follow income in Figure 12-10 up to point A where $c_t = y_t$. From there on it would follow the life-cycle path of Figure 12-6. In a cross section of the population, we would expect to find liquidity constraints most binding among the young. This expectation is borne out by empirical studies, such as the research of Hubbard and Judd. It also implies that the effect of cyclical fluctuations in income on consumption is felt most sharply by the younger segments of the working population.

The Duesenberry Approach: Relative Income

The model developed by Duesenberry in 1949 differs considerably from all the models we have presented in this chapter in that it does not begin with an entirely private utility function independent of the consumption of other persons. Instead, Duesenberry's analysis is based on two relative income hypotheses.

The first hypothesis is essentially that consumers are not so much concerned about their absolute level of consumption as they are with their consumption relative to that of the rest of the population. The Fisherian model is based on the solution to the problem of consumer choice when the consumer tries to maximize $u = u(c_0, \ldots, c_t, \ldots, c_T)$ subject to a present value constraint. In that case, only the absolute level of the individual's consumption enters the utility function. Duesenberry, however, writes the utility function as

$$U = U\left(\frac{c_0}{R_0}, \ldots, \frac{c_t}{R_t}, \ldots, \frac{c_T}{R_T}\right), \tag{37}$$

where the R's are a weighted average of the rest of the population's consumption. This says that utility increases only if the individual's consumption rises relative to that of the average.

This assumption leads to the result that the individual's c/y ratio will depend on his position in the income distribution. A person with an income below the average will tend to have a high c/y ratio because, essentially, he is trying to keep up with a national average consumption standard with a below-average income. On the other hand, an individual with an above-average income will have a lower c/y ratio because it takes a smaller proportion of his income to buy the standard basket of consumer goods.

This provides the explanation of both the cross-sectional result that $MPC < APC$ and the long-run constancy of c/y. If, as income grows along trend, the relative distribution of income is stable, there will be no reason for c/y to change. As people earn more along trend, they can increase their consumption proportionately to maintain the same ratio between their consumption and the national average.

Duesenberry's second hypothesis is that present consumption is not influenced merely by present levels of absolute and relative income, but also by levels of consumption attained in previous periods. It is much more difficult, he argues, for a family to reduce a level of consumption once attained than to reduce the portion of its income saved in any period. This assumption suggests that the aggregate ratio of saving to income depends on the level of present income relative to previous peak income, $\hat{y}$. Mathematically, in Duesenberry's formulation,

$$\frac{s}{y} = a_0 + a_1 \frac{y}{\hat{y}}, \tag{38}$$

where y is real disposable income. As present income rises relative to its previous peak, s/y increases, and vice versa. We can convert this Duesenberry saving function into a consumption function by observing that if y is disposable income, $c/y = 1 - (s/y)$, so that from (38) we can obtain

$$\frac{c}{y} = (1 - a_0) - a_1 \frac{y}{\hat{y}}. \tag{39}$$

As income grows along trend, previous peak income will always be last year's income, so that $y/\hat{y}$ would be equal to $1 + g_y$, where g_y is the growth rate of real income. If y grows at 3 percent along trend, $y/\hat{y}$ will be 1.03 and c/y will be constant, as required by the long-run data of Kuznets.

But as income fluctuates around trend, the c/y ratio will vary inversely with income, owing to the negative coefficient of $y/\hat{y}$ in (39). To compute the MPC, we can multiply the c/y ratio of (31) by y to obtain

$$c = (1 - a_0)y - a_1 \frac{y^2}{\hat{y}}.$$

The MPC, the partial derivative of c with respect to y, is then

$$MPC = \frac{\partial c}{\partial y} = (1 - a_0) - 2a_1 \frac{y}{\hat{y}}. \tag{40}$$

Comparison of equation (40) giving the *MPC* and equation (39) giving the *APC* shows that in the short run, with previous peak income fixed, the Due-senberry model implies *MPC* < *APC*.

This combination of short-run and long-run behavior of consumption gives us the *ratchet effect* shown in Figure 12-11. As income grows along trend, c and y move up along the long-run function of Figure 12-11 with a constant c/y ratio. But if, at some point like c_0,y_0, income falls off and the economy goes into a recession, c and y move down along a short-run function c_0c_0 with a slope given by the *MPC* in equation (40). Recovery of income back to its trend level, which is also the previous peak, will take c and y back up c_0c_0 to the initial c_0,y_0 point, where trend growth resumes along the long-run function. If another recession occurs at c_1,y_1, consumption and income will fall back along c_1c_1, and rise back to c_1,y_1 during the recovery. Thus, Duesenberry's model implies a ratchet effect in that when income falls off, consumption drops less than it rises as income grows along trend. We might note that this mechanism is formally the same as that suggested by wage rigidity in Chapter 10.

This completes our survey of the principal theories of the consumption function. Each theory improves our understanding of the consumption-saving-income relationships. The theories of Ando-Modigliani and Friedman, with the rational expectations extension by Hall, seem to be more successful than Duesenberry's, in terms of their present acceptance among economists. The strength of Friedman's theory is related to the acceptance by many economists of the proposition that people base current consumption-saving decisions on more than just current and past values of income and assets. The notion, common to both Ando-Modigliani and Friedman, of a basic permanent con-

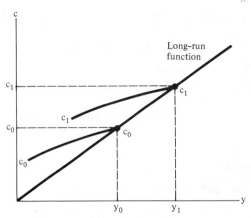

Figure 12-11 The ''ratchet effect'' in consumption.

sumption path that is tied to an expected income stream and is somewhat insensitive to temporary fluctuations in income, is persuasive. The Hall model is the most modern and uses expectations in a fully rational way. It is supported by the intuition that, with expected lifetime wealth available, only information influencing this expectation can affect consumption. On the other hand, it is useful to know what *does* cause fluctuations in current consumption, and the Ando-Modigliani model has a relative strength in its explicit inclusion of current income and assets in the explanation of consumption. Perhaps the best compromise is to explain consumption using the Ando-Modigliani model, but with reservations in cases of temporary income and asset fluctuations as suggested by the permanent income hypothesis.

CHOICE STRUCTURE AND DISEQUILIBRIUM

In Chapter 6 we modeled the worker-consumer as making a constrained optimal choice between income and leisure, given tastes and skills, the wage rate W, and the expected price level P^e. Thus, in deriving the economy's supply curve, we had a worker *choosing,* under the usual constraints, a level of income $y^e = w^e(T - S)$ [see equation (12), p. 116]. Now, in analyzing consumption and saving behavior, we take as given the income-leisure choice, so that consumption and saving depend on income.

Implicit in this treatment of income as predetermined in the consumption function is a model of the choice structure of the worker-consumer illustrated in Figure 12-12. Given time, tastes, skills, prices, and wages determined by the market, the worker makes a work-leisure decision. This was the starting point of Chapter 6. This decision will not be revised often. In the institutional context of most industrial economies, with union membership, long-term contracts, and skill and educational background "locking" people into labor market decisions for extended periods of time, the fundamental labor market decision is not going to be reviewed nearly as often as the saving-consumption decision.

The work-leisure decision yields a value for *permanent income* that is then split (after taxes, of course) into consumption and saving. This saving decision can be reviewed frequently. As the worker-consumer is occasionally surprised by the labor market outcome as national income fluctuates, we see

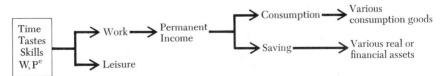

Figure 12-12 Worker-consumer choice structure.

consumption moving with income. This movement gave us the consumption functions of this chapter.

An alternative interpretation of the consumption function has gained support in the literature in the past 15 years or so. This interpretation derives the consumption function from a *constrained disequilibrium* situation. If we ignore the choice structure story above, and think of the worker-consumer as making a general equilibrium decision on work, leisure, consumption, and saving all at once, then consumption should depend only on the left-hand vector of time, tastes, skills, W, and P^e in Figure 12-12, without income intervening. In a timeless, general equilibrium world, each person looks at the entire price vector and then makes all decisions simultaneously, including consumption.

The alternative to the choice structure story justifying inclusion of income as a predetermined variable in the consumption function is an assumption that the worker-consumer is *constrained* in the quantity of labor he or she can sell at the going wage rate. This is the case of wage rigidity discussed in Chapter 10, and is the basis of the *disequilibrium* interpretation of the consumption function, as modeled, for example, by Robert Barro and Herschel Grossman.

If the wage rate is rigid in the downward direction, an exogenous drop in aggregate demand may throw a worker off his or her labor-supply curve, as discussed in Chapter 10. In this case a worker is rationed in the amount of labor he or she can sell, and consumption choices become constrained by the amount of income that can be earned, an amount less than optimal at the going wage. Income then becomes predetermined by the labor market constraint and is an independent variable in the consumption function.

This disequilibrium story also gives us an alternative interpretation of the consumption multiplier of Chapter 3. If a worker is constrained in the labor market because of wage rigidity, consumption expenditures are reduced by the income constraint. Thus, firms may face a sales constraint as consumer demand falls, if the going price level is also rigid. If the price level is rigid downward, the sales constraint will lead firms to reduce output and, consequently, employment. This feeds back into the labor market, reducing the demand for labor at the going rigid wage. The drop in demand for labor tightens the workers' income constraint, reducing their consumption expenditure, spilling back into the product market in the form of tightening constraint in sales. Thus, the feedback from the workers' labor market constraint to the firms' sales constraint multiplies the initial drop in demand that indicates the downward spiral.

This spillover disequilibrium story is fully consistent with the discussion of wage rigidity in Chapter 10 and the consumption function of this chapter. It is a useful interpretation of the short-term dynamics of the basic model when wage and price rigidities are present. We will return to this disequilibrium interpretation of the model in Chapter 13 on investment, and again in Chapter 18. There we pull together the elements of the disequilibrium interpretation from Chapters 10, 12, and 13 and present a full short-run static model with wage and price rigidity. Below we continue with the equilibrium interpretation of the basic model, staying in a framework of flexible wages and prices.

THE *MPS* MODEL

Beginning in 1967, a group of economists centered originally at the Federal Reserve Board, in Washington, and the Massachusetts Institute of Technology (MIT), in Cambridge, under the general direction of Ando and Modigliani, developed an econometric model of the U.S. economy. This research project was largely supported by the Federal Reserve Board (the Fed) and the Social Science Research Council (SSRC). The model is used for policy analysis and forecasting by economists at the Fed and in major centers of economic research. With the leaders of the project coming from the University of Pennsylvania (Ando) and MIT (Modigliani), the model has become known as the MIT-Penn-SSRC, or MPS model. Included in the model are consumption function estimates that are based on the original Ando-Modigliani work discussed earlier, and that introduce more clearly the difference between the concepts of *consumption* and *consumer expenditure* which are implicit in all the other models. Furthermore, this model deals explicitly with the dynamic nature of the multiplier by predicting how long it takes for a step increase in income to achieve its full impact on consumption.

The term *consumption* as we have been using it in most of this chapter means the *use* of a good rather than the expenditure on it in any one period. Durable goods have a lifetime of service. The present value of the services rendered by the good is equal to the original price of the good. Consumption is the amount of services of a good which is used up in any one period, while *consumption expenditure* is the expenditure on consumer goods in a period. The two values are usually different, unless all purchases of the services of durable goods are in the form of rents, or the economy is in a stationary state where all durable purchases are for replacement.

Considering the distinction between consumption and consumer expenditure, it can be seen that an increase in income in period 0 will lead immediately to an increase in *desired consumption,* given by the *MPC.* But to increase consumption services from durables, a person has to buy the entire capitalized stream of services in the current period. Thus, the increase in consumer expenditure resulting from an increase in income could greatly exceed the original income change. (Consider a tax cut of $300/month which leads to an auto purchase of $9000.)

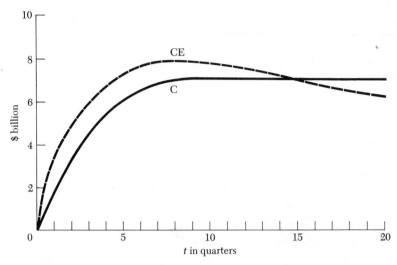

Figure 12-13 MPS model: consumption versus consumption expenditure.

The consumption function in the MPS model predicts the size of increases in both consumption and consumption expenditure following an exogenous change in income as well as the length of time needed before the new levels are fully reached, holding all other variables, for example, P and r, constant. This is illustrated in Figure 12-13, which shows the adjustment of both consumption and consumer expenditure to their new equilibrium levels following a one-time increase in income of $10 billion in period 0. This corresponds to the simplest multiplier effect of Chapter 3, where we are now looking at the *timing* of the effect. The solid line in Figure 12-13 represents the increased *consumption* resulting from the step increase in disposable income. It can be seen that it approaches the ultimate level c_N asymptotically. The dashed line represents actual *expenditures* on consumption goods. This increment to expenditures actually rises above the long-run consumption effect after 5 quarters and then declines to below that level after 15 quarters.

In the static model we have discussed, we have dealt only with the values for consumption, and we have observed only the two points c_0 and c_N. One virtue of the MPS model is that it permits us to see the time dimension of changes from c_0 to c_N and to relate changes in consumption to changes in consumer expenditure. The latter is the value that appears in the national income accounts, whereas the former is the consumption flow predicted by economic theory.

THE WEALTH EFFECT IN THE STATIC MODEL

We have now seen that the level of real household net worth—*wealth* or *assets*—has an effect on the level of consumption. In the original discussion of the effects of changes in consumption on the equilibrium of the money and product markets, we did not allow assets to enter into consideration. Now we will examine the implications for the general equilibrium analysis of including real assets in the consumption function.

We can begin with a general form of the Ando-Modigliani consumption function:

$$c = \alpha_0 y^L + \alpha_1 a, \tag{41}$$

where α_0 and α_1 are the positive coefficients that Ando and Modigliani estimated. An increase in either labor income or assets raises current consumption. The definition of assets at the beginning of the period that brought the a term into the function in the first place is

$$a_0 = \sum_0^T \frac{y_t^P}{(1 + r)^t} = y_0^P + \sum_1^T \frac{y_t^P}{(1 + r)^t}.$$

Thus, current property income y_0^P also enters the consumption function (41) positively through the assets term, and we can write the expanded consumption function in the general form

$$c = c(y - t(y), a); \qquad \frac{\partial c}{\partial (y - t(y))} > 0, \qquad \frac{\partial c}{\partial a} > 0. \tag{42}$$

Real consumption increases with an increase either in disposable income or in real assets.

Now if, at a given level of disposable income, an increase in real assets raises consumption, it must reduce saving since $s + c = y - t(y)$. This is not in violation of common-sense notions of saving. People save in order to accumulate assets or wealth. If there should suddenly be an exogenous increase in one's wealth, such as an inheritance, there is less need to save, and the saving rate will diminish. Thus, the saving function can be written as

$$s = s(y - t(y), a); \qquad \frac{\partial s}{\partial (y - t(y))} > 0, \qquad \frac{\partial s}{\partial a} < 0. \tag{43}$$

An increase in real assets reduces saving at a given level of disposable income.

The Composition of Real Assets

Net assets of the private sector, in money terms, can be defined as

$$A = K + R + B, \tag{44}$$

where $K \equiv$ the value of capital stock measured by the total value of stockholder's equity, that is, stock market shares, plus the value of the housing stock, land, and consumer durables,

$R \equiv$ the value of reserves held at the central bank, that is, the part of the money supply which is a private-sector claim on the government,

$B \equiv$ the money value of government bonds which are held by the public.

Here only that part of the money supply that is held as reserves at the central bank is included in assets, because the rest of the money supply represents the claims in the form of deposits of the nonbank public on the commercial banks. If the latter are included in the "public," this part of the money supply is a net zero asset, since the asset of the nonbank public is balanced by the liability of the banks. On the other hand, reserves and government bonds are included because they are claims of the private sector on an "outsider"—the government. The validity of including bonds is open to question, because they could be seen as future tax liabilities of the private sector. For the present, however, we will ignore that possibility and treat bonds as private claims on the government.

Net real assets a equal A/P, so that we have

$$a = \frac{K + R + B}{P}. \tag{45}$$

If the average price of real capital, that is, machines, buildings, land, and durable goods, moves with the price level, we can write the value of the capital stock as $K = Pk$, so that the first term in the real assets equation is Pk/P, or just k, the real capital stock. In the short-run analysis of the determination of income, we are holding the capital stock constant, so that k is fixed.

If we assume that all government bonds are very long term with a standard annual yield of \$1, then the total value of outstanding bonds is the number of bonds b divided by the interest rate. Thus, $B = b/r$. If, in fact, the standard yield is not \$1, but, say \$100, this just moves the decimal point in our measurement of b, not changing the qualitative analysis at all.

Now the expression for real assets can be rewritten as

$$a = k + \frac{R}{P} + \frac{B}{P} = k + \frac{R}{P} + \frac{b}{rP}. \tag{46}$$

Asset Effects and the *IS* Curve

From equation (46) we can see that inclusion of real assets in consumption flattens the slope of the *IS* curve as r changes, and also shifts the *IS* curve as R, b, or P change. We can look at the effects of movements of each of these variables in turn, to see the *direct* effects of movements in r, R, b, and P on the *IS* curve through the wealth effect on consumption.

A reduction in the interest rate increases the value of the outstanding stock of debt in the hands of the private sector by increasing bond prices.

Comparing equations (45) and (46), we see that a drop in r increases the value of B and a. The increase in real assets reduces saving and increases consumption. Thus, as r falls *both* investment and consumption rise along the *IS* curve. This flattens the *IS* curve; for a given drop in r, the effect on product market equilibrium y is increased by inclusion of the wealth effect on consumption.

The wealth effect thus opens another channel through which monetary policy affects income and output. As we saw in Part II an increase in the money supply, reducing the interest rate, increases investment; now we see that it also increases consumer spending. In Figure 12-14, flattening the *IS* curve from $I_0 S_0$ to $I_1 S_1$ increases the effect on y, for a given shift in the *LM* curve of $L_0 M_0$ to $L_1 M_1$. Without the wealth effect on consumption, y would increase to y_1. Including the wealth effect moves y up to y_2 as the *LM* curve shifts. This is a major additional channel for monetary policy in the MPS model.

An increase in b or R or a drop in P *shifts* the *IS* curve to the right, as shown in the four-quadrant diagram of Figure 12-15. With an initial asset level a_0, the *IS* curve is positioned at $I_0 S_0$. An increase in real assets to a_1, as b or R rises or P falls, shifts the saving function in the southeast quadrant from $s(a_0)$ to $s(a_1)$. Since $s + t$ is measured from the origin down on the vertical axis, this shift represents a decrease in saving at any given level of income; $\partial s/\partial a < 0$.

The downward shift in the saving function shifts the *IS* curve out to $I_1 S_1$ in Figure 12-15. The increase in real assets reduces saving and increases con-

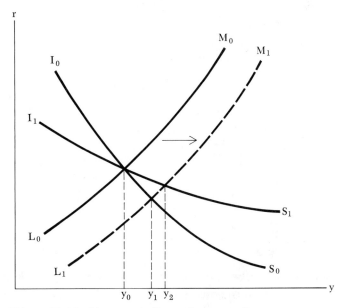

Figure 12-14 Monetary policy and consumption.

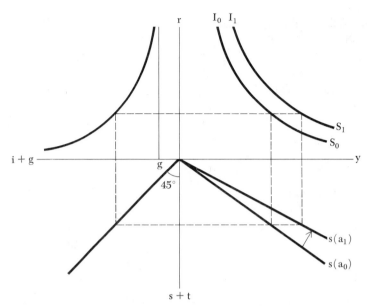

Figure 12-15   The asset effect shifting the IS curve.

sumption, raising equilibrium y in the product market at any given r. Thus, an increase in real assets as b, R, or P change shifts the IS curve.

Reserves R or government debt B in the hands of the private sector are increased by a government budget deficit. The government can finance this budget deficit by selling bonds to the public, by increasing B, or by selling bonds to the Fed in exchange for money balances. This becomes an increase in R when the government draws on its balance at the Fed to finance the deficit. Thus, through a continuing deficit, the IS curve shifts gradually right; a surplus would shift it left. This means that a static equilibrium with the budget *not* in balance implies a gradual movement in the IS curve over time. We return to these dynamic implications of budget imbalance in Chapter 21.

An open market increase in R, in which the Fed buys bonds from the public in exchange for money, simply swaps R for B, with $\Delta B = -\Delta R$. The Fed is buying bonds from the commercial banks, so when R goes up, B falls by the same amount, and vice versa when R goes down. This means that, as long as only the reserves part of the money supply is included in A in the first place, open market operations do not affect a, and thus do not *directly* shift the IS curve.

Price Level Changes and the Pigou Effect

An important result of the introduction of real assets into the consumption function is the effect of movements in the price level on the IS curve. A price

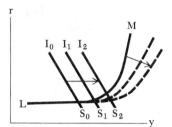

Figure 12-16 The "Pigou effect."

increase reduces the real value of assets, shifting the *IS* curve to the left. In Part II the adjustment of demand-side equilibrium output to changes in the price level came only through the money market, shifting the *LM* curve. Now it is clear that price level changes also shift the *IS* curve, and in the same direction as the *LM* curve; a price increase shifts both to the left. This makes demand-side equilibrium output more sensitive to price level changes, and flattens the economy's demand curve in the *P,y* space.

The main importance of the inclusion of real wealth in the consumption function from a historical point of view is that it eliminates the liquidity-trap inconsistency in the classical model which Keynes used to attack that model. According to Keynes, it was possible for interest rates to fall so low in the classical model that neither an expansionary monetary policy nor falling prices could ever increase the level of demand-side equilibrium output. Thus, with employment determined in the labor market and demand caught in the liquidity trap, the classical model had no solution. Professor A. C. Pigou, who responded to Keynes, pointed out that, in our terms, the price drop would shift the *IS* curve out. As prices fall the level of real assets rises, leading to downward shifts in the saving function.

These increases in real consumption that occur with falling prices would shift the *IS* curve out, raising the level demand-side equilibrium output as shown in Figure 12-16. Thus, the *Pigou effect* refuted the suggestion by Keynes that the so-called classical model was inconsistent in the liquidity-trap case.

CONCLUSION: SOME IMPLICATIONS FOR STABILIZATION POLICY

Our analysis of consumer behavior and the consumption function has two important implications for stabilization policy, which are briefly reviewed here. In Chapter 16 we take another thorough look at monetary and fiscal policy after we have further analyzed investment demand and the money market.

The first implication, mentioned several times already, is that how much reliance should be placed on using temporary tax changes for stabilization policy depends on how correct the permanent income hypothesis of Friedman is. It is quite possible that if there were a variable income tax surcharge set, say, every year by the President, people would soon calculate an average expected value for the surcharge and set their consumption pattern to fit disposable income with this average surcharge. Thus, fluctuations in the surcharge would be absorbed in the saving rate and have no effect on consumption. People would just shift saving between the public sector and the private sector.

This might be an extreme case of permanent income behavior counteracting fiscal policy, but it does seem clear that, in any case, temporary tax changes will be less effective than permanent ones of the same size, and small, explicitly temporary tax changes may have little or no effect on aggregate demand.

The second point is that inclusion of real assets as a determinant of consumer demand probably increases the effectiveness of monetary policy relative to fiscal policy through the interest rate effect on asset values, which flattens the *IS* curve. An expansionary monetary policy will reduce the interest rate. In addition to its effect on investment, the fall in the interest rate will increase the value of real assets in equation (40), stimulating consumption. Thus, the asset effect complements the effect of monetary policy and provides a link from monetary policy changes to consumer demand through the interest rate.

On the other hand, an expansionary fiscal policy tends to raise interest rates, reducing the real value of assets and consumption spending, partially offsetting the effect of the original fiscal policy expansion. In Figure 12-17 we show a given shift in two pairs of *IS* curves, the steep $I_0 S_0$ and $I_1 S_1$, and the

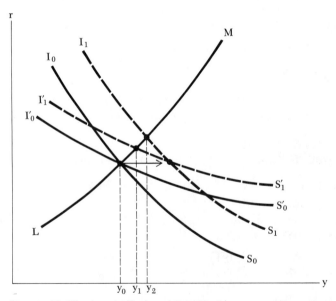

Figure 12-17 Asset effect and fiscal policy.

flat $I_0'S_0'$, as government spending is increased. With the steeper IS curves, omitting the asset effect, y rises from y_0 to y_2. With the flatter curves, including the asset effect, y only rises to y_1 with the postulated g increase. Thus, the asset effect, through the interest rate, creates a consumption demand change that complements the effects of monetary policy but tends to offset partially the effects of fiscal policy.

SELECTED READINGS

A. Ando and F. Modigliani, "The 'Life Cycle' Hypothesis of Saving: Aggregate Implications and Tests," *American Economic Review,* March 1963.

R.J. Barro and H.I. Grossman, "A General Disequilibrium Model of Income and Employment," *American Economic Review,* March 1971.

A.S. Blinder, "Temporary Taxes and Consumer Spending," *Journal of Political Economy,* February 1981.

J.S. Duesenberry, *Income, Saving and the Theory of Consumer Behavior* (Cambridge: Harvard University Press, 1949).

I. Fisher, *The Theory of Interest* (New York: Macmillan, 1930).

M. Flavin, "The Adjustment of Consumption to Changing Expectations About Future Income," *Journal of Political Economy,* October 1981.

M. Friedman, *A Theory of the Consumption Function* (Princeton, N.J.: Princeton University Press, 1957), chapters 1–3, 6, 9.

R.E. Hall, "Stochastic Implications of the Life Cycle—Permanent Income Hypothesis: Theory and Evidence," *Journal of Political Economy,* December 1978.

R.G. Hubbard and K.L. Judd, "Liquidity Constraints, Fiscal Policy, and Consumption," *Brookings Papers on Economic Activity,* vol. 1, 1986.

S. Kuznets, *National Product Since 1869* (New York: National Bureau of Economic Research, 1946).

F. Modigliani, "The Life Cycle Hypothesis of Saving Twenty Years Later," in M. Parkin, ed., *Contemporary Issues in Economics* (Manchester University Press: Manchester, 1975).

F. Modigliani and R.E. Brumberg, "Utility Analysis and the Consumption Function," in K.K. Kurihara, ed., *Post-Keynesian Economics* (New Brunswick, N.J.: Rutgers University Press, 1954).

C.R. Nelson, "A Reappraisal of Recent Tests of the Permanent Income Hypothesis," *Journal of Political Economy,* June 1987.

chapter *13*

Investment Demand

In Chapter 4 we introduced investment demand as a simple function of the interest rate, offering as a rationale the present value (*PV*) criterion for investment decisions. This simple function was sufficient for the purposes of Part II to expose and manipulate the basic interconnections between the product, money, and labor markets. But the $i = i(r)$ function is obviously not a good representation of the complex determinants of investment in the "real world." In fact, it is only in the past twenty years or so that empirical investigators have been able to obtain even barely reasonable empirical explanations of investment demand.

This chapter first reviews the basis in microeconomic theory for a macroeconomic view of investment demand, developing along the way the rationale for the *PV* rule and a comparison of this criterion with the concept of the *marginal efficiency of investment*. We then develop from a typical firm's intertemporal maximization problem a theoretical investment demand function that includes both replacement investment as a function of the *level* of output and the interest rate, and net investment as a function of *changes* in output—the accelerator principle—and the interest rate.

The alternative interpretation of the first-order conditions from the firm's maximization problem, known as Tobin's *q*-theory, emphasizes the role of the stock market evaluation of the firm and lags in adjustment of investment. This view is outlined after the discussion of the accelerator model.

The theoretical framework includes the *user cost of capital* as a variable explaining equilibrium capital stock. Discussion of the user cost takes us into the role of profits and liquidity as partial determinants of investment demand through the interest rate and user cost.

   After the theory of investment demand has been developed, we summarize the empirical results concerning the response of investment to changes in output and the cost of capital, in terms of both the size and time dimensions. Since the theory leads to an investment function in the static model of the form $i = i(r, y)$, where $\partial i/\partial y > 0$, the possibility is raised that the IS curve is positively sloped and the economy is unstable. The empirical findings suggest that the *marginal propensity to spend*—the sum of $\partial i/\partial y$ and the MPC out of GNP—is in fact less than unity so that the IS curve is negatively sloped. Finally, we end with some comments on monetary and fiscal policy, to be extended in Chapter 16. But the best place to begin is back with the present value criterion and the microeconomic theory of investment.

THE PRESENT VALUE CRITERION FOR INVESTMENT

In Chapter 4 we suggested that a firm should rank investment programs by the present discounted value of the projects' income streams,

$$PV_t = -C + R_t + \frac{R_{t+1}}{1+r} + \frac{R_{t+2}}{(1+r)^2} + \cdots + \frac{R_{t+n}}{(1+r)^n}, \tag{1}$$

where C is the cost of the project, and $R_t, \ldots, R_{t+n}$ is the stream of net returns. A natural starting point for a discussion of investment demand is the rationale of the PV criterion and its implications for the determinants of investment. To develop the rationale of the PV criterion, let us look at a simple firm owned by persons who want to maximize their utility as a function of a stream of real consumption as in Chapter 12,

$$U = U(c_0, c_1, \ldots, c_T), \tag{2}$$

where $c_0, \ldots, c_T$ is the consumption stream from time 0 to time T.

   The firm has the following kind of sales and income possibilities. With a given amount of resources in period 0, the firm can produce net output for sale in all the periods 0 through T. Its net revenues in each period can then be either disbursed to the owners as income, $y_0, \ldots, y_T$, or invested to produce a greater amount of output at some future date. Thus, by reducing current income, the owners can increase future income by investing the firm's retained earnings. An increase in income in any one period, y_t, requires a decrease in some other period. This decrease can come before period t in order to generate more total revenue in t, so that additional income can be withdrawn then without reducing income beyond period t. Or the decrease could come after t as a result of reduced investment in t.

From the point of view of the firm's owners, this situation can be expressed by an *income possibility curve,*

$$0 = \phi(y_0, y_1, \ldots, y_T). \tag{3}$$

If we hold all but two y's constant, then an increase in one y requires a decrease in the other. This must be true for any pair of y's. The problem, now, is for the firm to choose the set of y's, given its initial endowment of resources—cash or, in general, capital—that will permit the owners to maximize utility. In the two-period case, this income possibility curve is shown in Figure 13-1 as $0 = \phi(y_0, y_1)$. From a maximum income in time 0, y_0^{max}, which is equal to the total initial resource endowment, the firm's owners can trade income in time 0 for income in time 1 through the investment process, with diminishing returns. The slope of the income possibility curve of Figure 13-1 can be obtained by total differentiation of equation (3) in the two-period case:

$$0 = \frac{\partial \phi}{\partial y_0} dy_0 + \frac{\partial \phi}{\partial y_1} dy_1,$$

so that the *marginal rate of transformation (MRT)* of y_0 into y_1 is given by

$$\frac{dy_1}{dy_0} = - \frac{\partial \phi / \partial y_0}{\partial \phi / \partial y_1}. \tag{4}$$

The firm can produce any income stream y_0, y_1 on the income possibility curve of Figure 13-1, given its initial resources.

Once the firm chooses an income stream, such as point A in Figure 13-1, the owners can then borrow or lend to a consumption point along a budget constraint with slope $-(1 + r)$ in exactly the same fashion as we showed in Chapter 12. A set of such budget lines is shown in Figure 13-1. The problem

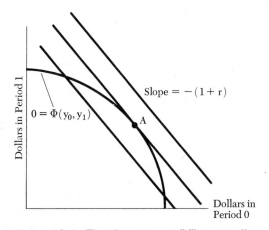

Figure 13-1 The "income possibility curve."

here is to choose an income stream y_0, y_1 along the income possibility curve that gets the owners to the highest possible budget line. As shown in Figure 13-1, the highest budget line that can be reached is the one just tangent to the income possibility curve, where $MRT = -(1 + r)$.

In Figure 13-2, we have added to the picture the owners' indifference curves from the utility function (2). These show rising levels of utility as one moves northeast, that is, $U_0 < U_1 < U_2$. As we saw in Chapter 12, the slope of an indifference curve can be derived from the utility function (2) in the two-period case:

$$0 = \frac{\partial U}{\partial c_0} dc_0 + \frac{\partial U}{\partial c_1} dc_1,$$

so that the *marginal rate of substitution (MRS)* of c_1 for c_0 is given by

$$\frac{dc_1}{dc_0} = -\frac{\partial U/\partial c_0}{\partial U/\partial c_1}. \tag{5}$$

Figure 13-2 shows that the owners reach their highest possible indifference curve by finding an indifference curve tangent to the *highest possible budget line.* So production is arranged by the firm to reach the highest budget line where $MRT = -(1 + r)$, for example, point A in Figure 13-2. The owners then transform this income stream into a utility-maximizing consumption stream by borrowing or lending to the highest possible indifference curve, where MRS is also equal to $-(1 + r)$. This gives us the condition for utility maximization in this case that combines both production and consumption decisions,

$$MRT = -(1 + r) = MRS. \tag{6}$$

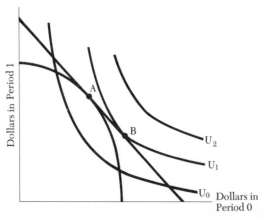

Figure 13-2 The investment and consumption decisions.

Now the intercept of the budget line on the horizontal period 0-axis is given by the present value of the y_0, y_1 income stream,

$$PV_0 = y_0 + \frac{y_1}{1 + r}, \tag{7}$$

as we also saw in Chapter 12. But this means that to reach the highest possible budget line, the firm should maximize present value—move to the budget line with the farthest-right time 0 intercept in Figures 13-1 and 13-2, given the location of the income possibility curve. Once this maximum PV line has been reached, the owners can worry about reaching the highest possible indifference curve independently of the production decision. Thus, the owners can insure that they can (but not will; this is a *necessary,* not *sufficient* condition) reach the maximum possible U level by giving the firm's manager the rule: Maximize present value! Following this rule will maximize the value of the firm and its owner's stock market shares.

The manager doesn't need any information on the shape of the owner's utility function and indifference curves: the production and consumption decisions are completely separate. Thus, the firm that is trying to maximize its owner's welfare will follow the rule: Maximize PV. In the economy this will result in equating the MRT along the production function to MRS along indifference curves, a basic condition for economic efficiency.

Now if the economy is populated by firms that are trying to maximize their owners' welfare in a competitive capitalist economy or directly to maximize the social value of output in a socialist economy—note that the first case may also maximize the social value of output—they will order investment plans to maximize the present discounted value of the income stream coming from the sum of all investment projects, that is, the capital stock. Any investment rule that is not consistent with maximizing PV will not achieve these ends, and thus will not be consistent with profit (or welfare) maximization in a competitive economy.

This kind of reasoning led us, in Chapter 4, to the investment rule that the firm should maximize its present value by investing in any project with positive PV, where PV is defined as in equation (1):

$$PV_t = -C + R_t + \frac{R_{t+1}}{1 + r} + \frac{R_{t+2}}{(1 + r)^2} + \cdots + \frac{R_{t+n}}{(1 + r)^n}.$$

Under the present value criterion, the firm computes a present value for each possible project it might undertake, and then ranks the projects in order of their PV's. This ranking is represented in Figure 13-3. The vertical axis measures the present value of each investment relative to its cost, and the horizontal axis gives the real value of the sum of all investment projects. In order to

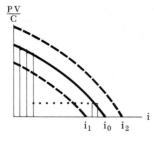

Figure 13-3 Ranking investment projects in order of their PV's.

maximize its present value, the firm should invest in all projects that have a $PV > 0$. This gives an equilibrium level of real investment for the firm of i_0, where the present value of the marginal project is zero.

As can be seen from the PV expression in equation (1), an increase in the market interest rate reduces the present value of each investment project. This causes a downward shift in the curve in Figure 13-3 and reduces the firm's equilibrium investment level to i_1. On the other hand, if the expected returns in each period increase, perhaps because of an increase in demand in the present period, which is expected to be fairly permanent, the curve shifts up, and a higher level of investment, i_2, results. This is the basic theory behind the simple investment function of Part II.

THE MARGINAL EFFICIENCY OF INVESTMENT

A different criterion for investment decisions was suggested by Keynes and has been used in macroeconomic texts ever since. This is the *marginal efficiency of investment* criterion. This criterion is very convenient as a teaching device but has its analytical weaknesses. The marginal efficiency of an investment project, m, is *defined* as the rate of interest that will discount the PV of the project to zero. Thus, m is defined by

$$0 = C + R_t + \frac{R_{t+1}}{1 + m} + \frac{R_{t+2}}{(1 + m)^2} + \cdots + \frac{R_{t+n}}{(1 + m)^n}. \qquad (8)$$

If, with any given C and R stream, we solve (8) for m, we have the interest rate that would discount the project's net returns back to zero.

Investment programs can be ranked by m, much as they were by PV. It would seem that a project with a "high" returns stream would have a "high" PV and thus require a "high" m to discount the net returns stream to zero. Thus, m can be plotted against i, as shown in Figure 13-4, much as PV was in Figure 13-3. As the size of the total investment program is increased, we go to projects with lower and lower R streams, so that as i rises, m falls.

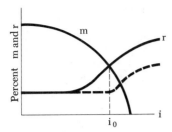

Figure 13-4 The "marginal efficiency of investment" criterion.

The Supply of Funds

This *m* function, representing investment demand, can now be confronted by a *supply-of-funds* schedule to determine the equilibrium level of investment, similar to i_0 in Figure 13-3. This supply schedule, *r*, is shown in Figure 13-4. It shows that up to a certain point the interest cost of financing investment is roughly constant. But as the size of the investment program goes beyond that point the cost of borrowing, or the opportunity cost of using retained earnings, begins to rise. Thus, the *r* curve in Figure 13-4 can be regarded as a supply-of-funds schedule. The *m* curve, which gives the interest rate at which each successive project could just break even, can be regarded as an investment demand schedule. The intersection of the *m* and *r* schedules determines i_0. To the left of i_0 all projects have positive *PV*'s since $m > r$.

As we will see in a moment, this model is not satisfactory as a general criterion for investment demand. However, it does have an advantage in that it points out that there may be more than one *cost of capital* or interest rate facing a firm, depending on the extent to which it draws on various sources of investment funds, and these various cost of capital levels affect the firm's decision to invest. For example, firms tend to *impute* a lower interest rate to funds that are available from retained earnings. Higher interest rates are imputed to external sources of funding such as bond issues because they represent a fixed liability that must be paid on time regardless of the financial position of the firm, or stocks because they dilute the management's degree of control over the firm.

The possible sources of internal financing, of course, consist of depreciation and retained earnings, after-tax profits less dividends. Since internal financing is imputed a lower interest rate, it can be visualized as the flat part of the *r* curve in Figure 13-4, borrowed from Duesenberry. As profits increase, the amount of internal funds which are available for investing increases, and the flat part of the *r* curve is extended, as is shown by the dashed line in Figure 13-4. Thus, an increase in profits will lead to an increase in investment by shifting out the supply-of-funds curve, *r* in Figure 13-4. Conversely, a lower profit rate shifts the supply curve left and reduces the level of investment.

The profit level, through the supply-of-funds schedule and the cost of capital, is undoubtedly an important determinant of investment demand, as we will see later in this chapter. But the marginal efficiency of investment is, nevertheless, not a very useful analytic device. The difficulty with the marginal efficiency of investment criterion is that it does not necessarily yield the same ranking of investment projects as the present value criterion. Intuitively, it should be clear that if we compare two projects, one of which has large returns in the distant future, the other with smaller returns coming sooner, the first will have a higher PV at some low interest rate, while the second project will have a higher PV at some higher rate that pushes down the PV of the distant returns of the first project.

Present Value and Marginal Efficiency

The important point here is that the PV ranking depends on the *market* rate of interest—the rate at which earnings can be reinvested—while the marginal efficiency of investment is not related to the market rate. So the PV rankings can be different from m rankings.

The best way to see this is to look at an example that can be easily generalized. Suppose we have two investment projects, both with cost $C = 1$ ($1000 perhaps). Both projects have zero return in period 1, when they are being built. Project 1 returns 0 in period 2, and 4 in period 3; project II returns 2 in period 2, and 1 in period 3. This information is summarized in the left-hand part of Table 13-1.

Now let's calculate the m values for these two projects. For project I we have

$$0 = -1 + 0 + \frac{0}{1 + m} + \frac{4}{(1 + m)^2}.$$

Solving this equation for m, we have $(1 + m)^2 = 4$, and $m = 1$, as shown in Table 13-1. For project II the m equation is

$$0 = -1 + 0 + \frac{2}{1 + m} + \frac{1}{(1 + m)^2}.$$

Moving the -1 to the other side of the equation and multiplying both sides by $(1 + m)^2$ gives

Table 13-1   MARGINAL EFFICIENCY AND PRESENT VALUE

	Cost	Return in period 2	Return in period 3	m	PV $r = 0$	PV $r = 1$
Project I	1	0	4	1	3	0
Project II	1	2	1	1.414	2	0.25

$$(1 + m)^2 = 1 + 2m + m^2 = 2 + 2m + 1,$$

where the middle term is just $(1 + m)^2$ written out. Subtracting $(1 + 2m)$ from both sides of the right-hand equation gives us $m^2 = 2$, or $m = 1.414$ for project II, again shown in Table 13-1. As the table shows, both projects have the same costs, but one has a very low return in period 2 and a high return in period 3, while the other has a moderate return in period 2 and a low return in period 3. The marginal efficiency of investment criterion indicates that project II is unequivocally better than project I, since $m_2 > m_1$.

However, under the present value criterion there is no unequivocally correct answer because the PV ranking depends on the market interest rate. With $r = 0$, project I has a present discounted value given by

$$PV = -1 + 0 + \frac{0}{1} + \frac{4}{1} = 3,$$

while project II has a PV given by

$$PV = -1 + 0 + \frac{2}{1} + \frac{1}{1} = 2,$$

so that at the (very) low rate $r = 0$, project I, with its high, but delayed, returns, is superior. With $r = 1$, project I has a PV given by

$$PV = -1 + 0 + \frac{0}{2} + \frac{4}{4} = 0,$$

while project II's PV is

$$PV = -1 + 0 + \frac{2}{2} + \frac{1}{4} = 0.25.$$

Thus, at a very high interest rate that discounts project I's returns heavily, project II is preferable. These PV results are shown in the last column of Table 13-1. They illustrate the deficiency of the marginal efficiency criterion for ranking investment projects. This criterion makes no reference to the market rate of interest, which measures the opportunity cost of investment.

The example we have just used can be generalized, as is shown in Figure 13-5, where the PV's of projects I and II are plotted as functions of the market interest rate. Table 13-1 shows that when $r = 0$, the PV of project I is 3, and the PV of project II is 2. The table also locates the PV's of the two projects where $r = 1$. Since at low r, $PV(I) > PV(II)$, while at a high r, $PV(I) < PV(II)$, there must be some r in between where the PV's are equal. To find this value of r, we set $PV(I) = PV(II)$:

$$0 - 1 + \frac{0}{1 + r} + \frac{4}{(1 + r)^2} = 0 - 1 + \frac{2}{1 + r} + \frac{1}{(1 + r)^2}.$$

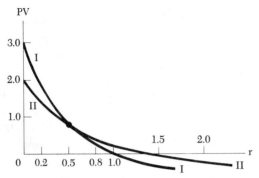

Figure 13-5   Present value and the market interest rate.

Dropping $(0 - 1)$ from both sides and multiplying through by $(1 + r)^2$ gives us

$$4 = 2r + 2 + 1 \quad \text{and} \quad r = 0.5.$$

At $r = 0.5$, the PV of both projects is 0.78, locating the equal PV point in Figure 13-5. At interest rates below 0.5, project I will have the higher PV; above 0.5, project II wins. Thus, a firm can obtain a true ranking of investment projects in terms of their opportunity costs by computing PV for each project at the relevant market rate of interest.

The *PV* Criterion and the Supply of Funds

In the discussion of the present value criterion at the beginning of this chapter, we assumed that the firm faces a competitive capital market, so that the interest rate at which it can borrow appears fixed. In that case, the firm invests until it reaches the marginal project with $PV = 0$, as shown in Figure 13-3. But then we saw that the firm might face a rising supply-of-funds schedule, shown in Figure 13-4. It was this likelihood that led to the use of the marginal efficiency of investment schedule as a demand curve. Now that we have seen why the marginal efficiency rule is not satisfactory, we must ask, how should a firm facing a rising supply-of-funds schedule jointly choose the level of the interest rate and the total amount of investment it should undertake applying the PV rule? The answer is fairly simple.

The firm can build a PV function in the following way. First, choose an initial low level of total investment, i_0. From Figure 13-4's supply-of-funds schedule, the interest rate needed to finance i_0 can be determined. This interest rate can then be applied to all possible projects to calculate PV's, and the maximum PV obtainable within i_0, PV_0, can be plotted as in Figure 13-6. As the firm then increases i, repeating this procedure, PV should first rise and then fall as the firm encounters a rising supply-of-funds schedule. The firm

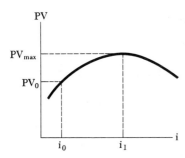

Figure 13-6 Determination of the level of investment.

should then select the level of investment, i_1, that maximizes PV at PV_{max} in Figure 13-6. The interest rate needed to finance this PV-maximizing level of investment can be obtained from the supply-of-funds schedule.

This procedure will yield an equilibrium level of investment for any given supply-of-funds schedule. An upward shift in that schedule, corresponding to an increase in the interest rate, will then raise the interest rate needed to finance any given level of investment, reducing the total PV that can be obtained with each i level. Thus, an increase in interest rates will shift the PV function of Figure 13-6 to the left and down, reducing the equilibrium level of investment under the PV rule. So with a rising supply-of-funds schedule, an increase in the interest rate r will reduce equilibrium i. This gives the $i = i(r)$ function of Part II.

What we now have developed is a static view of investment, in the following sense. Once the equilibrium level of investment has been reached, and if interest rates and expected returns do not change, there will be no net investment beyond the current period. Firms will have built the desired level of capital stock to produce the expected returns, or sales; all future investment will be to replace that part of the capital stock that wears out. There would be a further incentive to invest in future periods only if interest rates dropped or if there were an increase in expected sales. Either of these circumstances would raise to a level above zero the present value of projects which were rejected in previous calculations. Thus, the static PV model explains the amount of net investment that will bring the capital stock up to the optimum amount needed to produce a given level of output at a given interest rate. Once this desired capital stock is in place, there is no incentive for further net investment unless the level of output or the interest rate changes. It is the *growth* of output that induces continuing *net* investment. We can now turn to a more dynamic approach to the investment demand function that has been developed in the economics literature of the past twenty years.

INVESTMENT DEMAND AND OUTPUT GROWTH

The relationship between the *growth rate* of output and the *level* of net investment implied in the previous section is called the *accelerator principle* since it suggests that an increase in the growth rate of output—an acceleration—is needed to increase the level of investment. The *PV* criterion suggests that this relationship between output growth and net investment is not a fixed one, however. An increase in the interest rate should reduce the level of net investment associated with a given growth rate of output. This variable relationship between the growth rate of output and the level of net investment is frequently called the *flexible-accelerator* model, which we will develop in some detail in this section.

There are two distinct steps in the development of the flexible-accelerator model. The first step involves the determination of the desired level of the capital stock K^E. We will derive this level from the problem of the firm maximizing the present value of its expected profit stream. The labor-demand function of Chapter 6 will reappear as an output of this maximization problem. The second step is to translate movements in the desired, or equilibrium, capital stock into a flow of realized net investment. This involves an investment demand function that includes both net and replacement investment with the appropriate lags behind movements in the equilibrium capital stock. This second step shows how movements in actual investment are related to changes in the equilibrium capital stock ΔK^E. The development of investment demand in this section follows the pioneering work of Dale Jorgenson.

Equilibrium Capital Stock

The determinants of the desired capital stock can be derived from the present value maximization of a firm that looks to its expected future profit stream when it makes current investment decisions. This problem is quite similar to the problem of the consumer maximizing lifetime utility which we discussed in Chapter 12. Both are forward-looking, and both involve the effects of current decisions on future opportunities. The consumer's decision relates present to future via saving; the firm's decision does it through investment.

We can begin with the constraints facing the firm. The first is the technologically given production function, which we introduced in general form in Part II as

$$y_t = y(N_t, K_t); \qquad \frac{\partial y}{\partial N}; \qquad \frac{\partial y}{\partial K} > 0. \tag{9}$$

Here y_t is output per unit of time, N_t is worker-hours of input, and K_t is the capital stock—plant and equipment. Below we will shorten the notation for the two marginal products to $y_N \equiv \partial y/\partial N$ and $y_K \equiv \partial y/\partial K$. Implicitly, we assume here a constant rate of utilization of the capital stock, so that there is a one-to-one relationship between capital stock and machine-hour input. This assumption will be relaxed later.

The second constraint facing the firm is that its capital depreciates, so that it takes some investment—replacement investment—just to keep the effective capital stock constant. For simplicity, we will assume that a fixed proportion δ of the capital stock becomes obsolescent each period. Here δ is the *depreciation rate*. If total, or *gross,* investment at any time t is i_t, this means that the capital stock evolves according to

$$K_{t+1} = K_t + i_t - \delta K_t = (1 - \delta)K_t + i_t. \tag{10}$$

During any given quarter t, the firm takes its existing capital stock K_t as given. It uses up a fixed proportion δK_t in the production process during the quarter. Meanwhile, it also installs new investment i_t, which will not begin depreciating until the next quarter. So equation (10) gives the capital stock at the beginning of the next quarter $(t + 1)$.

The firm maximizes the present value of its future profit stream, subject to the constraints of equations (9) and (10). Profits are given by the value of sales, $P_t y_t$, less the wage bill $W_t N_t$, less expenditures on investment goods, $P_t^I i_t$. Here P^I is the price of plant and equipment—the plant and equipment deflator in the national income and product accounts. So the maximand is present value, given by

$$PV = (P_0 y_0 - W_0 N_0 - P_0^I i_0) + \frac{1}{1 + r}(P_1 y_1 - W_1 N_1 - P_1^I i_1)$$

$$+ \cdots + \frac{1}{(1 + r)} t(P_t y_t - W_t N_t - P_t^I i_t) + \cdots.$$

If the firm expects to continue in business indefinitely, this summation will go infinitely far into the future. Present value can be summed up as

$$PV_0 = \sum_0^\alpha \frac{1}{(1 + r)^t}(P_t y_t - W_t N_t - P_t^I i_t). \tag{11}$$

The analogous expression for the maximand in the consumer's problem is equation (9) in Chapter 12. To simplify the exposition here, we put aside considerations of uncertainty, so we do not write explicitly that future profits are *expected.* We also assume that the firm is *competitive;* it is a price-taker in all markets.

Now we can proceed to the firm's maximization problem, which is to maximize PV in equation (11), subject to the constraints given by equations (9) and (10). Because the production function (9) holds for all periods, we can substitute it into the present value expression to obtain

$$PV_0 = \sum_0^\alpha \frac{1}{(1 + r)^t}[P_t y(N_t, K_t) - W_t N_t - P_t^I i_t]. \tag{12}$$

The firm now faces the problem of choosing its inputs N_t and K_t and investment i_t to maximize PV in (12), given the period-by-period constraints in (10). This problem is usually written in the form

$$\max_{N_t,K_t,i_t} \sum_0^\alpha \frac{1}{(1+r)^t} [P_t y(N_t, K_t) - W_t N_t - P_t^I i_t],$$

subject to the constraints for each period t that

$$K_{t+1} = (1 - \delta)K_t + i_t.$$

Here we have a separate constraint for each period; in the consumer problem there was one overall lifetime budget constraint.

To solve this problem, we again use the method of *Lagrange multipliers*. Since the depreciation constraint is renewed each quarter, we need a new multiplier for each quarter. Thus, the *Lagrangean* expression that combines the objective and the constraint into one expression is

$$\max_{N_t,K_t,i_t,\lambda_t} L = \sum_0^\alpha \frac{1}{(1+r)^t} [P_t y(K_t, N_t) - W_t N_t - P_t^I i_t]$$

$$+ \sum_0^\alpha \lambda_t [i_t + (1 - \delta)K_t - K_{t+1}].$$

The constraint links capital stocks over time through investment.

A complete solution of the problem can now be obtained by partially differentiating with respect to all N's, K's, i's, and λ's, and setting these differentials to zero. This would give us the entire investment program and employment demand into the indefinite future. We can derive the equilibrium capital stock of the typical period by looking at each period's *first-order conditions:*

$$\frac{\partial L}{\partial N_t} = \frac{1}{(1+r)^t} (P_t y_N - W_t) = 0. \tag{13a}$$

$$\frac{\partial L}{\partial K_t} = \frac{1}{(1+r)^t} [P_t y_K + \lambda_t(1 - \delta) - \lambda_{t-1}] = 0. \tag{13b}$$

$$\frac{\partial L}{\partial i_t} \equiv -\frac{1}{(1+r)^t} P_t^I + \lambda_t = 0. \tag{13c}$$

$$\frac{\partial L}{\partial \lambda_t} = i_t + (1 - \delta)K_t - K_{t+1} = 0. \tag{13d}$$

One potentially puzzling point about equation (13b) is the presence of λ_{t-1}. This comes in because K_t is the end-of-period capital stock for period $t - 1$.

The expression in equation (13a) is simply the demand for labor from Chapter 6, setting the marginal product of labor equal to the real wage:

$$y_N(N_t, K_t) = \frac{W_t}{P_t}. \qquad (14)$$

Since implicitly labor is hired anew each period, each period's labor demand just depends on that period's real wage.

To solve for the desired capital stock, we combine equations (13b) and (13c). Equation (13c) says that

$$\lambda_t = \frac{P_t^I}{(1 + r)^t}.$$

Similarly, equation (13c) for period $t - 1$ would tell us that

$$\lambda_{t-1} = \frac{P_{t-1}^I}{(1 + r)^{t-1}}.$$

If we substitute these expressions into equation (13b) for λ_t and λ_{t-1}, we get

$$\frac{1}{(1 + r)^t} \left[P_t y_K + \frac{P_t^I(1 - \delta)}{(1 + r)^t} - \frac{P_{t-1}^I}{(1 + r)^{t-1}} \right] = 0. \qquad (15)$$

If we multiply the bracketed term in this expression by $(1 + r)^t$ and solve for the marginal product of capital y_K, we obtain

$$y_K = \frac{\delta P_t^I + r P_{t-1}^I - (P_t^I - P_{t-1}^I)}{P_t}. \qquad (16)$$

The numerator on the right-hand side of equation (16) is the *user cost of capital*, C_t. It is the cost per period of using the capital stock, the equivalent of a rental price, here implicit. The first term is the depreciation charge per unit of capital used in time t; to obtain this charge, multiply the depreciation rate δ times the cost of investment goods in that period. The second term is the interest charge for holding the capital stock valued at P_{t-1}^I at the beginning of period t. The last term is any capital gain on the capital stock from the beginning of the period. Equation (15) states that the capital stock should be expanded until the marginal product of capital equals its real user cost:

$$y_K(N_t, K_t) = \frac{C_t}{P_t} \equiv c_t. \qquad (17)$$

The implicit solution of equation (17) will give us the equilibrium capital stock K^E as a function of output, the user cost, and the price of output:

$$K^E = K^E(Y, C, P), \qquad (18)$$

with $\partial K^E / \partial y$ and $\partial K^E / \partial P$ both positive, and $\partial K^E / \partial C$ negative.

A Cobb-Douglas Example

Jorgenson first worked out investment demand assuming a Cobb-Douglas production function, named after its originators, Charles W. Cobb and (Senator) Paul H. Douglas. Cobb and Douglas specified their production function as

$$y = aK^\alpha N^{1-\alpha}. \tag{19}$$

This production function has the property that the exponents of the inputs add up to one, which gives constant returns to scale. If capital and labor inputs are doubled, output will also double. The marginal product of capital in the Cobb-Douglas function is given by

$$\frac{\partial y}{\partial K} = \frac{\alpha a K^\alpha N^{1-\alpha}}{K} = \frac{\alpha y}{K},$$

substituting y back in for $aK^\alpha N^{1-\alpha}$. Thus, with the Cobb-Douglas function, in equilibrium,

$$\frac{\partial y}{\partial K} = \frac{\alpha y}{K} = \frac{C}{P}. \tag{20}$$

The right-hand equation in (20) can be solved for the equilibrium level of the capital stock in the Cobb-Douglas function,

$$K^E = \frac{\alpha P y}{C} = \frac{\alpha y}{C/P}. \tag{21}$$

The equilibrium capital stock rises with an increase in y and falls with an increase in the real user cost of capital. Equation (21) gives the expression for K^E for a particular production function. It is a special form of the more general expression for K^E in equation (18) above.

The Investment Demand Function

So far we have derived an expression for the equilibrium capital stock, equation (18) for K^E, from the firm's maximization problem. Now we can derive an investment demand function from changes in K^E. We can begin by rearranging equation (10) to show the components of gross investment i^g:

$$i_t^g = K_{t+1} - K_t + \delta K_t. \tag{22}$$

Here we have added the superscript g to denote gross investment. On the right-hand side of (22), $K_{t+1} - K_t$ is net investment i^n, and depreciation δK_t is replacement investment i^r. So gross investment is the sum of net investment and replacement investment:

$$i^g = i^n + i^r. \tag{23}$$

(From here on we'll drop the time subscripts where they are not needed.)

Replacement investment is that part of gross investment needed to keep the capital stock at a constant level, and it is equal to the economic depreciation of the capital stock in any one period. Net investment is that part of gross investment that increases the level of capital stock. Thus, replacement investment is simply each period's depreciation of δK of the capital stock,

$$i^r = \delta K, \tag{24}$$

where δ is the depreciation rate, a number like one-tenth. Net investment, in the absence of lags in the adjustment process of actual capital stock to desired capital stock, would be

$$i^n = \Delta K^E, \tag{25}$$

where K^E is taken from equation (18). Thus, we can see that net investment depends on changes in the equilibrium level of the capital stock, whereas replacement investment depends on the level of the capital stock.

Let's look first at net investment. In the Cobb-Douglas production function, from equation (21)

$$i^n = \Delta K^E = \Delta\left(\frac{\alpha P y}{C}\right). \tag{26}$$

If we assume that the ratio of the user cost of capital to the price level, C/P, remains fairly constant over time, we can rewrite this equation as

$$i^n = \left(\frac{\alpha P}{C}\right)\Delta y.$$

This makes it clear that over the long run, with no trend in C/P, it is the growth of output, or demand, that gives us the level of net investment.

This relation between the *change* in output and the level of net investment is the *accelerator principle*. It introduces a basic dynamic relationship into the model of the economy. Thus, if net investment is related to Δy by (26), and net investment is also some given fraction—the net saving ratio s—of y,

$$i^n = sy,$$

then we have the basic growth relationship

$$sy = \left(\frac{\alpha P}{C}\right)\Delta y,$$

and

$$\frac{\Delta y}{y} = \text{growth rate of } y = \frac{s}{\alpha P/C}. \qquad (27)$$

Since investment *increases* the *supply* of output by increasing the capital stock, but is also associated with the *level* of *demand* through the multiplier, (27) gives the rate of growth of output that would maintain supply = demand. Growth models are discussed at length in Part V. Here we are just interested in exposing the link between investment and growth.

With the introduction of the accelerator, we have moved into the dynamics of the economy. We will soon see that the accelerator can create some difficult dynamic stabilization problems. But first let's look at total investment using the concepts of net and replacement investment which we have developed. From equations (23)–(25) we have

$$i^g = i^n + i^r = \Delta K^E + \delta K, \qquad (28)$$

putting aside, for the time being, the problem of lagged adjustment of actual to desired investment. In the general case, we can write the investment equation as

$$i^g = \Delta K^E(y, C, P) + \delta K. \qquad (29)$$

In the Cobb-Douglas example, i_g is given by

$$i^g = \Delta\left(\frac{\alpha Py}{C}\right) + \delta K,$$

and in the special case where the real user cost, c, is fairly constant, we have

$$i^g = \frac{\alpha}{c}\cdot \Delta y + \delta K,$$

the accelerator relationship.

The Accelerator and Stabilization Policy

The accelerator relationship in the gross investment function, equation (29), poses an interesting difficulty for short-run stabilization policy. The problem is illustrated in Figure 13-7, which shows, in essence, what happens to investment as output in the economy rises from one stable level to another. In Figure 13-7, we show two time periods, 0 to t_1, and t_2 on, and a transition period of unspecified length between the two. In the first period there is a given level of

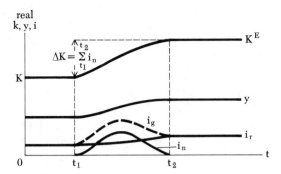

Figure 13-7 The "accelerator principle" of investment.

output y, which implies a given equilibrium capital stock K. At time t_1, the government increases government purchases g to stimulate demand, and output and equilibrium capital stock move to new, higher levels in the second period, from t_2 on. Since the capital stock is constant both before t_1 and after t_2, the level of net investment is zero in each period, and the level of i_r is positive in each.

In order for the capital stock to increase to its new higher level in the second period, there must be a positive level of net investment in the transition period. This is indicated by the bulge in i_n between t_1 and t_2. Since i_g is the sum of i_n and i_r, this means that, during the transition period, gross investment demand i_g also has this bulge, shown by the dashed line in Figure 13-7. Thus, total investment in each period is as follows:

$$\text{From 0 to } t_1, \quad i_g = i_r;$$

$$\text{From } t_1 \text{ to } t_2, \quad i_g = i_r + i_n;$$

$$\text{From } t_2 \text{ on}, \quad i_g = i_r.$$

From Figure 13-7 it is clear that in the first part of the transition period the growth rate of total investment i_g is greater than the growth rate of the economy as a whole given by the slope of y. Thus, if the economy is running at less than full employment, as it was in the early 1960s, a monetary or fiscal policy change designed to bring the economy up to the full-employment growth path runs the risk of temporarily overshooting the desired growth of demand. Initially, demand will grow at an apparently excessive and unsustainable rate because of the i_n buildup needed to increase the capital stock. But after this initial period of rapid growth, net investment will fall off again to its normal level in a growing economy. The important point to recognize is that the accelerator effect will produce a *temporarily* rapid growth of demand which will subside.

Capacity Utilization and the Accelerator

It should be clear that the accelerator relationship may not hold if the economy is operating with substantial excess plant capacity, that is, at a low capacity-utilization rate. In this case, the actual capital stock is greater than equilibrium, so that an increase in output can raise the equilibrium capital stock up toward the actual existing stock with little effect on net investment. Thus, to the extent that substantial excess capacity exists, fiscal policy can stimulate demand without encountering the difficulty described in the last section.

This qualification of the accelerator principle should be interpreted with care, however. Much of what appears to be excess capacity at any one time may actually be obsolete plant that embodies old, uneconomic technology. In this case, a major increase in demand could be temporarily met by bringing old plant back on the line, but after a while producers will replace this plant with newer plant embodying up-to-date technology. Thus, the accelerator effect might appear with a delay as an upsurge in replacement investment.

Demand Constraint and the Accelerator

In deriving the accelerator relationship between growth in output and investment, we began with a micro-level model of a firm that takes output y as predetermined when it makes the investment decision. This is clearly not the standard model of the competitive firm that we see in intermediate microeconomics. There the competitive firm faces given prices, wages, and capital costs, and makes output and input decisions simultaneously. This would give us an investment function that included all relative prices, but not output.

At the macro level, however, it is important to include output in the investment function. Total sales in the economy are constrained by aggregate demand; the equilibrium P,y point must be on the DD curve. One way to enter output into the investment demand function at the micro level is to drop the assumption that the firms involved are perfect competitors. In this case, the firm would face a downward-sloping demand curve relating its P and y. Then the P, y combination in equation (13), for example, would be determined. Thus, to the extent that U.S. firms follow a monopolist, oligopolist, or monopolistic competitor model, output could enter the investment demand function at the micro level.

Perhaps a better approach to inclusion of output in the investment equation is deriving the accelerator relationship from a constraint on total output. This has been suggested by Herschel Grossman. If total sales are constrained by the aggregate DD curve at the going price level, firms will see y as predetermined when making factor-input decisions. In this case output would enter the investment function. This interpretation of the accelerator relationship is analogous to the disequilibrium interpretation of the consumption function.

Here, if prices are slow to adjust, firms see a sales constraint along *DD*. In the consumption case, if wages are slow to adjust, worker-consumers see an income constraint along the labor-demand curve.

Again, the disequilibrium view gives us a new interpretation of the multiplier. Here, if there is an exogenous drop in demand, firms see demand-constrained sales fall at the existing price level. As they cut back in factor demand, this reduces investment directly and consumption through a drop in employment. This feeds back on sales, tightening that constraint, and so on. This is the fixed-price multiplier of Chapter 3.

Eventually, prices and wages do adjust, however, and the system moves to the equilibrium described in Part II. But the disequilibrium approach gives us a way to describe behavior out of equilibrium, and a useful view of both the accelerator and the consumption function. In Chapter 18 we will study in detail a full disequilibrium model with no wage or price adjustment. Here we continue in the flexible wage-and-price framework of the text.

THE *q*-THEORY OF INVESTMENT

Thus far, we have set aside three important aspects of the investment decision. First, we have the lags and adjustment costs inherent in selecting and implementing any capital investment project. A fully rational firm would take such things into account when choosing the amount and timing of investment; even the desired capital stock should be a function of these constraints. Second, we have skipped over the question of how expectations about future costs and payoffs are formulated. This point is intimately related to the first, if only because it may take time to form a clear opinion about the permanence and long-run effects of any change in the environment. The third aspect which has yet to be dealt with is the question of risk and its evaluation by the market. No one has really tackled all three problems at once, and even taken individually a full treatment of these problems is well beyond the scope of this text. However, we can sketch an approach to investment which hopes to deal with these complications. This is the approach known as Tobin's *q*-theory, after the research of James Tobin and by Tobin and William Brainard.

Let us start by multiplying the first-order condition for capital from our maximizing problem, the term in brackets in equation (15), through by $(1 + r)^t$. This gives us another version of that condition:

$$P_t y_K + P_t^I(1 - \delta) - P_{t-1}^I(1 + r) = 0. \qquad (30)$$

This can be rearranged (for reasons that will soon be clear) as the following expression:

$$\frac{[1/(1 + r)][P_t y_K + P_t^I(1 - \delta)]}{P_{t-1}^I} = 1. \qquad (31)$$

The expression on the left-hand side of equation (31) is Tobin's *marginal q*. The denominator is the cost of acquiring a small increment to the capital stock in period $t - 1$. The numerator is the increment from that acquisition to the value of the firm in period t, discounted back to $t - 1$. The term $P_t y_K$ is the increase in sales, and the term $P_t^I(1 - \delta)$ is the increase in the value of its capital in t. The sum is discounted back to $t - 1$ by dividing it by $(1 + r)$. So Tobin's marginal q is the ratio of the change in the value of the firm to the added capital cost for a small increment to the capital stock. If the firm is in equilibrium, the value of q is unity, as in equation (31). All investments that add more to the value of the firm than their cost have already been undertaken.

Under certain circumstances—roughly speaking, constant returns to scale which imply that average and marginal products are proportional—marginal q equals the ratio of the firm's total valuation to the total cost of its capital, which is known as *average Q*:

$$Q = \frac{PV}{P^I K}. \qquad (32)$$

This has the advantage of being, in principle, directly measurable, unlike the user cost or the expected marginal revenue product of capital.

How does q-theory help us when so far it seems to be a mere reformulation of the flexible-accelerator theory presented in the previous section of this chapter? To begin with, it is (relatively) easy to introduce adjustment costs into the story. Equation (31) suggests that investment will continue until marginal q is reduced to one. With adjustment costs, we can in principle derive a relationship between gross investment and the divergence of actual q from unity. If q happens to be above 1, then investing in capital more than pays for the costs of acquiring and installing the investment goods. If q is less than 1, then one should reduce the capital stock by disinvestment or letting depreciation take its course.

Now for the best aspect of q-theory: if we know the replacement cost of capital, then we can look up the stock market value of a firm and calculate its average Q directly. That observable value of the firm already contains the market's expectations about returns over all future periods, and it adjusts for risk. The economist does not have to make controversial assumptions about how expectations are formed or how uncertainties are evaluated, when the market does this for her. The market value of the firm should also already have allowed for lags and adjustment costs in investment. Thus, q-theory acknowledges the three problems with which we started this section, but conveniently it lets other people, that is, the stock market, provide a solution.

This emphasis on financial markets in q-theory is appealing, because the individual person or firm has a choice between investment in real or financial assets. This is an example of the simultaneity of markets which we have tried to emphasize ever since Chapter 4. One useful help to intuition about q-theory starts by imagining that a firm can choose either to invest in plant and machinery, or to acquire another firm. If the Q of the target firm is less than its equilibrium level, then it is cheaper to buy the company and use its capital than to purchase the equivalent capital goods. This means that the stock market tends to equalize the value of Q across firms, so that they are all likely to react similarly to aggregate shocks.

Let us note two qualifying points about q-theory. First, the link between marginal q and average Q can be complex. Consider, for example, an oil price shock that reduces the return on the capital stock in place, so that Q goes down. Meanwhile, the same shock will raise marginal q for investments in new energy-saving capital goods. The movement in average Q is the reverse of that of marginal q.

Second, there is an unclear story in the background about the "informational efficiency" of the stock market concerning who knows what and about who makes what choices. Managers who make a firm's investment decisions, as "insiders" do not normally play the stock market, but presumably for the sake of the shareholders they will want to keep the market informed of the firm's progress. One consequence of the efficiency of the stock market is that stock prices move very erratically and, indeed, are intrinsically unpredictable. Therefore, we cannot predict Q with any accuracy, and the theory is more a descriptive tool for explaining events *ex post,* than a predictive tool for foreseeing the level of investment to come.

THE USER COST AND LIQUIDITY EFFECTS

Let us return now to the concept of the real user cost of capital, $c,$ which was introduced earlier. It is through the user cost that both the interest rate and the level of profits enter our investment demand function.

We have already defined C as the nominal value of the implicit rental of capital services used in each period. This is not a measurable input price such as a wage rate or total compensation per worker-hour, since typically capital goods are bought in one period and then used over a length of time, not rented, as are labor services. This is the major difference between the market for capital goods and that for other inputs, including labor, that makes capital theory so complex and also makes measurement of capital inputs very difficult. In an economy free of slavery, firms do not buy labor, that is, workers themselves; firms rent labor services at a wage rate, a price stated as a payment per time unit of services rendered. On the other hand, since capital goods are generally bought at one point in time and then used by their owners over a long period, there is no direct measurement of the price of a machine-hour of service of a given quality. If all capital goods were owned by persons (or firms) that rented, or leased, the goods' services to other firms, and no firm used the capital goods it owned, we would have a satisfactory measure of the value of capital services—the user cost of capital—in the rental rate. But this is not the case, so we have to construct a measurement of the user cost C, using a large input of economic theory in the process.

Suppose that a machine is purchased at price P^I. We have seen that three components make up the user cost of the good to its owner in each period of its life.

1. The first is the interest cost of the capital good, which is the opportunity cost incurred by tying up funds. This is the interest rate r times P^I. If the firm buys a machine for, say, $100,000, and the interest rate it could have lent that sum at was 5 percent per year, then the firm is giving up an opportunity cost of $5,000 per year that it could have earned in interest.
2. Next is the amount the good depreciates in each period, δP^I. If the economic depreciation rate δ is 10 percent, then the firm loses 10 percent of the value of the machine a year in depreciation—$10,000 in the first year on the $100,000 machine.
3. Any change in the market price of the good once purchased enters into user cost. If the market price of a new machine of the same model is rising through time, this will pull the price of used machines up above the price dictated by the original purchase price less depreciation. This price increases as a *capital gain*—a negative cost equal dP_I/dt, the time rate of change of P_I.

If we consider time periods that are increasingly small, the user cost C in the numerator of equation (16) will become

$$C = rP_I + \delta P_I - \frac{dP_I}{dt},$$

or

$$C = P_I(r + \delta - \dot{P}_I), \tag{33}$$

where $\dot{P}_I$ is the proportional capital gain:

$$\dot{P}_I = \frac{dP_I/dt}{P_I}.$$

The three items in equation (16) or (33) are the three discussed just above.

Equation (33) can be rewritten as

$$C = P_I(r - \dot{P}_I + \delta),$$

to bring out the relationship of the user cost to the "real" rate of interest, $r - \dot{P}$. If lenders and borrowers are concerned about the real, or purchasing

nd liabilities, they will discount nominal interest rates
f inflation $\dot{P}$. If the annual interest rate on a loan is 9
nflation is 5 percent, the real rate of return, in terms
percent. If both r and $\dot{P}$ go up by the same amount,
ge, and lending, borrowing, and investing decisions
vill be the case if user cost is calculated as we show
equal increase in r and $\dot{P}$ leaves C unchanged so
stock is unaffected.

been dealt with in several ways in the empirical
that investors either don't know or don't care
gains will be when they consider purchasing a
$\dot{P}_I$ term can be eliminated from equation (33),

$$C = P_I(r + \delta). \tag{34}$$

son and collaborators in several early (1963–
ent behavior. Since these studies used data
e the inflationary period that began around
approximation. If there is little variance in
from a regression analysis will not harm

by Jorgenson and by Bischoff and others
ia-SSRC (MPS) model group has ap-
a lag distribution on past price changes.
n expectations of future price changes
es. In addition, the MPS formulation
only if $\dot{P}$ has exceeded some threshold
tion that inflation must reach some
. A rational expectations view would
economy, or approximate it from
sumption that on average they are

swered about the user cost is what
est, or opportunity, cost of capital
arlier, a firm can raise money for
using internal funds, by selling
n a world of perfect competition
each of these means of raising
fferential.
osts to funds borrowed outside
a bond sale or to the dilution
ins are likely to impute a lower rate
by retained earnings plus depreciation allowances

than to the other two sources of funds. Thus, the interest rate, or opportunity cost, used to compute the user cost of capital may be a weighted average of the interest rates which apply to these three different sources of funds, where the weights are the fractions of total funds raised from these alternative sources:

$$r = r_I\left(\frac{\text{internal funds}}{\text{total investment}}\right) + r_D\left(\frac{\text{bond issue}}{\text{total investment}}\right) + r_E\left(\frac{\text{equity issue}}{\text{total investment}}\right),$$

(35)

where $r_I \equiv$ the opportunity cost of lending the firm's retained earnings,

             $r_D \equiv$ an established bond rate such as Moody's Aaa corporate bond rate, and

             $r_E \equiv$ average earnings-price ratio on corporate equity.

Both r_D and r_E are assumed to be greater than r_I.

By breaking down r into these three components, we have introduced profits, or liquidity, into the investment function. As profits increase, the amount of internal funds available for investment increases. If the interest rate r_I imputed to internal funds is lower than the other rates, the increase in profits will reduce the weighted average of all interest rates, as is shown in equation (35) and this in turn will lower the user cost of capital as is shown in equation (33). A lower user cost means that more investment will be undertaken, so that we have established a link back from profits to the level of investment through the user cost.

In the data on investment, it is very difficult to see the effect of profits on investment because profits are highly correlated with changes in output. Yet surveys of businesspeople indicate that profits are important to their decisions to invest. Therefore, it seems reasonable that profits should be included as a determinant of investment demand.

LAGS IN INVESTMENT DEMAND

At this point, it may be useful to summarize the theory of investment demand we have developed. First, we have the investment demand function for gross investment given earlier as equation (29),

$$i^g = i^n + i^r = \Delta K^E(y, C, P) + \delta K,$$

(36)

still ignoring lags between changes in K^E and movements of i^n, one of the subjects to be dealt with in this section. Next, we have the definition in equation (33) of the user cost of capital, C,

$$C = P_I(r - \dot{P}_I + \delta),$$

which brings the interest rate into the picture. Finally, we have the expression for the interest rate as a weighted average of rates on the three principal sources of funds,

$$r = w_I r_I + w_D r_D + w_E r_E, \qquad (37)$$

where the w's are the fractions of funds raised internally (I), by bond issue (D), and by stock issue (E), and $\sum w = 1$. Here the profit level enters the picture since r_I is presumably lower than r_E and r_D. Up to now we have been dealing with a static situation, with no notion of the time lags involved in changing the level of capital stock. We will now take a more dynamic view of the investment process and look at some empirical results.

We can begin by regarding the demand for investment as a function of two things: the real user cost c of capital goods and the demand for the output of the firm, y. That is, if the cost of capital goes up relative to the cost of labor, for a given output we would expect a firm to use more labor and less capital in its production process, and we would also expect output to be reduced. On the other hand, for a given cost of capital, if the demand for output increases, we would expect a firm to increase its use of both capital and labor to produce more output.

Let us suppose that a firm decides to invest in a new plant. It will survey the various blueprints available for the new plant and choose the one that has a capital-labor ratio K/N that allows it to produce any given output at a minimum cost. Let us assume further that this new plant is a "putty-clay" investment. That is, the firm can choose between many blueprints with different K/N ratios, so that the K/N ratio is variable and K and N are substitutable *ex ante;* the capital stock is "putty" *ex ante.* But once the plant is built, capital and labor must be used in the fixed proportions to produce a given level of output as specified in the chosen blueprint; the capital stock turns into "clay" *ex post.* Thus, *ex ante* the firm's capital-output and capital-labor ratios are changeable; *ex post* they are fixed.

Now we want to see what effect changes in demand and changes in the cost of capital will have on the actual investment pattern of the firm, given the putty-clay production function. First, we look at changes in demand. Since the output of the existing plant is fixed *ex post,* if the firm expects the new level of demand to be permanent and wants to respond to it, it will have to add to its plant immediately in the absence of excess capacity. This response is shown in Figure 13-8. The increment to output eventually raises the equilibrium capital stock by ΔK^E, raising replacement investment gradually to $\Delta i^r = \delta(\Delta K^E)$. The increment to net investment along the i^n curve is added to the i^r curve to obtain the change in gross investment along the i^g curve in Figure 13-8. Within a short period the total capital stock is increased by an amount equal to the area under the i^n curve. Because there is now a higher equilibrium level of capital stock, there is an increase in the level of replacement investment by an amount Δi^r so that the path of total investment is shown by the i^g curve. The main point here is that these increases in i^n, i^r, and i^g all

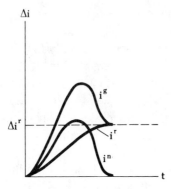

Figure 13-8 Sudden increase in the capital stock from an increase in product demand.

take place with a short lag owing to the *ex post* fixity of output capacity and the need to expand plant to meet demand.

Now let us suppose that the firm has the same original "clay" plant, but instead of a change in the demand for its product it sees a reduction in the relative cost of capital. The principal effect of this change will be that the firm will want to increase the amount of capital it uses relative to labor, that is, raise the K/N ratio. The firm will gradually replace its old plant with a new *kind* of plant—a more capital-intensive plant with a higher capital-labor ratio. The result is that with a change in the user cost of capital there is a much longer process of change than with an increase in demand; that is, there is a longer lag until the change is completed as is shown in Figure 13-9.

Simulations of the effects of changes in output and the cost of capital on investment expenditures on producers' durable equipment (i^g) are shown in Figures 13-10 and 13-11. These are taken from the MPS model; most of the investment equations there come from studies by Charles W. Bischoff. Figure 13-10 shows the effect of a sudden increase in output demanded by 10 percent. The effect on gross investment peaks at three quarters and levels off after five quarters. This is the empirical counterpart of the i^g path in Figure 13-8. Figure 13-11 shows the effect of a 10 percent decrease in the user cost. Gross invest-

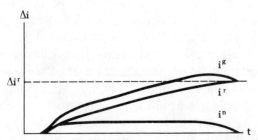

Figure 13-9 Gradual replacement of the capital stock as a result of a decline in the relative cost of capital.

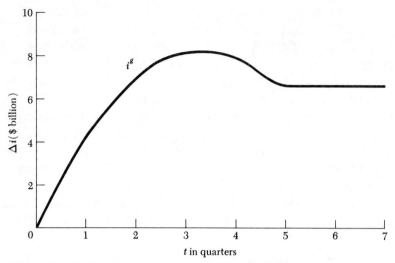

Figure 13-10 The effect of an increase in output demand on investment in equipment.

ment peaks at 20 quarters and levels off at 26 quarters or so. This is comparable to the i^g path in Figure 13-9.

A more recent study by Peter B. Clark suggests that investment reacts quite sharply to an increase in output; the effect peaks after about four quarters and remains strong for up to sixteen quarters. A fall in the user cost in capital, however, has rather little influence in the first quarter; it takes up to four years to work out the full consequences of this change.

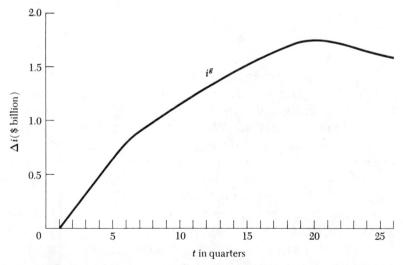

Figure 13-11 The effect of a 10 percent decrease in the cost of capital on investment in equipment.

As far as the long-run, steady-state response of investment demand to changes in its principal determinants, r and y, is concerned, Bischoff found that the long-run elasticity of investment demand with respect to changes in output is about unity, with a short lag. This implies a fairly constant capital-output ratio over the long run since, with a lag, the capital stock would grow at the same rate as output. Bischoff also found that the long-run elasticity of investment demand with respect to changes in the interest rate is about -0.5. In other words, if the interest rate on corporate bonds increases from 10 to 11 percent, a change of 10 percent, we could expect a 5 percent drop in investment over the long run, for example, from \$300 billion to \$270 billion, occurring gradually over a two- to three-year period. This is predicated, of course, on the assumption that investors see changes in the cost of capital as permanent, just as they assume that increases in demand now will continue into the future.

INVESTMENT IN THE STATIC MODEL

The investment demand function, equation (29), makes net investment a function of changes in the level of output and the interest rate. We analyzed the implications of this accelerator mechanism for stabilization policy earlier. The level of replacement investment i^r depends on the preexisting level of the capital stock. If the economy is in equilibrium with a given r and y, the existing capital stock may be about equal to equilibrium capital stock K^E, which in turn depends on the level of y and r. Thus, in the static model which determines equilibrium values of the variables, we can now write the investment function as

$$ i = i(r, y); \qquad \frac{\partial i}{\partial r} < 0, \qquad \frac{\partial i}{\partial y} > 0, \qquad (38) $$

replacing the $i = i(r)$ function of Part II. Here we are dealing with a *static* model, in which replacement investment is a function of the *level* of output and the interest rate. An increase in the interest rate reduces equilibrium capital stock K^E, reducing replacement investment, so that $(\partial i / \partial r) < 0$. An increase in output raises K^E, so that $(\partial i / \partial y) > 0$. We are not dealing with the accelerator discussed previously, since the accelerator depends on *rates of change* of income and we are dealing only with a change from one *level* of income to another.

By making i depend on y as well as r, we change the slope of the *IS* curve considerably. This is shown in Figure 13-12, which displays the four-quadrant *IS* diagram with $i = i(r,y)$. For every value of y, there is a different investment demand curve in the northeast quadrant of Figure 13-12. As income rises from y_0 to y_1, the investment demand curve shifts up from $i(y_0)$ to $i(y_1)$. This flattens the *IS* curve that gives r,y points that maintain product market equilibrium. With $i = i(r,y)$, a given interest rate drop will stimulate a greater increase in product market equilibrium output than with $i = i(r)$, because

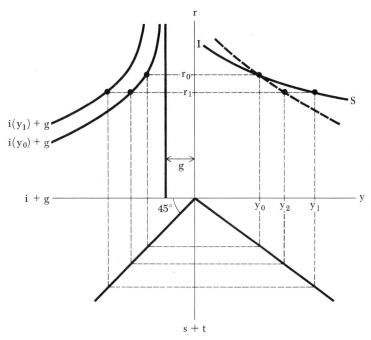

Figure 13-12 Modification of the IS curve: $i = i(r, y)$.

the initial y increase pulls i up, which further increases y. Thus, with $i = i(r,y)$, starting from r_0, y_0 in Figure 13-12 an interest rate drop to r_1 moves product market equilibrium y to y_1 along the solid *IS* curve, with the i function shifting up to $i(y_1)$. With $i = i(r)$, the equilibrium output level would have increased only to y_2 along the dashed *IS* curve.

A reduction in the interest rate now leads to an increase in investment, and that in turn leads to higher incomes which lead to yet higher investment because of the shift of the $i(y)$ function. We could even have an upward sloping *IS* curve if $i(r,y)$ were sufficiently responsive to increase in y. In Figure 13-12, if the increase from y_0 to y_1 caused the $i(y)$ curve in the northwest quadrant to shift much higher, it can be seen by tracing through the effects that the *IS* curve could be made to slope upward.

Fortunately, it seems from empirical evidence that the economy is stable; the *IS* curve in fact has a negative slope. The empirical estimates discussed in Chapter 12 suggest that the long-run marginal propensity to consume is equal to c/y, which is about 65 percent of GNP. Thus, $c'(1 - t')$ might be about 0.65. If the elasticity of investment demand with respect to output is unity, as suggested earlier in this chapter, then

$$1 = \frac{\partial i}{\partial y} \cdot \frac{y}{i},$$

so that

$$\frac{\partial i}{\partial y} = \frac{i}{y},$$

and we can measure $\partial i/\partial y$ by the investment–GNP ratio of about 0.15. Thus, the marginal propensity to spend might be about 0.80 $(= 0.65 + 0.15)$, and the *IS* curve is negatively sloped.

Fiscal Policy and Investment

In Part II, under the assumption that investment was a function only of the interest rate, $i = i(r)$, we saw that while an increase in government purchases raises both y and r, it reduces the level of investment since i', or $\partial i/\partial r$, is negative. Now that we have expanded the investment function to $i = i(r,y)$, the effect of an increase in government purchases on investment is no longer unambiguous. What are the conditions under which an increase in government spending will lead to an *increase* in investment?

Graphically, we can locate in the r,y space the sets of r,y points lying on trade-off lines—isoinvestment lines, conceptually similar to indifference curves—which hold investment at a constant level as r and y change. Two such lines are shown by i_0i_0 and i_1i_1 in Figure 13-13. The slope of the *ii* lines can be obtained by differentiating the investment function $i = i(r,y)$, holding i constant:

$$di = 0 = \frac{\partial i}{\partial r}\, dr + \frac{\partial i}{\partial y}\, dy,$$

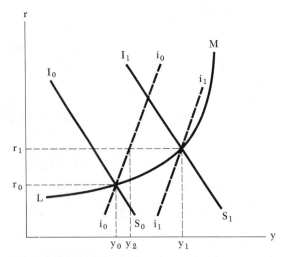

Figure 13-13 Effect of an increase in government spending on investment.

so that

$$\left.\frac{dr}{dy}\right|_{ii} = - \frac{\partial i/\partial y}{\partial i/\partial r}.$$

Since $\partial i/\partial y > 0$ and $\partial i/\partial r < 0$, we know that the slope of these ii lines is positive. An increase in investment is indicated by a movement rightward across the ii map—an increase in y with r held constant raises i since $\partial i/\partial y > 0$.

The rule which we can now state just by inspection of Figure 13-13 is that if at an initial equilibrium (y_0,r_0) the i_0i_0 line is steeper than the LM curve, an upward shift of the IS curve due to an expansionary fiscal policy will lead to a higher level of investment. In Figure 13-13 the shift of IS from I_0S_0 to I_1S_1 due to an expansionary fiscal policy action moves demand-side equilibrium from r_0,y_0 to r_1,y_1. Since the ii curve was steeper at r_0,y_0 than the LM curve, the new equilibrium is on an ii curve, i_1i_1, that gives a higher level of investment than at the original equilibrium. The reader should convince herself that the reverse is true if the ii curve is *flatter* than LM at the initial equilibrium.

In general, if an expansionary fiscal policy step is taken when the economy is slack and the initial equilibrium point lies along the relatively flat part of the LM curve, the movement from r_0,y_0 to r_1,y_1 will involve a large increase in y relative to r, and thus is likely to increase i. But if the expansion begins in the relatively steep part of the LM curve, the r increase will be large relative to the y increase, and investment is more likely to fall.

CONCLUSION: INVESTMENT DEMAND AND MONETARY AND FISCAL POLICY

In the last section we saw that whether replacement investment—and thus desired capital stock K^E—rises or falls with an expansionary fiscal policy action depends on the initial position of the economy. Thus, a fiscal policy stimulus in a period of relative slack in the economy, but reasonably high capacity utilization, will be complemented by an increase in investment. The effect of the r increase tending to decrease K^E will be offset by the effect of the y increase, so that K^E rises. This gives both a temporary accelerator effect boost to investment and a more permanent increase in replacement demand. On the other hand, when the economy is taut and interest rates are high, changes in government purchases will tend to be partially offset by opposite changes in investment demand as the movements in r dominate the movements in y.

This reinforces our previous view that fiscal policy will be relatively more effective at changing equilibrium output and unemployment when the economy is slack and unemployment is high, while monetary policy will be more effective when unemployment is very low and interest rates are high. This also reinforces the corollary to that view that the size of the multipliers depends on the initial state of the economy; a search for multipliers with "stable" or constant numerical values is likely to be fruitless.

SELECTED READINGS

A. Ando and F. Modigliani, "Econometric Analysis of Stabilization Policies," *American Economic Review,* May 1969.

C.W. Bischoff, "The Effect of Alternative Lag Distributions," in G. Fromm, ed., *Tax Incentives and Capital Spending* (Washington, D.C.: The Brookings Institution, 1971).

C.W. Bischoff, "Business Investment in the 1970's: A Comparison of Models," *Brookings Papers on Economic Activity,* vol. 1, 1971.

P.F. Clark, "Investment in the 1970s: Theory, Performance, and Prediction," *Brookings Papers on Economic Activity,* vol. 1, 1978.

J.S. Duesenberry, *Business Cycles and Economic Growth* (New York: McGraw-Hill, 1958), chapters 3–5.

H.I. Grossman, "A Choice Theoretical Model of an Income-Investment Accelerator," *American Economic Review,* September 1972.

F. Hayashi, "Tobin's Marginal q and Average q: A Neoclassical Interpretation," *Econometrica,* January 1982.

J. Hirscheifer, "On the Theory of Optimal Investment Decisions," *Journal of Political Economy,* August 1958.

D.W. Jorgenson, "Economic Studies of Investment Behavior: A Survey," *Journal of Economic Literature,* December 1971, with comments by R. Eisner and L.R. Klein in *Journal of Economic Literature,* March 1974.

D.W. Jorgenson and C. D. Siebert, "Theories of Corporate Investment Behavior," *American Economic Review,* September 1968.

J. Tobin and W.C. Brainard, "Pitfalls in Financial Model Building," *American Economics Association Papers and Proceedings,* May 1968.

chapter *14*

The Demand for Money

The demand for money was introduced in Chapter 4 as the demand for real money balances, $m = M/P$. There we suggested, in a fairly loose way, that the demand for real balances could be divided into a *speculative* demand component, inversely related to the interest rate, and a *transactions* demand component, positively related to income and inversely related to the interest rate. This gave us the demand-for-money function in Part II:

$$\frac{M}{P} = m = m(r, y) \approx l(r) + k(y), \tag{1}$$

where $\partial m/\partial r$ is negative and $\partial m/\partial y$ is positive.

Since the 1930s, economists have developed the theory underlying the demand for money along several different lines, each of which provides a different answer to the basic question: If bonds earn interest and money doesn't, why should a person hold money? While the way the various theories answer this question differs, in general they come down to a demand-for-money function similar to the one shown in equation (1).

In this chapter we will develop four prominent approaches to the demand for money. The first is the *regressive expectations* model attributed to Keynes and described by Tobin in his article on liquidity preference. This model essentially says that people hold money when they expect bond prices to fall, that is, interest rates to rise, and thus expect that they would take a loss if they were to hold bonds. Since people's estimates of whether the interest rate is likely to rise or fall, and by how much, vary fairly widely, at any given

319

interest rate there will be someone expecting it to rise, and thus someone holding money.

The obvious problem with this view is that it suggests that individuals should, at any given time, hold *all* their liquid assets either in money *or* in bonds, but not some of each. This is obviously not true in reality. The second approach, Tobin's model of liquidity preference, deals with this problem by showing that if the return on bonds is uncertain, that is, bonds are risky, then the investor worrying about both risk and return is likely to do best by holding both bonds and money.

A third approach to the demand for money is the inventory approach to transactions demand developed by both Baumol and Tobin. They show that there is a transactions need for money to smooth out the difference between income and expenditure streams, and that the higher the interest rate—the return on holding bonds instead of money—the smaller these transactions demand balances should be. Finally, we will look at Friedman's modern version of the quantity theory of money. Friedman analyzes the demand for money as an ordinary commodity. It can be viewed as a producer's good; businesses hold cash balances to improve efficiency in their financial transactions and are willing to pay, in terms of foregone interest income, for this efficiency. Money can also be viewed as a consumer's good; it yields utility to the consumer in terms of smoothing out timing differences between the expenditure and income streams and also in terms of reducing risk. This type of analysis brings Friedman to much the same demand-for-money function as that based on the other theories.

Our discussion of the demand for money initially focuses on the individual's decision concerning the composition of her liquid assets. We assume that she has a given amount of liquid wealth W which remains unchanged during the period under discussion. She must decide how much of that liquid wealth should be allocated to each of two kinds of assets: money (M), defined as currency plus demand deposits, which is riskless and does not earn interest; and bonds (B), which do earn interest and bear a liquidity risk. This is the risk that they might have to be sold at a capital loss if, when money is needed, bond prices are lower than they were when the bonds were purchased. Later in our analysis, we will see how the individual's preferences can be generalized into a community liquidity preference. We can begin with the regressive expectations model of the demand for money.

THE REGRESSIVE EXPECTATIONS MODEL

Our development of the regressive expectations model follows Tobin's analysis in his article on liquidity preference. A bond holder has an expected return on the bond from two sources: the bond's yield—the interest payment he receives; and a potential capital gain—an increase in the price of the bond from the time he buys it to the time he sells it. The bond's yield Y is usually stated as a percentage of the face value of the bond. The market rate of return on the bond r is the ratio of the yield to the price of the bond P_b. For example, if a $100 bond has a yield of $5, the percentage yield is 5 percent. If the price of the bond rises to $125, the $5 yield corresponds to a market rate r of 4 percent—$5/$125. Thus, the market rate is given by

$$r = \frac{Y}{P_b},$$

(2)

and, since the yield Y is a fixed amount stated as a percentage of the bond's face value, the market price of a bond is given by

$$P_b = \frac{Y}{r}.$$

(3)

The expected percentage capital gain g is the percentage increase in price from the purchase price P_b to the expected sale price P_b^e. This gives us an expression for the percentage capital gain, $g = (P_b^e - P_b)/P_b$. From equations (2) and (3), with a fixed Y on the bond, an expected price P_b^e corresponds to an expected interest rate, $r^e = Y/P_b^e$. Thus, in terms of expected and current interest rates, the capital gain can be written as

$$g = \frac{Y/r^e - Y/r}{Y/r}.$$

Canceling the Y terms and multiplying the numerator and denominator by r gives us

$$g = \frac{r}{r^e} - 1$$

(4)

as the expression for expected capital gain in terms of current and expected interest rates. For example, if the present market interest rate is 5 percent, and the purchaser of the bond expects the rate to drop to 4 percent, his expected capital gain will be

$$g = \frac{0.05}{0.04} - 1 = 1.25 - 1 = 0.25, \text{ or } 25 \text{ percent.}$$

The total rate of return on a bond—e for earnings—will be the sum of the market rate of interest at the time of purchase and the capital gains term.

Thus, $e = r + g$, and substituting for g from equation (4), we have an expression for the total rate of return

$$e = r + \frac{r}{r^e} - 1. \tag{5}$$

The Individual's Demand-for-Money Function

Now with an expected return on bonds given by e, and with a zero return on money, the asset holder can be expected to put his liquid wealth into bonds if he expects the return e to be greater than zero. If the return on bonds is expected to be less than zero, he will put his liquid wealth into money.

In the regressive expectations model, each person is assumed to have an *expected* interest rate r^e corresponding to some *normal* long-run average rate. If rates rise above this long-run expectation, she expects them to fall, and vice versa. Thus, her expectations are *regressive*. Initially, we will assume that her expected long-run rate doesn't change much with changes in current market conditions.

The asset holder's expected interest rate r^e, together with the observable market interest rate r, determines her expected percentage return e. Given this, we can compute the critical level of the market rate r, r_c, which would give her a net zero return on bonds, that is, the value of r that makes $e = 0$. When actual $r > r_c$, we would expect her to hold all of her liquid wealth in bonds. When $r < r_c$, she moves 100 percent into money. To find this critical value of r, r_c, we set the total return shown in equation (5) equal to zero:

$$0 = r + \frac{r}{r^e} - 1;$$

$$r(1 + r^e) = r^e;$$

and thus

$$r = \frac{r^e}{1 + r^e} = r_c. \tag{6}$$

Here r_c, the value of the market interest rate r that makes $e = 0$, is given by $r^e/(1 + r^e)$.

This relationship between the individual's demand for real balances and the interest rate is shown in Figure 14-1. Here we label the horizontal axis to show the demand for real balances, since later developments will show, as suggested in Chapter 4, that it is the demand for real balances, $m = M/P$, that depends on the interest rate. Since we are implicitly holding the general price level constant throughout this section, changes in real balances M/P correspond

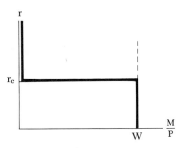

Figure 14-1 Individual's demand for money in the no-risk case.

to changes in M. Hence, the picture in Figure 14-1 will be the same whether we label the axis M or M/P.

In Figure 14-1, when r is greater than r_c, the asset holder puts all of W into bonds, so that her demand for money is zero. As r drops below r_c so that $e < 0$ and expected capital losses on bonds outweigh the interest yield, the asset holder moves her entire liquid wealth into money. This gives us a demand-for-money curve for an individual that looks like a step function. When r exactly equals r_c, $e = 0$ and the asset holder is indifferent between bonds and money. At any other value of r, the asset holder is either 100 percent in money or 100 percent in bonds.

Up to now, we have assumed that the individual has a *given* expected interest rate r^e that is not sensitive to changes in the market rate r. What would happen if the expected interest rate r^e depended positively on the current interest rate? Might an increase in present r raise r^e enough to raise r_c, thus *increasing* the demand for money?

Suppose $r^e = f(r), f' > 0$, so that from expression (6) for r_c we have

$$r_c = \frac{f(r)}{1 + f(r)} = h(r). \tag{7}$$

Then if $h' < 1$, we could plot r_c against r as shown in Figure 14-2, where the $h(r)$ curve has a slope less than unity. Where $h(r)$ crosses the 45° line, at $r = r_0$, r also is equal to r_c, and the person is indifferent between bonds and

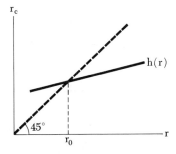

Figure 14-2 Critical interest rate, r_c, versus the actual interest rate, r.

money; she is on the horizontal segment of the demand curve of Figure 14-1. When r is greater than r_0, r is also greater than r_c along $h(r)$, and the person puts her entire liquid wealth into bonds. If r is less than r_0 in Figure 14-2, r is also less than r_c, and the individual is 100 percent in money. Thus, if $h' < 1$, the individual's demand-for-money function will look like that of Figure 14-1, even with $r^e = f(r)$.

What are the conditions under which $h' < 1$, that is, $dr_c/dr < 1$? Differentiating equation (7) with respect to r, we have

$$\frac{dr_c}{dr} = \frac{f'(r)}{1 + f(r)} - \frac{f(r)f'(r)}{[1 + f(r)]^2}.$$

Simplifying this gives us

$$\frac{dr_c}{dr} = \frac{[1 + f(r)]f'(r) - f(r)f'(r)}{[1 + f(r)]^2}$$

and

$$h'(r) = \frac{dr_c}{dr} = \frac{f'(r)}{(1 + r^e)^2}. \tag{8}$$

Since r^e is presumably positive, so that the denominator of (8) is greater than one, a sufficient condition for $h' < 1$ is that $f'(r) \equiv dr^e/dr$ is less than one. Thus, the individual's money demand function will resemble that of Figure 14-1 if $f'(r) < 1$, that is, if an increase in the current market rate r, raises r^e by less than the increase in r. Expectations must be sufficiently *regressive* that movements in the current market rate cause smaller movements in expected rates. If this is the case, the Figure 14-1 demand-for-money curve will hold in this no-risk model where expectations concerning r^e are held with certainty.

The Aggregate Demand-for-Money Function with Regressive Expectations

The individual demand curves can be aggregated for the entire money market as follows. Locate the individual with the highest critical interest rate, $r_c^{\max}$ in Figure 14-3. As the interest rate falls below that $r_c^{\max}$, she shifts all of her liquid wealth into money. As the interest rate drops, more individual r_c's are passed and more people shift from bonds to money. Eventually, r will drop far enough that no one will want to put liquid wealth into bonds, and the demand for money will equal total liquid wealth, ΣW.

Figure 14-4 shows the frequency distribution of the critical interest rates. The area under a frequency distribution equals 100 percent, and for any level of r_c, the area under the curve to the left of that r_c gives the proportion of people with r_c less than that r_c. The population average r_c is shown as $\bar{r}_c$ in

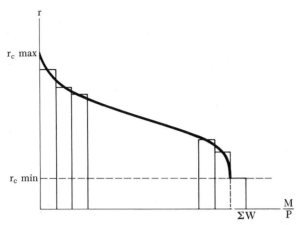

Figure 14-3 Aggregate demand for money in the no-risk case.

Figure 14-4. If r_c's are distributed among the population as shown in Figure 14-4, that is, few people having extreme r_c's and more people bunched around a central $\bar{r}_c$, then the aggregate demand-for-money curve will have the shape shown in Figure 14-3—more steeply sloped at the ends than in the middle for a given aggregate liquid wealth, $\Sigma\, W$.

Aggregate Wealth and the Interest Rate

It should be noted that the actual demand-for-money function would be flatter than the curve shown in Figure 14-3, which assumes $\Sigma\, W$ is independent of r. In fact, as interest rates go down, aggregate wealth increases, owing to an increase in bond prices through equation (3). Thus, we would observe for each drop in the interest rate a slightly greater shift into money than that shown in Figure 14-3 because each individual would have more "bond wealth" to change into "money wealth" as the rate falls. Each increase in the demand for money is due to a *wealth effect* as well as to an *interest rate effect*.

This point is illustrated in Figure 14-5. The curves d_0, d_1, d_2 are each drawn on the assumption of a *given* aggregate wealth $\Sigma\, W$, shown along the horizontal axis. Movement along any one demand curve shows the effect of

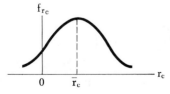

Figure 14-4 Frequency distribution of the critical interest rates.

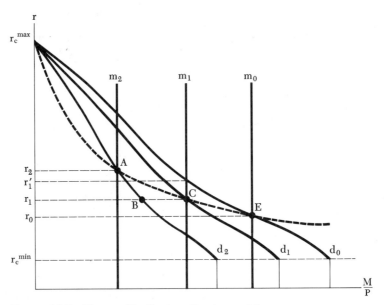

Figure 14-5 The wealth effect on the demand for money.

changes in the interest rate on the demand for money *directly,* but leaves out the effect through a change in $\Sigma\ W$. As interest rates fall, not only is there a shift of a given liquid wealth from bonds to money, but the amount of liquid wealth in the economy increases. Hence, there is a *further* expansion in the demand for money through a shift in the demand curve.

Suppose that at interest rate r_2 the demand for money is at point A. All people with a critical interest rate above r_2 hold money, and all people with critical rates below r_2 hold bonds, giving a demand for money at m_2. Suppose, now, that the interest rate drops to r_1. There is an increase in the price, or value, of bonds, since that value is inversely related to the level of interest rate, as shown in equation (3). Thus, the demand for money increases, *not* to B on the old demand curve d_2 but to C, on the new demand curve d_1.

We can now see how the true demand-for-money function is traced by following the effects of changes in the money supply. We have seen that the demand for money depends on the level of interest rate. Suppose there is an initial equilibrium point E where demand for money equals supply, and the interest rate is r_0. Now the government decides to reduce the supply of money to m_1 through action by the Federal Reserve Board. We know that this will raise the interest rate. On the old demand curve d_0 the interest rate would settle at r_1'. However, because interest rates are increasing, there is a *shift* in the demand curve to d_1. Interest rates rise from r_0 and at the same time demand shifts until a new equilibrium interest rate is reached at r_1, which equates demand and supply. This gives us a new equilibrium point, C. Should there be a further reduction in the money supply, the same process would be repeated until a new equilibrium level of r_c were reached at A. A reversal of the process, whereby the money supply shifted out from m_2 to m_1 to m_0, would give the same equilibrium points A, C, and E. Thus, by connecting all such equilibrium points, the demand-for-money curve which incorporates both interest rate and wealth effects can be described.

Figure 14-5 should make it clear that as the interest rate drops, there are continuing increments to liquid wealth, so that as the interest rate approaches zero, liquid wealth approaches infinity. In other words, the demand curve becomes flatter and flatter as r decreases, eventually approaching the minimum r_c value asymptotically in this static expectations model.

Thus, the regressive expectations model yields a demand-for-money function that looks much like the one we have been using so far in this book. As interest rates fall, the demand for money increases, and the demand curve is likely to be convex. That is, successive interest rate decreases of equal amounts will bring increasing increments in the demand for money.

There are two troublesome aspects of this analysis, however. In the first place, if the money market remained in equilibrium for a long enough period, people should begin to adjust their expected interest rates to correspond to the actual prevailing interest rate. They would all tend to adopt eventually the same critical interest rate as time passes, so that the aggregate demand curve for the entire money market would increasingly look like the flat curve of Figure 14-1, instead of the negatively sloped demand curve with a variety of critical rates shown in Figure 14-3. This implication of the regressive expectations model—that the elasticity of demand for money with respect to changes in the interest rate is increasing over time—is not supported by empirical studies.

Second, if we assume that people actually do have a critical interest rate as shown in Figure 14-2, then the clear implication of the model is that, in this two-asset world, individuals hold either all bonds or all money, never a mix of the two. The negative slope of the aggregate demand curve is due to the fact that people disagree about the value of r^e, and thus in their critical rates r_c. In fact, however, individuals do not hold portfolios consisting of just one asset. In general, portfolios hold a mixture of assets: they are *diversified*. An explanation of this result—that people hold both money and bonds at the same time—can be found in the portfolio balance approach to the demand for money developed by Tobin.

THE PORTFOLIO BALANCE APPROACH

The portfolio balance approach begins with the same expression for total percentage return e that we developed in the last section,

$$e = r + g. \tag{9}$$

In that section we assumed that the percentage rate of expected capital gain, given by

$$g = \frac{r}{r^e} - 1, \qquad (10)$$

is determined with certainty by the individual; she chooses r^e as a function of r, and no consideration of uncertainty, or risk, enters the problem. The basic contribution of the portfolio balance approach is to enter risk considerations explicitly into the determination of the demand for money.

The Probability Distribution of Capital Gains

Rather than some *fixed* expected capital gain, here we will assume that the asset holder has a whole spectrum of expected capital gains, each with a probability of its occurrence attached. Such a *probability*, or *frequency, distribution* of expected gains is shown in Figure 14-6. Each possible value of capital gain g has a probability f_g attached to it. If one asks the asset holder what the probability is of achieving a gain greater than $\bar{g}$, say, 15 percent, his answer will be the area under the probability distribution to the right of $\bar{g}$. Thus, the asset holder is not certain of the value of g he expects, but has an implicit distribution of these gains around some central value—the average, or *expected gain, $\bar{g}$*.

If the probabilities of capital gains are distributed "normally"—according to the familiar symmetrical bell-shaped distribution shown in Figure 14-6—then we have a natural measure of uncertainty, or risk. This measure is the *standard deviation, σ_g,* of the probability distribution of capital gains. To find the standard deviation of expected gains, σ_g, we can locate the two points symmetrically opposite each other on the normal probability distribution that have the following property: The area under the curve between these two points is two-thirds of the total area under the curve. Given the shape of the normal curve, these points are also the inflection points of the curve, where it turns from concave to convex. The standard deviation of the probability distribution, σ_g, is the distance between either of these two points and the mean of the distribution, $\bar{g}$. The statistical significance of σ_g is that, since two-thirds of the area under the curve is between the points $\bar{g} - \sigma_g$ and $\bar{g} + \sigma_g$, the

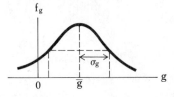

Figure 14-6 Probability distribution of expected gains.

asset holder has a 66.7 percent chance that the *actual g* will turn out between $\bar{g} \pm \sigma_g$. Thus, if $\bar{g} = 10$ percent, and $\sigma_g = 2$ percent, the investor has a two-thirds chance that actual g will be between 8 and 12 percent.

That the standard deviation is a natural measure of the riskiness of bonds can be seen by considering the two probability distributions, both with the same $\bar{g}$, shown in Figure 14-7. The narrow distribution, f_1, illustrates a case in which the asset holder is very *certain* of the gain—it has a small σ_g. The wider distribution f_2 shows a case in which, with the same central expected gain $\bar{g}$, the investor has a very uncertain estimate of the gain; thus, σ_{g2} is greater than σ_{g1}. If we can identify riskiness with uncertainty, σ_g is a measure of the risk of holding liquid assets in bonds.

Now in place of a return expected with certainty, e, we have an expected return, $\bar{e}$, where

$$\bar{e} = r + \bar{g}, \tag{11}$$

and $\bar{g}$ is the mean expected capital gain from the probability distribution of Figure 14-6. If the asset holder is putting B dollars of her liquid assets into bonds, her expected total return $\bar{R}_T$ is then

$$\bar{R}_T = B \cdot \bar{e} = B \cdot (r + \bar{g}). \tag{12}$$

Similarly, if the standard deviation of return on a bond is σ_g, a number like 2 percent, and all bonds are alike, then the total standard deviation of bond holdings is given by

$$\sigma_T = B \cdot \sigma_g. \tag{13}$$

The Individual's Portfolio Decision

Equations (12) and (13) give us the technical situation facing the asset holder—the budget constraint along which he or she can trade increased risk σ_T for increased expected return $\bar{R}_T$. They also give the investor a formula for deciding

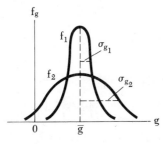

Figure 14-7 Different risks for bonds with the same expected gain.

how much funds to put into bonds to achieve a given risk-return mix along the budget line. From (13) we have

$$B = \frac{\sigma_T}{\sigma_g} = \frac{1}{\sigma_g}\,\sigma_T. \tag{14}$$

With σ_g fixed by the asset holder's probability distribution, (14) gives the total bond holdings B needed to attain any given level of risk σ_T. Using this expression to replace B in (12) gives us the budget constraint,

$$\bar{R}_T = \frac{\sigma_T}{\sigma_g}\,(r + \bar{g}) = \sigma_T\!\left(\frac{r + \bar{g}}{\sigma_g}\right). \tag{15}$$

Here r is a known current value, fixed, at least to the individual, by the bond market. The investor knows $\bar{g}$ and σ_g, at least implicitly, from the probability distribution of g's in Figure 14-6. Thus, the expression in parentheses in (15) is a given, determined number which gives the constant rate of trade-off between return $\bar{R}_T$ and risk σ_T. Differentiating (15) we have

$$\frac{d\bar{R}_T}{d\sigma_T} = \frac{r + \bar{g}}{\sigma_g}. \tag{16}$$

If r is, say, 5 percent, $\bar{g}$ is 10 percent, and σ_g is 5 percent, then $d R_T / d\sigma_T$ will be 3. In this case, an increase of one percentage point in the standard deviation in the total portfolio σ_T will buy a 3 percent increase in expected total return $\bar{R}_T$.

The budget constraint (15) for an individual asset holder is shown in the top half of Figure 14-8. The standard deviation of the total portfolio, σ_T, is shown on the horizontal axis. The vertical axis above the horizontal axis measures the expected rate of return on the portfolio, $\bar{R}_T$. The straight line in the top half shows the trade-off between risk and expected return which faces the individual. Its slope, derived from equation (16), is $(r + \bar{g})/\sigma_g$. Each of these terms, and thus the slope of the budget line, is fixed for each individual.

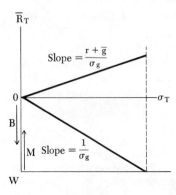

Figure 14-8 Budget constraint for individual trading increased risk for increased return.

The length of the vertical axis below the horizontal axis in Figure 14-8 is given by the total liquid wealth W of the individual. The distance from the origin along this axis gives total bond holdings B; the distance from W ($= W - B$) gives money holdings M. For any given value of σ_T we can locate the value of B by multiplying by $1/\sigma_g$ from equation (14), or reflecting it from the line with slope $1/\sigma_g$ in the bottom half of Figure 14-8. Thus, once we locate an optimum return-risk point along the budget line in the top half of Figure 14-8, knowing σ_2 we can determine the corresponding portfolio mix of B and M in the bottom half of the diagram.

In order to locate the individual's equilibrium risk σ_T and expected rate of return $\bar{R}_T$ we must confront the technical budget constraint of Figure 14-8 with the individual's utility-function trade-off between risk and return. These preferences are represented by indifference curves such as those used in our analysis of consumption and investment. The shape of the curve depends on the nature of the investor's preferences between risk and return.

Tobin distinguished three kinds of preferences that an individual might have. These are shown in Figures 14-9 through 14-12. The first three figures represent *risk averters*. In these cases, the indifference curves have positive slopes, indicating that the person demands more expected return in order to be willing to take more risk. Figure 14-12 shows the indifference curves of a person who might be called a *risk lover*. The slope of her indifference curves is negative, showing that the risk lover is willing to take less return in order to be able to assume more risk.

The indifference curves shown in Figure 14-9 are representative of a subclass of risk averters known as *diversifiers*. As risk increases by equal increments, the diversifier demands increasing increments of return, so that her indifference curves are convex to her budget line. As usual in this kind of analysis, the diversifier will attempt to reach as high an indifference curve as

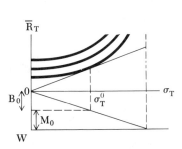

Figure 14-9 The "diversifier's" portfolio selection between risk and return.

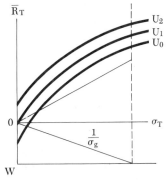

Figure 14-10 The "plunger's" portfolio selection: all money.

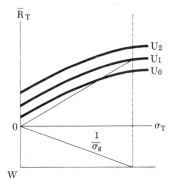

Figure 14-11 The "plunger's" portfolio selection: all bonds.

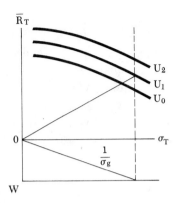

Figure 14-12 The "risk lover's" portfolio selection.

possible, given her budget constraint. Thus, the expected return and risk of her portfolio $\bar{R}_T$, σ_T will be determined by the point of tangency of the budget line with the highest possible indifference curve. Given the convex shape of her indifference curves, the diversifier is likely to reach an *interior equilibrium* at σ_T^0 holding both bonds B_0 and money M_0. Only part of this person's total wealth is put into bonds. This is why she is called a *diversifier*. Thus, in the case of the diversifier who demands increasing increments of return to induce her to take on constant increments of risk, the portfolio balance approach does away with the all-or-nothing version of the demand for money shown earlier in Figure 14-1.

Figures 14-10 and 14-11 show the indifference curves representative of a subclass of risk averters called *plungers*. The plunger will either not put her wealth into bonds at all or will put all of her wealth into bonds. In Figure 14-10, the plunger's indifference curves are steep relative to the budget line, so that she holds all money and no bonds. If her indifference curves are flat relative to the budget line as in Figure 14-11, she will hold all bonds, no money. This behavior would be consistent with the earlier regressive expectations model, but not with reality for most asset holders. Finally, Figure 14-12 shows the utility curve of the risk lover. She will attempt to maximize risk, and thus she, too, will put her entire wealth into bonds.

Since we observe empirically that the world is characterized by diversification, we can conclude that, in terms of the portfolio balance model, most asset holders are *diversifiers*. Thus, the situation shown in Figure 14-9, with indifference curves representing *increasing risk aversion,* is the basis for the portfolio balance model of the demand for money.

The Aggregate Demand for Money in the Portfolio Balance Model

We can now derive a demand function for money by varying the interest rate in Figure 14-9 and following the changes in the allocation of liquid wealth to bonds and money, particularly the latter. What happens in this model when interest rates rise? The result is shown in Figure 14-13. Since the slope of the budget line is $(r + \bar{g})/\sigma_g$, as r increases from r_0 to r_1 to r_2 the slope increases, and the line rotates upward. At any given level of risk, return will be increased as r rises. As r increases, the budget line touches successively higher indifference curves. This traces out the *optimum portfolio curve* connecting the points of tangency, shown in Figure 14-13. As r increases from a very low value, the diversifiers' tangency points move up and to the right, increasing both the expected rate of return and risk.

The progressively smaller increases in optimum risk from σ_T^0 to σ_T^1 to σ_T^2 in Figure 14-13 that come from continuing equal increases in r give successively smaller increases in the amount of wealth put into bonds. This is shown as B rises from B_0 to B_1 to B_2 in Figure 14-13. If, as r rises by constant increments, B rises by decreasing increments, then the demand for money must *decrease* by progressively smaller amounts as r increases, since $B + M$

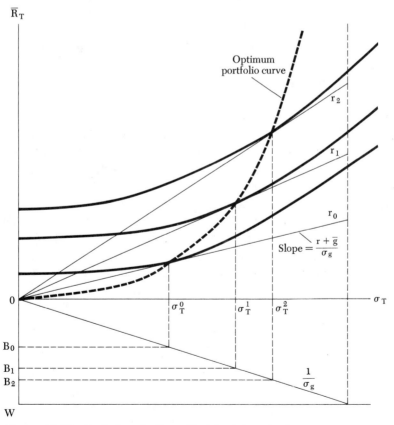

Figure 14-13 Portfolio selection with rising interest rates.

equals a fixed W. This relationship between M and r is shown in Figure 14-14, which is simply the same demand-for-money curve that we derived in Chapter 4. Along this demand-for-money function, a given drop in r, measured by Δr in Figure 14-14, gives a bigger increase in the demand for money at a low interest rate—from point two to point three—than at a high interest rate—from point zero to point one.

The demand-for-money function of Figure 14-14 is drawn as $m(y_0)$, assuming a given level of real income. This is because the portfolio balance model is basically a theory of the speculative demand for money. It analyzes the allocation of a given amount of liquid wealth to bonds and money, depending on interest rates and expectations concerning the return and risk on capital gains. No reference is made in the model to a transactions demand for money. Thus, the portfolio balance model gives us a more satisfactory theory of the speculative demand for money than does the regressive expectations model, particularly in its explanation of diversification. In the next section we will review the inventory-of-money approach to transactions demand that has been developed by Baumol and Tobin. But first, let us look at the effects of changes in expected capital gains $\bar{g}$ and risk estimates, σ_g in the portfolio balance model.

An increase in expected capital gains $\bar{g}$ will have the same effect as an increase in the interest rate, rotating the budget line up and increasing the amount of liquid wealth held in bonds, decreasing the demand for money at any given interest rate. This would shift the demand curve in Figure 14-13 to the left; at any r, the demand for money is decreased.

What happens if estimates of risk change? The standard deviation σ_g of the probability distribution of Figure 14-6 may increase as a result of increasing uncertainty. This increase would rotate the budget line in the upper half of Figure 14-13 down (smaller slope) and also rotate the line in the lower half up by reducing $1/\sigma_g$. Since $\sigma_T = B \cdot \sigma_g$, an increase in σ_g means that the amount of bonds B yielding any given total risk falls. The increase in σ_g thus reduces bond holdings B in two ways. In the upper half of Figure 14-13, the downward rotation of the budget line reduces desired risk σ_T. Even with the original σ_g value, a reduction in σ_T would cause a drop in B. But the additional effect of the increase in σ_g, rotating upward the $1/\sigma_g$ line in the bottom half

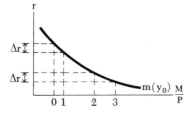

Figure 14-14 Demand for money.

of Figure 14-13, would further increase the drop in B needed to reduce total risk σ_T while risk per bond σ_g is rising.

Tobin's model of portfolio balance provides a much firmer ground for the speculative demand for money by explaining why rational individual asset holders might hold their portfolios distributed among several assets of differing riskiness and expected return. It also explains why the speculative demand for money should be inversely related to the interest rate, in the way that was assumed in Chapter 4. We will now turn to the transactions demand to see that it, too, should be sensitive to interest rate changes.

THE TRANSACTIONS DEMAND FOR MONEY

In Chapter 4 we suggested that one principal motive for holding money is the need to smooth out the difference between income and expenditure streams. This *transactions motive* lies behind the transactions demand for money which is related to the level of income. The alternative to holding money, which is the means of payment and earns no return, is bonds, which earn a return but also incur transactions costs—brokerage fees—as one moves from money received as pay to bonds and back to money to make expenditures. In Chapter 4 we suggested that the higher the interest rate bonds earn, the tighter transactions balances should be squeezed to hold bonds, giving the transactions demand some degree of sensitivity to interest rate changes. Here we can develop this point a bit more thoroughly, using a model of the *interest-elastic* transactions demand originally developed separately by William Baumol and James Tobin.

Suppose an individual is paid monthly and spends a total amount of real income y on purchases spread evenly throughout the month. He or she has the option of holding transactions balances in money or in bonds. Bonds yield a given interest rate r if held for a month, and proportionately less than r if they are held for a shorter period. Exchanges of bonds for money incur *transactions costs,* which prevent the person from continuously exchanging bonds into money as purchases are made. So initially, the person will exchange most of the paycheck for bonds or, more realistically, deposit it in an interest-earning account. Then, periodically, he or she will exchange an amount of bonds into money or withdraw funds from the interest-earning account, and then run down those cash balances as purchases are made, until the time comes for the next exchange of bonds into money. The more transactions from bonds to money that the person makes, the longer will be the average bond holding, and therefore interest earned. But since transactions are costly, increasing transactions increases cost. So the number of transactions, or trips to the broker or savings bank, that the person makes will be determined by a trade-off between interest earnings on bonds and costs of transactions. The individual's average money holdings, or demand for real balances, will be determined by the number of transactions made, and the aggregate demand for money will reflect this representative individual's demand. We will now describe a basic model of this cost-minimization problem which the individual faces, and then derive the interest-elastic transactions demand for real balances from it.

The Optimum Number of Transactions

Our consumer anticipates spending y in real income over a month of length T (30 days, if you like) in a smooth flow of purchases. Let's assume that n transactions take place. The first will be conversion of $(n-1)/n$ percent of y into bonds, or deposit of $(n-1)/n$ percent into the interest-earning account, leaving $1/n$ percent of y in money to be spent in the first part of the month. The rest of the transactions, $n-1$ of them, will each convert y/n into cash. This breaks the month into n intervals each T/n long, with the person beginning each interval with y/n in cash and ending it with zero cash, rushing off to the bank or broker.

The cash flow of our representative consumer i is shown in the sawtooth pattern of Figure 14-15. There we show time on the horizontal axis and money holdings on the vertical. For concreteness, we assume five bonds-to-money transactions after the initial conversion of 5/6 of the paycheck into bonds. This divides the period T into six subperiods. The consumer begins each subperiod with y/n in real balances and ends each with zero. The average money holdings in this sawtooth pattern is obviously $\bar{m}_i = y/2n$. The corresponding pattern of bond holdings is shown in Figure 14-16. Initially, the consumer holds $[(n-1)/n] \cdot y$ in bonds and exchanges y/n for money each subperiod, ending with zero. In the example here, $(n-1)/n$ is 5/6.

The consumer's problem now is to determine the optimal number of transactions. To solve for optimal n, we can write the cost of money-holding—both transactions cost and interest foregone—as a function of the number of

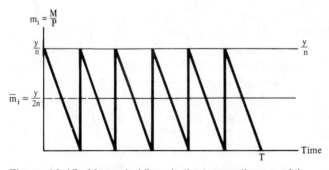

Figure 14-15 Money-holdings in the transactions model.

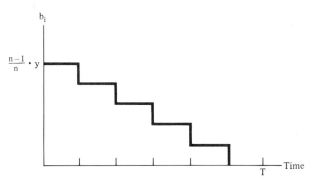

Figure 14-16 Bond holdings in the transactions model.

transactions n, and then find the cost-minimizing value of n. For simplicity, we assume that each transaction has a fixed cost a, so the transactions cost is na.

Calculation of the opportunity cost of foregone interest is a little more complicated. We assume that interest r is paid on bond or savings-account holdings proportional to the length of time they are held. Thus, the lost interest on money-holdings can be computed as follows. Initially, the consumer converts $[(n-1)/n] - y$ into bonds, keeping y/n in money. The interest lost on this money-holding is r for the full period T, or rTy/n. After one subperiod, another y/n is converted into money. That conversion out of bonds loses interest for $(n-1)/n$ percent of T, adding a loss of $rTy(n-1)/n$. The next conversion loses $rTy(n-2)/n$, and so forth. This gives us total interest lost as

$$\text{Interest cost} = \frac{rTy}{n} + \frac{rTy(n-1)}{n^2} + \frac{rTy(n-2)}{n^2} + \cdots$$

$$= \frac{rTy}{n}\left[1 + \frac{n-1}{n} + \frac{n-2}{n} + \cdots + \frac{1}{n}\right]. \qquad (17)$$

The last term in the expansion in brackets is $[n-(n-1)]/n = 1/n$.

The problem now is to find the convergent value for the expansion in brackets in equation (17). To do this, factor $1/n$ out of the brackets to obtain

$$\text{Interest cost} = \frac{rTy}{n^2}[n + (n-1) + (n-2) + \cdots + 1].$$

The expression in brackets is now the sum of all numbers from 1 to n. This is given by $n(n+1)/2$. So the final expression for the interest cost for n transactions, including the initial one *into* bonds, is

$$\text{Interest cost} = \frac{rTy}{n^2}\cdot\frac{n(n+1)}{2} = \frac{rTy}{2}\left(1 + \frac{1}{n}\right). \qquad (18)$$

We can now sum interest opportunity cost and transactions cost to obtain total cost TC:

$$TC = na + \frac{rTy}{2}\left(1 + \frac{1}{n}\right). \tag{19}$$

To solve for the cost-minimizing value of n, we set the partial derivative of total cost equal to zero:

$$\frac{\partial TC}{\partial n} = a - \frac{rTy}{2n^2} = 0.$$

Solving for optimal n, we obtain

$$n = \left(\frac{rTy}{2a}\right)^{1/2}. \tag{20}$$

The optimal number of transactions is the square root of $rTy/2a$. It increases with an increase in r, T, or y, and decreases with an increase in transactions cost a.

Individual and Aggregate Money Demand

Now that we have the solution for the number of transactions n, we can solve for the individual consumer's average money demand $\bar{m}_i$. From Figure 14-15, we have $\bar{m}_i = y/2n$. Using the optimal value of n from equation (20), we get for individual i's money demand

$$\bar{m}_i = \frac{y}{2}\left(\frac{2a}{rTy}\right)^{1/2} = \left(\frac{ay}{2rT}\right)^{1/2}. \tag{21}$$

The consumer's demand for real balances is the square root of $ay/2rT$. This is the well-known *square-root rule* of Baumol and Tobin. Transactions demand increases with the square root of y and decreases with the square root of r.

To move to aggregate money demand, we observe that for each representative consumer i whose money demand is given by equation (21), there must be someone on the other side of the money market. Suppose, for example, that consumer i buys goods from a representative firm, which periodically converts its money-holdings into bonds. This firm's pattern of bond and money-holdings would then mirror that of the consumer in Figures 14-15 and 14-16. In particular, we see that the firm's money-holdings would follow a sawtooth pattern exactly complementary to the consumer's pattern in Figure 14-15. This means that the firm's average money-holding would also be given by the square-root rule of equation (21).

Aggregate money demand in the transactions model is the sum of the individuals and that of the firms on the other side of the market. This means we must double $\bar{m}_i$ in equation (21) to get the aggregate demand for real balances m:

$$\frac{M}{P} = m = 2\left(\frac{ay}{2rT}\right)^{1/2} = \left(\frac{2ay}{rT}\right)^{1/2}. \tag{22}$$

Aggregate demand follows the Baumol-Tobin square-root rule. The elasticity of demand for real balances with respect to income is 0.5; with respect to the interest rate it is −0.5. These numbers are not inconsistent with the empirical evidence summarized later in this chapter. Transactions costs enter through the parameter a in equation (22).

To summarize, an increase in the interest rate should reduce the transactions demand for real balances, for any given level of the income stream, by an elasticity of −0.5. This takes us back to the demand-for-money function of Chapter 4,

$$\frac{M}{P} = m(r, y); \qquad \frac{\partial m}{\partial r} < 0, \qquad \frac{\partial m}{\partial y} > 0. \tag{23}$$

The transactions demand for money should respond to a change in the interest rate through a change in the number of bonds-to-money conversions. Thus, money demand is interest-sensitive even if all demand is for transactions. Any speculative component may add to this sensitivity, but speculative demand is not necessary for r to enter the money demand equation. One might even say that the division of money-holdings into speculative and transactions balances is largely a matter of analytic convenience.

Precautionary Demand in a Stochastic Setting

The transactions demand for money will exist if incomes and expenditures are not perfectly coordinated, whether or not they are deterministic. The *precautionary demand* is a fairly straightforward extension to a stochastic setting where the surplus or deficit of current income over expenditure is random. At each moment there may be a discrepancy between income and spending. Perhaps a worker's income rises because she has a chance to work overtime or falls because she is temporarily laid off. On the expenditure side, a shopper may come across a good "limited time only" offer, or her desired purchase may be out of stock.

On average, expenditure must be no more than income. The dilemma for the individual is that, on the one hand, it is costly if he or she does not have enough resources readily available to make a sudden purchase. Perhaps obtaining liquid funds by trading in bonds suffers a transaction cost, or the individual suffers a loss of utility when he or she cannot afford to pay for something on the spot (e.g., the acute embarrassment brought on when your date orders the most expensive item on the menu). This problem is alleviated by holding a stock of money as a sort of homemade insurance. One would hold more liquid funds if the cost of running short increased, or if the probability of doing so went up. Were the variability of the net surplus to increase with the expenditure, then money-holdings would also rise with income.

On the other hand, money pays little or no interest, so liquidity is achieved at an opportunity cost proportional to the size of the money stock and the interest rate. The money demand equation is the outcome of the trade-off between the expected losses from illiquidity and foregone interest, as in the transactions model.

We will now turn to another major perspective on the demand for money—Friedman's view of money as a consumer's and producer's good. This will lead us back again to the original demand-for-money equation (23).

MONEY AS A CONSUMER'S AND PRODUCER'S GOOD

The money demand models discussed so far, due mainly to Keynes and Tobin, draw an important distinction between transactions and speculative demands for money. Friedman, however, develops the demand for money within the context of the traditional microeconomic theories of consumer behavior and of the producer's demand for inputs. Consumers hold money because it yields a utility—the convenience of holding the means of payment rather than making frequent trips to the broker and risking losses on bonds. Their demand for money should be a demand for real balances, just as any consumer demand should be a demand for real consumer's goods, as opposed to their money value, in the absence of money illusion. This demand for real balances should depend on the level of real income. It should also depend on the returns to other ways of holding assets such as bonds or consumer durables, much as the demand for one kind of fruit should depend on the prices of other kinds.

Producers hold money as a productive asset that smooths payments and expenditure streams. Just as their demand for real capital services depends on the level of real output and the relative price of capital, as shown in Chapter 13, their demand for real balances should depend on real output (or income), and the relative returns on other ways of holding wealth.

The approach gives us a demand function for real balances,

$$\frac{M}{P} = m = m(y, r_1, \ldots, r_j, \ldots, r_J), \tag{24}$$

where $r_1, \ldots, r_J$ are the rates of return on all assets that are alternatives to money. If the ratio between the demand for real balances and real income is relatively trendless through time, and depends at any given point in time on the returns to alternative assets, we have Friedman's quantity theory version of (24):

$$\frac{M}{P} = k(r_1, \ldots, r_J) \cdot y, \qquad (25a)$$

or

$$\frac{m}{y} = k(r_1, \ldots, r_J). \qquad (25b)$$

In fact, as we will see shortly, the elasticity of m with respect to changes in y may well be about unity, so that the ratio between m and y is roughly constant along trend, and (25) is a good approximation to (24).

To fill out the demand function, we can include the rate of return on bonds and on durable goods as examples of the more complete list of alternative assets that might be relevant substitutes for money.

As we have already shown at some length in this chapter, as the rate of return on bonds rises, the demand for money falls. Rather than distinguish between transactions demand and speculative demand, we can simply note that as the expected total return on bonds rises, the demand for bonds should rise and the demand for money should fall. Earlier, we developed an expression for the expected return on bonds, equation (5):

$$e = r + \frac{r}{r^e} - 1.$$

Since bonds are a relevant substitute for money, we would insert r and r^e into the demand function (25). If $r^e = f(r)$, we can condense this expression of the dependency on the bond rate by simply including r in (25).

The Effect of the Rate of Inflation

Durable goods—producers' or consumers'—also serve as alternative assets to money. In Chapter 13, we saw that the real interest rate $(r - \dot{P})$ enters the demand function for purchases of producers' durables (investment demand). Here we explore the relation between consumer durables and money demand through the rate of inflation. As the price level rises, the value, or purchasing power, of a stock of durable goods remains roughly constant as durable goods prices rise along with the general price index. On the other hand, the purchasing power of money falls with an increase in prices, so that an increase in the *expected rate of inflation* should cause a shift out of money and bonds and into consumer durables. This should be interpreted carefully. In equation (19), a one-time increase in the price level will cause an increase in the nominal demand for money to keep M/P constant with y and all the r's in the k function unchanged. But an increase in the expected *continuing* rate of inflation will reduce the demand for real balances m.

Thus, compared with money, the rate of return on speculative holdings of consumer durables is the rate of inflation, $\dot{P} = (dP/dt)/P$, where as usual $\dot{P}$ stands for the proportional rate of change of prices. On the assumption that expected rates of inflation are positively related to the current rate, we can include $\dot{P}$ among the rates of return in (25).

With the rates of return of the two principal alternatives to money included, we now have the demand-for-money function,

$$\frac{M}{P} = m = m(y, r, \dot{P}). \tag{26}$$

The demand for real balances increases with an increase in y and falls with an increase in r or $\dot{P}$. In the modern quantity-theory version of (26), we would have

$$\frac{M}{P} = k(r, \dot{P}) \cdot y, \tag{27}$$

so that the ratio of m to y varies with changes in r and $\dot{P}$. The partial derivatives of k with respect to both r and $\dot{P}$ are negative.

This function is very close to the one we developed in Chapter 4. The only important difference is the inclusion of the rate of inflation, $\dot{P}$, in the demand function. It should be noted that (27) suggests that the *level* of the demand for real balances depends on the expected *rate* of inflation. Thus, if the economy shifts from a 2 percent rate of inflation to a 4 percent rate, the demand for money in the static model will shift down to a new level, and the demand for consumer goods will shift up. But once the demand function has shifted, the economy will reach a new static equilibrium unless there is another change in the *rate* of inflation. Thus, adding $\dot{P}$ to the demand function will not greatly affect the qualitative nature of the static model unless substantial *variations* in $\dot{P}$ are expected.

The Velocity of Money

From the demand-for-money equation (27), we can conveniently develop an expression for the income velocity of money, $v = y/m$. Replacing M/P in (27) by m and rearranging terms, we have the expression for velocity,

$$v = \frac{y}{m} = \frac{1}{k(r, \dot{P})} = v(r, \dot{P}). \tag{28}$$

Since $\partial k/\partial r$ and $\partial k/\partial \dot{P}$ are both negative, $\partial v/\partial r$ and $\partial v/\partial \dot{P}$ are both positive. An increase in either the interest rate or the rate of inflation should cause people to economize on money-holdings since these are the rates of return on the alternative assets, bonds, and durable goods. This would result in an increase in velocity as money demand falls relative to GNP.

In the long-run U.S. data, the velocity of money seemed, on balance, to decline along trend up to World War II. Since then it has risen, along with interest rates, fairly steadily. This suggests that, over the long run, the ratio of y to m is rather stable, as is the ratio of consumption to income, c/y. The question of the relative stability of the y/m ratio v and the $c - y$ relationship is, as we will see in Chapter 16, one of the points at the heart of the *Keynesian-Monetarist* controversy.

If the short-run elasticity of v with respect to changes in interest rates were very low, we could approximate $v(r, \dot{P})$ in (28) by a constant $\bar{v}$, giving a direct relationship between movements in m and y; $y = \bar{v}m$. However, there is substantial empirical evidence that the interest elasticity of the demand for money is not insignificant in the short run. This suggests, through equation (22), that the interest elasticity of velocity is not insignificant so that, in fact, both the product and money market equations are needed to predict movements in nominal and real GNP. We will return to this point in some detail in the discussion of monetary and fiscal policy in Chapter 16.

EMPIRICAL ESTIMATES OF INCOME AND INTEREST ELASTICITIES

In the absence of substantial shifts in expected rates of inflation, which are not fully compatible with a static model of income determination which deals with movements from one equilibrium price level to another, the demand-for-money function that emerges from the analysis of this chapter is the familiar

$$\frac{M}{P} = m = m(r, y) \tag{29}$$

of Chapter 4.

The y term in the demand function represents transactions demand or, in Friedman's terms, the increasing demand for money as a producer's and consumer's good, through an income effect, as income rises. The r term represents the interest elasticity of both the transactions demand for money and the speculative demand through Tobin's portfolio balance model. It also represents a potential substitutability against bonds in production and consumption decisions.

There have been many investigations into the values of the elasticities of the demand for *real money*—currency plus demand deposits, $M1$ or $M1$ plus time deposits, $M2$, deflated by the price level P as in equation (29)—with respect to interest rate and income changes. There are many continuing controversies concerning the values of these elasticities and the proper form of the demand-for-money function. However, representative elasticities of the demand for real balances from Goldfeld's 1973 article are about 0.7 with respect to changes in real income, and -0.25 with respect to changes in r. Here r is a short-term interest rate—a three-month commercial paper rate, a three-month treasury bill rate, or a time deposit rate. With the money stock $M1$ at about \$750 billion in 1987, GNP at about \$4.4 trillion, and the short-term interest rate at about 6 percent, these elasticities imply that a \$65 billion GNP increase—1.5 percent—would raise the demand for money by about \$8 billion, and a 1-point drop in short-term interest rates—17 percent—would increase the demand for money by about \$32 billion.

Most demand-for-money estimates suggest that demand changes lag slightly behind interest rate changes. Thus, if interest rates fell from 5 to 4 percent, causing an increase of \$30 to \$40 billion in the desired holdings of money, the estimates suggest that about 30 percent of the discrepancy between actual and desired money-holdings would be eliminated in one quarter, 50 percent in two quarters, and 75 percent in a year. This means that if an increase in y or decrease in r increases the level of desired equilibrium real balances from $(M/P)_0$ to $(M/P)^*$ at time t_0 in Figure 14-17, the path of actual holdings of $M/P = m$ will tend to follow the dashed adjustment path toward the final desired level of real balances, $(M/P)^*$.

This partial adjustment pattern leads to the same kind of overreaction of interest rates to changes in the money supply that we see in traditional microeconomic analysis, in which demand changes yield larger short-run than long-run changes in prices, and vice versa for output. In Figure 14-18 the demand-for-money curve $M(y_0)$ is the long-run curve reflecting the long-run interest elasticity mentioned above as about -0.25. The intersection of $M(y_0)$ with the given initial money supply, $(M/P)_0$, at point E_0, gives an initial equilibrium interest rate r_0. Through E_0 we can also draw a short-run demand function $m(y_0)$ that reflects the partial short-run adjustment mechanism of Figure 14-17. This shows the one-period reaction of demand to interest rate

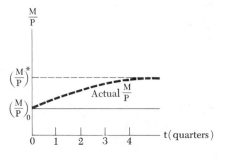

Figure 14-17 The adjustment path of actual holdings of M/P.

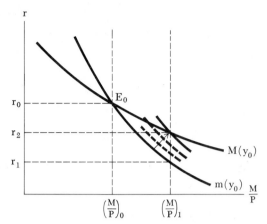

Figure 14-18 Long-run and short-run demand for money and effects of an increase in the money supply.

changes, while the $M(y_0)$ curve shows the long-run relationship between M/P and r.

Now if the money supply is increased to $(M/P)_1$ the interest rate will initially fall to r_1 along the short-run $m(y_0)$ function, holding y constant throughout this partial analysis, that is, assuming a vertical IS curve. As time passes, and the actual demand shifts up toward equilibrium along the dashed path of Figure 14-17, the interest rate will rise toward r_2, with the short-run demand function shifting up, shown as the dashed short-run functions of Figure 14-18. Eventually, holding y constant at y_0, the interest rate will settle at r_2, rising from the short-run level of r_1 but below the initial equilibrium r_0.

If the level of income has also risen during the process as the LM curve shifts along an actual nonvertical IS curve, the interest rate will end up higher than r_2, on a higher $M(y_1)$ function, but lower than the initial r_0. Thus, since the demand for money is less elastic in the short run than in the long run, owing to the partial adjustment process of Figure 14-17, we can expect an increase in the money supply to push interest rates down somewhat more in the short run, one quarter, than in the slightly longer run, one year.

Since this chapter's review of the several approaches to the demand for money has not substantially altered the demand function we began with in Chapter 4, there is no need to return to the static model of income determination here. This chapter has illustrated another kind of channel that economic research follows. In this chapter the emphasis has been on developing theoretical explanations—or, put more simply, ways to understand common empirical observations such as people holding positive amounts of two assets with different rates of return at the same time (diversification), and the interest elasticity of transactions balances. After we briefly discuss in Chapter 15 the supply of money—a quantity taken as given up to now—we will return to some of the important points in the analysis of the demand for money in Chapter 16.

SELECTED READINGS

W. J. Baumol, "The Transactions Demand for Cash: An Inventory Theoretic Approach," *Quarterly Journal of Economics,* November 1952.

F. De Leeuw and E. Gramlich, "The Federal Reserve-MIT Econometric Model," *Federal Reserve Bulletin,* January 1968, pp. 11–40.

M. Friedman, "The Demand for Money: Some Theoretical and Empirical Results," *Journal of Political Economy,* August 1959.

M. Friedman, "The Quantity Theory of Money—A Restatement," in M. G. Mueller, ed., *Readings in Macroeconomics* (New York: Holt, Rinehart and Winston, 1966).

S. M. Goldfeld, "The Demand for Money Revisited," *Brookings Papers on Economic Activity,* vol. 3, 1973.

S. M. Goldfeld, "The Case of the Missing Money," *Brookings Papers on Economic Activity,* vol. 3, 1976.

A. H. Hansen, *Monetary Theory and Fiscal Policy* (New York: McGraw-Hill, 1949), chapters 3–4.

F. Modigliani, R. A. Rasche, and J. P. Cooper, "Central Bank Policy, Money Supply, and the Short-Term Rate of Interest," *Journal of Money, Credit, and Banking,* May 1968.

R. L. Teigen, "The Demand for and Supply of Money," in W. L. Smith and R. L. Teigen, eds., *Readings in Money, National Income and Stabilization Policy* (Homewood, Ill.: R.D. Irwin, 1965).

J. Tobin, "The Interest-Elasticity of the Transaction Demand for Cash," *Review of Economics and Statistics,* September 1956.

J. Tobin, "Liquidity Preference as Behavior Toward Risk," *Review of Economic Studies,* February 1958.

chapter 15

The Supply of Money

In this chapter we will discuss the process that determines the money supply, which up to now we have taken as exogenously fixed by the Federal Reserve System—the Fed. The money supply that we will focus on has a *narrow* definition called $M1$ and an alternative *broad* definition called $M2$. The narrow definition $M1$ consists of currency—paper money and coins—in the hands of the nonbank public, plus checkable deposits in commercial banks and other depository institutions such as savings and loan associations. $M1$ was $730 billion at the end of 1986. The broader definition adds money market funds, savings deposits, and small-denomination time deposits to $M1$. $M2$ was $2.8 trillion.

The narrow set of liquid assets in $M1$ has two characteristics that separate them from other assets in the economy: They are the generally accepted means of payment, and they earn little or no interest. This was the most generally used definition of money until the 1980s. The introduction of money market funds during the deregulation of financial markets in the 1980s created a major part of $M2$ that can be used as a means of payment. Money market funds grew from near zero in 1978 to $750 billion in 1986.

The growth of money market funds has blurred the distinction between $M1$ and $M2$. Easy substitution on the part of deposit holders between checking accounts at commercial banks and money market funds made the mix between $M1$ and other components of $M2$ less stable in the 1980s. Thus, by 1987 the emphasis in analyzing monetary policy shifted to $M2$; in January 1987 the

Fed stopped reporting targets for $M1$ to the Joint Economic Committee of Congress.

All of the assets in $M2$ earn significantly lower interest than the next-liquid assets such as certificates of deposits (CDs) and are much more liquid. So there is now a natural separation between $M2$ as a liquid asset that is generally acceptable as a means of payment *and* earns low or no interest, and broader money concepts that include CDs. Within $M2$, the deposits in $M1$ are most liquid and earn the lowest return. Historically, analysis of money supply has been done in terms of $M1$; now the emphasis is shifting toward $M2$. Choice between the two concepts will not make much difference for the money supply analysis presented in this chapter, and most of the empirical work we discuss has been done on $M1$. Therefore, here we will retain a focus on $M1$ and note where this might make a difference.

In the following sections we first describe the instruments of monetary policy available to the Fed and a bit of the institutional apparatus of money supply determination. Second, we review the process of money supply expansion. Third, we develop a money supply model that makes clear the roles of the Federal Reserve, the public, and the banks in determining the actual money supply. Fourth, we review some empirical estimates of the interest elasticity of the money supply. Finally, we work this new money supply function into the static model by altering the LM curve to account for the sensitivity of money supply to the interest rate.

We conclude the chapter with a discussion of an important issue in monetary policy: whether the Fed should target the money supply or interest rates. This question arises when the Fed has to adopt a short-run decision rule for day-to-day policy in a situation where the actual movement of the economy becomes known only with a lag. If the Fed wants to stabilize GNP against private-sector shocks, should its *intermediate target* be the money stock or the interest rate?

THE INSTRUMENTS OF MONETARY POLICY

Up to this point, we have just assumed that the Federal Reserve System can change the level of the money supply when it chooses. The Fed controls the level of the money supply first by setting *reserve requirements* against deposits, and then by changing the amount of reserves it supplies, both on its own initiative and on the initiative of the banks. The reserve requirements state that commercial banks and other depository institutions like savings and loans must hold as reserves some fraction z, say 10 percent, of their total demand deposit liabilities, that is, of their customers' total checking account balances. These reserves are held in the form of deposits at Federal Reserve Banks. Thus, if the reserve requirement z is 0.1, and the commercial banks hold a total of

$30 billion in deposits at the Federal Reserve Banks, the banks' deposits cannot total more than $300 billion.

The Fed has three ways of changing the money supply, all operating through the reserve mechanism. First, it can increase reserves by *open market operations.* The Fed can buy, say, $100 million in federal government bonds in the market in New York, paying with checks drawn on itself. The sellers of the bonds will then deposit the checks drawn on the Fed in their banks. These checks become the banks' claims on the Fed, or *reserves* from the banks' point of view. The banking system can expand its demand deposit liabilities by $1 billion (= 100/0.1) by a technique that we describe in the next section. Open market operations of this sort—buying and selling in the bond market on the Fed's account—are handled by the Federal Reserve System's open market manager, usually a vice president of the Federal Reserve Bank of New York, under supervision of the System's Open Market Committee, made up of the seven members of the System's Board of Governors in Washington and five of the Federal Reserve Bank presidents. These open market operations are the Fed's normal policy tool for making day-to-day changes in the money supply.

Second, banks can obtain additional reserves by borrowing from the Fed at the *discount rate r_d,* usually set somewhat below short-term market rates such as the rate on three-month treasury bills. When a bank borrows at the Fed's *discount window,* a deposit at the Fed, in the amount of the borrowed reserves, is created in the bank's name. This is essentially the same procedure that a bank follows in making a loan to a private person; it credits his or her checking account with the amount of the loan. It should be noted here that, where reserve creation by open market operations comes at the Fed's initiative, an increase in borrowed reserves at the discount window comes at the bank's initiative. This distinction will be important in the money supply model we develop later in this chapter.

Both open market and discount window operations affect the money supply by changing the level of reserves with a given reserve ratio z. The Fed's third way to operate on the money supply is through changes in the reserve ratio itself. With z at 0.1, $30 billion in reserves will support a $300 billion money supply ($300 = 30/0.1$). An increase in the reserve ratio z to 0.15 would reduce the money supply supported by the $30 billion reserve base to $200 billion (= $30/0.15$). Thus, reserve ratio increases amount to what is called *effective reserve* changes, changing the money supply that can be supported by a given amount of reserves.

The Fed tends to use its three policy instruments—open market operations, the discount window, and the reserve ratio—for quite different purposes. Open market operations are used for day-to-day control of the money supply, or, more generally, credit conditions. If interest rates are rising faster or higher than the Open Market Committee desires, given the position of the economy, the manager of the open market account can buy bonds, shoring up bond prices and keeping interest rates down. This operation increases the money supply. Or, focusing on the money supply, if it is growing less rapidly than the Open Market Committee wishes, the manager can also buy bonds. These operations are conducted every day by the manager and provide the Fed with a continuing, relatively unpublicized, way of controlling the money supply.

Discount window operations provide banks with the opportunity to acquire reserves in a pinch, within the context of overall credit conditions set by the Fed. Discount operations thus contribute to the degree of control over the money supply exercised by the banks.

Finally, the Fed uses reserve ratio changes as an overt, well-publicized move to change effective reserves in a major way, as opposed to the normal, more continuous changes generated by open market operations. Thus, changes in the reserve ratio signal a major shift in the Fed's monetary policy and serve as a warning of the change to the financial community. This does not happen often: the last significant changes in reserve requirements were in 1986.

In general, banks create deposits on which no or low interest is paid, in order to make loans on which higher interest is earned. The deposits are created in the process of making the loans; a loan is credited to the borrower's account. Thus, the incentive to increase deposits lies in the possibility of making profitable loans. When loan demand by potential borrowers falls off, banks may not create deposits up to the full limit that reserves would support. Thus, they may, from time to time, have on hand *excess reserves.* On the other hand, when loan demand is particularly strong, banks may borrow reserves at the discount window to support the additional deposit creation that accompanies the increase in loans. This degree of freedom that the banks have to hold excess reserves or to borrow reserves makes the money supply responsive, to a certain extent, to loan demand and the interest rate. When loan demand is strong and interest rates are high, the banks will squeeze excess reserves and increase borrowing at the discount window, increasing the money supply supported by a given amount of *unborrowed reserves* supplied by the Fed. Thus, the money supply itself will have a positive elasticity with respect to the interest rate, reducing the slope of the *LM* curve—that is, flattening it. Before we develop a simple model showing the relationships between *free reserves* (*excess reserves* less *borrowed reserves*), the interest rate, and the money supply, we will briefly review the mechanism of money expansion in a fractional reserve system.

THE MECHANISM OF MONETARY EXPANSION

As we have defined it, the money supply consists of currency and demand deposits that are supplied by commercial banks. These banks have balance sheets made up of liabilities, including demand deposits, and assets, including loans and reserves. The Federal Reserve requires that commercial banks retain a certain percent z of their liabilities as reserves, mainly as deposits in the Federal Reserve Banks.

Suppose that the Open Market Committee decides to expand the money supply. The manager of the Fed's open market account buys, in the bond market in New York, a certain amount of treasury bonds, say, $100,000 worth, and issues a check, drawn on the Federal Reserve System, for $100,000 to the seller. The seller then deposits the check in his checking account in bank A, creating $100,000 in liabilities for the bank, the claim on the bank by the depositor, and also $100,000 in assets for the bank, the claim on Federal Reserve System. If there is a 10 percent reserve requirement, bank A can loan $90,000 of its increase in assets and must retain $10,000 as reserves, as shown in Table 15-1.

The borrower of the $90,000 presumably spends it, transferring the $90,000 to the seller's bank, bank B, which can in turn loan out $81,000. This amount is transferred to bank C, and the process continues. As a result, the total increase in the money supply from the $100,000 reserve increase is given by

$$\Delta M = \$100 + \$90 + \$81 + \cdots,$$

or

$$\Delta M = 100[1 + 0.9 + (0.9)^2 + \cdots] = 100 \frac{1}{1 - 0.9} = 1000.$$

Thus, in this simple example the change in the money supply is given by

$$\Delta M = \frac{1}{z} \Delta R, \tag{1}$$

where ΔR is the initial reserve increase and z is the reserve ratio. This is a *reserve multiplier* giving the effect of reserve changes on the money supply M, exactly analogous to the simple investment or government spending multipliers that we developed in Chapter 3, which give the effects of changes in these variables on output.

Table 15-1   BALANCE SHEET EFFECTS OF A $100,000 INCREASE IN RESERVES

Bank A		Bank B		Bank C	
Assets	Liabilities	Assets	Liabilities	Assets	Liabilities
$100	$100	$90	$90	$81	$81
($10 reserves		($9 reserves		($8.1 reserves	
$90 loans)		$81 loans)		$72.9 loans)	

The multiple increase in M came from each bank holding as reserves only a fraction z of its increased deposits—that is, liabilities—and lending out $1 - z$ percent of the increased deposits. Thus, from the point of view of each bank, it is simply lending out a fraction, $1 - z$, of its increased deposit inflow, but the system as a whole is increasing deposits by $1/z$ times the reserves increase.

This example contains two important oversimplifications. First, since the banks stay *loaned up*, excess reserves do not enter the picture so that the dependence of the money supply on the interest rate is obscured. Second, no provision is made for leakage into increased public holdings of currency, which would reduce the value of the reserves multiplier. We will now look at a more realistic model that incorporates these effects.

THE DETERMINANTS OF THE MONEY SUPPLY

The relationship between the money supply—currency in the hands of the public outside the banking system plus demand deposits—and unborrowed reserves provided by the Fed's open market operations depends on the public's preference between currency and demand deposits, and on the banks' holding of excess reserves or borrowing of reserves at the discount window. The latter activity will make the money supply a function of the interest rate and change somewhat our view of the LM curve. In this section we will develop a money supply model that follows fairly closely work done by Teigen. Then we will review some empirical results on the interest elasticity of the money supply obtained by Teigen, by Modigliani, Rasche, and Cooper in the MPS model, and by Hendershott and De Leeuw.

The money supply M is currency held by the public C_p plus demand deposits held by the public in the commercial banking system D_p:

$$M = C_p + D_p. \tag{2}$$

The public holds h percent of its money in currency and $1 - h$ percent in checking account deposits, so that

$$C_p = hM \tag{3}$$

and

$$D_p = (1 - h)M. \tag{4}$$

Earlier, we introduced the required reserve ratio z, which gives the fraction of demand deposits D_p that must be held as required reserves RR:

$$RR = z \cdot D_p = z(1 - h)M, \tag{5}$$

from equation (4). Total reserves can be divided on the one hand into the *sources* of reserves, and on the other hand into the *uses* of reserves. The Fed provides unborrowed reserves, RU, mainly by buying U.S. government securities in the bond market. It also supplies borrowed reserves, RB, by lending to the commercial banks through the discount mechanism. These reserves are allocated to three uses. The banks can allocate their reserves to required reserves RR or to excess reserves RE, which is defined as total bank reserves less RR. In addition, some of the reserves provided by the Fed through open market purchases of bonds will end up as currency in the hands of the public C_p. Since both sources and uses must sum to total reserves R, this gives us the basic reserves identity,

$$RU + RB \equiv R \equiv RR + RE + C_p. \tag{6}$$

The reserves identity also gives us an expression for the policy instrument that the Fed directly controls through open market operations,

$$RU = RR + RE - RB + C_p = RR + RF + C_p, \tag{7}$$

where *net free reserves, RF,* is defined as $RE - RB$. Free reserves should be sensitive to movements in the interest rate, as we will see shortly.

Equations (3) for C_p and (5) for RR can be combined with equation (7) for unborrowed reserves to yield an equation giving the money supply as a function of unborrowed reserves, controlled by the Fed, and free reserves, controlled by the commercial banks. Substituting from equations (3) and (5) for C_p and RR, respectively, into the right-hand side of (7), we have

$$RU = z(1 - h)M + RF + hM.$$

Solving this equation for M gives us the money supply equation,

$$M = \frac{RU - RF}{h + z(1 - h)} = \frac{RU - RF}{z + h(1 - z)}. \tag{8}$$

It should be apparent from equation (8) that $\partial M / \partial RU > 0$ and $\partial M / \partial RF$, $\partial M / \partial h$, and $\partial M / \partial z$ are all negative. The money supply rises as the Fed provides more unborrowed reserves and falls as free reserves increase, the public's preference for currency rises, or the Fed increases the reserve ratio. The banks, through decisions on excess reserves and borrowing at the discount window, determine RF, the Fed determines z directly and RU by open market operations, and the public's tastes between currency and checking deposits determine h. These variables taken together determine the money supply M.

Next, we can separate the right-hand term in (8) into two parts:

$$M = \frac{RU}{h + z(1 - h)} - \frac{RF}{h + z(1 - h)}. \tag{9}$$

The *RU* term in (9) gives the portion of the money supply determined mainly at the initiative of the Fed, which might be considered the exogenous portion of the money supply. Unborrowed reserves grew from about $19 billion in 1960 to $55 billion at the end of 1986.

The *RF* term in (9) gives the portion of the money supply which is mainly endogenously determined by the banking system in response to loan opportunities and interest rates. In tight credit conditions, when loan demand is high relative to the supply of unborrowed reserves from the Fed, we would expect free reserves to be negative, with banks squeezing excess reserves as tightly as possible and borrowing substantially at the discount window. When credit conditions are easier, *RF* will be positive.

Movements in *M1, M2, RU,* and *RF* are shown in Figure 15-1. In the early 1960s, as GNP grew up to potential from 1960 to 1965, and then excess demand developed after 1965, free reserves fell steadily from $0.7 billion at the end of 1960 to zero at the end of 1965, and then more erratically to −$0.8 billion at the end of 1969. From 1969 to 1974 free reserves were typically negative, fluctuating between zero and −$1.0 billion. In 1975 and 1976 they were positive, during a time of recession and slack demand. From 1977 to 1985 they were negative, reaching −$2.2 billion in 1984. This was generally a period of high interest rates and tight monetary policy. As monetary policy eased after 1985, free reserves again became positive. As credit demand increased during the 1960s, the banking system added perhaps $1.5 billion to reserves by squeezing excess reserves and increasing borrowings at the discount window. During the 1970s, free reserve fluctuations accounted for up to $2.2 billion of changes in total reserves. In the 1980s, these fluctuations reached $2.8 billion. In the depression days of the 1930s, free reserves were positive, standing at $3 billion at the end of 1935.

This response of free reserves to changes in credit conditions, which might be measured by interest rates, gives the money supply a positive elasticity with respect to the interest rate.

EMPIRICAL ESTIMATES OF INTEREST ELASTICITY

Banks lend at market interest rates, represented by r, and borrow reserves at the Fed's discount window at the discount rate r_d. As the market rate rises relative to the discount rate, banks will reduce excess reserves and increase their borrowing at the discount window to take advantage of the widening $r - r_d$ differential. Since free reserves *RF* equal excess reserves *RE* minus borrowed reserves *RB,* both of these effects tend to reduce free reserves as the differential increases. Thus, we can write *RF* as a function of the $r - r_d$ differential,

$$RF = f(r - r_d), \tag{10}$$

with *RF* falling as $r - r_d$ increases.

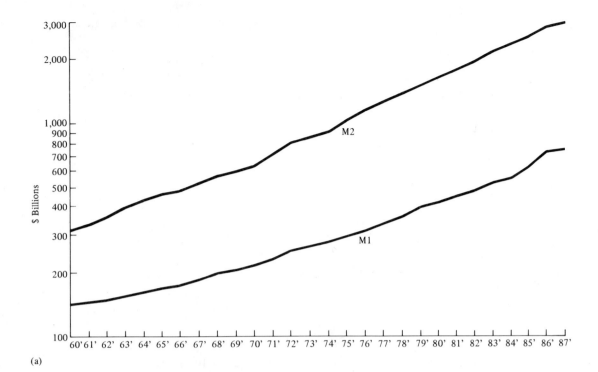

(a)

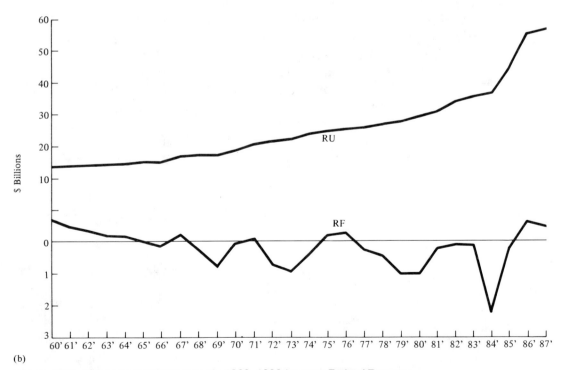

(b)

Figure 15-1 Reserves and money stock, 1960–1988 (source: Federal Reserve Bulletin). Source: 1988 Economic Report of the President and July 1986 Survey of Current Business.

With unborrowed reserves RU and the reserve ratio z determined exogenously by the Fed, and with h a parameter depending on the public's preferences between currency and demand deposits, the free reserves function in (10) makes the money supply also a function of $r - r_d$, given RU, z, and h:

$$M = \frac{RU - f(r - r_d)}{h + z(1 - h)} = M(r - r_d),\tag{11}$$

and M' is positive.

The most direct way to estimate the interest elasticity of the money supply is to estimate a version of the free reserve equation (10), and then calculate the effect of an r change on the money supply M through the money supply equation (11). Studies by Modigliani, Rasche, and Cooper, in developing the money market sector of the MPS model, and by Hendershott and De Leeuw, have estimated essentially linear versions of (10):

$$RF = a_0 - a_1(r - r_d).$$

Both studies estimate the coefficient a_1 of the interest differential to be about $500 million. Thus, an increase in the market interest rate r of one percentage point—from 8 to 9 percent, for example—will reduce free reserves by $500 million. With unborrowed reserves held constant, this gives an increase in $RU - RF$ of $500 million. Since $RU - RF$ ($= RU + RB - RE$ by the definition of RF) was about $34 billion in the mid-1970s, an increase in $RU - RF$ of $500 million is a 1.5 percent ($= 0.5/34$) change. With short-term rates at about 8 percent during the same period, a one-point change in the market rate is a 12.5 percent ($= 1/8$) change. Hence, during the mid-1970s, the elasticity of reserves to changes in the interest rate is about 0.12 ($= 1.4/12.5$); a 1 percent increase in the interest rate will increase $RU - RF$ by about 0.12 percent.

We can convert this interest rate elasticity of reserves into an interest elasticity of the money supply by observing that the money supply function, equation (8), can be written as

$$M = \frac{1}{h + z(1 - h)}(RU - RF).\tag{12}$$

With the denominator held constant, a 1 percent change in $(RU - RF)$ will yield a 1 percent change in M. Thus, if a 1 percent increase in the interest rate r raises reserves, $RU - RF$, by 0.12 percent, it also raises the money supply by 0.12 percent, so that the elasticity of the money supply with respect to changes in r is about 0.12 on the Modigliani-Rasche-Cooper and Hendershott-De Leeuw estimates.

A different approach to measurement of the interest elasticity was taken earlier by Teigen. He observed that in equation (9), repeated here,

$$M = \frac{RU}{h + z(1 - h)} - \frac{RF}{h + z(1 - h)},$$

the term with RU in the numerator is the portion of the money supply determined mainly by the Fed, while the term in RF is determined mainly by the banks. If the term in RU is defined as an exogenously determined M^*:

$$M^* \equiv \frac{RU}{h + z(1 - h)}, \tag{13}$$

then the ratio of actual M to exogenous M^* is a function of the $r - r_d$ spread. Dividing all the terms in equation (12) by M^*, as defined in (13), we have

$$\frac{M}{M^*} = 1 - \frac{RF(r - r_d)/[h + z(1 - h)]}{M^*} = g(r - r_d), \tag{14}$$

where the ratio M/M^* increases as $r - r_d$ increases since RF is a decreasing function of $r - r_d$; so that $g' > 0$.

Using the actual values of z and RU, we can construct an average value of h, M^* on a quarterly basis from (13). Then the ratio of actual M to constructed M^* can be related to $r - r_d$ in a linear regression,

$$\frac{M}{M^*} = b_0 + b_1(r - r_d),$$

to obtain an estimate of the interest sensitivity of M/M^*. Using this procedure, Teigen obtained estimates of the elasticity of the money supply with respect to changes in r ranging from 0.12 to 0.17, depending on the estimating technique used. For our purposes, this estimate is not at all different from the estimates coming from the direct relation of RF to $r - r_d$, discussed earlier. Thus, for a *typical* estimate of the interest elasticity of the money supply, culled from a small but rapidly growing literature on the subject, we can use 0.15. An increase of 1 percent (not percentage point) in the short-term interest rate will increase the money supply by about 0.15 percent.

THE MONEY SUPPLY IN THE STATIC MODEL

The interest sensitivity of the money supply can be worked into the static model in several ways. Figure 15-2 shows the supply and demand curves for real balances $m = M/P$. With an initial income level y_0, the demand-for-money curve is $m(y_0)$. With an initial real money supply m_0 ($= M_0/P$; we hold P constant throughout this analysis), the interest rate is r_0. Now suppose

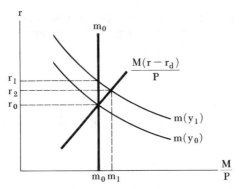

Figure 15-2 Interest-sensitive money supply.

income rises, due perhaps to an upward shift of the *IS* curve. Then the demand curve in Figure 15-2 shifts up to $m(y_1)$, and with a money supply fixed at m_0, as in Part II, the interest rate will rise to r_1.

But if the money supply is sensitive to changes in the interest rate, the money supply function through the initial equilibrium point r_0, y_0, m_0 looks like the positively sloped supply function $M(r - r_d)/P$ in Figure 15-2. In this case, the increased demand for money calls forth an increase in supply equal to $m_1 - m_0$ as the interest rate rises to r_2 instead of r_1. Thus, the interest elasticity of the money supply reduces the increase in r (from $r_1 - r_0$ to $r_2 - r_0$) needed to maintain money market equilibrium with a given increase in y, from y_0 to y_1, in Figure 15-2.

The last sentence says that with an interest-sensitive money supply, the slope of the *LM* curve is flatter than otherwise. This is shown in the four-quadrant *LM* diagram of Figure 15-3. At the initial interest rate r_0, the real money supply is equal to $M(r_0)/P$ in the southwest quadrant. If the interest rate rises to r_1, with the money supply fixed at $M(r_0)/P$, as we assumed in Part II, the level of income must rise to y_1 to maintain money market equilibrium. The interest rate increase reduces the speculative *and* transactions demands for money, as we saw in Chapter 12, freeing money to support an increase in y within the constraint of a given m.

If the money supply is not fixed, but is a function of the interest rate r:

$$M = M(r); \qquad M' > 0, \qquad (15)$$

then an increase in the interest rate from r_0 to r_1 shifts the money supply out from $M(r_0)/P$ to $M(r_1)/P$ in Figure 15-3. This increase in money supply will support an increase in income to y_2, as opposed to y_1. Thus, the *LM* curve with an interest-sensitive money supply looks like L_1M_1 in Figure 15-3— flatter than L_0M_0, which assumes a fixed real money supply.

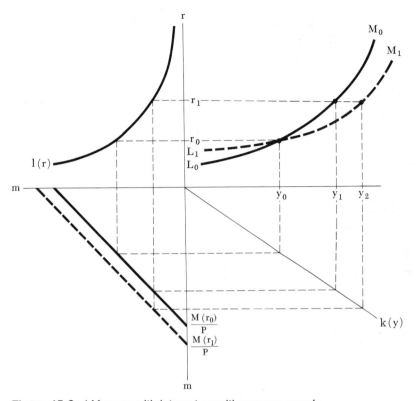

Figure 15-3 *LM* curve with interest-sensitive money supply.

We can derive the modified expression for the slope of the *LM* curve with an interest-sensitive money supply by returning to the equilibrium condition in the money market. As we saw in Chapter 12, the demand for money can be written as either

$$\frac{M^d}{P} = m(y, r); \quad \frac{\partial m}{\partial y} > 0, \quad \frac{\partial m}{\partial r} < 0, \tag{16a}$$

or

$$M^d = P \cdot m(y, r). \tag{16b}$$

The money supply function can now be written as

$$M^s = M(r); \quad \frac{\partial m}{\partial r} > 0. \tag{17}$$

Equilibrium in the money market requires that the demand for money equal the supply at the existing interest rate. This means $M^d = M^s$, or

$$P \cdot m(y, r) = M(r). \tag{18}$$

To obtain the slope of the *LM* curve with a given *P*, we can totally differentiate (18) to obtain

$$P\left(\frac{\partial m}{\partial y} dy + \frac{\partial m}{\partial r} dr\right) = M' dr.$$

Collecting the terms in *dy* and *dr,* we have

$$dr\left(P \frac{\partial m}{\partial r} - M'\right) = -P \frac{\partial m}{\partial y} dy.$$

This gives us the expression for the slope of the *LM* curve with an interest-sensitive money supply,

$$\left.\frac{dr}{dy}\right|_{LM} = -\frac{P \cdot \dfrac{\partial m}{\partial y}}{P \cdot \dfrac{\partial m}{\partial r} - M'}. \tag{19}$$

Since $\partial m/\partial y$ is positive, $\partial m/\partial r$ is negative, and M' is positive, this expression for the slope of *LM* is positive.

In Part II, with $M' = 0$, the slope of the *LM* curve was just $-[(\partial m/\partial y)/(\partial m/\partial r)]$. Addition of an interest-sensitive money supply with M' positive reduces the slope of the *LM* curve. That is, the *LM* curve is flatter with $M' > 0$ than it is with $M' = 0$.

In Chapter 14 we noted that if the interest elasticity of *demand* for money is small, the velocity of money may be taken as a constant. In this special case the *LM* equation can be reduced to

$$y = \bar{v}m, \tag{20}$$

where $\bar{v}$ is the fixed velocity of money. Equation (20) is then one equation in one exogenous unknown, *m.* A monetarist could use it to predict real GNP (*y*) changes without reference to any other part of our multimarket system.

If the money *supply* is sensitive to interest rate changes, then this position does not hold up even in the face of an interest elasticity of the *demand* for money equal to zero. Suppose the demand for real balances is given by

$$m^d = \frac{1}{\bar{v}} y, \tag{21}$$

with zero interest elasticity. If the money supply function, at a given price level, can be written as

$$m^s = m(r), \tag{22}$$

then the equilibrium condition in the money market, in this world of interest-insensitive demand for money, is

$$m(r) = \frac{1}{v} y. \tag{23}$$

Thus, if the money *supply* is sensitive to the interest rate, the money market equilibrium condition contains *both y* and *r,* regardless of the degree of interest elasticity of money demand. This means that both the *IS* and *LM* equations must play a role in the determination of equilibrium GNP, even in the extreme case where the demand for money is unrelated to interest rate changes.

INTERMEDIATE TARGETS AND THE PRACTICE OF MONETARY POLICY

The ultimate aims of macroeconomic policy, including monetary policy, include the stability of prices and real output and a reasonably high level of employment. Back in Chapter 9 we showed how these aims would be achieved through the use of policy instruments such as government spending and the money supply. But we now see that the money supply is *not* well defined, and the Fed directly controls only bank reserves via open market operations. The Fed will need a set of rules to conduct open market operations on a day-to-day basis when the "big" monetary aggregates like $M1$ are not immediately observable. Even if $M1$ statistics were promptly available, policy makers would still have a problem in pursuing their ultimate goals. There is inevitably a delay in assessing the state of the economy after any disturbance and in deciding what is to be done, and then there is another delay between the implementation of policy and its effect on output and prices. As explained in Chapter 4, the immediate impact is in financial markets, and then the effects work gradually through to the markets for goods and labor.

Given this lag between the conduct of policy and its perceptible effects on ultimate goals, it is useful to have intermediate targets. The idea is that, if the appropriate intermediate targets are met, then the behavior of those variables that are ultimately of concern will on the whole be acceptable. The adoption of intermediate targets is a practical measure for conducting policy. To be useful, they must, of course, be predictably related to the ultimate goals, and they must be readily and quickly observable. For the latter reason, prices or quantities in financial markets are especially suitable.

In the case of monetary policy, the problem of selecting an intermediate target is often presented as the choice between controlling the money supply or interest rates. Let's consider the alternatives of holding the money supply at a certain level and accepting the market-determined rate of interest, versus stabilizing the rate of interest by conducting whatever open market operations are necessary. The correct choice is the one which, on average, best serves to stabilize real income, which in turn depends on the source of the shocks to the economy. If the money supply is constant at $\bar{M}$, then we are always on the standard upward-sloping LM curve. If the interest rate is fixed at $\bar{r}$, then the LM curve is effectively flat. This contrast is shown in Figure 15-4.

For concreteness, we will illustrate the problem in the fixed price IS-LM framework of Chapter 5 with the addition of stochastic shocks of the kind introduced in Chapter 11. The example comes from the original work of William Poole. We assume that real GNP is unobservable at the time policy is formulated and that the choice is between fixing M or r. Algebraically, we have

$$IS: \quad y = c - ar + u, \tag{24}$$

and

$$LM: \quad M + v = y - br. \tag{25}$$

Here c is a constant in the IS curve, the price level is set at unity so we have y in the LM curve, and u and v are random disturbances in the goods and money markets, respectively. As usual, both the demand for goods [the right-hand side of equation (24)] and for money [the right-hand side of equation (25)] are negatively related to the rate of interest r.

Controlling the Supply of Money

Since the late 1970s, monetary authorities have become increasingly concerned about controlling the supply of money. In the extreme case, the money supply

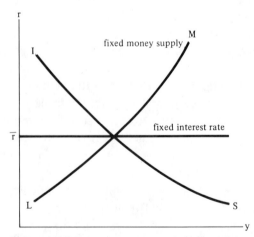

Figure 15-4 Money supply versus interest rate targets.

might be set at some predetermined level $\bar{M}$, which gives us from the *LM* equation (25),

$$r = -\frac{1}{b}(\bar{M} + v - y). \tag{26}$$

Substituting into equation (24), we obtain an equation with only y endogenous:

$$y = c + \frac{a}{b}(\bar{M} + v - y) + u.$$

After a little rearrangement, we get the expression reduced-form for y:

$$y = \frac{bc + a\bar{M}}{a + b} + \frac{av + bu}{a + b}, \tag{27}$$

where the elements in the first term on the right-hand side of (27) are all fixed and the second term is composed of the random shock components from the money and the goods markets. If the variance of v is σ_v^2 and the variance of u is σ_u^2, then the variance of y with M fixed is given by

$$\text{Var}(y) = \frac{a^2\sigma_v^2 + b^2\sigma_u^2}{(a + b)^2}. \tag{28}$$

This is the variance of real output y with M fixed by policy and random shocks in both *IS* and *LM*.

Controlling the Rate of Interest

For much of the postwar period, monetary policy was directed toward hitting target interest rates. If the rate is fixed at a target value $\bar{r}$, then the *LM* curve becomes irrelevant to the determination of real GNP, because monetary policy adjusts to hold r at the target. In this case, we can look just at the *IS* curve to determine y:

$$y = c - a\bar{r} + u.$$

Clearly, only demand shocks u affect real income, and its variance is given by

$$\text{Var}(y) = \sigma_u^2. \tag{29}$$

The variance of y in this case is determined by shocks to the *IS* curve shifting along the target $\bar{r}$ line in Figure 15-4.

Money Supply or Interest Rate Targets?

The problem facing the policy maker is to choose a usable target when the ultimate goal, the stabilization of real output, cannot be attacked directly. Will the variance of y be smaller if M or r is fixed by policy? Comparing the expressions for $\text{Var}(y)$ in equations (28) and (29), we find that a fixed money supply will result in lower real output variance if

$$\frac{a^2\sigma_v^2 + b^2\sigma_u^2}{(a+b)^2} < \sigma_u^2,$$

which can be simplified to

$$a^2\sigma_v^2 < (a^2 + 2ab)\sigma_u^2,$$

or to

$$\frac{a^2}{a^2 + 2ab} \cdot \sigma_v^2 < \sigma_u^2. \tag{30}$$

Thus, a money supply target is superior to an interest rate target depending on the relative magnitude of shocks in the money and goods markets (σ_v^2 and σ_u^2, respectively) and on the interest rate sensitivities of the money and goods demands (b and a). The choice is an empirical one related to the source of disturbances to the economy.

Suppose that there are no shocks in the money market, so that $\sigma_v^2 = 0$. Then a money supply target is certainly better than an interest rate target, as seen in equation (30) and shown in Figure 15-5. With $\sigma_v^2 = 0$, the LM curve

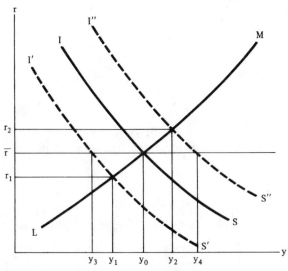

Figure 15-5 Money supply and interest rate targets with goods market shocks.

is fixed. Suppose the *IS* curve shifts between *I'S'* and *I"S"*. With the money supply constant, income varies between y_1 and y_2 around its average level y_0, while the interest rate will vary between r_1 and r_2. If, instead, the interest rate is held at $\bar{r}$, then the range over which y varies is greater, between y_3 and y_4. In this case, using an interest rate target entails procyclical movements in money supply which exacerbate the disturbances coming from the goods market.

What happens at the other extreme when there are only money market disturbances, that is, when $\sigma_u^2 = 0$? Then the interest rate is the superior intermediate target for stabilization. In Figure 15-6, the *IS* curve is fixed, and the *LM* curve varies between *L'M'* and *L"M"* as money demand shifts. The mean level of real output is y_0. With the interest rate held constant, the incipient *LM* shifts resulting from shocks to money demand are offset by changes in money supply. Therefore, the *LM* curve remains in its initial position. The interest rate target cuts off the transmission from the money market to the goods market. If, instead, the money supply were held constant, the *LM* curve could fluctuate between *L'M'* and *L"M"* in Figure 15-6, and these shocks would pass through to the goods market making real output between y_1 and y_2 while the interest rate ranged from r_1 to r_2.

In summary, targeting the money supply in the face of shocks to the goods markets makes use of the stabilizing effect of interest rate fluctuations on aggregate demand. A positive shock, shifting *IS* up, increases the interest rate along a given *LM* curve. This crowds out investment and partially offsets

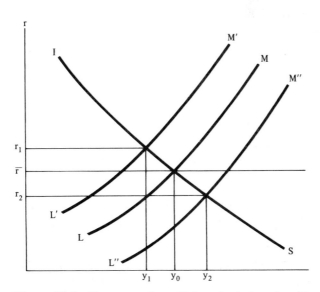

Figure 15-6 Money supply and interest rate targets with money market shocks.

the effects of the shock. If the interest rate were held constant by shifting the *LM* curve out, this would add to the effect of the initial shock. But the situation is reversed if the shock is to money demand. Then offsetting the shock by changing money supply to maintain a target *r* will leave *LM* unshifted and maintain the original equilibrium. Thus, the choice between targeting interest rates or money supply will come down to empirical estimates of the parameters of equation (30), including the relative variability of disturbances to the goods markets and financial markets.

SELECTED READINGS

L. V. Chandler, *Money and the National Economy* (New York: General Learning Press, 1971).

P. H. Hendershott and F. De Leeuw, "Free Reserves, Interest Rates, and Deposits: A Synthesis," *Journal of Finance,* June 1970.

F. Modigliani, R. Rasche, and J. P. Cooper, "Central Bank Policy, Money Supply, and the Short-Term Note of Interest," *Journal of Money, Credit, and Banking,* May 1970.

W. Poole, "Optimal Choice of Monetary-Policy Instruments in a Simple Stochastic Macro Model," *Quarterly Journal of Economics,* May 1970.

R. L. Teigen, "The Demand for and Supply of Money," in W. L. Smith and R. L. Teigen, eds., *Readings in Money, National Income, and Stabilization Policy* (Homewood, Ill.: R.D. Irwin, 1965).

J. Tobin, "Commercial Banks as Creators of 'Money'," in W. L. Smith and R. L. Teigen, eds., *Readings in Money, National Income and Stabilization Policy* (Homewood, Ill.: R.D. Irwin, 1965).

chapter **16**

Monetary and Fiscal Policy in the Extended Model

Chapters 12 through 15 have reviewed, in some detail, both the theoretical underpinnings and empirical results concerning the four important functions on the demand side of the economy—consumer demand, investment demand, the demand for money, and the supply of money. Wherever it seemed appropriate in these chapters, we briefly discussed the effect of the analysis on our view of monetary and fiscal policy. Here, we pull together the results of Chapters 12 through 15, and the rational expectations discussion of Chapter 11, to obtain a more comprehensive view of how monetary and fiscal policies affect the economy, and of some important current policy issues concerning the use of monetary and fiscal policy. In considering the effects of policy, we focus on the timing relationships discussed in Chapters 12–15—for example, the lags of consumer expenditure changes behind income changes and of investment demand behind changes in output and interest rates. Thus, here we add the timing elements on the demand side to the analysis of monetary and fiscal policy of Part II, which dealt mainly with changes from one equilibrium position to the next, with little discussion of the time path of the economy between equilibria.

In the first section of this chapter we summarize the basic static model as modified or extended by Chapters 12–15. Then we look at the general effects of fiscal and monetary policy changes in this extended model, focusing partly on timing effects and partly on the relationship between the labor market and supply curve assumptions and the effects of policy changes. This discussion leads naturally, in the next section, to consideration of the *monetarist-fiscalist* (or as it is sometimes called, *Keynesian*) debate that was a major focus of macroeconomic policy discussions in the 1970s, and the entry of the new classical view into that debate in the 1980s. Both the monetarist and fiscalist views on aggregate demand policy—that only money matters or money does not matter at all—and the new classical view that no systematic policy matters are extreme, and probably incorrect, cases of our basic static model. Starting from an implicit assumption that the interest elasticity of the demand for money is virtually zero, the monetarist position focuses on the use of a vertical *LM* curve to determine real output *y*. The fiscalist position, starting from the assumption that the interest elasticity of investment demand is virtually zero, focuses on the use of a vertical *IS* curve to determine *y*. The new classical position uses a vertical aggregate supply curve even in the short run to determine *y*.

In the fourth section of this chapter, we look at the relationship between tax rate changes and changes in the budget surplus. When *rates* are reduced, income generally rises, so the outcome for tax *revenues*—the tax rate times income—is uncertain. Whether tax revenues, and thus the budget surplus (or deficit), rise or fall with a tax cut depends on the initial state of the economy—that is, its position on the *LM* curve. The possibility that a reduction in tax rates could increase tax revenue was introduced into the U.S. political debate during the Kennedy Administration in the early 1960s. The assertion that it would increase tax revenue was the basis for the tax rate cuts in the Kemp-Roth-Reagan tax program enacted in 1981.

Finally, in the last section, we look briefly into the problem of debt management from the point of view of stabilization policy. Here we will see what difference it makes, in stabilization terms, *how* a deficit of a given size is financed. Roughly speaking, an increase in the deficit, financed by selling bonds to the public, shifts the *IS* curve up along a given *LM* curve with the money supply *M* held constant. But if the deficit is financed by selling bonds to the Federal Reserve, *M* is increased and the *LM* curve shifts out too. Thus, the size of the *y* increase, and whether the interest rate *r* rises or falls for a given increase in the deficit, depend partially on how it is financed.

THE STATIC MODEL EXTENDED

In Chapter 12 we saw that the consumption function of Part II must be extended at least to include real assets a ($=A/P$). In addition, we saw that consumer expenditure will probably react quickly to a change in disposable income that seems permanent to consumers—as opposed to the effect of a temporary tax rate change. Furthermore, the increase in consumer expenditure might exceed the increase in disposable income, at least in the short run, since the increase in desired *consumption* that follows the increase in income will reflect a disproportionate increase in purchases of consumer durables. The consumption function that emerged from Chapter 12 is repeated here:

$$c = c(y - t(y), a); \qquad \frac{\partial c}{\partial(y - t(y))}, \qquad \frac{\partial c}{\partial a} > 0, \qquad (1)$$

where real consumer net worth (assets) $a = A/P$.

The second modification of the components of the *IS* product market equilibrium condition came in Chapter 13, where we saw that investment should be a function of the level of output, as well as the interest rate. Here it should be noticed that, in a model of static equilibrium, *replacement investment* should depend on the *level* of output. *Net investment,* due to changes in interest rates or output, does not appear in the static model, but is an important factor in determining the path of the economy between equilibria.

Thus, in the static model we have a function for replacement investment, given the equilibrium level of capital stock:

$$i = i(r, y); \qquad \frac{\partial i}{\partial r} < 0, \qquad \frac{\partial i}{\partial y} > 0. \qquad (2)$$

In addition, to move from one equilibrium level of capital stock to another, net investment will appear as a function of the *change* in r or y. Thus, a drop in the interest rate r will increase the equilibrium capital stock. This will bring a transitory positive level of net investment as the capital stock is increased to its new equilibrium level. At that level, the static investment function of (2) will show a higher level of replacement investment as a function of the lower interest rate.

The *IS* Curve

These modifications of the consumption and investment functions give us a revised form of the product market equilibrium condition,

$$y = c(y - t(y), a) + i(r, y) + g, \qquad (3a)$$

or

$$s(y - t(y), a) + t(y) = i(r, y) + g, \qquad (3b)$$

shown as the *IS* curve in Figure 16-1.

In Figure 16-1, the position of the curve showing saving plus tax revenue—gross social saving—as a function of the level of real income is determined by the level of real consumer net worth a_0. A reduction in real net worth, normally due to a price increase in the short run, would reduce consumer expenditure, given the income level, and thus increase saving. This would rotate the $s + t$ curve in the southeast quadrant of Figure 16-1 down, or clockwise, increasing the level of saving corresponding to any given level of income y.

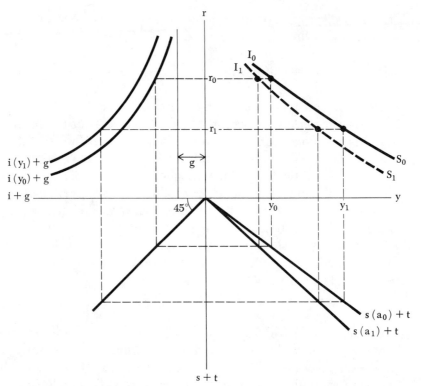

Figure 16-1   The *IS* curve in the extended model.

The investment function $i = i(r, y)$ gives us a family of investment curves in the northwest quadrant of Figure 16-1. As income rises from y_0 to y_1, the level of (replacement) investment associated with any given interest rate rises, so the investment demand curve shifts from $i(y_0)$ to $i(y_1)$ in Figure 16-1.

At an initial real-asset level a_0, which fixes an $s + t$ function in Figure 16-1, the *IS* curve giving the r, y points that maintain equilibrium in the product market can be traced using the appropriate $i(y)$ curves. As we saw in Chapter 13, introduction of the sensitivity of investment demand to the level of real output flattens the *IS* curve. For a_0, the *IS* curve $I_0 S_0$ is traced out as an illustration in Figure 16-2. Remember too from Chapter 12 that the effect of changes in the interest rate on consumption by way of real-asset values also flattens the *IS* curve.

Now if the real value of consumer net worth falls to a_1, due to a price increase, the *IS* curve will shift down to $I_1 S_1$ in Figure 16-1. At any given level of income there is a greater desire to save (*ex ante* saving is higher). Thus, at any given level of the interest rate, the equilibrium level of output in the product market will fall as the price level rises due to the falling level of consumer demand as the real value of assets is reduced. Recognition of the important role that real net worth plays in the determination of consumer expenditure and saving introduces real assets as a factor that shifts the *IS* curve in the r,y space of Figure 16-1, as the price level moves.

The *LM* Curve

In Chapter 14 we developed several different views of the demand for money, all of which came to the same function that we used in Part II. For a given stock of liquid assets, the speculative demand for real balances is negatively related to the interest rate; the transactions demand is positively related to the level of transactions, or income, and negatively related to the interest rate. The demand-for-money function can be written as

$$\frac{M}{P} = m(r, y) \approx l(r) + k(y), \tag{4a}$$

or

$$M = P \cdot m(r, y) \approx P \cdot l(r) + P \cdot k(y). \tag{4b}$$

Here $\partial m / \partial r < 0$ and $\partial m / \partial y > 0$.

As we saw in Chapter 15, for a given amount of unborrowed reserves supplied by the Fed, and given the public's preferences between money and currency, the supply of money is an increasing function of the interest rate,

$$M = M(r); \qquad M' > 0. \tag{5}$$

Equating money supplied to money demanded gives us the equilibrium condition for the money market,

$$\frac{M(r)}{P} = m(r, y) \approx l(r) + k(y). \tag{6}$$

This is the *LM* curve in Figure 16-2.

The $k(y)$ curve in the southeast quadrant gives the movement in the demand for real balances as y changes. The $l(r)$ curve in the northwest quadrant gives changes in demand—both speculative and transactions—as the interest rate changes. The 45° line in the southwest quadrant constrains the two components of demand to add to total supply of real balances, $M(r)/P_0$. Here P_0 is the given initial price level. As the interest rate changes, this supply of real balances changes.

To trace out the *LM* curve in Figure 16-2, we can begin with an initial interest rate r_0, which fixes the supply of real balances at $M(r_0)/P_0$. At r_0, the liquidity preference schedule $l(r)$ shows a speculative demand for money at $l(r_0)$ in Figure 16-2. With $M(r_0)/P_0$ fixed by r_0, this leaves $[M(r_0)/P_0]$

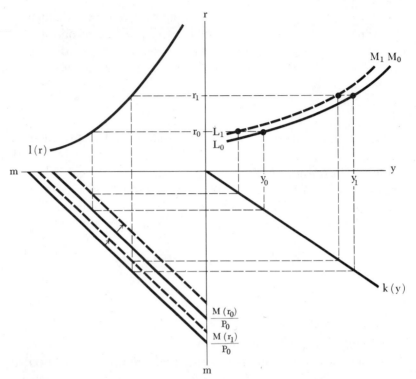

Figure 16-2   The *LM* curve in the extended model.

$- l(r_0) = k(y_0)$ for transactions balances, an amount that will support income level y_0. This establishes the r_0,y_0 point on the *LM* curve in the northeast quadrant in Figure 16-2.

At interest rate r_1 ($> r_0$), the supply of real balances expands to $M(r_1)/P_0$ due to shrinkage of free reserves in the banking system. Tracing counterclockwise around the four-quadrant diagram from r_1 to $M(r_1)/P_0$ to y_1, we can establish another money market equilibrium point r_1,y_1. The $L_0 M_0$ curve of Figure 16-2 can be drawn through the two points r_0,y_0 and r_1,y_1.

If the money supply were fixed at the level $M(r_0)$, then the money market equilibrium y level corresponding to r_1 would be less than y_1, since the trace from r_1 would bounce off the $M(r_0)/P_0$ money supply line instead of the $M(r_1)/P_0$ line. In this fixed money supply case the *LM* curve would then be steeper than that shown in Figure 16-2. Since an increase in r would not increase the money supply, for any given increase in r the increase in money market equilibrium y would be smaller than in the flexible money supply case where $M = M(r)$.

The $L_0 M_0$ curve of Figure 16-2 is drawn on the assumption of a given initial price level P_0. An increase in the price level will reduce the supply of real balances—or what amounts to the same thing, increase the demand for nominal balances at any given r and y—and shift the LM curve up and to the left. In Figure 16-2 a price level increase shifts each M/P line in toward the origin. As shown by the dashed lines in the southwest quadrant, this represents a reduction in M/P and a drop in the money market equilibrium y associated with any given r. Thus, a price increase shifts the LM curve up toward the $L_1 M_1$ curve in Figure 16-2.

The Aggregate Demand Curve

Given the money value of assets and the price level, the IS equation (3) and the LM equation (6) are two equations in two unknowns, r and y. These can be solved for equilibrium demand-side r and y, given P. The solution is shown graphically as the intersection of the $I_0 S_0$ and the $L_0 M_0$ curves in Figure 16-3, which are the $I_0 S_0$ and $L_0 M_0$ curves from Figures 16-1 and 16-2, based on the initial price level P_0.

As in Part II, we can derive the economy's aggregate demand curve by varying the price level and observing the movement of equilibrium demand-side y in Figure 16-3. An increase in the price level, we have seen, reduces real household net worth, increasing desired saving at any income level and rotating the $s + t$ line in Figure 16-1 downward. This reduction in consumption demand shifts the IS curve to the left, toward $I_1 S_1$ in Figure 16-3. As we saw in the previous section, a price level increase also shifts the LM curve left toward $L_1 M_1$ in Figure 16-3 by reducing the supply of real balances. Thus, as prices rise, both the IS and LM curves shift left in Figure 16-3, reducing the equilibrium level of output.

This relationship between equilibrium demand-side output and the price level is shown as the economy's demand curve $D_0 D_0$ in Figure 16-4. As the

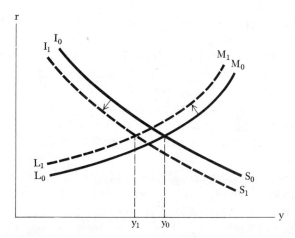

Figure 16-3 Equilibrium r and y on the demand side.

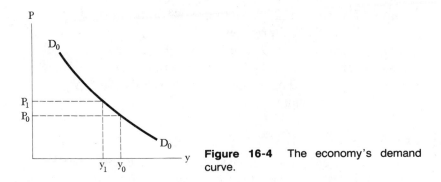

Figure 16-4   The economy's demand curve.

price level rises from P_0 to P_1, consumption demand is reduced directly due to the reduction in the real value of assets—our analog to the Pigou effect. As should be apparent from Figure 16-3, the drop in the real money supply, shifting *LM* left, tends to raise interest rates. On the other hand, the drop in income that follows the drop in consumer demand, shifting the *IS* curve left, reduces the demand for money, tending to reduce interest rates. Thus, the price increase may raise or lower interest rates, depending on the relative sensitivity to the interest rate of both the supply of and the demand for money, on the one hand, and of consumer demand to real assets, on the other.

    With investment demand a function of both real output and the interest rate, $i = i(r, y)$, the leftward movement of the *IS* and *LM* curves virtually assures a decrease in investment demand from one static equilibrium to the next with the price level rising. The interest rate may rise or fall as P rises from P_0 to P_1, but with the drop in income and output, the equilibrium capital stock will drop, reducing replacement investment in the new static equilibrium. There will also be a transitory negative net investment to reduce the capital stock between equilibria.

    The drop in consumption demand and investment demand following an increase in the price level from P_0 to P_1 moves equilibrium demand-side output from y_0 to y_1 in Figures 16-3 and 16-4. The reduction in *consumption demand* will come fairly quickly, probably within two to three quarters, certainly within a year, after the price increase. The speed of reaction of *consumer expenditure* will probably be more rapid than this, since, as we saw in Chapter 12, expenditure must overadjust to bring consumption of durables into line. The reduction in investment demand may come fairly rapidly as firms react to excess capacity by cutting net investment to reduce capital stock. After this transitory reduction of net investment, which reduces equilibrium capital stock, is completed over the period of perhaps one to two years, gross investment will rise to its new replacement investment level $i_1 = i(r_1, y_1)$, lower than the initial $i_0 = i(r_0, y_0)$ level but higher than gross investment during the transitory period of negative net investment.

Thus, the demand curve of Figure 16-4 reflects changes in equilibrium demand-side output due to the effect of price level changes on both consumption and investment demand. An increase in the price level from P_0 to P_1 will bring a reduction in equilibrium demand-side output from y_0 to y_1 over a period of a year or two. Because of the transitory drop in net investment demand, income may temporarily overshoot y_1; as gross investment revives, equilibrium demand-side output will then rise to y_1.

Labor Market Equilibrium

The supply-side equilibrium conditions are the same as those developed in Chapter 7, so we do not have to discuss them in detail here. Output y is linked to employment by the production function

$$y = y(N; \bar{K}). \tag{7}$$

The demand for labor by an individual firm sets employment at the level at which the real wage rate the employer pays equals the marginal product of labor. In the aggregate, this gives us a demand-for-labor function that can be written as the wage employers will offer as a function of the price level and the level of employment,

$$W^d = P \cdot f(N); \qquad f' < 0. \tag{8}$$

Here $f(N)$ can be thought of as the aggregate marginal product of labor (MPL), so that (8) equates the MPL to the real wage $w = W/P$. The labor-demand function (8) is shown in Figure 16-5, given the initial price level P_0.

On the supply side of the labor market, we have the supply function of Chapter 7 written as an equation giving the money wage along the supply function,

$$W^s = P^e \cdot g(N).$$

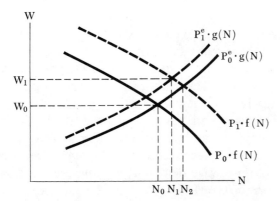

Figure 16-5 Labor market equilibrium.

The expected price level P^e is linked to the actual price level by the expectations function,

$$P^e = p(P).$$

Combining these gives us the labor-supply function linking nominal wage demands, the price level, and employment:

$$W^s = p(P) \cdot g(N). \tag{9}$$

Here an increase in the price level raises wage demands, that is, shifts the labor-supply curve up in the W,N space. The labor-supply function (9) is also shown in Figure 16-5 at the initial price level P_0, equal to P_0^e if initial expectations are correct. If $p' = 0$ in equation (9), we have the polar Keynesian case of Chapter 7, while if $p' = 1$ we have the polar classical case. If we think of the case in which $p' = 1$ represents a rationally anticipated price increase, then we have the new classical model of Chapter 11. In general, with $0 < p' < 1$, we have the model labeled the *general static* model in Chapter 7.

Equating the demand wage to the supply wage gives us the labor market equilibrium condition:

$$P \cdot f(N) = p(P) \cdot g(N). \tag{10}$$

For a given price level P_0, equation (10) can be solved for the equilibrium level of employment N_0. Since equilibrium employment is *defined* as that level of N that equates W^d and W^s, the equilibrium N_0, along with P_0, can be inserted into either equation (8) or (9) to obtain the equilibrium money wage rate. This solution of the labor market equilibrium equation is shown graphically in Figure 16-5, where the intersection of the supply and demand functions, at the initial price P_0 and expected price $P_0^e = P_0$, gives equilibrium employment N_0 and wage rate W_0.

The Aggregate Supply Curve

We can derive the aggregate supply curve by changing the price level in the labor market (Figure 16-5) and observing how supply-side equilibrium output changes. In the general static model, an increase in the price level from P_0 to P_1 shifts both the labor-demand and labor-supply curves up in Figure 16-5, demand more than supply, since $p' < 1$.

The price increase raises marginal revenue products for all firms, so they all want to expand employment and will offer a higher wage to attract workers. On the other hand, the price increase reduces the purchasing power of money wages, and thus should raise wage demands, shifting the labor-supply curve up. If price expectations do not fully adjust in the short run, so that labor supply is less sensitive to price changes than it is to wage changes, the upward shift of the labor-supply function to $P_1^e \cdot g(N)$ will be smaller than the demand function shift to $P_1 \cdot f(N)$, so that the price increase from P_0 to P_1 will raise equilibrium employment from N_0 to N_1 in Figure 16-5.

The increase in equilibrium employment from Figure 16-5 is translated into a change in supply-side equilibrium output by the production function in Figure 16-6. The increase of employment from N_0 to N_1 raises equilibrium output on the supply side from y_0 to y_1 in Figure 16-6. This, in turn, gives us the aggregate supply curve of Figure 16-7. The price increase from P_0 to P_1 in Figure 16-5 raised equilibrium employment from N_0 to N_1. This increase in employment yields an increase in supply-side equilibrium output from y_0 to y_1 in Figure 16-6, so that we have the supply curve relationship between the price level and equilibrium output on the supply side shown as $S_0 S_0$ in Figure 16-7. As P rises from P_0 to P_1, supply-side output rises from y_0 to y_1.

In the polar classical case or the new classical model, with $p' = 1$, a price level increase would shift the labor-supply and -demand functions up by the same amount in Figure 16-5, so that equilibrium employment would remain unchanged. In this case the supply curve of Figure 16-7 would be vertical. In the polar Keynesian case, with $p' = 0$, the price increase would not shift the labor-supply function at all, so that the price increase from P_0 to P_1 would raise employment to N_2 in Figure 16-5, raising equilibrium output on the supply side to y_2 in Figures 16-6 and 16-7. Thus, in the polar Keynesian case the supply function would be the flatter $S_1 S_1$ curve in Figure 16-7.

Equilibrium in the Extended Model

In Figure 16-8 we bring together the demand curve of Figure 16-4 and the supply curve of Figure 16-7 to determine equilibrium price and output, P_0, y_0. Given equilibrium P_0 and y_0 we can trace back through the system to determine the equilibrium values of the other variables.

On the supply side, y_0 gives us equilibrium employment N_0 through the production function of Figure 16-6. With N_0 and P_0, we can determine W_0 in Figure 16-5. Going back on the demand side, the equilibrium price level P_0

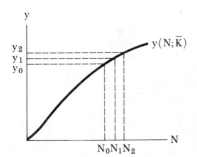

Figure 16-6 The production function.

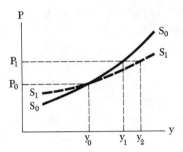

Figure 16-7 The aggregate-supply curve.

gives us the position of the $I_0 S_0$ curve in Figures 16-1 and 16-3. Combining equilibrium y_0 and the position of the IS curve gives us equilibrium r_0 in Figure 16-3. With r_0 we can determine the level of the money supply $M(r_0)$, which, combined with P_0, fixes the position of the LM curve at $L_0 M_0$ in Figure 16-3. Thus, the four-equation system of the IS equation (3), the LM equation (6), the production function (7), and the labor market equation (10) give us the equilibrium values of the key variables y, r, P, and N. Given r we can determine the value of M, and given N we can determine the value of w. Next, we can briefly follow through the effects of a fiscal policy change in this system, focusing on the likely timing effects suggested by the empirical work reviewed in Part III.

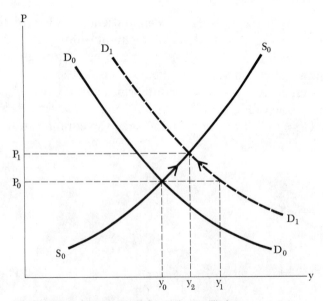

Figure 16-8 Demand and supply equilibrium.

THE EFFECTS OF FISCAL POLICY CHANGES

As usual, a fiscal policy increase in government purchases g or cut in tax rates shifts the *IS* curve in Figure 16-9 out to $I_1 S_1$ and shifts the economy's demand curve in Figure 16-8 out to $D_1 D_1$. The demand increase raises equilibrium output demanded at the initial price level to y_1 in Figures 16-8 and 16-9 creating excess demand measured by $y_1 - y_0$, which pulls the price level up.

Adjustment in the Labor Market

On the supply side of the economy, the excess demand and price increase will shift the demand-for-labor curve up fairly rapidly, toward $P_1 \cdot f(N)$ in Figure 16-10, so that employment and output respond quickly to the increase in demand. The upward shift in the labor-supply curve toward $P_1^e \cdot g(N)$ due to the workers perceiving a cut in purchasing power and as a result, raising wage demands, will come more slowly and with a lag that depends on the speed of adjustment of expectations and the degree of contract rigidity in wages. Thus, there is a possibility of an overadjustment of employment on the supply side, with the price increase initially raising employment along the original

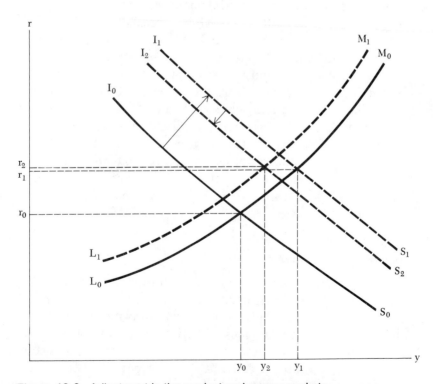

Figure 16-9 Adjustment in the product and money markets.

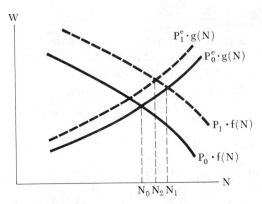

Figure 16-10   Adjustment in the labor market.

$P_0^e \cdot g(N)$ labor-supply curve to N_1. Then, once adjustment seems complete, the labor-supply curve will begin shifting up toward tending to reduce employment toward N_2 in Figure 16-10.

The Effect on Consumer Demand

The increase in income, on the demand side, should be reflected fairly quickly in a rise in consumer demand. This is especially true for consumer durables, as consumers increase purchases to adjust their future stream of consumption of services from the durables upward. The increase in consumer expenditure on nondurable goods and on services should rise more gradually, over a period of two quarters to a year. Thus, the increase in consumer demand in response to the increase in income generated by the initial g change should come rapidly and be initially weighted toward an increase in purchases of consumer durables.

    The price rise generated by the excess demand shown in Figure 16-8 will reduce the real value of household net worth, tending to increase saving and reduce consumption somewhat. The price increase thus shifts the IS curve back from $I_1 S_1$ toward $I_2 S_2$ in Figure 16-9, partially offsetting the effects of the initial g increase.

The Effect on Investment Demand

If the increase in demand comes at a time when the economy is operating near full capacity, perhaps above 85 percent on the Federal Reserve index, investment demand should respond within two or three quarters through the accelerator mechanism. This will bring a spurt of net investment to increase the capital stock to a new equilibrium level. Once this is completed, after a year or so, investment demand should taper off toward the continuing replacement requirements of the larger capital stock. This level of investment demand is represented in the static $i = i(r, y)$ investment function and is reflected in the slope of the *IS* curves of Figure 16-9.

But the accelerator mechanism creates the likelihood of overadjustment on the demand side. The *g* increase raises output. This increase generates a spurt of new investment which further raises output. This spurt of net investment could be represented by a further temporary shift in the *IS* curve out beyond $I_1 S_1$ in Figure 16-9. Then after a period of perhaps two years, investment demand will fall off to replacement level, shifting the *IS* curve back down to $I_1 S_1$ or to $I_2 S_2$ if the asset effect on consumer demand has taken hold.

Adjustment in the Money Market

The price rise generated by the excess demand shown in Figure 16-8, and the increase in income as *y* and *N* rise, both increase the demand for money, pulling interest rates up. The interest rate increase works to eliminate the excess demand in the money market both by reducing demand $(\partial m/\partial r < 0)$ and by increasing the money supply $[M'(r) > 0]$.

The rise in interest rates due to the increase in transactions demand following the increase in income and output, and the money supply response to the interest rate increase, are both built into the slope of the *LM* curve, as is shown in Figure 16-2. Thus, these money market adjustments are represented in Figure 16-9 by the rise in *r* from r_0 along the initial *LM* curve $L_0 M_0$.

The effect of the price increase, raising the demand for nominal balances or reducing the supply of real balances, is reflected in a leftward shift of the *LM* curve toward $L_1 M_1$ in Figure 16-9. Thus, at the *initial* price level P_0, equilibrium demand-side output rises to y_1 as a result of the *g* increase. The subsequent price increase shifts both *IS* and *LM* left, reducing equilibrium demand-side output toward y_2 in Figure 16-9.

Demand and Supply in the New Equilibrium

The movement of demand-side equilibrium output back toward y_2 as the price level rises is shown as a movement along the new demand curve $D_1 D_1$ in Figure 16-8. At the same time, equilibrium supply-side output is increasing with the increase in employment toward N_2 in Figure 16-10. This is represented by a movement along the initial supply curve from y_0 to y_2 in Figure 16-8. The price level continues to rise until excess demand is eliminated at P_1, y_2.

For a significant increase in *g*, or cut in tax rates, movement from P_0, y_0 to P_1, y_2 might take two or three years in the U.S. economy. The recovery that began in 1983 in the United States followed increases in defense spending and tax cuts that began in 1982, and went on to 1986 or so. As we have seen, it is quite possible that the economy will overshoot the final y_2 level, both because of the net investment spurt that shifts IS temporarily beyond I_1S_1 in Figure 16-9, and because of the lag in the shift of the labor-supply curve up toward $h(P_1, N)$. Thus, in reality we are likely to see a cyclical movement from the initial y_0 to the final y_2, with real output first rising above y_2 and then falling back to the final equilibrium. This will be the case regardless of which fiscal policy instrument is used to stimulate the economy. By 1986, forecasters in the United States were worrying that the recovery had run out of steam, and the possibility of recession appeared. In the event, the economy was supported by export demand, following the depreciation of the dollar after 1985. This minimized the slowdown as the effect of the fiscal stimulus ended.

THE EFFECTIVENESS OF AGGREGATE DEMAND POLICY: MONETARISTS, FISCALISTS, AND NEW CLASSICALS

In the static model, monetary policy affects the economy by shifting the LM curve and, as a result, shifting the economy's demand curve. Fiscal policy works by shifting the IS and demand curves. In the general static model with $p' < 1$, with lagged adjustment of expectations or wage rigidities, the economy's supply curve has a positive slope, so that a shift of the demand curve changes the level of output.

In the original classical case, with $p' = 1$ and no wage rigidity, the economy's supply curve is vertical. In this case, fiscal policy changes affect the allocation of total output by changing the price level and the interest rate. Monetary policy changes affect only the price level, leaving the interest rate and composition of output unchanged. Thus, in the classical case both monetary and fiscal policies affect the price level and nominal GNP, $Y = P \cdot y$. In addition, fiscal policy changes affect the composition of output. In the new classical model with rational expectations and no wage rigidities, which we discussed in Chapter 11, the short-run aggregate supply curve is vertical with anticipated shifts in monetary or fiscal policy, but is positively sloped if the shift in policy is unanticipated. Eventually in this case, the supply curve becomes vertical as the effects of the policy change become apparent.

A different distinction from the one between the classical or new classical and Keynesian poles on the supply side was of great importance in debates about macroeconomic policy in the 1960s and 1970s, and is still alive today. It concerns relative effectiveness of monetary and fiscal policies on the demand side. On one side of this distinction is a group of economists generally known as *monetarists,* whose position, taken to an extreme, seems to be that as between aggregate fiscal and monetary policies, only monetary policy can shift the aggregate demand curve and affect the level of nominal GNP, with the division between changes in the price level P and output y determined by the slope of the aggregate supply curve. On the other side is a group dubbed by David Fand as the *fiscalists.* Their position, taken to an equal extreme, seems to be that only fiscal policy can shift the aggregate demand curve.

The difference between the two views lies in differing estimates of two key elasticities in our static model. The fiscalist position, which generally tends to be imputed by monetarists to no one economist in particular, is that the interest elasticity of investment demand is very small, or even zero, in the short run. This makes the *IS* curve vertical, so that changes in monetary policy shift the *LM* curve along the vertical *IS* curve, changing r but not y. A change in a fiscal policy variable, however, will shift the vertical *IS* curve, changing y. The extreme monetarist position is that the interest elasticities of the demand for and supply of money are zero, so that the *LM* curve is vertical. In this case, fiscal policy changes the composition, but not the level of national output, while monetary policy, shifting a vertical *LM* curve, can change the level of output.

Both positions can thus be viewed as special cases of our general model with certain elasticities set at zero. The empirical estimates of these elasticities mentioned in Chapters 14 to 16, all definitely not zero, suggest that neither special case is, in fact, very relevant to actual economic conditions. But it will be useful to develop these two models more thoroughly in the next two sub-sections. This will give the reader a fuller insight into the analysis behind what remains a matter of controversy in the public press between the two extreme positions. The models do serve as extreme cases in the analysis of the relative effectiveness of monetary and fiscal policies.

The Fiscalist Model

The fiscalist model takes us back essentially to the simple multipliers of Chapter 3. There we assumed that investment demand is given exogenously. Then given any level of investment and a stable relationship between consumer expenditure and income, it is changes in government purchases g, or tax rates t, that change real output.

This is the extreme fiscalist position. It is very hard to find an economist who actually holds this view; rather it became the straw man set up by the monetarists in public debate. The fiscalist position is frequently called *Keynesian* by its opponents. This seems to be not so much because Keynes held this simplistic view, but more because the simple multiplier analysis, which accords literally no role to monetary policy, was the way the introductory texts introduced Keynes' analysis of income determination to the public. It should be clear that, at any rate, this author regards the fiscalist position as a mildly interesting, if improbable, extreme case of the general model and a handy straw man for attack in debate by the monetarist view, not a position actually taken seriously by any practicing economist. With this preamble, let us proceed to the analysis.

Suppose investment demand is given exogenously in the product market equilibrium condition,

$$y = c\left(y - t(y), \frac{A}{P}\right) + i + g. \tag{11}$$

Here tax revenue depends on the level of real income, and consumption and saving depend on disposable income and real household net worth. For any given i, g, tax schedule, and level of real assets, equation (11) determines the level of y independently of the money market. Determination of the level of y in the fiscalist model is shown in Figure 16-11, which should be familiar from Chapters 3 and 4.

For a given initial price level P_0, the saving function is fixed as $s(A/P_0)$, and equilibrium income is y_0 in Figure 16-11. An increase in the price level to P_1 reduces real household net worth, increasing desired saving at any given level of income. This shifts the saving function up to $s(A/P_1)$, and reduces equilibrium y to y_1. To translate this into an IS curve in r,y space, we notice that, for any given price level, equilibrium y is determined independently of the interest rate. Thus, with $P = P_0$, $y = y_0$ at any interest rate, and the IS curve is the vertical I_0S_0 curve of Figure 16-12.

The demand side of the fiscalist model can be completed by adding the usual money market equilibrium condition,

$$\frac{M(r)}{P} = m(r, y), \tag{12}$$

which gives us the initial L_0M_0 curve in Figure 16-12 at the initial price level P_0. The product market equation (11) determines y_0, given P_0. The money

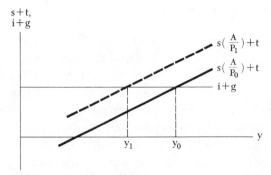

Figure 16-11   Income determination in the fiscalist model.

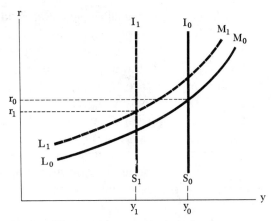

Figure 16-12 *IS* and *LM* in the fiscalist model.

market equation (12) then determines r_0, as is shown in Figure 16-12. If the price level rises, the *IS* curve shifts left due to the real-asset effect on the consumption function, toward $I_1 S_1$ which is vertical at the y_1 level in Figures 16-11 and 16-12. At the same time the price increase shifts *LM* left toward $L_1 M_1$, giving a new equilibrium r_1.

The economy's demand curve, in the fiscalist model, can be derived from either Figure 16-11 or Figure 16-12. A price increase reduces real assets, increasing saving and reducing consumer expenditure and real income. This gives us the negatively sloped demand curve $D_0 D_0$ in Figure 16-13. This can

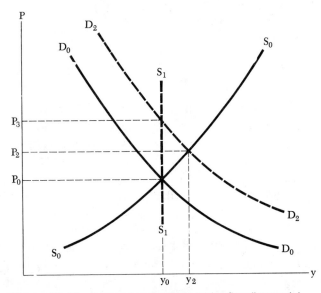

Figure 16-13 Demand and supply in the fiscalist model.

be confronted by the aggregate supply curve of our general model, $S_0 S_0$, or of the classical case, $S_1 S_1$, to determine equilibrium P_0, y_0. Given P_0 and y_0, we can determine r_0 from the LM equation, as shown in Figure 16-12.

What are the effects of policy in this model? An increase in g or a cut in t will shift the IS curve to the right in Figure 16-12 and the demand curve to the right to $D_2 D_2$ in Figure 16-13. If the policy change were fully anticipated and wages perfectly flexible, the relevant supply curve would be the dashed $S_1 S_1$ in Figure 16-13, output would not change, though its composition would, and the price level would rise to P_3. This is the classical case. If one of these conditions does not hold, we are in the general static model with $p' < 1$. In this case, real output will rise to y_2 and the price level will rise to P_2 along the $S_0 S_0$ supply curve in Figure 16-13.

On the other hand, an M increase in this model will shift only the LM curve in Figure 16-12, with no shift of the demand curve in Figure 16-13. There is no effect on either the price level or output; the shift of the LM curve will reduce interest rates, but since investment demand is not sensitive to interest rate changes, there is no effect on demand or the price level.

Thus, the fiscalist view cuts the link between monetary policy and the rest of the economy, including the price level, by assuming that investment demand does not respond to interest rate changes. In general, the empirical studies reviewed in Chapter 12 do not support this assumption. Business investment responds to a change in the cost of capital within a year, and residential construction activity responds even more quickly. The extreme fiscalist model may be relevant in deep depression conditions, with expected returns from investment sufficiently depressed that a reduction in the cost of capital will have no effect on investment. But it does not seem particularly relevant in an economy that is operating near full employment.

The Monetarist Model

The fiscalist model made the product market the sole determinant of equilibrium demand-side output by assuming that investment demand is insensitive to interest rate changes, so that the IS curve is vertical. The monetarist model assumes that the demand for money is insensitive to interest rate changes, making the LM curve vertical.

The demand-for-money function of Chapter 13 can be written as

$$M^d = P \cdot m(r, y). \tag{13}$$

If the elasticity of demand for real balances with respect to real income is about one, we can write (13) in Friedman's quantity-theory form,

$$M^d = P \cdot y \cdot k(r). \tag{14}$$

Frequently, this demand-for-money equation is written to include the income velocity of money, $v(r)$, which is the inverse of $k(r)$ in equation (14),

$$M^d = P \cdot y \cdot \frac{1}{v(r)}. \qquad (15)$$

The monetarist model assumes that the demand for money is insensitive to changes in the interest rate. This means that $k(r)$ in (14), and the income velocity v, are not really functions of r, so that the demand function can be written as

$$M^d = P \cdot y \cdot \frac{1}{v} = \frac{P}{v} \cdot y, \qquad (16)$$

with a fixed income velocity v. With the money supply given exogenously as $M^s = \bar{M}$, the money market equilibrium condition in the monetarist model can be written as

$$\bar{M} = \frac{P}{v} \cdot y. \qquad (17)$$

For a given initial price level P_0, this equation determines equilibrium y as a function of $\bar{M}$, with no reference to the product market equilibrium condition. This is shown in Figure 16-14, which is analogous to Figure 16-11 which shows a product market equilibrium in the fiscalist model. At the initial price level P_0, the demand for money is given by $(P_0/v)y$, and demand equals supply at y_0. An increase in the price level to P_1 shifts the demand for money up to $(P_1/v)y$ in Figure 16-14, reducing equilibrium y to y_1.

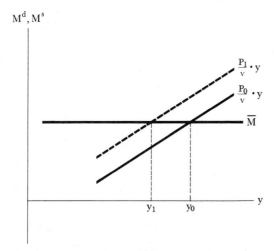

Figure 16-14 Income determination in the monetarist model.

To translate this into an LM curve in r,y space, note that, given $\bar{M}$ and P_0, equilibrium y is determined in the money market independently of the interest rate. At P_0, $y = y_0$ in Figure 16-14 at any interest rate level, and the LM curve is the vertical $L_0 M_0$ line in Figure 16-15. To complete the demand side of the monetarist model, we can add the usual $I_0 S_0$ curve with initial price level P_0. In this case, the IS curve serves to determine the interest rate r_0, with y_0 fixed in the money market.

A price level increase from P_0 to P_1 reduces money market equilibrium y to y_1 in Figure 16-14, shifting the vertical LM curve to $L_1 M_1$ in Figure 16-15. This relationship between P and y in Figures 16-14 and 16-15 gives us the normal negatively sloped demand curve of Figure 16-16, $D_0 D_0$. The price increase, of course, also shifts the IS curve left to $I_1 S_1$ in Figure 16-15. This affects the interest rate, but not the level of income, in the monetarist model.

Again, we can confront the demand curve $D_0 D_0$ in Figure 16-16 with the supply curve—either $S_0 S_0$ in the general model or $S_1 S_1$ in the classical case. The intersection of the demand and supply curves determines equilibrium P_0, y_0, and y_0 can be traced back to the $ISLM$ diagram of Figure 16-15 to determine r_0.

In this model, of course, the implications of policy changes in the fiscal instruments g or t or in the money supply $\bar{M}$ are just reversed from the fiscalist model. An increase in g or a cut in t will shift the IS curve up in Figure 16-15, but leave the vertical $L_0 M_0$ curve unchanged. There is no change in equilibrium demand-side y, so no shift of the demand curve in Figure 16-16. The upward shift of the IS curve in Figure 16-15 raises interest rates, reducing investment enough to just offset the g increase or the policy-induced consumer expenditure increase. Thus, in the monetarist model, a fiscal policy change alters the composition of final output but leaves both equilibrium P_0 and y_0

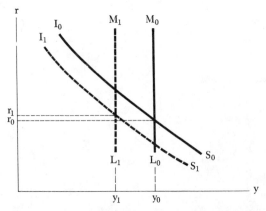

Figure 16-15 *IS* and *LM* in the monetarist model.

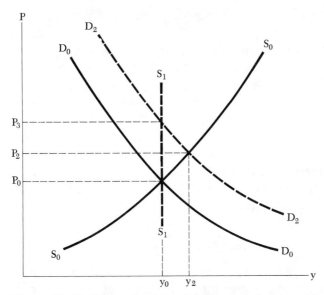

Figure 16-16 Demand and supply in the monetarist model.

unchanged. This result occurs whether the economy's supply curve is positively sloped or vertical.

The monetarist model is not the same as the classical or new classical case on the supply side. The monetarist result of no change in P or y with a fiscal policy change holds in both the general model with $p' < 1$ and the classical case with $p' = 1$. On the other hand, in the classical case with a normal negative interest elasticity of demand for money, a fiscal policy change affects P but not y.

An increase in the money supply $\bar{M}$ will shift the vertical LM curve of Figure 16-15 out in the monetarist model. This will shift the demand curve of Figure 16-16 out to $D_2 D_2$. If the labor supply follows our general model with $p' < 1$, or if there are widespread price rigidities, the price level and output will rise along the $S_0 S_0$ curve to P_2, y_2. On the other hand, if the classical case with $p' = 1$ holds, y will remain at y_0 and P will rise to P_3. Thus, in the monetarist model, an increase in $\bar{M}$ will raise nominal GNP, $P \cdot y$. Whether the increase is all in P or is split between P and y depends on the labor market assumption. This was the focus of Friedman's 1970 statement of the monetarist position.

In the fiscalist model, the results of fiscal policy changes are about the same as in the general model, but the assumption that the interest elasticity of investment is zero cuts off any effect of changes in $\bar{M}$ on P or y. Similarly, in the monetarist model, the effects of $\bar{M}$ changes are about the same as in the general model, but the assumption that the demand for, and supply of, money are sensitive to interest rate changes cuts off any effect of g or t changes on P or y.

Again, the monetarist model is an extreme special case of our general model with the interest elasticity of demand for money, and also of the supply of money, for that matter, set at zero. Empirical studies of the money supply and demand functions suggest that this assumption is not generally correct. At very high interest rates where almost the entire money stock is used for transactions purposes, that is, velocity is near a technical maximum, the monetarist model would be relevant as a special case. But in general the interest elasticity of the excess demand for money—demand less supply—may be around −0.4 measured over three quarters, so that the strict monetarist model also will not generally hold.

The Effectiveness of Monetary and Fiscal Policy

The monetarist and fiscalist models are two extreme cases of our general model. In the monetarist case the economy is operating in the near vertical section of the LM curve, at r_0, y_0 in Figure 16-17. In that case the limit on output is the transactions need for money. An attempt to increase output by, for example, raising g and shifting the IS curve up will just raise interest rates and reduce investment demand. If we write the monetarist's money market equilibrium condition (17) as

$$P \cdot y = Y = v\bar{M}, \tag{18}$$

we see that in this case nominal GNP is limited by the money supply. With interest rates very high, speculative balances have been reduced to a minimum,

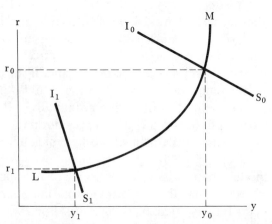

Figure 16-17 Monetarist and fiscalist poles of the general model.

and velocity v is at a technical maximum. Thus, to change nominal GNP a change in $\bar{M}$ is required.

In the fiscalist case with the $I_1 S_1$ curve in Figure 16-17 nearly vertical and interest rates low, the limit on output is aggregate demand. With interest rates extremely low, an increase in the money supply won't reduce them much—LM is flat—and even if interest rates were to fall, investment demand wouldn't rise because of depressed expectations. In this case, it is an increase in g or a cut in t, shifting IS to the right, that will raise both real and nominal GNP.

Thus, the fiscalist model might be relevant in predicting changes in GNP when the economy is very slack—when interest rates are low and unemployment is high—but in an economy with a very high level of both capital and labor utilization and high interest rates, the money supply will be the restraining factor and the monetarist model might be the best predictor of GNP movements. But neither model will be applicable in general in an economy operating near full employment. Both key interest elasticities will then be nonzero, money will matter, and so will fiscal policy. How much each will matter will depend on the exact situation. The economist trying to forecast GNP changes or to simulate the effects of policy changes needs a model that includes both the IS and the LM sectors—both monetary and fiscal variables—not a simple polar-case model that will be wrong most of the time.

TAX RATE CHANGES AND THE BUDGET DEFICIT

The two remaining topics in this chapter are, first, the relationship between tax rate changes, or fiscal policy changes in general, and changes in the budget deficit; and, second, whether, and how, it matters *how* the deficit is financed. The possibility of a tax cut reducing the budget deficit was raised by the Council of Economic Advisors (CEA) in the Kennedy Administration, as they argued for the 1964 tax cut. The idea that a cut in tax rates could raise tax revenue and reduce the budget deficit was the key concept in the "supply-side" economics of the Reagan Administration's tax cuts that began in 1982. The issue remains relevant in 1989, as the new Administration tries to reduce the budget deficit. The question of whether a tax cut increases or decreases the deficit is closely connected to the last section of the preceding chapter; the answer is that it depends on where the economy is on the LM curve.

Assuming a proportional tax system, tax revenues T can be given as

$$T = \tau Y = \tau P y, \tag{19}$$

where τ is, as in Chapters 3, 5, and 9, the tax rate. A permanent tax cut—a reduction in τ—tends to raise nominal GNP, Y, in both the classical and Keynesian models, and in the general static model it will raise both P and y.

Thus, with τ falling and P and y rising, the effect on revenues T is not clear. And if government purchases are set at $G = P \cdot g$, it is not clear then whether the deficit,

$$D = G - T, \tag{20}$$

will rise or fall with a tax cut.

From equation (19) it is clear that the larger the rise in y resulting from a given tax cut, the higher the probability of T rising instead of falling, so that the deficit is reduced by the tax cut. But the increase in y depends on the initial conditions in the economy.

Figure 16-18 shows the effect of a tax cut of a given magnitude, causing an outward shift of the $I_0 S_0$ curve to $I_1 S_1$. This increase raises equilibrium y from y_0 to y_1. The first thing to notice is that if the initial IS curve had been flatter than $I_0 S_0$—like the dashed IS curves in Figure 14-18—the y increase would have been smaller—to y_2 instead of y_1. Thus, the flatter the IS curve, the smaller the increase in y resulting from a given tax cut. Since the expression for the slope of the IS curve always has a term $\partial i / \partial r$ in the denominator, the bigger this term, the larger the interest elasticity of investment, and the smaller

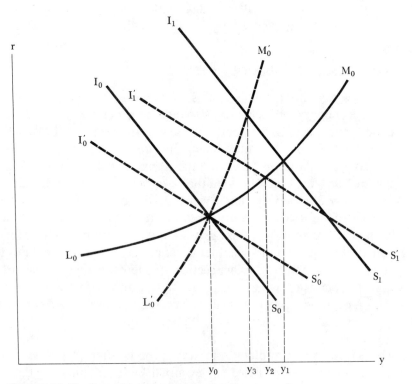

Figure 16-18 Tax cut and income increase.

the increase in y. Second, if the LM curve at the initial y_0 point had been steeper—like the dashed LM curve in Figure 16-18—the increase in y would have also been smaller—to y_3 instead of y_1. Thus, the steeper the LM curve, that is, the greater the r increase needed to maintain money market equilibrium with a given y increase, the smaller the equilibrium y increase. A tax cut, raising income, raises interest rates along the LM curve, and this increase tends to reduce investment demand, limiting the income increase. The more interest rates rise, and the more sensitive investment demand is to interest rates, the smaller the income increase will be.

This can be made more explicit by going back to the tax rate multiplier of Chapter 5. Holding the price level P constant, from the tax revenue equation (19) we have

$$dT = P \cdot [\tau \, dy + y \, d\tau],$$

so that

$$\frac{dT}{d\tau} = P \cdot \left[\tau \frac{dy}{d\tau} + y \right].$$

If tax revenue T is to rise with a tax cut, $dT/d\tau$ must be negative. The only way this is possible is if $\tau(dy/d\tau) + y$ is negative, since P is positive. Thus, we have for the condition under which a tax cut will increase revenue,

$$\frac{dT}{d\tau} < 0 \quad \text{if} \quad \tau \frac{dy}{d\tau} + y < 0,$$

or the negative elasticity of output with respect to a change in the tax rate is greater than one in absolute value:

$$\frac{dT}{d\tau} < 0 \quad \text{if} \quad \frac{\tau}{y} \frac{dy}{d\tau} < -1. \tag{21}$$

The next step is to obtain the tax rate multiplier $dy/d\tau$. To simplify the problem without changing the qualitative results much, we can hold prices constant and thus leave the asset term out of the consumption function, and also assume M is fixed at $\bar{M}$ by the Fed.

The product market equilibrium condition is then

$$y = c(y - \tau y) + i(r, y) + g. \tag{22}$$

Totally differentiating (22) and holding g constant, we have

$$dy = c' \cdot (dy - \tau \, dy - y \, d\tau) + \frac{\partial i}{\partial r} dr + \frac{\partial i}{\partial y} dy$$

and

$$dy\left[1 - c'(1 - \tau) - \frac{\partial i}{\partial y}\right] = \frac{\partial i}{\partial r}\, dr - c'y\, d\tau. \tag{23}$$

The money market equilibrium condition is

$$\frac{\bar{M}}{P} = m = m(r, y) \approx l(r) + k(y). \tag{24}$$

Differentiation, holding m constant, gives us

$$0 = l'\, dr + k'\, dy \quad \text{and} \quad dr = -\frac{k'}{l'}\, dy.$$

Substitution of this term, the change in r with a given change in y along LM, back into equation (23) for dr, yields,

$$dy\left[1 - c'(1 - \tau) - \frac{\partial i}{\partial y}\right] = \frac{\partial i}{\partial r} \cdot \left(-\frac{k'}{l'}\, dy\right) - c'y\, d\tau, \tag{25}$$

so that the tax rate multiplier is given by

$$\frac{dy}{d\tau} = \frac{-c'y}{1 - c'(1 - \tau) - \dfrac{\partial i}{\partial y} + \dfrac{\partial i}{\partial r} \cdot \dfrac{k'}{l'}}. \tag{26}$$

The last term in the denominator is positive; it gives the reduction in investment due to the increase in interest rates along the LM curve.

Substituting this expression for the tax rate multiplier back into the inequality shown in (21), we see that for $dT/d\tau < 0$,

$$\frac{-\tau c'y}{1 - c'(1 - \tau) - \dfrac{\partial i}{\partial y} + \dfrac{\partial i}{\partial r} \cdot \dfrac{k'}{l'}} + y < 0.$$

Subtracting y from both sides of the inequality and then dividing by $-y$ and reversing the inequality, we have

$$\frac{\tau c'}{1 - c' + \tau c' - \dfrac{\partial i}{\partial y} + \dfrac{\partial i}{\partial r} \cdot \dfrac{k'}{l'}} > 1$$

and

$$\tau c' > 1 - c' + \tau c' - \frac{\partial i}{\partial y} + \frac{\partial i}{\partial r} \cdot \frac{k'}{l'}.$$

Next, subtracting $\tau c'$ from both sides gives us

$$1 - c' - \frac{\partial i}{\partial y} + \frac{\partial i}{\partial r} \cdot \frac{k'}{l'} < 0,$$

or

$$c' + \frac{\partial i}{\partial y} - \frac{\partial i}{\partial r} \cdot \frac{k'}{l'} > 1 \quad \text{for} \quad \frac{dT}{d\tau} < 0. \tag{27}$$

The term $[(\partial i/\partial y) - (\partial i/\partial r) \cdot (k'/l')]$ is the *net* change in investment from one equilibrium point to another. Thus, the condition for a tax cut leading to an increase in tax revenue is that the marginal propensity to consume plus the net marginal propensity to invest, including the effect of the endogenous interest rate change along *LM,* is greater than one. The *MPC* in this case is out of *disposable* income, not *gross* income, since we began by defining consumption as a function of disposable income, $c = c(y - \tau y)$, and c' is the slope of this function.

The fact that tax revenue may increase with a decrease in tax rates does not imply an unstable situation, as might appear to be the case at first glance. The *MPC* out of disposable income is about 0.9, while the *MPC* out of gross income is only about 0.65. Thus, if the marginal propensity to invest, $[(\partial i/\partial y - (\partial i/\partial r) \cdot (k'/l')]$, is between 0.1 and 0.4, $dT/d\tau$ can be negative and the *IS* curve can still have a negative slope. With total investment running about 15 percent of GNP, $\partial i/\partial y$ may be about 0.15; so, in fact, the condition for $dT/d\tau < 0$ may frequently be on the borderline of being met in the United States. The last term in inequality (27), $(\partial i/\partial r) \cdot (k'/l')$, gives the effect on investment resulting from an expansionary fiscal policy raising interest rates along the *LM* curve. k'/l' is the slope of the *LM* curve—the increase in r that will maintain money market equilibrium with a given increase in y—and $\partial i/\partial r$ converts this into a drop in i.

If the economy is operating at a point where the *LM* curve is very flat, the term k'/l' will be very small; if the *LM* curve is perfectly flat, this term will be zero. In this case a reduction in tax rates is likely to bring about an increase in tax revenue, since the term $(\partial i/\partial r) \cdot (k'/l')$ will not detract significantly from the positive value of $c' + \partial i/\partial y$. On the other hand, if the economy is operating where the *LM* curve is steep, k'/l' is likely to be large, and an increase in tax revenue is not likely to result from a cut in tax rates.

Thus, a tax rate decrease is the more likely to *increase* tax revenue the more slack the economy is when taxes are cut. That is, if interest rates are relatively low and the *LM* curve is *flat* at the initial equilibrium, when tax rates are cut the interest rate effect of the tax cut is likely to be low, investment will rise, and the income increase will outweigh the tax rate cut and increase T, reducing the budget deficit.

FISCAL STIMULUS AND DEFICIT FINANCING

The last topic we will cover in this chapter is the question of how the method of financing a budget deficit affects its expansionary effect. Here we follow the analysis in a Council of Economic Advisers' memorandum reprinted by Smith and Teigen.

Suppose a tax cut is used to stimulate the economy at a time when interest rates are high, but substantial excess capacity and unemployment exist. In this case, the LM curve is likely to be fairly steep, and the marginal propensity to invest $\partial i / \partial y$ is likely to be fairly low due to excess capacity, so the tax cut will increase the federal budget deficit.

Deficit Financing and the *LM* Curve

The tax cut and the attendant increase in the deficit have two major stimulative effects. First, obviously the tax cut directly increases disposable income. Second, if the deficit is increased, there is an increase in net private-sector financial assets. This follows from the equilibrium condition of Chapter 3,

$$I + G = S + T, \tag{28}$$

which can be rewritten as

$$G - T = S - I. \tag{29}$$

The left side of (29), $G - T$, is the government deficit. If a tax cut reduces T, it increases the deficit, and thus must increase net private saving, $S - I$. This increase in net private saving is the increase in private-sector financial assets corresponding to the public-sector increase in liabilities due to the deficit.

The stimulative effect of the tax cut and deficit increase, per se, is represented by the upward shift of the IS curve from $I_0 S_0$ to $I_1 S_1$ in Figure 16-19. Obviously, the expansionary effect of the shift in the IS curve will depend on whether the LM curve stays at $L_0 M_0$, or shifts to the right along with IS. The movement of the LM curve in this case depends on how the deficit is financed. If the financing technique does not increase reserves provided to the commercial banking system by the Fed, it does not increase the money supply and the LM curve remains at $L_0 M_0$. If additional reserves are created, the money supply increases and the LM shifts right, adding to the expansionary effect of the deficit.

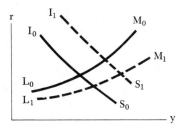

Figure 16-19 Deficit financing and shifts of the *LM* curve.

Methods of Financing the Deficit

The Treasury has five ways to finance an increase in the deficit. As we saw earlier, each of these ways must end up increasing net financial assets in the private sector by the amount of the deficit.

First, the Treasury can sell bonds to the nonbank public. This does not affect reserves and thus leaves the *LM* curve unshifted. When the Treasury spends the proceeds of the bond issue, it restores the public's holdings of money, which results in an increase in the public's net financial assets by the amount of the bond sale.

Second, the Treasury can sell bonds to the commercial banks. This operation, in itself, does not change reserves and thus leaves the *LM* curve unshifted. To make room in their asset portfolios for the additional government securities, the banks will have to reduce lending to the private sector.

These two financing techniques involve no change in reserves and thus leave the *LM* curve unshifted at $L_0 M_0$ in Figure 16-19. As a result, the upward *IS* shift tightens the money and credit markets. In the first case, income and output are raised with no increase in the money supply, creating excess demand for money which raises interest rates along $L_0 M_0$ in Figure 16-19. In this first case, the increased supply of bonds by the Treasury depresses bond prices, raising interest rates initially in the bond market. This leaves the public with more bonds and less money than they want to hold, so their demand for money rises and interest rates rise in the money market along $L_0 M_0$. In the second case, the commercial banks must sell other assets—say corporate bonds—to make room for additional government securities. This pushes up interest rates on bonds and again leads to a rise in money market rates along $L_0 M_0$. The key fact about each of these two cases is that reserves are unchanged and the *LM* curve is not shifted. Thus, the increase in interest rates along $L_0 M_0$ tends to reduce investment demand, partially offsetting the stimulative effect of the *IS* shift.

A third way to finance the deficit would be for the Treasury to draw down its demand deposits—checking account balances—at the commercial banks. This directly increases money held by the public. Since demand deposits held by the public are counted as part of the money supply, and deposits held by the government are not, the result is an increase of the money supply by the amount of the increase of the deficit. Reserves remain unchanged, however, so there is no multiple expansion of money and credit. The *LM* curve shifts out in this case, but less than in the next two cases, where reserves are increased.

The fourth way the Treasury could finance the deficit is by selling bonds to the Federal Reserve System in exchange for deposits at the Fed. The Treasury then would spend these funds by transferring ownership of the deposits to the public, who would then transfer them to their banks in exchange for a demand deposit at the bank. Thus, the ownership of the deposits at the Fed would find its way to the commercial banks. These deposits would then become additional reserves to the banks, and the money supply could expand by a multiple of the reserve increase.

The fifth way the Treasury can finance the deficit is by drawing down its balances at the Fed. This would also result in an increase in reserves through the channel described just above.

The last two cases, then, increase the reserve base and the money supply by transferring ownership of deposits at the Fed from the Treasury to the commercial banking system. This is represented by an outward shift of the *LM* curve toward L_1M_1 in Figure 16-19. The money supply increase reinforces the expansionary effect of the tax cut by holding interest rates down, preventing the offsetting drop in investment demand.

The procedure of financing a deficit by selling bonds to the monetary authority is frequently referred to as *monetization of the debt*. If we view the Treasury and the Fed as one unit, it is apparent in this case that the Treasury is financing the deficit by creating deposits on the central bank, that is, by *printing money*. The deficit in this case is financed by additional money creation.

Summary on Deficit Financing

If a deficit is financed by selling bonds to the nonbank public, or by selling bonds to commercial banks with no new creation of reserves, the effect is to tighten the money market and raise interest rates. This partially offsets the expansionary effect of the increase in the deficit by reducing investment. If, on the other hand, the deficit is financed through a creation by the central bank of additional reserves, expanding the money supply, there will be no tightening of the money market and thus no offset to the expansionary effect of the deficit increase. The former case amounts to a shift of the *IS* curve *along* a fixed *LM*. The latter *shifts LM* out by increasing *M*.

In reality, none of these "clean" cases is likely to appear. Any given increase in the deficit is likely to be financed by a mixture of these methods. The Treasury, for example, may sell bonds to the public and to the commercial banks on the New York market. If the money market is already tight and interest rates are high, the Fed may decide to prevent them from rising by buying some of the bonds. By buying the bonds, the Fed provides reserves through what is essentially an open market operation to keep interest rates down. Thus, in this case the Fed adds to the reserve base, shifting *LM* out and monetizing at least part of the deficit, through its normal open market operations.

Even in these mixed cases, however, the policy changes can be broken down into a decision by the Administration to change the degree of fiscal stimulus in the economy, shifting the *IS* curve, and a decision by the independent Fed either to allow interest rates to change along the *LM* curve by holding reserves constant, or to hold interest rates more or less constant by open market operations that shift the *LM* curve and reinforce the effect of the fiscal decision.

SELECTED READINGS

Council of Economic Advisers, "Financing a Federal Deficit" and "Fiscal Policy in Perspective," in W. L. Smith and R. L. Teigen, eds., *Readings in Money, National Income and Stabilization Policy* (Homewood, Ill.: R. D. Irwin, 1965).

R. Eisner, "What Went Wrong," *Journal of Political Economy,* May/June 1971.

R. Eisner, "Fiscal and Monetary Policy Reconsidered," *American Economic Review,* December 1969.

M. Friedman, "Theoretical Framework for Monetary Analysis," *Journal of Political Economy,* March/April 1970.

M. Friedman, "Comments on the Critics," *Journal of Political Economy,* Sept./Oct. 1972.

M. Friedman, "Monetary Policy: Theory and Practice," *Journal of Money, Credit and Banking,* February 1982.

W. W. Heller, "CEA's Stabilization Budget Policy after Ten Years," in R. A. Gordon and L. R. Klein, eds., *Readings in Business Cycles* (Homewood, Ill.: R. D. Irwin, 1965).

C. D. Romer, "Is the Stabilization of the Postwar Economy a Figment of the Data?," *American Economic Review,* June 1986.

R. L. Teigen, "A Critical Look at Monetarist Economics," *Federal Reserve Bank of St. Louis Review,* January 1972.

J. Tobin, "Friedman's Theoretical Framework," *Journal of Political Economy,* September/October 1972.

K. D. West, "Targeting Nominal Income: A Note," *Economic Journal,* December 1986.

chapter 17

The Foreign Sector and the Balance of Payments

Up to this point we have ignored the foreign sector of the economy, essentially developing the theory of income determination in a closed economy. In this chapter we describe the relationship between the foreign sector and the domestic economy, beginning with a discussion of how domestic developments affect the balance of payments, and then shifting the focus so the feedback of the foreign sector onto determination of the equilibrium level of income, the price level, and the interest rate. The U.S. economy is growing increasingly sensitive to foreign economic developments, through increased trade, international capital flows, and the effects of changes in world prices on U.S. prices. Many smaller and more open industrial economies, such as the United Kingdom and the Netherlands, have always been very sensitive to external developments. Thus, there is an obvious benefit to be gained by extending our discussion of income determination to include the foriegn sector in terms of understanding macroeconomic developments in most of the industrialized world. The cost of such an extension is low, since the foreign sector can be fitted into the *ISLM* apparatus very conveniently.

The international balance of payments is divided into two major accounts. The *current account* records income from the sale of currently produced goods and of services such as shipping, insurance, transportation of foreign tourists on U.S. airlines, and the use of U.S. technology and capital abroad. Income from provision of these capital services comes in the form of royalties and investment income. Total receipts for these sales of currently produced goods and services appear as exports, X, in the national income and product accounts. The current account also records payments for the import of similar goods and services from abroad. These appear as imports, M, in the national income accounts. Thus, the net exports term $X - M$ in the GNP identity,

$$\text{GNP} \equiv Y = C + I + G + (X - M), \tag{1}$$

from Chapter 2 is the current account balance in the balance of payments. It measures net receipts from the sale of currently produced U.S. goods and services abroad less payments for U.S. purchases of foreign-produced goods and services including payments for debt service to foreigners.

The second major account in the balance of payments is the *capital account*. This account measures the flow of funds from the United States to purchase assets from foreigners—U.S. firms' purchases of plant and equipment in Europe, U.S. investors purchasing stocks and bonds from foreigners, and so on—and the flow of funds into the United States as foreigners purchase assets here. The balance on capital account measures the net outflow of funds to purchase assets abroad. This has no direct relation to GNP, since the capital account involves asset transfers, not current production.

There is a minor third account in the balance of payments—net transfer payments to foreigners. This includes transfers by the private sector, R_f in Chapter 2, and government transfers such as Agency for International Development (AID) grants and government pension payments to foreign citizens. These government transfers are in the T component of the GNP identity,

$$C + I + G + (X - M) \equiv \text{GNP} \equiv C + S + T + R_f. \tag{2}$$

The reader will recall from Chapter 2 that in computing T, we subtracted transfer, interest, and subsidy payments to *U.S. citizens* from gross tax receipts. Thus, government transfers to foreigners are included in T as taxes collected but are neither spent on purchases of currently produced goods and services, G, nor returned to the U.S. income stream as transfer, interest, or subsidy payments.

The balance-of-payments surplus B is then net exports less the net private capital outflow F, less net transfers to foreigners R,

$$B = (X - M) - F - R, \tag{3}$$

where R is total government transfers plus private transfers, R_f in (2). Equation (3) defines roughly the "Official Settlements Balance" in the U.S. balance-of-payments statistics. This is the net change in the country's official reserve position.

The interaction between the foreign and domestic sectors of the economy, as described in this chapter, goes roughly as follows. Exports enter the product market equilibrium condition, the *IS* equation, in about the same way as government purchases G—as exogenous expenditures for U.S. output. One difference is that exports should depend on the U.S. price level. As U.S. prices go up—holding foreign prices constant—U.S. exports should fall. Imports enter the *IS* equation in about the same way as saving or tax receipts—as withdrawals from the domestic income stream. Imports should rise with income and with an increase in U.S. prices relative to foreign prices. In the first section of this chapter we will build these relationships into the *IS* equation.

The capital account net outflow should depend on the level of U.S. interest rates, holding foreign rates constant. Combining the relationship of the current account, $X - M$, to the level of income—$\partial(X - M)/\partial Y < 0$—and the net outflow of capital to the interest rate—$\partial F/\partial r < 0$—we will, in the second section of this chapter, locate a line in the r,y space along which the balance-of-payments surplus $B = 0$ in equation (3), that is, a balance-of-payments equilibrium line. The position of an internal equilibrium r_0,y_0 point relative to the $B = 0$ line will tell us whether at that r_0,y_0 point the economy is running a balance-of-payments surplus or deficit.

In the third section we will develop the feedback of the surplus or deficit with fixed exchange rates on the domestic economy through the money supply. A balance-of-payments surplus, for instance, adds reserves to the banking system, increasing the money supply and shifting the *LM* curve right. The system will not really be in equilibrium until the *LM* curve stops shifting and $B = 0$.

Next, we will look at the actual techniques used to maintain balance-of-payments equilibrium, still within the context of fixed exchange rates. Countries have at times used monetary and fiscal policy to maintain balance-of-payments equilibrium. This means, in our terms, moving the *IS–LM* intersection onto the $B = 0$ line. On the other hand, if this involves reducing real output or raising interest rates beyond politically acceptable limits, countries have shifted the $B = 0$ line by various means—import taxes, capital outflow taxes, import quotas, and so on. In addition, during the period of fixed exchange rates up to 1971, they occasionally changed exchange rates to change the price relationship between foreign and domestic goods.

In the fifth section of this chapter we will look further into this obvious way to maintain balance-of-payments equilibrium by permitting the exchange rate to float, continuously moving the $B = 0$ line to the *IS–LM* intersection. During the period 1971–1973, after the dollar was declared inconvertible into gold by President Nixon in August 1971, the major currencies shifted to a floating system against the U.S. dollar. These include the Canadian dollar, the German deutschemark, the Japanese yen, and the British pound sterling. Most other currencies maintain a fairly fixed relationship to one of the major ones, but the basic structure of the monetary system has shifted to floating rates among major currencies.

In a floating-rate system, the balance-of-payments equation (3) can be reinterpreted as a fourth equilibrium condition—supply equals demand in the foreign exchange market—in our multimarket static equilibrium model.

Through the first five sections we take prices as determined within the domestic economy, and translated into foreign exchange terms by the exchange rate. This is probably an approximately correct assumption for the United States, which might be considered a *price-setter* in world markets. However, most smaller countries are *price-takers* in world markets. They face world prices that are approximately fixed in foreign exchange, or dollar, terms. Their exchange rate translates foreign prices into domestic prices. In the sixth section of the chapter we modify the model to allow for the *small-country* assumption in which causality runs from foreign prices to domestic prices through the exchange rate. Finally, we will conclude with some comments on how the balance-of-payments and exchange rate adjustment mechanism is likely to develop in the next few years. We begin by introducing the foreign sector into the product-market equilibrium condition, the *IS* equation.

THE CURRENT ACCOUNT AND PRODUCT MARKET EQUILIBRIUM

Exports will enter the product market equilibrium equation in a way analogous to government purchases; imports enter in a way similar to saving. For a given level of aggregate foreign demand and prices, real exports x will depend on the U.S. price level P and the exchange rate e, which is measured in units of foreign currency per dollar. The foreign price of U.S. goods is given by $P^f = P \cdot e$. If the price of 1 U.S. dollar is 5 French francs so that $e = 5$, a good that sells for \$10 will sell for 50 F. Thus, for a given level of foreign demand and prices, our export function can be written as

$$x = x(P, e). \tag{4}$$

An increase in either the U.S. price P or the exchange rate e will raise the foreign price of U.S. goods and reduce exports. Thus, $\partial x / \partial P$ and $\partial x / \partial e$ are both negative.

Imports m will depend on the U.S. level of income y, the exchange rate e which translates foreign prices into U.S. prices, and the price of competing U.S. goods P. An increase in the exchange rate e will reduce the U.S. price of foreign goods at a given foreign price level, tending to increase imports. An increase in the U.S. price level P will raise the price of U.S. goods that compete with imports, also tending to raise m. Thus, the import function is

$$m = m(y, P, e). \tag{5}$$

Here $\partial m / \partial y$, $\partial m / \partial P$, and $\partial m / \partial e$ are all positive. The reader should notice that the letters M and m are now doing double symbolic duty, representing both imports and money supply. This is unfortunate, but this notation is well entrenched in the economics literature. The text below will try to make it clear which meaning should be attached to the letters in each context.

Product Market Equilibrium

We can now expand the product market equilibrium condition to include the foreign sector:

$$c + i + g + x - m = c + s + t + r_f, \tag{6a}$$

or

$$i + g + x = s + t + m + r_f. \tag{6b}$$

Since we might expect private transfer payments to foreigners r_f to rise with income, we can merge the r_f term in (6) into the import term to write the *IS* equilibrium equation as

$$i(r) + g + x(P, e) = s\left(y - t(y), \frac{A}{P}\right) + t(y) + m(y, P, e). \tag{7}$$

Here foreign purchases of U.S. goods x inject income into the income stream, and U.S. imports m withdraw income. To keep the analysis as uncomplicated as possible and still get the basic qualitative points across, we will leave y out of the investment function. Inclusion of it would just flatten the *IS* curve somewhat.

The product market equilibrium condition (7) is shown for a given exchange rate and initial price level P_0 as the $I_0 S_0$ curve in the four-quadrant diagram of Figure 17-1. In the southeast quadrant $m(P_0)$ has been added to

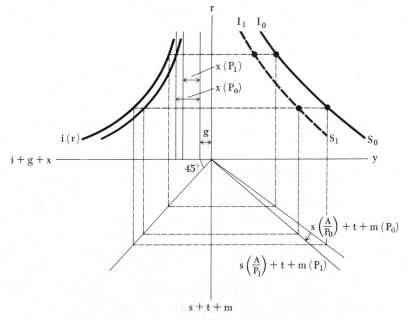

Figure 17-1 *IS* curve including the foreign sector.

the $s + t$ function; in the northwest quadrant $x(P_0)$ has been added to the $i + g$ function.

An exogenous increase in exports due, say, to a general increase in foreign demand, will increase $x(P_0)$ and shift the IS curve out to the right in Figure 17-1. An exogenous upward shift in the import function due, say, to a change in consumer tastes between U.S. and European autos, will rotate the $s + t + m$ function downward and shift the IS curve left in Figure 17-1.

The slope of the IS curve can be derived by differentiating the equilibrium condition (7) holding e, P, and g constant. Totally differentiating (7), we have

$$i'\, dr = \frac{\partial s}{\partial(y - t(y))} \cdot (1 - t')dy + t'\, dy + \frac{\partial m}{\partial y}\, dy$$

and

$$\left.\frac{dr}{dy}\right|_{IS} = \frac{\dfrac{\partial s}{\partial(y - t(y))} \cdot (1 - t') + t' + \dfrac{\partial m}{\partial y}}{i'}. \tag{8}$$

The slope of the import function has been added to the numerator of (7), making the IS curve steeper than the closed-economy IS curve. A drop in the interest rate r will stimulate investment and raise y through the multiplier process, but the increase in y will be smaller in the open economy than in the closed economy due to the import *leakage*. This can be seen in the Chapter 3 simple multiplier expression for a change in g that we can obtain by differentiating (7) holding r constant:

$$dy = \frac{1}{\dfrac{\partial s}{\partial(y - t(y))} \cdot (1 - t') + t' + \dfrac{\partial m}{\partial y}}\, dg.$$

Inclusion of $\partial m / \partial y$ reduces the value of the simple multiplier.

The Effect of a Price Change on the *IS* Curve

An increase in the domestic price level P from P_0 to P_1 increases both saving— through the real balance effect—and imports, rotating the $s + t + m$ line down in Figure 17-1. The price increase also shifts the $i + g + x$ function in Figure 17-1 to the right as exports are reduced. All of these effects work to shift the IS curve to the left toward I_1S_1 in Figure 17-1. The price increase reduces domestic income-related spending both by increasing saving to restore real assets and by redirecting expenditures to imports, which become relatively cheaper. It also reduces exports—spending on domestic output by foreigners—

by making foreign goods relatively cheaper. This reduces the equilibrium income that goes with any given $i(r) + g$, shifting IS left.

An increase in the exchange rate will have the same effect on exports and imports as a P increase, but will not directly affect saving. Thus, a 10 percent exchange rate increase will shift the IS curve to the left a little less than a 10 percent increase in domestic prices relative to foreign prices.

The modified IS curve of Figure 17-1 can be combined with the usual LM curve representing the money market equilibrium condition

$$\frac{M(r)}{P} = m(r, y), \tag{9}$$

to determine internal equilibrium r_0 and y_0 on the demand side of the economy. To see whether that r_0, y_0 combination will yield a balance-of-payments surplus or deficit we can develop the $B = 0$ balance-of-payments line in the r,y space, introducing the capital account into the analysis.

THE CAPITAL ACCOUNT AND BALANCE-OF-PAYMENTS EQUILIBRIUM

International capital *flows* result from the international purchase and sale of assets. In Chapter 14 we reviewed Tobin's portfolio distribution view of the demand for money in which persons with a given amount of liquid assets split their holdings between money and bonds as a function of the level of the interest rate. By completely analogous reasoning, we can see that a person will divide his holdings of assets between foreign and domestic assets depending on the level of interest rates at home and abroad. For a given set of interest rates he will reach an equilibrium distribution of his portfolio of assets between domestic and foreign assets. At any given asset level, a change in interest rates will produce a redistribution of assets, creating capital flows.

As total assets grow, the allocation of additions to portfolios among foreign and domestic assets will depend on interest rate levels. Thus, as U.S. wealth grows, U.S. citizens will put a bigger fraction of additions to their portfolios into foreign assets, the higher the level of foreign interest rates relative to U.S. rates. And as foreign wealth grows, foreign investors will put a smaller fraction of increments to their portfolios into U.S. assets, the higher are foreign rates relative to U.S. rates. Thus, at given foreign interest rate levels, the net outflow of capital F—net U.S. purchases of foreign assets less net foreign purchases of U.S. assets—will be a decreasing function of the U.S. interest rate,

$$F = F(r); \qquad F' < 0. \tag{10}$$

As the U.S. rate rises, the equilibrium net outflow from additions to portfolios falls.

The Balance-of-Payments Equation

We can now complete the balance-of-payments equation by subtracting the net capital outflow F from net exports less transfer payments, measured in current U.S. dollars. Exports are measured at the U.S. price level; the dollar value of imports is given by the foreign price P^f divided by the exchange rate e. Thus, the balance on current account, in money terms, is given by

$$X - M = P \cdot x(P, e) - \frac{P^f}{e} \cdot m(y, P, e), \tag{11}$$

and the balance-of-payments surplus B is

$$B = P \cdot x(P, e) - \frac{P^f}{e} \cdot m(y, P, e) - F(r). \tag{12}$$

Here again we have merged transfers to foreigners into the import function. For the balance-of-payments surplus to be zero, net exports must equal the net capital outflow.

In a system of fixed exchange rates, equation (12) gives the balance-of-payments surplus or deficit at the existing exchange rate e. This surplus or deficit must be absorbed by the central bank's (the Fed's) reserves, in order to maintain the fixed rate. This movement of reserves provides the principal automatic mechanism of adjustment in the fixed-rate system, as we see below. An alternative use of equation (12) is as the excess demand function in the foreign exchange market with a floating exchange rate. In this case, the Fed does not permit reserves to change, refusing to buy or sell in the foreign exchange market. Then with floating rates $B = 0$, and equation (12) determines the equilibrium value of e that sets $B = 0$. Thus, the balance-of-payments equation (12) gives reserve movements with fixed exchange rates *or* determines the exchange rate at $B = 0$ with floating rates.

We can find the slope of a line in r,y space that holds B at any given level including zero. An increase in y reduces net exports, requiring an increase in r to reduce F if an unchanged surplus is to be maintained. This can be seen by totally differentiating (12) holding $dB = 0$ and all prices and the exchange rate constant:

$$dB = 0 = - \frac{P^f}{e} \cdot \frac{\partial m}{\partial y} \, dy - F' \, dr$$

and

$$\left. \frac{dr}{dy} \right|_{dB=0} = \frac{\frac{P^f}{e} \cdot \frac{\partial m}{\partial y}}{F'}. \tag{13}$$

Since $\partial m/\partial y$ is positive and F' is negative, the slope of the family of BP lines in r,y space, along which $dB = 0$, is positive.

Internal Equilibrium and the Balance-of-Payments Surplus

We can derive the BP line along which $B = 0$ from equation (12) by setting net exports equal to the net capital outflow, as is shown in Figure 17-2. At a given foreign price level and exchange rate, and a given initial U.S. price level P_0, net exports are shown as a decreasing function of y in the southeast quadrant of Figure 17-2. The net capital outflow is shown as a decreasing function of r in the northwest quadrant. The 45° construction line in the southwest quadrant represents the constraint that $B = 0$; net exports equal net capital outflow.

Starting with an initial income level y_0, we can trace around the four-quadrant diagram to find the interest rate r_0 that equates the net capital outflow to net exports. This gives us an r_0,y_0 point where $B = 0$. The line connecting all such r_0,y_0 points which maintain $B = 0$ is shown as the B_0P_0 line in Figure 17-2. This is the balance-of-payments equilibrium line in the r,y space. Any r,y point below the line will yield a balance-of-payments deficit. At point A,

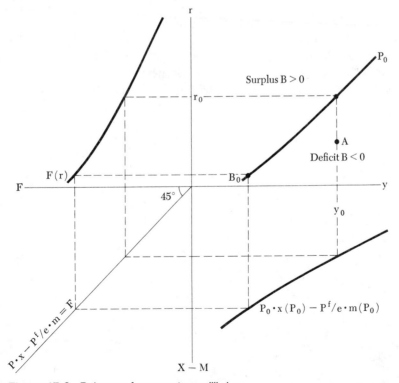

Figure 17-2 Balance-of-payments equilibrium.

for example, the interest rate below r_0 yields a capital outflow in excess of the net exports level corresponding to y_0. Conversely, any r,y point above the $B_0 P_0$ line will yield a balance-of-payments surplus.

To determine whether any given internal equilibrium r,y point determined by the intersection of the IS and LM curves will yield a balance-of-payments surplus of deficit, we can simply superimpose the BP line on the $ISLM$ diagram, as shown in Figure 17-3. There the equilibrium r_0, y_0 point lies below the $B_0 P_0$ line, so that at the existing price level P_0, which maintains equilibrium between demand and supply in the domestic economy, the balance of payments is in deficit. At income level y_0, the interest rate would have to be raised to r_1 in order to reduce the net capital outflow enough to eliminate the deficit. We will turn to questions of balance-of-payments adjustment after analyzing the effect of a domestic price change on the position of the BP line.

Price Changes and Balance-of-Payments Equilibrium

The current account in the balance of payments, in money terms, is given by

$$CA = X - M = P \cdot x(P, e) - \frac{P^f}{e} \cdot m(y, P, e). \qquad (14)$$

This expression is shown in the southwest quadrant of Figure 17-2 for a given exchange rate, foreign price level, and initial domestic price level P_0. An increase in the domestic price level will increase real imports—$\partial m / \partial P > 0$—as foreign goods are substituted for domestic goods. With a given foreign price level and exchange rate, this will also increase the U.S. dollar value of imports, M.

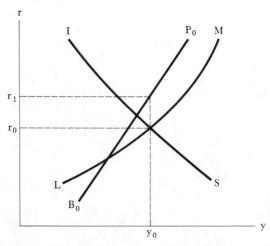

Figure 17-3 Balance-of-payments deficit.

Similarly, an increase in P will reduce real exports, $\partial x / \partial P < 0$. But whether the money value of exports X rises or falls depends on whether the decrease in real exports outweighs the increase in price—that is, on the elasticity of foreign demand for exports. Starting with $X = P \cdot x(P, e)$, we can differentiate with respect to P to obtain

$$\frac{\partial X}{\partial P} = x + P \frac{\partial x}{\partial P} = x\left(1 + \frac{P}{x} \frac{\partial x}{\partial P}\right).$$

The last term in parentheses is the price elasticity of demand for exports, $E_x = (\partial x / x)/(\partial P / P)$, which is negative since a price increase reduces sales volume along a negatively sloped demand curve. Thus, the expression for $\partial X / \partial P$ can be written as

$$\frac{\partial X}{\partial P} = x(1 + E_x). \tag{15}$$

If the demand for exports has an elasticity greater than unity in absolute value, that is, $E_x < -1$, $\partial X / \partial P$ will be negative and a price increase will reduce the money value of exports. In this case, where $E_x < -1$, a price increase reduces

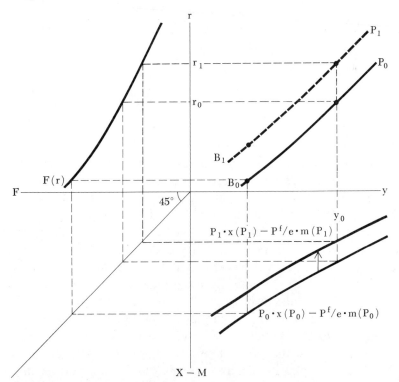

Figure 17-4 Price effect on balance-of-payments equilibrium.

X and increases M, clearly reducing net exports, CA in equation (14), at any given y level. Thus, with $E_x < -1$, a price increase will shift the net export line in the southeast quadrant of Figure 17-4 up, shifting the BP line up toward B_1P_1. If a price increase reduces net exports at the initial income level y_0, an increase in the interest rate from r_0 to r_1 is required to reduce the net capital outflow enough to eliminate the balance-of-payments deficit.

Even if the absolute value of E_x is less than unity so that a price rise *increases* export revenue X, the increase in X would have to be large enough to offset the increase in M if the price increase is to shift the BP curve down instead of up in Figure 17-4. Thus $E_x < -1$ is a sufficient, but not a necessary, condition for a domestic price increase to reduce net exports and shift the BP line up in Figure 17-4.

The full statement of the condition on demand elasticities for a domestic price increase to reduce net exports is that the sum of the import and export elasticities be less than -1. Empirically, this condition is most probably met. For example, Houthakker and Magee found that the overall price elasticity of demand for U.S. exports is about -0.5, and that U.S. import demand has a price elasticity of about -1.5. Thus, while it is theoretically possible that a price increase would increase net exports, $X - M$, the empirical studies suggest that, in fact, this is not the case.

The Effect of a Change in the Exchange Rate

Returning to the expression for net exports

$$X - M = P \cdot x(P, e) - \frac{P^f}{e} \cdot m(y, P, e), \qquad (16)$$

we can see that an increase in the exchange rate—that is, an up-valuation of the dollar—will reduce real exports, $\partial x/\partial e < 0$, and increase real imports, $\partial m/\partial e > 0$. The real export drop will reduce X at a given U.S. price level. But for a given foreign price level P^f, the e increase reduces the dollar price of imports, P^f/e. Thus, an increase in e reduces the dollar price of imports and increases real imports m. Again, whether M rises or falls with an e increase depends on the U.S. price elasticity of demand for imports in a way exactly analogous to the previous case concerning the effect of a change in P on X.

If the import elasticity E_m has an absolute value greater than one, the e increase will reduce net exports $X - M$ and shift the BP curve up in Figure 17-4. And even if $E_m > -1$ so that $dM/de < 0$, the e increase can reduce $X - M$ due to the reduction in export earnings. Since the empirical studies generally suggest that E_m is substantially greater than one in absolute value, it seems clear that, in fact, an "up-valuation"—an increase in e—will reduce net exports and shift BP up. Conversely, a devaluation—a decrease in e—will shift *BP* down in Figure 17-4. In a 1972 survey of the evidence on devaluation, Branson found that a U.S. devaluation of about 7 percent as in 1971 would increase U.S. exports by about $3.3 billion and reduce imports by about $2.6 billion, over a period of two years or so. From 1971 to 1973, in fact, the merchandise trade balance improved by about $3.2 billion. This, of course, suggests the obvious way to handle the deficit situation in Figure 17-3 if the r_0, y_0 combination is right from the point of view of internal domestic needs. This takes us to the important question of the balance-of-payments adjustment process.

BALANCE-OF-PAYMENTS ADJUSTMENT AND THE *LM* CURVE

A balance-of-payments surplus situation with fixed exchange rates is shown in Figure 17-5. The internal equilibrium interest rate and real income point corresponding to the *IS–LM* intersection r_0, y_0 lies above the *BP* line. This means that at y_0 the interest rate r_0 is so high that net exports exceed the net capital outflow. It would take a reduction of the interest rate from r_0 to r_1 to reduce the surplus to zero.

The balance-of-payments surplus, $B > 0$, means that both the commercial banks and the central bank—the Federal Reserve System—are accumulating reserves. With a surplus, the business sector's receipts from foreigners exceed payments. This means, essentially, that on balance the commercial banks in the United States are receiving for deposit checks denominated in foreign currencies. Either U.S. citizens are, on balance, receiving foreign currency checks and depositing them, or foreigners are buying U.S. currency from the banks, paying in foreign currency checks, and then paying their bills in dollars.

In either case, the commercial banks are in net receipt of foreign currency deposits, which they then deposit at the Fed, which credits them with the appropriate amount in dollars. At that point the Fed has an increase in foreign exchange reserves, and the commercial bank has an increase in unborrowed reserves, deposits at the Fed.

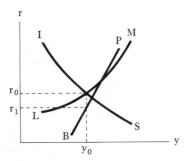

Figure 17-5 Balance-of-payments surplus.

The Fed can essentially do two things with its increment to foreign exchange assets. First, it can lend them to the foreign country by buying, say, a treasury bill of the foreign government. The bill is then held as an increase in U.S. official reserves. Or, the Fed can buy gold from the foreign central bank. The gold then becomes an addition to reserves.

Surpluses and the Money Supply

The more interesting result of the surplus, from the balance-of-payments adjustment point of view, is the effect on commercial bank reserves. When the commercial banks deposit foreign exchange at the Fed, their reserves go up by the amount of the surplus B. This represents an increase in unborrowed reserves, and, all other things equal, expands the money supply by

$$\Delta M = \frac{B}{h + z(1 - h)}, \tag{17}$$

where h is the fraction of the money supply the public holds as currency, and z is the reserve ratio, as developed in Chapter 15.

Thus, the situation shown in Figure 17-5 cannot be a full equilibrium situation because the surplus is increasing the money supply, shifting the LM curve to the right. As long as the IS–LM intersection is not on the BP line, the surplus or deficit tends to shift the LM curve toward the intersection of the IS and BP lines.

Adjustment Through Shifts of the *LM* Curve

In the absence of central bank open market operations to counter the external reserve increase, the LM curve thus shifts right with a balance-of-payments surplus and left with a deficit as the money supply changes. Figure 17-6 shows the area around r_0, y_0 in Figure 17-5 blown up so we can follow the adjustment process.

As the money supply increases, the LM curve shifts right from $L_0 M_0$. As usual, the LM shift increases demand in the economy, creating excess demand and raising prices. The price level increase moderates the LM shift, since with P rising the real money supply $m = M/P$ increases less rapidly than the nominal money supply M. The price level increase also shifts the IS curve left from $I_0 S_0$ due to both the asset effect in the consumption function and the reduction in real net exports.

If the price increase is raising equilibrium output and employment on the supply side of the economy, then the internal equilibrium point A in Figure 17-6 is moving down and to the right, as indicated by the arrow from A. The point here is that since the price increase, resulting from excess demand, is raising supply-side output, the internal equilibrium point must move to the

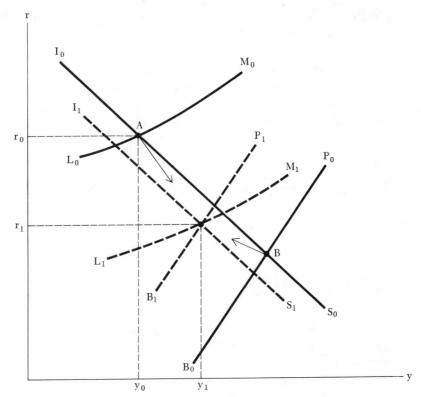

Figure 17-6 Balance-of-payments adjustment through a shift in *LM*.

right in Figure 17-6; the *IS* and *LM* shifts resulting from the price increase cannot overbalance the *LM* shift due to the initial *M* increase and shift the internal equilibrium point *A* to the left.

At the same time that the surplus is raising output and the price level internally by increasing *M*, the price level increase is also shifting *BP* up from B_0P_0, as we saw in the previous section. With the *IS* curve shifting left, this moves the *IS–BP* intersection at point *B* up and to the left, as shown in Figure 17-6.

With the internal equilibrium point *A* sliding *down* the shifting *IS* curve and *B* moving *up* it, eventually equilibrium will be reached both internally and externally at r_1, y_1 in Figure 17-6, where all three lines cross. Since the *A* point is moving to the right, the final equilibrium y_1 exceeds the initial internal equilibrium y_0. The balance-of-payments surplus eliminates itself by increasing the money supply and the price level in the economy, which increases y and reduces r, both of which act to reduce the surplus *B*.

Thus, in a fixed exchange rate system, balance-of-payments surpluses and deficits tend to be self-liquidating through the monetary mechanism. A surplus increases the money supply, expanding demand, output, and imports and reducing r which increases the net capital outflow. A deficit reduces the money supply with just the opposite results.

This is the adjustment mechanism underlying the *monetary approach* to balance-of-payments analysis. The approach focuses on predicted money flows internationally to forecast balance-of-payments developments, rather than trying to add up current account and capital account predictions. It also recognizes that full equilibrium requires $B = 0$ for the money stock to be constant.

Sterilization of the Surplus

The central bank can prevent this kind of adjustment, at least temporarily, in one of two ways. In the case of a surplus, the central bank can simply refuse to credit foreign exchange deposits as reserves. The commercial banks can obtain domestic deposits or currency for foreign exchange, but these may not be counted as reserves. This is sometimes called *sterilization of the surplus*—insulating the domestic economy from its effects.

The other way to counter the effect of B on reserves is through open market operations, selling bonds to the banks to absorb reserves. This procedure will also work in the reverse situation of a deficit. The central bank can then sell reserves, buying bonds, to the commercial banks to replace their losses as they convert deposits at the central bank into foreign exchange to send abroad.

Both of these techniques are stopgap measures taken to insulate the economy from the effects of the deficit or surplus while other policies work to bring the economy into full external and internal equilibrium. For example, if in the deficit situation of Figure 17-3 the r_0,y_0 point was considered the optimum from a domestic point of view—full employment and interest rates low enough to meet an investment target—the government would not wish to let the adjustment process work to raise r and reduce y. Or in the surplus situation of Figures 17-5 and 17-6 the government may feel threatened politically by the prospect of a price level increase—an inflation. In these cases, the monetary authorities would counter the effects of the surplus or deficit while policies to shift the BP line to the desired position were undertaken. Herring and Marston provide evidence that up to 90 percent of international reserve flows among the large industrial countries were sterilized during the fixed-rate regime of the 1960s.

BALANCE-OF-PAYMENTS ADJUSTMENT POLICY WITH FIXED RATES

Suppose the policy maker finds the economy at the internal equilibrium r_0,y_0 point A in Figure 17-7, running a payments deficit since point A is below the B_0P_0 curve. The monetary adjustment process would normally involve some reduction in y and increase in r in the direction of the arrows from

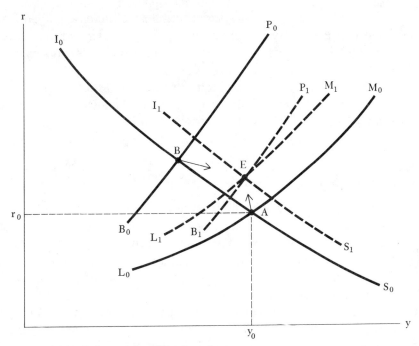

Figure 17-7 Balance-of-payments policy.

points A and B in Figure 17-7. But suppose further that the policy maker wants to establish full equilibrium at point E with only a slight drop in y, but a larger increase in interest rates than would be attained by the normal adjustment process.

The problem, then, is to shift $B_0 P_0$ to $B_1 P_1$ and to use monetary and fiscal policy to shift $L_0 M_0$ to $L_1 M_1$ and $I_0 S_0$ to $I_1 S_1$. Thus, we can divide the policy problem into two parts. First, the normal monetary and fiscal policy tools can be used to move the IS and LM curves to an intersection at E in Figure 17-7. Then, some direct action specific to the balance of payments must be taken to move BP to $B_1 P_1$. The first part of this process—the change in the monetary-fiscal policy mix to move internal equilibrium from point A to point E—is already familiar. It is the policy that shifts the BP line that is of interest here.

Exchange Rate Adjustment

The most obvious way to shift the BP line and eliminate a deficit or surplus without much disturbing internal equilibrium is to change the exchange rate e. An increase in e—an up-valuation of the domestic currency—will raise the foreign price of exports and reduce the domestic price of imports, reducing net exports and the balance-of-payments surplus at any given interest rate and income combination. In graphical terms an e increase will shift the BP line up, so that a country in the surplus position illustrated in Figures 17-5 and 17-6 can eliminate its surplus and restore full equilibrium by up-valuing its currency.

A decrease in e—a devaluation of the domestic currency—will increase the current account balance and reduce a balance-of-payments deficit. A country in the deficit position illustrated in Figures 17-3 and 17-7 could thus restore full equilibrium by devaluing, shifting the BP line down.

Direct Measures Affecting the Current Account

Instead of changing the exchange rate, the government can change the current account surplus by manipulating tariffs, import quotas, taxes, or subsidies. For example, an increase in an import tariff will reduce the dollar value of imports if the price elasticity of demand is greater than one in absolute value. This would shift the BP line down and reduce a deficit. Similarly, an import quota will reduce imports to the quota level, again shifting BP down. Both of these techniques of adjustment run counter to the General Agreement on Tariffs and Trade (GATT), to which most nations are parties. The GATT basically rules out unilateral tariff changes and allows quota impositions only in extreme cases. This is because all countries realize that both tariffs and quotas reduce the gains in efficiency and welfare that are obtained by free trade. In addition, most countries understand that if one country violates the rules of the game established under GATT and erects import barriers, other countries will retaliate, cutting off the first country's exports and leaving everyone worse off.

A more politically acceptable direct current-account measure is the use of taxes and rebates to influence trade flows. For example, several European countries rebate, to producers and sellers, taxes they pay on production of items shipped abroad, and apply to imports taxes equivalent to those paid in domestic manufacture of the item. Changes in the degree to which these subsidies and taxes are applied will shift the BP curve. Frequent manipulation of these taxes and subsidies is generally considered to be bad international behavior, since such action really is just a way around the GATT prohibition on tariff manipulation. Thus, countries tend to justify the institution of such schemes as long-run structural tax changes and to leave them in place once they are established.

Direct Measures Affecting the Capital Account

The balance-of-payments surplus can be affected, and the BP line shifted, by direct measures affecting the net capital outflow, as well as the current account. The most prominent use of these measures in the 1960s was the interest equalization tax (IET) and the foreign credit restraint (FCR) program instituted by the United States to stem its capital outflow in the mid-1960s.

The IET was a tax on U.S. purchases of foreign stocks and bonds, initially imposed in 1964. The tax reduced the return on foreign portfolio investment, and thus reduced the fraction of additions to U.S. assets that went abroad. The FCR program, begun in 1965, limited the outflow of capital first through lending by banks and nonfinancial institutions such as insurance companies. As the years passed to 1970, corporate financing of direct investment abroad was brought under this program. These techniques all served to shift the U.S. *BP* line down during a period of chronic balance-of-payments deficit. These capital control programs were eliminated during the years 1971–1973 as the international monetary system shifted toward floating exchange rates for the major currencies. With exchange rates providing for balance-of-payments adjustment, there was no longer any need for direct measures.

FLEXIBLE EXCHANGE RATES

Direct measures influencing the current and capital accounts were usually used under the post-World War II Bretton Woods system to avoid exchange rate adjustment in the case of a balance-of-payments disequilibrium. There are several reasons for this reluctance to change exchange rates.

First, at the International Monetary Conference held at Bretton Woods, New Hampshire, in 1944, which set up the International Monetary Fund (IMF), the industrial countries agreed that changes in exchange rates should be made only in cases of *fundamental disequilibrium.* This fixity of exchange rates was considered necessary to minimize uncertainty in order to encourage international trade. The fundamental disequilibrium notion was generally interpreted as ruling out frequent exchange rate changes, leading countries to resort to direct measures. The second and closely related reason is that the international monetary system under Bretton Woods was biased toward devaluation. A country running a surplus—suitably sterilized—and accumulating reserves had no incentive, other than international disapproval of its behavior, to eliminate its surplus. But on the other side of the coin, the country running the corresponding deficit had to take some action before it ran out of reserves. The natural step was devaluation, which is politically unpopular for two kinds of reasons. First, in a country dependent on imports for basic staples of living, like the United Kingdom, a devaluation will be unpopular because it raises the price of imported foodstuffs. And the bigger and more obvious the devaluation, the more unpopular it will be. Second, there seems to be a loss of national "face" when the currency is devalued. Since most voters do not understand the issues involved very well, it is easy for an opposition politician to score points by decrying the "cheapening of our money."

Thus, in the Bretton Woods system, exchange rate changes tended to be infrequent. Since they came late they generally had to be large, and this exposed the government that devalued to severe political problems. As a result, exchange rate changes were used as a last resort after all the other ways of manipulating the *BP* line to restore equilibrium had been tried under Bretton Woods.

The Shift to Flexible Exchange Rates

During the period 1971–1973 the Bretton Woods system broke down under the pressure of enormous U.S. balance-of-payments deficits. By the end of the 1960s the U.S. trade balance had shrunk to zero under the pressure of excess demand and an overvalued dollar. The current account balance became negative in 1968 and was −$3.9 billion in 1971. With monetary policy easing in 1970–1971 following the recession of 1969–1970, the U.S. Official Settlements Balance was −$9.8 billion in 1970 and −$29.8 billion in 1971.

To keep exchange rates fixed, foreign central banks had to buy this outflow of dollars; this caused them sterilization difficulties, and they felt that their domestic money supplies were running out of control. In the face of the huge deficit in 1971, and the shrinkage of the U.S. gold stock from $15 billion in the mid-1960s to $10 billion in 1971, as foreign central banks exchanged dollars for gold, the Nixon Administration ended gold sales in August 1971. This cut the Bretton Woods tie of the dollar to gold and clearly put the choice to the European countries and Japan: absorb the dollars flowing out through the U.S. payments deficit, or permit exchange rates to float.

A new set of rates was negotiated at the Smithsonian Institute in Washington on December, 1971, with the dollar devalued by about 7 percent on average. These rates held, more or less, through 1972, with another $10.4 billion flowing to foreign central banks through the U.S. deficit. As this deficit continued into early 1973, foreign central banks, especially the Deutsche Bundesbank and the Bank of Japan, gave up on holding the new parities and floated their exchange rates against the dollar. The monetary system has seen the major currencies floating since 1973, with the European currencies joining in the European Monetary System (EMS), essentially pegged to the Deutschemark, and smaller countries pegging their currencies to one or another of the major countries.

Determination of the Exchange Rate

The polar opposite case from the Bretton Woods system is a completely free exchange rate system, with rates determined by supply and demand in the foreign exchange market. This provides continuous exchange rate changes, always maintaining the *BP* line passing through the intersection of the *IS* and *LM* curves and eliminating the balance-of-payments problem.

The foreign exchange market can be understood by viewing the BP equation,

$$B = P \cdot x(P, e) - \frac{P_f}{e} \cdot m(y, P, e) - F(r),\qquad(18)$$

as the foreign exchange market equilibrium condition with $B = 0$.

Demand in the foreign exchange market is generated by U.S. exports, $P \cdot x(P, e)$. These earn foreign exchange receipts, which exporters then take to the foreign exchange market to obtain dollars. The greater the total value of exports, the greater the demand for dollars. At the same time, foreigners are receiving dollars due to U.S. imports and net capital outflow. They supply these dollars to the foreign exchange market. The greater the value of imports and capital outflow, the greater the supply of dollars.

Thus, we have the supply of dollars to the foreign exchange market,

$$S = \frac{P_f}{e} \cdot m(y, P, e) + F(r),\qquad(19)$$

where $\partial S / \partial e$ is positive. An increase in the exchange rate increases import earnings if import demand has a price elasticity greater than unity. The demand for dollars is given by

$$D = P \cdot x(P, e);\qquad \frac{\partial D}{\partial e} < 0.\qquad(20)$$

The equilibrium price of the dollar—the exchange rate—is established where demand equals supply, at e_0 in Figure 17-8. Equating demand and supply gives us the foreign exchange market equilibrium condition,

$$P \cdot x(P, e) = \frac{P^f}{e} \cdot m(y, P, e) + F(r),\qquad(21)$$

which is the same as equation (18) with B set at zero.

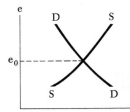

Dollars   **Figure 17-8**   The foreign exchange market.

Internal and External Equilibrium

With a given foreign price level P^f, the foreign exchange market equilibrium condition (21) can be combined with our usual equilibrium equations for the product, money, and labor markets and the production function to yield simultaneous equations in five key variables, y, N, P, r, and e, the exchange rate.

The foreign exchange market equation (21) is represented by the BP line in the r,y space for any given e. A change in e, as we have seen, shifts the BP line. If e continually changes to clear the foreign exchange market so that the supply and demand of dollars in Figure 17-8 are always equal given the internal equilibrium r and y, then the e changes continually shifting the BP line to pass through the IS–LM intersection.

In Figure 17-9 the effect of monetary policy on the exchange rate is illustrated. Beginning with an initial equilibrium at point A, suppose the money stock is increased, so the LM curve shifts out to L_1M_1. The internal equilibrium point moves to B. What happens to the exchange rate e? It must change to shift the BP curve to B_1P_1, which passes through the new internal IS–LM equilibrium B. This implies an immediate drop in e to shift the BP curve down. The force behind the drop in e can be understood in Figure 17-8. As the interest rate falls, there is an increased capital flow $F(r)$, increasing the supply of dollars to the foreign exchange market. This shifts the supply curve out in Figure 17-8, reducing the equilibrium value of e. This movement is reinforced by the increase in y in Figure 17-9, which also shifts the supply curve in Figure 17-8 by increasing imports. Thus, an expansionary monetary policy will lead quickly to a devaluation in the floating exchange rate e, and a contractionary monetary policy will lead to an up-valuation.

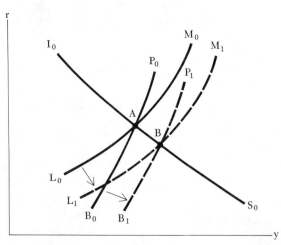

Figure 17-9 Monetary policy and the exchange rate.

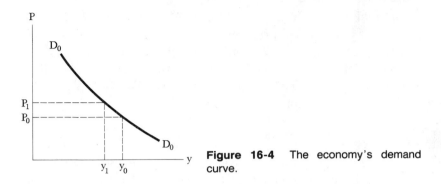

Figure 16-4 The economy's demand curve.

price level rises from P_0 to P_1, consumption demand is reduced directly due to the reduction in the real value of assets—our analog to the Pigou effect. As should be apparent from Figure 16-3, the drop in the real money supply, shifting *LM* left, tends to raise interest rates. On the other hand, the drop in income that follows the drop in consumer demand, shifting the *IS* curve left, reduces the demand for money, tending to reduce interest rates. Thus, the price increase may raise or lower interest rates, depending on the relative sensitivity to the interest rate of both the supply of and the demand for money, on the one hand, and of consumer demand to real assets, on the other.

With investment demand a function of both real output and the interest rate, $i = i(r, y)$, the leftward movement of the *IS* and *LM* curves virtually assures a decrease in investment demand from one static equilibrium to the next with the price level rising. The interest rate may rise or fall as P rises from P_0 to P_1, but with the drop in income and output, the equilibrium capital stock will drop, reducing replacement investment in the new static equilibrium. There will also be a transitory negative net investment to reduce the capital stock between equilibria.

The drop in consumption demand and investment demand following an increase in the price level from P_0 to P_1 moves equilibrium demand-side output from y_0 to y_1 in Figures 16-3 and 16-4. The reduction in *consumption demand* will come fairly quickly, probably within two to three quarters, certainly within a year, after the price increase. The speed of reaction of *consumer expenditure* will probably be more rapid than this, since, as we saw in Chapter 12, expenditure must overadjust to bring consumption of durables into line. The reduction in investment demand may come fairly rapidly as firms react to excess capacity by cutting net investment to reduce capital stock. After this transitory reduction of net investment, which reduces equilibrium capital stock, is completed over the period of perhaps one to two years, gross investment will rise to its new replacement investment level $i_1 = i(r_1, y_1)$, lower than the initial $i_0 = i(r_0, y_0)$ level but higher than gross investment during the transitory period of negative net investment.

nominal balances at any given r and y—and shift the LM curve up and to the left. In Figure 16-2 a price level increase shifts each M/P line in toward the origin. As shown by the dashed lines in the southwest quadrant, this represents a reduction in M/P and a drop in the money market equilibrium y associated with any given r. Thus, a price increase shifts the LM curve up toward the L_1M_1 curve in Figure 16-2.

The Aggregate Demand Curve

Given the money value of assets and the price level, the IS equation (3) and the LM equation (6) are two equations in two unknowns, r and y. These can be solved for equilibrium demand-side r and y, given P. The solution is shown graphically as the intersection of the I_0S_0 and the L_0M_0 curves in Figure 16-3, which are the I_0S_0 and L_0M_0 curves from Figures 16-1 and 16-2, based on the initial price level P_0.

As in Part II, we can derive the economy's aggregate demand curve by varying the price level and observing the movement of equilibrium demand-side y in Figure 16-3. An increase in the price level, we have seen, reduces real household net worth, increasing desired saving at any income level and rotating the $s + t$ line in Figure 16-1 downward. This reduction in consumption demand shifts the IS curve to the left, toward I_1S_1 in Figure 16-3. As we saw in the previous section, a price level increase also shifts the LM curve left toward L_1M_1 in Figure 16-3 by reducing the supply of real balances. Thus, as prices rise, both the IS and LM curves shift left in Figure 16-3, reducing the equilibrium level of output.

This relationship between equilibrium demand-side output and the price level is shown as the economy's demand curve D_0D_0 in Figure 16-4. As the

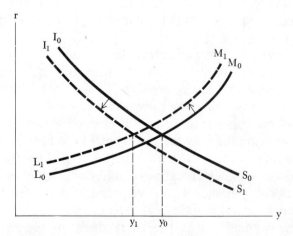

Figure 16-3 Equilibrium r and y on the demand side.

Next, subtracting $\tau c'$ from both sides gives us

$$1 - c' - \frac{\partial i}{\partial y} + \frac{\partial i}{\partial r} \cdot \frac{k'}{l'} < 0,$$

or

$$c' + \frac{\partial i}{\partial y} - \frac{\partial i}{\partial r} \cdot \frac{k'}{l'} > 1 \quad \text{for} \quad \frac{dT}{dr} < 0. \tag{27}$$

The term $[(\partial i/\partial y) - (\partial i/\partial r) \cdot (k'/l')]$ is the *net* change in investment from one equilibrium point to another. Thus, the condition for a tax cut leading to an increase in tax revenue is that the marginal propensity to consume plus the *net* marginal propensity to invest, including the effect of the endogenous interest rate change along *LM*, is greater than one. The *MPC* in this case is out of *disposable* income, not *gross* income, since we began by defining consumption as a function of disposable income, $c = c(y - \tau y)$, and c' is the slope of this function.

The fact that tax revenue may increase with a decrease in tax rates does not imply an unstable situation, as might appear to be the case at first glance. The *MPC* out of disposable income is about 0.9, while the *MPC* out of gross income is only about 0.65. Thus, if the marginal propensity to invest, $[(\partial i/\partial y) - (\partial i/\partial r) \cdot (k'/l')]$, is between 0.1 and 0.4, dT/dr can be negative and the *IS* curve can still have a negative slope. With total investment running about 15 percent of GNP, $\partial i/\partial y$ may be about 0.15; so, in fact, the condition for $dT/dr < 0$ may frequently be on the borderline of being met in the United States. The last term in inequality (27), $(\partial i/\partial r) \cdot (k'/l')$, gives the effect on investment resulting from an expansionary fiscal policy raising interest rates along the *LM* curve. k'/l' is the slope of the *LM* curve—the increase in *r* that will maintain money market equilibrium with a given increase in *y*—and $\partial i/\partial r$ converts this into a drop in *i*.

If the economy is operating at a point where the *LM* curve is very flat, the term k'/l' will be very small; if the *LM* curve is perfectly flat, this term will be zero. In this case a reduction in tax rates is likely to bring about an increase in tax revenue, since the term $(\partial i/\partial r) \cdot (k'/l')$ will not detract significantly from the positive value of $c' + \partial i/\partial y$. On the other hand, if the economy is operating where the *LM* curve is steep, k'/l' is likely to be large, and an increase in tax revenue is not likely to result from a cut in tax rates.

Thus, a tax rate decrease is the more likely to *increase* tax revenue the more slack the economy is when taxes are cut. That is, if interest rates are relatively low and the *LM* curve is *flat* at the initial equilibrium, when tax rates are cut the interest rate effect of the tax cut is likely to be low, investment will rise, and the income increase will outweigh the tax rate cut and increase T, reducing the budget deficit.

FISCAL STIMULUS AND DEFICIT FINANCING

The last topic we will cover in this chapter is the question of how the method of financing a budget deficit affects its expansionary effect. Here we follow the analysis in a Council of Economic Advisers' memorandum reprinted by Smith and Teigen.

Suppose a tax cut is used to stimulate the economy at a time when interest rates are high, but substantial excess capacity and unemployment exist. In this case, the LM curve is likely to be fairly steep, and the marginal propensity to invest $\partial i/\partial y$ is likely to be fairly low due to excess capacity, so the tax cut will increase the federal budget deficit.

Deficit Financing and the LM Curve

The tax cut and the attendant increase in the deficit have two major stimulative effects. First, obviously the tax cut directly increases disposable income. Second, if the deficit is increased, there is an increase in net private-sector financial assets. This follows from the equilibrium condition of Chapter 3,

$$I + G = S + T, \qquad (28)$$

which can be rewritten as

$$G - T = S - I. \qquad (29)$$

The left side of (29), $G - T$, is the government deficit. If a tax cut reduces T, it increases the deficit, and thus must increase net private saving, $S - I$. This increase in net private saving is the increase in private-sector financial assets corresponding to the public-sector increase in liabilities due to the deficit.

The stimulative effect of the tax cut and deficit increase, per se, is represented by the upward shift of the IS curve from I_0S_0 to I_1S_1 in Figure 16-19. Obviously, the expansionary effect of the shift in the IS curve will depend on whether the LM curve stays at L_0M_0, or shifts to the right along with IS. The movement of the LM curve in this case depends on how the deficit is financed. If the financing technique does not increase reserves provided to the commercial banking system by the Fed, it does not increase the money supply and the LM curve remains at L_0M_0. If additional reserves are created, the money supply increases and the LM shifts right, adding to the expansionary effect of the deficit.

With unborrowed reserves RU and the reserve ratio z determined exogenously by the Fed, and with h a parameter depending on the public's preferences between currency and demand deposits, the free reserves function in (10) makes the money supply also a function of $r - r_d$, given RU, z, and h:

$$M = \frac{RU - f(r - r_d)}{h + z(1 - h)} = M(r - r_d), \qquad (11)$$

and M' is positive.

The most direct way to estimate the interest elasticity of the money supply is to estimate a version of the free reserve equation (10), and then calculate the effect of an r change on the money supply M through the money supply equation (11). Studies by Modigliani, Rasche, and Cooper, in developing the money market sector of the MPS model, and by Hendershott and De Leeuw, have estimated essentially linear versions of (10):

$$RF = a_0 - a_1(r - r_d).$$

Both studies estimate the coefficient a_1 of the interest differential to be about $500 million. Thus, an increase in the market interest rate r of one percentage point—from 8 to 9 percent, for example—will reduce free reserves by $500 million. With unborrowed reserves held constant, this gives an increase in $RU - RF$ of $500 million. Since $RU - RF$ ($= RU + RB - RE$ by the definition of RF) was about $34 billion in the mid-1970s, an increase in $RU - RF$ of $500 million is a 1.5 percent ($= 0.5/34$) change. With short-term rates at about 8 percent during the same period, a one-point change in the market rate is a 12.5 percent ($= 1/8$) change. Hence, during the mid-1970s, the elasticity of reserves to changes in the interest rate is about 0.12 ($= 1.4/12.5$); a 1 percent increase in the interest rate will increase $RU - RF$ by about 0.12 percent.

We can convert this interest rate elasticity of reserves into an interest elasticity of the money supply by observing that the money supply function, equation (8), can be written as

$$M = \frac{1}{h + z(1 - h)} (RU - RF). \qquad (12)$$

With the denominator held constant, a 1 percent change in $(RU - RF)$ will yield a 1 percent change in M. Thus, if a 1 percent increase in the interest rate r raises reserves, $RU - RF$, by 0.12 percent, it also raises the money supply by 0.12 percent, so that the elasticity of the money supply with respect to changes in r is about 0.12 on the Modigliani-Rasche-Cooper and Hendershott-De Leeuw estimates.

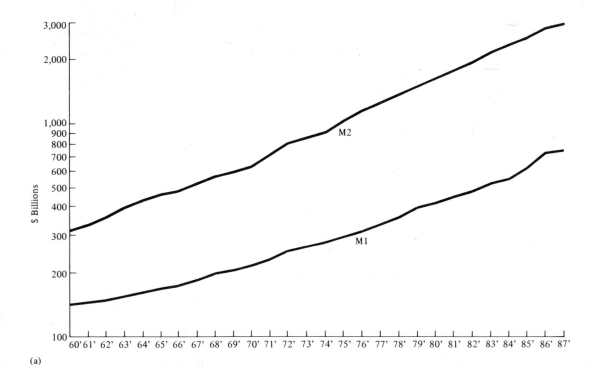

(a)

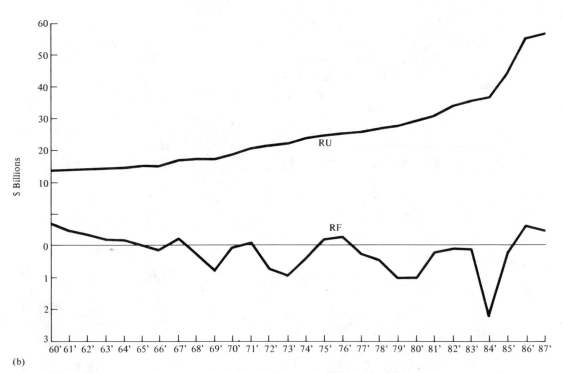

(b)

Figure 15-1 Reserves and money stock, 1960–1988 (source: Federal Reserve Bulletin). Source: 1988 Economic Report of the President and July 1986 Survey of Current Business.

demand is represented in the static $i = i(r, y)$ investment function and is reflected in the slope of the IS curves of Figure 16-9.

But the accelerator mechanism creates the likelihood of overadjustment on the demand side. The g increase raises output. This increase generates a spurt of new investment which further raises output. This spurt of net investment could be represented by a further temporary shift in the IS curve out beyond I_1S_1 in Figure 16-9. Then after a period of perhaps two years, investment demand will fall off to replacement level, shifting the IS curve back down to I_1S_1 or to I_2S_2 if the asset effect on consumer demand has taken hold.

Adjustment in the Money Market

The price rise generated by the excess demand shown in Figure 16-8, and the increase in income as y and N rise, both increase the demand for money, pulling interest rates up. The interest rate increase works to eliminate the excess demand in the money market both by reducing demand $(\partial m/\partial r < 0)$ and by increasing the money supply $[M'(r) > 0]$.

The rise in interest rates due to the increase in transactions demand following the increase in income and output, and the money supply response to the interest rate increase, are both built into the slope of the LM curve, as is shown in Figure 16-2. Thus, these money market adjustments are represented in Figure 16-9 by the rise in r from r_0 along the initial LM curve L_0M_0.

The effect of the price increase, raising the demand for nominal balances or reducing the supply of real balances, is reflected in a leftward shift of the LM curve toward L_1M_1 in Figure 16-9. Thus, at the *initial* price level P_0, equilibrium demand-side output rises to y_1 as a result of the g increase. The subsequent price increase shifts both IS and LM left, reducing equilibrium demand-side output toward y_2 in Figure 16-9.

Demand and Supply in the New Equilibrium

The movement of demand-side equilibrium output back toward y_2 as the price level rises is shown as a movement along the new demand curve D_1D_1 in Figure 16-8. At the same time, equilibrium supply-side output is increasing with the increase in employment toward N_2 in Figure 16-10. This is represented by a movement along the initial supply curve from y_0 to y_2 in Figure 16-8. The price level continues to rise until excess demand is eliminated at P_1, y_2.

For a significant increase in g, or cut in tax rates, movement from P_0, y_0 to P_1, y_2 might take two or three years in the U.S. economy. The recovery that began in 1983 in the United States followed increases in defense spending and tax cuts that began in 1982, and went on to 1986 or so. As we have seen, it is quite possible that the economy will overshoot the final y_2 level, both because of the net investment spurt that shifts IS temporarily beyond I_1S_1 in Figure 16-9, and because of the lag in the shift of the labor-supply curve up toward $h(P_1, N)$. Thus, in reality we are likely to see a cyclical movement from the initial y_0 to the final y_2, with real output first rising above y_2 and then falling back to the final equilibrium. This will be the case regardless of which fiscal policy instrument is used to stimulate the economy. By 1986, forecasters in the United States were worrying that the recovery had run out of steam, and the possibility of recession appeared. In the event, the economy was supported by export demand, following the depreciation of the dollar after 1985. This minimized the slowdown as the effect of the fiscal stimulus ended.

THE EFFECTIVENESS OF AGGREGATE DEMAND POLICY: MONETARISTS, FISCALISTS, AND NEW CLASSICALS

In the static model, monetary policy affects the economy by shifting the LM curve and, as a result, shifting the economy's demand curve. Fiscal policy works by shifting the IS and demand curves. In the general static model with $p' < 1$, with lagged adjustment of expectations or wage rigidities, the economy's supply curve has a positive slope, so that a shift of the demand curve changes the level of output.

In the original classical case, with $p' = 1$ and no wage rigidity, the economy's supply curve is vertical. In this case, fiscal policy changes affect the allocation of total output by changing the price level and the interest rate. Monetary policy changes affect only the price level, leaving the interest rate and composition of output unchanged. Thus, in the classical case both monetary and fiscal policies affect the price level and nominal GNP, $Y = P \cdot y$. In addition, fiscal policy changes affect the composition of output. In the new classical model with rational expectations and no wage rigidities, which we discussed in Chapter 11, the short-run aggregate supply curve is vertical with anticipated shifts in monetary or fiscal policy, but is positively sloped if the shift in policy is unanticipated. Eventually in this case, the supply curve becomes vertical as the effects of the policy change become apparent.

A different distinction from the one between the classical or new classical and Keynesian poles on the supply side was of great importance in debates about macroeconomic policy in the 1960s and 1970s, and is still alive today. It concerns relative effectiveness of monetary and fiscal policies on the demand side. On one side of this distinction is a group of economists generally known as *monetarists*, whose position, taken to an extreme, seems to be that as between aggregate fiscal and monetary policies, only monetary policy can shift the aggregate demand curve and affect the level of nominal GNP, with the division between changes in the price level P and output y determined by the slope of

The effect of fiscal policy on the exchange rate is unclear, however. An increase in government purchases pulls up interest rates, reducing the capital outflow, but also increases real income y, increasing imports. The direction of the supply curve shift in Figure 17-8 then depends on the relative strength of these two effects. In Figure 17-9, with B_0P_0 steeper than L_0M_0, an expansionary fiscal policy move, shifting IS up, would require a downward shift in BP, and thus a devaluation of e, to restore external equilibrium. But if BP were flatter than LM at the start, the opposite results would hold.

Empirical results from the 1960s and early 1970s suggested that the slopes of the BP and LM curve were about the same in Canada and the United States. However, the increase in financial market integration since the 1970s has flattened the BP curve for the United States considerably, so that by the 1980s it was certainly flatter than the LM curve. The evidence for this is summarized in Branson (1988). The large tax cut and increase of defense spending in the early 1980s in the United States shifted the IS curve up and produced a major appreciation of the dollar, an upward movement of e, that continued to 1985.

Comparing monetary and fiscal policy effects on the exchange rate, we see that a shift in monetary policy has a clear and probably quick effect on the exchange rate, while the sign of the effect of fiscal policy is unclear. Thus, in designing policies to maintain internal and external balance, it would make sense to assign fiscal policy to the internal output or employment target, with monetary policy eliminating any effects on the exchange rate. Or, if an active exchange rate policy is to be pursued, this should be done mainly through monetary policy, which has a comparative advantage in influencing the exchange rate.

THE DOMESTIC ECONOMY AS A PRICE-TAKER

Up to now, we have taken the price relationship $P^f = e \cdot P$ as translating a domestically determined price level P into foreign terms. This implicitly assumes that the economy is large in terms of world markets, so that the foreign exchange, or world, prices of its goods are determined by internal cost and demand conditions. For the U.S. economy, this is probably a good assumption.

For smaller industrial economies, however, the causation probably runs the other way. In the literature on international trade, the small country is usually considered to be a *price-taker* on world markets. If we consider the extreme simplifying example of a small industrial country that produces only goods that are traded on the world market, it faces given world prices P^f for these goods. The exchange rate e then translates the world price index P^f into home prices as

$$P = \frac{P^f}{e}. \tag{22}$$

In the extreme small-country case, the world price is fixed at P^f and the domestic price level is just P^f/e.

This gives us a horizontal aggregate supply curve at $P = P^f/e$ for the small country, as shown in Figure 17-10. The point of intersection with the usual downward-sloping aggregate demand curve gives the equilibrium level of output y_0 and the domestic price level $P_0 = (P^f/e)_0$. In the small-country case, the usual IS–LM analysis fixes the demand curve. But the price level is determined in the world market, and the intersection of the normal demand curve with the world-market supply price determines output.

Effects of an Increase in P^f

The small-country model gives us a good interpretation of the effects of an exogenous increase in world prices. An example is the oil price increase in 1973–1974. We previously analyzed this case in terms of domestic supply in Chapters 7 and 8. Here we short-cut that analysis with the small-country assumption.

As P^f rises, to take a pertinent recent example, the domestic price level (supply curve) rises to $P_1 = P_1^f/e_0$ in Figure 17-10. With the demand curve unshifted, output falls to y_1. In the IS–LM diagram implicit in the background, the price increase from P_0 to P_1 has reduced equilibrium output demanded from y_0 to y_1. The exogenous increase in the world price level both raises the internal price level and reduces output in the smaller industrial countries. This is a good illustration of the effects of the oil price increase in most European economies in 1974–1976.

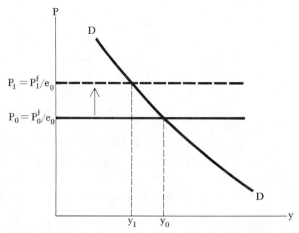

Figure 17-10 Supply and demand in the small-country case.

The results of an increase in P^f on the current account are unclear. If the increase were on all goods, strictly speaking the price-taking small country would see no current account effects. Prices of imports and exports would rise by the same amount. But if the price increase were only on a specific import such as energy, then the effect would depend on the price elasticity of demand E_m. If it were less than -1 in absolute value ($0 > E_m > -1$), then import payments would rise. This was clearly the case with the oil price increase, where substitution possibilities were severely limited in the short run. In that case the inflation and falling output in the European economies and Japan were accompanied by increased current account deficits. This analysis can be easily extended to changes in export prices and to tariffs on exports or imports as well.

Exchange Rate Fluctuations and the Policy Mix

Movements in exchange rates give results that are symmetrically opposed to those due to changes in P^f. This should be apparent in Figure 17-10. The upward movement in the domestic price level from P_0 to P_1 could follow from a reduction in e, as well as from an increase in P^f. Thus, a devaluation with e falling can raise the internal price level of a small country and reduce the level of output. An up-valuation would have the opposite effect.

This feedback from the exchange rate to the domestic price level, coupled with the effects of monetary policy on the exchange rate, discussed above, makes management of monetary policy a difficult task in the small open economy. Figure 17-11 shows the effects of an expansionary monetary policy action

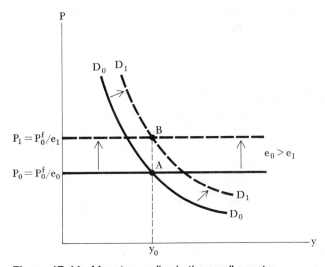

Figure 17-11 Monetary policy in the small country.

in this context. A monetary expansion shifts the demand curve out from $D_0 D_0$ to $D_1 D_1$. In the closed-economy analysis of Chapters 4–16 this is clearly expansionary. But we saw in Figures 17-8 and 17-9 that a monetary expansion reduces the exchange rate e. This shifts the internal price level in Figure 17-11 up to $P_1 = P_0^f / e_1$. The result for the price level is clear; the exchange rate effect raises it. The result for real output is unclear. Whether the new value for real output at point B exceeds y_0 at point A depends on the entire structure of the economy. Thus, in the small open economy, monetary policy can influence the price level directly through the exchange rate, while the effects on real output may be unclear. Empirical evidence supporting these results has been presented by Dornbusch and Krugman.

This ambiguity does not exist for fiscal policy. In the small open economy, the *BP* curve is approximately horizontal at the world rate of interest. So a fiscal expansion will generate an up valuation and a reduction in the domestic price level in Figure 17-11. Thus the effect of fiscal policy on output is unambiguous. An expansion shifts *DD* in Figure 17-11 up and reduces the domestic price level via up valuation of e.

Thus, the small-country results reinforce our earlier conclusions in the use of monetary and fiscal policy. The comparative advantage of fiscal policy lies in influencing domestic output. Monetary policy has the comparative advantage in moving the exchange rate. In the small country, this gives monetary policy a clear target on the price level or the rate of inflation, with fiscal policy aimed at output.

Small Countries and Large Countries

The small-country analysis above shows us a direct link from monetary policy to inflation. This link exists to some degree in large countries, even in the United States. So the message for management of the policy mix with flexible exchange rates is to look for the short-run effects of monetary policy on the exchange rate and the price level. With a flexible instead of a fixed exchange rate system, fiscal policy is likely to have a more predictable effect on output and a less predictable effect on the price level.

As we move across the spectrum from large to small industrial countries, the separation between monetary policy as an instrument moving P via e and fiscal policy moving y becomes greater. But even for U.S. policy, an increased awareness of the exchange rate effects of monetary policy would be a good idea.

SELECTED READINGS

W. H. Branson, "The Trade Effects of the 1971 Currency Realignments," *Brookings Papers on Economic Activity,* vol. 1, 1972.

W. H. Branson, "Sources of Misalignment in the 1980s," in R. C. Marston, ed. *Misalignment of Exchange Rates: Effects on Trade and Industry* (Chicago: The University of Chicago Press, 1988).

R. Dornbusch and P. Krugman, "Flexible Exchange Rates in the Short Run," *Brookings Papers on Economic Activity,* vol. 3, 1976.

W. J. Ethier, *Modern International Economics,* 2nd Ed., (New York: W. W. Norton & Co., 1988), Chapter 2.

J. Frenkel, "Flexible Exchange Rates, Prices, and the Role of 'News': Lessons from the 1970s," *Journal of Political Economy,* August 1981.

H. S. Houthakker and S. P. Magee, "Income and Price Elasticities in World Trade," *Review of Economics and Statistics,* May 1969.

R. A. Mundell, "The Appropriate Use of Monetary and Fiscal Policy for External and Internal Balance," *IMF Staff Papers,* March 1962.

M. Obstfeld, "Floating Exchange Rates: Experience and Prospects," *Brookings Papers on Economic Activity,* vol. 2, 1985.

M.v.N. Whitman, "Global Monetarism and the Monetary Approach to the Balance of Payments," *Brookings Papers on Economic Activity,* vol. 3, 1975, with discussion by W. H. Branson.

chapter 18

Macroeconomics When Markets Do Not Clear*

We have now given a full account of the static equilibrium model and its extensions, which represents the mainstream of post-Keynes macroeconomics. This model uses the *ISLM* framework introduced by Hicks. It is often called the "neoclassical synthesis," because in a simple, general equilibrium setting, the framework appears to be consistent with traditional microeconomic analysis in terms of supply and demand. Behavioral equations at the macro level are obtained by adding up the behavioral equations of individuals whose information about market events is limited to prices. Our purpose in this chapter is to present an alternative view of macroeconomics and its microfoundations.

THE REAPPRAISAL OF THE FOUNDATIONS OF MACROECONOMICS

The question now arises: is the neoclassical synthesis an adequate representation of Keynes' *General Theory* and its underlying vision? This question has provided the motivation for a significant proportion of macroeconomic research in the last ten years.

We set up the basic general equilibrium framework in our skeletal closed economy model with the four unknowns: output, employment, the interest rate, and the price level. As Chapter 8 explained, the solution can be obtained from the three equilibrium conditions, respectively, in the product market, the money market, and the labor market, and the remaining equation, which is the production function linking output and employment. The equilibrium conditions in the general case reflect an equilibrium in which each market clears.

Keynes and the Neoclassical Synthesis

One of Keynes' central preoccupations was to explain how widespread involuntary unemployment can exist and persist when the labor market does not clear. As we have seen, in the neoclassical synthesis this can arise only in special circumstances, so the *General Theory* could be seen merely as a special case of a more general theory. With the liquidity trap appearing rather implausible, only money wage rigidity remains as a possible cause of involuntary unemployment. This cause of involuntary unemployment can operate whether we make the classical assumption about price expectations, $P^e = P$, or the extreme Keynesian one where P^e does not adjust fully to changes in the current price P. One can well ask whether the "Keynesian Revolution" was merely about institutional wage rigidities.

Of course, we still have Keynes' concepts of the consumption function, the speculative demand for money and the marginal efficiency of investment, but the centerpiece of the analysis, the role of insufficient effective aggregate demand, has been relegated to the sidelines, where it now only suggests one possible policy response to observed unemployment.

Dissent from this view of Keynes was scattered and generally unfocused for many years. Some questioned whether the synthesis took adequate account of "the dark forces of time and ignorance" but did not explain where in the model these omissions were critical. Others even attacked the principle of constructing macroeconomics from microeconomic relationships, without suggesting how else macrofunctions might be derived. Certainly Keynes did not express a clear and fully consistent account of the microfoundations for the *General Theory*. But since the mid-1960s a promising new approach, beginning with exegesis of Keynes, has led to a fundamental reappraisal of the foundations of macroeconomics.

The Importance of Markets not Clearing

One element of this reappraisal emerged with Patinkin's analysis of the demand for labor, though he did not generalize his insight to the rest of his model. Patinkin noted that if a positive excess supply of goods developed, so that firms could not sell all they wished, their demand for labor would fall. The general point that if one market did not clear there would be repercussions in other markets was made much more explicit by Clower. He took the consumption function as his example: involuntary unemployment in the labor market is reflected in a lower level of demand in the goods market. This is implicit in Keynes' analysis of the consumption function, and integrating it into the rest of the neoclassical synthesis poses a serious logical problem. In traditional microeconomic analysis, when markets clear, quantities demanded and supplied are functions of initial endowments and prices (and expected future prices, if the analysis is intertemporal). So indeed were the labor demand and supply curves of Chapter 6, though these functions were inverted to make the wage a function of the quantity of labor. Yet Keynes' consumption function, to which he himself attached central importance, is defined on *realized income,* not wage rates and time endowments. But at a given wage when a worker becomes unemployed, his or her time endowment is unaltered while realized income is reduced. In other words, Keynes' consumption function takes into account the repercussion on the demand for goods of the labor market not clearing, which really puts it outside the framework of traditional microeconomic analysis, where demand functions take no account of such effects.

If a market does not clear, the amount that individuals are able to trade may be less than the amount they would like to trade. This constraint on the quantity traded will then enter the demand or supply functions defined on other markets. Therefore, *quantity signals* as well as prices enter the analysis, and there can be quantity interactions between markets that are direct, not transmitted through price changes. The presence of quantity signals implies a radically different view of the efficiency of the "invisible hand"—the information-disseminating and organizing role of decentralized markets. Clower and Leijonhufvud stress the informational failures that are implicit in the *General Theory.* The effective demand for goods of an unemployed worker is constrained by his or her realized income and not given by the "notional" demand that corresponds to the prevailing wage rate, prices, and his or her time endowment. Workers thus do not signal to firms the demand that they would express if they were employed, which in turn would support their employment. Thus, excess supply on goods and labor markets is mutually reinforcing. Keynes diagnosed another important reason for such informational failures—the intertemporal nature of many decisions. The existence of durable goods and assets and of lags in production causes decision makers to take into account trades in the future. But markets do not exist where such trades can be agreed now. For example, excess demand for future consumption cannot be adequately signaled to producers. All that can be signaled is an excess supply for current consumption, which is unlikely to make producers invest more in order to be able to produce more goods for future consumption.

Connections with Earlier Chapters

In earlier chapters, we have already had several foretastes of these themes of
the reappraisal of macroeconomics, and much of our earlier analysis will be
illuminated by their development. One very important example is the expenditure multiplier analysis of Chapter 3, for which we will now be able to provide
a systematic microeconomic story that connects what happens in product and
labor markets. This will be related to the microeconomic foundation of the
consumption function as discussed in Chapter 12, which, for example, in
Ando and Modigliani's empirical formulation explicitly includes employment
as a variable. In Chapter 12, in the analysis of intertemporal choice, illustrated
by the two-period case on p. 245, current and expected labor incomes were
taken as exogenous; together with the slope of the intertemporal budget line,
they determine current consumption demand. This use of indifference curves
defined on this and the next period's real consumption contrasts with that of
Chapter 7, where indifference curves defined on real consumption and leisure
are used to analyze current labor supply decisions. We will see that both kinds
of behavioral relationships can be obtained from the same household objectives
but involve different assumptions about the state of the labor market. We will
also be able to utilize the notion of excess capacity discussed in Chapter 8 in
a wider context, with excess capacity in product markets playing the role of
involuntary unemployment in labor markets. And connecting with the discussions of the demand for money in Chapter 14 and investment demand in
Chapter 13, our discussion of money balances and inventories will reveal how
durable assets or goods permit intertemporal shifting of purchasing power and
the consequences for production, employment, and consumption decisions.
In the case of investment demand, our discussion of the accelerator was another
example of the relevance of current and expected quantity constraints in demand functions.

SOME ANALYTIC PRELIMINARIES FOR THE "REAPPRAISAL" MODEL

Before we proceed to the exposition of the underlying macroeconomics of
demand and supply in markets for labor and goods, and the resulting behavior
of the "reappraisal" model of market interaction with nonclearing markets,
we must define a few basic concepts and relate the variables of the model to
the national income accounts. These preliminaries are dealt with in this section.

The Concept of Equilibrium and Quantity Rationing

We must contrast the concept of equilibrium in macroeconomic models where
markets always clear, as assumed (with some exceptions) in Part II, with equilibrium in models where markets do not clear. In order for prices always to

adjust to clear markets, there would have to be a highly centralized, costless system of processing information and organizing transactions. In models of pure theory, this system is run by an auctioneer who receives information on aggregate supplies and demands at each set of prices. He raises the prices of goods for which there is positive aggregate excess demand and lowers prices for goods in excess supply. He then gets new information on demands and supplies and continues this iterative process until it converges to an equilibrium where in each market, excess demand is zero.

In this story, trading does not take place until the equilibrium is reached. But in a decentralized economy, this is obviously unrealistic, and even with an auctioneer, it might take a long time to reach a market-clearing set of prices. And if transactions take place at prices that do not clear the market, then either some buyers or some sellers will not be able to trade what they wish at these prices. There will be some more or less systematic way of allocating among buyers a good in excess demand (or allocating among sellers the purchases of a good in excess supply). Individuals will thus be *rationed,* and it is unlikely that they will continue to assume that they can transact whatever their initial endowments permit at parametrically given prices. Hence, the rationing they encounter on one market will affect their behavior in another.

This is the crucial difference between models of general market-clearing equilibrium and general equilibrium where markets may *not* clear. In our version of the latter, we will assume that individuals view quantity "rations" as well as prices as exogenous parameters, though over time their views of these parameters can change. This exogeneity assumption is the simplest way of modeling responses to nonclearing markets; we will briefly discuss alternatives at the end of the chapter. The concept of equilibrium here is one that involves quantity signals as well as price signals.

Models in which markets do not clear are often called "disequilibrium" models, but we agree with Malinvaud and Hahn that this usage is misleading. The analysis is concerned with a sequence of short periods. Within each period, although markets do not clear, we assume that agents have adjusted their behavior in the light of perceived price and quantity signals so that their actions are mutually consistent. It makes perfectly good sense to call the resulting state of rest a short period equilibrium, as argued in Chapter 8. This does not, of course, imply that each short period equilibrium will be the same as the preceding one. Note that in this concept of equilibrium, individuals may well be *off* the supply and demand curves which, as in Chapter 8, do not take quantity signals into account (being defined only on prices and initial endowments).

In our analysis, the quantity signals and quantity interactions between markets will be the focus of attention. This does not mean that we assume wages and prices to be institutionally rigid. We define, as a simplifying analytical device, a notion of the short-run period in which individuals take wages and prices to be exogenous and only quantities change. Between periods, wages and prices can change too. We will suggest reasons why in the absence of an auctioneer, market forces and not just institutional imperfections might make wages and prices adjust more slowly.

The National Accounts

Since market interactions are made more complicated by the operation of quantity signals, we want to keep the analysis as simple as possible in other dimensions. Therefore, we will assume that there is no bond market; though as Barro and Grossman show in their book, a bond market can be added without much difficulty if it can be assumed that it always clears. We will begin with a closed economy which we introduce by extending a little the national accounts considered in Chapter 2.

The output of firms equals sales of goods plus inventory change in (final) goods: $y = x + \Delta inv$. Sales are made to consumers or to the government (where exogenous investment can be thought of as part of g): $x = c + g$. We will assume that the government can never be rationed; so if the demand for goods exceeds the supply, it is consumers who will be rationed. The savings flow of households, income minus expenditure, equals dividend payments D received from firms at the beginning of the period, plus labor income WN minus consumer expenditure Pc. We will assume that the only asset available to households is money balances, so that all saving adds to money balances. Thus, $S = D + WN - Pc = \Delta M^h$, which is the change in households' money balances. The profits of firms R are sales income minus wage costs: $R = Px - WN$. The change in firms' money balances ΔM^f is profits minus dividend payments: $\Delta M^f = R - D$. Now we can check easily enough that the value of government expenditure must balance the change in money holdings by firms and households: $\Delta M = \Delta M^h + \Delta M^f = D + WN - Pc + Px - WN - D = P(x - c) = Pg$. This just says that government expenditures are financed by issuing money, in our simplified model.

We could include transfer payments by government to households and taxes on firms and households. Then g would be financed by ΔM plus taxes minus transfers. This would not change the substantive analysis that follows; so we omit taxes and transfers to keep the structure as simple as possible. Also, for simplicity, we will assume that dividend payments are governed by some rule of thumb that makes them independent of current profits (e.g., pay out all of last period's profits).

It is assumed that transactions take place through money on two markets. On one, firms pay workers in money and on the other, households buy goods with money. The importance of this is that it reflects the decentralization of a market economy and specialization in production. This means that workers cannot be paid in terms of the goods they themselves produce. Thus, c should be thought of as an aggregate quantity index which reflects a detailed list of goods produced and consumed.

The Income-Expenditure Model in Consumption-Employment Space

We now illustrate these national accounts and use the diagrams to foreshadow the diagrammatic apparatus that is central to the subsequent exposition. In Figures 3-2 to 3-8, we saw that the saving-investment balance $c + i + g = y = c + s + t$ could be represented graphically. For simplicity, but without any real loss of generality, we are in this chapter absorbing investment in g and assuming taxes t are zero, thus giving Figure 18-1. Another way of seeing exactly the same balance is with the income-expenditure diagram common in elementary texts. It is Figure 18-2 in our case. Although superficially this represents only the goods market, if we can use the production function from Chapter 7 to link output y and employment N, here we have an implicit story about the labor market. This is easy enough to picture if we translate the output axis into units of N using the production function. To get just consumption on the vertical axis we subtract g from $c + g$ in Figure 18-2. Remember, the government is never rationed, so we can safely eliminate g in this way. Making both changes transforms Figure 18-2 into Figure 18-3, and

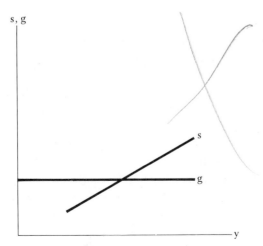

Figure 18-1 The saving-investment balance.

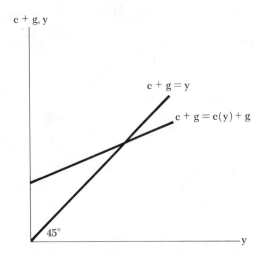

Figure 18-2   The income-expenditure balance.

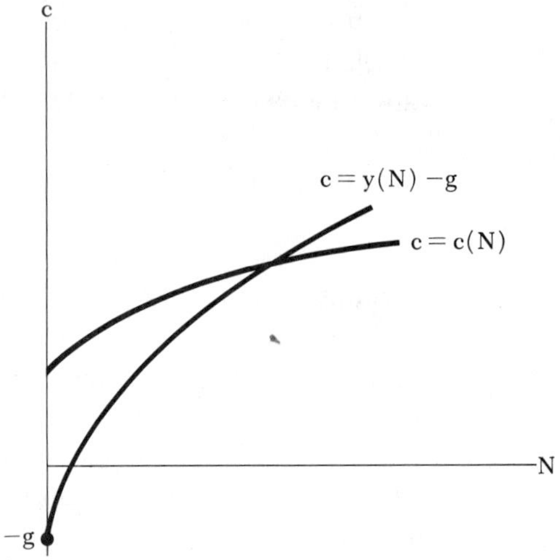

Figure 18-3   The income-expenditure balance in consumption-employment space.

in the future the diagrams in which we will investigate the interactions of goods and labor markets will be in the same c,N space.

Rationing and the Minimum Conditions

Now we must distinguish the different concepts of supply and demand for each market. *Notional* or *unrationed* demand and supply depend only on initial current (and expected) endowments and current (and expected) prices; they are independent of any quantity rations experienced on other markets. In contrast, *rationed* or *quantity-constrained* demand or supply also depend on quantity rations experienced on other markets. These ration levels refer to *other* markets, not to the market for which demand or supply has been defined. This is because we want a concept of demand and supply in each market that is separate from the quantities traded on that market. Whether the notional or the rationed demand will be *effective* depends on whether or not quantity constraints are actually encountered in other markets. If not, effective demand will be the notional demand. If there are quantity constraints in other markets, effective demand will be the rationed demand conditional on the rations from other markets. This *switch* in the effective demand function is the essential point of what Clower calls "the dual decision hypothesis." To illustrate, the demand for goods by a worker who can choose his or her hours of employment depends on the wage rate, prices, and the time endowment, while if the worker is rationed in employment, this ration will enter the demand function for goods.

To recapitulate, the concepts of supply and demand we have defined can be outlined as follows:

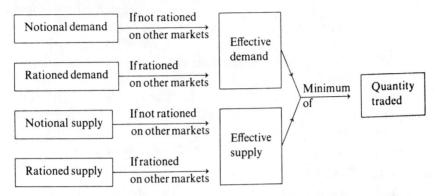

An equilibrium with rationing must satisfy some basic properties. First, the total quantity sold must equal the total quantity purchased. This does *not,* of course, mean that notional demand equals notional supply. Second, exchange must be voluntary, so no individual can be forced to sell more than his or her effective supply or less than his or her effective demand. This ensures that the "minimum condition" holds: the quantity traded is the minimum of the effective demand and the effective supply.

This is illustrated for a single market by Figure 18-4. To be concrete, let us take this to be the labor market as in Figure 10.4. Clearly, at the wage W_1, N_1^D is less than N_1, so that it is the demand by firms that is traded, leaving some workers unemployed. At the wage W_2, there is positive excess demand, and the supply by households is the quantity traded. It should

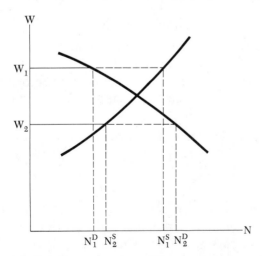

Figure 18-4 The min condition in a single market.

be noted that this diagram ignores any feedbacks through goods markets, which we will deal with shortly.

The third basic property of an equilibrium with rationing is that there cannot be both rationed buyers and rationed sellers on the same market. Conditions two and three are quite strong. We will return below to the question of whether condition two is consistent with the presence of inventories. Condition three is seemingly contradicted by the simultaneous observation of unfilled vacancies and unemployment. The way out, which is to say that there are many local labor markets between which conditions vary, would change the subsequent analysis, so we will assume that there is only a single labor market and return to this point at the end of the chapter.

Rationing in a Two-Market Model

With just two markets, the minimum conditions are:

in the consumer goods market $c = \min(c^D, c^S)$

in the labor market $N = \min(N^D, N^S)$

We will distinguish rationed and unrationed (notional) functions by putting a bar over the former and including as an explicit argument the ration level on which they are conditional. For example, $c = \bar{c}^D(N;\cdot)$ is the rationed consumer goods demand function, which is conditional on the rationed level of employment N, while $c = c^D(\cdot)$ is the unrationed demand function. With two markets there are four possible constraint regimes, which we will discuss in greater detail later.

Sellers rationed in both markets (Keynesian unemployment)

$$\begin{cases} c^D < c^S, & \text{so that} \quad c = \bar{c}^D(N;\cdot) \\ N^D < N^S, & \text{so that} \quad N = \bar{N}^D(c;\cdot) \end{cases} \tag{1}$$

Here there is excess supply on both the labor market—involuntary unemployment—and the goods market. Therefore, the quantities traded are the effective demands on each market, where these are given by the rationed demand functions, reflecting the fact that workers are rationed in employment and firms in sales of goods.

Buyers rationed in both markets (repressed inflation)

$$\begin{cases} c^D > c^S, & \text{so that} \quad c = \bar{c}^S(N;\cdot) \\ N^D > N^S, & \text{so that} \quad N = \bar{N}^S(c;\cdot) \end{cases} \tag{2}$$

Here there is excess demand on both markets; so the quantities traded are effective supplies. Households are rationed in the goods market, and firms are rationed in the labor market. The term *repressed inflation* makes sense because an increase in the wage rate and price level would reduce or eliminate the excess demands.

Buyers rationed in goods market, sellers rationed in labor market
(classical unemployment)

$$\begin{cases} c^D > c^S, & \text{so that} \quad c = c^S(\cdot) \\ N^D < N^S, & \text{so that} \quad N = N^D(\cdot) \end{cases} \tag{3}$$

Firms are willing to trade less than households in each market, so their notional supply and demand prevail. Here the wage is so high that firms do not find it profitable to employ more workers or sell more goods—hence *classical unemployment*.

Sellers rationed in goods market, buyers rationed in labor market
(underconsumption)

$$\begin{cases} c^D < c^S, & \text{so that} \quad c = c^D(\cdot) \\ N^D > N^S, & \text{so that} \quad N = N^S(\cdot) \end{cases} \tag{4}$$

Here the wage is so low that there is excess supply in the goods market and excess demand in the labor market.

MICROECONOMIC FOUNDATIONS FOR THE REAPPRAISAL MODEL

Before we discuss in detail what is going on at a macroeconomic level in each of the four cases, we must investigate the microeconomic origins of the various functions. Even with only two markets, the interactions between markets look a little complicated. However, we will introduce some diagrams similar to Figure 18-4 that should make things clear. We will derive them in some detail from the intertemporal microeconomic theory of household and firm behavior, which itself has many insights to offer.

An Intertemporal Model of Household Behavior

We will generalize the analysis of labor supply in Chapter 6 and the two-period model of the consumption function discussed in Chapter 12 by introducing current and future leisure as well as current and future consumption into the model and by explicitly considering the form of the constraints when there is rationing. Money balances have the role of a store of value by permitting purchasing power to be shifted between the current period and the future, and we *derive* this role from the future part of the objective function. To introduce this very fundamental notion in the simplest possible way, let's briefly return to the two-period problem considered in Chapter 12.

The problem there was to maximize $U(c_0, c_1)$ subject to the intertemporal constraint. Assuming that the price level is the same in both periods but an interest rate r can be earned on lending (or paid on borrowing), we see that the constraint implies that saving in period 0, $s_0 = y_0 - c_0$, becomes $(1 + r)s_0$ at the beginning of period 1, so that $(1 + r)s_0 + y_1 = c_1$ is the amount that can be spent next period. By substituting for c_1 in the utility function the problem becomes

$$\max U(c_0, (1 + r)s_0 + y_1) \quad \text{subject to} \quad s_0 + c_0 = y_0.$$

We have *derived* a role for saving s_0 in the utility function that clearly comes from the utility of future consumption.

In what follows, there is no interest rate, and saving is an increase in money balances. Thus, our derived utility of money balances comes from the utility of future activities, where we explicitly analyze both consumption and labor supply and the constraints that may be ruling in each market. As we will see, the constraints that are expected to prevail make a critical difference to the derived utility of money balances. For example, a household that expects that it cannot sell labor next period clearly has a quite different need for money balances than one which expects to be rationed in the goods market.

Suppose the utility function is

$$U = U(c_0, T_0 - N_0, c_1, T_1 - N_1) \tag{5}$$

which is increasing in all four arguments and where, as in Chapter 12, c_0 and c_1 are consumption in periods 0 and 1. $T_0 - N_0$ and $T_1 - N_1$ are leisure hours in periods 0 and 1. Notice that this also generalizes the static leisure versus income choice considered in Chapter 6. If we hold c_1 and $T_1 - N_1$ constant, (5) implies indifference curves in $c, T - N$ space (cf. Figure 6-8); if we hold $T_0 - N_0$ and $T_1 - N_1$ constant, it implies indifference curves in c_0, c_1 space (cf. Figure 12-4).

Consider a household planning for the second period given its decisions for period 0, which entail some levels of $c_0 \geq 0$, $T_0 \geq N_0 \geq 0$ and $M_0 \geq 0$. If no money balances are planned to be held at the end of period 1, the period 1 budget constraint is

$$M_0 + D_1 + W_1 N_1 = P_1 c_1, \tag{6}$$

(unless, exceptionally, the ration level on c_1 is so low that even by working zero hours exogenous spending power exceeds spending: $M_0 + D_1 > P_1 c_1$). W_1 and P_1 are the expected money wage and price level in period 1, and D_1 is exogenous nonlabor income (dividends and/or a government transfer). Equation (6) needs to be supplemented by the respective ration levels of the four alternative constraint regimes which in principle the household could expect for period 1. It could be unrationed in both markets; rationed only in the labor market, which we denote by $N_1 = \bar{N}_1$—rationed only in the goods market, $c_1 = \bar{c}_1$; or rationed in both (which, however, could only arise if there were a further period or an inheritance motive for wanting money balances at the end of period 1). For each case we could write down the optimal levels of c_1 and $T_1 - N_1$. For example, with no rationing, c_1 and N_1 would depend on exogenous purchasing power $M_0 + D_1$, the wage W_1, the price level P_1, the time endowment T_1, and the levels of c_0 and $T_0 - N_0$, which have been taken as given. In contrast, with rationing in the labor market, $N_1 = \bar{N}_1$ and by (6) we have $c_1 = (M_0 + D_1 + W_1\bar{N}_1)/P_1$. For each of the possible cases we can write down the utility function with the future part substituted out. For example, with rationing in the labor market,

$$U = U\left(c_0, T_0 - N_0, \frac{M_0 + D_1 + W_1\bar{N}_1}{P_1}, T_1 - \bar{N}_1\right). \qquad (7)$$

Notice that here it is quite explicit that the marginal utility of money balances M_0 is conditional on the expected price level, wage level, and employment ration. The form of the function will be different for different constraint regimes. In practice, households are unlikely to know for sure in which constraint regime they will be next period and what P_1, W_1 and the ration levels will be. However, given their recent experience which, as in the Chapter 7 discussion of the expected price level, influences these expectations, they can attach weight to the probability of each of the possible outcomes. So we can imagine households taking some kind of weighted average of the different utility functions corresponding to different outcomes in period 1. (Formally, this can be done through a model of "expected utility" in which the diminishing marginal utility of c_1 and $T_1 - N_1$ determines the attitude to risk, which will significantly influence the desired level of money balances.) Having done this, we can write the resulting objective function as

$$V_H = V(c_0, T_0 - N_0, M_0, \theta). \qquad (8)$$

Here θ is a catch-all list of variables which includes future endowments of time and (because of their reffect in forming expectations) recent experience of the price and wage levels and recent ration levels, to the extent that these are not already represented by the arguments c_0 and $T_0 - N_0$. Thus, we have derived a current period utility function that represents the indirect utility of money balances, taking into account the future states of labor and goods markets as these affect the household. In doing so, we have explicitly faced up to the fact that the future cannot be perfectly forecasted. The structure of the argument that led to (8) is easily extended to a model with many periods.

Now we can turn to the choices that have to be made in period 0. The budget constraint is

$$M_{-1} + D_0 + W_0 N_0 - P_0 c_0 = M_0; \qquad c_0 \geq 0, \qquad T_0 \geq N_0 \geq 0, \qquad (9)$$

where M_{-1} is the inherited level of money balances. Substituting (9) into (8), we can write the objective function as a function of c_0 and N_0, the two endogenous variables:

$$V_H = V(c_0, T_0 - N_0, M_{-1} + D_0 + W_0 N_0 - P_0 c_0, \theta). \qquad (10)$$

We can sketch in c,N space (dropping period 0 subscripts) the resulting constant V_H contours. Unless preferences and the expectations-generating mechanism are a bit peculiar, one would expect this to result in contours similar to those in Figure 18-5. At the point H, there is no rationing. The tangency of the iso-V_H curves with various vertical lines such as $N = \bar{N}$, representing employment ration levels, traces out the employment-constrained consumption demand function $\bar{C}^D(N;\cdot)$, the curve AH. This will be a function of $\bar{N}$ through purchasing power $M_{-1} + D_0 + W_0 \bar{N}_0$ and, in general, a function of $\bar{N}$ separately because the employment constraint can affect the intertemporal consumption trade-off and expectations. This consumption demand function should by now be a familiar concept. It is the rigorous form at a microlevel of the familiar Keynesian consumption function. Analogously, the effect of goods rationing can be seen from the tangency of the iso-V_H curves with various horizontal lines, such as $c = \bar{c}$, that represent goods ration levels. These tangencies trace out the goods-rationed labor supply function $\bar{N}^s(c;\cdot)$, the curve HB. As one would expect, the fewer goods the consumer is allowed to purchase, the less is the incentive to supply labor.

Thus, in terms of the notation used above to distinguish rationed and unrationed (notional) functions, H represents the consumption and employment levels given by the notional demand function $c = c^D(\cdot)$ and the notional

we plot the is

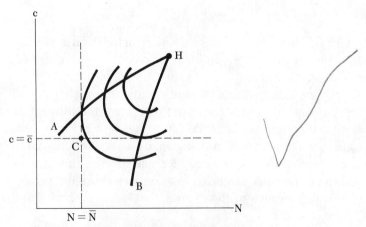

Figure 18-5 The household's rationed demand and supply function derived from iso-V_H contours.

supply function $N = N^S(\cdot)$. Points on AH represent the rationed consumption demand function $c = \bar{c}^D(N;\cdot)$, where $N = \bar{N} < N^S(\cdot)$; points on BH represent the rationed labor-supply function $N = \bar{N}^S(c;\cdot)$ where $c = \bar{c} < c^D(\cdot)$; and finally, at a point such as C where the two constraints $c = \bar{c}$ and $N = \bar{N}$ meet, the household is rationed on both sides, so $c = \bar{c} < \bar{c}^D(\bar{N};\cdot)$ and $N = \bar{N} < \bar{N}^S(\bar{c};\cdot)$. In this last case, the household is accumulating money balances $M_0 = M_{-1} + D + W\bar{N} - P\bar{c}$. However, these money balances are not without utility: if they were, labor supply would be cut so that the labor ration $\bar{N}$ would no longer be effective.

The reason why the AH, BH wedge represents demand and supply functions on axes that *both* represent quantities, rather than with a price along one axis, should be clear by now. It pictures the quantity signals that are the distinguishing feature of models with nonclearing markets. And it is the quantities that are being emphasized in our analysis; we do not discuss an explicit theory of price-setting.

We conclude our discussion of the household with some general remarks about saving and money balances. Treating the change in money balances as synonymous with saving, and hence representative of the change in assets in general, reminds us at least that it is an important element in saving. But this means that the variables in the consumption function which include proxies for price, wage, and unemployment expectations ought to be relevant for the demand for money too, and this complements the discussion in Chapter 14 of money as a consumer's and producer's good. Second, it must be pointed out that saving (and particularly the money component in saving) acts as a buffer stock, absorbing unanticipated shocks. This role is in part already implicit in the theory: each period the household replans in the light of new information and can sequentially take correcting action for past mistakes. The question is: can the concept of equilibrium which is being used accommodate such buffer stock behavior *within* the period? Superficially it seems not, since the concept of equilibrium requires that the perceived ration coincides with the actual ration, so that neither buyers nor sellers have any incentive to change. However, we can think of a sequence of very short periods in which the current ration levels are interpreted as perceived levels that may start differently from the actual ration levels but converge to them by the end of the sequence. The process that is working itself out here is part of the familiar multiplier process.

An Intertemporal Model of the Firm

Formally, this model will be very similar to that of the household, with inventories playing a role analogous to that of money balances for households. Consider a firm that, having made decisions for period 0, inherits a stock of inventories inv_0 at the beginning of period 1. If it wishes to have no inventories at the end of period 1 and if there are no inventory-holding costs, the period 1 budget constraint is

$$inv_0 + y(N_1) = x_1 \tag{11}$$

(unless, exceptionally, the ration level on sales x_1 is so low that even with zero production, $inv_0 > x_1$). The period 1 profit level is

$$R_1 = P_1 x_1 - W_1 N_1. \tag{12}$$

This is to be maximized subject to (11), supplemented by the various ration levels which can arise in the different constraint regimes. For example, if the firm is unrationed on both sides, maximizing (12) subject to (11) gives the optimal level of employment as a function of W_1/P_1 and inv_0, while if the firm is sales rationed to the level $\bar{x}_1$, $y(N_1) = \bar{x}_1 - inv_0$, which can be solved for employment N_1. Depending on which constraint regime applies, the optimal period 1 profit level can be calculated. Given that the firm has some views on the likelihood of different values of P_1, W_1, ration levels, and constraint regimes, one can imagine it constructing some weighted average of the different levels of R_1 that are possible. Risk aversion can be built in by taking a weighted average of $f(R_1)$, where $f(R_1)$ is a concave function so that $f' > 0$, $f'' < 0$: this makes low or negative profit levels count more heavily relative to high levels and hence puts a premium on strategies that avoid them. Let this weighted average of the different R_1's or $f(R_1)$'s that can arise be represented by $f^*(inv_0, \Psi)$, where Ψ is a list of variables including N_0, x_0, P_0, and W_0 (because they condition expectations of P_1, W_1), ration levels and constraint regimes, and sources of such expectations. As one would expect, the usefulness of inventories depends very much on whether the firm thinks it is more likely to be sales or labor constrained. If it expects to have difficulty in selling next period, there is little point in accumulating inventories now. It is the possibility of holding inventories which, of course, makes the model intertemporal and makes expectations so important.

The period 0 maximization problem then is to maximize

$$V_F = P_0 x_0 - W_0 N_0 + f^*(inv_0, \Psi) \tag{13}$$

subject to

$$inv_0 = inv_{-1} + y(N_0) - x_0, \qquad inv_0 \geq 0, \qquad y_0 \geq 0, \qquad x_0 \geq 0 \tag{14}$$

and the various ration levels that arise in the different regimes. In carrying out this maximization, it should be remembered that Ψ includes N_0 and x_0. By substituting for the level of inventories from (14) in (13), V_F can be expressed in terms of the two endogenous variables, sales x_0 and employment N_0. In Figure 18-6, which is analogous to the household's Figure 18-5, we plot the iso-V_F contours in sales–employment space. Analogously to Figure 18-5, the

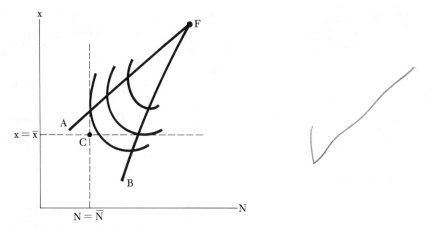

Figure 18-6 The firm's rationed demand and supply functions derived from iso-V_F contours.

point F represents the unrationed (notional) goods supply and labor demand. The line FA represents the labor-rationed supply function of goods $\bar{x}^s(N;\cdot)$, FB the goods-rationed demand function for labor $\bar{N}^D(x;\cdot)$, and a point such as C the case where both sales and labor are rationed. Note that with $x = c + g$, we can go from x,N space to c,N space and write $\bar{c}^S(N;\cdot)$ and $\bar{N}^D(c;\cdot)$.

Given sales x_0 and employment N_0, which determines output y_0, the inventory level inv_0 is determined as well. Like planned sales and employment, planned inventory holdings depend on the exogenous variables in the objective function V_F and the constraints: inv_{-1}, P_0, W_0, ration levels, and expectational proxies. It is such variables that one would expect in the investment demand function if the model were extended to investment. Note that the accelerator model of investment can be interpreted as being based on expected levels of sales rations, though it would be relevant only when firms expected to be sales rationed.

Now we can discuss the buffer stock role of inventories which was emphasized in Chapter 3. As was pointed out there (see p. 38), if households suddenly decide to increase their expenditure, the increase causes an unexpected drop in inventories as sellers meet the unexpected demand increase by selling from inventories. This parallels our discussion of the buffer stock role of money balances for households. If we interpret $\bar{x}_0$, for example, as the *perceived* sales ration in the current period, the theory of the firm as formulated can accommodate an error in this perception: the firm will then have made an error in its employment and inventory plans. Information on this error materializes from the inventory levels which, if $\bar{x}_0$ underestimated demand, will be unexpectedly low. In the next short period, plans will be made in the light of actual inventory holdings and of revised views on the sales ration.

Such a process is likely to converge quickly to an equilibrium in which the perceived sales ration is the true one. The Keynesian multiplier process involves both such unplanned inventory changes and unplanned changes in money balances. Thus, we can see how the buffer stock role of both money balances (saving) and inventories is important for analysis of the very short run. While such a process is working itself out in the very short run, we can say that the economy is "in disequilibrium," and this is really the only sense in which this class of models can be said to be about disequilibrium.

THE COMPLETE MODEL

We must now aggregate the behavioral functions of households and of firms in order to analyze market interaction in the reappraisal model. Aggregation from the micro to the macro level is always a bit tricky, so it is worth a few paragraphs before we move on to the macro analysis.

The simplest way to aggregate is to assume that all households are identical and when rationed, identically so, and the same for firms. But the same basic diagrams will work if we allow other rationing schemes, though the slopes of the functions may be different and the microeconomic story will differ between households and firms.

For example, let's suppose there is involuntary unemployment and consider how the available work might be rationed to households. We might have an equal labor ration $\bar{N}$ for each household. In this case, if initial money balances plus exogenous income $M_{-1} + D_0$ differ across households and labor supply falls with $M_{-1} + D_0$, some affluent households will offer less than $\bar{N}$ and not be rationed. Then the aggregate labor-rationed consumption function will be a weighted average of the rationed microfunctions of the less affluent and the unrationed microfunctions of the more affluent. Even with the simplest linear functions and all households having the same tastes, different distributions of exogenous purchasing power give different aggregate behavior.

A similar result follows if unemployment always takes on an all-or-nothing form—zero hours or no constraint on hours at all. This might occur under "efficient" rationing of labor, where less efficient plants are the first to be closed as effective demand drops and production and employment are cut back. Another all-or-nothing rationing rule is "last hired, first fired." Here the less well paid would probably bear the brunt of a rise in unemployment, so the consumption reduction per worker would be smaller than if the incidence of unemployment were random. Clearly, the precise shape of the labor-rationed consumption function depends on the particular way in which the demand for labor is rationed among households. Quantity rationing in either the labor or the product market makes it even more important to look at how our macrorelations are derived by aggregating microbehavior.

"Efficient" rationing has the advantage of giving a unique association between aggregate sales, aggregate labor demand, and implied aggregate inventory demand. But although rational behavior of this kind might be plausible within a multiplant firm, for the economy as a whole it assumes a lot of coordination between firms. This doesn't fit very well with our emphasis on the informational problems responsible for the failure of markets to clear. There are, however, other, more realistic rationing schemes which might justify our asumption of a unique relation between aggregate sales and aggregate labor demand.

The Four Regimes in the "Double Wedge" Diagram

We can now set out the complete two-market model, which Barro and Grossman first put together, integrating the work of Patinkin and Clower. For goods and for labor, we have a demand function, a supply function, and a *min condition* telling us which is actually realized. But the form taken by the demand and supply functions in one market depends on what is going on in the other market—whether buyers or sellers are being rationed there, that is, which is the minimum of demand and supply there.

Thus, we have

$$c^D = \begin{cases} c^D(\cdot) & \text{if } N = N^S \le N^D \\ \bar{c}^D(N;\cdot) & \text{if } N^S > N^D = N \end{cases} \tag{15}$$

$$c^S = \begin{cases} x^S(\cdot) - g & \text{if } N^S \ge N^D = N \\ \bar{x}^S(N;\cdot) - g & \text{if } N = N^S < N^D \end{cases} \tag{16}$$

$$c = \min(c^D, c^S) \tag{17}$$

$$N^D = \begin{cases} N^D(\cdot) & \text{if } c = c^S \le c^D \\ \bar{N}^D(c;\cdot) & \text{if } c^S > c^D = c \end{cases} \tag{18}$$

$$N^S = \begin{cases} N^S(\cdot) & \text{if } c^S \ge c^D = c \\ \bar{N}^S(c;\cdot) & \text{if } c = c^S < c^D \end{cases} \tag{19}$$

$$N = \min(N^D, N^S). \tag{20}$$

In each of equations (15), (16), (18), and (19), there is a *switching condition:* for example, in (15) we see that if households are not rationed in the labor market ($N = N^S \le N^D$), their effective aggregate consumption demand is given by the notional function $c^D(\cdot)$, independent of N; but with involuntary unemployment ($N^S > N^D = N$), we *switch* to the labor-rationed consumption function $\bar{c}^D(N;\cdot)$. The min conditions express the possibility of quantity rationing, while the switching conditions tell us for each market whether *effective* demand and supply are given by the notional or the quantity-constrained functions. These conditions express the direct interaction through quantities of markets that do not clear.

Now we turn to the alternative quantity-constrained regimes. If both markets clear, we have a familiar general market-clearing equilibrium. Translating Figure 18-6 into c, N space and putting it together with Figure 18-5, we may represent this equilibrium in Figure 18-7. This is the first of the "double wedge" diagrams we will use to portray the various possible equilibria generated by different constraint regimes.

The equilibrium is where H and F coincide, and neither households nor firms are rationed in either market. The relative slopes assumed for the households' and firms' constrained demand and supply functions in Figure 18-7 and the other diagrams to follow will be discussed later.

General market-clearing equilibrium is clearly a very special case, because any change in any of the arguments of any of the notional demand or supply functions—P, W, M_{-1}, inv_{-1}, g, expectations—would shift H or F, or both. Disregarding for the moment other borderline cases in which one market clears but the other doesn't, we have the four possible constraint regimes (types of equilibria) set out in equations (1)–(4). We'll start with *Keynesian Unemployment* (K), which we see in Figure 18-8. The equilibrium is at K, where the labor-constrained demand function for consumption goods intersects with the consumption sales-constrained demand function for labor. Households can't sell as much labor as they would like, and firms can't sell as much goods as they would like, and the two constraints interact and reinforce each other. There is *excess effective supply* in both markets, which we have indicated on the axes.

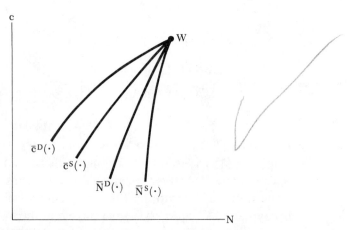

Figure 18-7   Walrasian equilibrium in quantity space.

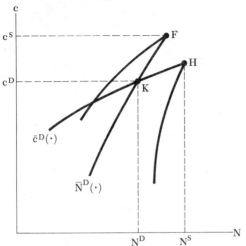

Figure 18-8 Keynesian unemployment in quantity space.

What might cause Keynesian Unemployment? Any of the forces that might result in F being to the northwest of H in the diagram. We will discuss comparative statics more fully later, but it's easy to see, for example, that starting from the position of Figure 18-7, a fall in g shifts F upward and gives an outcome like Figure 18-8. Remembering that investment can be regarded as part of g, this fall in g can be interpreted as a fall in investment. This can occur because the *rate of growth* of demand for consumption goods has fallen off, which through the accelerator reduces investment, or because of the petering out of a wave of innovation as increased competition drives down rates of profit. Alternatively, lower M_{-1} will mean lower $c^D(\cdot)$ and higher $N^S(\cdot)$, thus shifting H down and to the right. In either case, the demand multiplier operates: as the demand for goods falls, the demand for labor falls, which further reduces the demand for goods.

Repressed Inflation (R) is the equilibrium in Figure 18-9, where the consumption goods-constrained labor-supply function intersects the labor-constrained supply function for consumption goods. The diagram shows the excess effective demands in both markets. Households can't get all the goods they would like to buy (so there must be some formal or informal rationing scheme) and therefore reduce their labor supply below the notional level, an effect that very much concerned wartime managers of the domestic economy. Firms can't get all the labor they'd like and so can't produce their notional supply. And again, the quantity constraints interact. For example, if some exogenous change shifts F southeast in the diagram, the fall in consumption goods supply reduces labor supply, which further cuts the supply of goods.

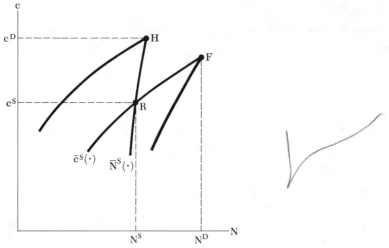

Figure 18-9 Repressed inflation in quantity space.

Barro and Grossman call this the "supply multiplier," and it is indeed entirely symmetrical to the demand multiplier.

In *Classical Unemployment* (C), as Figure 18-10 shows, households would like to trade more than firms on both markets. Thus, the equilibrium is at F, where firms' notional demands are realized. There is excess effective demand for goods, but firms won't hire more labor to satisfy it because this wouldn't be profitable—the real wage is too high. Consequently, raising gov-

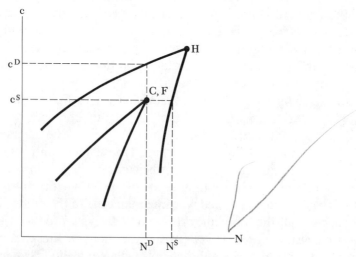

Figure 18-10 Classical unemployment in quantity space.

ernment expenditure (shifting F down) would merely *increase* the imbalance in the product market *without* raising the demand for labor, although unemployment might fall somewhat if households reduced their labor supply in response to more severe goods rationing.

The converse case, *Underconsumption* (U), is seen in Figure 18-11, where firms would like to trade more than households on both markets, and the equilibrium is at H. Here the real wage is too low, so excess supply of goods coexists with excess demand for labor. Firms believe it would be worthwhile to produce more for inventory, but they can't get the extra labor.

Later we will discuss the likelihood of these cases appearing in reality. To do that seriously, we need to bring in foreign trade. Meanwhile, note that we could never observe intersections of $\bar{N}^D(c)$ and $\bar{N}^S(c)$, or of $\bar{c}^D(N)$ and $\bar{c}^S(N)$, with both sides rationed on the same market.

Desired and Undesired Savings and Inventory Accumulation

Voluntary exchange requires that households be on or within the wedge formed by $\bar{c}^D(\cdot)$ and $\bar{N}^S(\cdot)$ and that firms be on or within the wedge formed by $\bar{c}^S(\cdot)$ and $\bar{N}^D(\cdot)$. As noted earlier, to be within the wedge means partly undesired savings or inventory accumulation (in C and U, respectively). This is an important difference between R and C for households, and between K and U for firms.

In R, households facing goods rationing *adjust* their labor-supply and saving behavior. They move along $\bar{N}^S(\cdot)$, substituting leisure and future con-

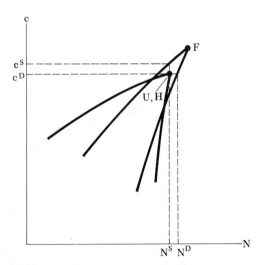

Figure 18-11 Underconsumption in quantity space.

sumption for the present consumption they can't get. The supply multiplier process is assumed to work itself out within the unit period; so in equilibrium they are supplying the amount of labor and accumulating the amount of assets they desire, given the constraint facing them. Although there is "forced saving" in the sense that they are saving more than they would without the constraint, this saving is *desired* to finance future consumption, given their expectations about future constraints in the goods market. If it weren't, they would reduce labor supply still further. In C, however, this option is not open: they are already constrained to sell less labor services than they would like, even taking into account the rationing in the goods market. Given the level of employment, they can't consume as much as they would like and are accumulating some undesired money balances (which they would rather spend this period than next, though they would rather have them for next period than work even less).

For firms, we have a similar contrast between K and U. In K, they can adjust employment downwards to reach their desired level of inventory accumulation, given the sales constraint facing them (the demand multiplier process is assumed to work itself out). In U they cannot, but given the labor supply available, they are selling less this period than they would like (though it is nevertheless profitable to produce for sale next period).

Unemployment

The excess supply of labor in C and K is involuntary unemployment. In both cases, households are off their labor-supply curves. But the overall positions are quite different between the two cases. In C, a money wage cut, by shifting F northeast and H (normally) southwest, will reduce both the unemployment and the excess demand for goods. In K, however, a money wage cut, with the same effects on F and H, will increase the excess supply of goods and may have little or no effect on unemployment (while $N^S(\cdot)$ is falling, K is also moving back down $\bar{N}^D(c)$, as the money wage cut reduces effective aggregate demand). This of course ignores effects on expectations, to which we'll return.

Even if the real wage is "correct," we might still have involuntary unemployment. Suppose we start from the general market-clearing equilibrium of Figure 18-7 and raise W and P by the same percentage. The real wage stays at the level that previously cleared the market, but the real balance effect takes the economy into a Keynesian Unemployment equilibrium, as H moves down. Symmetrically, equiproportionate reduction in W and P would shift H up and result in Repressed Inflation. Here too, employment would fall, as households move back along $\bar{N}^S(c)$. Clearly, there is no unique relation between the real wage and the level of employment, because what is happening in the product market directly affects the labor market.

The reduction of employment in Repressed Inflation below $N^S(\cdot)$ is a kind of *voluntary* unemployment different from that discussed in Chapter 8. There, voluntary unemployment was labor voluntarily withheld from the market because the expected real wage wasn't high enough. Thus, households could be at H, where there is no involuntary unemployment, but if an increase in the expected real wage would shift H to the right, increasing the notional supply of labor, then not all the total labor force is being used. In Repressed Inflation, however, the voluntary reduction of labor supply is a response to current and expected shortages of consumption goods rather than the expected real wage. To say it is "voluntary" simply means that households are on their supply curve.

The Model in *W,P* Space

The double wedge diagrams in c,N space neatly represent the various configurations of the two-market system and how these endogenous quantity variables interact. Another aspect of what is going on can be seen in W,P space. Consider Figure 18-12. Here each of the curves traces out W, P pairs that maintain equilibrium between notional supply and demand in each market. They are in this sense quite similar to *IS* and *LM* curves. Both curves must slope upward. For example, if W rises, then $c^D(\cdot)$ rises and $c^S(\cdot)$ falls; so to maintain notional equilibrium, P would have to rise, reducing $c^D(\cdot)$ and increasing $c^S(\cdot)$. Thus, W and P must increase together as we move along

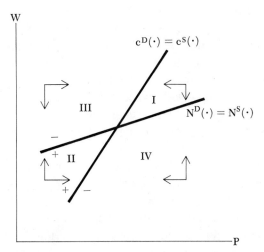

Figure 18-12 Curves of notional equilibrium.

$c^D(\cdot) = c^S(\cdot)$. We could also totally differentiate the equilibrium condition: from $N^D(\cdot) = N^S(\cdot)$, we get

$$\frac{\partial N^D}{\partial W} \, dW + \frac{\partial N^D}{\partial P} \, dP = \frac{\partial N^S}{\partial W} \, dW + \frac{\partial N^S}{\partial P} \, dP,$$

so

$$\left. \frac{dW}{dP} \right|_{N^D=N^S} = \frac{\partial N^S/\partial P - \partial N^D/\partial P}{\partial N^D/\partial W - \partial N^S/\partial W}.$$

If $\partial N^S/\partial P \leq 0$ and $\partial N^S/\partial W \geq 0$, this expression will be positive. The signs on either side of each curve indicate regions of excess demand ($+$) and supply ($-$). We take the product-market equilibrium curve to be steeper for two reasons. First, this makes region I have general excess supply and region II have general excess demand, so that low W and P have a positive real balance effect on demand. Second, if we assume that the money wage rate would rise (fall) with excess demand (supply) in the labor market, and that the price level would respond similarly to conditions in the goods market, we can draw the arrows for a dynamic process as shown (compare Figure 4-11), and we find that the system would converge on the intersection of the two curves. If the labor market equilibrium curve were steeper, this point would not be stable.

Now consider the *effective* demands and supplies. Excess supply in the labor market will reduce effective demand in the goods market relative to the notional demand there, and excess supply in the goods market will reduce effective demand in the labor market relative to the notional demand there. Thus, the region of general excess *effective* supply (which we denote by K) must *contain* that of general excess *notional* supply. A similar argument applies for general excess demand. Hence, when we go from notional to effective demands, regions I and II expand, so regions III and IV must contract, and we get Figure 18-13. The curves are now those along which effective demand equals effective supply, and they divide wage-price space into regions corresponding to those defined by (1) to (4). For example, the equilibrium denoted by K in Figure 18-8 would correspond to a particular point in region K in Figure 18-13.

This type of diagram has some advantages in comparative statics, since one can see immediately toward which constraint regime (region in Fig. 18-13) a given change in W and/or P will move the system. For example, starting in C at a sufficiently high W and increasing P will eventually take the system to the boundary between C and K, on which the goods market clears but there is excess effective supply of labor, and then into K itself, where there is excess effective supply in both markets. A fairly complicated comparative

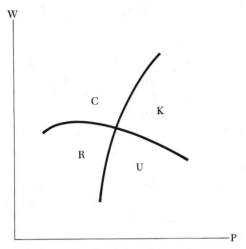

Figure 18-13 Regions of quantity-constrained equilibrium.

statics exercise in quantity space is to increase W and P equiproportionately, keeping the real wage constant; here this is simply represented by giving out along a ray from the origin. But Figure 18-13 doesn't show the process by which a quantity-constrained equilibrium is actually attained and the interaction of markets through quantity signals, which is the main point of this chapter. So we'll continue to work directly with the endogenous quantity variables, where the action is.

THE MODEL IN A SMALL OPEN ECONOMY

Although the model as developed so far may be applicable at the level of the world economy or perhaps to the United States, it does not apply to small economies open to trade. Following the approach of Dixit, consider a small open economy, for which labor is immobile but goods are tradeable. Let the exchange rate be fixed, and suppose for the moment that the economy faces perfectly elastic world demand and supply schedules for goods (assuming there is no quantity rationing at the level of the world economy). The economy is a *price taker* on world markets, as described in Chapter 17, pp. 423. The given world price then prevails in the domestic market, and foreign supply or demand meets any gap between effective domestic demand and supply for goods, so there can be no repercussions from the goods market on the labor market. If there is unemployment, the real wage is too high; if there are unfilled vacancies, it is too low. So the only kind of unemployment is of the classical variety.

Incorporating net exports b (balance of trade) in our accounting framework, we have $x = c + g + b$. If $N^S > N^D(\cdot)$, we have $c = c^D(N)$ and $x = x^S(\cdot)$; so

$$b = x^S(\cdot) - g - c^D(N). \tag{21}$$

Thus, exogenous demand g affects b but not employment. A change in the exchange rate, however, is equivalent to changing P, which enters both $x^S(\cdot)$ and $c^D(N)$; it therefore affects both b and N.

If $N^D > N^S = N^S(\cdot)$, we have $x = \bar{x}^S(N)$ and $c = c^D(\cdot)$; so

$$b = \bar{x}^S(N) - g - c^D(\cdot). \tag{22}$$

Again, g affects only b. Figures 18-14–18-17 show the possible combination of unemployment or excess demand in the labor market with balance of trade deficit or surplus. Clearly, shifting F up or down has no effect on employment (nor, therefore, on output).

THE IMPORTANCE OF TIME AND THE FUTURE

It is important to see that time plays an essential role in the macromodel of this chapter. We could have proceeded with an atemporal model of the firm, as does Malinvaud. Here there are no inventories, and the only asset is household money balances. Then there can be no equilibrium of type U. For if firms cannot carry inventories forward for sale in the future, and they face excess supply of goods, they will not seek to hire more labor than they already employ, just to accumulate more stocks of unsaleable goods. Instead, they will

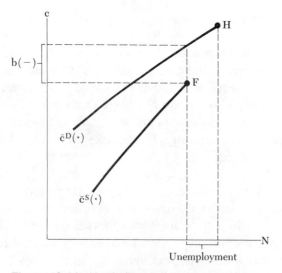

Figure 18-14 Unemployment and trade deficit.

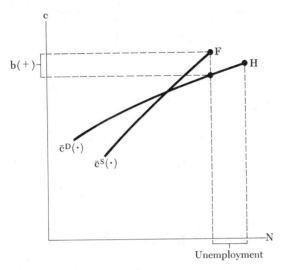

Figure 18-15 Unemployment and trade surplus.

cut back on labor use until production is no greater than what they can sell now (in the current—the only—period). In this case, the goods-constrained demand for labor function is the inverse of the labor-constrained supply of goods function, which makes the distinction between them less obvious; the wedge collapses to a single curve, the production function shifted downward by g. Disregarding borderline cases, we have the remaining three possible equilibria, and Figure 18-18 shows the Keynesian case.

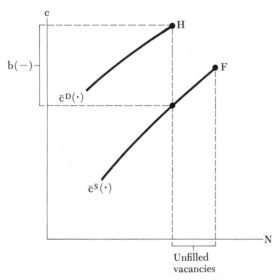

Figure 18-16 Excess demand for labor and trade deficit.

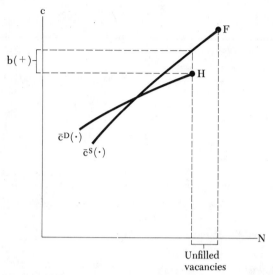

Figure 18-17 Excess demand for labor and trade surplus.

If we now consider a *fully* atemporal model, however, we find that the interaction of markets through quantity constraints generates inconsistencies. Analogously to the argument above, we can rule out the possibility of regime *C*. Suppose households hold no money balances at the end of the period, because there is no future in which they could be used. If they face excess

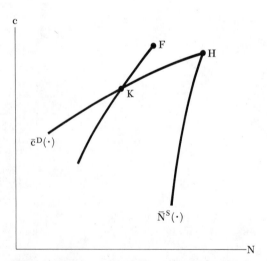

Figure 18-18 Keynesian unemployment in quantity space with an atemporal model of the firm.

demand for goods, they will not seek to sell more labor merely to accumulate unusable money balances; they will instead withdraw labor until they are earning no more than they can spend. Their goods-constrained labor-supply function is now the inverse of their employment-constrained goods demand function, and in c,N space $\bar{N}^S(c)$ coincides with $\bar{c}^D(N)$. Our diagram is now Figure 18-19. This looks like the income-expenditure diagram, Figure 18-3, but now it seems to represent simultaneous determination of interacting quantity-constrained equilibria in *both* the goods and labor markets. The trouble is that it's really saying too much.

Consider Figure 18-19. Here voluntary exchange implies that any realized position must lie on both curves, that is, at their intersection. Starting from the notional positions H and F, we see that everywhere to the right of (above) the intersection, we have the firms on the short side of the labor market and households on the short side of the goods market. Thus, $N = \min(N^D, N^S) = N^D$ and $c = \min(c^D, c^S) = c^D$, and at their intersection the curves are to be interpreted as $\bar{c}^D(N)$ and $\bar{N}^D(c)$. This of course gives a Keynesian unemployment equilibrium with excess effective supply in both markets.

We could, however, interpret the intersection in Figure 18-19 quite differently. Everywhere to the left of (below) it, households wish to supply less than firms demand on the labor market, and firms wish to supply less than households demand on the goods market. Thus, $N = \min(N^D, N^S) = N^S$ and $c = \min(c^D, c^S) = c^S$, and at their intersection the curves may be interpreted

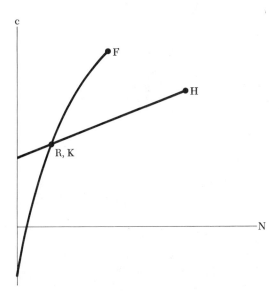

Figure 18-19 Quantity space with atemporal models of firms and households.

as $\bar{N}^S(c)$ and $\bar{c}^S(N)$. This gives a *repressed inflation* equilibrium, with excess effective demands in both markets.

Clearly, we cannot have both types of equilibria with the same data at the same (c, N). This is the inconsistency mentioned earlier. It has arisen because we have tried to integrate behavior in the goods and labor markets in a model without time. For if the labor-supply function is the inverse of the demand function for goods, and the labor-demand function is the inverse of the supply function for goods, the system is underdetermined. We have two markets and only one independent equilibrium condition. The system is underdetermined because behavior is overdetermined: neither households nor firms have the extra degree of freedom offered by the opportunity to hold an asset for future use. Our macromodel with quantity rationing cannot be given a consistent micro foundation without an essential role for assets and the future.

In the atemporal context, we cannot even tell the standard Keynesian story of adjustment within the period, because "the" equilibrium is unstable. Starting from the right in Figure 18-20, the demand multiplier process will not stop at the intersection. A slight further displacement down and to the left brings into play the supply multiplier, and output falls to zero.

COMPARATIVE STATICS, MULTIPLIERS, AND DYNAMICS

We have already done some informal comparative statics with our double wedge diagram. Since one of the main points of this chapter is to give a con-

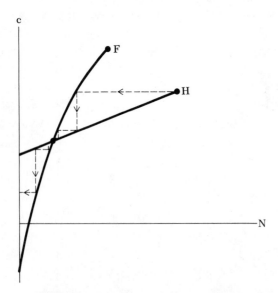

Figure 18-20 Unstable equilibrium with atemporal models of firms and households.

sistent microeconomic basis for a Keynesian theory of effective demand, we ought to look at the multiplier in this context. Starting in Keynesian unemployment, an increase in government expenditure shifts F upward, and the intersection of $\bar{N}^D(c)$ with $\bar{c}^D(N)$ moves up and to the right along $\bar{c}^D(N)$. Excess effective supply falls in both markets. To derive the multiplier, we must recall that, although we have been writing simply $\bar{N}^D(c)$ when holding everything else constant, the sales-constrained, labor-demand function expressed more fully is $\bar{N}^D(x, P, W, inv_0, \Psi) = \bar{N}^D(c + g; \cdot)$. Thus, in regime K we have $c = \bar{c}^D[\bar{N}^D(c + g)]$. Differentiating, we get

$$dc = \frac{\partial \bar{c}^D}{\partial N} \frac{\partial \bar{N}^D}{\partial c} (dc + dg),$$

so

$$dc = \frac{(\partial \bar{c}^D/\partial N)(\partial \bar{N}^D/\partial c)}{1 - (\partial \bar{c}^D/\partial N)(\partial \bar{N}^D/\partial c)} dg. \tag{23}$$

Note that $dx = dc + dg$, so dx is just the initial expenditure change divided by $(1 - MPC)$, as we expect. Here the marginal propensity to consume is represented as the product of the labor-demand response to an increase in sales of goods and the consumption demand response to an increase in sales of labor. The distinction between these two elements is especially important when the labor-demand function contains lags. Working in c,N space gives a direct view of the interaction between quantity constraints on which multiplier analysis is based. Note also that planned inventories play a significant role here, absorbing some of the increase in demand and thereby reducing the multiplier. The multiplier is an increasing function of $\partial \bar{N}^D/\partial c$, which for any c is normally less than its analogue without inventories, which would be the slope of the labor requirements function (inverse of the production function).

A different multiplier, with a different microeconomic basis, comes into play in Repressed Inflation. Here an increase in government expenditure takes output away from consumption (recall that we assume exogenous expenditure is never rationed), and this results in a reduction of labor supply, so output falls (and consumption falls further). Diagrammatically, F shifts downward, and the intersection of $\bar{c}^S(N)$ with $\bar{N}^S(c)$ moves down and to the left along $\bar{N}^S(c)$. Algebraically, we have $c = \bar{x}^S[\bar{N}^S(c)] - g$, so

$$dc = \frac{\partial \bar{x}^S}{\partial N} \frac{\partial \bar{N}^S}{\partial c} dc - dg.$$

Since $\partial \bar{x}^S/\partial N = \partial \bar{c}^S/\partial N$, we get the supply multiplier

$$dc = -\frac{1}{1 - (\partial \bar{c}^S/\partial N)(\partial \bar{N}^S/\partial c)} dg, \tag{24}$$

with corresponding expressions for the changes in sales and employment. Here we have a "marginal propensity to produce," composed of a labor-supply response to consumption goods availability and a goods supply response to a change in the amount of labor available.

Equations (23) and (24) immediately suggest stability conditions. The denominators must be positive so as to ensure positive but finite multipliers. This requires that

$$0 \leq \frac{\partial \bar{c}^D}{\partial N} < \frac{1}{\partial \bar{N}^D / \partial c} \tag{25}$$

$$0 \leq \frac{\partial \bar{c}^S}{\partial N} < \frac{1}{\partial \bar{N}^S / \partial c} , \tag{26}$$

so the goods-constrained demand-for-labor curve must intersect the labor-constrained demand-for-goods curve from below, and the goods-constrained supply-of-labor curve must intersect the labor-constrained supply of goods curve from below. This is, of course, how we have drawn them in our diagrams.

Stability of Multipliers

By shifting the H and F systems appropriately, we can investigate the effects of changes in any of the exogenous variables P, W, M_{-1}, inv_{-1}, g, and other determinants of the shapes and positions of the curves (productivity, tastes, etc.), starting from any one of the four types of equilibrium. But our microeconomic analysis, with its stress on intertemporal and expectational effects, suggests some caution. We have here not only price expectations, but also quantity expectations, and they will often greatly amplify (or sometimes reverse) the simple contemporaneous effects. In a multiplier expansion process, for example, falling excess supply of labor may lead households to revise optimistically their expectations about future unemployment, reduce their precautionary need for real balances to carry forward, and hence increase current demand for goods. Meanwhile, producers are also revising optimistically their expectations about future demand for goods, so they increase their demand for labor. If expectations are fairly sensitive to observed rationing, this may generate a good deal of instability or, conversely, insensitivity to policies designed to shift the existing equilibrium, depending on whether and how these affect expectations.

Indeed, compared with our earlier models with only price expectations, here the power of quantity expectations and their interactions with each other and with current variables tends to give the analysis much more of a "bootstraps" character. This refers to the idea that one might pull oneself up by one's own bootstraps; here, the economy might be in a given equilibrium mainly because of expectations that it will be in that kind of equilibrium. If the expectations in different markets are self-reinforcing through quantity signals, exogenous changes might not have much effect unless they change the expectations themselves. The "bootstraps" element appears even stronger when we recognize that the expectational variables in each of our demand and supply functions are defined with respect to the initial positions of households and firms. There is no ahistorical, abstract consumption function; the function will be different depending on the starting point and the expectations it creates.

This limits the value of standard comparative statics exercises, but some experience with the mechanics of shifting the curves about will still be useful, and it will suggest two important general points. First, starting in a given constraint regime (type of equilibrium), the regime toward which a given exogenous change moves the system will differ according to precisely where the system is at the outset. For example, starting in Keynesian Unemployment, an increase in g might move the system toward Classical Unemployment or Underconsumption (depending in particular on how high the money wage is at the start). Second, a single policy instrument cannot in general simultaneously bring both the product and the labor market to equilibrium. A single instrument might reduce the size of excess effective demand or supply in both markets, but there is always the danger of overshooting, and some policies reduce excess demand in one market at the cost of aggravating it in the other.

Dynamics

In going from one period to the next, the government may have new productive assets and new liabilities (ΔM), while firms' inventory levels and households' money balances will in general have changed ($\Delta inv,\ \Delta M^h$), and this period's dividend payments may differ from those of last period. These are endogenously generated changes in quantities; we might also wish to consider price and wage adjustment, if we believe that this will follow upon quantity rationing. Again, we may represent these dynamic phenomena in c,N space by shifting the H- and F-systems or moving in W,P space when appropriate. Barro and Grossman work out some dynamic paths, but any such analysis will find it difficult to take account of the full range of intertemporal changes in asset holdings outlined above, as well as expectational effects. Clearly, a great deal of work is to be done before we have realistic dynamic representations of the quantity-constrained macromodel of this chapter.

THE MODEL AND ACTUAL ECONOMIES

We can try to introduce a bit of realism into the reappraisal model by asking when and where we might observe each of the various types of equilibria in real economies.

The case of Keynesian unemployment, or insufficient aggregate effective demand, is familiar enough, but we can say a little more about it. We've seen how in our equilibrium of type K, there is excess supply in both goods and labor markets (the latter being involuntary unemployment), and they reinforce each other. This provides some justification for the assumption of sticky wages and prices and for the persistence of this type of unemployment equilibrium in the absence of expansionary government policies. With excess supply in *both* markets, there is less likelihood of an adjustment of the *relative* price of labor and goods—the real wage—sufficient to clear the markets. Moreover, with the demand for labor determined by the demand for goods and the marginal product of labor already greater than the real wage, offers to work at still lower money (and hence real) wages won't get jobs for any additional workers.

We also have an explanation for the empirical observation (contrary to the theoretical discussion in Chapter 8) that the real wage often moves procyclically—up for at least a substantial part of a period of economic expansion, down in a contraction. For as we saw, when the labor market doesn't clear, there need be no unique relation between the real wage and the level of employment. For a given level of employment, determined by demand conditions in the goods market, the real wage may be anywhere between the demand price of employers (the marginal product of labor) and the supply price of workers. In an upswing with the demand for labor and average productivity rising, employers may be willing to raise money wages, while prices may be fairly sticky until costs start to rise and order books lengthen. There will be nothing to stop the resulting rise in the real wage until it approaches the marginal product of labor (which will itself be falling).

In the small open economy facing perfectly elastic foreign demand, the goods market will clear (ignoring nontradeables), so Keynesian Unemployment becomes just excess supply of labor, which then *is* due to an excessively highly real wage. But in reality, although a small open economy may well face a very elastic *supply* of goods from abroad, it may be fairly specialized as an exporter and therefore be unable to sell all it likes. This asymmetry may explain why, although excess supply of both goods and labor seems fairly common, we do not observe Classical Unemployment very often. The excess demand for goods in this case simply sucks in imports, so we are left with only excess supply of labor. It has been suggested, however, that in France in 1968, when money wages rose very sharply and suddenly, the unemployment that followed for some time fit our picture of regime C. Another case might have been the recession of 1974. The oil price increase brought a substantial fall in the terms of trade of the major industrialized countries. Workers got money wage increases to try to maintain their real incomes in the face of price increases, so real wages didn't fall as much as the real marginal product of labor. Profits fell, and firms cut output and employment, while there was also some reduction in the demand for goods as price increases ate away households' real balances. This same effect would be likely to make households want to work more to restore real balances. So in our double wedge diagram, we can think of F moving southwest and H moving southeast, though probably not by as much. The net effect is likely to have been Classical Unemployment.

Again, the possibility of meeting excess demand for goods through imports would appear to make Repressed Inflating fairly rare. The standard case is wartime, but any economy in which there are strong pressures to increase output and some control over foreign trade might have general excess demand. A frequently cited example is the case of centrally planned economies applying maximum pressure for rapid growth. But there is some controversy over whether these economies have in fact had sustained excess demand for consumer goods. Underconsumption seems a curious case at first sight, but perhaps the Japanese economy, with its relatively low real wage and high demand for labor, might be an example. Here, however, firms do a fairly good job of selling abroad the goods for which there is insufficient domestic demand.

CONCLUSION: SOME FUTURE RESEARCH IN MACRO THEORY

Finally, we discuss briefly four important respects in which the model needs to be qualified or extended. First, markets for fixed investment and financial assets should be added. Barro and Grossman take a significant step in this direction. Assuming, as they do, that financial markets always clear and that investment goods are perfect substitutes in supply for consumption goods, there is only one significant extra dimension, the endogenous interest rate. A more complicated alternative would be a two-sector model with the possibility of rationing in both consumption and investment goods markets. This would be a natural extension of Leijonhufvud's work.

More fundamental in many ways, because it may change the very notion of equilibrium with which one works, is the question: who sets prices and wages? One possible answer is unions, industry price leaders, government. If these decisions are taken by a set of agents different from households and firms, the kind of microeconomic analysis carried out above remains valid though incomplete. An alternative possibility is to pursue Arrow's recognition that markets which do not clear are not perfectly competitive and attempt to model explicitly individuals' demand and supply schedules in imperfect competition. If these schedules are kinked, our analysis holds, though as with the kinked oligopoly demand curve, the kinks may only explain why prices stay where they are for the time being and not why they change when they do. It seems likely that a proper microeconomic analysis will need to combine the insights of recent models of monopolistic competition and those of market behavior under imperfect information.

A third important question concerns international trade. We briefly examined the consequences of making our economy a small economy in a world where the goods market clears. But this is a special case, and we mentioned the case in which the economy faces a perfectly elastic supply schedule for tradeable goods but faces excess supply as a seller. If nonmarket clearing is possible at the level of the world economy, a more general model is needed to analyze open economies.

Finally, we come to questions of aggregation and "spillovers." Taken literally, the model of this chapter postulates discrete switching between distinct regimes. This framework is also characteristic of the applied econometric work on nonclearing markets started by Fair and Jaffee. One difficulty with this approach arises in aggregating, as for example over labor markets, where it seems more plausible that some submarkets are in excess demand and others in excess supply, but that the relative dominance of the different regimes can change. A similar problem arises when there is excess demand for "the" consumer good. In reality, with a range of consumer goods, the excess demand for some will spill over into markets for others. There will be "forced substitution" from those goods in excess demand to those in excess supply at the given nonmarket-clearing prices. Thus, there will be different intensities of rationing, depending on the elasticities of substitution and how far consumers are forced to switch, and the very concept of aggregate excess demand becomes hard to define.

These phenomena of aggregation and spillovers imply that aggregation can smooth out some of the discrete switching in our simple model. This could affect the empirical and statistical forms taken by macroeconometric models constructed in the spirit of the theory we have presented. But in either case, such models are likely to be rather different from the macroeconometric models that are currently popular, whether one represents the theory in the form of discrete switching between regimes, as we have done here, or attempts to aggregate explicitly over submarkets in different regimes.

SELECTED READINGS

R. Barro and H. Grossman, *Money, Employment and Inflation* (Cambridge, England: Cambridge University Press, 1976).

J. P. Benassy, *Macroeconomics: An Introduction to the Non-Walrasian Approach* (Orlando: Academic Press, 1986).

R. Clower, "The Keynesian Counterrevolution," in F. Hahn and F. Brechling, eds., *The Theory of Interest Rates* (London: Macmillan, 1965).

A. Dixit, "The Balance of Trade in a Model of Temporary Keynesian Equilibrium," *Review of Economic Studies* 45, 1978.

R. Fair and D. Jaffee, "Methods of Estimation for Markets in Disequilibrium," *Econometrica,* May 1972.

F. Hahn, "Keynesian Economics and General Equilibrium Theory: Reflections on Some Current Debates," in G.C. Harcourt, ed., *The Microeconomic Foundations of Macroeconomics* (New York: Macmillan, 1978).

A. Leijonhufvud, *On Keynesian Economics and the Economics of Keynes* (London: Oxford University Press, 1968).

E. Malinvaud, *The Theory of Unemployment Reconsidered* (Oxford: Blackwell, 1977).

D. Patinkin, *Money, Interest and Prices* (New York: Harper and Row, 1st ed. 1956, 2nd ed. 1965).

R. E. Quandt and H. S. Rosen, "Unemployment, Disequilibrium and the Short Run Phillips Curve: An Econometric Approach," *Journal of Applied Econometrics,* July 1986.

four

MEDIUM-TERM DYNAMICS: BETWEEN STATIC EQUILIBRIUM AND LONG-RUN GROWTH

chapter 19

Inflation, Productivity, and Income Distribution

This chapter begins the transition from the static models of income determination of Parts II and III, which focused on the determination of the *level of actual output* and employment at any given time, to models of the dynamic development of the economy from one short-run equilibrium to the next. The five chapters of Part IV on *medium-term dynamics* discuss various aspects of the dynamic adjustment of the economy from an initial short-run equilibrium toward the long-run potential growth path. In Part V we will move to the theory behind the determinants of that potential growth path.

In this chapter and the next we focus on inflation. The following sections begin with a discussion of the nature of inflation—a general increase in the price level—in the static model. A distinction is drawn between demand-pull inflation, which is due to a shift in the economy's demand curve, and cost-push inflation, which has its impetus in an upward shift of the supply curve. Next, we develop the relationship between wage rate and productivity increases that leave the economy's supply curve undisturbed. This gives us the basic rule for noninflationary wage increases: Wage rates can rise at the same rate as labor productivity without generating a cost-push inflation. Development of this *wage–price–productivity* arithmetic then takes us into a discussion of the Council of Economic Advisers' wage-price guideposts, which were based on that arithmetic. The guidepost arithmetic was also behind the wage-price freeze of 1971, and the operation of the Council on Wage and Price Stability of the Nixon-Ford years. In the next chapter we turn to the question: what determines the rate at which the labor supply function *actually* shifts up?

INFLATION IN THE STATIC MODEL

In Parts II and III we developed the static equilibrium model of income determination that is illustrated in Figures 19-1 and 19-2. Equilibrium output *demanded* by consumers, businesses, and the government is determined in the static model by the intersection of the IS and LM curves of Figure 19-1(a). To derive the economy's demand curve we can ask what happens to equilibrium output demanded as the price level P rises. A price increase shifts the LM curve left by reducing the supply of real money balances. It shifts the IS curve left by reducing the real value of household net worth and, in an open economy, reducing real net exports. Thus, a price increase will shift both the IS and LM curves left, so that on the demand-side equilibrium real output y falls as P rises, due to the drop in consumption and investment demand. This inverse relationship between y and P gives us the demand curve $D_0 D_0$ of Figure 19-2.

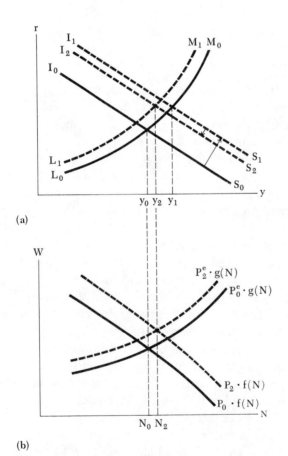

(a)

(b)

Figure 19-1 Demand shift and inflation.

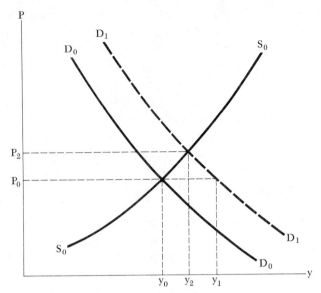

Figure 19-2 Demand-pull inflation.

The equilibrium output *supplied* by producers in the static model is given by the economy's production function, $y = y(N; \bar{K})$, combined with the equilibrium intersection in the labor market of Figure 19-1(b), which determines employment N_0. To derive the economy's aggregate-supply curve, we can ask what happens to equilibrium employment as the price level rises. A price increase from P_0 to P_2 shifts the labor-demand curve of Figure 19-1(b) up from $P_0 \cdot f(N)$ to $P_2 \cdot f(N)$. It also shifts the supply curve up from $P_0^e \cdot g(N)$ to $P_2^e \cdot g(N)$. If the general assumption that $P^e = p(P)$, with $p' < 1$, holds, then the shift in the demand curve will be larger than the supply curve shift, increasing equilibrium employment from N_0 to N_2 in Figure 19-1(b). This action increases equilibrium output on the supply side from $y_0 = y(N_0; \bar{K})$ to $y_2 = y(N_2; \bar{K})$ along the production function. This positive relationship between P and y on the supply side is shown as the $S_0 S_0$ supply curve in Figure 19-2.

The Effect of a Demand Increase: Demand-Pull Inflation

In Parts II and III we analyzed the operation of the static model in terms of a shifting demand curve. Any shift in a demand or supply function underlying the *IS* or *LM* curve will, in general, result in a shift in the demand curve of Figure 19-2. For example, if the saving function shifts down—reflecting less saving at any given income level—so that there is an exogenous increase in consumer demand, the *IS* curve in Figure 19-1(a) will shift up toward $I_1 S_1$, and the demand curve of Figure 19-2 will shift up to $D_1 D_1$.

In this case, at the initial price level, P_0, the equilibrium output on the demand side of the economy rises to y_1 in Figures 19-1(a) and 19-2. This creates excess demand measured by $y_1 - y_0$, and prices begin to rise. The price increase shifts both the IS and LM curves left, reducing output demanded toward y_2 along the new demand curve $D_1 D_1$.

The reduction of demand due to the price increase comes from three factors. First, the price increase reduces the supply of real balances, raising interest rates and eventually reducing investment demand. Second, the price increase reduces the real value of assets, shifting the saving function up and reducing consumer demand. Third, the price increase reduces real net exports. All these effects tend to reduce excess demand from the demand side of the economy.

While demand is falling from y_1 toward y_2 in Figure 19-2, the price increase also raises equilibrium output on the supply side from y_0 toward y_2. With the labor-demand curve shifting more than the supply curve in Figure 19-1(b), employment and output rise, reducing excess demand from the supply side. When the price level has risen to P_2 in Figure 19-1(b) and Figure 19-2, excess demand is eliminated and the economy is at a new equilibrium level of output, y_2, and of employment, N_2.

The price increase generated by an upward shift in the economy's demand curve is frequently called *demand-pull inflation.* A general price increase is an inflation, and one caused by a demand shift is identified as demand-pull inflation. This is in contrast with a *cost-push inflation* which has its impetus on the supply side of the economy.

The Effect of a Supply Shift: Cost-Push Inflation

Inflation can also result from an upward, or inward, shift of the supply curve, as illustrated in Figures 19-3 and 19-4. The upward shift of the supply curve creates excess demand at the initial price level, P_0, raising prices but bringing a *reduction* in equilibrium output, as opposed to the demand-pull case where the price increase *raises* output.

In Figure 19-3(b) we show an exogenous upward shift in the labor-supply curve from $P_0^e \cdot g^0(N)$ to $P_0^e \cdot g^1(N)$. This may result from an increase in wage demands in a highly unionized economy, or from a shift in tastes toward leisure. The upward shift in the labor-supply function reduces equilibrium employment at the initial price level. In other words, the economy's supply curve shifts back to $S_1 S_1$ in Figure 19-4.

The shift of the supply curve creates excess demand measured by $y_0 - y_1$ in Figure 19-4. At the initial price level, P_0, producers want to supply y_1, but consumers, business, and government want to buy y_0. As usual, excess demand raises the price level.

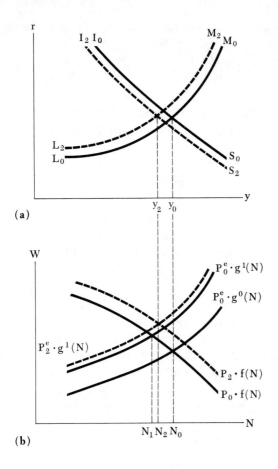

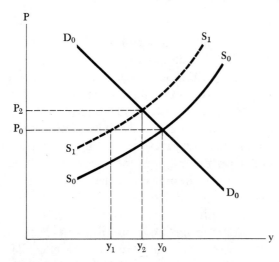

Figure 19-4 Cost-push inflation.

On the demand side of the economy, the price increase reduces equilibrium output from y_0 toward y_2 along the original demand curve D_0D_0. This movement is shown in Figure 19-3(a) by the leftward shifts of the IS and LM curves. At the same time, the price increase raises equilibrium output on the supply side from y_1 toward y_2 along the new supply curve S_1S_1 in Figure 19-4. In Figure 19-3(b) the labor-demand curve shifts up toward $P_2 \cdot f(N)$, whereas the price increase induces a further upward shift in the labor-supply function toward $P_2^e \cdot g^1(N)$.

The price increase thus reduces the excess demand gap by reducing demand along the D_0D_0 curve and increasing supply along the S_1S_1 curve in Figure 19-4. Equilibrium is restored at P_2 in Figures 19-3(b) and 19-4, where the excess demand is eliminated and output has fallen to y_2. Inflation due to an upward shift of the supply curve is generally called *cost-push inflation.* The increase in wage demands, represented as an upward shift in the labor-supply curve of Figure 19-3(b), raises costs and causes producers to cut back output and raise prices.

In Chapter 7 we saw that the economy's supply curve can also be shifted up by a drop in the marginal productivity curve, $f(N)$. This also raises costs at a given wage rate, reducing equilibrium employment and output and raising prices. It should further be clear that a productivity *increase,* shifting $P_0 \cdot f(N)$ up in Figure 19-3(b), will tend to shift the supply curve out in Figure 19-4. Thus, a productivity increase will tend to balance an increase in wage demands in terms of the net effect on the economy's supply curve. We will return to this point shortly.

The Effects of Inflation on Output and Employment

The effects of inflation on output, at least in the short run, depend on whether the initial impulse is cost-push or demand-pull. In Figure 19-4 we see that the cost-push impulse leads to a rise in the price level and a drop in output along the demand curve. A demand-pull impulse would shift the demand curve up, resulting in a rise in the price level but an *increase* in output along the supply curve. The 1965–1968 period in the United States was mainly one of demand-pull inflation with output rising more rapidly than trend growth; the 1973–1975 period had a large cost-push element from agriculture and oil, and brought a drop in output. In the 1980s, the major event was the reduction of inflation brought about by a restriction of demand that led to the steep recession in 1982. This was a demand-induced *disinflation.*

The effect of demand-pull inflation on employment is clear. The rise in the price level shifts the demand-for-labor curve up more than the supply curve in Figure 19-1(b), increasing employment. The effect of a cost-push inflation on employment is less clear. In Figures 19-5 and 19-6 we show an

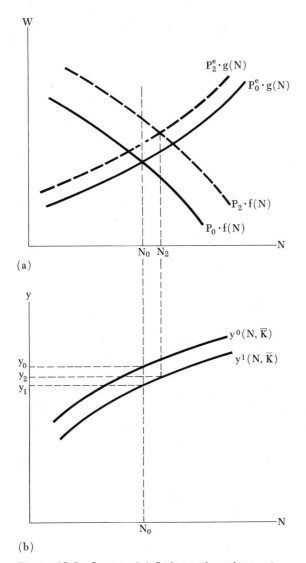

Figure 19-5 Cost-push inflation and employment.

extreme case, mentioned in Chapter 7, in which the shift in the production function does not shift the demand-for-labor curve, which is derived from the marginal product of labor (MPL)—the slope of the production function. If the production function shifts down so the slope is the same at the initial level of N, this will be the case. An example would be a production function in which raw materials or energy E enter additively with capital and labor, which in turn produce value-added:

$$y = y(N;K) + bE.$$

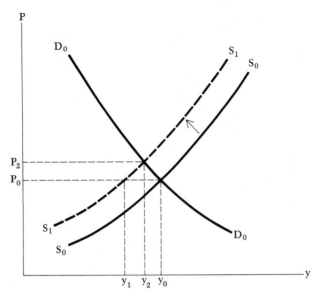

Figure 19-6 Cost-push inflation.

Here b is a fixed energy-output coefficient, and the *MPL* does not depend on E.

In this unusual case, shown in Figure 19-5, the price increase that follows the supply shift will increase employment! In Figures 19-5 and 19-6 we see that the price rise increases employment from N_0 to N_2, partly cushioning the output drop. Essentially, as the supply of energy inputs is reduced, employers try to substitute labor for energy in production, so production does not fall as much as it would if the labor input were fixed. Equilibrium output y_2 must lie between y_0 and y_1, as in Figure 19-6.

Normally, we would expect a decrease in the supply of a cooperating factor of production to reduce the marginal product of labor, as well as the average product. If this were the case, the $f(N)$ function in Figure 19-5 would shift down along with the $y(N;\bar{K})$ function. The initial equilibrium level of employment would then drop along the $P^e \cdot g(N)$ labor-supply curve. The subsequent price increases would tend to restore some of the drop in employment. Whether it would get employment back up to the initial N_0 level depends on the values of the elasticities of the curves in Figures 19-5 and 19-6.

The main point here, however, is that the effects of inflation on *output* are fairly clear, but while demand-pull tends to increase *employment,* cost-push may not, in itself, reduce it.

The Self-Liquidating Nature of Inflation

In the static model, inflation is caused by excess demand in the product market. Excess demand can, however, come from an upward shift in the demand curve which generates demand-pull inflation, or from an upward shift in the supply curve which generates cost-push inflation. Both types of inflation are characterized by excess demand.

With either demand-pull or cost-push inflation, the excess demand means that at the initial price level and interest rate level, aggregate demand exceeds supply in the economy. The ensuing price increase from P_0 to P_2 in both the demand-shift and supply-shift cases works on both the demand and supply sides of the economy to eliminate excess demand.

As we have seen, the price increase reduces investment demand through the money market effect on r; it reduces consumer demand by reducing real household net worth; and it reduces real net exports by making U.S. goods more expensive relative to foreign goods. On the supply side, the price increase raises equilibrium output and employment in the short run in our general model, while in the long run with $p' = 1$ all the adjustment comes on the demand side. In either case, inflation is a self-liquidating phenomenon in the static model. Price increases are caused by the appearance of excess demand and tend to eliminate that excess demand as long as the *IS* and *LM* curves are not shifted by the government to counter the effects of the price increase in changing employment and real output.

If the government is committed to maintain full employment, a cost-push inflation can become more or less continuous, due to a policy reaction known as *validation*. In Figure 19-3(b) the upward shift in the labor-supply curve reduces the equilibrium level of employment to N_2 from N_0, presumably increasing measured unemployment. In Figure 19-4 this is represented by the output drop to y_2. A full-employment policy, rigorously pursued, would lead the government to shift the demand curve in Figure 19-4 out by monetary or fiscal policy measures, in order to restore the full-employment level of output y_0.

The price increase associated with this demand increase could, in turn, bring another upward shift of the labor-supply curve, followed by another *validating* increase in demand, and so on. This kind of mechanism could produce a continuing upward pressure on prices through the reaction of government policy to cost-push inflation. Thus, while inflation is self-liquidating in the static model, it may be fairly continuous or even accelerating if there is a tendency for the labor-supply curve to shift up faster than productivity at full employment, with aggregate-demand policy validating the cost push.

Identification of Demand-Pull and Cost-Push Inflation

In practice, it is extremely difficult to separate demand-pull from cost-push inflation. All that the price and wage data show is an unending sequence of price and wage increases. If we choose a wage increase as the initial departure from equilibrium, then the subsequent inflation may be labeled *cost-*

push. But if a price increase is taken as the initial departure, the inflation is *demand-pull.*

In addition, with labor union bargaining the picture is more complicated. With a union contract period of three years, an initial burst of demand-pull inflation can leave the union asking for a wage increase to compensate not only for the past lag of wages behind prices, but also for the *expected* price increase. In this case the labor-supply function may shift up in anticipation of an expected demand-pull price rise.

WAGES, PRICES, AND PRODUCTIVITY

It was pointed out earlier that while an upward shift in the labor-supply curve will tend to shift the economy's supply curve up, creating cost-push inflation, an upward shift in the labor-demand curve due to an increase in the marginal productivity of labor will tend to shift the economy's supply curve down, so that the two movements—in wages and in productivity—tend to cancel each other out. A case in which the two effects just balance each other is shown in Figure 19-7(a). There at the initial price level, P_0, equilibrium supply-side employment remains at N_0 as $g(N)$ and $f(N)$ both shift up. This shows a noninflationary wage increase with real wages rising as fast as productivity, leaving equilibrium employment at N_0 and the equilibrium price level undisturbed.

In Figure 19-7(b), we see that the increase in productivity represented by the upward shift of $f(N)$ in Figure 19-7(a) shifts the production function up. At any employment level N, output y is greater along $y^1(N;\bar{K})$ than on $y^0(N;\bar{K})$, and the slope of the production function $\partial y/\partial N = f(N)$ is also steeper, that is, greater.

Thus, the increase in productivity represented by the shift from $f^0(N)$ to $f^1(N)$ in Figure 19-7(a) raises equilibrium output supplied at any given level of employment. At the initial equilibrium P_0, N_0 level, equilibrium output on the supply side rises from y_0 to y_1 in Figure 19-7(b); with wages and marginal productivity of labor growing at the same rate, the economy's supply curve in the P,N space is undisturbed, while the supply curve in the P,y space shifts out.

This relationship between the two supply curves is shown in the four-quadrant diagram of Figure 19-8. In the northeast quadrant of this figure is the supply curve in the P,N space, as derived, for example, from the labor market diagram of Figure 19-1(b). The production function in the southeast quadrant of Figure 19-8 translates employment into output supplied; $y_0(N,\bar{K})$ is the production function of Figure 19-7(b) turned upside down. The 45° line in Figure 19-8 transfers y to the horizontal axis. Starting with equilibrium P_0, N_0 in the northeast quadrant of Figure 19-8, the same P_0 and N_0 as in Fig-

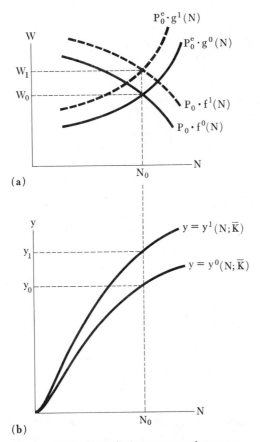

Figure 19-7 Noninflationary wage increase.

ure 19-7, we can obtain y_0 from the production function. P_0, y_0 in the north-west quadrant of Figure 19-7 is a point on the aggregate-supply curve in the P,y space, $S_0 S_0$.

If labor productivity and the wage rate now rise by an equal amount, equilibrium P_0 and N_0 will be retained with W rising from W_0 to W_1 in Figure 19-7(a). Equilibrium output will rise to y_1 in Figure 19-8, shifting the aggregate-supply curve in the P,y space to $S_1 S_1$. The initial employment level and price level are now consistent with a higher wage rate W_1 and level of output y_1, due to the productivity increase. Thus, to maintain equilibrium in the economy at P_0, N_0, y_1, demand-side equilibrium output must also be expanding, with the economy's demand curve shifting out. This requires the *IS–LM* intersection to shift out, as shown in Figure 19-9, to maintain supply-demand balance at the equilibrium price level P_0. If the labor-supply curve shifts up as shown in Figure 19-7(a), raising wages along with productivity, the initial employment level, N_0, will remain the equilibrium employment level at price level P_0. As

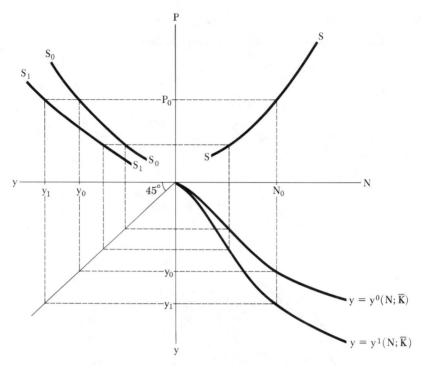

Figure 19-8 Supply-side equilibrium with a productivity increase.

a result, the economy will remain in equilibrium with output, productivity, and the wage rate rising, and employment and the price level constant.

This basic wage–price–productivity relationship can be derived from a version of the labor market equilibrium condition,

$$W = P \cdot f(N). \tag{1}$$

For any given N, the price level is given by

$$P = \frac{W}{f(N)}. \tag{2}$$

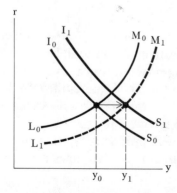

Figure 19-9 Equilibrium demand-side output with an increase in productivity.

If the money wage W and the marginal productivity of labor $f(N)$ grow at the same rate, there will be no change in equilibrium P. For example, starting from

$$P_0 = \frac{W_0}{[f(N)]_0},$$

assume that both W and $f(N)$ grow at 5 percent per year, so that $W_1 = W_0(1.05)$ and $[f(N)]_1 = [f(N)]_0 \cdot (1.05)$. Then for P_1 we have

$$P_1 = \frac{W_1}{[f(N)]_1} = \frac{W_0(1.05)}{[f(N)]_0(1.05)} = \frac{W_0}{[f(N)]_0} = P_0.$$

In logarithmic terms, (2) can be written as

$$\ln P = \ln W - \ln f(N). \tag{3}$$

(See the appendix to this chapter for a brief introduction to logarithms.) Since the differentials of logarithms are percentage changes, differentiation of (3) with respect to time gives us

$$\dot{P} = \dot{W} - [\dot{f}(N)]. \tag{4}$$

Here we introduce the notation to be used throughout Parts IV and V: a dot over a variable denotes the percentage rate of growth of the variable. Thus, we define

$$\dot{P} \equiv \frac{\dfrac{dP}{dt}}{P},$$

and in general, for variable X:

$$\dot{X} = \frac{\dfrac{dX}{dt}}{X}.$$

Thus, if W and $f(N)$ in equation (4) grow at the same rate so that $\dot{W} = [\dot{f}(N)]$, $\dot{P}$ will be 0, that is, the equilibrium price level will remain unchanged.

Another way to look at equation (4) is to note that since the real wage w is just W/P, the growth rate of the real wage is given by

$$\dot{w} = \dot{W} - \dot{P}. \tag{5}$$

If money wages grow as fast as productivity, and P remains unchanged so that $\dot{P} = 0$, (5) combined with (4) gives us

$$\dot{w} = \dot{W} - \dot{P} = [\dot{f}(N)]. \tag{6}$$

Thus, another way to state a noninflationary rule for wage increases is that the real wage rate can grow as fast as productivity with no change in the equilibrium price level.

Illustration: The Cobb–Douglas Production Function

In the Cobb–Douglas production function, introduced in Chapter 13,

$$y = aK^{\alpha}N^{1-\alpha}, \tag{7}$$

and

$$\frac{\partial y}{\partial N} \equiv f(N) = (1 - \alpha)\frac{aK^{\alpha}N^{1-\alpha}}{N} = (1 - \alpha)\frac{y}{N} \tag{8}$$

is the expression for the MPL, $f(N)$. Then since $W = P \cdot f(N)$,

$$W = P \cdot (1 - \alpha)\frac{y}{N}, \tag{9}$$

so that

$$P = \frac{W}{(1 - \alpha)\dfrac{y}{N}}. \tag{10}$$

In logarithmic terms, equation (10) is

$$\ln P = \ln W - \ln \frac{y}{N} - \ln(1 - \alpha). \tag{11}$$

Since total differentiation of logs gives percentage changes, equation (11) gives us

$$\dot{P} = \dot{W} - (y/N), \tag{12}$$

as in the general case.

Thus, an increase in the money wage rate and productivity of the same percentage amount leaves the equilibrium price level unchanged. In terms of the labor-supply and -demand curves of Figure 19-7(a), an increase of both wages and productivity at the same rate can come from both supply and demand shifting up by the same amount, keeping P_0, N_0 unchanged.

Unit Labor Cost and the Labor Share

This line of analysis can be carried further. We can define the unit labor cost (ULC)—the labor cost per unit of real output—as

$$ULC = \frac{WN}{y} = \frac{W}{\frac{y}{N}}, \tag{13}$$

where N is the total labor force employed. Taking logs, we have

$$\ln ULC = \ln W - \ln \frac{y}{N}. \tag{14}$$

This tells us that if the money wage rate and productivity increase at the same rate—$\dot{W} = (y/N)$—then unit labor cost remains constant.

The labor share of total output S_L can be written as

$$S_L = \frac{WN}{Py} = \frac{w}{\frac{y}{N}}. \tag{15}$$

We have seen that if the real wage w and productivity y/N grow at the same rate, the equilibrium price level can remain unchanged. Taking logs of equation (15) and differentiating, we see that

$$\dot{S}_L = \dot{w} - (y/N). \tag{16}$$

Thus, if w and y/N grow at the same rate, the labor share of output remains constant: $\dot{S}_L = 0$. If the capital share of output is just $1 - S_L$, then this implies that if w and y/N grow at the same rate, so that W can grow as fast as y/N with P constant, the capital share of output will also remain constant.

THE WAGE-PRICE GUIDEPOSTS AND INCOME DISTRIBUTION

The wage–price–productivity artithmetic we have just reviewed says that if money wage rates W grow as fast as average labor productivity, y/N, and the average price level P remains constant, then the relative shares of capital and labor—the distribution of output to the factors of production—will remain constant and unit labor costs will also remain constant. This is the fundamental arithmetic behind the Council of Economic Advisers' wage-price guideposts, first published in the *Economic Report of the President* in January 1962, and behind subsequent attempts at incomes policy in the United States and Europe.

The CEA's general guidepost for wages was that the rate of increase of wage rates, including fringe benefits in all industries, should equal the economy-wide trend rate of productivity increase. Adherence to this guidepost would maintain a constant average unit labor cost in the economy. The general guidepost for prices was that in industries where productivity rose faster than average, prices should fall, and in industries where productivity rose slower than average, prices should rise, maintaining average price stability.

This formulation of the guideposts would have all wages growing at about the same rate. If we put bars over variables to indicate economy-wide averages, the wage guidepost says

$$\dot{W}_i = (\overline{\dot{y}/N}). \tag{17}$$

Wages in each industry i grow as fast as *average* labor productivity. If this is the case, unit labor costs in any given industry i will grow at the rate:

$$\dot{ULC}_i = \dot{W}_i - (\dot{y}/N)_i = (\overline{\dot{y}/N}) - (\dot{y}/N)_i. \tag{18}$$

So if industry i has productivity growing faster than average, its unit labor costs will be falling and the price guidepost says that it should reduce prices at the rate of ULC decrease to preserve constant relative shares. Conversely, if the industry's productivity is growing slower than average, ULC_i will be rising, and prices must rise to preserve relative shares. On average, adherence to the price guidepost will maintain a constant price level.

Political Difficulties with the Guideposts

The CEA's guideposts came under fairly heavy political fire from the beginning, aimed both at the substance of the guideposts and at the way they were enforced. The guideposts, if followed, would maintain constant relative shares of output going to capital and labor, so that labor's aggregate share of total output would grow as fast as capital's share along trend growth in y. While this may seem to be the best neutral prescription for a functional income distribution policy, it is not satisfactory to either management or labor, both of which want to raise their relative shares. Thus, the guideposts were not accepted by either business or labor as an income distribution prescription.

In addition, the guideposts had no legal standing, so that enforcement in cases of price or wage increases by individual companies, unions, or industries was left to public exposure by the CEA or the President, followed by public pressure generated by the President to roll back the price or wage increase in question. Business naturally resented this kind of selective political pressure. To some this also seemed to be an arbitrary exercise of power in an extralegal fashion by the White House, although it was clear that the price increases that were subjected to scrutiny represented the exercise of monopoly power by industry.

Economic Difficulties with Incomes Policy

From 1962 to 1965 wages and prices, by and large, followed the guidepost prescription. Whether this wage and price behavior was due to the guideposts, or whether it was due to the slackness of the economy and unusually rapid productivity increases that permitted substantial wage increases without disturbing unit labor costs is another matter.

Beginning in 1965, the guideposts broke down due to their two major economic weaknesses. First, an incomes policy can be effective only in the monopolistic sectors of the economy. The policy prescribes how people should *set* prices and wages; firms and individuals in competitive markets have no control over their prices and so cannot observe the guideposts. Thus, as excess demand appeared and increased beginning in 1965, prices rose in competitive sectors of the economy, making it more and more difficult to require the monopolistic sectors to hold the line.

The second major problem is that the policy does not prescribe behavior for wages when prices violate their guidepost, and vice versa. With productivity rising at about 2 percent per year, the wage guidepost prescribes wage increases of 2 percent per year. If prices are rising, violating their guidepost, then real wages are rising slower than productivity and the labor share is falling relative to the profit share. If prices rise faster than 2 percent per year, as they did after 1965, real wages would fall if the guideposts were respected. Thus, as prices rise it becomes unreasonable to ask labor to follow the wage guidepost; therefore, wages begin to rise, making it hard to hold prices to the price guidepost in turn.

As a result of excess demand pressure, combined with the lack of a remedy for bad price behavior, the guideposts broke down in the late 1960s. In its *Annual Report* of January 1969, the CEA, while repeating the indisputable correctness of the wage–price–productivity arithmetic underlying the guideposts, recognized that excess demand pressures had made them unenforceable, at least for the time being, and did not publish a set of numerical wage and price guides for the next year.

In August 1971, with the inflation rate down to about 2.5 percent, after the excess demand explosion of the late 1960s and the recession of 1969–1970, the Nixon Administration imposed wage and price controls that implicitly followed the guidepost formulas. The excessive stimulus to demand that followed in 1971 and 1972 led to another round of inflation when price controls became unmanageable in 1973. Subsequently, the Council on Wage and price Stability and the Council of Economic Advisers tried to use "moral suasion" and any pressure tactics they had available to induce business and organized labor price and wage decisions to follow guidepost behavior.

Although the guideposts and wage and price controls broke down under excess demand pressure, it is quite possible, even likely, that the guideposts are useful in holding down cost-push inflation in a situation where there is no general excess demand and prices have been fairly stable so that wages can reasonably follow the wage guidepost. The U.S. economy experienced such conditions from 1961 to 1965, again in 1971, and also coming out of the 1974–1975 recession. Some form of wage-price policy may be useful if U.S. growth continues into the 1990s.

SELECTED READINGS

Council of Economic Advisers, *Annual Reports* (Washington, D.C.: Government Printing Office), 1962 and 1969.

R.J. Gordon, "Understanding Inflation in the 1980s," *Brookings Papers on Economic Activity,* vol. 1, 1985.

R.J. Gordon, "The Response of Wages and Prices to the First Two Years of Controls," *Brookings Papers on Economic Activity,* vol. 3, 1973.

G.L. Perry, "Wages and the Guideposts," *American Economic Review,* September 1967.

L.S. Seidman, "Tax-Based Incomes Policies," *Brookings Papers on Economic Activity,* vol. 2, 1978.

Appendix: The Uses of Logarithms

THE NATURAL CONSTANT *e*

The first step in the derivation and uses of logarithms is the development of a natural constant, which is generally denoted by the letter "*e.*" We can begin by looking at the difference between discrete and continuous compounding of interest or growth.

Suppose a sum of money y_0 is invested at interest rate r compounded annually. Then, at the end of t years, y_0 will have grown to

$$y_t = y_0(1 + r)^t. \tag{1}$$

If the interest or growth is compounded twice a year, then

$$y_t = y_0\left(1 + \frac{r}{2}\right)^{2t}. \tag{2}$$

Equations (1) and (2) can be generalized to compounding at n times a year with

$$y_t = y_0\left(1 + \frac{r}{n}\right)^{nt}. \tag{3}$$

We can rewrite equation (3) as

$$y_t = y_0\left[\left(1 + \frac{r}{n}\right)^{n/r}\right]^{rt}.$$

This equation can be simplified by defining $m \equiv n/r$ and substituting:

$$y_t = y_0\left[\left(1 + \frac{1}{m}\right)^{m}\right]^{rt}. \tag{4}$$

In the case of continuous compounding or growth $n \rightarrow \infty$. From the definition of m, we see that as n approaches infinity (for any finite rate r) m also goes to infinity. Therefore, for continuous compounding equation (4) can be written as

$$y_t = \lim_{m \rightarrow \infty} y_0 \left[\left(1 + \frac{1}{m} \right)^m \right]^{rt}.$$

But it can be shown that

$$\lim_{m \rightarrow \infty} \left(1 + \frac{1}{m} \right)^m = 2.71828 \equiv e.$$

Thus, as $m \rightarrow \infty$, and we use continuous compounding,

$$y_t = \lim_{m \rightarrow \infty} y_0 \left[\left(1 + \frac{1}{m} \right)^m \right]^{rt} = y_0 e^{rt}. \tag{5}$$

Thus, $y_t = y_0 e^{rt}$ is the continuous compounding analogue to the discrete compounding equation (1), $y_t = y_0 (1 + r)^t$.

NATURAL LOGARITHMS

The natural logarithm (ln) of a number is defined as the power to which e must be raised to obtain that number; that is, if $y = e^x$, then $\ln y = x$, or $y = e^{\ln y}$.

Logarithms have the following convenient algebraic properties.

1. *Products:* By the definition of the natural logarithm, we have

$$xz = e^{\ln xz} = e^{\ln x} e^{\ln z} = e^{\ln x + \ln z},$$

since $x = e^{\ln x}$ and $z = e^{\ln z}$. This gives us the rule for products that

$$\ln xz = \ln x + \ln z. \tag{6}$$

2. *Exponentiation:* Again, by the definition of the natural logarithm,

$$x^\alpha = [e^{(\ln x)}]^\alpha = e^{\alpha \ln x}.$$

Thus, the rule for exponentiation is given by

$$\ln x^\alpha = \alpha \ln x. \tag{7}$$

Furthermore, from equation (7) for exponentiation and equation (6) for products, we can see that if

$$y = x^\alpha z^\beta,$$

then we have

$$\ln y = \alpha \ln x + \beta \ln z. \tag{8}$$

3. *Quotients:* To handle quotients in logarithmic terms, we simply note that

$$\frac{x}{z} = xz^{-1}.$$

This gives us the quotient rule that

$$\ln \frac{x}{z} = \ln xz^{-1} = \ln x - \ln z. \tag{9}$$

4. *Derivatives:* The derivative of the function $x = \ln t$ is

$$\frac{dx}{dt} = \frac{d}{dt}(\ln t) = \frac{1}{t}. \tag{10}$$

It is useful to prove this equality. We can do this by substituting $(x + \Delta x)$ for x and $(t + \Delta t)$ for t in the original equation.

$$x + \Delta x = \ln(t + \Delta t),$$

$$\Delta x = \ln(t + \Delta t) - x,$$

$$\Delta x = \ln(t + \Delta t) - \ln t.$$

From the quotient rule,

$$\Delta x = \ln\left(\frac{t + \Delta t}{t}\right) = \ln\left(1 + \frac{\Delta t}{t}\right).$$

Dividing both sides by Δt gives us

$$\frac{\Delta x}{\Delta t} = \frac{1}{\Delta t} \cdot \ln\left(1 + \frac{\Delta t}{t}\right) = \frac{1}{t}\left(\frac{t}{\Delta t}\right) \ln\left(1 + \frac{\Delta t}{t}\right).$$

From the exponent rule, we have

$$\frac{\Delta x}{\Delta t} = \frac{1}{t} \ln\left(1 + \frac{\Delta t}{t}\right)^{t/\Delta t}.$$

If we let $m = t/\Delta t$, then

$$\frac{\Delta x}{\Delta t} = \frac{1}{t} \ln\left(1 + \frac{1}{m}\right)^{m}.$$

As $\Delta t \to 0$, $m \to \infty$. Therefore,

$$\lim_{\Delta t \to 0} \frac{\Delta x}{\Delta t} \equiv \frac{dx}{dt} = \lim_{m \to \infty} \frac{1}{t} \ln\left(1 + \frac{1}{m}\right)^{m}.$$

As noted above

$$\lim_{m \to \infty} \left(1 + \frac{1}{m}\right)^{m} = e.$$

Therefore,

$$\frac{dx}{dt} = \frac{1}{t} \ln e = \frac{1}{t},$$

since $\ln e = 1$.

If $x = f(t)$, we can take the natural logarithm of both sides of the equation,

$$\ln x = \ln(f(t)).$$

We can also differentiate both sides with respect to time:

$$\frac{d}{dt}(\ln x) = \frac{d}{dt}\ln(f(t)) = \frac{1}{f(t)} \cdot \frac{df(t)}{dt}.$$

Thus, we have

$$\frac{d}{dt}(\ln x) = \frac{f'(t)}{f(t)}, \tag{11}$$

where $f'(t) = (d/dt)f(t)$.

The right-hand side of equation (11) is seen to be the instantaneous proportional rate of change (or growth rate) of x. As a specific example, consider the Cobb–Douglas production function,

$$y = K^\alpha L^{1-\alpha}, \tag{12}$$

where y is real output, and K and L are capital and labor inputs. In logarithmic form, (12) can be written as

$$\ln y = \alpha \ln K + (1 - \alpha) \ln L.$$

Application of the rule given by equation (11) for differentiation with respect to time gives us

$$\frac{\frac{dy}{dt}}{y} = \alpha \frac{\frac{dK}{dt}}{K} + (1 - \alpha) \frac{\frac{dL}{dt}}{L}, \tag{13}$$

so that the proportional growth rate of y is a weighted average of the proportional growth rates of K and L.

POINT ELASTICITIES

These concepts can be applied more generally in the notion of the point elasticity of a function. If x is a function of, say, L that does not represent time, then the expression

$$\frac{\frac{dx}{x}}{\frac{dL}{L}} = E_{xL} \tag{14}$$

is the ratio of the instantaneous percentage change in x to the accompanying instantaneous percentage change in L. We can write

$$x = f(L).$$

If we let $j = \ln x$, $h = \ln L$ so that $L = e^h$, then

$$\frac{d(\ln x)}{d(\ln L)} = \frac{dj}{dh}.$$

Multiplying by $(dx/dx) \cdot (dL/dL)$ and rearranging gives us

$$\frac{d(\ln x)}{d(\ln L)} = \frac{dj}{dh} = \frac{dj}{dx}\frac{dx}{dL}\frac{dL}{dh} = \left(\frac{d}{dx}\ln x\right)\left(\frac{dx}{dL}\right)\left(\frac{d}{dh}e^h\right)$$

$$= \frac{1}{x}\frac{dx}{dL}e^h = \frac{L}{x}\frac{dx}{dL} = \frac{\dfrac{dx}{x}}{\dfrac{dL}{L}}.$$

Therefore, we see that the point elasticity of x with respect to L, E_{xL} can be given by

$$E_{xL} = \frac{d(\ln x)}{d(\ln L)}. \qquad (15)$$

Again, in the case of the Cobb–Douglas production function, where

$$\ln y = \alpha \ln K + (1 - \alpha) \ln L,$$

holding L constant, we have the elasticity of y with respect to K given by

$$E_{yK} = \frac{d \ln y}{d \ln K} = \alpha.$$

Similarly, holding K constant, we have

$$E_{yL} = \frac{d \ln y}{d \ln L} = (1 - \alpha).$$

Thus, the coefficients of the Cobb–Douglas function are the partial elasticities of output with respect to changes in the K and L inputs.

SELECTED READING

A.C. Chiang, *Fundamental Methods of Mathematical Economics,* 3rd Ed. (New York: McGraw-Hill, 1984), Chapter 10.

chapter 20

Inflation and Unemployment: The Phillips Curve

The 1980s began in the United States with an inflation rate of over 10 percent. The disinflation policy that was already in effect brought the unemployment rate to its post–World War II peak of 10.6 percent. It was also successful in bringing the rate of inflation down to less than 3 percent by 1986. The dynamics of this disinflation are discussed in this chapter, building on the analytical apparatus developed in Part II. The macroeconomic events of the last decade, while a painful experience for many, provide the economist with the equivalent of the scientist's laboratory experiment.

In the first section of this chapter, we review the basic analytics of inflation. The short-run Phillips curve relating the rate of wage increase to the unemployment rate is developed first. It is then augmented by a price equation and the adaptive price expectations mechanism of Chapter 7 to obtain the long-run Phillips curve. This gives us the basic model of wage and price dynamics. Next, we go on to discuss the three inflation cycles since 1960, applying this analytical apparatus.

The principal point of this chapter is that the experience of inflation and unemployment in the U.S. economy since the 1960s can be understood quite readily in the framework of the macroeconomic analysis of Part II. The inflation came from overstimulative demand policy and from supply shocks. The rise in unemployment resulted from anti-inflationary policy and from changes in the composition of the labor force. By 1986, after three years of expansion, there was reason to expect that the economy was back on a stable path. However, as the expansion continued to 1988, the inflation rate picked up again.

495

THE BASIC ANALYTICS OF INFLATION AND UNEMPLOYMENT

The wage–price–productivity arithmetic of Chapter 19 shows that if money wage rates rise as fast as productivity, in general there is no reason for the equilibrium price level to rise. That discussion, which assumed that the labor-supply curve—the workers' money wage demands—shifts up through time, focused on conditions for noninflationary wage increases. The question remains: What determines the rate at which the labor-supply curve shifts upward? That is, what moves the money wage rate? The answer to this question will lead us into a discussion of the Phillips curve—the relationship between the rate of increase of money wages W and the unemployment rate u.

The Theoretical Basis for the Phillips Curve

From the labor market diagram of Figure 20-1, we can see that an increase in the demand for labor—an outward shift in the $P \cdot f(N)$ curve—will bring an increase in the money wage rate, due to the appearance of excess demand in the labor market. In Figure 20-1 at wage rate W_0 there is excess demand for labor measured by $N_0^d - N_0^s$. This excess demand bids the wage rate up from W_0. The first assumption in construction of the Phillips curve is that the percentage rate of increase of the wage rate, W, depends on the magnitude of the excess demand for labor, $N^d - N^s$. That is,

$$\dot{W} = f(N^d - N^s); \qquad f' > 0. \tag{1}$$

Figure 20-1 shows that both labor demand and labor supply depend, in turn, on the level of the wage rate.

A complete model of the labor market would include empirical estimates of the labor-demand curve, the labor-supply curve, and the wage adjustment function, equation (1). Empirical estimates of labor-demand and -supply functions are very difficult to obtain, but the wage adjustment equation is more manageable and can be estimated independently of the demand and

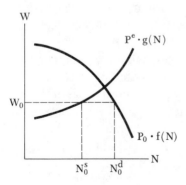

Figure 20-1 Excess demand for labor.

supply functions. Obtaining this estimate involves transforming the excess demand expression in (1) into the unemployment rate. The British (but New Zealand-born) economist A. W. Phillips introduced the inverse relationship between the rate of wage increase and unemployment into the economics literature in 1958.

To begin with, we can note that excess supply in the labor market, $N^s - N^d$, is just the negative of excess demand, that is,

$$\text{Excess supply} = N^s - N^d = -(N^d - N^s). \tag{2}$$

Using this relationship, we can rewrite the wage adjustment equation (1) as

$$\dot{W} = -f(N^s - N^d). \tag{3}$$

The next step is to introduce the unemployment rate $u = U/L$ as a proxy for excess supply. As excess supply rises, the unemployment rate rises, as shown in Figure 20-2. From the discussion of search unemployment in Chapter 10, we recall that there generally is positive unemployment even when the labor market is in equilibrium, that is, when excess supply is zero. Thus, the excess supply–unemployment rate function of Figure 20-2 crosses the horizontal axis at a positive level of unemployment.

Substituting the unemployment rate for excess supply in equation (21) gives us the wage adjustment equation,

$$\dot{W} = g(u); \qquad g' < 0. \tag{4}$$

Since $\dot{W}$ falls with an increase in excess supply, it also falls with an increase in u. Thus, as unemployment rises, the rate of increase of wages falls, and vice versa as unemployment falls. Equation (4) is the basic short-run Phillips curve equation relating $\dot{W}$ to u.

Figure 20-3 shows this Phillips curve, equation (4). We expect that the $g(u)$ function should have the convex shape shown in Figure 20-3, for the following reasons. As unemployment is reduced by constant amounts, the wage rate will rise at an increasing rate, with $\dot{W}$ approaching infinity as u approaches 0. In other words, a negative unemployment rate is not observable. On the other hand, there must be some institutional lower boundary below

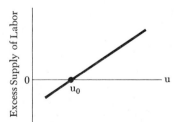

Figure 20-2 Unemployment and excess labor supply.

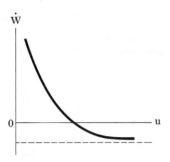

Figure 20-3   The Phillips curve.

which $\dot{W}$ cannot fall. It takes time to change wage rates, especially to reduce them, so that $\dot{W}$ cannot approach $-\infty$ as the unemployment rate grows larger and larger, but rather reaches some stable rate of decrease of wages. Thus, as u approaches 100 percent, $\dot{W}$ approaches the lower bound shown in Figure 20-3. These features give the curve its convex shape. Although these arguments are not really compelling, the empirical estimates generally support the convexity proposition. An early econometric study by George Perry specified the convexity of the U.S. Phillips curve by estimating it as

$$\dot{W} = -\alpha + \beta \cdot \frac{1}{u}.$$

Perry's estimate of the coefficient β was 14.7. We will use this estimate later to help determine the value of the "natural" or equilibrium unemployment rate.

The convex shape of the Phillips curve suggests that, on average, the economy will experience less inflation if the level of unemployment has narrow fluctuations about some average $\bar{u}$ than if the fluctuations are wider with the same mean $\bar{u}$. If unemployment is fluctuating symmetrically about the 6 percent level, for example, the average pressure on prices goes up more below the 6 percent level than it goes down above 6 percent, because of the convex nature of the curve. Thus, the broader the fluctuation in unemployment levels at any given average unemployment rate, the greater will be the cost-push inflationary pressure on the economy.

Unemployment and Price Expectations

The Phillips curve of equation (4) makes the rate of change of money wages simply a function of the unemployment rate. This is analogous to assuming that the extreme Keynesian model of Chapter 7 holds: money wage demands do not respond to expectations of price increase. To move to the more general model, we should add inflation expectations to the Phillips curve. For a given level of the unemployment rate u, the faster prices are expected to rise, the faster money wage demands will rise. This expectations-augmented Phillips curve can be written as

$$\dot{W} = g(u) + \dot{P}^e. \tag{5}$$

Later, we will discuss how inflation expectations are formed, and we will come back to the adaptive and rational cases of Chapter 7. For now, let us take $\dot{P}^e$ as given exogenously.

The Phillips curve of equation (5) is shown in Figure 20-4. There we see that as $\dot{P}^e$ rises from $\dot{P}^e_0$ to $\dot{P}^e_1$, the entire curve shifts up. Each individual Phillips curve for a given $\dot{P}^e$ is a "short-run" Phillips curve. Below we will derive a "long-run" curve by combining the price equation determining $\dot{P}$ with equation (5).

A reduction in labor supply due to an increase in demand for leisure would shift each short-run Phillips curve up; $g(u)$ would rise. Employers would have to offer larger wage increases to obtain the same amount of labor as before the change in tastes. Similarly, if the composition of the labor force changed with an increase in the proportion of workers with less than average attachment to the labor market and higher than average unemployment—second earners in a family, for example—the short-run $g(u)$ Phillips curve would shift up. For a given movement of wages, unemployment would rise because the composition shifted toward people with generally higher unemployment rates. As we see later in this chapter, this factor has been at work in the United States since the mid-1960s.

THE LONG-RUN PHILLIPS CURVE

The price equation that preserves constant income shares from Chapter 19 is

$$\dot{P} = \dot{W} - (y/N) + \epsilon, \tag{6}$$

where the additional term represents cost-push disturbances. Normally, we expect $\epsilon = 0$. When there is a major crop shortfall or drop in oil supply, ϵ

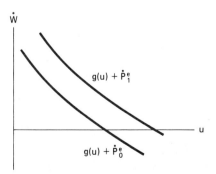

Figure 20-4 Short-run Phillips curves.

becomes positive for a time. For example, Joel Popkin has estimated that in 1973, these two elements increased the U.S. consumer price index (CPI) by 4.5 percent. In that case, for 1973, $\epsilon = 0.045$.

If shares do remain fairly constant over time, as we will see is the case in Chapter 22, and if there are no persistent nonwage cost-push disturbances ($\epsilon = 0$), then equation (6) gives us a link between wages and prices, so that the Phillips curve can be stated in terms of prices as well as wages. The Phillips curve relationship between the rate of price increase and unemployment is shown in Figure 20-5. If productivity grows at about 2 percent per year, roughly the U.S. average growth rate since 1970, then, with constant shares, a zero rate of price increase corresponds to a 2-percent rate of wage increase. Thus, for any given level of unemployment, we can read off the rate of increase of wages on the vertical axis to the left of Figure 20-5 and the rate of price increase on the vertical axis to the right.

Combining equations (5) and (6), we can see how the price-wage spiral works and derive the long-run Phillips curve. Suppose an initial cost-push disturbance $\epsilon > 0$ pushes the price level up, so $\dot{P} > 0$. This increases wage demands—$\dot{W}$ becomes positive—and in turn feeds back on $\dot{P}$ through equation (6), and so on. If the initial impulse were demand-pull, we would first see a drop in the unemployment rate u in (5), raising $\dot{W}$. This would push up $\dot{P}$ in (6), giving a further increase in wage demands in (5), and so on.

The effect of a change in the unemployment rate, or a continuing cost-

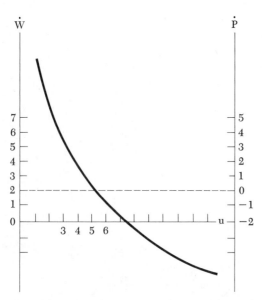

Figure 20-5   The Phillips curve: linking prices and wages.

push pressure with $\epsilon > 0$, can be obtained by combining equations (5) and (6). Substitution of (5) for $\dot{W}$ into equation (6) gives us the price-inflation version of the Phillips curve,

$$\dot{P} = g(u) + \dot{P}^e - (y/N) + \epsilon, \qquad (7)$$

where the supply disturbance term ϵ is normally zero.

In any long-run equilibrium with a constant rate of inflation, eventually the expected rate of inflation $\dot{P}^e$ will be equal to the actual rate $\dot{P}$. Of course, the short-run disturbance factor ϵ will be zero. Putting these assumptions into the price-inflation Phillips curve of equation (7) gives us a vertical long-run Phillips curve. With $\dot{P} = \dot{P}^e$ and $\epsilon = 0$, equation (7) becomes

$$\dot{P} = g(u) + \dot{P} - (y/N), \quad \text{or}$$

$$g(u) - (y/N) = 0. \qquad (8)$$

For a given rate of productivity growth (y/N), equation (8) gives us the "natural" unemployment rate u_n. As an example of the calculation of u_n, let's take Perry's estimate of $g(u) = 14.7/u$, and the long-run productivity growth rate of the late 1960s in the United States of 3.0 percent per year. Then we have

$$\frac{14.7}{u_n} = 3.0, \quad \text{or} \quad u_n = 4.9.$$

This is about the same as Robert J. Gordon's estimate of the 1960s natural rate of 5 percent.

The family of short-run Phillips curves from Figure 20-4 is combined with the long-run vertical Phillips curve of equation (8) in Figure 20-6. There each short-run curve corresponds to a given expected inflation $\dot{P}^e$, with $\dot{P}_0^e < \dot{P}_1^e < \dot{P}_2^e$. Since the natural rate is calculated assuming that actual inflation $\dot{P}$ equals $\dot{P}^e$, the point where each short-run curve crosses the long-run u_n is where $\dot{P}$ on the right-hand vertical axis is equal to the $\dot{P}^e$ attached to the short-run curve.

Actual and Expected Inflation

The long-run Phillips curve was derived by setting $\dot{P} = \dot{P}^e$ and $\epsilon = 0$ in equation (7). Then we calculated the natural unemployment rate u_n by solving equation (8), $g(u) = (y/N)$ for u. This tells us that at any point to the left of u_n in Figure 20-6, actual inflation $\dot{P}$ must exceed expected inflation $\dot{P}^e$, and to the right of u_n, $\dot{P} < \dot{P}^e$. Let's see why this is true. From equation (7), we can see that the difference between actual and expected inflation (with $\epsilon = 0$), is given by

$$\dot{P} - \dot{P}^e = g(u) - (y/N). \qquad (9)$$

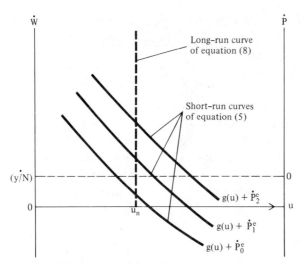

Figure 20-6   Long-run and short-run Phillips curves.

To the left of u_n, $u < u_n$ and $g(u) > g(u_n)$, because of the negative slope of the short-run Phillips curve ($g' < 0$). Therefore, left of u_n, $g(u) - (y/N)$ is positive; this is because at u_n this expression is zero in equation (8). So, along any short-run curve, left of u_n, $\dot{P} > \dot{P}^e$, and vice versa to the right of u_n.

This makes sense in terms of the basic static model of Part II. We calculated u_n as the unemployment rate where $\dot{P} = \dot{P}^e$. If expansionary demand policy raises employment and reduces unemployment below u_n, it must do so by increasing P more than P^e. In terms of the Phillips curve, this means $\dot{P} > \dot{P}^e$. Similarly, if a contraction of demand reduces employment and raises the unemployment rate above u_n, then P must fall more than P^e. This means $\dot{P} < \dot{P}^e$ right of u_n.

Simply by the way we obtained the natural rate, we can see that below u_n, actual inflation exceeds expected inflation, and above u_n, it is less than expected. This should tell us intuitively that when $u < u_n$, inflation would be rising, as $\dot{P}^e$ begins to catch up to $\dot{P}$. When $u > u_n$, inflation would be falling, as $\dot{P} < \dot{P}^e$. This means that left of u_n, inflation itself would be increasing, so the price level would be accelerating. To the right of u_n, inflation would be falling, so the price level would be decelerating. This characteristic of the model led James Tobin to label u_n the NAIRU—the nonaccelerating inflation rate of unemployment. We will use this terminology from here on.

Validation of Inflation

We will make this intuition on accelerating inflation more precise shortly by introducing the explicit assumption of adaptive expectations. But we can see the problem it poses for demand management by looking at the example of Figure 20-7. Suppose that initially the economy is at point A in Figure 20-7, with a zero rate of price inflation and wages growing as fast as productivity. Initially, the unemployment rate is at the NAIRU, u_n.

At point A, suppose that an expansionary shift in monetary or fiscal policy moves the economy up the short-run Phillips curve to point B. This could happen if the government decided that the cost of inflation at point A was less than the gain from reducing unemployment. In this case the inflation rate would become positive and unemployment would fall to u_B. In the supply-demand diagram of Figure 20-8, the economy has moved from point A to point B. But with a positive inflation rate from Figure 20-7, we know that in Figure 20-8 the aggregate supply curve is shifting up with the economy at point B. This is the price-wage spiral at work. Aggregate demand therefore has to continue to expand to hold the unemployment rate at u_B and output at y_B in Figures 20-7 and 20-8. In the economics literature this is known as *validation of inflation.*

Now the question is: Can demand policy hold the economy at u_B, y_B in Figures 20-7 and 20-8 by a steady expansion of demand that maintains the rate of inflation at point B in Figure 20-7? The answer is no. Recall that the expected inflation rate that positioned the short-run Phillips curve through points A and B was zero. This is the actual inflation intercept of the curve at u_n. But at point B the actual inflation rate is positive, greater than zero. So at point B actual $\dot{P}$ exceeds expected $\dot{P}^e$, and the expected inflation rate will adjust upward toward the actual. This means that at point B in Figure 20-7 the short-run Phillips curve shifts up as $\dot{P}^e$ rises, toward a point like C. Because the inflation rate is rising at u_B, the supply curve in Figure 20-8 is shifting up

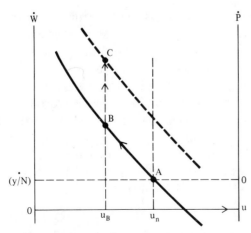

Figure 20-7 Accelerating inflation below the NAIRU.

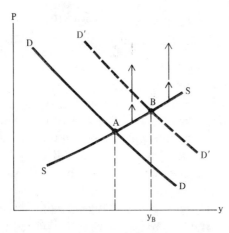

Figure 20-8 Price-wage spiral.

at an increasing rate. This is the acceleration of the price level. If policy makers want to hold the economy at u_B, y_B, demand will have to expand at an *increasing rate.*

This dilemma resulted from attempts at expansionary policy in the 1960s and 1970s in the United States. To hold the economy at a point where the unemployment rate is below the NAIRU, u_n, demand has to expand at an increasing rate, resulting in an accelerating inflation. This eventually proved to be unacceptable policy, and the disinflation of the 1980s followed. We will return to the story of U.S. unemployment and inflation since the 1960s shortly, but first we should make the discussion of expectations adjustment more precise by reintroducing the model of adaptive expectations from Chapter 7.

ADAPTIVE EXPECTATIONS IN THE PHILLIPS CURVE

One reasonable way to form expectations is by an error-correction mechanism: Adjust your expectations by a proportion of your most recent error. This can be a good procedure if you are not certain about the process that governs the variable of interest. In that case, when a realized value turns out differently from the expectation, it may be due to a random event or to a change in the underlying process. If a random event was responsible, you should not change expectations at all. If it was due to a change in the underlying process, you should adjust the way you form expectations fully. If you are uncertain, you should adjust partially. This error-correction procedure results in the adaptive expectations formation process that was introduced in Chapter 7. Here we can apply it to the expected rate of inflation $\dot{P}^e$.

Specifying Adaptive Expectations

To make the discussion precise, we have to use the before-and-after time subscripts of Chapter 7, now applied to the inflation rate. So in this section, we replace the general idea expressed in $\dot{P}^e$ by $_{t-1}\dot{P}_t$, the expectation formed in period $(t - 1)$ of inflation in period t. In general, we can imagine inflation expectations formed in any previous period $(t - i)$ for any period after it $(t - i + j)$. This would be $_{t-i}\dot{P}_{t-i+j}$.

The mechanism for adjusting expectations can be written as

$$_t\dot{P}_{t+1} - _{t-1}\dot{P}_t = \lambda(\dot{P}_t - _{t-1}\dot{P}_t). \tag{10}$$

This says that I adjust my expectations by a fraction $\lambda (0 < \lambda < 1)$ of my recent error. I had an expectation for this period's inflation, $_{t-1}\dot{P}_t$. I see the actual value for this period, $\dot{P}_t$. So expectations for the next period, $_t\dot{P}_{t+1}$, are expectations for this period, plus a fraction λ of this period's error. Equation (10) here is written in the form that is common in the economics literature on adaptive expectations. Equation (8) in Chapter 7 was written in the form that is more familiar from the engineering literature on error correction. You might check to see that the two are algebraically the same. The only difference is that the positions of the weights λ and $1 - \lambda$ are reversed from Chapter 7 to here.

From equation (10), we can obtain two informative ways to express expected inflation $_t\dot{P}_{t+1}$. The first comes simply from moving $_{t-1}\dot{P}_t$ to the right-hand side to get

$$_t\dot{P}_{t+1} = \lambda\dot{P}_t + (1 - \lambda) _{t-1}\dot{P}_t. \tag{11}$$

This says that expected inflation today is a weighted average of this period's expected and actual inflation. Here we see that the parameter value of the parameter λ should depend on what we think about the likely source of this period's error. If it was a permanent shift in the process forming $\dot{P}$, then we set $\lambda = 1$ so that $_t\dot{P}_{t+1} = \dot{P}_t$. This is *static expectations:* tomorrow's inflation is expected to be the same as today's. If we think today's error was just due to a random event, we set $\lambda = 0$, so there is no adjustment, and $_t\dot{P}_{t+1} = _{t-1}\dot{P}_t$. In general, the value of λ will depend on the variability of the process forming $\dot{P}$ relative to the sheer randomness of $\dot{P}$ itself relative to that process.

The other useful way to look at adaptive expectations is to slip the indexes in equation (11) back one period to get

$$_{t-1}\dot{P}_t = \lambda\dot{P}_{t-1} + (1 - \lambda) _{t-2}\dot{P}_{t-1}, \tag{12}$$

and then substitute this back into (11) for $_{t-1}\dot{P}_t$ to obtain for this period's expectation

$$_t\dot{P}_{t+1} = \lambda\dot{P}_t + \lambda(1 - \lambda)\dot{P}_{t-1} + (1 - \lambda)^2 _{t-2}\dot{P}_{t-1}. \tag{13}$$

Doing this substitution repeatedly gives us

$$_t\dot{P}_{t+1} = \lambda\dot{P}_t + \lambda(1 - \lambda)\dot{P}_{t-1} + \lambda(1 - \lambda)^2 \dot{P}_{t-2}$$
$$+ \lambda(1 - \lambda)^3 \dot{P}_{t-3} + \cdots \tag{14}$$

The infinite sum on the right-hand side of equation (14) can be written more compactly to give us

$$_t\dot{P}_{t+1} = \sum_{i=0}^{\infty} \lambda(1-\lambda)^i \, \dot{P}_{t-i}. \tag{15}$$

Given that $0 < \lambda < 1$, with adaptive expectations the current expectation is an infinite regress on all past realizations. Adaptive expectations look infinitely far back into the past to form today's expectation.

The NAIRU and Inflation Dynamics

We can return to the discussion of inflation dynamics by substituting equation (12) for $_{t-1}\dot{P}_t$ into the price version of the Phillips curve given in equation (7) to obtain

$$\dot{P}_t = g(u) - (y/N) + \lambda\dot{P}_{t-1} + (1-\lambda) \, _{t-2}\dot{P}_{t-1}, \quad \text{or} \tag{16}$$

$$\dot{P}_t = g(u) - (y/N) + \sum_{i=1}^{\infty} \lambda(1-\lambda)^{i-1} \, \dot{P}_{t-i}. \tag{17}$$

Recall that the NAIRU is the unemployment rate u_n that satisfies the condition

$$g(u) - (y/N) = 0.$$

This condition is met, and the economy is at u_n in Figure 20-9 if

$$\dot{P}_t = \lambda\dot{P}_{t-1} + (1-\lambda) \, _{t-2}\dot{P}_{t-1} = \, _{t-1}\dot{P}_t,$$

that is, if inflation expectations are realized. If, however, aggregate demand policy holds u at some level u_0 below u_n in Figure 20-9, then actual inflation

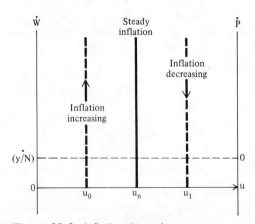

Figure 20-9   Inflation dynamics.

exceeds expected inflation by an amount that we can calculate from equation (16) as

$$\dot{P}_t - \lambda \dot{P}_{t-1} - (1 - \lambda)_{t-2}\dot{P}_{t-1} = g(u_0) - g(u_1) \approx g' \cdot (u_0 - u_n). \qquad (18)$$

Remember that $g' < 0$, so with $u_0 < u_n$, this is positive. If actual inflation exceeds expected, with adaptive expectations actual inflation must be rising, since the current actual rate feeds into the future expected rate.

We can calculate how fast the actual rate rises by subtracting and adding $\dot{P}_{t-1}$ from the left-hand side of (18) to get (using the approximation in equation 18)

$$\dot{P}_t - \dot{P}_{t-1} + (1 - \lambda)(\dot{P}_{t-1} - {}_{t-2}\dot{P}_{t-1}) = g' \cdot (u_0 - u_n).$$

If u_0 is held constant by demand policy, then the actual less expected inflation in period $(t - 1)$ was also given by $g' \cdot (u_0 - u_n)$, so we have

$$\dot{P}_t - \dot{P}_{t-1} + (1 - \lambda)(g' \cdot (u_0 - u_n)) = g' \cdot (u_0 - u_n).$$

Thus, the increase in the rate of inflation over time is given by

$$\dot{P}_t - \dot{P}_{t-1} = \lambda \cdot g' \cdot (u_0 - u_n). \qquad (19)$$

If $\lambda = 1$, expectations adjust immediately, so the actual rate of inflation must rise by the full amount

$$\dot{P}_t - \dot{P}_{t-1} = g' \cdot (u_0 - u_n).$$

At the other extreme, if $\lambda = 0$ expectations never adjust. Thus, any reduction in u and increase in $\dot{P}$ will create a permanent gap between actual and expected inflation, and there will be no necessary increase in actual inflation to keep actual ahead of expected. In this case, we are back to the short-run Phillips curve with exogenous $\dot{P}^e$ and no NAIRU.

The same analysis, with the sign reversed, applies to the right of u_n in Figure 20-9. If $u > u_n$, then from equation (16)

$$\dot{P}_t < {}_{t-1}\dot{P}_t = \lambda \dot{P}_{t-1} + (1 - \lambda)_{t-2}\dot{P}_{t-1},$$

and the speed at which the inflation rate falls is given by equation (19) with $u > u_n$. Only where $u = u_n$ does expected inflation equal actual, and the actual inflation rate can remain constant.

So with adaptive expectations, we have the map of inflation dynamics shown in Figure 20-9. At the NAIRU, any inflation rate can be a steady equilibrium rate, as long as it is validated by demand policy. In particular, a policy of $\dot{M} = \dot{P}$ will hold real balances constant and keep the aggregate demand curve shifting up as fast as aggregate supply in Figure 20-8. If demand policy wants to hold $u < u_n$, it has to expand at an increasing rate to keep actual inflation ahead of expected. To reduce the rate of inflation, demand policy can tighten, letting u rise above u_n. Then the inflation rate decreases, and slowing demand growth keeps actual inflation below expected. After a brief discussion of the case of rational expectations, we will use the map of inflation dynamics to analyze the inflation cycles of 1960–1985 in the U.S. economy.

Rational Expectations

The main alternative to adaptive expectations is rational expectations, with unbiased forecasts of inflation taken from the model. In this case, from Chapter 11, we have

$$\dot{P}_t = {}_{t-1}\dot{P}_t + \eta_t$$

where η_t is the random forecast error. This means that the $\dot{P}^e$ term in equation (7) can be replaced by

$$_{t-1}\dot{P}_t = \dot{P}_t - \eta_t, \tag{20}$$

so that the short-run Phillips curve becomes

$$g(u) - (y/N) + \epsilon - \eta = 0. \tag{21}$$

The expected value of the unemployment rate, when $\epsilon = \eta = 0$, is simply the NAIRU. With rational expectations, all but random inflation is anticipated, so all deviations from the NAIRU are random.

The rational expectations hypothesis applied to the inflation rate collapses the long-run vertical Phillips curve into the short run. Since any inflation or deflation generated by systematic government policy is anticipated in this case, the government cannot move the economy along a short-run Phillips curve. Because the effects of persistent shocks to private demand also become anticipated, they influence unemployment only when they first appear. Consequently, there is no role for stabilization policy in the rational expectations case.

The hypothesis of rational expectations is not very convincing when it is applied to inflation. A glance ahead at Figure 20-10 will show you the long swings in unemployment in the United States since 1960, strongly correlated with movements in demand. We will discuss those movements shortly. Given the evidence, we have to conclude that for inflation, adaptive expectations is a better working hypothesis. Perhaps seeing *is* believing.

INFLATION AND UNEMPLOYMENT 1960–1986

The period 1960–1986 in the United States can be viewed as one long inflation cycle, or it can be broken into three subcycles. The data on inflation and unemployment are presented in Figure 20-10. The solid line shows the path of the inflation rate, and the dashed line the unemployment rate. We can use the Phillips curve model to analyze the data and the data to illustrate the Phillips curve analysis.

Inflation in Figure 20-10 is measured by the percentage increase in the GNP deflator this quarter over the same quarter last year. Therefore, these are four-quarter percentage increases, giving annual rates. The formula is

$$\dot{P}_t = [(P_t/P_{t-4}) - 1] \cdot 100,$$

to give rates of inflation in percentage units. Unemployment is measured by unemployed persons as a percentage of the total civilian labor force.

The sense of one long inflation cycle comes from focusing on the inflation chart in Figure 20-10. There we see inflation near zero in 1960, rising erratically to around 6 percent in 1968–1971, and then dipping to 4 percent in 1972. It rose rapidly to a peak of over 10 percent in early 1974, following the oil price increases of 1973, subsided to less than 6 percent in 1977, and then jumped to another peak above 10 percent in late 1980, following the second round of oil price increases. From 1981 to 1986, tight monetary policy brought inflation back down to the range of 3 to 4 percent, which prevailed in the early 1960s.

The movement of the unemployment rate is harder to characterize. We see a fairly steady decrease from the early peak of 1961 to a bottom below 4 percent in 1969. Then it rises irregularly with recessions in 1970, 1974, 1980,

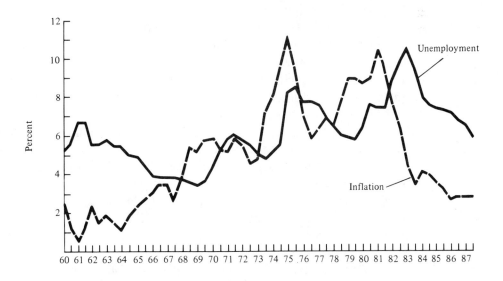

Figure 20-10 Inflation and unemployment since 1960.

and 1982 to peak at over 10 percent in the last recession. Since 1982 it has fallen steadily to below 6 percent.

These movements of inflation and unemployment have come from an irregular sequence of demand and supply shocks hitting the economy, with their initial impulses propagated by the wage-price dynamics of the Phillips curve. Demand shocks shift the aggregate demand curve and move the economy along the short-run Phillips curve. This effect was illustrated in Figures 20-7 and 20-8. Supply shocks shift the aggregate supply curve and appear as temporary nonzero values of ϵ in the price equations (6) and (7). A positive value for ϵ, shifting the aggregate-supply curve up, increases $\dot{P}$ for any given unemployment rate. This feeds into $\dot{W}$ via price expectations $\dot{P}^e$, and the rise in $\dot{W}$ feeds back into $\dot{P}$ in equation (6). If demand policy validates, that is, shifts aggregate demand up enough to hold y and u constant, the inflationary spiral continues. The economy has moved to a higher point on the vertical long-run Phillips curve. If demand does not validate, the unemployment rate rises and the inflation subsides.

Three Inflation Cycles, 1960–1986

We can distinguish three inflation cycles in the data presented in Figure 20-10—in1960–1967, 1972–1976, and 1977–1986—by referring to combinations of these demand and supply disturbances. The first cycle was a classic case of a demand-pull inflation, touched off by the jump in defense spending in early 1966. This cycle moved into the price-wage spiral phase around 1968. The first Nixon Administration ended validation in 1969, generating the recession we can see in 1970 in the unemployment data of Figure 20-10. This cycle was already coming to an end in 1971 when the administration resorted to price and wage controls.

The second cycle combined demand-pull and cost-push impulses. There was a rapid expansion of demand worldwide in 1972–1973. This can be seen in the falling unemployment rate after 1971 and rising inflation from 1972 in Figure 20-10. It was caused mainly by expansionary policy in the major countries, magnified by international trade multiplier effects. Meanwhile, a shortfall in world agricultural output in 1972 provided a cost-push element. On top of this shortfall came the reduction of oil output by OPEC and the subsequent increase in energy prices beginning in 1974. The result was the first inflation peak above 10 percent, at the beginning of 1975. By the end of 1975 the administration's policy of no (or even negative) validation had reduced demand enough that the rate of inflation slowed substantially. In 1976 a cautious expansion began again, with aggregate-demand policy aiming at a gradual reduction of the unemployment rate without an increase in the rate of inflation. By mid-1977 the unemployment rate was down from the 1975 peak of 9 percent to under 7 percent, and the rate of inflation was about 6 percent.

The third cycle also combined demand and supply factors. Continued expansion through 1979 pushed unemployment below 6 percent and inflation up to 9 percent. The second oil price increase led to the second inflation peak above 10 percent at the end of 1981. By then, the Federal Reserve had already shifted to a tightening of monetary policy, with unemployment beginning to rise in 1979. The unemployment rate hit a postwar peak of over 10 percent in the recession of 1982–1983, and the inflation rate came down rapidly. By 1986 inflation was in the 3 to 4 percent range, and unemployment was back to 6 percent, about equal to the current estimates of the NAIRU. The disinflation of the 1980s is a dramatic example of the Phillips curve in action.

The Increase in the NAIRU

Since the early 1960s, the estimated NAIRU in the United States has increased from 5 to 6 percent, according to the research of Robert J. Gordon. This is due mainly to the changing composition of the U.S. labor force.

The labor force can be separated into primary and secondary workers. Primary workers are usually defined as the first, or major, wage-earners in a family unit; other wage earners are defined as secondary labor force participants. Given the working habits of American families, primary workers are generally males over age 20; females and persons under age 20 are more often secondary participants.

Primary workers tend to be more skilled, to be more committed to the labor force, and to earn higher wages than secondary workers. Unemployment rates are higher among secondary workers. In 1987, when the overall unemployment rate was 6 percent, it was 4 percent for men and 9 percent for women with families and 16 percent for persons 16 to 19 years of age. Since primary workers are more committed to the labor force, a given amount of unemployment among primary workers, say, 100,000 persons, is likely to put more downward pressure on the wage rate than the same amount of unemployment among secondary workers. So a shift in the composition of the labor force that increases the number of secondary workers relative to primary workers will tend to raise the rate of wage increase associated with any given level of unemployment and increase the NAIRU.

Since the mid-1960s the composition of the U.S. labor force has shifted toward secondary workers. In 1965 secondary workers accounted for 40 percent of the labor force. This fraction rose to 45 percent by 1975 and 48 percent in 1986. Two factors account for this shift. First, the ratio of population aged 16 to 19 years to the total population rose from 6.9 percent in 1965 to 7.8 percent in 1975 and then fell to 6.1 percent in 1986. This increased the weight of young people in the labor force in the earlier period. Second, the labor force participation rate of women (the ratio of women in the labor force to total female population aged 16 and up) rose from 39.3 percent in 1965 to 55.3 percent in 1986. This increased the weight of women in the labor force.

These factors have increased the NAIRU by about 1 percentage point, from 5 to 6 percent, based on Gordon's estimates. This accounts for the rising unemployment trend in Figure 20-10 and for the contributions of excessively expansionary demand policy to the inflation episodes of the 1970s. As the NAIRU increased, policy makers were shooting at old estimates, which contributed an inflationary bias to demand policy then. In the 1980s the estimated NAIRU of about 6 percent was widely accepted, and so the economy's performance on inflation improved.

Phillips Curve Analysis of 1963–1986

The general movements of unemployment and inflation during the period since 1960 can be readily interpreted using the Phillips curve and aggregate demand and supply diagrams. The key thing to remember is that as long as the economy is above the $\dot{P} = 0$ level in the Phillips curve diagram, the aggregate-supply curve is shifting up. If the unemployment rate is at the NAIRU, it is shifting up at a constant rate. If $u < u_n$, $\dot{P}$ is increasing. If $u > u_n$, then $\dot{P}$ is decreasing.

Precise econometric analysis of inflation during this period has been presented in the work of George Perry and Robert Gordon. Here the point is to illustrate how the Phillips curve analysis explains the broad movements in the variables over the period. During this period, productivity growth slowed and the NAIRU increased. Including these changes in the analysis would make it messy without adding to understanding. We will therefore leave them aside and assume that the productivity growth rate is 2 percent, the average over the 1970–1985 period, and that the NAIRU is 6 percent, the 1980s number. Based on these assumptions, the story begins at points 0 in Figures 20-11 and 20-12, with $\dot{P} = 0$, $u = u_n$, and $y = y_n$. This was roughly the situation around 1963–1964 in the United States. We can now analyze the large inflation cycle from 1963 to 1987 using the two diagrams.

The initial expansionary phase of the cycle is represented by the move from points 0 to 1 in Figures 20-11 and 20-12. This is the long demand expansion of the Kennedy-Johnson years, with unemployment falling from 7.0 to 3.4 percent and inflation rising from near zero to 6 percent. The initial price increase along the supply curve in Figure 20-12 comes from the fall in productivity and the rise in unit labor costs as output expands along the economy's aggregate production function in the initial expansion. At the beginning of the expansion, unemployment was actually above the NAIRU, so inflation began in earnest only in 1964, as we can see in Figure 20-10. In addition, with a noninflationary history since the Korean War in 1950–1953, actual inflation influenced expectations with a lag. Hence, the acceleration phase was delayed. Eventually, however, expectations began to adjust. The Phillips curve shifted

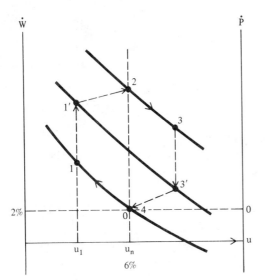

Figure 20-11 Inflation cycle: Phillips curve.

up in Figure 20-11, and the rate of inflation increased. This shifted the aggregate supply curve up in Figure 20-12 at an increasing rate. Demand had to expand at an increasing rate to hold the unemployment rate at u_1. The result is illustrated by the movement to points $1'$ in the two figures. In the data of Figure 20-10, this is the jump in inflation from around 3 percent in 1967 to 6 percent in 1969, while unemployment was held under 4 percent, well below the NAIRU.

The next phase is characterized by the end of demand validation of the *rising* inflation. This came in the first Nixon administration. With demand growth slowed, the economy moved to points like 2 in Figures 20-11 and 20-12. The unemployment rate went up to 6 percent by 1971, and inflation stabilized at around 6 percent, as we can see in Figure 20-10. The major idea to understand here is that at points 2 in Figures 20-11 and 20-12 inflation is positive. In Figure 20-12, the supply curve is shifting up. To hold unemployment u_n, demand policy must validate the steady rate of inflation at point 2 in Figure 20-11. Thus, from points 1 to 2, demand policy stops validating the *rise* in inflation, but at points 2, back at the NAIRU, the system has an inflation momentum that demand policy has to validate unless it is willing to let unemployment rise above the NAIRU. So while the economy remains at point 2 in Figure 20-11, with validation of a steady $\dot{P}$, it moves to point $2'$ in Figure 20-12.

The demand expansion and supply shocks of 1972–1973 pushed inflation to a temporary peak in 1975, from which it fell back to around 6 percent as unemployment was allowed to rise above the NAIRU. Another demand ex-

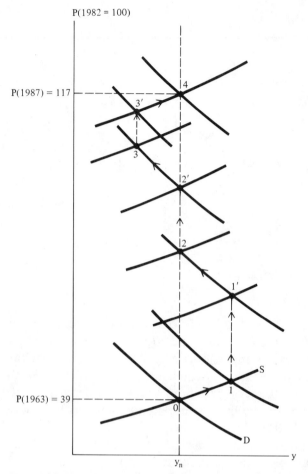

Figure 20-12   Inflation cycle: supply and demand.

pansion and supply shock produced another peak in inflation in 1980. These are evident in Figure 20-10. Rather than hopelessly complicating Figures 20-11 and 20-12 with these shifts, let's pick up the action at points 2 in Figure 20-11 and 2′ in Figure 20-12, around 1980 in the actual data of Figure 20-10.

In 1979 the Federal Reserve, in the person of Chairman Paul Volcker, decided to end validation of the inflation and accept the consequences. These took the form of a recession, with unemployment rising far above the NAIRU, which itself had risen since the 1960s. This decision was taken partly under pressure from European central banks, which were threatening to stop support of the dollar. In 1979 the unemployment rate was at about the NAIRU of 6 percent, but the second oil price increase sent the inflation rate above 10 percent in 1980.

The Fed stepped on the brakes beginning in 1979. The unemployment rate jumped to 7.5 percent in 1980, paused, and then rose to over 10 percent at the bottom of the recession in early 1983. The inflation rate would have subsided somewhat anyway, as the oil price rise of 1970–1980 faded. But with unemployment so far above the NAIRU, the inflation rate came down rapidly. The Fed's action is represented by the movements from points 2 and 2′ to points 3 in Figures 20-11 and 20-12. Unemployment rose above u_n, the economy went into a recession, and the inflation rate fell.

The extreme rise in unemployment and the Fed's evident determination to keep monetary policy tight seem to have convinced wage- and price-setters that inflation was coming down. This reduced expectations, shifting the Phillips curve back down in Figure 20-11 and moving the economy from points 3 to 3′ in Figures 20-11 and 20-12. The rapid disinflation of 1981–1983 is evident in Figure 20-10. It was aided by the appreciation of the dollar during 1981–1985, which reduced import prices.

By 1983 the Reagan tax cuts were providing fiscal stimulus to the economy, and the Fed relaxed monetary policy, with inflation below 4 percent. This is the move from points 3′ toward 4 in Figures 20-11 and 20-12. Demand expanded gradually until the unemployment rate reached the NAIRU of 6 percent in 1987, with the inflation rate back down to the 3 to 4 percent range. The disinflation of the 1980s was a clear example of the operation of the Phillips curve dynamics, and of the effectiveness of a credible monetary policy. It showed how monetary policy can stabilize a disequilibrium situation if it is determined and thereby becomes credible.

SELECTED READINGS

M. Friedman, "The Role of Monetary Policy," *American Economic Review,* March 1968.

R. J. Gordon, "Recent Developments in the Theory of Inflation and Unemployment," *Journal of Monetary Economics,* April 1976.

R. J. Gordon, *Macroeconomics,* 4th Ed. (Boston: Little, Brown and Company, 1987), chapter 11 and Appendix B.

G. L. Perry, "Changing Labor Markets and Inflation," *Brookings Papers on Economic Activity,* vol. 3, 1970.

G. L. Perry, *Unemployment, Money Wage Rates, and Inflation* (Cambridge: MIT Press, 1966), chapters 1–3.

E. S. Phelps, et al., *Microeconomic Foundations of Employment and Inflation Theory* (New York: W. W. Norton, 1970), Part II.

A. W. Phillips, "The Relation Between Unemployment and the Rate of Change of Money Wage Rates in the United Kingdom, 1861–1957," *Economica,* Nov. 1958.

J. Popkin, "Commodity Prices and the U.S. Price Level," *Brookings Papers on Economic Activity,* vol. 1, 1974.

J. Tobin, "Inflation and Unemployment," *American Economic Review,* March 1972.

chapter 21

Introduction to Stock-Adjustment Dynamics

The short-run equilibrium of Parts I–III determined values for the key variables y, N, r, and P for given values of the money stock M, the level of government purchases g, and the tax schedule $t(y)$. In Part III we introduced wealth into the demand functions for consumption and (implicitly) money. The Tobin model of demand for money as a riskless asset in Chapter 14 showed how wealth is allocated between bonds and money as a function of the interest rate and the riskiness of bonds. If we integrate wealth into the consumption and money demand functions, then we see that the short-run equilibrium of Chapter 16 implicitly holds constant the other asset stocks that are counted as wealth, K and B. So the short-run equilibrium of Parts I–III gives equilibrium values for y, N, r, and P, taking as given the values of the various asset stocks in the economy.

While asset stocks, inherited from history, are given at any point in time, they are also changing at each point in time. In the short-run equilibrium we determine a value for investment; this gradually moves the capital stock. We also determine a value for the government budget surplus or deficit. As we saw in Chapter 16, financing the surplus or deficit means that the money stock or the government debt is gradually changing. In an open economy, the balance-of-payments surplus or deficit also changes the money stock in the absence of sterilization, as we saw in Chapter 17.

Thus, implicit in the short-run equilibrium solution of Parts I–III are values for the *rates of change* of the stocks that were taken as given in the analysis of the short-run equilibrium. Movement of these stocks through time moves the short-run equilibrium y, N, r, and P over time; the supply and demand curves, IS, and LM move gradually as stocks accumulate. In a stable economy, movements in these stocks are taking the economy toward a *balanced growth path*, where all asset stocks grow at the same rate.

In Chapter 22, we will describe the short-run equilibrium as it moves along such a balanced growth path. Then in Part V which focuses on growth models, we will look at the convergence of the economy toward a balanced growth path, assuming that the monetary and fiscal policy maintains full employment. Here in Chapter 21, we study a few simple examples of how asset stock accumulation moves the short-run equilibrium toward a long-run stock equilibrium, corresponding to the balanced growth path of Chapter 22. We only look at some simple cases, rather than a full-blown differential equation model, because the latter would be too complex to be readily understandable; simple cases highlight the important channels of adjustment. Thus, the simple cases will give us an intuitive "feel" for how the economy moves through time, and will take us near the frontier of research in the field.

In the first section we will study the effects of finance of the government deficit by printing money (selling bonds to the Fed, or "monetizing" the deficit) in a simple case with no wealth effects. This will give us a good look at the basic adjustment mechanism involved in moving the short-run equilibrium. Then we introduce wealth effects into the system, moving from the skeletal model of Chapter 9 to the extended model of Chapter 16. This discussion permits us to study the effects of bond finance of the budget deficit and the phenomenon known as "crowding out" in the macroeconomic literature. In the fourth section we look again at balance-of-payments effects on the money stock, from Chapter 17, as analogous to money finance of the budget deficit, and we end the chapter with a general schematic picture of the stock adjustment mechanism.

MONEY FINANCE OF THE BUDGET DEFICIT

In the skeletal model of Part II, we determined short-run equilibrium values for the key variables y, N, r, and P, holding constant the money stock M, government purchases g, and the tax schedule $t(y)$. The short-run equilibrium value for y determined a level of tax revenue $t(y)$, and together with g this gave a budget surplus or deficit in real terms,

$$d = g - t(y) \tag{1}$$

To begin our analysis of stock adjustment dynamics, suppose the government finances the budget deficit or surplus by printing or destroying money, M. In Chapter 16 we described the mechanics of this operation; the Treasury sells its bonds to the Fed, and the balances created become reserves. In order to avoid unnecessary complications, we will assume here that the required reserve ratio is unity, so reserves *are* the money stock, and vice versa.

Short-Run Equilibrium

In the short-run *IS–LM* equilibrium of Part II, the level of income y is determined by the values of M and g, given supply-side conditions and the tax schedule. Since the story in this chapter is about demand-side adjustment as stocks change, we will take supply-side conditions as given, and even summarize them in a constant price level. Since we have already shown how to calculate equivalent changes in the tax schedule and in government purchases ($dg = c'y\, dt$ from Chapter 5), we will hold the tax schedule constant and look at the effects of changes in g. With these assumptions, the short-run equilibrium level of income is just a function of M and g,

$$y = y(M, g). \tag{2}$$

The value of M positions the *LM* curve, and g positions the *IS* curve in Figure 21-1. The equilibrium value of y (and r) results.

The partial derivatives of the *reduced-form* equation (2) for y are the familiar multipliers of Chapter 5. They are the effects on y of changes in M and g, respectively, holding the other variable constant (as well as the price level and the tax schedule). Thus, the partial derivatives of (2) are given by

$$\frac{\partial y}{\partial g} = \frac{1}{1 - c'(1 - t') + i'k'/l'} > 0;$$

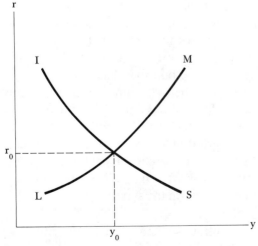

Figure 21-1 Short-run equilibrium.

and

$$\frac{\partial y}{\partial M} = \frac{1}{1 - c'(1 - t') + i'k'/l'} \cdot \frac{i'l'}{P} > 0. \qquad (3)$$

These are the multipliers of Chapter 5; they give the effect on equilibrium y in Figure 21-1 of a change in M or g. They will be important in the dynamic analysis below.

The short-run equilibrium in Figure 21-1 is, technically speaking, an *instantaneous* equilibrium. It is conditional on a given value of the money stock M, but as we will see shortly, it also determines a rate of change of that money stock. So the instantaneous equilibrium is also a *moving* equilibrium; as the money stock changes the LM curve shifts, moving the short-run equilibrium r_0, y_0 point. We want to ask, is this dynamic process stable, and what are the properties of the equilibrium to which it leads, if it is stable?

Adjustment of the Money Stock

Suppose the short-run equilibrium r_0, y_0 of Figure 21-1 results in a budget deficit, $g - t(y) > 0$, which is financed by money creation; the Treasury sells bonds to the Fed. In this case, at the initial equilibrium r_0, y_0 based on an initial value of the money stock M_0, the money stock is growing. This is shifting the LM curve of Figure 21-1 out, raising y. Where is the process likely to end? In Figure 21-2 we show the y^* value where the budget is balanced. At y^*, $g - t(y^*) = 0$. With a given g and tax schedule, when $y < y^*$, $t(y) < t(y^*)$, and $g - t(y) > 0$; there is a budget deficit, and M is growing. When $y > y^*$ there is a surplus, and M is contracting.

At the initial equilibrium r_0, y_0 in Figure 21-2, y_0 is smaller than the y^* that would balance the budget. So at r_0, y_0 there is a budget deficit and the money stock is increasing, shifting the LM curve out from $L_0 M_0$. As the LM curve shifts, y increases; this raises tax revenue $t(y)$ and reduces the size of the budget deficit. This movement continues until the LM curve reaches $L_1 M_1$ where equilibrium $y = y^*$, and the budget is balanced; $g - t(y^*) = 0$. When the short-run equilibrium has reached y^*, with the budget balanced the money stock is no longer changing. Thus, the point r^*, y^* is a *full stock equilibrium* in this simple model. Since the budget surplus moves the money stock, which in turn moves the short-run equilibrium, when we get to a short-run equilibrium where the budget is balanced, there is no further tendency for the money stock to change. This particular short-run equilibrium is also a long-run equilibrium, in the sense that the stocks in the system, only M in this simple model, are in equilibrium.

If the initial *ISLM* equilibrium had been to the right of y^* in Figure 21-2, there would have been a budget surplus at that starting point. In that

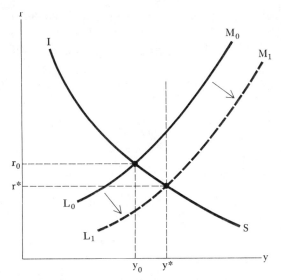

Figure 21-2 Money stock adjustment.

case the Treasury would be retiring debt from the Fed, reducing reserves and shrinking the money stock. This would shift the *LM* curve left, reducing *y* toward *y**, where the system would again be in full stock equilibrium. Thus, the initial budget deficit or surplus, by moving the money stock, tends to move the economy toward a position where the budget is balanced. The economy is in short-run equilibrium at each point in time; it is only when the underlying asset stocks are at rest, however, that the economy is in a full stock equilibrium.

Stability of Stock Adjustment

The discussion of adjustment above should have shown the reader that the adjustment process is stable in this simple model. Consider the stock equilibrium value of *y*, that is, *y** in Figure 21-2. If the initial, historically given, money stock is small enough that $y_0 < y^*$, the budget will be in deficit and the money stock will increase. If the initial value of *M* is large enough that $y_0 > y^*$, the budget will be in surplus and the money stock will shrink. Thus, through budget dynamics, a small money stock grows and a large money stock shrinks, both toward the *M** value where $y = y^*$, given *g, t,* the price level, and the supply-side parameters.

We can analyze the stability of this adjustment process a bit more carefully by writing out the dynamics explicitly. The budget deficit *is* the time rate of change of the money stock:

$$\frac{dM}{dt} \equiv DM = P \cdot [g - t(y)]. \tag{4}$$

Here we introduce the notation that the time rate of change of a variable is denoted by D: $dX/dt \equiv DX$. The rate of change of the money stock is given by the price level times the real value of the deficit in (4). When $y = y^*$ so that $g - t(y^*) = 0$, $DM = 0$. From equation (2) above, in the reduced form of the short-run system $y = y(M, g)$, and from (3), $\partial y/\partial M > 0$. Thus, we can rewrite (4) as

$$DM = P \cdot \{g - t[y(M, g)]\}. \tag{5}$$

Given P, g, and the tax function, equation (5) shows the rate of change of M, DM, as a function of M itself. If $\partial(DM)/\partial M < 0$, this system is stable:

$$\frac{\partial(DM)}{\partial M} = -Pt' \frac{\partial y}{\partial M} < 0. \tag{6}$$

Stability of the adjustment process can also be seen in the phase diagram of Figure 21-3, which represents the adjustment equation (5). At $M = M^*$, the budget is balanced (again given g and the tax function t). Where $M < M^*$, $y < y^*$ in Figure 21-2, and the budget is in deficit with $DM > 0$. When $M > M^*$, $DM < 0$. If we begin with the value of $M_0 < M^*$ in Figure 21-3, the budget deficit increases M along the phase line. The increase in y shrinks the deficit; so M grows at a decreasing rate toward M^*, where $DM = 0$. If we begin with $M > M^*$, M would shrink at a decreasing rate toward M^*. Thus, the stock adjustment mechanics of the system, working through the budget deficit or surplus, are stable.

The clear-cut stability of this model depends partially on the simplifying assumption that P is constant throughout the adjustment process. From the discussion of supply-side relationships in Chapter 7, we know that P generally

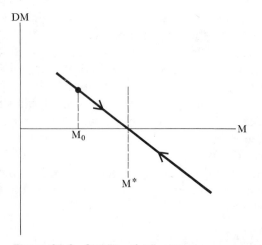

Figure 21-3 Stability of adjustment.

increases with y, given the supply-side parameters. If P increases fast enough, we can see from (5) that adjustment could become unstable. If we began with $M_0 < M^*$, the budget deficit would increase M. This would raise y, which would reduce the *real* value of the deficit, $g - t(y)$. But it would also increase P along the supply curve, which would tend to increase the *nominal* deficit $P \cdot [g - t(y)]$. If P rose fast enough, the nominal deficit, which is DM, could be increasing as M increases, making adjustment unstable.

If we include adjustment of P in (5), we have

$$DM = P[y(M, g)] \cdot \{g - t[y(M, g)]\}. \tag{7}$$

Then the shape of the phase line is given by

$$\frac{\partial (DM)}{\partial M} = P\left(-t \frac{\partial y}{\partial M}\right) + (g - t)P'\left(\frac{\partial y}{\partial M}\right),$$

which simplifies to

$$\frac{\partial (DM)}{\partial M} = \frac{\partial y}{\partial M}[P'(g - t) - Pt']. \tag{8}$$

If we begin with $M < M^*$, so that $(g - t) > 0$, then the slope of the phase line is indeterminate; the effect through y, $-Pt'$ is negative, but the price effect $P'(g - t)$ is positive. The system is stable with a growing money stock only if the price movement is slow compared to the adjustment in real income y. This is a basic assumption in the Keynesian tradition. Monetarists would question it.

On the other side of M^*, with a budget surplus so that $(g - t) < 0$, the system is stable. Both falling y and falling P shrink the nominal surplus, reducing DM. Thus, with sluggish price adjustment, the money finance system in this simple model is stable. Rapid price adjustment might render it unstable when initial conditions give a budget deficit.

Effects of Fiscal Policy

The fiscal policy multiplier $\partial y / \partial g$ of equation (3) assumed no change in the money stock. It is the short-run multiplier of Part II. Now we see that if the system began from a full stock equilibrium with $y = y^*$ in Figure 21-2, an increase in g would most likely lead to an initial budget deficit. This would yield a subsequent increase in the money stock and a further expansion of y. The multiplier between stock equilibria y^* where $g - t(y^*) = 0$ is easy to derive. From

$$g - t(y^*) = 0, \tag{9}$$

we have

$$dg - t' \, dy^* = 0,$$

and

$$\frac{dy^*}{dg} = \frac{1}{t'}. \tag{10}$$

Between stock equilibria, an increase in g induces a money stock change that continues until budget balance is restored. That is, y must increase until $t' \, dy = dg$. Thus, (10) is the multiplier endogenous adjustment of the money stock.

We can calculate the effect of an increase in g on the money stock by expanding equation (9) to the stock equilibrium condition

$$g - t[y(M, g)] = 0. \tag{11}$$

The total differential of this equilibrium condition is

$$dg - t' \frac{\partial y}{\partial M} dM - t' \frac{\partial y}{\partial g} dg = 0.$$

This gives us, for dM/dg:

$$\frac{dM}{dg} = \frac{1 - t' \dfrac{\partial y}{\partial g}}{t' \dfrac{\partial y}{\partial M}}. \tag{12}$$

If $t'(\partial y/\partial g) < 1$, this is positive. How should we interpret this condition? If $t'(\partial y/\partial g) < 1$, the increase in g results in a budget deficit in the short-run equilibrium. The expression $t'(\partial y/\partial g)$ is simply the short-run increase in tax revenue resulting from the increase in y following upon the increase in g, holding M constant. Thus, in the normal circumstance in which an increase in g, from an initial position of budget balance, leads to a budget deficit, M rises, giving a further increase in y. This case is illustrated in Figure 21-4.

There the increase in g raises y^* from y_0^* to y_2^*, with the increase given by the fiscal policy multiplier (10). In the short-run equilibrium, income rises from y_0^* to y_1, with the increase given by the short-run multiplier $\partial y/\partial g$ of (3). This leaves a budget deficit at point 1; so the money stock increases, and the LM curve shifts out until the full stock equilibrium is reached at point 2, where $y = y_2^*$. The increase in the money stock is given by the multiplier of equation (12), including the assumption of Figure 21-4 that $y_1 < y_2^*$ implies $dM/dg > 0$.

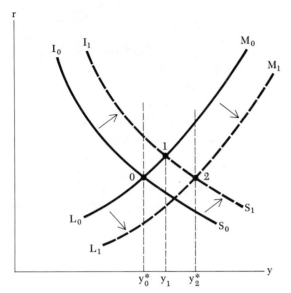

Figure 21-4 Effect of increase in g.

In Chapter 16 we saw that under some very special conditions an increase in g could lead to a budget surplus in the short run. In that case the short-run equilibrium point 1 in Figure 21-4 would be to the *right* of y_2^*, and the money stock would *decrease* in the movement to equilibrium. This case would imply $t'(\partial y/\partial g) > 1$, and $dM/dg < 0$ in equation (12).

This initial look at the stock-adjustment mechanism in the simplest case uncovers one channel of dynamic adjustment from the short-run equilibrium toward a stock equilibrium, which is the balanced growth path of Part V. It is instructive because it shows the longer run dynamic implications of short-run stabilization policy. Even in this simplest model, the possibility of instability (and runaway inflation) appear. Thus, even at this early stage there is a message of caution for policy: look to the implicit dynamics created by the effects of short-run policy. We now go on to complicate the story.

INTRODUCTION OF WEALTH EFFECTS

In the simple model we have been using to analyze the stock-adjustment dynamics of a money-financed budget imbalance, there were no assets or wealth effects in the demand functions of the system. The money finance model was the skeletal model of Chapter 9, in which the only source of dynamic adjustment was through the money supply. The restriction placed on the use of this model by the absence of wealth effects can be seen if one tries to use it to analyze the case of a bond-financed deficit. Suppose the economy is in an initial equilibrium position such as r_0, y_0 of Figure 21-5, with $y_0 < y^*$ so the budget is in deficit. We saw above that if the deficit is money-financed, the *LM* curve will shift out, moving y_0 toward y^* and eliminating the deficit. But if the deficit is financed by bond sales, there is no movement in either the *IS* or *LM* curve in the skeletal model of Chapter 9, and therefore no movement of y. Without wealth effects in the system, the growth of government debt in the hands of the public would continue indefinitely, seemingly with no effect on private behavior, as expressed by the demand functions of the model.

This implausible lack of dynamic adjustment simply results from an attempt to use the skeletal money finance model to analyze a problem for which it is unsuited. To study the case of bond finance of budget imbalances, we need to move to a model including wealth effects, an extension of the model of Chapter 16.

Wealth Effects in the *IS* Curve

In Chapter 12 we introduced wealth into the *IS* curve through the consumption function. Net real wealth a was defined there [equation (45), p. 278] as the sum of the real values of equity K, government debt B, and reserves R:

$$a = \frac{K + B + R}{P}. \tag{13}$$

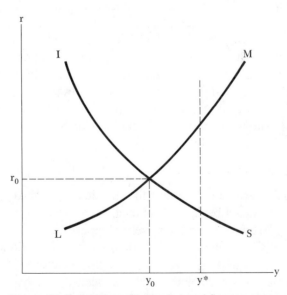

Figure 21-5 Initial equilibrium in bond-finance case.

Real wealth a enters the consumption function positively, so that now

$$c = c(y - t(y), a); \qquad \frac{\partial c}{\partial a} > 0.$$

With real assets in the consumption function, an increase in R or B financing an initial budget deficit as shown at r_0, y_0 in Figure 21-5 will shift the IS curve out. As the public's net worth rises, consumer spending goes up, increasing demand and output at the initial level of the interest rate.

Inclusion of real assets in the consumption function, as in Chapter 12, thus adds a channel of dynamic adjustment to the skeletal model. If the economy begins with an initial equilibrium $y_0 < y^*$ as in Figure 21-5, the growth of real assets through money finance *or* bond finance of the deficit will shift IS out, moving y toward y^* and reducing the deficit. Inversely, if the initial $y > y^*$, the budget surplus will be reducing a, either through shrinkage of the money stock or retirement of government debt, shifting IS left. This will again move y toward y^*, this time reducing the surplus.

In the money finance case, the additional channel of wealth effects in the IS curve adds to the dynamic stability of adjustment. With both LM and IS shifting in the same direction with budget imbalance, the key partial derivative in the stability condition (6), $\partial y / \partial M$, is greater than in the skeletal model.

The wealth effect in the IS curve also contributes to stability in the bond finance case. In the initial equilibrium of Figure 21-5, the budget is in deficit since $y_0 < y^*$. As bond finance of the deficit increases a, it shifts IS right, moving y toward y^*. If the initial equilibrium $ISLM$ intersection had been right of y^*, so $y_0 > y^*$, the surplus would reduce a through debt retirement, again moving y toward y^*. Thus, the IS channel of wealth effects contributes to a stable dynamic process in both cases. We will look at the bond finance case more closely after we introduce wealth effects into the LM curve.

Wealth Effects in the *LM* Curve

Whether wealth effects play a role in the LM sector is a subject of uncertainty in monetary economics. A strict transactions demand view of the demand for money will omit wealth effects from the LM curve. This is the case, for example, in the MPS model's financial sector. On the other hand, the portfolio-balance approach to the demand for money will include wealth effects on the LM curve. This can be seen in Tobin's model of the financial sector. The crucial question is whether or not wealth, or assets A, enters the demand function for money. If the answer is positive, as is the case in Tobin's view, then *how* a deficit is financed—by bond or money issue—becomes potentially very important for the dynamic behavior of the economy through its effects on the

LM curve. If the answer is no, as in the MPS model, the composition of financing is a less important question.

In the portfolio-balance model of Chapter 14, asset-holders distribute their demands across the available menu of assets, optimizing a risk-return trade-off. Money enters the portfolio-demand problem as the riskless asset. While money earns no return, it also offers no risk of capital loss, compared to other assets such as bonds or equities. Thus, inclusion of money in the total portfolio reduces overall risk. In the portfolio-balance approach, individuals with a given total wealth or assets express a demand for each asset that depends on risk estimates, the rates of return on all the assets, and total wealth. As wealth increases, the demand for all assets, including money, increases.

As an example of the portfolio-balance approach, let us look at a model with three assets, equities K, bonds B, and reserves or "outside money" R. These sum to total wealth A. The rate of return on equities is r_k and that on bonds is r_b. The equilibrium conditions determining r_k and r_b can then be written as follows:

Supply   Demand

$$\frac{R}{P} = m\left(r_k, r_b, y, \frac{A}{P}\right); \tag{14}$$

$$\frac{B}{P} = b\left(r_k, r_b, y, \frac{A}{P}\right); \tag{15}$$

$$\frac{K}{P} = k\left(r_k, r_b, y, \frac{A}{P}\right). \tag{16}$$

The sum of asset demands is constrained to equal total wealth, as given in equation (13),

$$A = R + B + K.$$

Given this balance-sheet constraint, there are just two independent demand equations in (14)–(16): holding equilibrium amounts of any two assets implies holding an equilibrium amount of the third.

From our point of view the important feature of this model is the inclusion of $A/P \equiv a$ in the money demand function (14). As total assets a increase, the demand for money rises. In general, this gives us an expanded money market equilibrium condition:

$$\frac{M}{P} = m(r, y, a); \qquad 0 < \frac{\partial m}{\partial a} < 1. \tag{17}$$

As a increases, the demand for money rises, but by less than the original wealth increase. Why? Because the wealth increase is spread across all the assets.

Now consider the effect of an increase in A, due to a budget deficit, on the LM curve through (17). If the deficit is money-financed, the *supply of money* goes up by ΔM, while the *demand* goes up by $(\partial m / \partial a) < \Delta M$. Since $\partial m / \partial a < 1$, the increase in M causes excess supply in the money market, shifting the LM curve down for a given value of y. But if the deficit is bond-financed, the supply of money is unchanged, while the demand rises by $(\partial m / \partial a) < \Delta B$. This results in excess demand in the money market, shifting the LM curve up. Thus, in the portfolio-balance model with wealth on the money demand function, *money finance* of the deficit shifts LM *down; bond finance* shifts LM up. This is illustrated in Figure 21-6. An initial position of budget surplus would reverse the movement of LM; reduction of M would shift LM up, while $\Delta B < 0$ would shift it down.

Inclusion of wealth effects in the LM curve does not change qualitatively the dynamics of the money finance case; IS and LM both shift out. But in the bond finance case, LM shifts up (or left) while IS shifts out. The possibility of instability in this case should be clear. We will come back to this after considering the argument against wealth effects in LM.

Consider a financial system that includes assets that are virtually riskless but yield a return, such as savings account deposits or treasury bills. In the case of savings account deposits there may be limitations in the frequency of withdrawal; for treasury bills there are small fluctuations in market prices. But these risk elements are very small compared to long debt or equities. In a system with a riskless asset earning a return, money is "dominated" by the other riskless assets. There is no portfolio-balancing demand for money since

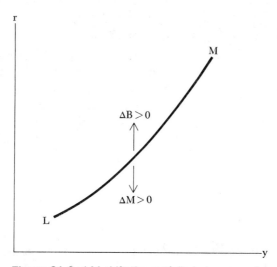

Figure 21-6 LM shifts in portfolio-balance model.

the other asset plays money's risk-reducing role *and* yields a higher overall rate of return.

In this situation, the demand for money is reduced to a pure transactions basis. As shown in Chapter 14, the transactions demand is responsive to the interest rate on the dominating riskless asset, which is the opportunity cost of holding money. But rates of return on other risky assets are then not relevant for money demand. The portfolio decision is split into two: money demand as a function of the rate of return on the other riskless asset, and demands for other assets dependent on the whole sector of returns and total wealth less money. As wealth increases in this case, all of the increased demand goes to nonmonetary assets since money is dominated by the riskless asset for portfolio-balancing purposes.

In this pure transactions demand model, we would exclude A/P from the demand functions (14) and (17). This would imply in the portfolio-balance model specified in equations (13)–(16) that $\partial b/\partial a + \partial k/\partial a = 1$. In addition, only the rates of return on the dominating asset and income would enter the demand function for money. Then with P and y given from the "real" sector and M fixed by the Fed, our standard money market equilibrium condition

$$\frac{M}{P} = m(r, y)$$

would determine r. Movements in wealth would not shift the LM curve in this pure-transactions model.

To summarize, in a model with a strict transactions basis for the demand for money, there are no wealth effects on the LM curve. But if we go to the portfolio-balance model, wealth effects enter the LM curve. In this case, an increase in the money stock shifts LM down (or right), and an increase in government debt shifts LM up (or left).

The empirical evidence, as summarized by Stephen M. Goldfeld, favors the transactions demand model. Once income is included in the money demand function, it is hard empirically to detect an independent role for wealth. This result is in sharp contrast with the empirical evidence on wealth effects on the *IS* curve. Through the consumption function, it is clear that an increase in real assets a shifts *IS* out. For our purposes here, the results of this balance of empirical evidence are two: (1) in the extended model of Chapter 16 we include wealth effects in *IS* but not *LM*, and (2) with bond finance of a deficit in the following analysis we assume the *IS* shift dominates the *LM* shift, so that y increases as B increases.

BOND FINANCE OF THE DEFICIT AND CROWDING OUT

With wealth effects in the *IS* and *LM* curves, we can now look more carefully at the dynamic effects of bond finance of an unbalanced budget. Taking the Tobin model of equations (13)–(16) as our starting point, we can see that the short-run equilibrium level of y now depends on all the stocks in the system. So equation (2), for equilibrium income with M the only stock in the system, is replaced by

$$y = y(M, B, g; K).$$ (18)

As before, $\partial y/\partial M > 0$. Both the IS and LM curves shift right as M increases. In addition, we still have $\partial y/\partial g > 0$ through the usual fiscal policy multiplier. But following from our discussion of wealth effects on IS and LM, the sign of $\partial y/\partial B$ is unclear. An increase in B shifts the IS curve right. If the demand for money has a pure-transactions basis, then there are no wealth effects on LM, so $\partial y/\partial B > 0$. This is illustrated in Figure 21-7. There the initial income level $y_0 < y^*$, where the budget would be balanced. At y_0 the budget is in deficit, and with bond finance the B stock is increasing. In the pure-transactions model, only the IS curve is shifting under these circumstances. Thus, $\partial y/\partial B > 0$ and y increases toward y^*.

If there are wealth effects on LM, as in the portfolio-balance model, an increase in the stock of government debt will shift LM up (or left), giving an unclear result for movement in y. This is illustrated in Figure 21-8, with both IS and LM shifting. With LM shifting up, there is a clear possibility that y could fall from y_0 as the B stock increases. The effects on investment from rising interest rates could more than offset the effects on consumption from rising wealth. In this case, $\partial y/\partial B < 0$. Thus, the central question with bond finance of a deficit is whether or not the rise in public debt B increases income y, moving y_0 toward y^*.

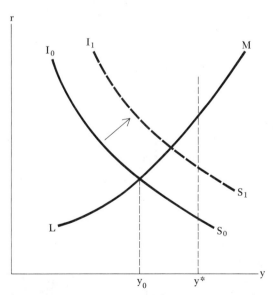

Figure 21-7 Bond finance with no wealth effects in LM.

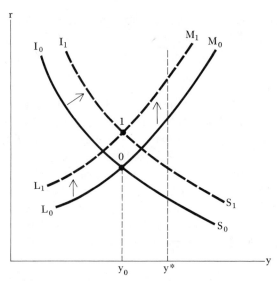

Figure 21-8   Bond finance with wealth effects in *LM*.

Stability of Dynamic Adjustment

With bond finance of budget imbalances, the movement in the bond stock is given by

$$\frac{dB}{dt} \equiv DB = Pd = P\{g - t[y(M, B, g; K)]\}. \tag{19}$$

If the deficit d is positive, B is increasing and vice versa. Again if we hold P constant for simplification, we see that this system is stable if

$$\frac{\partial(DB)}{\partial B} = -Pt'\frac{\partial y}{\partial B} < 0, \tag{20}$$

with bond finance of the budget imbalance. Clearly then, the condition for stability of the stock-adjustment process is $\partial y/\partial B > 0$. If this holds, when $y_0 < y^*$ and B is increasing, the rise in B moves y toward y^* where the deficit is eliminated and B comes to rest. But if $\partial y/\partial B < 0$, the initial deficit reduces y and increases the deficit, leading the system away from equilibrium. Thus, $\partial y/\partial B > 0$ is essential for stability of stock-adjustment dynamics with bond finance. This is the basic presumption from the MPS model and Goldfeld's empirical results.

Effects of Fiscal Policy

The stock equilibrium effects of a change in government spending g are the same with bond finance as with money finance. The stock equilibrium condition again is that the real deficit is zero, so that $DB = 0$. This gives us equations (9) and (10) for changes in y^* following changes in g, regardless of the method of finance. In both cases,

$$\frac{dy^*}{dg} = \frac{1}{t'}.$$

The difference between the two cases is in the potential instability of dynamic adjustment. While the change in long-run equilibrium y^* is the same with money finance and bond finance, in the latter case the economy might move away from the equilibrium, rather than converging toward it. This possibility is shown in Figure 21-9. At the initial full equilibrium point 0, with $y = y_0^*$, g is increased. This shifts IS to $I_1 S_1$ and y^* to y_1^*. The IS shift increases y to y_1, where there is a budget deficit. As the deficit increases B, if $\partial y/\partial B < 0$, so the system is unstable, y begins to fall from y_1, moving away from y_1^*. This is shown in the movement from equilibrium point 1 to 2, with LM shifting more than IS as B increases. Thus, while the movement in the long-run equilibrium y^* following a change in g may be independent of the method of financing, whether the economy moves toward the equilibrium can depend crucially on financing. Under the MPS–Goldfeld results, stability is ensured; with the Tobin model it is not.

Crowding Out of Investment By Deficit Spending

The potentially negative effect on equilibrium income of a bond-financed budget deficit is one version of a phenomenon labeled *crowding out* in the recent literature. In general, the term *crowding out* refers to the tendency for an increase in government spending, or a tax cut, to reduce private investment.

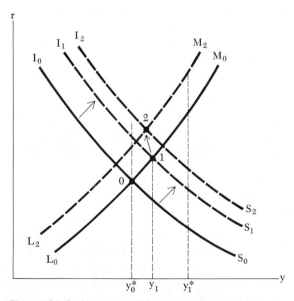

Figure 21-9 Unstable adjustment with g increase.

This tends to offset the effects of the original increase in g, or cut in t, on y. The potentially destabilizing effects of bond finance are one type of dynamic crowding out. Here we summarize the various aspects of crowding out which we have seen in this text, following the taxonomy set by Willem H. Buiter.

At the simplest level, crowding out appears on the demand side of the static model of Chapter 5; an increase in g raises r, reducing investment. We saw in Chapter 5 that the multiplier for g is smaller when we endogenize the interest rate than when it is held exogenous. In Chapter 16, the *monetarist* model provides an example of full crowding out on the demand side. With a vertical *LM* curve, an increase in g pulls up the interest rate enough to provide an offsetting decrease in i: $i' \Delta r = -\Delta g$. This is a first stage of crowding out, which determines how far the aggregate demand curve shifts for a given Δg.

The second level of crowding out involves the aggregate supply curve and the price reaction to the shift in demand. Suppose the economy follows the basic model on the demand side so that an increase in g shifts the aggregate-demand curve, but combine this with the classical supply model of Chapter 6, with $p' = 1$, or the new classical model of Chapter 11. In this case, the aggregate supply curve is vertical, and the increase in demand simply pulls the price level up enough to restore the original equilibrium value of y. With the basic demand-side model and a vertical aggregate supply curve, the price increase following the shift in aggregate demand raises the interest rate enough that again $i' \Delta r = -\Delta g$ and the fiscal policy increase is fully crowded out.

Above we have introduced a third level of crowding out. In Figure 21-9, the movement from equilibrium position 0 to position 1, with the implicit background change in the price level, reflects partial crowding out at the first two levels. The initiating increase in g moves income from y_0^* to y_1, where there is a budget deficit. Here the third level of dynamic crowding out comes in. If the *LM* shift from point 1 due to $DB > 0$ exceeds the *IS* shift, investment is reduced more than consumption is increased by *DB*, and y falls. If the *IS* shift exceeds the *LM* shift, y increases toward y_1^* where $dB = 0$. The effect of *DB* on the *LM* curve is to crowd out investment by raising the interest rate r, thus tending to reduce y. As Buiter aptly puts it, this is balanced by a "crowding in" effect on consumption as *DB* increases wealth. Only if the investment effect outweighs the consumption effect is the result an unstable net crowding out in the dynamic model.

INTERACTION BETWEEN THE GOVERNMENT BUDGET AND THE BALANCE OF PAYMENTS

The dynamic mechanism in the money finance case of Figure 21-2 is the budget deficit feeding the money stock. As long as the budget is out of balance, the money stock is changing, moving the *LM* curve. In the money finance case of Figure 21-2, movement of the *ISLM* intersection is toward the equilibrium value y^*, where the budget is balanced and $DM = 0$.

This adjustment mechanism has a close analogue in the relationship between the balance of payments and the money stock in a fixed exchange rate regime. As we saw in Chapter 17, if the balance of payments B is not zero, the money stock will tend to move, depending on the degree of sterilization by the monetary authorities. (Here we use B to represent balance of payments. Since we are discussing money finance cases, this should not cause any confusion with the previous B = bonds notation.) Thus, in Figure 17-6, as long as the balance of payments B is nonzero, the money stock moves the *ISLM* intersection toward the *BP* curve where $B = 0$. So we now have two dynamic adjustment mechanisms moving the money stock: the government deficit and the balance-of-payments surplus.

Money Stock Adjustment

Both the balance of payments and the government deficit move the money stock. Thus, in the open-economy, fixed exchange rate model, the rate of change of the money stock is given by

$$DM = P[g - t(y)] + B = Pd + B. \qquad (21)$$

A budget deficit, $d > 0$, or a balance-of-payments surplus, $B > 0$, contributes to $DM > 0$, so the money stock increases. There are clearly two kinds of possibilities for full equilibrium.

The least restricted equilibrium is one in which $Pd = -B$, so that any payments imbalance is just offset by a government imbalance, and $DM = 0$. Adjustment to this equilibrium is illustrated in Figure 21-10. At the initial equilibrium point r_0, y_0, international payments are in balance ($B = 0$), but the government budget is in deficit ($Pd > 0$). Thus, at r_0, y_0, the money stock is increasing and *IS* and *LM* are shifting right. As the money stock rises, the budget deficit shrinks, and a balance-of-payments deficit develops. The budget deficit increases M, while the payments deficit reduces it. As M increases and the *ISLM* intersection moves to the right, a point is reached where the budget deficit just equals the payments deficit: $Pd = -B$. At that point, illustrated by y_1, in Figure 21-10, $DM = 0$ and equilibrium is reached, in the sense that the money stock M is no longer increasing.

This equilibration mechanism is illustrated in Figure 21-11, which is coordinated with Figure 21-10. At the initial value of M, M_0, which positions $I_0 S_0$ and $L_0 M_0$ in Figure 21-10, the budget deficit is $-Pd_0$, and international payments are in balance with $-B = 0$. As M increases since $DM > 0$, the budget deficit shrinks along $Pd(M)$ and a balance-of-payments deficit appears along $-B(M)$. At M_1, where the two curves cross, $Pd_1 = -B_1$, and the system is in equilibrium.

The equilibrium of Figures 21-10 and 21-11 is an odd one, however. At y_1 the money stock is constant because the balance-of-payments deficit just

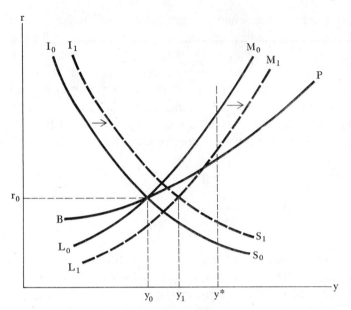

Figure 21-10   Adjustment with budget and payments imbalances.

matches the government budget deficit. Money is flowing *into* the domestic private sector at a rate given by Pd_1, and an equal amount is flowing *out* at the rate $-B_1$. Thus, at the y_1, M_1 equilibrium of Figures 21-10 and 21-11, foreign asset holders are accumulating home money at the rate B. This is a situation that cannot continue indefinitely, since the accumulation of home

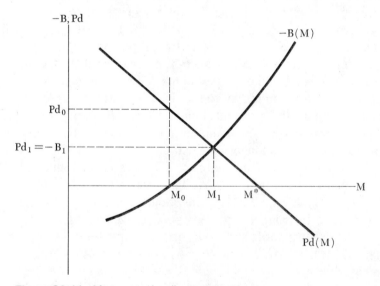

Figure 21-11   Money stock adjustment.

money in the portfolios of foreign asset holders will unbalance their portfolios. Eventually, this growing unbalance of dollar holdings will lead to increasing selling pressure in the foreign exchange markets. At some point reserve losses will force the Central Bank—the Fed if the United States is the "home country" in the example—to permit the exchange rate e to fall, devaluing the home currency. This could be managed in a gradual way, or the adjustment could come in one large jump if the Fed were to float the dollar. In either case, the devaluation shifts the BP line down in Figure 21-10, moving the equilibrium position to an equilibrium where $Pd = -B = 0$.

Exchange Rate Adjustment

Exchange rate adjustment from the temporary equilibrium position y_1, M_1 is shown in Figures 21-12 and 21-13, which extend 21-10 and 21-11. In Chapter 17 we saw that as the exchange rate e falls, the BP curve of Figure 21-12 shifts down. This reduces the payments deficit at the initial equilibrium y_1, making $DM > 0$ since now $Pd_1 > -B$. With $DM > 0$ the IS and LM curves begin to shift to the right, as shown in Figure 21-12, reducing the budget deficit. Movement of all three curves continues until a full stock equilibrium intersection of IS, LM, and BP is reached at y_2. There the budget deficit and the payments

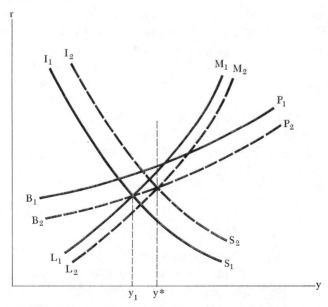

Figure 21-12 Interaction of exchange rate and money stock adjustment.

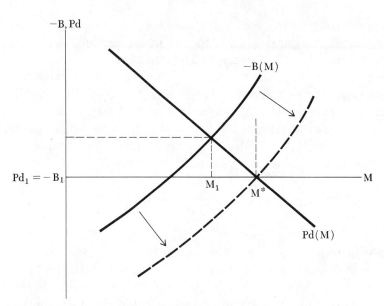

Figure 21-13 Exchange rate adjustment.

balance are both zero, and the money stock is at rest. The condition that the real deficit is zero in full equilibrium determines the y value, y^*:

$$0 = g - t(y^*).$$

Given y^* and, in the background, equilibrium values of the price level P and interest rate r, the exchange rate adjusts to an equilibrium value e^* where $B = 0$ and the BP curve passes through the $ISLM$ intersection at y^*.

Adjustment of the money stock to the M^* value where IS and LM intersect at y^* is shown in Figure 21-13. As the exchange rate falls, the balance-of-payments deficit for any given value of the money stock falls, shifting the $-B(M)$ curve in Figure 21-13 down. The exchange rate falls until the $-B(M)$ curve intersects $Pd(M)$ at M^*, where both $y = y^*$ and $Pd = -B = 0$. Thus, the system reaches a full equilibrium vector y^*, M^*, e^*, with background values of r and P, both the payments balance and budget deficit at zero, and the money stock constant.

A GENERAL VIEW OF ASSET STOCK ADJUSTMENT

This chapter has studied the dynamics implicit in budget imbalance and international payments imbalance for movement of an initial short-run equilibrium to a full stock equilibrium. Thus, we have focused on adjustment of financial stocks, B and M. In Chapter 13, we discussed investment as the mechanism that moves the capital stock toward a desired, or equilibrium, value corresponding to a desired capital-output ratio. Here we will simply sketch the full system of stock-adjustment dynamics that leads a stable economy from an initial short-run equilibrium with asset stocks arbitrarily given by history to a balanced growth path with all stocks growing at the same rate. These are the growth paths that are studied in Part V.

We can aggregate the stocks in the economy into four categories: money M, government debt B, capital K, and net foreign assets F. At any point in time, the initial values of M, B, K, and F are given by history. They, along with other parameters such as the level of government purchases and the tax structure $t(y)$, determine short-run equilibrium values for the interest rate r, income y (and from the supply curve P, and the production function N), and the exchange rate e. This is the short-run equilibrium solution of Part III. But the short-run solution for y, r, and e also determines investment, which is the rate of change of the capital stock K, the government deficit, which is $DM + DB$, and the current account in the balance of payments, which is DF with flexible exchange rates. Thus, the short-run equilibrium solution determines the rates of change of the initially given stock variables. This is summarized schematically in Figure 21-14. There we see the stock-adjustment system as a feedback loop, essentially a system of first-order differential equations. The stocks and other parameters determine, through the short-run equilibrium system, their own rates of change, which then feed back to move the stocks and the short-run equilibrium through time.

In this chapter, we looked at the financial aspect of this adjustment process. In general, if the entire system is stable, it will move the economy from an arbitrarily given set of initial stocks toward the balanced growth paths of Part V.

Another useful view of this system can be achieved by looking at the IS equation as an equilibrium condition for accumulation. Writing the IS equilibrium condition with only S on the left-hand side, we have

$$S = I + (G - T) + (X - M). \tag{22}$$

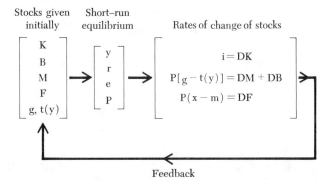

Figure 21-14 Stock adjustment system.

In Parts II and III, we concentrated on the flow, or goods-market equilibrium aspect of the *IS* equation. But translating from Figure 21-14, we can also see it as an accumulation equilibrium condition:

$$DA = DK + DB + DM + DF. \tag{23}$$

Saving is the growth in *demand* for total assets *A*. The items on the right-hand side of (23) are the growth in *supply* of the various categories of assets summing to *A*. Investment is the growth in supply of *K*. The government deficit and the financing decision control growth in supply of *B* and *M*. The current account balance is the growth in supply of *F* with flexible rates; with Fed intervention in exchange markets $(X - M)$ is split between *DF* and *DM*.

Thus, the short-run equilibrium solution on the *IS* curve determines values for (y, r, e) such that the desired growth in total assets $(S = DA)$ is just equal to the growth in supply of these assets. If the system is stable, this pattern of accumulation will take the economy to a growth path where all asset stocks grow at about the same rate. This is the growth path that is described in Chapter 22, and analyzed in Part V.

SELECTED READINGS

A. S. Blinder and R. M. Solow, "Does Fiscal Policy Matter?" *Journal of Public Economics,* November 1973.

W. H. Branson and R. L. Teigen, "Flow and Stock Equilibrium in a Dynamic Metzler Model," *Journal of Finance,* December 1976.

W. H. Buiter, " 'Crowding Out' and the Effectiveness of Fiscal Policy," *Journal of Public Economics,* July 1977.

C. F. Christ, "On Fiscal and Monetary Policies and the Government Budget Restraint," *American Economic Review,* September 1979.

S. M. Goldfeld, "The Demand for Money Revisited," *Brookings Papers on Economic Activity,* vol. 3, 1973.

D. J. Ott and A. Ott, "Budget Balance and Equilibrium Income," *Journal of Finance,* March 1965.

W. L. Silber, "Fiscal Policy in IS-LM Analysis: A Correction," *Journal of Money, Credit and Banking,* November 1970.

G. Smith, "Monetarism, Bondism, and Inflation," *Journal of Money, Credit and Banking,* May 1982.

J. Tobin, "A General Equilibrium Approach to Monetary Theory," *Journal of Money, Credit and Banking,* February 1969.

J. Tobin and W. H. Buiter, "Long Run Effects of Fiscal and Monetary Policy on Aggregate Demand," in J. L. Stein, ed., *Monetarism* (Amsterdam: North-Holland, 1976).

chapter 22

Trend Growth in the Static Model

By introducing such factors as wage and price inflation, growth in labor productivity, and accumulation of financial assets into the Part II model of income determination, Chapters 19–21 have taken us away from a purely static model of the economy to a more dynamic view. In Part V we analyze growth models that *assume* that aggregate demand policy keeps demand equal to potential output. This justifies concentration on movements of the *potential* output path in growth models.

In this chapter we pull together strands from Chapters 19–21 to analyze movements of policy variables such as government purchases, tax rates, money supply, and budget deficit d that are needed to keep aggregate demand equal to potential output as the latter grows. We take as given the growth path of potential output—that's the subject of Part V—and ask what configurations or combinations of policy variables will keep demand growing on the same path?

The relationship between actual and potential output is shown in Figure 22-1, which reproduces Figure 1-1(a). The potential line in Figure 22-1 shows the economy's potential output path, which is fairly smooth given the trend growth of labor force and productivity. This is also the *trend path* of full-employment output. It gives the level of output that could be attained at any given time with the unemployment rate at the NAIRU, u_n, of about 5 percent in the 1960s and 6 percent in the 1980s, and labor productivity at its trend value.

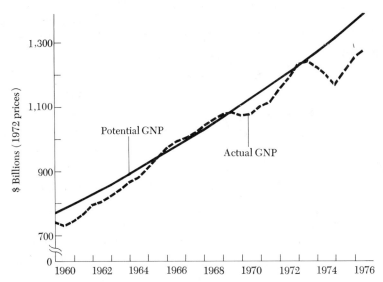

Figure 22-1 Actual and potential GNP.

The actual output line in Figure 22-1 shows actual measured real GNP. When actual output is below potential, unemployment is above u_n and real output is lost. When actual output is above potential, as in 1968–1969 when the unemployment rate fell below 3.5 percent, additional output above potential is gained, but only at the cost of a rate of inflation that is widely thought to be unacceptable. The potential output path in Figure 22-1, then, does not represent an absolute physical maximum of level of output. Rather, it gives the level of output associated with the NAIRU of about 6 percent in the 1980s. Thus, the potential output path of Figure 22-1 can also be considered as a feasible trend path for actual output; monetary and fiscal policies should be set to maintain actual output as close to potential output as possible.

The stabilization policy measures discussed in Parts II and III are steps that can be taken to close the gap between the potential and actual output paths and maintain actual output near its potential level. Of course, when we considered time lags in Part III we recognized that once an output gap appeared, movement toward the trend line cannot be instantaneous and complete. But the static model has shown how manipulation of such variables as government purchases, tax rates, or the money supply can close the gap between actual and potential output. Thus, if investment or consumer expenditure falls below its trend level associated with potential output and income, the government can take fiscal or monetary policy steps to counterbalance the effects of that exogenous drop in investment or consumer expenditure to keep the level of output up to its potential.

In Part V we assume that the government is doing its stabilization job well. That is, it is reasonably successful in keeping the economy growing close to the trend, or potential output, line. There will be, of course, fluctuations around the trend line. Consumption and investment will fluctuate around their trend levels, and fiscal and monetary policy will react only with a lag. But when private demand deviates from its trend level, we assume that the government responds well enough to correct the deviations within a reasonable period, say, a year. Thus, *on average,* the actual growth path of the economy is represented by the trend line.

Assuming this, our interest in Chapters 23–27 is focused on what determines the nature of the trend line: How are its slope and height determined? How can the economy move from one trend line to another? In other words, what determines the potential rate and level of growth of the economy?

Before taking up these questions, we summarize the *long-run trend* nature of fiscal and monetary policy that will keep the economy growing along the trend path. To repeat, in the short run there will always be fluctuations in private demand—higher or lower levels of investment or consumption—which require higher or lower levels of government spending, tax rates, or money supply to maintain actual output close to potential. But *on average,* over the long run, monetary and fiscal policy will exhibit certain *trend* characteristics as the economy grows along its trend path.

ASSUMPTIONS UNDERLYING TREND GROWTH

As the economy grows along its full-employment trend path, the government's monetary and fiscal policy variables will be moving to counteract changes in private demand. To find the required trends in these policy variables, we assume that the economy grows along a path with the unemployment rate at some given average level, perhaps 6 percent, which we define as *full employment.*

To describe the trends in monetary and fiscal policy variables along the full-employment path, we make some further assumptions, each of which, as we see in Chapter 23, is roughly consistent with the historical facts.

1. Interest rates are trendless, that is, they fluctuate around some mean level.
2. The rates of labor force growth, $\dot{L} = [(dL/dt)/L]$, and of average labor-productivity growth, $\dot{y/L} = [(d(y/L)/dt)/(y/L)]$, are fairly steady.
3. The capital-output ratio, K/y, is roughly constant.
4. The relative shares of labor and capital in output are roughly constant.

Here we are switching from a focus on employment N to the labor force L. If the unemployment rate u is constant, both N and L will grow at the same rate. The unemployment rate u is defined as

$$u = \frac{U}{L} = \frac{L-N}{L} = 1 - \frac{N}{L}, \tag{1}$$

where U is the number of persons unemployed. Thus, if u is constant, the employment rate, N/L, is constant, and N and L both grow at the same rate $\dot{L}$.

In this chapter, we explore the implications of these "facts" for equilibrium growth in the static model. Then in Chapter 23 we begin to explain why these are indeed the facts, in the context of growth models. To draw the implications of balanced growth for static equilibrium, we examine first the labor market to find the implied rate of growth of output, wages, and prices on average along trend. Then we find the average growth rate of the money supply that will keep the money market in equilibrium with real income growing and the price level rising, and interest rates remaining constant along trend. Finally, we see what full-employment product market equilibrium implies for the average level of the government deficit and debt.

TREND GROWTH OF OUTPUT AND PRICES

Our assumptions concerning the growth rates of the labor force and productivity can be combined to give the growth rate of potential output. We can define potential output as average labor force productivity y/L times the total labor force L:

$$y = \frac{y}{L} \cdot L. \tag{2}$$

Taking logarithms of equation (2) gives us

$$\ln y = \ln \frac{y}{L} + \ln L,$$

and differentiation with respect to time gives us the potential growth rate equation

$$\dot{y} = \dot{y/L} + \dot{L}, \tag{3}$$

where $\dot{x}$ is the percentage rate of growth of x:

$$\dot{x} \equiv \frac{dx/dt}{x}.$$

Thus, the two assumptions give us the rate of growth of potential output. In the United States, in the 1980s, with total productivity growing along trend at about 1.0 percent per year and available work-hours in the labor force growing at 1.5 percent, the growth rate of potential output y was about 2.5 percent.

As we saw in Chapter 17 the assumption that relative shares remain constant along trend implies that the rate of growth of the price level is equal to the rate of growth of the money wage rate less that of productivity,

$$\dot{P} = \dot{W} - y/L. \tag{4}$$

The rate of growth of productivity is given by assumption 2 above. The rate of growth of wages and prices depends on demand growth, as we saw in Chapter 20. With the unemployment rate at the NAIRU, any steady rate of inflation is possible. For the late 1980s, a rate of wage growth of about 4 percent seems to be a reasonable possibility. Thus, with productivity growing at about 1 percent, we could expect $\dot{P}$ to be about 3 percent along trend, with relative shares remaining constant.

Nominal GNP Growth

Adding the growth rate of real output y to the growth rate of prices P, we can obtain the trend growth rate of money GNP, Y. Since $Y = y \cdot P$, we have

$$\dot{Y} = \dot{y} + \dot{P}. \tag{5}$$

Substituting the equation (3) expression for trend $\dot{y}$ and equation (4) for trend $\dot{P}$ gives us

$$\dot{Y} = y/L + \dot{L} + \dot{W} - y/L = \dot{L} + \dot{W}. \tag{6}$$

Along trend, with relative shares constant, the growth rate of nominal GNP will be the sum of the rates of growth of the labor force, $\dot{L}$, and of the money wage rate, $\dot{W}$. From equation (4) the money wage growth rate that maintains constancy of relative shares is

$$\dot{W} = \dot{P} + y/L, \tag{7}$$

so that the $\dot{W}$ term in equation (6) simply represents productivity growth plus the rate of increase of prices, and the $\dot{L}$ term adds in the rate of growth of the labor force.

If zero inflation were attained, so that $\dot{Y} = \dot{y}$, the rate of growth of money wages would simply represent productivity growth. Thus, with zero inflation,

$$\dot{Y} = \dot{L} + y/L = \dot{y}. \tag{8}$$

Equilibrium Growth on the Supply Side

Equations (3) and (4), which give the growth rates of output and the price level along the potential GNP path, can be conveniently interpreted as the conditions for equilibrium growth on the supply side. Given the growth rates of the labor force and productivity, equation (3) shows the growth rate of output that will maintain constant employment and unemployment rates. The assumed unemployment rate then fixes the rate at which wage rates increase—the rate at which the labor-supply curve shifts up.

With the *rate of growth of output* which will maintain a given rate of unemployment and the *rate at which the labor supply curve shifts up* both fixed, equation (4) gives the rate of increase of the price level, P, that will keep the supply side of the economy in equilibrium. The next step in the analysis of trend growth in the static model is to determine the monetary and fiscal policies that will shift the economy's demand curve out along trend at just the rate that will maintain both demand and supply equilibrium along the growth path of y and P described by equations (3) and (4).

The problem is illustrated in Figure 22-2 (which is essentially the same as the northwest quadrant of Figure 19-8). Starting from an initial equilibrium P_0, y_0 point, where y_0 is potential output at time 0, the growth of the labor force and productivity raise y to y_1 and y_2 in time periods 1 and 2, following equation (3). With unemployment maintained at the NAIRU as y moves to y_1 and y_2, the labor-supply curve shifts up faster than productivity growth, so that the price level must rise from P_0 to P_1 to P_2 to maintain equilibrium on the supply side.

This analysis fixes points 0, 1, and 2 in Figure 22-2 as the equilibrium P,y points on the supply side as y and P grow according to equations (3) and (4). This means that the economy's supply curve is shifting out from $S_0 S_0$ to $S_1 S_1$ to $S_2 S_2$ in Figure 22-2 as the economy grows along trend. The problem

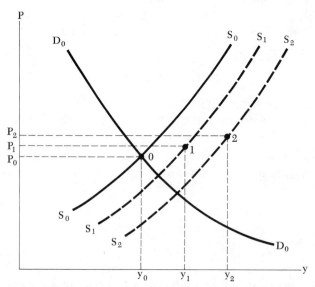

Figure 22-2   Growth of potential output on the supply side.

now is to find the path of the demand-side variables, especially the money supply M and the government budget deficit $d = g - t(y)$, that will shift the demand curve $D_0 D_0$ of Figure 22-2 out just fast enough to pass through points 1 and 2, so that the economy remains in equilibrium as y and P grow according to equations (3) and (4).

TREND GROWTH OF THE MONEY SUPPLY

We will begin on the demand side by finding the trend rate of growth of the money supply that will hold interest rates constant along trend as y and P grow according to equations (3) and (4). Then we can determine the movements of the government's fiscal policy variables that will maintain the product market in equilibrium. These results can then be modified by assuming that interest rates are not constant along trend. This will change the M path and the movement of investment along trend, changing the fiscal policy path that will maintain product market equilibrium.

The equilibrium condition in the money market from Part III is

$$\frac{M}{P} = m(r, y). \qquad (9)$$

In logarithmic form this can be written as

$$\ln \frac{M}{P} = \ln M - \ln P = \alpha_0 + \alpha_1 \ln y - \alpha_2 \ln r, \qquad (10)$$

where α_1 is the long-run elasticity of demand for real balances with respect to changes in real income and α_2 is the elasticity with respect to changes in the interest rate.

In Chapter 14 we suggested that α_1 is about 1.0, and α_2 is about 0.25, so that the money market equilibrium condition is

$$\ln M - \ln P = \alpha_0 + 1.0 \ln y - 0.25 \ln r. \qquad (11)$$

The trend rate of growth of the money supply M that will maintain money market equilibrium as y and P grow according to equations (3) and (4) can be obtained by moving $\ln P$ to the right-hand side of (11) and differentiating with respect to time. This operation gives us

$$\dot{M} = \dot{y} + \dot{P} - 0.25\dot{r}, \qquad (12)$$

for trend growth in the money supply M as y, P, and r all change.

Growth in nominal income, $\dot{y} + \dot{P}$, increases the demand for money. To hold interest rates constant, that is, to hold $\dot{r} = 0$, the money supply must grow at the same rate as nominal income along trend. Thus, if interest rates are roughly constant along trend, the trend growth in the money supply should follow the rule

$$\dot{M} = \dot{Y} = \dot{y} + \dot{P}. \tag{13}$$

If nominal income grows at 5 percent or so along trend, the money supply also must grow at about 5 percent with a unitary income elasticity of demand for money to keep the money market in equilibrium with constant r. This money supply behavior will also hold velocity $v = Y/M$ constant as the economy grows along trend.

Equation (13) gives the growth in the money supply that will shift the *LM* curve of Figure 22-3 out fast enough to maintain money market equilibrium as y grows according to equation (3) with r constant. As y grows at rate $\dot{y}$, the *LM* curve must shift out at the same rate to maintain money market equilibrium at the initial interest rate r_0. To shift the *LM* curve out at that rate, the money supply must grow at the rate $\dot{Y} = \dot{y} + \dot{P}$, given by equation (13), to supply the increased transactions demands stemming from both the P and y increase.

This section has given us the rule for trend growth in the money supply. *To keep the money market in equilibrium at constant—or, more precisely, trendless—interest rates with y and P growing along the trends given by equations (3) and (4), the trend growth rate of the money supply should be about the same as that of nominal GNP.* If the price level grows at about 2 to 3 percent per year, this indicates a trend money supply growth rate of about 5 percent, since $\dot{y}$ is about 2.5 percent. If prices are constant, the money supply should show a trend growth rate of about 2.5 percent to hold interest rates constant. Again, we should note that this is the rule for the long-run average, or trend, growth in the money supply to keep the economy near its potential

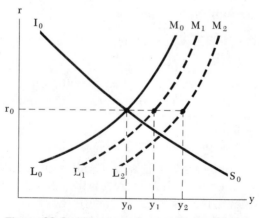

Figure 22-3 Money supply growth along trend.

growth path. As private demand fluctuates about its long-run trend, policy variables will also have to fluctuate to maintain total demand at the full-employment level, as we saw in Parts II and III. Here we are developing the long-run average outcome for the policy variables given the trend growth in private demand. Now we can turn to the fiscal policy prescription that shifts the *IS* curve out just fast enough to maintain demand-side equilibrium as y grows from y_0 to y_1 in Figure 22-3.

PRODUCT MARKET EQUILIBRIUM AND THE BUDGET

The equilibrium condition in the product market can be written as

$$c + i + g = c + s + t, \tag{14a}$$

or

$$i + g = s + t. \tag{14b}$$

Here each variable is set at its *ex ante,* or planned level; product market equilibrium is maintained where planned $i + g$ = planned $s + t$. Equation (14b) can be divided through by y to obtain the product market equilibrium condition, with all items stated as fractions of real output,

$$\frac{i}{y} + \frac{g}{y} = \frac{s}{y} + \frac{t}{y}. \tag{15}$$

Rearranging the terms in equation (15), we obtain the necessary equality between net private-sector saving $s - i$, and net public-sector expenditure, the deficit $d = g - t$, to maintain the product market in equilibrium:

$$\frac{g - t}{y} = \frac{d}{y} = \frac{s - i}{y}. \tag{16}$$

This just restates the fact that in equilibrium the government deficit d must equal the excess of private saving over investment in the economy. If the saving fraction s/y and the investment fraction i/y have fairly stable trend values, equation (16) will give us the trend ratio of the deficit to output that will be needed to keep the product market in equilibrium as the economy grows along trend.

The Saving-Income Ratio

In Chapter 12 we saw that the long-run data on consumption and income and the three main theories of the consumption function all say that the ratio of real consumption to real income is roughly constant over the long run. If c/y is roughly constant along trend and the tax structure is proportional so that $t(y) = ty$, then the ratio of planned saving to income must also be constant along trend.

One way to write the product-market equilibrium condition is

$$y = c + s + t, \tag{17}$$

so that the ratios of c, s, and t to income must add to unity,

$$1 = \frac{c}{y} + \frac{s}{y} + \frac{t}{y}. \tag{18}$$

If c/y and t/y are constant, then s/y must also be constant. A permanent increase in tax rates, raising t/y, will reduce both c/y and s/y, presumably in the same proportions that consumption and saving come out of disposable income. Thus, in the fiscal policy equation (16) s/y will be roughly constant with any given tax structure which determines t/y. An increase in t/y will yield a smaller decrease in s/y, as perhaps 10 percent of the t increase comes out of saving.

The Investment-Income Ratio

In Chapter 13 we found that empirical estimates show a long-run elasticity of investment demand with respect to changes in output of unity. This implies a constant ratio of investment to real output along trend, as increases in output call forth equal percentage increases in investment.

This result can also be obtained by assuming that the capital-output ratio, K/y, is constant, as shown in assumption 3 above. If K/y is equal to a constant v (here v is the capital-output ratio), then we have

$$\text{Net investment} = i_n = \frac{dK}{dt} = v \cdot \frac{dy}{dt},$$

as an expression for net investment, which is just the rate of increase of the capital stock. Dividing the net investment expression by y yields

$$\frac{i_n}{y} = v \cdot \frac{dy/dt}{y} = v \cdot \dot{y}. \tag{19}$$

If both v and $\dot{y}$, the trend growth rate of output, are constant along trend, then the ratio of net investment to output will also be constant along trend.

Replacement investment is generally assumed to be a fraction δ of the capital stock K, so that replacement investment is given by

$$i_r = \delta K = \delta v y, \tag{20}$$

and the ratio of replacement investment to output, along trend, will just be the constant δv. If both net and replacement investment are roughly constant fractions of output, then total investment i will also be a constant fraction of y along trend.

Both net and replacement investment, in equations (19) and (20), depend on the capital-output ratio v. This gives the desired capital stock at any given level of y. The *level* of this stock then determines replacement investment through δ and *the rate of growth* of this stock is net investment. Thus, equations (19) and (20) show that for any given v there is a constant long-run average ratio of investment to output.

As we saw in Chapter 13, the desired capital-output ratio should, in turn, depend on the interest rate through the cost of capital. The higher the interest rate, the lower the desired capital-output ratio v. Thus, if the economy moves from one roughly constant level of the interest rate r_0 to another lower level r_1, there will be a corresponding increase in the capital-output ratio v from v_0 to v_1 and an increase in the investment-output ratio from $(i/y)_0$ to $(i/y)_1$. This says that for any given level of interest rates there will be given equilibrium capital-output and investment-output ratios. A change in rates will change the ratios to new equilibrium levels.

The Government Budget Along Trend

We can now return to the equilibrium rule for the government budget given earlier by equation (16):

$$\frac{g-t}{y} = \frac{d}{y} = \frac{s-i}{y}.$$

If s/y and i/y are constant along trend, (16) gives the long-run trend in the budget position that is needed to maintain product market equilibrium. The saving ratio is determined by trend real income and the tax rate; the investment ratio is at least partially determined by the level of interest rates.

If private-sector full-employment saving tends to exceed investment demand, $s > i$, and a government deficit equal to the difference will be needed on average over the long run to maintain equilibrium full-employment growth. Conversely, if $s < i$, a surplus will be needed. This is the rule that will keep the *IS* curve of Figure 22-4(a) and the demand curve of Figure 22-4(b) shifting out just fast enough to maintain static equilibrium in the economy as potential output grows from y_0 to y_1 to y_2, with the interest rate constant at r_0 and the price level rising steadily from P_0 to P_1 to P_2.

The long-run equilibrium deficit or surplus, then, depends on the long-run tendencies of the s/y and i/y ratios. The s/y ratio can be affected by tax rate changes, and the i/y ratio can be changed somewhat by interest rate changes, but there is no particular reason to expect the two ratios to be the same so that the government budget can be just balanced over the long run.

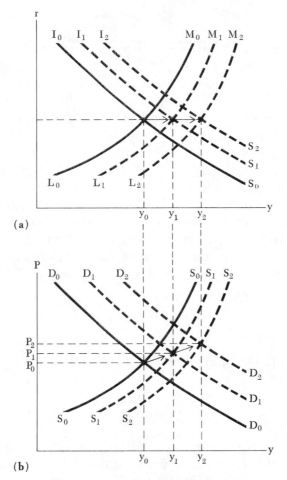

Figure 22-4 Static equilibrium with full-employment output growth.

THE MONETARY-FISCAL POLICY MIX ALONG TREND

Equation (16), giving the full-employment budget surplus or deficit needed to maintain equilibrium along trend, is a useful point of departure for a final discussion of the long-run allocation implications of the monetary-fiscal policy mix. Assume that stabilization policy is maintaining the economy near its potential growth path by balancing exogenous deviations from long-run trend behavior in s/y and i/y by short-run changes in government purchases, tax rates, or the money supply. In other words, the government counters exogenous short-run shifts in private demand components by changing its own demand, changing consumer demand through tax rate changes, or changing investment demand through deviations from trend money supply growth. These policy actions keep the economy close to the potential growth path so that the remaining monetary-fiscal policy question concerns the mix of output along trend.

The Trend Mix of Output

Presumably, the long-run desired output mix—the c, i, and g combination as y grows along its potential path—should be determined by balancing the marginal social gain of additional units of real consumer, investment, and government expenditures within the constraint that they can add up to no more than potential output. This decision concerning the long-run mix is a political decision to be taken with the understanding that current investment may affect the future potential growth rate, as we will see in Chapters 23 and 27.

Once the mix decision is reached by weighing the marginal social benefits of increases in each kind of expenditure, equation (16) shows how to implement that decision. First, the interest rate *level* should be set to obtain the desired i/y ratio. This will involve an initial period of higher-than-trend M growth to reduce rates, or lower-than-trend growth to raise them. This sets the trend i/y ratio.

Next, given the desired g/y ratio, tax rates must be set to yield the ratios of tax revenue and saving to income that just balance supply and demand in the economy. The determination of this equilibrium tax rate is shown in Figure 22-5. The $[\bar{g} - t(y)]/y$ line in Figure 22-5 shows the relationship between the tax rate and the ratio of the government deficit at potential output to potential y itself as tax rates rise. With g fixed at $\bar{g}$ by the balancing of marginal social benefits of expenditures, as tax rates rise to increase $t(y)$, $[\bar{g} - t(y)]/y$ falls fairly sharply.

The $(s - \bar{i})/y$ line in Figure 22-5 shows the relationship between the tax rate and the ratio of net private saving at potential output, $s - \bar{i}$, to potential output. Here $\bar{i}$ is the desired investment level at potential output. An increase in the tax rate reduces saving, reducing $s - \bar{i}$, but by less than it increases $t(y)$, since most of the $t(y)$ increase comes out of consumption.

With $\bar{i}/y$ and $\bar{g}/y$ set by policy along trend, Figure 22-5 shows the tax rate t_0 that will equate net private saving and the deficit at potential output. In Figure 22-5, the tax rate t_0 yields a negative deficit—a surplus—along trend, measured by $-(d/y)_0$. In that example, the desired investment level $\bar{i}$ is large enough that the $s - \bar{i}$ line is low enough to intersect the $\bar{g} - t(y)$ line below the horizontal axis, giving a required surplus as the economy grows along trend.

There is no way to determine *a priori* whether the potential output equilibrium intersection of Figure 22-5 will be above or below the horizontal axis, that is, whether a deficit or surplus will be required to maintain the economy

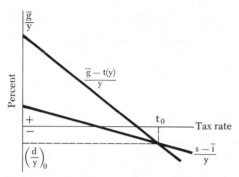

Figure 22-5   Net private saving and the surplus at potential output.

near its potential output path. Monetary policy can shift the $s - \bar{i}$ curve by adjusting the level of interest rates. The government budget can shift the $g - t(y)$ line by changing g. In the end, the equilibrium deficit will be to a large extent determined by these policy decisions concerning the output mix.

Two Interpretations of the Product Market Equilibrium Condition

Equation (16) giving the necessary budget position along trend can be viewed in two ways. First, if we take the level of interest rates and the tax rate as given, we can use it to determine the possible level of government purchases and the deficit. If, in

$$\frac{g - t}{y} = \frac{s - i}{y}, \tag{21}$$

we take interest rates as given, then i/y is fixed. Potential output and the tax structure determine both s and t. This leaves only g/y to be determined as

$$\frac{g}{y} = \frac{s}{y} + \frac{t}{y} - \frac{i}{y}. \tag{22}$$

If $s > i$, g will be greater than t and there will be a deficit; if $s < i$, then there will be a surplus with $g < t$.

Second, if we determine the level of the interest rate needed to achieve some target investment level, fixing i/y by policy, and then fix g/y to equate the marginal social benefits of public versus private spending, equation (21) can be used to determine the tax rate needed to maintain static equilibrium as the economy grows along its potential output path.

Summary of Equilibrium Growth in the Static Model

This completes our exposition of the behavior of the static model as the economy grows along its potential path. The rates of growth of productivity and the labor force determine the rate of growth of potential output,

$$\dot{y} = y\dot{/}L = \dot{L}. \tag{23}$$

The Phillips curve gives us the rate of growth of wages $\dot{W}$, and this, combined with the assumption of constant relative income shares, gives us the growth rate of the price level,

$$\dot{P} = \dot{W} - y\dot{/}L. \tag{24}$$

To maintain money market equilibrium at any given level of the interest rate, along trend we have M growing at the same rate as nominal GNP,

$$\dot{M} = \dot{Y} = \dot{y} + \dot{P}. \tag{25}$$

To raise interest rates, $\dot{M}$ should be temporarily lower than $\dot{Y}$ and vice versa to lower interest rates.

The level of interest rates determines the investment ratio i/y, and the tax structure determines the tax and saving ratios t/y and s/y, leaving the product market equilibrium condition,

$$\frac{g - t}{y} = \frac{s - i}{y},$$

to determine the necessary values of g and the deficit $(g - t)$ that keep the economy near its potential growth path. If s, t, and i are all roughly constant fractions of y, then g/y will also have to be roughly constant; that is, g must grow as fast as y to maintain product market equilibrium along this balanced-growth path.

We can now move on in Chapter 23 to a brief review of the facts of economic growth in the United States and then to the development of models that explain the trend growth path of the economy. Here we have seen how the economy can be kept in static equilibrium along its trend growth path, assuming such a path exists. In Chapters 23–27 we look at explanations of why such a growth path does exist and what determines its level and slope, the rate of growth. Before moving on, it is convenient to discuss very briefly two questions of interest raised by this exposition of equilibrium growth—the notion of fiscal drag and the relationships between the deficit, the national debt, and potential output.

FISCAL DRAG AND THE FULL-EMPLOYMENT SURPLUS

The product market equilibrium condition with the economy growing along its potential output path is

$$\frac{g - t(y)}{y} = \frac{s - i}{y} = \frac{d}{y} = \text{a constant,} \qquad (26)$$

on average, over time.

For that to hold true with a given tax structure, the level of government purchases g must grow at the same rate as output y. If g does not grow as fast as y, the tax rate must be continually reduced to keep $g - t(y)$ growing at the same rate as y. If both g and the tax rate were to stay constant, then as potential y grows the deficit would shrink, and the economy would begin to slow down, falling off the full-employment path. This phenomenon is known as "fiscal drag" and is illustrated in Figure 22-6. Let us assume in Figure 22-6 that the deficit, given by (26), needed to maintain product market equilibrium at potential output is zero, with the initial *level* of government purchases fixed at g_0 and the proportional tax structure given by $t_0 y$. Under these assumptions, the economy initially is in equilibrium at the full-employment level of output y_F^0.

As potential output grows with g_0 and t_0 fixed, the full-employment surplus increases with $t_0 y$ rising and g_0 constant, violating the equilibrium con-

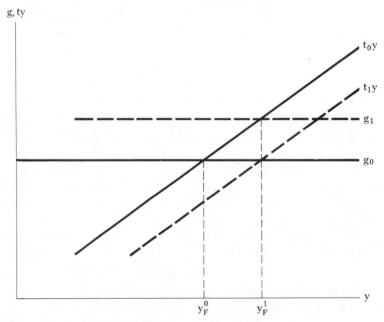

Figure 22-6 "Fiscal drag."

dition for full-employment trend fiscal policy, putting increasing downward pressure on the economy, and increasing unemployment.

To avoid fiscal drag, one of two things must occur. Either the tax rates must be reduced as income grows, shifting the ty line from $t_0 y$ to $t_1 y$, in Figure 22-6, or the level of government expenditure must be increased from g_0 to g_1 in Figure 22-6 as full-employment output rises from y_F^0 to y_F^1.

The point here is just that budget procedures fix the *level* of government purchases and tax *rates*. Thus, as y grows, revenues grow automatically, but increases in government purchases have to be legislated. T' means that a neutral budget position, over time, must involve steady incr ases in g or steady cuts in tax rates to maintain the product market equilibrium condition (26) as the economy grows along trend.

PUBLIC DEBT WITH TREND GROWTH

One final question is raised by the product market equilibrium condition given in equation (26). Suppose along trend private saving exceeds investment, so that the fiscal rule says that $g > t$ and the deficit-income ratio d/y must be positive. If the government must persistently run a deficit as the economy grows along trend, what happens to the ratio of debt to income? Will the public debt—the accumulated deficit—grow relative to income, or will it tend to some stable ratio to income? The answer is that the debt-income ratio will tend toward a constant given by $(d/y)/\dot{y}$. The problem is the same as that of the investment-output ratio implied by a constant capital-output ratio; in that case investment was the rate of change of the capital stock. Here the deficit is the rate of change of the debt. In the capital stock case we went from a constant capital-output ratio to a constant investment-output ratio by differentiation; here we will go from a constant deficit-output ratio to a constant debt-output ratio by integration.

Suppose the deficit-income ratio is given by δ, so that the deficit in time t is given by

$$d_t = \delta y_t = \delta y_0 e^{\dot{y}t}, \tag{27}$$

where y grows at the rate $\dot{y}$. Then the debt at any time T, D_T, is given by the integral of all deficits from time zero to time T:

$$D_T = \int_0^T d_t \, dt = \int_0^T \delta y_0 e^{\dot{y}t} \, dt. \tag{28}$$

Integration of this expression gives us

$$D_T = \delta y_0 \left| \frac{e^{\dot{y}t}}{\dot{y}} \right|_0^T = \frac{\delta y_0}{\dot{y}} (e^{\dot{y}T} - 1).$$

With $y_T = y_0 e^{\dot{y}T}$, the debt-income ratio is then

$$\frac{D_T}{y_T} = \frac{\delta}{\dot{y}}\left(1 - \frac{1}{e^{\dot{y}T}}\right). \tag{29}$$

As time passes and T becomes larger and larger, the second term in the parentheses tends toward zero, so that

$$\frac{D_T}{y_T} \to \frac{\delta}{\dot{y}} \quad \text{as} \quad T \to \infty. \tag{30}$$

Thus, if the deficit is reduced to about 1 percent of GNP along trend, so that $\delta = 0.01$, and the growth rate of real output is about 2.5 percent, so that $\dot{y} = 0.025$, the debt-income ratio will tend toward 40 percent as time passes.

With the U.S. GNP running about $5 trillion, a 1 percent deficit would be about $50 billion. The arithmetic of deficits and debts in a growing economy thus says that if the United States continually ran deficits of this magnitude relative to GNP, in the long run the public debt would stabilize at about one-half of GNP. This is hardly any cause for alarm, no matter what one's theory is concerning the burden of the public debt.

SELECTED READINGS

M. N. Baily and R. J. Gordon, "Measurement Issues, the Productivity Slowdown, and the Explosion of Computer Power," *Brookings Papers on Economic Activity,* vol. 2, 1988.

A. S. Blinder and R. M. Solow, "Analytical Foundations of Fiscal Policy," in Blinder, et al., *The Economics of Public Finance* (Washington, D.C.: The Brookings Institution, 1974).

R. Eisner and P. Pieper, "A New View of the Federal Debt and Budget Deficits," *American Economic Review,* March 1984.

D. W. Jorgenson and Z. Griliches, "The Explanation of Productivity Change," *Review of Economics and Statistics,* July 1967.

five

LONG-RUN GROWTH WITH FULL EMPLOYMENT

chapter *23*

Introduction to Growth Models

The theory of economic growth generally deals with the economy's long-run trend, or potential, growth path. Assuming that the monetary and fiscal authorities are successful in keeping the economy near full employment, we can ask what determines the height and slope of the potential growth path, shown in Figures 22-1 and 1-1. As we saw in Chapter 22, the *slope* of the long-run growth path—the rate of growth of potential output—is related to the rates of growth of the labor force and of productivity. The *height* of the growth path, on the other hand, is related to the amount of accumulated capital per worker in the economy and to the saving rate. Most of the remaining chapters of this book are devoted to the analysis of the precise relationships between the slope and height of the growth path and the rates of productivity and labor force growth and the saving rate.

The growth models of Chapters 23–27 will deal with relationships between capital and labor inputs, real output, real investment and consumption demand, the real wage rate and the profit rate. Since we are dealing with only real variables here, it will be convenient to change notation so that capital letters stand for aggregate real magnitudes and small letters denote per capita real magnitudes. Thus, for the remainder of the book:

$L \equiv$ labor input, in terms of worker-hours per unit of time.
$K \equiv$ capital input, in terms of machine-hours per unit of time.
$Q \equiv$ real output per unit of time, and, in general, $Q = F(K, L)$.
$W \equiv$ total real wages.

$k \equiv$ amount of capital per person—the capital-labor ratio $K/L = k$.
$q \equiv$ output per worker, or productivity, so that $Q/L = q$.
$w \equiv$ wage rate, that is, $w = W/L$.

In general, we will also assume that the rates of utilization of the labor force and the capital stock are constant, so that we can use L to represent either the labor force or worker-hour input, and K to represent either the capital stock or machine-hour input.

We will find it useful—indeed, necessary—to distinguish between four kinds of growth in Chapters 23–27. These are illustrated in Figure 23-1, which shows two long-run equilibrium growth paths q_1q_1 and q_2q_2, and the path of output per person in a hypothetical economy from point 0 at time t_0 to point 2 at time t_2.

Long-run growth paths q_1q_1 and q_2q_2 represent trend growth paths of output per worker with a slope given by the rate of growth of labor force productivity $\dot{q}$, which is the same as the (y/L) variable of Chapter 22. Long-run growth path q_1q_1 has a lower saving rate and thus is below long-run path q_2q_2. The dashed path AB shows the *full-employment* growth path of the hypothetical economy as it grows up to its long-run trend path q_1q_1. As we will see in Chapter 24, if an economy with a long-run path like q_1q_1 starts off below that path, at a point like A, its potential output will tend to grow toward that long-run path as full employment is maintained by stabilization policy.

The solid path from point 0 to point 2 in Figure 23-1 shows the movement of the hypothetical economy from an initial point of less than potential output, first up to full employment as it joins the AB path, then to a long-run steady-state growth path q_1q_1, which it joins at point B. At time t_1 we assume that the economy's saving rate increases so that its long-run path shifts up to q_2q_2.

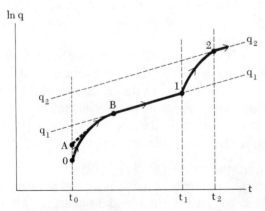

Figure 23-1 Four kinds of economic growth.

Maintaining full employment, the economy then follows path 1-2 to reach the new long-run path at time t_2.

This scenario thus shows four different kinds of growth. The first, illustrated by the movement from point 0 up to path AB, is growth that accompanies the elimination of unemployment. The first three parts of this book dealt with this stabilization question—how to keep the economy on its full-employment growth path.

The second kind of growth is shown by the movement along the full-employment path AB toward a long-run steady-state path like q_1q_1. Part IV of the book described several aspects of the dynamics of this path. We continue the analysis of this path from medium-term to long-term equilibrium here. One of the major questions dealt with in the growth models of the next few chapters is whether a full-employment economy will, both in fact and in theory, tend toward a steady-state path like q_1q_1.

The third kind of growth is movement along the steady-state path once the economy gets onto the path at point B. A second major theme of the growth models of the next few chapters is investigation of the characteristics of the steady-state path. It should be noticed that two separate questions are involved in growth from A to B and then along path q_1q_1 from B. The first is the question of what path q_1q_1 looks like, assuming the economy gets on it at point B. The second is whether the economy tends toward a path like q_1q_1, assuming that it starts at a full-employment point off the path, like point A.

The fourth kind of growth involves movements between two steady-state paths, normally as a result of a change in the saving rate. This is illustrated by the movement from point 1 to point 2 in Figure 23-1. This kind of growth is quite similar to that from point A to point B. When the saving rate changes and shifts the long-run steady-state path from q_1q_1 to q_2q_2, the economy is then off the steady-state path (and at full employment) at point 1 much as it was at point A.

As mentioned above, the first kind of growth that comes from moving to a position of full resource utilization was discussed in Parts I to III. Parts IV and V deal with the second and third kinds of growth—to and along the steady-state path, maintaining full employment. Chapter 27 concludes with a discussion of the fourth kind of growth between full-employment steady-state paths.

In the following sections, we first review the "stylized facts" of economic growth. These are rough and approximate empirical observations of the characteristics of long-run growth in industrial countries, relating the observed growth rate of output to growth rates in inputs and patterns of change in factor input prices to factor income shares. These stylized facts are the approximate empirical reality that growth models attempt to explain.

Next we discuss the three basic assumptions underlying most one-sector growth models. These are the usually exogenously determined rate of growth of the labor force, $g_L = (dL/dt)/L$; the production function, $Q = F(K, L)$; and the saving–investment–capital formation relationship, $S = I = dK/dt$. These functions, taken together, give us a fairly simple intuitive description of the growth process.

Finally, we develop the first simple model of capital accumulation and output growth generally attributed to Evsey D. Domar and Sir Roy Harrod. This model develops the implications of the fact that on the demand side of the economy investment is an important determinant of the *level* of output through the multiplier, while on the supply side investment is an important determinant of the *rate of increase* of potential output by increasing the capital stock. Thus, there will be one investment path along which the capital stock will be fully employed, with the level of demand just sufficient to absorb the total output produced by the capital stock. This path is given by the Harrod–Domar condition, which is a basic equilibrium condition in one-sector growth models.

THE STYLIZED FACTS OF GROWTH

The stylized facts, introduced by Nicholas Kaldor in 1958, refer to the long-term regularities in the relationships that seem to appear in most industrial countries—between growth rates of output and capital and labor inputs, and between factor prices and relative income shares. These are the facts that a growth model must explain. This section summarizes these stylized facts and gives some rough numerical estimates for their values in the United States since World War II.

Labor Force and Output Growth

The growth rate of available worker-hours in the labor force is fairly steady over time, that is, $\dot{L} = (dL/dt)/L$ is roughly constant. Through the 1950s and the first half of the 1960s the labor force grew at a rate of about 1.2 percent per year. Subtracting 0.2 percent for a shrinking work week gave a growth rate of available worker-hours of about 1 percent per year during that period. During the late 1960s, as the people born during the post–World War II "baby boom" began to enter the labor force, the rate of labor force growth picked up. In addition, the participation rate of women in the labor force also began to rise in the late 1960s. These effects raised the growth rate of the labor force by about half a percentage point, so that in the 1970s the labor force was growing by about 1.7 percent per year. With the work week still shrinking by about 0.2 percent per year, this gave a trend $\dot{L}$ growth rate of about 1.5 percent in the 1970s. These trends continued in the 1980s, maintaining the growth rate of L at about 1.5 percent per year.

The rate of growth of labor productivity in the private sector of the economy fluctuates with the business cycle. Along trend in the United States it was fairly steady at about 2.9 to 3.2 percent per year in the early 1960s. The growth rate was at the upper end of this range from 1960 to 1965 as the unemployment rate fell and resource utilization rose. From 1966 to 1970 the rate of growth of productivity was lower as the economy reached full employment and then went through a period of excess demand pressure followed by a recession. Beginning with the recession of 1969–1970, and accentuated by the recession of 1974–1975, the rate of growth of productivity was reduced. It seems from the vantage point of 1988 that the reduction in productivity growth was permanent, or at least indefinite. Thus the Council of Economic Advisers estimates trend productivity growth in the private sector of about 1.2 percent in the late 1980s. With the private sector producing about 85 percent of total real output, this yields a growth rate of economy-wide average labor productivity of about 2 ($\approx 0.85 \cdot 2.5$) percent per year.

Total potential output in the economy can be defined as the product of average labor productivity, Q/L, and total labor force,

$$Q_t = \left(\frac{Q}{L}\right)_t \cdot L_t. \tag{1}$$

The growth rate of output, $\dot{Q}$, is then the sum of the growth rates of labor input and productivity:

$$\dot{Q} = (Q\dot{/}L) = \dot{L}. \tag{2}$$

Thus, the trend growth rates of productivity and available worker-hours give us the trend growth rate of potential output, $\dot{Q}$.

In the 1950s and early 1960s, with labor productivity growing at a rate of about 2.7 percent annually and available hours growing at about 1 percent, the growth rate of potential output was about 3.7 percent per year—somewhat lower in the early part of the period and rising in the later part of the period. As the growth rate of the labor force, in terms of available hours, rose from about 1 percent to the rate of about 1.5 percent in the early 1970s, the growth rate of potential output, $\dot{Q}$, rose from 3.7 percent to 4.2 percent. The productivity growth slowdown of the early 1970s has reduced the estimate of productivity growth to about 2 percent. Thus, in the late 1970s, we experienced labor-supply growth $\dot{L}$ of about 1.5 percent per year, potential output growth $\dot{Q}$ of about 3.5 percent per year, and growth of output per worker-hour input, $\dot{q}$, of about 2 percent per year. In the 1980s productivity growth slowed to about 1.0 percent, so potential output growth slowed to 2.5 percent.

Capital Stock Growth

The second set of stylized facts concerns the rate of growth of the capital stock and the capital-labor ratio $k = K/L$. In general, the rate of growth of the capital stock seems to be fairly steady and greater than the rate of growth of the labor force. Thus, the capital-labor ratio k is rising through time. Table 23.1 gives the compound rate of growth of the net capital stock for all U.S. industries for the period 1960–1985.

The sluggish performance of the economy in the late 1950s pulled the rate of growth of the capital stock down to 3.4 percent during 1955–1960. As the economy slowly picked up after 1961, the rate of growth of the capital stock, $\dot{K}$, rose to 3.9 percent in the period 1960–1965, and as an excess demand boom developed in the late 1960s, $\dot{K}$ rose even further. The economic slowdown that started in 1969 and carried over to 1975 leveled off investment demand and reduced $\dot{K}$. In the 1970s, the capital stock grew by 3.3 percent. However, the crowding-out effects of the budget deficit and the recession in 1982 reduced investment, so capital growth slowed to 2.6 percent in 1980–1985. Unless the deficit is reduced substantially, capital stock growth could remain at 2.5 percent or so in the 1990s.

The long-term rate of growth of the capital stock from 1960 to 1985 was about 0 percent, roughly equal to the growth rate of potential output, and greater than the growth rate of the labor force. If the capital stock grows at about 2.5 percent per year in the 1990s, the rate of growth of capital per worker-hour, k, will be about 1 percent per year.

The Capital-Output Ratio

Historically, the ratio of capital K to output Q has been a central variable in growth theory. This will become clear when we discuss the Harrod–Domar condition later in this chapter. In the first part of this section we saw that the rate of growth of potential output has fallen from about 3.7 percent in the 1950s and early 1960s to about 2.5 percent in the 1970s. With the capital stock growing at about 2.5 percent annually, this would give a roughly constant capital-output ratio, K/Q.

The Profit Rate and Relative Income Shares

The last important stylized fact is that the profit rate ρ, defined as the ratio of profits P to the value of the capital stock K, shows no perceptible long-run

Table 23.1

	1960–1965	1965–1970	1970–1975	1975–80	1980–85
$\dot{K}(\%)$	3.9	5.2	3.3	3.3	2.6

Source: Survey of Current Business, November 1987, Table 4, p. 37.

trend. In other words, $\rho \equiv (P/K)$ is roughly constant in the long run, although it shows substantial variation over the business cycle.

If both the profit rate ρ and the capital-output ratio are constant, then the relative share of profits in output must be roughly constant in the long run. Since the profit share in income P/Q can be written as

$$\frac{P}{Q} = \frac{P}{K} \cdot \frac{K}{Q}, \tag{3}$$

if ρ and K/Q are constant, so is the profit share P/Q. Furthermore, if the wage share W/Q is simply $1 - P/Q$, then a constant profit share implies a constant wage share and a constant long-run relative distribution of output. It should be clear that this follows from the two stylized facts of (a) a constant K/Q ratio and (b) a constant profit rate in the long run.

Figure 23-2 shows the net profit rate—measured by the ratio of net profits to total stockholder's equity value of capital—in the U.S. corporate manufacturing sector since 1950. There is no apparent trend in the profit rate, although it does show a clear pattern of cyclical fluctuation. If we allow for the redefinition of the series in 1973, we observe that this last stylized fact stands up fairly well in the U.S. data.

Summary of the Stylized Facts

Here we can provide a brief summary of the stylized facts, or rough empirical observations, that growth models must explain.

1. The growth rates of potential output and labor input are fairly steady, with $\dot{Q} > \dot{L}$, so that $\dot{q} > 0$.
2. The growth rate of the capital stock is also fairly steady, with $\dot{K} > \dot{L}$, so that $\dot{k}$ is also positive.
3. The growth rate of the capital stock is about the same as the

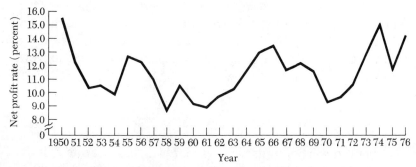

Figure 23-2 Net profit rate in the United States, 1950–1977. (*Source:* CEA Annual Report, January 1978.)

growth rate of output, so that $\dot{K} = \dot{Q}$, and the K/Q ratio is fairly constant.

4. The profit rate, $\rho = P/K$, is fairly constant in the long run. Combined with a constant capital-output ratio, this implies a constant long-run relative distribution of output between wages W and profits P.

We can now go on to a brief discussion of the basic assumptions that go into all of the one-sector growth models, and then to the Harrod–Domar condition.

BASIC ASSUMPTIONS OF ONE-SECTOR GROWTH MODELS

Growth models are generally based on a combination of three assumptions or assumed functional relationships. The first is usually an exogenously determined labor supply, which grows at some given rate $g_L = \dot{L}$. The second is a production function, which converts labor and capital inputs at any given time into output. The third is a saving and investment relationship, which determines how much of current output will be saved and invested to add to the capital stock.

Labor Force Growth

Labor force growth is usually taken as exogenously determined. The labor force grows at some given percentage rate of growth g_L. The labor force at time t is therefore given by

$$L_t = L_0 e^{g_L t}. \tag{4}$$

In the United States in the 1980s the rate of growth of the labor force, $g_L = \dot{L}$, is about 0.5 percent per year.

When we introduce technical progress in Chapter 24, in the form of growing labor productivity, we will introduce it through the notion of an *effective labor unit*. If, over time, each worker is becoming more productive at the rate λ, this can be viewed as if each worker is able to work an increasing number of *effective worker-hours*. Then if E_t is the *effective labor force* at time t, we have

$$E_t = L_t e^{\lambda t} = L_0 e^{(g_L + \lambda)t}, \tag{5}$$

and effective labor units per person, E_t/L_t, grow at rate λ. If this is interpreted as the rate of increase of average labor productivity, λ in the United States is about 2 percent per year.

The Production Function

The second relationship basic to growth models is the production function which converts K_t and L_t inputs into Q_t output:

$$Q_t = F(K_t, L_t). \tag{6}$$

Both marginal products $\partial F/\partial K$ and $\partial F/\partial L$ are assumed to be positive and decreasing as the relevant input increases.

In general, we will assume that the production function is homogeneous of degree one in K and L. This means that we assume constant returns to scale so that output per person, q, depends only on capital per person, k. Formally, a function is homogeneous to degree h if, for any arbitrary positive number a, we have

$$a^h Q = F(aL, aK). \tag{7}$$

First-degree homogeneity means that

$$aQ = F(aK, aL).$$

If this is the case, we can set a equal to $1/L$ to obtain the labor-intensive production function,

$$q_t = \frac{Q}{L} = F\left(\frac{K}{L}, 1\right) = f(k_t); \tag{8}$$

$$f' > 0, \qquad f'' < 0.$$

The labor-intensive production function is shown in Figure 23-3. Its slope is positive and decreasing, so that $f' > 0$ and $f'' < 0$.

Investment and Capital Formation

The last basic building block in growth model construction is the saving-investment relationship. Since we are dealing with full-employment growth paths, the static equilibrium equation of saving and investment holds:

$$S + T = I + G.$$

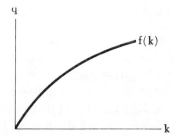

Figure 23-3 Labor-intensive production function.

From the point of view of the growth process, this equilibrium condition gives us the link between current social saving $S + T$—the amount of income not spent on consumption—and total investment, which is just the rate of increase of the capital stock. If we view $I + G$ as total social investment I, which is the time rate of change of the capital stock, dK/dt, then we have

$$S_t = I_t = \frac{dK}{dt}, \tag{9}$$

as the equation relating saving S to capital formation dK/dt.

The simplest saving function is obtained by assuming that a constant fraction s of output is saved and invested. In this case the capital formation relationship would be

$$\frac{dK}{dt} = I_t = S_t = sQ_t. \tag{10}$$

Each period sQ_t is saved and invested, raising K by that amount from period t to $t + 1$.

The Simple Dynamics of Growth

We can combine the three basic functions reviewed above to give a simple intuitive explanation of the growth process. The labor force assumption given by equation (4) or (5) determines labor input for any given time period t. This labor input, combined with the capital stock inherited at the beginning of period t, produces a flow of output Q_t via the production function. The saving function then determines what fraction of output is invested in period t through an equation like (10), and this investment adds to the inherited capital stock to give the larger capital stock that is passed on to the next period, $t + 1$. That capital stock then combines with the larger labor force in $t + 1$ to produce an increased level of output Q_{t+1}. The question for the growth models of Chapters 24–26 is whether this process naturally settles down to a stable growth path as seems to be described by the stylized facts.

THE HARROD–DOMAR CONDITION FOR EQUILIBRIUM GROWTH

Equilibrium growth requires that both the labor force and the capital stock be fully employed as the economy grows. Rising unemployment of labor would, by definition, violate the full-employment growth assumption, and it would probably also be accompanied by deficient demand and falling prices. On the other hand, underutilization of the capital stock would drive profits and investment incentives down, reducing investment and the demand for output.

The requirement that the capital stock be fully utilized as the economy grows brings us to the basic dynamic process pointed out by Sir Roy Harrod and Evsey Domar in the early 1940s. The level of investment is associated with the *level* of output through the multiplier, while it is also associated with the *rate of growth* of output through changes in the capital stock. The implications of this relationship for the equilibrium growth rate of the economy can be derived in the context of a simple growth model using the *fixed-coefficients production function*.

The Fixed-Coefficients Production Function

If the economy has a fixed-coefficients technology, so that α units of labor L and v units of capital K are required to produce one unit of output Q, then the production function can be written as

$$Q_t = \min\left[\frac{K_t}{v}, \frac{L_t}{\alpha}\right].$$
(11)

This production function is shown in the (K,L) space of Figure 23-4. With fixed coefficients v and α, the production isoquants showing levels of output Q are right-angled with corners along the ray from the origin with slope v/α. If both capital and labor are fully employed, then output Q is equal to both K/v and L/α, so that $K/v = L/\alpha$ and $K/L = v/\alpha$. If we locate the isoquant showing one unit of output, $Q_0 = 1$, we can measure v and α as shown in Figure 23-4.

If the ratio of capital to labor in the economy is greater than v/α, there will be excess capital stock, zero profits, and no investment. If K/L is less than v/α, there will be unemployed labor in the economy.

Saving, Investment, and the Warranted Rate of Growth

To investigate the supply and demand relationship leading to the growth rate that will maintain full employment of the capital stock, we can introduce a

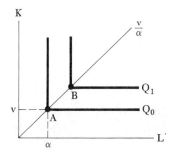

Figure 23-4 Harrod–Domar production function: fixed coefficients of production.

net saving function that makes saving a constant fraction s of output. This gives us a capital formation equation

$$I_t = \frac{dK}{dt} = S_t = sQ_t. \tag{12}$$

This relationship can be used to determine output demanded in the economy as $Q_t = I_t/s$, so that increments to output demanded are given, as usual, by the multiplier

$$\frac{dQ}{dt} = \frac{1}{s}\frac{dI}{dt}, \tag{13}$$

on the demand side.

If capital is to be fully employed, then from production function (11), we obtain $Q_t = K_t/v$. Changes in output from the supply side—the increments that would be produced by a growing capital stock—are then given by

$$\frac{dQ}{dt} = \frac{1}{v}\frac{dK}{dt} = \frac{1}{v}I_t, \tag{14}$$

on the supply side.

With full employment of the capital stock, the growth in output *demanded* through the growth in investment, given by equation (13), should be equal to the growth in output *supplied* due to capital stock growth, given by equation (14). Thus, for full employment of the capital stock as the economy grows, we have

$$\frac{dQ}{dt} = \frac{1}{s}\frac{dI}{dt} = \frac{1}{v}I_t, \tag{15}$$

so that the necessary growth rate of investment is given by

$$\dot{I} \equiv \frac{dI/dt}{I} = \frac{s}{v}. \tag{16}$$

If the ratio of I to Q is a constant, namely s, then I and Q must grow at the same rate. This means that the rate of growth of output that will maintain full employment of the capital stock is given by

$$\dot{Q} = \dot{I} = \frac{s}{v}. \tag{17}$$

To maintain full employment of capital in this model, output must grow at the rate s/v. This is the rate of growth that will cause investors' expectations to be realized, or, as Harrod put it, "warranted." Thus, s/v gives the *warranted rate of growth* that maintains full employment of the capital stock.

Labor Force Growth

The rate of growth of output that will maintain full employment of the labor force can be obtained almost directly from the production function (11) plus the assumption that the rate of labor force growth is exogenously given as g_L. To maintain full employment, or any constant unemployment rate, of the labor force, output Q_t must be equal to L_t/α. Thus, the ratio L_t/Q_t is fixed at α, and the growth rate of output must be equal to the growth rate of the labor force, g_L. So, to maintain full employment of the labor force,

$$\dot{Q} = \dot{L} = g_L. \tag{18}$$

If we replace L_t in the production function, equation (11), with *effective labor*, E_t, then the production function can be written as

$$Q_t = \min\left[\frac{K_t}{v}, \frac{E_t}{\alpha}\right]. \tag{19}$$

If this is the case, to maintain full employment of the labor force Q_t must grow at the same rate as effective labor input, so that

$$\dot{Q} = g_L + \lambda, \tag{20}$$

where, as discussed earlier, λ is the rate of growth of average labor productivity. The rate of effective labor force growth, $g_L + \lambda$, is frequently called the *natural rate,* following Harrod.

The Harrod–Domar Condition

The difficulty with this one-sector growth model with both a fixed-coefficients production function and a fixed saving rate should now be apparent. For capital to be fully employed, output must grow at the *warranted* rate: $\dot{Q} = s/v$. But for labor to be fully employed in the case with growing productivity, output must grow at the *natural* rate: $\dot{Q} = g_L + \lambda$. Thus, for both capital and labor to be fully employed as the economy grows, we have the Harrod–Domar condition,

$$g_L + \lambda = \frac{s}{v}. \tag{21}$$

But since $g_L + \lambda$, s, and v were all fixed independently by assumption to begin with, the possibility of equilibrium growth with full employment of both capital and labor, that is, that $g_L + \lambda = (s/v)$, is almost nil. If the natural rate $g_L + \lambda$ exceeds the warranted rate s/v, there will be increasing unemployment of labor, violating the initial equilibrium assumption. If $g_L + \lambda < (s/v)$, on the other hand, excess capital will develop, driving the marginal productivity of capital—the profit rate in equilibrium—to zero, discouraging investment, and throwing the economy out of equilibrium. The Harrod–Domar condition has been characterized as a "knife-edge" case in which if $g_L + \lambda$ just happens to equal s/v, all is well, but if not, the model moves away from full-employment equilibrium.

The reason for this instability in this model is that the initial assumptions are too rigid. In order to *explain* growth with a roughly constant capital-output ratio v, it is *assumed* that v is fixed *a priori*. Combining this assumption of fixed coefficients with a fixed saving ratio s, and fixed effective labor force growth rate $g_L + \lambda$, leaves no freedom for movement toward equilibrium in the model; it is *overdetermined*.

This rigidity can be relieved by (a) changing the production function to allow substitution between capital and labor, thus permitting the equilibrium v to be determined by the growth process itself; (b) making the saving ratio itself a function of the profit rate or the distribution of income between capital and labor, thus permitting the equilibrium saving ratio to be determined by the growth process; or (c) a combination of (a) and (b).

We will now move to the basic neoclassical growth model of Robert Solow, which employs option (a) above, permitting capital and labor substitution in the production function.

SELECTED READINGS

E. D. Domar, "Expansion and Employment," *American Economic Review,* March 1947.

Z. Griliches, "Productivity, R & D, and Basic Research at the Firm Level in the 1970's," *American Economic Review,* March 1986.

R. F. Harrod, "Domar and Dynamic Economics," *Economic Journal,* September 1959.

N. Kaldor, "Economic Growth and Capital Accumulation," in F. Lutz and D. C. Hague, eds., *The Theory of Capital* (London: Macmillan, 1961).

chapter 24

The Basic Neoclassical Growth Model

In Chapter 23 we saw that the basic inputs to—or assumptions underlying—growth models, that is, models of economies that produce a single output Q which can be either consumed or saved and invested, are as follows:

1. First, we require an assumption concerning the rate of growth of the labor force—usually that it is given exogenously, so that $L_t = L_0 e^{g_L t}$.
2. Next, we must specify a production giving output Q as a function of the capital and labor inputs, K and L, so that $Q_t = F(K_t, L_t)$.
3. Finally, we need an explanation of saving and investment behavior that gives the *change* in the capital stock, investment, as a function of the *level* of output. One simple saving-investment function assumes saving is a constant fraction, s, of output, so that $dK/dr = I_t = S_t = sQ_t$.

With a given capital stock and labor force at some initial time t_0, the production function of assumption 2 gives the level of output. The investment behavior of assumption 3 gives the increase in K from t_0 to t_1 as a function of the t_0 level of output, and the labor force growth of assumption 1 gives the change in L from t_0 to t_1. These new values of K and L in t_1 give a new level of full-employment output in t_1, and so on. Thus, the entire model of growth is embedded in the three assumptions concerning labor force growth, the production function, and investment behavior. Formulating a growth model in terms of these assumptions amounts to drawing the implications of the assumptions for an array of questions such as these: Do long-run equilibrium values of output per person, $Q/L = q$, and capital per person, $K/L = k$, exist?

575

If so, are these equilibrium values stable? What are the equilibrium levels of consumption and investment? What is the distribution of output between profit and wages in equilibrium?

This chapter will develop the basic neoclassical growth model formulated by Robert W. Solow, based on the following assumptions:

1. The labor force growth rate is given exogenously as g_L.
2. The production function is $Q = F(K, L)$, with properties to be discussed shortly.
3. Investment and saving are a fixed fraction of output.

The first section will develop the properties of the production function that are important to the analysis of the growth model. The basic requirement is that the function exhibit constant returns to scale.

Next, we will study the neoclassical growth model under conditions of no technical progress. The analysis of the model is exactly the same with or without the assumption that effective labor units E are growing relative to the labor force L, and the initial exposition is much clearer if we omit this complication.

In studying the neoclassical model, we first see that the model tends toward a long-run equilibrium capital-labor ratio k^* (a star* denotes the equilibrium value of any given variable) at which output per worker is also in equilibrium at q^*, and Q, K, and L all grow at the rate g_L. Then we investigate the distribution of output between consumption and investment and the implications of the model for factor payments—the wage and profit rates—and income shares.

In the next section we will introduce technical progress in the form of *effective* labor units, $E_t = L_t e^{\lambda t}$. The analysis will follow exactly the same lines as that of the model without technical progress with E replacing L throughout. Finally, we can, in a nonrigorous fashion, relax the assumptions of constant returns to scale and of exogenously determined population growth to illustrate cases of multiple equilibria. These include the case of the *low-level equilibrium trap* which may be relevant to underdeveloped countries.

THE CONSTANT-RETURNS PRODUCTION FUNCTION

The neoclassical growth model is built on a production function with constant returns to scale, capital and labor substitutability, and diminishing marginal productivities. The production function,

$$Q = F(K, L), \tag{1}$$

is homogeneous of first degree, or, to put it another way, it exhibits constant returns to scale. This means if all inputs are changed proportionately, then output will change by the same proportion. In other words, the function can be written as

$$aQ = F(aK, aL). \tag{2}$$

If K and L are doubled ($a = 2$), then output will also double. This is what is meant by the assumption of constant returns to scale.

With this assumption, we can write the production function in a very handy per capita form. If we let $a = 1/L$, then we have

$$q \equiv \frac{Q}{L} = F\left(\frac{K}{L}, 1\right) = f\left(\frac{K}{L}\right) = f(k). \tag{3}$$

This gives output per person as a function of capital per person *alone*. Increasing the scale of operations by increasing K and L proportionately will not change Q/L. Thus, there is no gain in Q/L from increasing both labor and capital as long as the K/L ratio k is the same *because* the production function exhibits constant returns to scale. The per capita production function (3) is shown in Figure 24-1. The marginal productivity to increasing the K/L ratio is positive, but diminishing. That is, $f'(k) > 0, f''(k) < 0$.

An example of a constant returns to scale, diminishing the marginal-productivity function, is the familiar Cobb–Douglas function:

$$Q = bK^\alpha L^{1-\alpha}. \tag{4}$$

Here homogeneity of degree one, or constant returns to scale, is ensured by making the coefficients of K and L sum to unity. The reader should verify this by seeing what happens to Q if K and L are multiplied by 2. This production function can be put in per capita terms:

$$q = \frac{Q}{L} = \frac{bK^\alpha L^{1-\alpha}}{L} = \frac{bK^\alpha}{L^\alpha} = b\left(\frac{K}{L}\right)^\alpha = bk^\alpha. \tag{5}$$

We can compute the marginal productivity of k:

$$MPk = \frac{\partial q}{\partial k} = bak^{\alpha-1}, \tag{6}$$

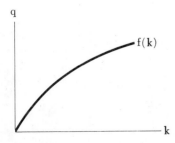

Figure 24-1 Per capita production function.

which is positive. The second derivative,

$$\frac{\partial(MPk)}{\partial k} = \frac{\partial^2 q}{\partial k^2}$$

$$= b\alpha(\alpha - 1)k^{\alpha-2}, \tag{7}$$

is negative since $\alpha < 1$. This shows that the MPk is *decreasing* with additions to k; that is, the production function of Figure 24-1 is concave downward, as shown.

Introduction of the neoclassical production function with the possibility of substitution between capital and labor inputs gives us a way to *vary* the capital-output ratio as the growth process proceeds. Each point on the production function of Figure 24-1 determines a ratio of q to k:

$$\frac{q}{k} = \frac{Q/L}{K/L} = \frac{Q}{K}, \tag{8}$$

which is the inverse of the capital-output ratio v. Thus, the slope of a ray from the origin to any point on the production function determines the capital-output ratio at that point; the slope of the ray is given by $1/v$. As the economy moves out along the production function with k increasing from k_0 to k_1 to k_2 in Figure 24-2, the capital-output ratio increases from v_0 to v_1 to v_2. This is because the labor-intensive production function of Figures 24-1 and 24-2 shows diminishing returns to increases in k.

Recall from Chapter 23 that the basic difficulty with the Harrod–Domar model is that it is overdetermined; s, v, and q_L are all given exogenously, so that only by coincidence could the equilibrium growth condition $g_L = s/v$ be met. Introducing the neoclassical production function gives us a way to allow

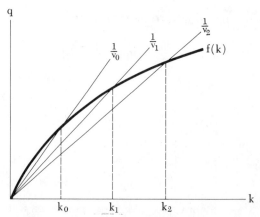

Figure 24-2   The relationship of k and v.

v to vary as k changes, thus eliminating the rigidity of the Harrod–Domar model.

EQUILIBRIUM GROWTH IN THE NEOCLASSICAL MODEL

We can now ask whether the production function described in labor-intensive form in equation (3), taken together with the exogenous growth of the labor force,

$$L_t = L_0 e^{g_L t}, \tag{9}$$

and the saving-investment assumption,

$$\frac{dK}{dt} \equiv I_t = S_t = sQ_t, \tag{10}$$

yields a dynamic system that tends toward equilibrium values of the capital-labor ratio k, output per person q, and the capital-output ratio v. We begin by developing the equation for the growth rate of the capital-labor ratio k.

The Equilibrium Capital-Labor Ratio

Focusing on the capital-labor ratio, we want to see if there is an equilibrium K/L ratio k^* toward which the economy moves, whatever initial capital-labor ratio k_0 it begins with. If there is, this implies that the economy moves toward an equilibrium growth path as it moves toward that K/L ratio k^*, and then grows along that growth path if that k^* is a stable equilibrium. Along that growth path, the values of k and q would be constant at k^* and q^*, so that both capital and output would grow at the same rate as the labor force.

Writing the k ratio in logarithmic form gives us

$$\ln k_t = \ln K_t - \ln L_t. \tag{11}$$

Differentiation of this expression gives us the equation for the proportional growth rate of the capital-labor ratio,

$$\dot{k}_t \equiv \frac{dk/dt}{k} = \frac{dK/dt}{K} - \frac{dL/dt}{L} \equiv \dot{K}_t - \dot{L}_t, \tag{12}$$

where, as usual, a dot over a variable denotes the proportional growth rate of that variable.

Since the numerator of the $\dot{K}$ term in equation (12) is investment which is in turn equal to sQ, and $\dot{L}$ is given exogenously as g_L, we can rewrite (12) as

$$\dot{k} = \frac{sQ}{K} - g_L.$$

Dividing both Q and K by L then gives us

$$\dot{k} = \frac{sq}{k} - g_L = \frac{sf(k)}{k} - g_L \tag{13}$$

as the fundamental differential growth-rate equation in terms of the capital-labor ratio k. This equation gives $\dot{k}$, the *rate of growth* of k, in terms of the *level* of k itself.

The equilibrium capital-labor ratio is that value of k which makes $\dot{k}$ equal to zero in equation (13). If k reaches that value, it will remain there, since $\dot{k}$ will then be zero. We can find the equilibrium value, k^*, by setting $\dot{k}$ in (13) equal to zero, so that

$$\frac{sf(k^*)}{k^*} = g_L \tag{14}$$

defines k^*.

The solution of equation (13) for the equilibrium value k^* is shown in Figure 24-3(a). The equilibrium condition (14) can be rewritten as

$$q^* = f(k^*) = \frac{g_L}{s} k^*. \tag{15}$$

Figure 24-3(a) shows the production function, $q = f(k)$, and a ray through the origin with slope g_L/s. At the k value where the two lines cross,

$$f(k) = \frac{g_L}{s} k \quad \text{or} \quad \frac{sf(k)}{k} = g_L,$$

so that $\dot{k} = 0$, and that value of k is the equilibrium value k^*. It remains to be determined whether that equilibrium point is a stable one. Will the economy move to that k^* point and stay there, if it begins at a different K/L ratio? The answer is yes.

By inspection of Figure 24-3(a), we can see that to the left of k^*, where $k < k^*$, $f(k) > [(g_L/s)k]$. This means that

$$\frac{sf(k)}{k} > g_L,$$

and from equation (13) we can see that in this case $\dot{k} > 0$, so that k is increasing if $k < k^*$. To the right of k^*, where $k > k^*$, and

$$\frac{sf(k)}{k} < g_L,$$

$\dot{k} < 0$ and k is decreasing.

Thus, the economy will indeed move toward the k^* equilibrium where $\dot{k} = 0$ from any initially given capital-labor ratio k_0. This stability is shown

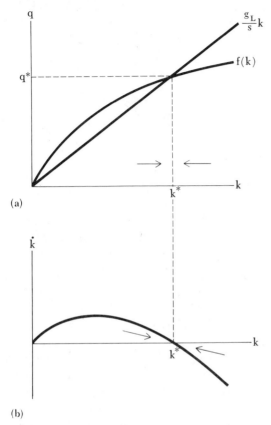

Figure 24-3 Neoclassical growth equilibrium.

by the phase diagram in Figure 24-3(b), which plots $\dot{k}$ against k. To the left of k^*, $\dot{k} > 0$ and k is increasing. To the right of k^*, $\dot{k} < 0$ and k is decreasing. At k^*, $\dot{k} = 0$, so that the economy stays at k^*. Thus, the system is stable.

This analysis shows that an economy that maintains full employment of capital and labor and is characterized by our three assumptions concerning labor force growth, the production function, and investment behavior will move toward some equilibrium capital-labor ratio k^* from its initial k ratio. Once it reaches its k^* value, which is determined by g_L, s, and the shape of the production function $f(k)$, capital will grow as fast as labor to maintain k at k^*.

One way to describe this movement graphically is shown in the capital-labor space of Figure 24-4. There the equilibrium capital-labor ratio k^* is described as a ray from the origin with slope k^*. If the economy begins with $k_0 < k^*$, for example, at point A, as labor grows at its exogenously determined rate, investment is sufficiently large to raise the capital-labor ratio toward k^*

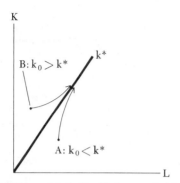

Figure 24-4 Equilibrium capital-labor ratio.

as both K and L grow. When the capital-labor ratio reaches k^*, the capital stock is large enough that it takes all of the investment generated by sQ to keep it growing at the same rate as the labor force, so k stays at k^*. If the economy somehow began at point B, the investment generated by sQ would not even suffice to keep K growing as fast as L; so k would fall toward k^* as K and L grew. Eventually, the economy would reach equilibrium k^* where the capital-labor ratio would be constant and $\dot{K} = \dot{L} = g_L$.

From the production function we see that when k reaches k^*, output per person q also reaches an equilibrium level q^*. With output per person constant at q^*, output is also growing as fast as the labor force, so that $\dot{Q} = \dot{L} = g_L$ also. This model therefore explains the convergence of the economy toward a steady growth path where $\dot{Q} = \dot{K}$ and the capital-output ratio v is constant, but it is not consistent with the stylized fact that both $\dot{Q}$ and $\dot{K}$ are greater than $\dot{L}$. This discrepancy can be eliminated by adding a technical progress factor to labor force growth, giving an *effective labor force* growing faster than L. We will return to this point after completing the development of the basic no-technical-progress model.

The Equilibrium Capital-Output Ratio

The equilibrium condition (14) can be rewritten as

$$\frac{g_L}{s} = \frac{f(k^*)}{k^*} = \frac{1}{v^*} . \tag{16}$$

This is because $f(k^*)$ is just equilibrium output per person; dividing it by capital per person gives equilibrium Q/K, the reciprocal of the equilibrium capital-output ratio v^*. Thus, the neoclassical model with a production function that allows v to vary explains how the economy moves toward the equilibrium capital-output ratio v^*, which then tends to remain constant through time.

Again rewriting the equilibrium condition, we have

$$g_L = \frac{s}{v^*}, \tag{17}$$

the Harrod–Domar condition for balanced full-employment growth. By allowing v to vary, the neoclassical model explains how the economy will tend toward a growth path along which the Harrod–Domar condition is met. Thus, the observed, roughly constant, capital-output ratio v^* can be viewed as the *result* of an equilibration process that brings it equal to s/g_L, rather than as a necessary technological assumption.

The Role of the Saving Rate

The equilibrium condition shown in Figures 24-3 and 24-4 assumes a given saving rate, which fixes, along with g_L, the slope of the g_L/s line in Figure 24-3 and thus determines the equilibrium k^*. Figure 24-5 shows the effect on k^* of an increase in the saving rate from s_0 to s_1. The g_L/s line is rotated down, increasing k^* from k_0^* to k_1^*.

With k at the initial equilibrium level k_0^*, the increase in the saving rate from s_0 to s_1 increases investment—presumably the government eases monetary conditions to increase I to match the exogenous drop in C—above the level needed to keep K growing as fast as L at k_0^*. Thus, the capital-labor ratio begins to rise toward the new equilibrium k_1^* level, where, once again growth of that larger capital stock at the rate g_L will absorb $s_1 Q$ of investment.

The departure from one equilibrium level of k, k_0^*, and movement toward another, k_1^*, means moving from one trend growth path toward another. This is illustrated in Figure 24-6, which shows the growth path of Q

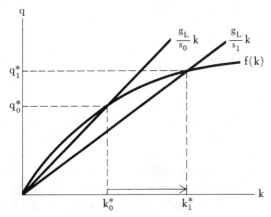

Figure 24-5 The saving rate and k^*.

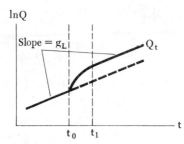

Figure 24-6 Equilibrium growth path: increase in the saving rate.

through time. At time t_0 there is an increase in the saving rate from s_0 to s_1. This causes the system to begin moving toward a higher equilibrium k^*, k_1^*, which in turn brings a higher q^*. Thus, the saving rate increase shifts the equilibrium growth in path in Figure 24-6 up, bringing a transitory period of output growth at a faster rate than q_L as output per person rises from q_0^* toward q_1^* in Figure 24-5. The new equilibrium k_1^* is reached at time t_1, and the economy moves along a new trend growth path with the same slope, or growth *rate,* as the earlier one, equal to the growth rate of the labor force, but one with a higher *level* of Q due to the saving rate increase.

Investment and Consumption in Equilibrium

To study the implications of the neoclassical model for investment and consumption, we can rewrite the equilibrium condition, (14), as

$$sf(k^*) = g_L k^*. \tag{18}$$

All we have done is to multiply both sides of equation (15) by the same constant, s, which in graphical terms means simply shifting the two functions $f(k)$ and $(g_L/s)k$ down by the same proportion s, as shown in Figure 21-7.

Since $I = sQ$, and $q = f(k)$, we know that investment per person, I/L, is given by

$$\frac{I}{L} = \frac{sQ}{L} = sq = sf(k). \tag{19}$$

Thus, the $sf(k)$ curve in Figure 24-7 shows investment per person for any given level of k. Then if $f(k)$ gives output per person and $sf(k)$ gives investment per person, the difference between the $f(k)$ and $sf(k)$ curves in Figure 24-7 must be equal to consumption per person at any given k.

The $g_L k$ line in Figure 24-7 gives the investment per person needed to increase the capital stock rapidly enough to preserve any given capital-labor ratio, such as k_0, with a growing labor force. This is true for all levels of k, not just equilibrium k^* levels. This can be seen by noting that to maintain k

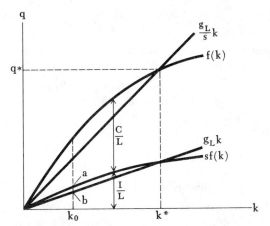

Figure 24-7 Equilibrium per capita investment and consumption.

constant, K must grow as fast as L, or $\dot{K} = g_L$. But $\dot{K}$ is given by I/K, so that to maintain k constant—again, for any given k—we require that

$$g_L = \frac{I}{K},$$

or

$$I = K \cdot g_L.$$

Dividing by L converts this condition into

$$\frac{I}{L} = \frac{K}{L} g_L = g_L k,$$

so that the $g_L k$ line shows investment per person needed to maintain any given capital-labor ratio k.

At k_0 in Figure 24-7, total investment per person, $sf(k)$, is generated at level a, while investment per person required to *maintain* k_0, $g_L k$, is at level b. Thus, at k_0 investment per person is greater than that required to keep k_0 constant so that k is rising; $\dot{k} > 0$. As k increases, the amount of investment needed to maintain k increases *proportionately*. But since there are diminishing returns to increasing k, and investment is proportional to q ($I/L = sq$), as k increases total investment per person rises *less than proportionately*. Thus, as k rises, the gap between $sf(k)$ and $g_L k$ in Figure 24-7—which is the investment per person available to increase the k ratio—diminishes. Eventually, the economy reaches the level of k where it takes all the investment generated by $sf(k)$ to keep $\dot{K} = g_L$, so that $sf(k) = g_L k$, and k has reached the equilibrium level k^*.

An increase in the saving rate would shift the $sf(k)$ function of Figure 24-7 up and the $(g_L/s)k$ function down, increasing k^*. With a higher s, investment per person would be greater than that required to maintain the old k^*, so the economy would move toward a new, higher k^*, that is, toward a higher trend growth path. Eventually, however, diminishing returns cause the economy once again to reach a point where $\dot{k} = 0$, and $\dot{K} = \dot{Q} = \dot{L} = g_L$ along the higher growth path of Figure 24-6.

Wages, Profits, and Relative Shares

Finally, we can develop the implications of the neoclassical model for the price constellation—the profit rate ρ and real wage rate w—and distribution of output to factor income shares with competitive pricing assumptions.

The constant-returns-to-scale production function can be written as

$$Q = Lf\left(\frac{K}{L}\right) = Lf(k), \tag{20}$$

as was shown earlier in equation (3). The profit rate, or return to capital, ρ, in a competitive economy with constant returns is equal to the marginal product of capital, the MPK. Thus, for the profit rate ρ we have

$$\rho = MPK = \frac{\partial Q}{\partial K} = Lf'\left(\frac{K}{L}\right) \cdot \frac{1}{L},$$

or, canceling the L terms,

$$\rho = f'(k). \tag{21}$$

That is, the profit rate is simply the slope of the per capita production function.

The return to labor, or real wage rate, in a competitive economy, is equal to the marginal product of labor, the MPL. Thus, we have

$$w = MPL = \frac{\partial Q}{\partial L} = Lf'\left(\frac{K}{L}\right) \cdot \left(-\frac{K}{L^2}\right) + f\left(\frac{K}{L}\right),$$

or

$$w = f(k) - kf'(k). \tag{22}$$

This simply says that

$$\frac{\text{Wages}}{\text{Person}} = f(k) - kf'(k).$$

But $f(k)$ is output per person, k is capital per person, and the profit rate is profits per unit of capital, so that (22) says that

$$\frac{\text{Wages}}{\text{Person}} = \frac{\text{output}}{\text{person}} - \frac{\text{capital}}{\text{person}} \cdot \frac{\text{profits}}{\text{capital}},$$

or

$$\frac{\text{Wages}}{\text{Person}} = \frac{\text{output}}{\text{person}} - \frac{\text{profits}}{\text{person}},$$

which must be true if wages and profits add up to total output.

The relative income shares of capital and labor in equilibrium at k^*, q^* are shown in Figure 24-8. In equilibrium at $k^* = (K/L)^*$, output per person is given by $(Q/L)^*$. Profits per person, P/L, are the product of K/L and P/K, but P/K, the profit rate ρ, is given by the slope of the production function at k^*, q^*. Thus, the graphical representation of $(K/L) \cdot (P/K)$ is given by the difference between $(Q/L)^*$ and the q-axis intercept of the tangent to the production function at k^*, q^*, which has slope ρ. In equilibrium at k^*, q^*, profits per person are given by P/L in Figure 24-8. The difference between Q/L and P/L is wages per person W/L, as we just saw. This gives us the equilibrium distribution of output between profits and wages shown in Figure 24-8. Once the economy reaches the equilibrium k^*, q^* point, the distribution of output per person between profits per person and wages per person is constant. Thus, the neoclassical model without technical progress explains the constancy of relative income shares. We will see shortly that this is also the case after we introduce technical progress into the model.

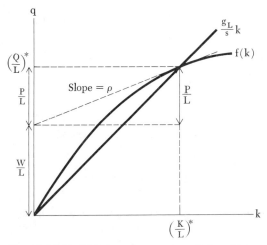

Figure 24-8 Relative shares of capital and labor in equilibrium at k^*, q^*.

THE NEOCLASSICAL MODEL WITH TECHNICAL PROGRESS

Earlier, we saw that the basic neoclassical growth model without technical progress produces the result that when the economy is growing along the long-run trend equilibrium growth path, output and capital grow at the same rate as the labor force, that is,

$$\dot{Q} = \dot{K} = \dot{L} = g_L.$$

These results, however, are not in accord with the stylized facts of growth which indicate that capital and output tend to grow at the same rate, but faster than the labor force, so that in fact,

$$\dot{K} = \dot{Q} > \dot{L} = g_L.$$

To reconcile this difference, we can introduce technical progress into the picture in the form of a rate of increase in labor productivity, exogenously determined. Thus, we can redefine the labor force in the neoclassical Solow model as the *effective labor force E,* including not only the number of workers but also an element of technical improvement. Assume that the labor force grows at the rate g_L, and effective labor units per person grow at the rate λ. This gives us

$$E_t = L_t e^{\lambda t} = L_0 e^{g_L t} e^{\lambda t} = L_0 e^{(g_L + \lambda)t}. \tag{23}$$

Effective worker-hours E_t grow at the rate $g_L + \lambda$, and the ratio of E_t / L_t grows at the rate λ.

Next, we can restate the production function in terms of K and E:

$$Q_t = F(K_t, E_t), \tag{24}$$

where all the properties for $F(K, L)$ still hold, except that E is now substituted for L.

Growth Equilibrium with Technical Progress

We can now repeat the entire analysis of the growth process substituting E for L. Beginning with the production function, we have

$$q = \frac{Q}{E} = \frac{Q}{L e^{\lambda t}} = f\left(\frac{K}{L e^{\lambda t}}\right) = f(k), \tag{25}$$

where k is now defined as K/E. Next, since $k = K/E$, we obtain the expression for the growth rate of k,

$$\dot{k} = \dot{K} - \dot{E}. \tag{26}$$

Since $E = Le^{\lambda t} = L_0 e^{(g_L+\lambda)t}$, the growth rate E is exogenously given as $g_L + \lambda$, so that (26) can be rewritten as

$$\dot{k} = \frac{sQ}{K} - (g_L + \lambda) = \frac{sq}{k} - (g_L + \lambda) = \frac{sf(k)}{k} - (g_L + \lambda). \qquad (27)$$

The equilibrium value of k, k^*, is again obtained by setting $\dot{k}$ in equation (27) equal to zero, so that at k^*,

$$\frac{sf(k^*)}{k^*} = g_L + \lambda. \qquad (28)$$

We can locate equilibrium k^* graphically in Figure 24-9 by rewriting the equilibrium condition (28) as

$$f(k^*) = \frac{g_L + \lambda}{s} k^*. \qquad (29)$$

The ray from the origin in Figure 24-9 now has a slope $(g_L + \lambda)/s$, while in Figure 24-3 the slope was g_L/s since there it was assumed that $\lambda = 0$. The point of intersection of $f(k)$ and $[(g_L + \lambda)/s]k$ in Figure 24-9 gives us the stable equilibrium values for $k^* = (K/E)^*$ and $q^* = (Q/E)^*$.

At the equilibrium value k^*, the ratio of capital to E is constant, so that along the equilibrium growth path,

$$\dot{K} = \dot{E} = g_L + \lambda, \qquad (30)$$

and the ratio of capital to labor grows at the rate λ. Equilibrium k^* determines an equilibrium value of output per *effective* worker q at q^* in Figure 24-9. If the ratio of Q to E is constant along the equilibrium growth path, then

$$\dot{Q} = \dot{E} = g_L + \lambda = \dot{K}. \qquad (31)$$

Thus, with E defined as $Le^{\lambda t}$, we explain the stylized fact that $\dot{Q}$ and $\dot{K}$ are equal, and both exceed $\dot{L}$ by λ, which is now recognized as the rate of growth of labor productivity.

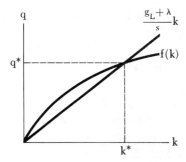

Figure 24-9 Growth equilibrium with technical progress.

The analysis of the distribution of output between investment and consumption is the same here as in the model without technical progress. The result that the stability of the equilibrium k^*, q^* solution comes basically from the fact that the level of investment needed to maintain any given k ratio grows proportionately with k, while the actual level of investment increases less than proportionately with k since $f''(k) < 0$, is also the same. The fact that the relative income shares of labor and capital are constant in the model with technical progress probably requires some elaboration, however.

Income Shares with Technical Progress

Turning to the relative shares of capital and labor, we find that this technical progress model leads us back to the wage-price guideposts discussed in Chapter 19. The production function given in equation (25) can be written as

$$Q = Ef\left(\frac{K}{E}\right) = Le^{\lambda t}f\left(\frac{K}{E}\right) = Le^{\lambda t}f(k). \tag{32}$$

Differentiation of the middle version of (32) with respect to K gives us the MPK, or, under competitive conditions, the profit rate,

$$\rho = \frac{\partial Q}{\partial K} = Le^{\lambda t}f'\left(\frac{K}{Le^{\lambda t}}\right) \cdot \frac{1}{Le^{\lambda t}} = f'\left(\frac{K}{Le^{\lambda t}}\right) = f'(k), \tag{33}$$

so that the profit rate is equal to the slope of the production function in Figure 21-9, which is *constant* in equilibrium.

The wage rate is given by differentiation of Q with respect to L:

$$w = \frac{\partial Q}{\partial L} = Le^{\lambda t}f'\left(\frac{K}{Le^{\lambda t}}\right) \cdot \left(-\frac{K}{e^{\lambda t}L^2}\right) + e^{\lambda t}f(k).$$

Simplification of this expression gives us

$$w = e^{\lambda t}[f(k) - kf'(k)] \tag{34}$$

for the real wage w.

In equilibrium, the value of k is constant at k^*, so that the real wage rate grows at the rate λ, which is the rate of growth of average labor productivity, $\dot{Q} - \dot{L}$. Thus, the wage guidepost that the aggregate real wage rate should grow at the same rate as productivity is consistent with a neoclassical growth equilibrium with technical progress.

The capital share of income is given by the product of the profit rate ρ and the capital stock K, while $w \cdot L$ gives the labor share. Thus, to see whether income shares are constant in the technical progress model, we can ask whether the ratio of ρK to wL is constant. In equilibrium we found

$$\frac{K}{E} = \frac{K}{Le^{\lambda t}} = k^*,$$

a constant. This means that $K/L = k^* e^{\lambda t}$, and, as we have seen, the capital-labor ratio grows at the rate λ in equilibrium. Combining this with expressions (33) and (34) for the profit and real wage rates, respectively, and noticing that the ratio of the capital share to the labor share is given by $\rho K/wL = (\rho/w) \cdot (K/L)$, we have

$$\frac{S_K}{S_L} \equiv \frac{K \text{ share}}{L \text{ share}} = \frac{f'(k^*)}{e^{\lambda t}[f(k^*) - k^* f'(k^*)]} \cdot k^* e^{\lambda t}. \tag{35}$$

Canceling out $e^{\lambda t}$ yields the result that the ratio of the capital share to the labor share is constant at the equilibrium K/E ratio k^*. If the ratio of the wage rate to the profit rate grows as fast as the ratio of K to L, the two movements cancel each other out and relative shares remain constant.

Thus, by adding a factor for technical progress, we have explained all of the stylized facts of growth. Capital and output grow at the same rate, $g_L + \lambda$, so the capital-output ratio is constant. Both the K and Q growth rates exceed L by λ, so that both K/L and Q/L grow at the rate λ. The profit rate is roughly constant, while the real wage grows at rate λ. This leaves relative income shares constant.

MULTIPLE EQUILIBRIA IN THE NEOCLASSICAL MODEL

As noted earlier, the neoclassical model, suitably modified to take account of technical progress, seems to be generally relevant to the developed, or industrial, economies, since the assumption of constant returns to scale and the maintenance of full employment, at least since the 1940s, may be generally valid in those economies. However, we know that not all economies share these characteristics. In developing economies there is a much wider scope for increasing returns to scale. This would change the shape of the production function and lead to the possibility of multiple equilibrium positions. It is also possible that the rate of growth of the population may depend on the level of per capita income, so that g_L depends on q and k. This would also lead to the possibility of multiple equilibria.

Increasing Returns to Scale

Earlier in this chapter, we saw that the equilibrium k^* is stable because the production function cut from above the g_L/s ray from the origin. Since the production function assumed diminishing q returns to increases in capital per person k as k grew, investment grew less than proportionately while the level of investment required to maintain k grew proportionately. Thus, eventually the economy, with diminishing returns to k increases, moved to a stable equilibrium, k^*.

If the production function exhibits increasing returns to scale, owing, perhaps, to the need to provide *social overhead capital*—roads, dams, and so on—the production function could have the shape shown in Figure 24-10(a). Output per person could grow with increasing returns to the capital-labor ratio k at low k levels—$f''(k) > 0$—and as k rises eventually reach a point of diminishing returns where $f''(k) < 0$. Thus, the production function could have two intersections with the g_L/s line, cutting it from below at a low k level, k^{**}, and from above at a higher k level, k^*. This gives us two possible equilibrium k levels, but only one is stable.

Where $k < k^{**}$ in Figure 24-10(a), $f(k) < [(g_L/s)k]$. Thus,

$$\frac{sf(k)}{k} < g_L,$$

and we know from equation (13) that $\dot{k} < 0$. Using similar reasoning for each portion of the production function, we can derive the phase diagram shown

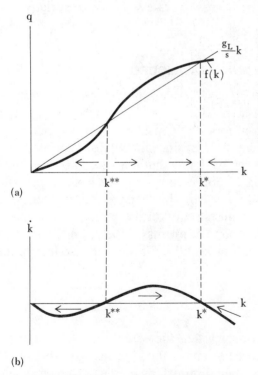

(a)

(b)

Figure 24-10 The neoclassical model: increasing returns to scale and phases of growth.

in Figure 24-10(b). The implication of the phase diagram is that, if the economy begins at a point where $k < k^{**}$, k will decrease toward zero and the economy will, in some sense, disappear. This point, k^{**}, is a *low unstable equilibrium point*. If somehow the economy could be pushed over that point, it could then move to the higher, *stable* equilibrium level at k^*. This model suggests that if the saving ratio could be increased temporarily, the low unstable equilibrium point could be done away with, and the economy would grow toward the upper, stable, equilibrium k^*.

Variable Population Growth

A more interesting model can be developed by introducing systematic variation in the rate of population growth as q and k change. We will assume that at a low level of output, g_L is very low. As output begins to grow above a subsistence level, g_L begins to increase quite rapidly. At a yet higher level of output, g_L begins to slow again. This pattern of g_L variation is shown by the curve with slope g_L/s in Figure 24-11(a), which also shows the original production function, $q = f(k); f''(k) < 0$.

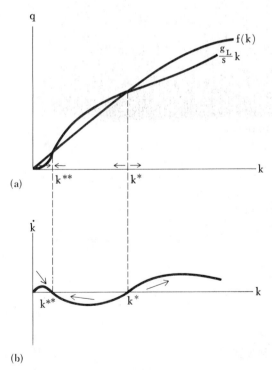

(a)

(b)

Figure 24-11 Variable population growth rates and the "low-level equilibrium trap."

Again the model has at least two equilibrium points, k^{**} and k^*. By examining the two functions with reference to the equilibrium condition given by equation (13), we can derive the phase diagram of Figure 24-11(b). It tells us that the low-level equilibrium k^{**} is now stable. This is what Richard Nelson has called the *low-level equilibrium trap*. If the economy begins with any k lower than k^*, rapid population growth with rising income ensures that k will move to the stable equilibrium level k^{**}. But if the economy can initially rise above k^*, getting out of the trap, it will continue to expand indefinitely, unless there is a third equilibrium point associated with superaffluence and higher population growth rates.

This model gives a basic rationale for the theory of the *big push* in economic development. If saving rates could just be increased sufficiently, if the production function could be shifted up, or if a "windfall" of capital could be obtained, so that k is increased above k^*, the low-level trap could be bypassed and the economy would enter a phase of self-sustaining growth. These variations on the basic neoclassical model do not offer any new insights into the real problems of economic development. Rather, they provide a description of a problem—a way of viewing the situation that the underdeveloped countries are in.

SELECTED READINGS

R. G. D. Allen, *Macro-Economic Theory* (New York: St. Martin's Press, 1967), chapters 13–14.

J. Buttrick, "A Note on Professor Solow's Growth Model," *Quarterly Journal of Economics,* November 1958.

H. Leibenstein, *Economic Backwardness and Economic Growth* (New York: John Wiley and Sons, 1963).

R. R. Nelson, "A Theory of the Low Level Equilibrium Trap in Underdeveloped Economies," *American Economic Review,* December 1956.

E. S. Phelps, "The New View of Investment: A Neoclassical Analysis," *Quarterly Journal of Economics,* November 1962.

R. M. Solow, "A Contribution to the Theory of Economic Growth," *Quarterly Journal of Economics,* February 1956.

R. W. Solow, *Growth Theory* (Oxford: Oxford University Press, 1970).

chapter 25

The Basic Model Extended: Varying Saving Assumptions

In Chapter 24 we saw that the basic neoclassical growth model with a technical progress factor augmenting the effective labor force tends toward a long-run equilibrium growth path on which the ratio of capital to effective labor units $K/E = k$, and the ratio of output Q to E, q, approach equilibrium k^*, q^* values, so that both capital and output tend to grow as fast as the effective labor force E. With the effective labor force E defined as

$$E_t = L_t e^{\lambda t} = L_0 e^{(g_L + \lambda)t}, \tag{1}$$

E grows at the rate $g_L + \lambda$, so that in equilibrium at k^*, q^*,

$$\dot{Q} = \dot{K} = g_L + \lambda, \tag{2}$$

giving a growth rate of output per person and capital per person equal to λ, the *technical progress factor*. In long-run equilibrium the profit rate is constant, and the real wage rate grows at the rate λ. With K/L growing at the same rate λ, relative shares of output are constant in equilibrium, since

$$\frac{K \text{ share of output}}{L \text{ share of output}} = \frac{\rho K}{wL} = \text{constant}, \tag{3}$$

with w/ρ and K/L both growing at the same rate. Finally, we saw that the equilibrium growth path is *balanced*, with both investment and consumption growing at the *natural* rate $g_L + \lambda$.

These results came from the simplest one-sector (meaning that the economy has only one output that can be either invested or consumed) neoclassical growth model built on the following three basic assumptions:

1. The effective labor force E_t grows at the rate $g_L + \lambda$, as shown in equation (1).
2. Total output Q_t depends on capital K_t and effective labor E_t inputs according to the production function,

$$Q_t = F(K_t, E_t). \qquad (4)$$

The production function is homogeneous of degree one, or exhibits constant returns to scale, so that we can divide by E_t to obtain the labor-intensive production function,

$$q_t \equiv \frac{Q_t}{E_t} = f\left(\frac{K_t}{E_t}\right) \equiv f(k_t). \qquad (5)$$

3. Saving, which equals investment by the assumption of full employment, is a constant fraction s of output. Thus,

$$\frac{dK}{dt} = I_t = S_t = sQ_t. \qquad (6)$$

These three basic assumptions are combined in Chapter 24 to obtain the basic dynamic equation of the neoclassical growth model,

$$\dot{k} = \frac{sf(k)}{k} - (g_L + \lambda). \qquad (7)$$

This equation can be solved for a stable equilibrium k^* value for k where $\dot{k} = 0$. This equilibrium k^* value can be obtained by setting $\dot{k}$ in equation (7) equal to zero, so that

$$f(k^*) = \frac{g_L + \lambda}{s} k^*$$

defines the equilibrium k^*. This solution to equation (7) is shown graphically in Figure 25-1. The production function, $f(k)$, in Figure 25-1(a), gives the level of q for each value of k. The straight line showing $[(g_L + \lambda)/s]k$ for each value of k has the following economic interpretation.

At any given k level, for example k_0 in Figure 25-1(a), the amount of investment per effective worker needed to maintain k_0 is equal to $(g_L + \lambda)k_0$. Why is this so? To maintain a given K/E ratio k_0 with E growing at $g_L + \lambda$, K must grow at $g_L + \lambda$. But this says that *to maintain any given k,*

$$\frac{dK/dt}{K} = (g_L + \lambda).$$

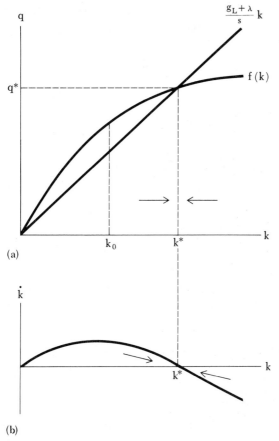

Figure 25-1 Neoclassical growth equilibrium.

Since $I = dK/dt$, this means that $I/K = g_L + \lambda$, so that $I = (g_L + \lambda)K$, and

$$\left.\frac{I}{E}\right|_{\bar{k}} = (g_L + \lambda)\frac{K}{E}$$

$$= (g_L + \lambda)k, \tag{8}$$

where we write $\left.\dfrac{I}{E}\right|_{\bar{k}}$ to denote the I/E ratio which holds k constant.

Now if $I = sQ$, so that $Q = I/s$ and $q = [(I/E)/s]$, and if investment per effective worker needed to maintain any given value of k is given by (8), the level of output per effective worker needed to maintain any given k can be found by dividing (8) by s:

$$\left.\frac{Q}{E}\right|_{\bar{k}} = \frac{1}{s}\cdot\left.\frac{I}{E}\right|_{\bar{k}} = \frac{g_L + \lambda}{s}k. \tag{9}$$

Thus, the q values given along the $[(g_L + \lambda)/s]k$ function give the output per effective worker needed to maintain the corresponding k ratios constants as E grows through time.

This analysis shows why the equilibrium k^*, q^* is stable. Left of k^*, output per effective person q exceeds the output level needed to maintain the k ratio constant. Thus, to the left of k^* there is enough investment both to equip each new E unit with the existing K/E ratio and to increase the K/E ratio; in that case $\dot{k} > 0$ and k grows. To the right of k^*, there is not even enough output per effective worker to outfit each new worker, or, to be precise, E unit, at the existing K/E ratio, given s, so k falls. At k^*, the q^* level actually produced is the q which yields just enough investment, given s, to maintain k constant as E grows. Thus, at k^*, $\dot{k} = 0$, and the system has reached a stable equilibrium. This stability is shown in the phase diagram of Figure 25-1(b).

Once we have found an equilibrium k^*, q^* that is stable, we can, assuming that the economy is competitive, differentiate the production function with respect to L and K to obtain the marginal products that will be equal to the real wage and profit rates. These rates, combined with equilibrium K/L, give the relative shares of output. Observing that

$$\frac{I}{E} = sf(k) \quad \text{and} \quad \frac{\text{Consumption}}{E} \equiv (1 - s)f(k),$$

we can obtain the distribution of output between consumption and investment at the equilibrium k^* level.

This chapter will investigate the consequences of changing the saving assumption 3, above. The basic neoclassical model assumed that saving is a constant fraction of output: $S = sQ$. Here we will consider three different saving assumptions. The first is the classical saving function in which $s = s(\rho)$; $s' > 0$. In this case the saving ratio declines as the profit rate, which measures the future return to saving, falls. The second alternative assumption is the Kaldor saving function, in which

$$S = s_w W + s_p P; \qquad 1 > s_p > s_w > 0.$$

Here the percentage of profits P which is saved, s_p, exceeds the percentage of wages W which is saved, s_w. Finally, we will consider the saving behavior implicit in the Ando–Modigliani consumption function,

$$C = \alpha_0 W + \alpha_1 K; \qquad 1 > \alpha_0 > \alpha_1 > 0.$$

In this case, consumption depends on labor income and consumer net worth, which in this simple model is the capital stock.

Each of these saving functions, combined with the E growth assumption and the production function, will yield a stable equilibrium k^*, q^* which is consistent with the stylized facts of Chapter 23. Seeing how the models are developed and what role the saving ratio plays in each will improve our understanding both of how the growth models work and of useful ways to view and manipulate the models.

THE CLASSICAL SAVING FUNCTION

The classical saving function makes the saving ratio s a function of the profit rate ρ. If the reason for saving and investing is to increase future consumption possibilities, one might expect that as the rate of return on investment—which equals saving in full-employment equilibrium—falls with a rising K/E ratio, the rate of saving will fall since the future consumption payoff will be reduced. We should note that this assumes that the substitution effect of a lower return on saving outweighs the income effect that would tend to increase saving to maintain a given future consumption stream. Under this assumption, the classical saving function can be written as

$$s = s(\rho); \qquad s' > 0. \tag{10}$$

The Equilibrium K/E Ratio

Combining this saving function with the constant-returns production function in K and E,

$$q = f\left(\frac{K}{E}\right) = f(k), \tag{11}$$

and the exogenously determined rate of growth of effective labor E_t given by

$$\dot{E} = g_L + \lambda, \tag{12}$$

we can construct the expression for the rate of growth of the K/E ratio, k:

$$k = \dot{K} - (g_L + \lambda) = \frac{sQ}{K} - (g_L + \lambda) = \frac{s(\rho)f(k)}{k} - (g_L + \lambda). \tag{13}$$

It is important to notice here that the key saving variable is the *ratio* of saving to output, given in equation (10) as $s(\rho)$. Later, when we introduce more complicated saving functions, we will see that the main analytical trick is to manipulate the saving function into a form where the saving *ratio* is a function of k. This has already been done in equation (13), since $\rho = f'(k)$.

Equation (13) can be solved for the equilibrium K/E ratio, k^*, by setting $\dot{k} = 0$ to obtain

$$\frac{s(\rho)f(k^*)}{k^*} - (g_L + \lambda) = 0,$$

or

$$f(k^*) = \frac{g_L + \lambda}{s(\rho)} k^*, \tag{14}$$

as the equation which determines k^*. This equilibrium condition is similar to that of the basic neoclassical model:

$$f(k^*) = \frac{g_L + \lambda}{s} k^*,$$

except that in equation (14) s is an increasing function of the profit rate. How does this change affect the determination of the *existence* and *stability* of the equilibrium k^*?

This question is answered graphically in Figure 25-2. There, in Figure 25-2(a) the $q = f(k)$ function is the same as that of Figure 25-1. But the $[(g_L + \lambda)/s]k$ function is now convex instead of a straight line. This is because as k increases, $\rho = f'(k)$, the slope of the production function, falls due to diminishing marginal returns. This decreasing ρ causes s to fall as k rises, since $s'(\rho) > 0$. The falling saving rate in turn causes the $(g_L + \lambda)/s$ slope to rise with increasing k, giving a convex shape to the $[(g_L + \lambda)/s]k$ function, as shown in Figure 25-2(a).

Earlier, we saw that at successively higher values of k, it takes proportionately higher levels of I/E to maintain the existing k ratio. But if the saving ratio is falling with increasing k, it will take increasing increments to Q/E to

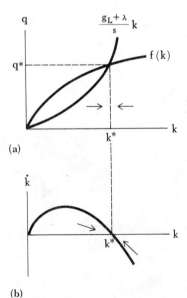

(a)

(b)

Figure 25-2   Equilibrium with classical saving function.

provide the proportional increases in I/E needed to maintain the existing k as E grows. Thus, the $[(g_L + \lambda)/s(\rho)]k$ function, which gives the output per effective worker needed to preserve any given k, has an increasing slope due to the falling s as k rises and ρ falls. Since the $f(k)$ function has a decreasing slope throughout—it is concave downward—and the $[(g_L + \lambda)/s(\rho)]k$ function has an increasing slope, they intersect once at the equilibrium k^*, q^* point shown in Figure 25-2(a).

This classical saving function ensures the existence of a stable equilibrium k^*, q^* in the one-sector model, as Figure 25-2(b) shows. To the left of k^*, where $k < k^*$,

$$f(k) > \frac{g_L + \lambda}{s(\rho)} k \quad \text{and} \quad \frac{s(\rho)f(k)}{k} > g_L + \lambda,$$

so that $\dot{k} > 0$, and k is increasing, as is shown in Figure 25-2(b). With the opposite results for $k > k^*$, it is clear that k^* is a stable equilibrium. Thus, in steady-state growth with the classical saving function, we have a constant k^* and q^*, so that

$$\dot{Q} = \dot{K} = g_L + \lambda, \tag{15}$$

and both output per person and capital per person grow at the rate λ.

Factor Returns and Income Shares

The values of the profit and wage rates can, as usual, be obtained from the production function, equation (5), which can be written as

$$Q = Le^{\lambda t} f\left(\frac{K}{Le^{\lambda t}}\right). \tag{16}$$

To obtain the profit rate, P/K, assuming the economy is competitive, we can differentiate (16) with respect to K:

$$\frac{P}{K} \equiv \rho = \frac{\partial Q}{\partial K} = Le^{\lambda t} f'(k) \cdot \frac{1}{Le^{\lambda t}} = f'(k). \tag{17}$$

Again the profit rate is given by the slope of the production function. At $k = k^*$, the profit rate is constant at $\rho^* = f'(k^*)$.

Next, to obtain the real wage rate w, we can differentiate (16) with respect to L:

$$\frac{W}{L} \equiv w = e^{\lambda t}\left[Lf'(k) \cdot \left(-\frac{K}{L^2 e^{\lambda t}}\right) + f(k)\right]$$
$$= e^{\lambda t}[f(k) - kf'(k)] = e^{\lambda t}f(k) - e^{\lambda t}kf'(k)$$
$$= \frac{\text{output}}{\text{person}} - \frac{\text{capital}}{\text{person}} \cdot \frac{\text{profits}}{\text{capital}}. \tag{18}$$

At $k = k^*$, $w = e^{\lambda t}[f(k^*) - k^*f'(k^*)]$, so that w grows at the rate λ with $f(k^*) - k^*f'(k^*)$ constant.

Thus, in long-run growth equilibrium, with the classical saving function and the neoclassical production function, the profit rate is constant and the wage rate grows at the rate of growth λ of output per person. Two things should be noted concerning this result.

First, this model yields the expected result that in equilibrium wages grow as fast as productivity, giving constant relative shares of output. Again, the relative distribution of output is determined by k^* and the shape of the production function, as shown in Figure 25-3. Profits per effective person, P/E, can be measured along the q-axis as the product $\rho^* k^*$. The rest of total q^* goes to wages per effective worker. Multiplying both P/E and W/E by E_t at any given time would give the distribution of Q_t between P_t and W_t. Second, once we have established that a stable equilibrium k^*, q^* exists, the propositions concerning the equilibrium values of ρ and w and the capital share and the labor share follow solely from differentiation of the production function under the assumption of a competitive economy that equates $w = MPL$ and $\rho = MPK$.

THE CHARACTERISTIC EQUATIONS OF A ONE-SECTOR GROWTH MODEL

By now we have seen that the equilibrium solution to a one-sector growth model is, in general, characterized by the following three simultaneous equations:

$$f(k^*) = \frac{g_L + \lambda}{s} k^* \quad \text{or} \quad g_L + \lambda = \frac{sf(k^*)}{k^*} = \frac{s}{v^*}, \qquad (19)$$

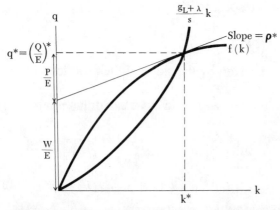

Figure 25-3 Classical saving function: relative shares of output.

where v, the capital-output ratio, is equal to both K/Q and k/q. Thus,

$$v^* = \frac{k^*}{f(k^*)} . \tag{20}$$

Finally, we have

$$\rho^* = f'(k^*), \tag{21}$$

which gives us the factor prices and the distribution of output to factor incomes.

In the basic neoclassical model with $(g_L + \lambda)$ and s fixed, the equilibrium solution of the model could be determined in a particularly simple way. From (19), given $(g_L + \lambda)$ and s, we can obtain equilibrium v^*. Given equilibrium v^*, k^* can be obtained from equation (20), as shown in Figure 25-4, where the production function and the ray with slope $1/v^*$ determine the location of k^*. Then, given k^*, we can obtain ρ^* from equation (21).

In the classical model, and in the Kaldor and Ando–Modigliani models to follow, solution of the simultaneous equilibrium equations (19)–(21) is not that simple because the saving ratio s is not *given*, but is a function of other variables in the system. In the classical model $s = s(\rho) = s[f'(k)]$. Substituting (21) and (20) into (19) gives us the equilibrium condition

$$g_L + \lambda = \frac{s[f'(k^*)]f(k^*)}{k^*} , \tag{22}$$

which is one equation in one variable k^*. This is the equilibrium condition expressed in equation (14) earlier.

The important points to be noticed here are the following:

1. From the basic assumptions concerning labor input growth, the production function, and saving behavior, we can obtain a basic dynamic equation in the form

$$\dot{k} = \frac{sf(k)}{k} - (g_L + \lambda),$$

where s is the ratio of saving to output.

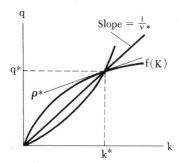

Figure 25-4 Equilibrium with a classical saving function.

2. This equation yields an equilibrium k^* where $\dot{k} = 0$, and there are generally a set of simultaneous equations such as (19)–(21) to describe the k^*, q^*, v^*, and price constellation in equilibrium.
3. These simultaneous equilibrium equations will be interrelated to the degree that the variables s, v, and k are interdependent. We might even, as in Chapter 24, consider g_L or λ to be a function of k.

With this growth model summary in mind, we now turn to the Kaldor and Ando–Modigliani saving functions.

THE KALDOR SAVING FUNCTION

Nicholas Kaldor suggested a saving function that makes the saving ratio a function of profit rate ρ and capital-output ratio v. Kaldor's basic saving function is

$$S = s_w W + s_p P. \tag{23}$$

Here wage income W plus profit income P add to output Q, and Kaldor assumes that the saving ratio out of profits, s_p, is greater than that out of wages, s_w. That is, it is assumed that $1 > s_p > s_w > 0$.

The overall saving ratio $s = S/Q$ can be derived from (23) as follows. First, since $W + P = Q$, we can write S as

$$S = s_w(Q - P) + s_p P = s_w Q + (s_p - s_w)P.$$

Dividing by Q to obtain the saving ratio s gives us

$$s \equiv \frac{S}{Q} = s_w + (s_p - s_w)\frac{P}{Q} = s_w + (s_p - s_w)\frac{P}{K}\cdot\frac{K}{Q}.$$

Noting that $P/K = \rho$ and $K/Q = v$, this expression can be rewritten to give s in terms of ρ, v, and the fixed ratios s_w and s_p:

$$s = s_w + (s_p - s_w)\rho v. \tag{24}$$

The expression for the growth rate of the K/E ratio k is, as usual, given by

$$\dot{k} = \frac{sf(k)}{k} - (g_L + \lambda). \tag{25}$$

Substituting the saving ratio from equation (24) into this expression for $\dot{k}$ gives us

$$\dot{k} = \left[s_w + (s_p - s_w)\rho\,\frac{k}{q}\right]\frac{q}{k} - (g_L + \lambda),$$

or

$$\dot{k} = s_w \frac{q}{k} + (s_p - s_w)\rho - (g_L + \lambda), \tag{26}$$

as the basic equation for the growth rate of k.

What does expression (26) for $\dot{k}$ tell us about the existence, and stability, of an equilibrium k^* where $\dot{k} = 0$? The answer can be determined as follows. At "low" values of k, such as k_0 in Figure 25-5, q/k and ρ are both "high," so that there is some low value of k, where

$$s_w \frac{q}{k} + (s_p - s_w)\rho > g_L + \lambda \quad \text{and} \quad \dot{k} > 0,$$

so that k is increasing. As k rises from that low value, both q/k and ρ fall, so that the difference between $[s_w(q/k) + (s_p - s_w)\rho]$ and $(g_L + \lambda)$ diminishes. Eventually, as k rises, it will reach a level—k^*—at which

$$s_w \frac{q}{k} + (s_p - s_w)\rho = g_L + \lambda$$

and

$$\dot{k} = 0.$$

For any k beyond that level k^*, where $k > k^*$,

$$s_w \frac{q}{k} + (s_p - s_w)\rho < g_L + \lambda$$

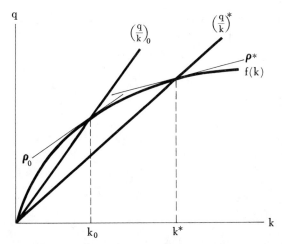

Figure 25-5 Kaldor saving function with neoclassical production function.

and

$$\dot{k} < 0,$$

so that k is decreasing.

Thus, the neoclassical growth model with the Kaldor saving function has a stable *equilibrium* $k*, q*$, which, in turn, yields results consistent with the stylized facts. Kaldor's saving function makes both the capital-output ratio v and the saving ratio s functions of the capital-labor ratio k, increasing both the freedom and the complexity of the model.

The expression for the saving ratio, equation (24), can be rewritten as

$$s = s_w + (s_p - s_w)f'(k) \cdot \frac{k}{f(k)}, \qquad (27)$$

using equation (21) for ρ, so that s is seen to be a function of k. Substitution of this expression, plus equation (20) for $v*$, back into the basic equilibrium condition given by (19), reproduced here as

$$f(k*) = \frac{s}{v*}, \qquad (28)$$

gives one equilibrium condition in one unknown, $k*$.

As we have seen, this $k*$ solution is stable, giving equilibrium growth at a stable $k*, q*$ point. Again, equilibrium factor prices and income shares can be derived from the production function in exactly the same fashion as in the basic neoclassical and classical models.

THE ANDO–MODIGLIANI (A–M) CONSUMPTION FUNCTION

The consumption function of Ando and Modigliani provides yet another important variant of the neoclassical one-sector growth model. The A–M consumption function also provides a conceptual link with the static models discussed in Parts II and III.

Derivation of the Saving Ratio

The A–M function makes consumption depend on labor income W and consumer net worth, which is given by K in our simple growth models. Thus, Ando and Modigliani posit a consumption function in which

$$C = \alpha_0 W + \alpha_1 K; \qquad 1 > \alpha_0 > \alpha_1 > 0. \qquad (29)$$

This can be converted into a saving function, assuming $S + C = Q$, as follows. First, we can write

$$S = Q - C = Q - \alpha_0 W - \alpha_1 K.$$

Since total labor income $W = Q - P$, this can be written as

$$S = Q - \alpha_0(Q - P) - \alpha_1 K = (1 - \alpha_0)Q + \alpha_0 P - \alpha_1 K.$$

Recognizing that $P = \rho K$, we have

$$S = (1 - \alpha_0)Q + \alpha_0 \rho K - \alpha_1 K$$

and

$$S = (1 - \alpha_0)Q - (\alpha_1 - \alpha_0 \rho)K, \tag{30}$$

as the basic form of the A–M aggregate saving function in a growth model context. If, as Ando and Modigliani assume, $\partial S/\partial K < 0$, then the expression $(\alpha_1 - \alpha_0 \rho)$ is positive. Dividing both sides of (30) by Q will give us an expression for the saving ratio s,

$$s \equiv \frac{S}{Q} = (1 - \alpha_0) - (\alpha_1 - \alpha_0 \rho)v, \tag{31}$$

since $K/Q = v$. Thus, (31) is the expression for the saving ratio s in terms of ρ and v implicit in the A–M consumption function.

The Equilibrium K/E Ratio

The expression for the growth rate of k is given by

$$\dot{k} = \frac{sf(k)}{k} - (g_L + \lambda), \tag{32}$$

so that k^*, where $\dot{k} = 0$, is given by the usual equilibrium condition:

$$f(k^*) = \frac{g_L + \lambda}{s} k^*. \tag{33}$$

The per capita production function, $f(k)$, can be plotted as usual in Figure 25-6. But what is the shape of the $[(g_L + \lambda)/s]k$ function, which gives the levels of output per effective person needed to maintain any given k? We can answer this question by determining how s varies with changes in k. If s falls

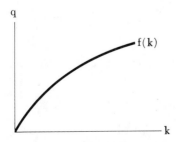

q

f(k)

k

Figure 25-6 Per capita production function.

as k rises, then the $[(g_L + \lambda)/s]k$ function will look like that of the classical model of Figure 25-2(a). If $\partial s/\partial k > 0$, the $[(g_L + \lambda)/s]k$ function will have a decreasing slope, and the model might not have an equilibrium k^*, q^* point because the $f(k)$ and $[(g_L + \lambda)/s]k$ lines might never cross. This seems intuitively unlikely because the A–M function basically assumes, with life-cycle saving behavior, that s falls as k rises, and if $(\alpha_1 - \alpha_0\rho)$ is, indeed, positive, this will be the case. But we can improve on this intuitive conclusion by determining directly the conditions under which $\partial s/\partial k < 0$ from expression (31) for s.

Since the capital-output ratio v rises as k rises along the Figure 25-6 production function, we can concentrate on the sign of $\partial s/\partial v$, translating to $\partial s/\partial k$ at the end. Differentiation of equation (31) with respect to v yields

$$\frac{\partial s}{\partial v} = -(\alpha_1 - \alpha_0\rho) + v\alpha_0 \frac{\partial\rho}{\partial v}. \tag{34}$$

Since ρ falls and v rises as k rises, $\partial\rho/\partial v < 0$. Thus, $\partial s/\partial v$—and $\partial s/\partial k$—could be positive only if $\alpha_0\rho > \alpha_1$, that is, if $\alpha_1 - \alpha_0\rho < 0$, contrary to the basic A–M assumption, as noted earlier.

The condition under which $\partial s/\partial v$ is negative can be developed much more precisely, however. We see from equation (34) that

$$\frac{\partial s}{\partial v} < 0 \quad \text{if} \quad -(\alpha_1 - \alpha_0\rho) + v\alpha_0 \frac{\partial\rho}{\partial v} < 0.$$

This condition can be rewritten as

$$\frac{\partial s}{\partial v} < 0 \quad \text{if} \quad \frac{\alpha_1}{\alpha_0\rho} - \frac{v}{\rho}\frac{\partial\rho}{\partial v} > 1. \tag{35}$$

Condition (35) for $\partial s/\partial v$ and $(\partial s/\partial k) < 0$ in the A–M model has an interesting interpretation. Consider that the capital share of output, S_K, is given by

$$S_K = \frac{\rho K}{Q} = \rho v,$$

so that

$$\ln S_K = \ln \rho + \ln v.$$

Then, remembering that increases in v accompany decreases in ρ, we have an expression for percentage changes in S_K:

$$\frac{dS_K}{S_K} = \frac{d\rho}{\rho} + \frac{dv}{v}.$$

If the elasticity of substitution in the underlying production function is unity—as in the Cobb–Douglas function—then S_K is constant $(dS_K/S_K = 0)$, as ρ and v change. This means that if the elasticity of substitution is unity,

$$\frac{d\rho}{\rho} = -\frac{dv}{v} \quad \text{and} \quad \frac{v}{\rho}\frac{d\rho}{dv} = -1.$$

If this is the case, then condition (35) for $\partial s/\partial v < 0$ reduces to $\alpha_1/\alpha_0\rho > 0$, which is obviously fulfilled. Thus, if *increases* in the capital-output ratio v are accompanied by equal percentage *decreases* in the profit rate ρ, then the share of capital in output will remain unchanged, and $(v/\rho)(d\rho/dv) = -1$. If the underlying production function has an elasticity of substitution equal to one, then condition (35) for $\partial s/\partial k < 0$ is met and the $[(g_L + \lambda)/s]k$ function is convex, similar to that of the Figure 25-2 classical model, so that an equilibrium k^*, q^* is ensured with the A–M consumption function.

But if the capital share tends to rise with rising v, implying that the drop in ρ does not offset the rise in v, then the factor $(v/\rho)(\partial\rho/\partial v)$ in (35) is between -1 and 0, and it is possible that at high values of ρ and low values of k and v, $\partial s/\partial k > 0$ in equation (35). This possibility need not overly concern us, however, since from (35) it is clear that, if the elasticity of substitution is fairly constant throughout the range of k, that is, if $(v/\rho)(\partial\rho/\partial v)$ isn't very sensitive to k, then as k rises and ρ falls, condition (35) has an increasing probability of being met, since with falling ρ, the term $\alpha_1/\alpha_0\rho$ will become dominant.

This gives us two possibilities for the shape of the $[(g_L + \lambda)/s]k$ function in the A–M model, illustrated in Figure 25-7. The solid $[(g_L + \lambda)/s]k$ function shows the normal case where $\partial s/\partial k < 0$ throughout. The dashed $[(g_L + \lambda)/s]k$ function shows a case where the elasticity of substitution is small enough that $[(g_L + \lambda)/s]k$ is concave initially, but becomes convex eventually as the term $\alpha_1/\alpha_0\rho$ comes to dominate the left-hand side of condition (35). With the likelihood that the elasticity of substitution runs between, say, 0.8 and 1.0 in industrial economies, the latter possibility is not a serious problem.

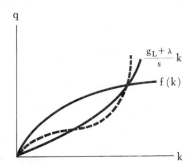

Figure 25-7 Equilibrium growth with the A–M consumption function.

As usual, in the case of the A–M consumption function, once a stable k^*, q^* has been located, the implications for prices and relative shares can be drawn from the production function, and the equilibrium levels of consumption and investment can be obtained from q^* and the saving ratio. All of the alternative saving functions considered here give stable equilibrium ratios of capital to effective labor and thus are consistent with the stylized facts. In the next chapter, we will consider briefly some issues concerning *which* growth path, that is, which k^* a rational growth policy would choose assuming it could manipulate the saving ratio through tax policy.

SELECTED READINGS

R. G. D. Allen, *Macro-Economic Theory* (New York: St. Martin's Press, 1967), chapter 16.

R. Findlay, "The Robinsonian Model," *Economica,* February 1963.

N. Kaldor, "Alternative Theories of Distribution," *Review of Economic Studies,* no. 61, 1955–1956.

F. Modigliani, "Comment," in *Behavior of Incomes Shares,* National Bureau of Economic Research (Princeton, N.J.: Princeton University Press, 1964).

J. Robinson and R. Findlay, "Comments," *Economica,* November 1963.

R. M. Solow, "Comment," *Review of Economic Studies,* June 1962.

chapter 26

The Golden Rule and an Introduction to Optimal Growth Models

In Chapters 24 and 25 we saw that the neoclassical growth model with technical progress embodied in the labor force tends to a long-run growth path with equilibrium values for output per effective person, $q^* = (Q/E)^*$, and capital per effective person, $k^* = (K/E)^*$, under a wide variation of theories of saving behavior. Along the long-run equilibrium growth path, output, consumption, and investment all grow at the same rate, as, of course, do output, consumption, and investment per capita. Thus, the growth path gives *balanced growth* with the division of output between consumption and investment on the output side and between profits and wages on the income side stable through time.

The *rate of growth* of output, consumption, and investment in long-run equilibrium is determined by the growth rate of the labor force, g_L, plus the exogenous growth of labor productivity, λ. The *level of the growth path*, given by the equilibrium k^* and q^* levels, is determined jointly by the natural growth rate, $n = g_L + \lambda$, and by saving behavior. Note that here we are introducing a specific notation for the natural growth rate, $n = g_L + \lambda$. This is introduced purely to simplify notation and facilitate presentation of the models.

We saw in Chapter 25 that an *increase* in the saving ratio s raises the equilibrium values of k^* and q^*, shifting the economy to a *higher* equilibrium growth path. The question then naturally arises: If the government (or society in general) can control the saving ratio s, which of the many possible equilibrium growth paths, each corresponding to a different s, should it choose? At what level should the *control variable* s be set? This chapter analyzes this question in the context of equilibrium growth models and outlines some of the answers proposed by optimal growth theories.

First, we review the solution of the basic neoclassical model with technical progress, focusing on the role of the saving ratio in determining the level of the growth path. Next, we derive Phelps' *golden rule of accumulation*. It says that the long-run equilibrium growth path that maximizes consumption per capita in all periods, once the economy has reached its equilibrium path, is determined by the k^* level at which $f'(k) = g_L + \lambda = n$. This is the k^* point where the slope of the production function $q = f(k)$ is equal to the slope of the $(g_L + \lambda)k$ line in, for example, Figure 25-1.

Next, we briefly describe optimal growth turnpike theorems. These suggest that an economy that wants to maximize the integral of social welfare, or utility, over time, on the assumption that utility is a function of consumption per capita, should move toward a path like the golden rule path as it grows. This discussion will introduce the readers to one of the "frontier" areas of macroeconomic theory.

THE BASIC NEOCLASSICAL MODEL ONCE MORE

Discussion of optimal growth and the role of the saving rate is based on the neoclassical model developed in Chapter 24. The model is built on the following assumptions concerning the structure of the economy:

1. The labor force, L, grows at an exogenously determined rate g_L. The *effective labor force*, $E_t = L_t e^{\lambda t}$, grows at the rate $g_L + \lambda$. This is the *natural growth rate* of the economy, $n = g_L + \lambda$.

2. Output, Q_t, depends on capital and effective labor inputs, K_t and E_t. The production function is written as

$$Q_t = F(K_t, E_t). \qquad (1)$$

   The production function is homogeneous of degree one, so that we can write it as

$$q_t \equiv \frac{Q_t}{E_t} = F\left(\frac{K_t}{E_t}, 1\right) = f(k_t); \qquad f' > 0, \qquad f'' < 0. \quad (2)$$

3. Investment, which equals saving, is a given fraction, s, of total output. Thus, capital formation is given by

$$\frac{dK}{dt} = I_t = S_t = sQ_t. \qquad (3)$$

   In this chapter, we will treat the saving rate s as the government's *control* or policy variable. By changing s, presumably by changing taxes, the government can move the economy's growth path from one equilibrium level to another.

These assumptions can be combined to obtain the key expression for the growth rate of the ratio of capital to effective labor units, $k = K/E$. The growth rate of k is definitionally given by

$$\dot{k} = \dot{K} - \dot{E}. \tag{4}$$

The growth rate of the capital stock, $\dot{K}$, is simply

$$\dot{K} = \frac{dK/dt}{K} = \frac{I}{K} = \frac{sQ}{K} = \frac{sq}{k} = \frac{sf(k)}{k}. \tag{5}$$

From assumption 1, the growth rate of effective labor, E_t, is just

$$\dot{E} = g_L + \lambda = n, \tag{6}$$

the economy's natural rate of growth. Thus, the expression for the growth rate of k can be written as

$$\dot{k} = \frac{sf(k)}{k} - (g_L + \lambda) = \frac{sf(k)}{k} - n, \tag{7}$$

which gives the growth rate of k as a function of the level of k itself. Equation (7) has an equilibrium value for k where $\dot{k} = 0$. This equilibrium value $k*$ can be obtained by setting $\dot{k} = 0$ in equation (7), so that $k*$ is determined by

$$f(k*) = \frac{g_L + \lambda}{s} k*. \tag{8}$$

This solution is shown graphically in Figure 26-1(a), which plots both $f(k)$, actual output per effective person, q, as a function of k, and $[(g_L + \lambda)/s]k$, which gives the level of q needed to maintain the corresponding k as E grows at the rate $g_L + \lambda$.

Starting with $k_0 < k*$ in Figure 26-1(a), output per effective person exceeds that needed to maintain k_0, so there is investment "left over" to raise k toward $k*$. When k reaches $k*$ this "*excess investment*" becomes zero and k stops rising. Thus, the equilibrium value of k, $k*$, is a stable equilibrium, as shown in the phase diagram of Figure 26-1(b).

If the economy tends toward a stable equilibrium $k*$ in the long run, this implies that $\dot{K} = \dot{E} = g_L + \lambda$ in the long run, since $k* = (K/E)*$ is constant. Similarly, with q tending toward $q*$, we have $\dot{Q} = \dot{E} = g_L + \lambda$ in the long run, so that in *long-run growth equilibrium*

$$\dot{K} = \dot{Q} = g_L + \lambda = n, \tag{9}$$

and

$$(\dot{Q/L}) = (\dot{K/L}) = \lambda.$$

Both the capital-labor ratio and output per person grow at the technical progress rate λ.

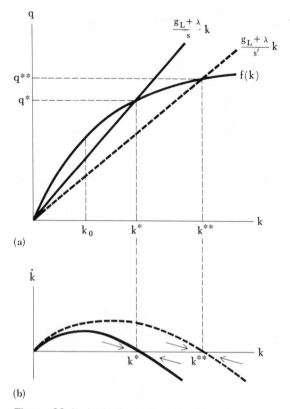

(a)

(b)

Figure 26-1　An increase in the saving ratio.

Figure 26-2 shows the long-run equilibrium growth path of output per person given by the k^*, q^* equilibrium point of Figure 26-1. With the ratio of output to effective labor fixed at q^* in equilibrium, we have

$$\left(\frac{Q}{E}\right)^* = \left(\frac{Q_t}{L_t e^{\lambda t}}\right)^* = q^*,$$

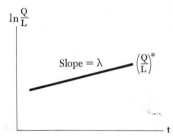

Figure 26-2　Long-run equilibrium path of output per worker.

so that

$$\left(\frac{Q_t}{L_t}\right)^* = q^* e^{\lambda t},$$

and the growth rate of Q/L is equal to λ, as shown in Figure 26-2, since q^* is constant in equilibrium.

What happens if saving ratio s increases to s'? In Figure 26-1 this rotates the $[(g_L + \lambda)/s]k$ ray down to $[(g_L + \lambda)/s']k$. At any given level of k, since the saving ratio has risen, it takes less output to generate the investment needed to maintain that k. At the old k^*, $f(k^*) > [(g_L + \lambda)/s']k^*$, so $\dot{k} > 0$, as is shown in the dashed phase diagram of Figure 26-1(b). Thus, k and q begin to rise toward the new k^{**}, q^{**}. But if k is growing, $\dot{K} > \dot{E} = g_L + \lambda$, and $(\dot{K/L}) > \lambda$. Similarly, with growing output per effective person q, $\dot{Q} > \dot{E}$, and $(\dot{Q/L}) > \lambda$. Thus, while q grows from q^* to q^{**}, the growth rate of output per person exceeds λ, the slope of the long-run equilibrium growth path in Figure 26-2.

When k and q reach the new equilibrium k^{**}, q^{**}, however, q stops growing, so $\dot{Q}$ falls back to equal $\dot{E}$ and the growth rate of output per person again falls to λ. This is illustrated in Figure 26-3. There the saving rate is increased from s to s' at time t_0, causing output per person to begin to grow at a rate faster than λ. As q approaches q^{**} in Figure 26-1, corresponding to the $(Q/L)^{**}$ path of Figure 26-3, the growth rate of Q/L slows to λ again, reaching the equilibrium long-run k^{**}, q^{**} path at time t_n.

The increase in the saving ratio s has moved the economy from one long-run growth path to another. Each of these equilibrium paths has a slope, or growth rate, given by the technical progress rate λ. It is only in the period while q is moving from q^* to q^{**} that the growth rate of Q/L exceeds λ.

As long as, in Figure 26-1, $f'(k) > 0$, that is, the marginal productivity of increases in the K/E ratio is positive, an increase in s will *raise* equilibrium

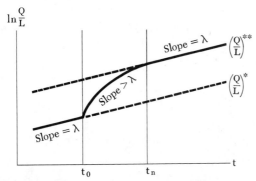

Figure 26-3 A change in the saving ratio that shifts the growth path.

k and q and thus *raise* the growth path of Q/L in Figure 26-3. But this does not mean that policy should be directed toward increasing the saving rate to raise the growth path. If the aspect of economic activity that enters the society's welfare function is consumption, not output, then perhaps the policy maker should seek the value of s that gives the highest path of C/L, not of Q/L. This suggests that we now examine more closely the relation of the saving ratio to the level of consumption.

SAVING AND CONSUMPTION IN GROWTH EQUILIBRIUM

The level of investment and saving per effective person, I/E, *at any level of* k is given by

$$\frac{I}{E} = \frac{sQ}{E} = sq = sf(k),$$ (10)

which is plotted in Figure 26-4. Consumption per effective person *at any given* k (not just equilibrium k^*) is then given by $(Q/E) - (I/E)$,

$$\frac{C}{E} \equiv \frac{C}{Le^{\lambda t}} = \frac{Q}{E} - \frac{sQ}{E}$$

$$= f(k) - sf(k),$$ (11)

and is the difference between $f(k)$ and $sf(k)$, shown as $(C/E)_0$ at k_0 in Figure 26-4. Again, equation (11) gives the level of consumption at any k, given the saving ratio s. We can now rewrite equation (11) to give the value of consumption per capita, C/L, at any value of k,

$$\frac{C}{L} = e^{\lambda t}[f(k) - sf(k)].$$ (12)

From the equilibrium condition for k^*, equation (8), we see that, in equilibrium

$$sf(k^*) = (g_L + \lambda)k^*.$$ (13)

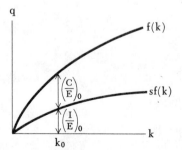

Figure 26-4 Consumption and investment with disequilibrium k.

Thus, the equilibrium value of k^* is the same at the upper intersection of Figure 26-5, given by equation (8), as at the lower intersection, given by equation (13). Inserting the expression for $sf(k^*)$, given by equation (13), into equation (12) for consumption per person, C/L, we obtain an expression for C/L in equilibrium,

$$\left(\frac{C}{L}\right)^* = e^{\lambda t}[f(k^*) - sf(k^*)]$$

$$= e^{\lambda t}[f(k^*) - (g_L + \lambda)k^*]. \qquad (14)$$

The substitution of $(g_L + \lambda)k^*$ for $sf(k^*)$ can be made *only* in the expression for $(C/L)^*$—long-run equilibrium C/L. This substitution in (14) simply reflects the lower intersection in Figure 26-5. The crucial points here are the following:

1. For any given s, as k varies, C/E is given by $f(k) - sf(k)$, and thus the difference between $f(k)$ and $sf(k)$ in Figure 26-4 traces out the value of C/E.
2. But in equilibrium, $(C/E)^*$ must equal $f(k^*) - (g_L + \lambda)k^*$, so that as s varies (due to government manipulation, perhaps) *equilibrium* $(C/E)^*$ is traced by the difference between $f(k)$ and $(g_L + \lambda)k$ in Figure 26-6. Here the reader should note that since $(C/L)^* = e^{\lambda t}(C/E)^*$, maximization of $(C/E)^*$ is equivalent to maximization of $(C/L)^*$, so that we can discuss the choice of a value of s to maximize consumption per person in terms of either $(C/L)^*$, as in (14), or $(C/E)^*$ as in the last two paragraphs.
3. Thus, while C/E for any given k is given by $f(k) - sf(k)$, to analyze how C/E (or C/L) differs among different *long-run*

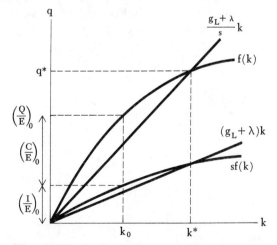

Figure 26-5 Saving and consumption.

equilibrium growth paths, we must focus on the difference between $f(k)$ and $(g_L + \lambda)k$ in Figure 26-6.

The relationship between $f(k)$, $(C/E)^*$, and $(g_L + \lambda)k$ is analyzed in Figure 26-7. There we see that the various possible $(C/E)^* = c^*$ equilibrium values, corresponding to various values of s, are given by the difference between $f(k)$ and $(g_L + \lambda)k$.

If the saving ratio is set at s_0 in Figure 26-7, equilibrium will be reached at k_0^*, q_0^*. Consumption per effective person at equilibrium k_0^*, q_0^* will be $c_0^* = (C/E)_0^*$. Furthermore, with s set at s_0, consumption per person in equilibrium will be given by

$$\left(\frac{C}{L}\right)^*_0 = e^{\lambda t}\left(\frac{C}{E}\right)^*_0 = e^{\lambda t}c_0^* = e^{\lambda t}[f(k_0^*) - (g_L + \lambda)k_0^*]. \qquad (15)$$

As the saving ratio s is increased from s_0 to s_1 and s_2 in Figure 26-7, the difference between $f(k)$ and $(g_L + \lambda)k$, which is equal to $(C/E)^*$, first rises, then falls. At which value of k^* is equilibrium per capita consumption at a maximum? Clearly, at the value of k^* where the slope of $f(k)$ is equal to the slope of $(g_L + \lambda)k$, that is, where $\rho \equiv f'(k) = g_L + \lambda$. Once we have located this $k^* - k_1^*$ in Figure 26-7, varying s from s_1 in either direction will reduce $(C/E)^*$, and thus reduce $(C/L)^*$.

The reason why there exists a k^* that maximizes $(C/E)^*$ is simply diminishing returns. With increases in q diminishing with increases in k, but increases in q that are *needed to maintain equilibrium* k^* growing proportionately with increases in k^*, as s rises a k^* value is reached beyond which we would have to reduce consumption per effective person to provide enough investment per effective person to maintain any greater k^* equilibrium value.

The existence of a maximum $(C/E)^*$ in Figure 26-7 shows that, in Figure 26-8, as we increase the saving ratio, raising the equilibrium $(Q/L)^*$ path, the $(C/L)^*$ paths first shift up and then down. The highest $(C/L)^*$ path is

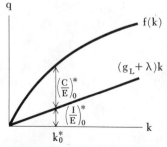

Figure 26-6 Consumption and investment with equilibrium k^*.

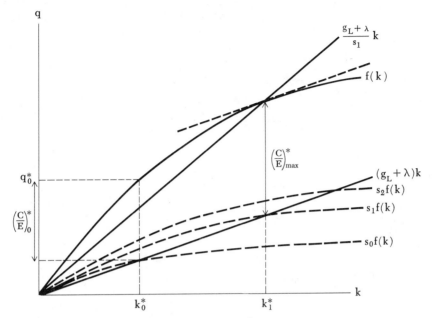

Figure 26-7 Maximum equilibrium consumption per person.

attained when s is set to give $k*$ equilibrium at the level where $f'(k) = g_L + \lambda$, k_1^* in Figure 26-7.

PHELPS' GOLDEN RULE OF ACCUMULATION

It is important to notice that all of the $(C/L)*$ paths of Figure 26-8 are parallel; they all have the same slope equal to the technical progress factor λ. This follows from the expression given in equation (14) for equilibrium C/L,

$$\left(\frac{C}{L}\right)^* = e^{\lambda t}[f(k^*) - (g_L + \lambda)k^*]. \tag{16}$$

Since each of the $(C/L)*$ paths in Figure 26-8 represents a long-run growth equilibrium, each has a corresponding value of $k*$ which is constant in equilibrium. Thus, in equilibrium the term in brackets in equation (16) is constant, so that the growth rate of $(C/L)*$ for any equilibrium value of $k*$ is λ.

If all equilibrium $(C/L)*$ paths are parallel, the one that maximizes $(C/L)*$ at any arbitrarily chosen time period t_i will maximize $(C/L)*$ for *all* time periods. Thus, the argument of the previous section, which showed that maximum $(C/L)*$ is reached at the $k*$ value where $f'(k) = g_L + \lambda$, can be developed rather simply mathematically. The problem is, given equation (16) for $(C/L)*$, what value of $k*$ maximizes $(C/L)*$? To find that $k*$, we dif-

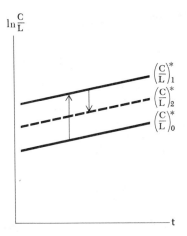

$\ln \frac{C}{L}$

$\left(\frac{C}{L}\right)^*_1$

$\left(\frac{C}{L}\right)^*_2$

$\left(\frac{C}{L}\right)^*_0$

t

Figure 26-8 Long-run equilibrium C/L: increasing the saving ratio.

ferentiate the expression for $(C/L)^*$ with respect to k^* and set that derivative equal to zero:

$$\frac{\partial (C/L)^*}{\partial k^*} = e^{\lambda t}[f'(k^*) - (g_L + \lambda)] = 0. \qquad (17)$$

Since $e^{\lambda t} \neq 0$, this means that maximum maintained $(C/L)^*$ is obtained at the value of k^* where

$$f'(k^*) - (g_L + \lambda) = 0,$$

or

$$f'(k^*) = g_L + \lambda. \qquad (18)$$

That is, the s should be chosen that sets k^* at the level where the profit rate $\rho = f'(k)$ is equal to the *natural growth rate,* $n = g_L + \lambda$.

This is Edmund Phelps' golden rule of accumulation, and we will give several interpretations of it shortly. But first we should make clear what is involved here. The golden rule k^* describes the growth path which, once the economy attains it, will give a higher level of per capita consumption than any other growth path for all time. We should note that the golden rule discriminates between long-run equilibrium paths in terms of their equilibrium $(C/L)^*$ values on the assumption that the economy can choose freely among these paths. But clearly, if an increase in saving is required to move to the golden rule path, the present generation would have to sacrifice consumption for the benefit of future generations of consumers. Thus, the golden rule path would be a *target growth path* only if, in a sense, the costs of moving toward the path were small relative to the longer run benefits that come from reaching it. We will soon return to this point, which is central to the turnpike theorems of optimal growth.

It should also be noted that we are choosing among consumption paths that all have constant (but different) equilibrium K/E ratios. The paths are thus *golden rule paths* in that each generation must pass on the same K/E ratio that it inherited. It would not be fair eating up some of the K you received or sacrificing to build up K/E and pass the benefit on.

Solow has given an excellent common-sense explanation of the golden rule result. Imagine an economy that can receive capital free—that is, it can freely choose the level of its growth path—with the proviso that it must, for all time, keep the same K/E ratio that it initially chooses. Then for each increment of capital, ΔK, it accepts, it receives an increment of output equal to

$$\Delta Q = f'(k)\Delta K. \tag{19}$$

To maintain the K/E ratio k, the capital stock must grow at the rate of growth of E, $g_L + \lambda$. Thus, investment needed to maintain any given k ratio is given by

$$\frac{I}{K} = (g_L + \lambda) \quad \text{and} \quad I = (g_L + \lambda)K. \tag{20}$$

This means that the increase in *investment* needed to maintain the increase in K/E that comes from accepting an additional increment of K is given by

$$\Delta I = (g_L + \lambda)\Delta K. \tag{21}$$

As long as the increment to output, ΔQ, exceeds the increment to investment, ΔI, the ΔK increment gives an increase in consumption ΔC. But $f'(k)$ decreases as k increases, so eventually the economy reaches a point where

$$\Delta Q = \Delta K f'(k) = \Delta I = \Delta K(g_L + \lambda). \tag{22}$$

At this point, taking on more free capital will increase the level of investment needed to maintain k more than it increases output. That is, it would imply a reduction of C to maintain the K/E ratio. Thus, the optimal amount of free capital to accept under golden rule conditions is the K that equates the profit rate to the natural rate of growth:

$$f'(k) = g_L + \lambda. \tag{23}$$

There are two other interesting interpretations of the golden rule condition. First, multiplying both sides of (23) by K/Q, we have

$$\frac{f'(k)K}{Q} = (g_L + \lambda)\frac{K}{Q} = \frac{I}{Q} = s, \tag{24}$$

from the fact that $I = (g_L + \lambda)K$ in equilibrium. While the right-hand side of equation (24) is the ratio of investment (= saving) to output, the left-hand side of equation (24) is the profit rate ρ [$= f'(k)$] times K/Q:

$$\frac{\text{Profits}}{\text{Capital}} \cdot \frac{\text{capital}}{\text{output}} = \frac{\text{profits}}{\text{output}}.$$

Thus, the golden rule equates the share of profits in output to the ratio of investment to output. So the golden rule could be stated as "invest your profits, consume your wages." This is just another way of selecting the saving ratio s that yields the golden rule k^*.

The final interpretation of the golden rule also follows from equation (24). The term $f'(k)K/Q$ can be converted into the elasticity of output with respect to capital input as follows:

$$\frac{f'(k)K}{Q} = \frac{f'(k)k}{q} = \frac{\partial q}{\partial k} \cdot \frac{k}{q}.$$

Then equation (24) can be rewritten as

$$\frac{\partial q}{\partial k} \cdot \frac{k}{q} = \frac{I}{Q} = s. \tag{25}$$

This says that the saving ratio s should be set equal to the elasticity of output with respect to capital input to move the economy to the golden rule path.

These are all various ways of stating the same golden rule condition. To attain the k^* that gives the highest long-run equilibrium consumption per capita $(C/L)^* = e^{\lambda t}(C/E)^*$, set the control variable s, so that, at the equilibrium k^*, the slope of the production function $\rho = f'(k)$ is equal to $g_L + \lambda$, the natural growth rate. The k^* equilibrium value that results will then be the golden rule k_g^* shown in Figure 26-9. The golden rule determines the equilibrium growth path that maximizes consumption per person over all time, once the economy reaches that path.

OPTIMAL GROWTH TURNPIKES

In the preceding two sections, we have seen that we can find one equilibrium k_g^* value that gives the highest possible equilibrium growth path for per capita consumption, $(C/L)_g^*$. Since all growth paths are parallel with slope = $g_L + \lambda$, this highest equilibrium consumption path, once attained, gives the highest possible per capita consumption to each future generation, assuming the golden rule is followed. This is the assumption that each generation maintains the inherited k_g^* ratio, so that all paths are, in fact, parallel.

Now suppose the economy begins at an equilibrium k^* lower than k_g^*, perhaps due to having a saving ratio s lower than that associated with k_g^*.

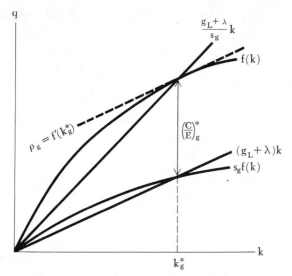

Figure 26-9 Golden rule k^* and C/E.

Moving toward the golden rule k_g^* then would involve raising the saving rate. Then the movement to the golden rule $(C/L)_g^*$ path would involve the present generation's *building up* capital, and the K/E ratio, in order that future generations could gain the benefit of traveling along the golden rule growth path. Thus, movement toward the golden rule path from an initial low k^* involves a cost paid by the present (and near-future) generations in exchange for the benefit to future generations of moving along the golden rule path. Should the present generation—of planners, or society, or politicians—be willing to accept that cost?

Rather than try to answer this question categorically, we can consider two cases. First, suppose that the initial k^* value is close to k_g^*, so that only a "small" cost is involved in moving to k_g^*. Suppose further that the planner's (or society's) time horizon is very long, so that he or she can consider the benefits to many future generations of being on the golden rule path. In this case the optimal policy would be to move quickly toward the golden rule path. On the other hand, if the initial k^* were far below k_g^* so that a substantial sacrifice of present consumption to increase s and build up the capital-labor ratio would be required to get to k_g^*, and the planner's time horizon were fairly short, optimal policy would suggest arching only gently toward the golden rule path.

These kinds of considerations underlie the *turnpike theorems* of optimal growth as developed, for example, by Roy Radner and Paul Samuelson. Essentially, these say that the longer the time horizon, the smaller the percentage of time that should be spent away from the turnpike (here the golden rule) growth path. Thus, given a starting $k* < k_g^*$, the longer the planning horizon, the relatively faster should be the movement toward the turnpike, since the longer the planning horizon, the more the benefits of being near the turnpike outweigh the costs of getting to it. In Figure 26-10, the longer time horizon, the faster the economy should move from $(C/L)_0^*$ to $(C/L)_g^*$. By now, the reason for the terminology "turnpike theorem" should be clear. A person taking a long trip will gain by incurring some initial cost to get onto a turnpike, while it might not pay to go to the turnpike for a shorter trip.

The Golden Rule Path as an Undiscounted Turnpike Path

Turnpike theorems, stating that an optimal growth path should spend all but an arbitrarily small percentage of its time in the neighborhood of a given turnpike path, like our k_g^*, as the planning time horizon becomes longer and longer, come generally from the solution of the following kind of problem. Suppose the economy has the structure of the neoclassical growth model (the *constraints* of the problem), and one wants to maximize the integral of social utility (the *objective function* of the problem) as a function of per capita consumption from time 0 to time T. What growth path should the economy follow from some arbitrarily selected initial K/E ratio?

The first step in the solution of this problem is to state consumption per effective person, C/E, as a function of the level and rate of growth of the K/E ratio. From equation (11), the C/E ratio can be written as

$$\frac{C}{E} = f(k) - \frac{I}{E}. \tag{26}$$

Noting that $I/E = (I/K) \cdot (K/E) = \dot{K}k$, and that since $K = k \cdot E$, $\dot{K} = \dot{k} + \dot{E}$, we can rewrite (26) as

$$\frac{C}{E} = f(k) - k(\dot{k} + \dot{E}) = f(k) - nk - k\dot{k}. \tag{27}$$

Here we are using $n = g_L + \lambda$ as the growth rate of E just to simplify the notation. Next, we introduce the notation that $dX/dt = DX$, and $d^2X/dt^2 =$

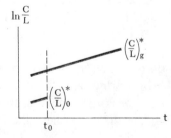

Figure 26-10 The turnpike theorem: per capita consumption growth.

$D^2 X$. Since $k\dot{k}$ in (27) is just $k \cdot [(dk/dt)/k]$, we can then rewrite equation (27) in its final form,

$$\frac{C}{E} = f(k) - nk - Dk. \quad \text{\tiny ''} \quad (28)$$

Now, recognizing that the equilibrium growth path that maximizes C/E also maximizes C/L, we can state the problem as maximizing the integral from the present, time 0, to a future time T of social utility U which is a function of C/E:

$$U = U\left(\frac{C}{E}\right); \qquad U' > 0, \qquad U'' < 0. \qquad (29)$$

Thus, the problem is to maximize the integral

$$\int_0^T U\left(\frac{C}{E}\right)dt = \int_0^T U(f(k) - nk - Dk)dt = \int_0^T F(k, Dk)dt. \qquad (30)$$

The right-hand term in (30) is introduced to show that this problem is one of maximizing an integral of a function of k and Dk, one that is easily handled by the Euler equation of the calculus of variations. The Euler equation is the analogue in a case where variables are time-dependent to the ordinary rules for finding a maximum in a static case where all partial derivatives are set equal to zero. In the dynamic case given by (30), the Euler equation

$$\frac{\partial F}{\partial k} - \frac{d[\partial F/(\partial Dk)]}{dt} = 0 \qquad (31)$$

will identify the equilibrium k value that maximizes the integral

$$\int_0^T U\left(\frac{C}{E}\right)dt,$$

with Dk and $D^2 k = 0$.

Taking the derivatives in the specific case of (30) gives us

$$0 = U' \cdot (f'(k) - n) - \frac{d(-U')}{dt}$$

$$= U' \cdot (f'(k) - n) + U'' \cdot (f'(k)Dk - n\,Dk - D^2 k) \qquad (32)$$

as the equilibrium condition identifying the k path that maximizes the integral in (30). If the economy is at an equilibrium k^* value, then Dk and $D^2 k = 0$, and, since U' is positive, condition (32) boils down to

$$0 = f'(k^*) - n, \quad \text{or} \quad f'(k^*) = n = g_L + \lambda \qquad (33)$$

as the condition identifying the $k*$ value that maximizes

$$\int_0^T U\left(\frac{C}{E}\right) dt.$$

Thus, the golden rule growth path is also the turnpike path in the case where the objective is to maximize social welfare as an undiscounted function of consumption per capita over a long planning horizon. This should have been clear from the outset, since the golden rule was obtained by asking what path maximizes C/L or C/E, for all periods, once the path is reached, with no reference to discounting future income and consumption.

A More General Turnpike Model

We can analyze a much more general optimal growth turnpike problem by introducing a discount rate into the social welfare integral. Suppose future income and consumption are discounted at the rate r, so that a discounting factor e^{-rt} is introduced into the welfare integral given in (30). In this case the problem is to maximize

$$\int_0^T F(k, Dk)dt = \int_0^T e^{-rt}U(f(k) - nk - Dk)dt \qquad (34)$$

to find the $k*$ value with Dk and $D^2k = 0$ that maximizes discounted future utility.

The Euler equation in this case gives us

$$0 = e^{-rt} \cdot U' \cdot (f'(k) - n) - \frac{d(-e^{-rt}U')}{dt} ;$$

$$0 = e^{-rt} \cdot U' \cdot (f'(k) - n) + e^{-rt} \cdot U'' \cdot (f'(k)Dk - n\,Dk - D^2k)$$
$$+ U'(-re^{-rt}).$$

Setting Dk and $D^2k = 0$ and dividing out U' and e^{-rt}, both positive, gives us

$$0 = [f'(k**) - n] - r, \quad \text{or} \quad f'(k**) = n + r = g_L + \lambda + r \qquad (35)$$

as the equilibrium condition identifying the turnpike $k**$ value that maximizes the discounted social welfare integral of (34).

Since r is positive in this case, the discounted turnpike path would involve a lower saving rate and lower $k**$ level than k_g^*, as shown in Figure 26-11. This results, of course, from reducing the current estimate of the value of future income and consumption by a discount rate, thus reducing the value of current saving to increase future consumption.

The common-sense explanation of this result follows directly from that which Solow offered for the golden rule result. Consider again an economy

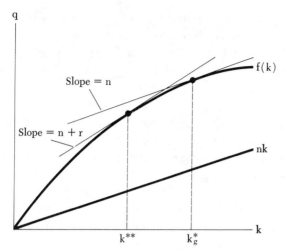

Figure 26-11 Undiscounted and discounted turn-pike paths.

that is free to accept a capital gift on the condition that it must maintain forever the K/E ratio it initially accepts. In this case the present value of future output gained by accepting an increment of capital is given by

$$\Delta Q = f'(k)\Delta K - r\,\Delta K = [f'(k) - r]\Delta K, \qquad (36)$$

since future output increments are discounted by r. On the other hand, to maintain the K/E ratio as E grows at rate $n = g_L + \lambda$, an increment to K will require an increment to I given as before by

$$\Delta I = n\,\Delta K = (g_L + \lambda)\Delta K. \qquad (37)$$

Now the economy with a discounted social welfare integral will want to accept capital with diminishing $f'(k)$ until $\Delta Q = \Delta I$, giving us

$$f'(k) - r = n = g_L + \lambda, \qquad (38)$$

the turnpike condition with future income discounted at rate r. The economy with a long planning horizon should set its saving rate to move fairly rapidly to an equilibrium growth path along which the marginal productivity of capital—correctly measured to include such negative outputs as pollution—is equal to the natural rate of growth plus the social discount rate, if these can be correctly measured.

CONCLUSION

This chapter completes our discussion of theoretical models of long-run equilibrium growth. It should be clear that these models are still highly theoretical, corresponding to the static models of Part II of this book. The empirical work analogous to that on short-run macroeconomics, reported in some detail in Part III, has yet to be done on long-run growth models. Thus, it is not yet certain what their full contribution to practical economic policy will be.

But two obvious gains in our understanding of the long-run workings of the economy have already resulted from the study of growth models. First, the distinction between medium-term and long-run growth has become clear. We cannot expect a perpetually higher growth rate as a result of an increase in the saving rate; rather, the effect is to shift the economy to a higher growth path. And it is foolish to try to *maximize* the rate of growth, at least in an advanced economy. Increased growth incurs costs, in terms of current consumption, so that we should seek an *optimum,* rather than a maximum, rate of growth that balances the gains to future generations against the losses to the current generation. There are both benefits and costs to growth, and they must be balanced to reach an optimal growth path.

SELECTED READINGS

E. S. Phelps, "The Golden Rule of Accumulation: A Fable for Growth Men," *American Economic Review,* September 1961.

E. S. Phelps, "Second Essay on the Golden Rule of Accumulation," *American Economic Review,* September 1965.

R. Radner, "Paths of Economic Growth That Are Optimal with Regard Only to Final States: A Turnpike Theorem," *Review of Economic Studies,* January 1961.

P. A. Samuelson, "A Catenary Turnpike Theorem," *American Economic Review,* June 1965.

P. A. Samuelson, "A Turnpike Refutation of the Golden Rule," in K. Shell, ed., *Essays on the Theory of Optimal Economic Growth* (Cambridge: MIT Press, 1967).

chapter *27*

Medium-Term Growth and "the Measure of Our Ignorance"

In moving from the analysis of static models of income determination, which focused on the problem of maintaining full employment, to the analysis of long-run equilibrium growth models, we noted that the distinction should be made between four different kinds of growth. First, we studied in Parts I–III the growth involved in moving the economy from a position of slack demand and high unemployment to full employment. Here we call this type of growth *short-run growth*. This type of growth cannot be a continuing process; once the economy is utilizing its resources fully, it can only grow as fast as the expansion of those resources—growth of the capital stock and the labor force—and technological progress permit.

The second type of growth that we noted is growth with full employment toward a long-run equilibrium growth path. In this case, while maintaining full employment, the economy increases its ratios of capital and output to effective labor input, moving toward the long-run equilibrium k^*, q^* point, in the language of Chapters 23–26. This second type of growth we will call *medium-run growth*. In Part IV we looked at some aspects of medium-run growth on the demand side. But medium-run growth on the supply side was left to this chapter. The third kind of growth that we noted is long-run equilibrium growth at the economy's k^*, q^*—the balanced-growth path of the neoclassical growth models. This third type of growth, which was the subject of Chapters 23–26, we call *long-run growth*.

These three types of growth can be described in terms of two familiar diagrams. In Figure 27-1, expansion to full employment with a growing labor force can be described as a movement to the production function from a point, like 0, at which the economy is not producing the potential output, q_A, that it could, given its capital per effective person, k_A. Thus, moving to full employment involves growth from point 0 to the production function at some point between A and B in Figure 27-1. This is what we mean by short-run growth.

Once full employment is reached, the economy grows along the production function $f(k)$ toward the long-run equilibrium point B. This second kind of growth involves *capital-deepening*—increasing the amount of capital per effective worker, k—as well as *capital-widening*—providing new workers with capital at the existing k ratio. This type of growth we call intermediate-run growth. Eventually, as we have seen in Chapters 24–26, the economy reaches a ratio of capital to effective labor at which all the investment at that ratio, given the saving rate, is required just to widen capital—to provide each new *effective worker* with capital at the existing k^* ratio. At this point, B in Figure 27-1, the k ratio stops changing, and the economy is in a long-run growth equilibrium with k^* and q^* fixed.

These three types of growth—from 0 to the AB path to B—are also shown in Figure 27-2, which is similar to Figure 23-1. It plots the natural log of output per worker against time. The movement from point 0 to the AB path involves eliminating unemployment and moving to the economy's production possibility curve. The movement along that function to point B in Figures 27-1

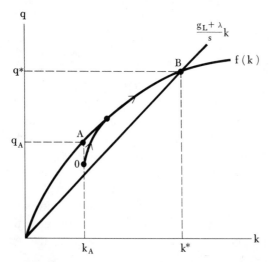

Figure 27-1 Expansion to full-employment equilibrium.

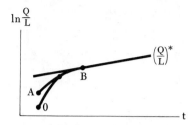

Figure 27-2 Expansion to full-employment equilibrium growth path.

and 27-2 involves full-employment growth toward the long-run balanced-growth path. After point B, the economy is on the equilibrium growth path of the neoclassical model.

In Chapter 26 we discussed the question of what long-run path the economy should want to be on. Choosing this *optimal growth path* involved setting the government's control variable—the saving ratio—at a level that gives in some sense the *best* k^*, q^* point. Thus, changing the saving ratio from s_0 to s_1 in Figure 27-3 increases equilibrium k from k^* to k^{**}, giving a period of intermediate-run growth from time t_0 to time t_1 in Figure 27-4, as the economy moves from the initial long-run equilibrium $(Q/L)^*$ path to the new long-run $(Q/L)^{**}$ path. This is the fourth type of growth that we distinguished in Chapter 23, and Figure 27-4 reproduces Figure 23-1 with a slight change in labels. This fourth kind of growth is also intermediate-run growth, with the economy moving between long-run growth paths, maintaining full employment all the while. This type of growth process is the focus of this chapter.

In particular, in this chapter we ask how sensitive the growth rate of output is to changes in the ratio of investment to output in the intermediate run. This question can be posed in one of two ways. Assuming that a given change in the saving rate (saving = investment) will move the long-run equilibrium growth path from $(Q/L)^*$ to $(Q/L)^{**}$ in Figure 27-4, we can ask either how *long* is the period from time t_0 to time t_1 that we're defining as *intermediate*

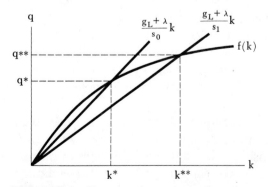

Figure 27-3 Changing the saving ratio.

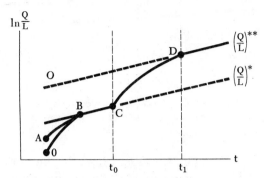

Figure 27-4 Shifting the equilibrium growth path.

run, or we can ask how *steep* is the growth path from point C to point D in Figure 27-4. That is, how much does the actual growth rate of output respond to a given change in s? The longer the period from t_0 to t_1, the flatter will be the growth path from C to D, given the $(Q/L)^*$ and $(Q/L)^{**}$ levels.

The *steepness* of the intermediate-run growth path depends on the sensitivity of the growth rate of full-employment output to changes in the growth rate of the capital stock. If the growth rate of output is highly sensitive, or elastic, to changes in the growth rate of capital, then a given increase in the saving ($=$ investment) ratio, with full employment maintained, initially increasing the growth rate of K, will give a greater initial increase in the growth rate of output—that is, a steeper intermediate-run growth path—than if this elasticity were small.

So, although the economy will eventually settle onto a new $(Q/L)^*$ path after an increase in the investment ratio, for an intermediate-run period the rate of growth will exceed the long-run natural rate of growth, $n = g_L + \lambda$. How much the growth rate will increase—or how long the intermediate run is—will depend on how elastic the growth rate of output, $\dot{Q}$, is with respect to changes in the growth rate of the capital stock, $\dot{K}$. In turn, as we will see shortly, this elasticity depends on the source of technical progress in the economy. If it is embodied in the capital stock, then increasing investment will yield not only *more* capital, but newer, *better,* and more productive capital as well, increasing the elasticity of $\dot{Q}$ with respect to $\dot{K}$. At the other extreme, if all technical progress is embodied in the labor force—more education leading to better skills, and so on—then increasing investment will give a smaller $\dot{Q}$ response.

To introduce the discussion of these issues, we first develop the growth relationships implicit in the production function $Q = F(K, L)$ in some detail. This gives us a relationship between the growth rates of output Q and of the capital and labor inputs, K and L, as the economy moves along its production function between equilibrium long-run growth paths. We then see how the sensitivity of $\dot{Q}$ with respect to changes in saving, investment, and $\dot{K}$ depends on whether technological advance must be embodied in new capital stock or appears in the form of a pure upward shift in the production function or a simple augmentation of the effective labor force in the fashion assumed in Chapters 24–26.

OUTPUT GROWTH, INPUT GROWTH, AND THE CONSTANT-RETURNS-TO-SCALE PRODUCTION FUNCTION

To develop the relationships between the growth rates of capital and labor inputs and of output, we can begin with a familiar general production function that is homogeneous to degree one:

$$Q_t = F(K_t, L_t). \tag{1}$$

We will now derive from (1) an expression for the growth rate of output $\dot{Q}$ in terms of the growth rates of the inputs, $\dot{K}$ and $\dot{L}$. Differentiating the production function with respect to time gives us

$$\frac{dQ}{dt} = \frac{\partial F}{\partial K}\frac{dK}{dt} + \frac{\partial F}{\partial L}\frac{dL}{dt},$$

and dividing through by Q gives us an expression for the proportional growth rate $\dot{Q}$,

$$\frac{dQ/dt}{Q} \equiv \dot{Q} = \frac{\partial F}{\partial K}\frac{1}{Q}\frac{dK}{dt} + \frac{\partial F}{\partial L}\frac{1}{Q}\frac{dL}{dt}. \tag{2}$$

Next, we can multiply the right-hand terms of (2) by K/K and L/L, respectively, to obtain

$$\dot{Q} = \frac{\partial F}{\partial K}\frac{K}{Q}\frac{dK}{dt}\frac{1}{K} + \frac{\partial F}{\partial L}\frac{L}{Q}\frac{dL}{dt}\frac{1}{L},$$

and recognizing that $[(dK/dt)/K] = \dot{K}$, and similarly for L, we can rewrite this last expression to give $\dot{Q}$ in terms of $\dot{K}$ and $\dot{L}$:

$$\dot{Q} = \frac{\partial F}{\partial K}\frac{K}{Q}\dot{K} + \frac{\partial F}{\partial L}\frac{L}{Q}\dot{L}, \tag{3}$$

or

$$\dot{Q} = \eta_K\dot{K} + \eta_L\dot{L}, \tag{4}$$

where $\eta_K \equiv (\partial F/\partial K)\cdot(K/Q)$ and $\eta_L \equiv (\partial F/\partial L)\cdot(L/Q)$. Thus, if $\dot{K}$ rises, $\dot{Q}$ will increase by η_K times the $\dot{K}$ increase, and similarly for $\dot{L}$ changes.

Output Elasticities and Relative Shares

The coefficients η_K and η_L in equation (4) have two interesting interpretations. First, they should be recognized as the elasticities of output with respect to changes in input. With L held constant, for example, the elasticity of output with respect to changes in capital input, E_K, is given by

$$E_K = \frac{\partial Q}{\partial K} \cdot \frac{K}{Q} = \eta_K,$$

and similarly, with K held constant, $E_L = \eta_L$. Looking back at equation (4), this says that the growth rate of output, $\dot{Q}$, equals the sum of the growth rates of inputs, each multiplied by its elasticity.

The second interesting interpretation follows if we assume competitive pricing of factor inputs. For example, with competitive pricing the real wage rate w is equal to the marginal product of labor $\partial F/\partial L$. If this is the case, η_L also gives the labor share of output:

$$\eta_L = \frac{\partial F}{\partial L} \cdot \frac{L}{Q} = \frac{W}{Q} = \text{labor share.}$$

Similarly, η_K is equal to the capital share. Thus, with competitive pricing, the η_K and η_L coefficients give the shares of capital and labor in output.

Now if the original production function is homogeneous to degree one, this means that an equiproportionate increase in K and L will give the same proportional increase in Q. For example, if both K and L increase by 5 percent, that is, $\dot{K} = \dot{L} = 0.05$, then Q must increase by 5 percent, $\dot{Q} = 0.05$. But this says that with $\dot{Q}$, $\dot{K}$, and $\dot{L}$ all equal to 0.05, from equation (3),

$$0.05 = \eta_K(0.05) + \eta_L(0.05)$$

and

$$1 = \eta_K + \eta_L. \tag{5}$$

Thus, if the production function is homogeneous to degree one, the η elasticity/ share coefficients must sum to unity. This ensures that if a production function is homogeneous to degree one *and* the economy has competitive factor pricing, *then* the competitively earned shares of output will sum to one, that is, exhaust output.

It is sometimes suggested that the identification of η coefficients with output elasticities and relative factor shares under competitive pricing can be made only with a Cobb–Douglas production function. However, the foregoing analysis shows that these relations hold with any production function that is homogeneous to degree one in a competitive economy. The Cobb–Douglas function does, however, provide a useful example that may make these relationships more clear.

The Cobb–Douglas function is written as

$$Q = bK^{\alpha}L^{1-\alpha}, \tag{6}$$

or in logarithmic form,

$$\ln Q = \ln b + \alpha \ln K + (1 - \alpha) \ln L.$$

From this we can see that in the Cobb–Douglas case,

$$\dot{Q} = \alpha\dot{K} + (1 - \alpha)\dot{L}, \tag{7}$$

so that the elasticity coefficients η_K and η_L of equation (4) are just α and $1 - \alpha$ here and clearly sum to one.

Differentiating the production function (6) with respect to L and assuming competitive factor pricing gives us

$$w = \frac{\partial F}{\partial L} = (1 - \alpha)\frac{Q}{L},$$

so that the labor share is given by

$$\frac{W}{Q} = (1 - \alpha)\frac{Q}{L} \cdot \frac{L}{Q} = (1 - \alpha),$$

which is the η_L elasticity coefficient in equation (7). A similar relation holds for capital; the capital share is given by α, so that the shares are identified with the elasticities and the sum to one.

The "Residual" Factor in U.S. Growth

We can now use the production function expression for $\dot{Q}$,

$$\dot{Q} = \eta_K\dot{K} + \eta_L\dot{L}, \tag{8}$$

to interpret the "stylized facts" of U.S. growth, which were presented in Chapter 23. There we saw that in the U.S. economy, along trend, the capital stock and output are growing at about 2.5 percent per year, and the labor force is growing at about 1.5 percent. Thus, along trend, $\dot{Q} = \dot{K} = 0.025$, and $\dot{L} = 0.015$. We also know from Chapter 2 that, depending on how proprietor's income is split between capital and labor income, the labor share of national income is about 75 percent, where the capital share is about 25 percent. Thus, $\eta_L = 0.75$ and $\eta_K = 0.25$.

Inserting the values for factor-input growth rates and relative shares into the growth equation (8) gives us, on the assumption that the economy's production function exhibits constant returns, an explained output growth of

$$\eta_K\dot{K} + \eta_L\dot{L} = 0.25(0.025) + 0.75(0.015) = 0.0175.$$

But in fact output grows along trend at about 0.025 or 2.5 percent per year! Thus, only 70 percent of the growth in output is explained by input growth. The unexplained growth in output is the *residual:*

$$\dot{Q} - \eta_K \dot{K} - \eta_L \dot{L} \approx 0.75 \text{ residual.}$$

This residual factor in economic growth is the growth of output that cannot be explained simply by input growth with a constant-returns production function. It is what Edward Denison has called "the measure of our ignorance."

A large, and sometimes controversial, literature centered on the works of Denison, Kendrick, Solow, and Jorgenson and Griliches has developed since the late 1950s over the explanation of the residual factor in economic growth. In general, if inputs are being correctly measured and the production function at any given moment is homogeneous to degree one, then the residual will come from the existence of technical progress. In other words, the production function will be shifting up through time as a result of (a) improvements in organization, (b) improvements in capital goods, or (c) improvements in the labor force. Whether this technical progress factor *augments* specific inputs or simply shifts the production function in a neutral way, and whether it must be *embodied* in new inputs, as opposed to augmenting both old and new inputs alike, will affect both the rate of technical progress that is compatible with a residual factor of a given size, and the sensitivity of output growth to changes in input growth rates.

A given rate of technical progress, if it simply shifts the production function up, will generate a larger residual than if it augments just the labor force, in which case it affects $\dot{Q}$ only through the labor input elasticity η_L. It will give a residual that is smaller yet if it has to work through the capital elasticity η_K. To put the point another way, to explain a residual factor of 0.75 percent per year, the rate of technical progress must be larger if it works through the labor elasticity η_L than if it shifts the entire production function up, and larger yet if it works through η_K. In addition, if technical progress must be embodied in one or another of the factors, the sensitivity of output growth to investment in these factors will be increased. Again, if technical progress must be embodied in new machines, an increase in saving and investment will raise output growth by producing not only *more* machines, but also *newer* and *better* machines.

The next three sections will bring these points out by studying the cases of, first, neutral disembodied technical progress in the form of production function shifts, then labor-augmenting disembodied technical progress of the $E_t = L_t e^{\lambda t}$ form of Chapters 23–26, and finally, capital-embodied technical progress which raises the elasticity of $\dot{Q}$ with respect to investment.

Whichever one of these assumptions is correct—or whatever mixture of them—should have an important bearing on intermediate-run growth policy. If the last one, capital-embodied technical progress, were correct, there would be a higher growth payoff, for example, to an investment tax credit than if either of the other two were correct.

NEUTRAL DISEMBODIED TECHNICAL PROGRESS

The simplest technical progress assumption, introduced by Solow in 1957, is that progress consists of organizational improvements that just shift the production function up through time. This kind of technical progress, it is assumed, just floats costlessly down on the economy. In this case the production function can be written

$$Q_t = A_t \cdot F(K_t, L_t), \tag{9}$$

where $F(K_t, L_t)$ is our original constant-returns production function. If A_t is a *steady* autonomous upward shift in the production function, we can write it as

$$A_t = A_0 e^{\lambda t}. \tag{10}$$

We can now derive a new expression for $\dot{Q}$ as a function of input growth and the rate of technical progress from equation (9). First, differentiation with respect to time gives us

$$\frac{dQ}{dt} = F(K, L)\frac{dA}{dt} + A\frac{\partial F}{\partial K}\frac{dK}{dt} + A\frac{\partial F}{\partial L}\frac{dL}{dt} .$$

Next, the same kind of substitutions that led to equations (3) and (4) earlier yields the growth equation

$$\dot{Q} = \dot{A} + \eta_K \dot{K} + \eta_L \dot{L}. \tag{11}$$

Here the residual has been defined as the growth rate of A, the autonomous technical progress shift factor. If (10) holds, then we have as a measurement of the residual,

$$\dot{A} = \dot{Q} - \eta_K \dot{K} - \eta_L \dot{L} = \lambda, \tag{12}$$

and the residual is equal to the growth rate of A.

Graphically, we now have a per capita—but not necessarily per *effective worker*—production function that is shifting up through time. Dividing the production function (9) through by L, remembering F's first-degree homogeneity, we have

$$\frac{Q}{L} = A_t \cdot f\left(\frac{K}{L}\right), \tag{13}$$

so that in Figure 27-5 the per capita production function shifts up through time at the rate λ, the growth rate of A.

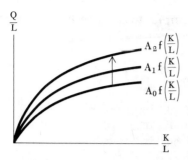

Figure 27-5 Per capita production function shifting up through time.

Substituting our stylized facts into (12), we have, in the case of neutral disembodied technical progress,

$$\lambda = \dot{A} = 0.025 - 0.25(0.025) - 0.75(0.015) \approx 0.0075.$$

Thus, under this assumption the *rate of technical progress* is defined as the residual, about 0.75 percent per year. Substitution of this value of $\dot{A}$ back into the expression for $\dot{Q}$ in this simple case gives us

$$\dot{Q} = 0.0075 + 0.25\,\dot{K} + 0.75\,\dot{L}. \tag{14}$$

Since technical progress is not embodied in the capital stock, a 1 percent increase in the growth rate of capital, $\dot{K}$, will, in the intermediate run, increase $\dot{Q}$ by only about 0.25 percent. There is no special technological benefit from increasing $\dot{K}$ since the technical progress gains float down on old machines as well as on new.

On the other hand, a 1 percent increase in $\dot{L}$ will raise $\dot{Q}$ by 0.75 percent, even without any embodiment of technical progress in labor, since, if income shares are a reasonable measure of elasticities, the elasticity of output with respect to labor is about 0.75, while that with respect to capital is only about 0.25. Next, we will see the results of assuming that all technical change is labor-augmenting but still disembodied.

LABOR-AUGMENTING DISEMBODIED TECHNICAL PROGRESS

Development of the expression for $\dot{Q}$ under the assumption of labor-augmenting technical progress, used in the development of the neoclassical growth model, is fairly simple. Suppose technical progress comes through improvements in the labor force due to such things as improving skills and that all workers share equally in these improvements. In this case, we have the production function

$$Q_t = F(K_t, E_t), \tag{15}$$

which is homogeneous to degree one in capital K and effective labor E, which is defined as $E_t = L_t e^{\lambda_L t}$. The growth rate of E is given by

$$\dot{E} = \dot{L} + \lambda_L = n, \qquad (16)$$

the natural rate of growth.

The expression for the growth rate of Q from equation (15) is now

$$\dot{Q} = \eta_K \dot{K} + \eta_E \dot{E} = \eta_K \dot{K} + \eta_E(\dot{L} + \lambda_L). \qquad (17)$$

If the share of output going to effective labor is still 0.75, we can compute the value of λ_L, the rate of technical progress under the assumption of labor-augmenting technical progress from the following expression:

$$0.025 = 0.25(0.025) + 0.75(0.015 + \lambda_L).$$

Solving this equation for λ_L yields a value of 1 percent, which is simply the difference between the growth rate of output, 2.5 percent, and the growth rate of labor input, 1.5 percent. Thus, in the labor-augmenting case, λ_L is the exogenous rate of growth of labor productivity.

Since in this model, technical progress operates through the elasticity of output with respect to labor, 0.75, the technical progress parameter, λ_L, is 0.01, as opposed to $\lambda = 0.0075$ in the disembodied case. If the size of the residual to be explained in both cases is the same, 0.0075, the parameter λ will have to be larger in the case where it has less "leverage" on $\dot{Q}$.

The expression for the growth rate of output, however, is still

$$\dot{Q} = 0.0075 + 0.25\dot{K} + 0.75\dot{L}, \qquad (18)$$

since the labor-augmenting technical progress is not embodied. There is no additional benefit to labor force growth beyond the simple addition of more labor to the production process.

CAPITAL-EMBODIED TECHNICAL PROGRESS

Both Solow and Nelson have developed simple models that embody technical progress in the capital stock through the assumption that new machines are more efficient than old ones. In this case, an increase in investment will reduce the average age of the capital stock, giving an increase in the rate of technical progress. This increase in the rate of technical progress associated with a drop in the average age of the capital stock will, in turn, increase the rate of growth of output beyond the increase associated with a simple increase in the number of machines available. Thus, as long as investment is sufficient to reduce the average age of the capital stock, the growth rate of output will rise both because there is more capital and because the average machine is becoming younger. Once the capital stock reaches its equilibrium average age for a given ratio of investment to output, this additional "kick" to output growth from capital stock growth will disappear, and the growth rate of output will settle down to its long-run value.

Here we will develop the model with capital-embodied technical progress following Nelson. The capital-embodied production function can be written as

$$Q_t = F(J_t, L_t), \tag{19}$$

with F homogeneous to degree one in labor and *capital jelly, J,* inputs. The growth rate of output is now determined by the growth rates of technologically enriched capital—capital jelly, J—and the labor force:

$$\dot{Q} = \eta_J \dot{J} + \eta_L \dot{L}. \tag{20}$$

Capital jelly is defined as the aggregate capital stock with each machine weighted by a technical progress factor reflecting its newness. Thus, we can write J as

$$J_t = \sum_{v=0}^{t} K_{vt}(1 + \lambda_K)^v. \tag{21}$$

Here K_{vt} is the capital stock of vintage v that is in operation at time t. Vintage is defined such that the oldest machine in use at time t has $v = 0$. K_{vt} with $v > 0$, then, is the capital built v years after the oldest machine still in operation at time t. λ_K is the technical progress factor, a constant growth rate per year, so that $(1 + \lambda_K)^v$ gives the technical progress adjustment that converts each vintage K_{vt} into equivalent current units of capital jelly.

From (21) we can see that if the capital stock is constant, so that net investment is zero and each year's gross investment just replaces dying machines with new ones, then the growth rate of J will be λ_K. Each year the technologically enriched capital stock will be more efficient by a factor of λ_K due to replacement. If the capital stock itself is growing at a constant rate, as it would in long-run growth equilibrium, then the expression for the growth rate of capital jelly is

$$\dot{J} = \dot{K} + \lambda_K. \tag{22}$$

This gives the growth rate of J in the long-run steady state with a given ratio of investment to output.

Now a constant growth rate of the capital stock also implies a constant average age of the capital stock. What would happen if the investment ratio were increased so that the average age would fall? If suddenly each machine in the capital stock became one year younger, so that $\Delta \bar{a}$, the change in the average age, $\bar{a}$, were -1, then the growth rate of J would go up by λ_K, since suddenly each machine would be one year more efficient. This tells us that to introduce the effect of changing $\bar{a}$ into equation (22) for $\dot{J}$ we should add $(-\lambda_K \, \Delta\bar{a})$ to it. Then if $(-\Delta\bar{a})$ is, say, one-half year, $\dot{J}$ will rise by half of a year's increase in productivity. This yields as an expression for $\dot{J}$ with average age changing,

$$\dot{J} = \dot{K} + \lambda_K - \lambda_K \, \Delta\bar{a}. \tag{23}$$

For the growth rate of output, this gives us

$$\dot{Q} = \eta_J(\dot{K} + \lambda_K - \lambda_K \, \Delta\bar{a}) + \eta_L \dot{L}. \tag{24}$$

Next, we should examine the relation between the rate of growth of the capital stock, which is the policy variable in this analysis, and the change in the average age. This relationship will give us the effect of increasing investment on Q *through* increasing the rate of technical progress.

Nelson shows that we can approximately express $\Delta\bar{a}$ as

$$\Delta\bar{a} = 1 - (\dot{K} + \delta)\bar{a}, \tag{25}$$

where δ is the percentage depreciation rate of the capital stock. If gross investment I_g is the sum of net investment I_n plus depreciation δK,

$$I_g = I_n + \delta K,$$

then the expression in parentheses in (25) is

$$\dot{K} + \delta = \frac{I_n}{K} + \delta = \frac{I_g}{K},$$

the ratio of gross investment to the capital stock. Thus, (25) says that if *gross* investment is zero, that is, $\dot{K} + \delta = 0$, then the average age of the capital stock will increase by one year, since no old capital is being replaced. If *net* investment equals zero so that only the dying capital is being replaced, then

$$\Delta\bar{a} = 1 - \delta\bar{a} = 0,$$

since the average age of the capital stock is approximately the inverse of the depreciation rate so that $\delta\bar{a}$ equals one. Finally, the greater $\bar{a}$, the more a given increase in gross investment will reduce the average age. For example, if the existing capital stock consisted entirely of 100 machines, all ten years old, so that $\bar{a}$ were equal to 10, then gross investment of 100 new machines would reduce $\bar{a}$ to 5, so that $\Delta\bar{a}$ would be 5. If the existing stock had been 20 years old, the same amount of gross investment would have reduced $\bar{a}$ to 10, so that $\Delta\bar{a}$ would be 10.

Substituting equation (25) for $\Delta\bar{a}$ into the expression for $\dot{Q}$ gives us

$$\dot{Q} = \eta_J\{\dot{K} + \lambda_K - \lambda_K[1 - (\dot{K} + \delta)\bar{a}]\} + \eta_L \dot{L}.$$

Combining terms within the braces yields

$$\dot{Q} = \eta_J[\dot{K} + \lambda_K(\dot{K} + \delta)\bar{a}] + \eta_L\dot{L}, \qquad (26)$$

as the expression for $\dot{Q}$ in the case of capital-embodied technical progress. We can now use the representative U.S. data to estimate λ_K—the rate of technical progress in the capital-embodied model that explains a residual of 1.5 percent per year. We have already estimated that $\dot{Q} = \dot{K} = 0.025$, $\dot{L} = 0.015$, $\eta_J = 0.25$, and $\eta_L = 0.75$. We can estimate δ at about 0.10, that is, depreciation is about 10 percent of the capital stock, and $\bar{a}$ at about 10 years. Inserting these values into equation (26) gives us

$$0.025 = 0.25[0.025 + \lambda_K(0.125)10] + 0.75(0.015).$$

Solution of this equation for λ_K yields a value of 0.024, or 2.4 percent. Thus, with capital-embodied technical progress, the residual to be explained is still 0.0075, but since λ_K works on $\dot{Q}$ only through the small capital elasticity η_J, it must take on a larger value than λ or λ_L to explain the same residual.

We can rewrite the expression for $\dot{Q}$ with capital-embodied technical progress at the rate of 2.4 percent per year to find the sensitivity of $\dot{Q}$ with respect to $\dot{K}$ in this model:

$$\dot{Q} = 0.25[\dot{K} + 0.024(\dot{K} + 0.10)10] + 0.75\dot{L},$$

so that

$$\dot{Q} = 0.006 + 0.31\dot{K} + 0.75\dot{L}. \qquad (27)$$

Assuming that technical progress is embodied in new machinery increases the intermediate-run sensitivity of $\dot{Q}$ with respect to $\dot{K}$ from 0.25 in the disembodied and labor-augmenting models to 0.31 here. This increase is a measure of the effect of investment, giving the economy not just *more* capital, as in the first two models, but also *newer* capital.

Thus, assuming all technical progress is embodied in new capital raises the estimate of the sensitivity of $\dot{Q}$ to changes in $\dot{K}$ to about 0.3—a fairly small return on a program of, for example, subsidy of capital investment. A similar model embodying progress in the labor force would probably increase the η_L coefficient to perhaps 0.8 or 0.85, making human capital programs much more attractive in terms of growth policy.

Denison's Sources of Growth

Another explanation of U.S. growth was attempted by Edward Denison. He analyzed what occurred between 1929 and 1957, two years in which output was reasonably near its potential level, and later extended the study to 1982. Although conventional in many of his assumptions such as the use of income shares to measure factor productivity, his analysis differs from that of Solow and Nelson in a number of important and interesting respects. His categorization of factor inputs is sufficiently broad to associate some sources of growth with particular inputs rather than assign them to the residual. This is particularly true with respect to changes in the quality of the labor force. Furthermore, he disaggregates the inputs, labor and capital, to allow separate estimates of the effect of the changing age and sex composition of the labor force and of various forms of capital. Finally, he attempts to disaggregate even his reduced residual so that it is not all attributed to technical change. Of particular importance, he abandons the assumption of constant returns to scale and replaces it with the assumption of increasing returns to scale.

Denison's accounting of growth between 1929 and 1982 is shown in Table 27-1. There we see that real national income grew by an average annual rate of 2.92 percent over this period. Of this growth, Denison atttributes 1.9 percent per year to growth of inputs and 0.26 percent per year to economies of scale. In Denison's accounting, the residual is reduced to 0.76 percent out of a growth rate of output of 2.92 percent.

Denison's growth figures differ from the stylized facts because of differences in the time periods used and method of analysis. However, it is interesting to note the differences in the relative importance of different sources of growth,

Table 27-1 ALLOCATION OF GROWTH OF TOTAL OUTPUT, 1929–1982
(annual growth rates)

REAL NATIONAL INCOME				2.92
INCREASE IN INPUTS				1.90
Labor			1.34	
Employment		1.12		
Impact of shorter hours		−0.27		
Annual hours	−0.51			
Quality impact	0.24			
Education		0.40		
Change in age-sex composition		−0.18		
Unallocated		0.17		
Land			0.00	
Capital			0.56	
Nonfarm residential structures		0.20		
Other structures and equipment		0.30		
Other		0.06		
INCREASE IN OUTPUT PER UNIT OF INPUT				1.02
Advance of knowledge			0.66	
Economies of scale			0.26	
Other			0.10	

Source: Trends in American Economic Growth, 1929–82, p. 111.

Table 27-2   RELATIVE IMPORTANCE FOR GROWTH

	Labor	Capital	Technical change
Neutral Disembodied Model	45%	25%	30%
Capital-Embodied Model	45%	31%	24%
Denison	46%	19%	23%

since they imply different policies to encourage growth (Table 27-2). Growth in the capital stock is most important if we assume that technical change has its impact through new capital stock. Capital growth is less important in Denison's analysis where improvement in the quality of labor is stressed. In the neutral, disembodied technical progress model with which we began, neither factor is as important as the fact of technical change, and less can be expected of policies that alter the growth rate of labor or capital. Whether growth policies should be oriented toward capital investment or toward improvement of the labor force through education, for example, will depend on important assumptions regarding embodiment of technical progress in capital or labor. In addition, the Solow-Nelson results are pessimistic about the ability of policy to change the growth path, while Denison's are more optimistic. But none is very certain; this remains a major area for research in macroeconomics.

These rough guesses reflect the state of knowledge of growth models and their relation to economic growth in reality. Presumably, the effect of a policy encouraging capital investment, such as accelerated depreciation or investment tax credits, will raise the rate of growth of output, in the intermediate run—but, of course, not at all in the long run—by between 20 and 30 percent of the attendant increase in the ratio of growth of the capital stock. More than this cannot be said at the current state of empirical knowledge of economic growth relationships.

SELECTED READINGS

M. Abramowitz, "Review of Denison," *American Economic Review,* September 1962.

E. F. Denison, *The Sources of Economic Growth in the United States and the Alternatives Before Us* (New York: Committee for Economic Development, 1962).

E. F. Denison, "The Unimportance of the Embodied Question," *American Economic Review,* March 1964.

E. F. Denison, "Sources of Postwar Growth in Nine Western Countries," *American Economic Review,* May 1967.

E. F. Denison, Trends in American Economic Growth, 1929–82 (Washington: The Brookings Institution, 1985).

D. W. Jorgenson and F. Griliches, "The Explanation of Productivity Change," *Review of Economic Studies,* July 1967.

R. R. Nelson, "Aggregate Production Functions," *American Economic Review,* September 1964.

R. M. Solow, "Technical Change and the Aggregate Production Function," *Review of Economics and Statistics,* August 1957.

R. M. Solow, "Investment and Technical Progress," in K. J. Arrow, S. Karlin, and P. Suppes, eds., *Mathematical Methods in the Social Sciences* (Stanford, Calif.: Stanford University Press, 1960).

INDEX